MARKETING

MARKETING

SECOND EDITION

Carl McDaniel, Jr.

The University of Texas, Arlington

HARPER & ROW, PUBLISHERS, New York
Cambridge, Philadelphia, San Francisco,
London, Mexico City, São Paulo, Sydney

To my parents, Martha and Carl McDaniel

Sponsoring Editor: *Arthur Sotak*
Development Editor: *Mary Lou Mosher*
Supervisor of Editing: *Rhonda Roth*
Designer: *Frances Torbert Tilley*
Production Manager: *Jeanie Berke*
Photo Researcher: *Jo-Anne Naples*
Compositor: *Ruttle, Shaw & Wetherill, Inc.*
Printer and Binder: *The Murray Printing Company*
Art Studio: *Eric Heiber Technical Services*

MARKETING, Second Edition

Library of Congress Cataloging in Publication Data

McDaniel, Carl D.
   Marketing.

   Rev. ed. of: Marketing, an integrated approach,
c1979.
   Includes indexes.
   1. Marketing—United States.   2. Marketing—United
States—Case studies.   I. Title.
HF5415.1.M38 1982   658.8'00973   81-7148
ISBN 0-06-044359-6   AACR2

Contents

One

**The nature
of marketing**

Two

**Understanding
the marketplace**

6 Industrial organization: behavior and management 146

7 Marketing information systems and marketing research 177

Three

Product concepts

Four

The nature of pricing

Five

Distribution structure

Six

Promotion concepts

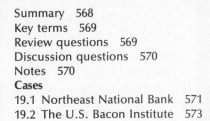

Seven

Marketing
management

Eight

**Marketing in
a changing world**

Preface

The decade of the '80s presents unique opportunities and challenges in marketing. Careers in marketing are expanding and will continue to offer rewarding futures. The challenges, however, will be formidable, as a result of inflation, shortages, fickle consumers, shifting markets, rapidly changing technology, and stiff domestic and international competition. This dynamic environment demands an understanding of marketing philosophy and the ability to make decisions. The goal of *Marketing,* Second Edition, and the principles of marketing course for which it is intended, is to provide the student with a firm foundation upon which this understanding and this skill can be built.

In essence, this second edition can be viewed as a new book; the content has been vastly changed, with only 30 percent of the first edition being retained. This new edition also provides a much stronger and expanded theoretical base, with topics presented from a decision-making perspective. This change is nowhere more evident than in Chapter 5, ''The Decision-Making Process in Consumer Buying,'' which has been rewritten with a decision-making model as its foundation. Marketing management and strategic planning are introduced in Chapter 2 and developed throughout the text. Since most decision making is tactical rather than strategic, many tactical approaches—such as tactics for segmenting a market, setting a price, creating a promotional plan, and developing a distribution channel—are explained.

Another major feature of this edition is the balanced treatment of macro and micro marketing. All too often, macro marketing is given secondary treatment in a basic text. But today's marketing personnel must cope with the total marketing environment and not just with a particular industry or firm. Macro marketing is defined and discussed in Chapter 1, and then further examined throughout the text.

Other structural changes have been made. All chapters have been expanded to allow a more in-depth treatment of the topics. A first edition chapter on planning and control has been broadened into two chapters: Chapter 21 covers planning and forecasting, and Chapter 22 deals with marketing organization and control. This material has been designed so that it may be taught much earlier in the course if desired. New chapters have been added on the marketing environment (Chapter 3), industrial organization behavior and management (Chapter 6), and marketing in nonbusiness organizations (Chapter 24). The text concludes with a short epilogue on the future of marketing, and an appendix that explores career opportunities in marketing.

Building on the success of the first edition, I have tried to make the second edition livelier and more interesting. Each chapter opens with objectives that alert the reader to what should be gained from the chapter, and a vignette designed to whet the student's appetite for the topic to be discussed. At the end of every chapter is a summary, a list of key terms, review questions, discussion questions, reference notes, and two cases. A major case is presented at the end of each part. The cases provide a basis for learning to define marketing problems and developing courses of action.

Although a number of new chapters have been added and others expanded, the text length is still within the parameters of coverage of the principles course. Control of the book's size has been accomplished by eliminating a chapter on the product/service classification system and incorporating those key points into Chapter 8 on product and service management. The roles of demand and cost in price determination now occupy one chapter rather than two. Similarly, personal selling and sales management are covered in a single chapter.

Preparing a complete revision of a text and its supplements required the help of many individuals. A special debt of thanks goes to John Woods and Ann Ludwig, who helped develop the original plan for this project; and to Mary Lou Mosher and Art Sotak, who "fine-tuned" the project.

I also extend my gratitude to the writers of the supplemental materials: Ron Bush, Louisiana State University, and Robert Brobst, The University of Texas at Arlington, who wrote *Marketing Simulation: Analysis for Decision Making*, Second Edition; Robert Hoel, Colorado State University, who developed *The Dynamics of Marketing: Current Happenings in the Marketplace;* Lee D. Dahringer, Emory University, who prepared the study guide and the test bank; and Eric Pratt, New Mexico State University, who prepared the instructor's manual. I am also indebted to Ron Michman, Shippensburg State College, for preparing the part cases.

A special thanks goes to the reviewers who offered many comments and suggestions along the way: Lee D. Dahringer, Emory University; Homer Dalbey, San Francisco State University; Del Hawkins, University of Oregon; Robert Hoel, Colorado State University; Alfred R. Manduley, Manhattan College; Ron Michman, Shippensburg State College; Constantine Petrides, CUNY-Borough of Manhattan Community College; Bruce Stern, Portland State University; Paul Thistlethwaite, Western Illinois University; and Sumner White, Massachusetts Bay Community College.

Finally, I would like to thank those who have worked behind the scenes to make this book a reality: Melinda Preston, my "right-hand person," who gathered countless research materials from varied (and sometimes obscure) sources; Melanie Callahan, who arrived later in the development of the project and was of invaluable assistance; Michelle Bock, who typed and retyped many chapters; and Debbie Farmer, my secretary, who typed part of the manuscript and, more importantly, performed many of the routine administrative chores of the marketing department, freeing me to write.

CARL McDANIEL, JR.

PART One

The nature of marketing

1 The marketing function

OBJECTIVES

To understand the importance of studying marketing.

To define marketing.

To understand the basic elements of the philosophy of marketing.

To become aware of the variables that make up the marketing mix.

To learn the functions of marketing.

To describe the broadened marketing concept.

To present a preview of the book.

Why study marketing?

Think about the number of transactions required every day to feed, clothe, and shelter the people of New York City, Chicago, or Paris. It is enormous—and yet the system works, usually quite well, day after day and year after year. What makes it work? Marketing. It is marketing that gets the output of farms and factories to us in a convenient, economical, and sanitary way. Look at Figure 1.1 on page 2. It shows the food consumption of one family of four in just one year—2.5 tons! Marketing makes food available when you want it, in economic quantities, at accessible locations, in sanitary and convenient packages and forms (such as instant and frozen foods). Food, of course, is just one of the many products that are part of our standard of living. The quantity of goods and services available to a nation's population defines its standard of living.

One function of marketing is to provide the delivery system for a standard of living. Without marketing, life as we know it in the industrialized nations would be far different. The level of efficiency of the marketing system also affects the quality of life. In some countries, for example, prices of products are high because of the large number of people (wholesalers and retailers) who handle a product before it reaches the final consumer. A significant amount of merchandise arrives broken, spoiled, or out-of-date because of lack of storage and physical handling equipment. But a standard of living like ours is not achieved without significant expense. One study estimates that marketing costs take about 50 cents out of every dollar you spend.[1] This may seem high to you. Look at Figure 1.1 again and think of the costs that would be involved if you had to go to the agricultural producer and pick up the goods yourself. Nevertheless, marketing managers are continually striving to find new ways of lowering marketing costs while delivering the same standard of living or an even higher one. For improving the efficiency of marketing can save literally billions of dollars.

Another reason for understanding the functions and principles of marketing is that it is one of the basic components of a business enterprise. As a college graduate entering the business world

1

Source: Courtesy of Du Pont Company, Public Affairs Department, Wilmington, Delaware 19898.

you will need to know how marketing relates to production, finance, engineering, and other business functions, no matter what your specific job or specialty. If a firm does not perform the marketing function properly the results can be disastrous. The stakes get higher every year. By the time you read this paragraph, Super Bowl commercials will probably cost more than a half-million dollars for 30 seconds of air time. If a company has the wrong message, the wrong product, or reaches the wrong audience, a lot of money has been wasted.

A classic example of a marketing mistake is Du Pont's Corfam, discussed below. Du Pont was lucky because it was large enough to withstand a $100 million loss. Many smaller companies and even some larger ones no longer exist because of marketing mistakes; others hang on, but they are not effective competitors. Around 1900 the household cleanser Bon Ami was a favorite product of most homemakers. The product was symbolized by a baby chick emerging from its shell and the slogan, "Hasn't scratched yet." In its heyday Bon Ami held 85 percent of the cleanser market. A failure to understand the importance and function of marketing coupled with aggressive marketing efforts by competitors left it with a 1 percent market share in the mid-1960s. Bon Ami mistakes ran the gamut from failure to maintain distribution in food stores to ineffective promotion.

What filled the gap when Bon Ami's market share declined? Products like Comet, Comet Liquid, Mr. Clean, Spic and Span, and Top Job. These brands have one thing in common; they are all made by one very aggressive marketer — Procter and Gamble. The firm also makes these laundry and cleaning products: Bold, Cascade, Cheer, Dash, Dawn, Dreft, Duz, Era, Gain, Ivory Liquid, Ivory Snow, Joy, Oxydol, Tide, Biz, Camay, Coast, Lava, Safeguard, and Zest. Firms cannot make marketing mistakes and compete with marketers like Procter and Gamble.

Du Pont introduced Corfam for spring 1964 footwear at New York's National Shoe Fair in October 1963, as a "step into tomorrow." Corfam was a man-made material that resembled leather. Through an intensive, multimillion-dollar promotion campaign Corfam was presented to consumers as an ideal shoe material. Corfam shoes were said to have shape retention, breathability, water repellency, durability, scuff resistance, and little or no need to be shined. What went wrong? Du Pont made several marketing mistakes. It emphasized durability when people were demanding shoes that were designed to be worn for a short period of time. They expected to buy the latest fashions next season. The concept of quality as meaning longevity was an irrelevant marketing idea for most potential buyers.

Another claimed advantage of Corfam was its ability to snap back into its original shape after being worn. What this really meant was that the shoe had to be broken in every time it was worn. Du Pont lost sight of the fact the consumers expect shoes to be comfortable after they are worn a few times.

Finally, Du Pont projected a huge increase in footwear consumption by the 1980s, plus a big gap in the availability of leather. It failed to forecast the growth of imported inexpensive leather and shoes. In short, marketing mistakes cost Du Pont $100 million.

You also need to understand marketing because it will be continually evaluated and debated during your lifetime. Sometimes society dictates what marketing can and cannot do through legislation and regulations. For example, it required Detroit to make cars safer; cigarette advertising was banned from television; and some states have outlawed disposable bottles and cans. Among the controversial issues in marketing are these:

1. Should marketing be used to "sell" birth control?
2. Is it right to advertise to young children?
3. Should high public officials running for election be marketed like a bar of soap or any other product?
4. How aggressive should the marketing efforts of multinational firms be in de-

veloping nations? How much power should giant multinationals be allowed to possess?

5. Do the poor pay more because of inefficient marketing?
6. Do various branches of government, such as the Postal Service and the military, have a right to promote and market their services?
7. Are there too many products differentiated only on a superficial basis such as brand name or color?
8. Is there too much advertising on television?

By understanding the nature and philosophy of marketing you will be able to examine both sides of these and other controversial aspects of marketing.

Marketing can help alleviate the plight of the world's hungry. In developing nations a large section of the population must depend upon agriculture for a living. Those who live in urban areas will spend two-thirds or more of their income on food.[2] One reason for the high cost of food and indeed starvation is rudimentary storage and distribution systems. In India, insects reportedly cause postharvest losses of at least 10 percent of cereals; rodents are reputed to cause an added loss of 10 to 20 percent of stored grains. A United Nations report on Brazil places losses of stored grain at 15 to 20 percent annually. In comparison, losses on stored grain in the United States average about one-half of 1 percent.[3] In tropical areas, as much as 50 percent of fruits and vegetables is lost from spoilage in the harvest season.[4] The application of modern marketing technology could help overcome some of these problems.

What is marketing?

Let us begin our examination of marketing with some definitions. I prefer the broad definition: **marketing** is human activity directed at satisfying needs and wants through the exchange process.[5] **Exchange** occurs when there are at least two parties and each has something of potential value to the other. When the two parties can communicate and have the ability to deliver the desired goods or services, exchange can take place. In the United States, exchange typically involves one party offering money and the other a product or service. For example, when you obtained this book, you probably exchanged cash for the text at the bookstore.

Not all exchanges involve money. You may swap a text you have already used with a student who has completed the basic marketing course. In order for exchange to occur, both parties (or at least one party) must feel they are better off than they were previously. You often pass up items in a store because you feel you are better off keeping your cash. Not all exchanges are profit-oriented, yet they are still part of marketing. A politician offers promises and hope in exchange for votes; the army offers training, excitement, travel, and being part of a team in exchange for enlistment; and the Salvation Army offers support for the needy in exchange for public support and donations. (I will return to the nonprofit aspects of marketing later in the chapter.) Both profit and nonprofit organizations want to facilitate the exchange process. If a manufacturer does not sell what it produces (engage in exchange), it soon goes out of business. If the March of Dimes does not effectively fight birth defects (in the minds of donors and supporters), it will cease to exist. An organization must engage in exchange in order to survive.

How do marketing managers attempt to create exchange? They follow the *right* principle. They attempt to get the right goods or services to the right people at the right place at the right time at the right price using the right promotion techniques. This principle tells you that marketing managers control many factors that ultimately determine marketing success. Think about this principle and the last exchange you made. What if the price had been 30 percent higher? What if the store, vending machine, catalog, or other source of goods and services had not been as accessible? Exchange probably would not have occurred.

MARKETING: A MACRO PERSPECTIVE

Marketing can be divided into two broad categories—macro and micro. Macro marketing begins with the study of broad marketing systems, of aggregate units of marketing activity. They are studied to discover how goods and services go from producer to consumer within a country and to compare one country's marketing system with that of another.

To appreciate the concept of movement of goods and services from producer to consumer in the American economy, you need to understand how our economic system works. The American economic system is essentially decentralized and based on free enterprise. The allocation of goods and services is not done by a central planning arm of government; instead, individual consumers direct the flow of goods and services. Our system is a free enterprise one because we are free to enter any occupation or business we choose. The decision of what to produce can be conceptualized as a voting process. When you buy a product such as a General Electric color television, you are voting for that product to continue to be produced. If enough people share your feelings, General Electric will receive a sufficient return on its investment and will have incentive to continue to offer the television to the marketplace. Moreover, the monies collected will enable General Electric to buy the resources to produce more sets. The reverse is also true. A product that does not receive dollar "votes" means that money does not flow back to the producer. Thus capital is not available to produce more units in the long run even if the firm wanted to produce them. Our economic system is market-directed. The buyer ultimately determines what is produced, and money and prices form the basis for allocating output.

A macro marketing system examines the transactional flows that decide a society's standard of living. In **barter** economies, products and services are exchanged without the use of money. A bunch of bananas may be exchanged for a dozen eggs. Historically, central markets have developed once societies have moved beyond the subsistence level, where each family produces and consumes its own output. A central market offers a place where transactions for goods and services can take place. As societies grow in complexity and begin to industrialize, the market system also becomes more intricate and complicated.

The marketing system and society. Macro marketing also involves the analysis of how a marketing system affects a society. Does the system, for example, aid or hinder economic development? The rebuilding of Western Europe's transportation system after World War II, along with new and modern storage and physical handling equipment, provided great impetus for economic growth. Conversely, in some South American countries wholesaling has been carried on in the same way for centuries. One family will physically move the product two or three miles and resell it to another family. They in turn move the merchandise a few miles and resell it to a different family acting as wholesalers (merchants who buy for resale to retailers or institutions). A product may travel through eight or more wholesalers and physically move less than a hundred miles. This system is deeply ingrained in the culture and has been extremely difficult to modernize. It has definitely retarded economic development.

Another example of how a marketing system affects a society is by how well it meets the social needs of the country. One by-product of the American market system, for example, is the tremendous litter problem caused by packaging. Each American family discards about a ton of empty packages a year. Another is that poor people in America often pay more for identical goods and services than other consumers because they lack mobility and therefore cannot get to stores that sell quality merchandise at reasonable prices. Other aspects of social responsibility will be discussed in Chapter 23.

A third broad dimension of macro marketing is how society influences the marketing system. In America we have decided that products and services should at least meet minimum safety standards. Congress created the Consumer Product Safety Commission (CPSC) to remove unsafe merchandise from the market and counsel us on proper use of products and services. Gone from the market are paints that can cause lead poisoning, children's pajamas that were highly flammable, and trouble lights that could cause severe shock. Society, acting through government, has also changed the safety features of automobiles, banned cigarette commercials on television, and made certain drugs available only by prescription. Government has even changed some forms of distribution, for example by outlawing pyramiding schemes. This is a plan where one person is sold territorial rights, who in turn sells part of the territory to others but retains a commission on sales. The second party resells to others and the pyramiding process continues. Society, again acting through government, allows some forms of entertainment only in certain geographic areas, such as gambling in Nevada and Atlantic City. So society can have a profound impact on the marketing system.

Macro marketing defined. We are now ready to bring the various aspects of macro marketing together in a definition. **Macro marketing** refers to the study of (1) marketing systems, (2) the impact and consequence of marketing systems on society, and (3) the impact and consequence of society on marketing systems.[6] Macro marketing is thus a multidimensional concept. Consumers are not passive recipients of a standard of living; they actively construct their life styles. The way you and I determine what we are in our purchases of services and products influences what is produced. For example, when the weekend athlete buys jogging suits and shoes, racquetball gear, and a new set of golf clubs, he or she helps determine the nature of what is produced. In planned economies, by contrast, central planning boards determine what will be the components (goods and services) of a standard of living.

Consumers and businesses also help construct a macro marketing system in a free enterprise economy by their votes for legislators they feel will vote for or against economic and consumer legislation. Pressure on legislators, consumer movements, and even protest activities help mold and shape the marketing system.

MICRO MARKETING

Micro marketing is the study of the individual units within the macro system. It is the analysis and examination of (1) individual consumers, (2) business organizations, and (3) industries. The focus of this text is primarily on micro marketing. Specifically, we will study how managers effectively utilize the techniques, philosophies, and principles of marketing to help an organization achieve its objectives.

The marketing concept

In order to accomplish their goals, firms today have adopted what is called the **marketing concept.** It is based on (1) a consumer orientation, (2) a goal orientation, and (3) a systems approach.

Consumer orientation. **Consumer orientation** means that firms strive to identify that group of people (or firms) most likely to buy their product (the target audience) and to produce a product or offer a service that will meet the needs of the target audience most effectively. Being consumer-oriented often involves research to explore consumer needs or to obtain reactions to new product ideas and concepts. Consumer orientation does not stop there however; it should be a philosophy that is practiced throughout the organization. An example of consumer orientation is shown below.

Sharp Electronics, manufacturers of everything from calculators to videotape cameras, spends a great deal of time and effort in researching and developing new technologies. Yet, Sharp does not force a product onto the market just because it is state of the art. The company tests prototypes with potential purchasers to discover underlying attitudes toward the product concept. If the general attitude is favorable, Sharp examines what features the consumers want on the product.

At both IBM and Digital Equipment, top management spends at least 30 days a year conferring with top customers. Both computer manufacturers also use customer satisfaction surveys as a partial determinant of a manager's pay. Management trainees at Johnson and Johnson are required to make customer sales calls. A young accountant couldn't understand the logic of such training. He was told that it would help ensure that he had empathy with a customer's financial situation.

Companies like IBM, Digital Equipment, and Johnson and Johnson find that consumer orientation becomes a culture for the company. Nearly every IBM employee has stories about how he or she took great pains to solve a customer's problem.

Goal orientation. The second tenet of the marketing concept is **goal orientation.** The firm must be consumer-oriented but only to the extent that it accomplishes corporate goals. These goals in profit-making firms usually center on financial criteria, such as a 15 percent return on investment. Sears marketing executives might be aware that telephone and catalog shoppers would like free home delivery. The costs of this service, however, would not enable Sears to meet its corporate objectives. Caterpillar Tractor Company attempts to meet its consumer service objective of "24-hour parts delivery anywhere in the world" and usually does. The manufacturer is aware that Caterpillar equipment owners have huge sums of money tied up in that equipment. Caterpillar owners would like "six hours or less parts delivery anywhere in the world." The cost to Caterpillar of additional strategically placed parts warehouses in numerous countries plus the expense of a much larger inventory would mean that it could not achieve its corporate financial goals. Caterpillar is a well-managed, consumer-oriented firm that recognizes the limits of feasible and practical service. Another example of goal orientation is shown below.

While Philip Morris U.S.A. certainly would not object to being the nation's No. 1 cigarette company, its marketing plans are focused on profitability, not on taking that position away from archrival R. J. Reynolds.

The company's executive vice-president, marketing, observed: "Being No. 1 means nothing to us as long as we continue to perform successfully with our products. Who the hell wants to be No. 1 and not growing? Besides, consumers generally don't know who makes the cigarettes they smoke, much less who the nation's No. 1 marketer is." At Philip Morris the clear-cut objective is profitability.[7]

Systems orientation. The third component of the marketing concept is a **systems orientation.** A system is an organized whole—or a group of diverse units

that form an integrated whole—functioning or operating in unison. It is one thing for a firm to say it is consumer-oriented and another actually to be consumer-oriented. Systems must be established to find out what consumers want and identify market opportunities. Next, this information must be fed back to the firm. Without feedback from the marketplace, a firm is not truly consumer-oriented. Also, internal systems must be established to make sure the "right" goods and services are produced, promoted, distributed, and sold to meet the needs of the target audience (see Figure 1.2). Chapter 2 will explain in detail the nature of a firm's marketing system. The point to remember here is that the marketing concept requires a well-planned and coordinated set of systems to make things work smoothly and efficiently.

EVOLUTION OF THE MARKETING CONCEPT

The marketing concept may sound so logical that you may assume organizations have always done things this way. The answer is that they have not. As businesses have evolved since the Industrial Revolution in America (from 1850 to 1915), different facets of the firm have received more emphasis than others. Several philosophies of doing business have been followed.

Production orientation. During and immediately after the Industrial Revolution managers focused on how to raise output and how to produce an item of uniform quality. Such inventions as standardization of parts and interchangeability of parts meant that products no longer had to be custom made. This led to mass production, the assembly line, and ultimately lower unit costs. The production orientation philosophy is that buyers wish to obtain merchandise at the lowest price possible. It assumes that price is the critical variable in the purchase decision and that buyers are aware of prices of competing brands.

But price is not the only component of the production orientation. It is basically an internal philosophy in that it focuses on the internal capabilities of the firm rather than the desires and needs of the marketplace. Production orientation means that management assesses its resources and asks the questions "What can we do best?" "What can engineering design?" "What is economical and easy to produce given our equipment?" In the case of a service organization, the question is "What services are most convenient to offer and where do our talents lie?"

There is nothing wrong with assessing a firm's capabilities; in fact it is a major consideration in strategic planning (see Chapter 2). Production orientation falls short because it does not consider whether what the firm produces most efficiently also meets the needs of the marketplace. Production orientation does not doom a company to failure—particularly in the short run. Sometimes what a firm can best produce is exactly what the market wants. Some scholars would argue that such a firm is not production-oriented, since management attempts to produce what it thinks the market wants. Others would say that since there was no formal, systematic assessment of target customer needs, the firm did not truly have the marketing concept.

Even up to the 1960s, the textile industry was production-oriented. This was also true of most apparel manufacturers; they decided what was fashionable and what they could best produce. Munsingwear, Inc., is a 94-year-old clothing maker best known for its Penguin brand golf shirts and Vassarette lingerie. Through the 1960s sales increased at a steady but unspectacular rate. Management's philosophy was "if you produce a quality product, it will sell itself."[8] Reliance on production orientation brought disastrous results. In the 1970s competitors began determining what customers wanted and altered their product lines accordingly. Munsingwear did not conduct market studies and did very limited promotion. It rolled out its standard product line and its old styles. By 1980 its market share and profitability had decreased dramatically, and it was uncertain whether or not the firm could survive. It is true that there are still many production-oriented organizations left today. But, like Munsingwear in 1980, the long-run prognosis is not good.

Sales orientation. The improvement of production technology and application of scientific management principles led to a change to a sales orientation by the 1920s. Many firms were attempting to cope with the huge output generated by mass production. A sales orientation assumes that buyers resist purchasing things that are not essential. It is also predicated on the idea that people will buy more goods and services if aggressive sales techniques are used, and that high sales mean high profits.

Not only were sales to the final buyer emphasized, but also promotion to wholesalers and retailers to get middlemen to push the manufacturer's product more aggressively. The fundamental problem with a sales orientation is again the lack of understanding of the needs of the marketplace. Companies that were sales-oriented found that regardless of how good their sales force was, if the market did not want the product or service, it could not be sold. In some cases, aggressive selling of inferior merchandise meant there were never any repeat sales.

Just as many firms are still production-oriented, there are many that still follow a sales orientation. For example, retail car and appliance dealers are still basically sales-oriented. The same can be said for those pushing lake lots, retirement villages, encyclopedias, carpet cleaning services, and a host of other products and services consumers rarely seek out. A number of high-technology electronics and computer firms are either sales or production oriented. As competition stiffens in the 1980s, however, more of them are moving to the marketing concept.

Marketing orientation. The problems with both the sales and the production orientation led firms such as Pillsbury, General Electric, General Foods, and General Mills to begin implementing the marketing concept in the early 1960s. Their success quickly resulted in other companies jumping on the bandwagon. By the mid-1970s utilization of the marketing concept had spread to virtually every industry producing consumer and industrial products. Generally speaking, however, consumer goods firms embraced the concept more quickly than industrial goods firms. And as difficulties continue to arise from the old ways of doing business, more companies are shifting to the marketing concept. One such firm is the Wolverine Shoe Company, discussed in the example below.

Wolverine is an old line work boot and glove manufacturer that first stumbled into the pigskin business about 35 years ago. At that time, supplies of horsehide, then Wolverine's primary raw material, were becoming increasingly scarce, and a solution seemed to be to turn to pigskin to make boots. But the company soon discovered that this was not a very practical idea. It has always been exceedingly difficult to tan pigskin to a smooth leather finish. And the company learned that few farmhands and other heavy-duty boot customers liked the cheaper alternative of brushed pigskin suede, since a suede boot tends to get clogged with dirt and dust when worn in the field.

As a result of these misjudgments of the market, Wolverine's pigskin business floundered throughout most of the fifties—until someone at the company's headquarters in Rockford, Michigan, came up with the notion of fashioning pigskin suede into a casual everyday shoe. Since pigskin is more porous and thus more ''breathable'' than cowhide, the company calculated that some customers might willingly trade in their tennis shoes for more versatile footwear. The shoes thus inspired were the original Hush Puppies. One of the first products aimed directly at the burgeoning leisurewear market, they scored a dazzling success. By 1965, the company was selling more than eight million pairs annually.

The late sixties brought new adversity, however, as dozens of other large manufacturers began to shoehorn in on the casual-footwear market. Sales of the humble Hush Puppies went into a long, slow slide. By 1972 the company decided to attempt to revive Hush Puppies but through the use of the marketing concept. Marketing research found that the average Hush Puppy customer was pushing 50, and getting older. This was because the design of this shoe had not been changed in fifteen years. The marketing team decided to go after a younger market. Also more emphasis was placed on women's shoes since women buy twice as many as men do. By 1980 the women's line contained 28 styles and the men's over 40 styles. New designs were based upon what the younger market said it wanted. Use of the marketing concept launched the firm on a new wave of prosperity.[9]

IMPLEMENTING THE MARKETING CONCEPT

When a company like Wolverine decides to implement the marketing concept, it is not always easy or done overnight. It is a philosophy of doing business and must be accepted and believed in by all members of the organization. If top management is not convinced that the marketing concept is necessary, implementation will surely fail. Simply changing the sales manager's title to marketing manager will be of little or no use. A system must be set up to recognize consumer needs and to react to them in a timely fashion.

Changes in authority and responsibility. Changing to the marketing concept often requires major revisions in authority and responsibility relationships within the firm. People who have been making "marketing" decisions, such as a production manager who decides what products are produced, may suddenly find their authority in the product area is gone. By contrast, new personnel in areas such as marketing research may find that they have considerable authority.

One way of gaining acceptance for the marketing concept is to get everyone who will be affected by it to participate in the planning process. Some human relations problems are inevitable during a period of change. Implementing the marketing concept by degree rather than in a revolutionary fashion normally smoothes the transition.

False starts. Sometimes companies fool themselves into thinking they have the marketing concept when they really do not. Management may concentrate on the "trappings" of marketing, such as:

Declarations of support from top management—speeches, annual reports.
Creation of a marketing organization—appointment of a marketing head and product or market managers, transfer to marketing of the product development and service function, salesmen reassigned around markets, advertising function strengthened.
Adoption of new administrative mechanisms—formal marketing planning approaches, more and better sales information, reporting system restructured around markets.
Increased marketing expenditures—staffing, training and development, advertising, research.[10]

Such "trappings" are no guarantee of success. Successful implementation of the marketing concept requires a basic shift in thinking throughout the organization toward the three basic elements of the concept—consumer orientation, goal orientation, and a systems approach.

Old production-focused ideas and habits are not easy to change. When a person has been doing something a certain way for many years, change often comes very hard. Consider the following:

In one capital-goods company, management had historically focused on selling the largest, highest powered, most maintenance-free units possible, with the thought that this approach favored the company's manufacturing economics. However, user needs had shifted toward smaller, less costly units without the rugged engineering characteristics required for maintenance-free operation.

Since this trend was clear, and the company was losing its market leadership position, marketing had recommended a major redesign of the product line. However, the company's manufacturing and engineering executives, who were acknowledged industry experts, argued convincingly that the current product design and cost structure were still superior to any competitor's, and all that was needed was a better selling effort.

Faced with these conflicting points of view, top management decided to stick with the original product concept and put pressure on the marketing group for a more aggressive selling effort. It was not until the company lost substantial market share and its entire profit structure was threatened that the president could bring himself to fly in the face of the expert opinion of his engineering and manufacturing executives and force the redesign through.[11]

The marketing mix

Establishing the marketing concept is the first step in developing a marketing-oriented organization. Within the marketing department, a marketing mix must be created. The unique blend of pricing, promotion, product offerings, and a distribution system designed to reach a specific group of consumers is called the firm's **marketing mix** (see Figure 1.3). Each factor is important in achieving

◀ **FIGURE 1.3 The marketing mix.**

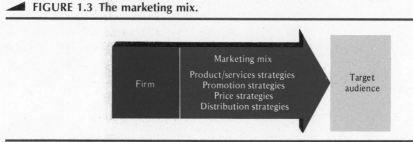

the firm's marketing objectives. An excellent product with a poor distribution system is often doomed to failure. The essence of marketing management is developing a successful marketing mix for a target audience.

Every market requires a unique marketing mix. Kool-Aid is not marketed like Coke, for example, yet both are nonalcoholic beverages. Their promotional themes differ; they appeal to different audiences; Kool-Aid has to be mixed with water while Coke does not; Kool-Aid is rarely, if ever, sold through fountain dispensers; and so on. You can see that each product requires its own distribution system, price strategy, and promotional themes. (The marketing mix will be discussed further in Chapter 2.)

Even similar products require different marketing mixes. Marlboro and Winston are both filter cigarettes that appeal to essentially the same market. Yet their manufacturers spend millions of dollars convincing the consumer that the two brands are different. Is it wrong to create mental distinctions between products? We will delve into this important issue later in the book.

PRODUCT/SERVICE STRATEGIES

The elements of the marketing mix are called the firm's controllable variables. These are activities the marketing manager can plan, organize, and control. For example, he or she can develop a strategy for a new product. But the marketing manager cannot control competitors' actions, inflation, foreign imports, buyer whims, and a host of other things (uncontrollable variables).

Throughout the text I will often use the word *product* in a broad sense to mean product or service. The heart of the marketing mix is a firm's product and/or service offerings. Marketers view products in a much larger context than you might imagine. For example, we say that a product includes not only the physical unit but package, warranty, service subsequent to sale, brand and company image, and a host of other factors. The names Yves St. Laurent and Gucci create additional value for everything from cosmetics to bath towels. It is interesting that you and I buy things not only for what they will do, but also for what they mean.

In the product section of the text we will discuss the various types of branding strategies a manager can use. One chapter is devoted to how new products are developed and how decisions are made to drop old ones. Management of the product line is also discussed.

The late 1970s ushered in an era of greater concern for product safety. The Consumer Products Safety Commission was instrumental in fostering this movement, as was greater social concern by marketing executives. Product recall became commonplace. Later in the text you will learn how product recalls are managed and how safety audits attempt to minimize their occurrence.

DISTRIBUTION

A second controllable element within the marketing mix is distribution. In the marketing mix distribution is sometimes referred to as *place* so that there are four Ps — product, place, price, and promotion. Distribution is essentially the study of how a product flows from producer to consumer. In this book we will look at why distribution channels are important and what functions they perform. The theory of channels will be discussed. You will also learn about channel systems and how a manager selects a channel of distribution.

Two chapters are devoted to the institutions between producer and consumer. We will examine the nature of wholesaling and how wholesaling institutions are changing to meet the challenges of the 1980s. The retailing chapter discusses the management of retail institutions, how store locations are determined, and how retail institutions have evolved. Another chapter discusses physical distribution. Physical distribution has a goal of minimizing the time between when an order is placed and when the merchandise is delivered as ordered. In addition to providing good service, however, physical distribution managers attempt to minimize costs. Naturally there are some tradeoffs between the two. You will see how a distribution manager attempts to provide good service and also meet cost control objectives.

PRICE

The third variable of the marketing mix is price. Price is essentially determined by two factors, demand for the good or service and cost. In addition, some special considerations can influence the general level of price. Sometimes, for example, a special introductory price is used to get people to try a new product. The factors that affect price will be discussed in the first pricing chapter.

The second pricing chapter will introduce marketing strategies and tactics. You will learn why some manufacturers enter a market with very high prices and then lower them over a period of time, such as with pocket calculators. You will also understand why a firm such as Texas Instruments penetrated the digital watch market with a new product priced at $20, which was far below the prices of the competition. Price tactics such as odd pricing ($9.99 rather than $10), geographic pricing, and others will be examined.

PROMOTION

Many people feel that the fourth controllable element of the marketing mix is the most exciting. Promotion covers personal selling, advertising, sales promotion, and publicity. A good promotion campaign can sometimes dramatically increase a firm's sales. Each element of promotion is coordinated and managed with the others to create a promotional blend. An advertisement, for example, helps a buyer "get to know" a company. It paves the way for a successful sales call.

The first promotion chapter will cover communications theory as it applies to promotion — how the promotional blend is created and what factors influence that blend. Two chapters cover advertising and advertising management. You will also learn about the special role of publicity in the organization. Bad publicity is free. Good publicity, such as a story on television or in a magazine about a firm's new product, is usually the result of considerable time, money, and effort being spent by an organization's public relations department. You will also learn how sales promotion helps stimulate sales. Sales promotion includes things such as trade shows, catalogs, contests, games, premiums, coupons, and special offers. The last two chapters of the promotion section introduce sales and sales management. Careers in professional selling, salesperson and potential buyer interaction, and sales procedures are discussed. The sales management chapter explains how a sales manager hires, trains, motivates, and controls the sales force.

Functions of the marketing department

So far we have discussed major areas of marketing responsibility—pricing, distribution, promotion, and the product. Now we take a closer look at the specific functions of the marketing department. Figure 1.4 shows the functions for which marketing is normally responsible.

The various work functions have been subdivided into two areas: those concerned with generating demand or sales, and those concerned with servicing the demand after it has been created. Several tasks, such as general marketing administration, financing, and marketing research, support all the other activities necessary to generate and service demand.[12]

STIMULATING DEMAND

Stimulating demand for a good or service is a function of many things. Advertising, for example, can create awareness for a product or service. Often you will see ads for Pioneer stereo receivers and systems in college newspapers because college students represent part of the target audience for Pioneer products. Or you may have read an article about a new Pioneer system in an audio magazine. The material for the article probably came from a news release by Pioneer's public relations department.

If you happen to be planning to buy a new stereo, the Pioneer ad may motivate you to visit an audio specialty store. Upon entering, you might notice a special display of the Pioneer system advertised. It is a "cutaway" model showing the special features of the internal components. Such a model is a form of sales promotion created to help stimulate demand for the Pioneer product. As you stand looking at the display, a salesperson may walk over and ask if you have any questions about the system. It is the job of the salesperson to provide product knowledge that will help you get the stereo that best suits your needs. It is also his or her job to close the sale. The salesperson informs you that the new system has a special introductory price discount of 15 percent off. That may be the clincher that closes the sale.

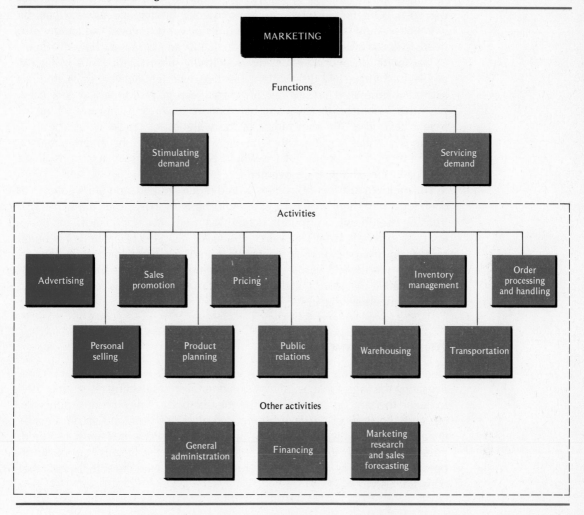

Source: Adapted from Richard Lewis and Leo Erickson, "Marketing Functions and Marketing Systems: A Synthesis," *Journal of Marketing,* 33 (July 1969): 12. By permission of the American Marketing Association.

SERVICING DEMAND

Selling the product or service is only half the task. Marketing managers must also service demand. Sufficient inventory must be on hand. If, for example, the shop happened to be temporarily out of the new system, the salesperson, eager for a sale, may convince you to buy another brand instead. Pioneer must provide the store with enough systems to meet anticipated demand but avoid having too many on the shelves. The latter condition increases inventory carrying costs. Orders must be processed quickly and efficiently so that the warehouse knows when to ship more units of various types. The factory also needs to know what models are selling so that it can plan production schedules.

Transportation and warehousing are closely interrelated. Pioneer, for example, might have as a distribution objective overnight delivery of its products to a retail store after a restocking order has been placed. One way to accomplish this would be to have one distribution center and ship everything air freight beyond a 500-mile radius of the warehouse. Trucks would be used within 500 miles. On the other hand, twelve distribution centers could be placed around the country. Each would be positioned so that a truck could reach all retail audio stores overnight.

The multiple distribution centers would require duplication of inventories at each location. There would be labor and building costs, plus a much larger trucking fleet. If one distribution center was used, inventory, labor, and delivery fleet expenses would be lower. However, the cost of air freight is much more expensive per pound shipped than train, truck, or any other form of transportation. It is the task of marketing management to calculate the total costs of all alternative distribution systems and install the one that is least costly and that also meets service objectives.

OTHER MARKETING ACTIVITIES

Financing marketing activities, such as the purchase of advertising and compensating the sales force, must also be undertaken. Marketing research is used to define the target market, determine the feasibility of new product concepts, measure the level of recall of a proposed advertisement, and so on. Finally, general administrative duties must be performed. Personnel must be hired, trained, motivated, and controlled. Strategic plans and strategies must be developed, and marketing activities must be coordinated with the activities of other departments.

RESEARCH ON MARKETING FUNCTIONS

Recent research has revealed several things about marketing functions:

1. Actual responsibilities within marketing departments vary widely from company to company.
2. Promotion is the most common marketing function in consumer goods corporations.
3. Sales forecasting and customer relations are the functions most frequently assigned to marketing in industrial goods organizations.
4. Inventory management and warehousing are the areas most likely to be delegated to other departments, regardless of the type of organization.[13]

The nature of the market (dispersed vs. concentrated, large customers vs. small customers, sophisticated buyers vs. uninformed purchasers), the availability of qualified personnel, the firm's management philosophy, and tradition can all influence how the marketing concept is applied and the specific functions carried out by a marketing department.

The broadened concept of marketing

The marketing concept we have been discussing was broadened during the 1970s to include nonbusiness and social marketing as well. It was recognized that the marketing concept would be just as valuable for nonprofit organizations in attempting to reach their goals. It was also argued that marketing people must develop a social consciousness: they should become involved in vital social issues and provide important public services. Let us look first at the **broadened marketing concept** as it applies to nonbusiness organizations.

NONBUSINESS MARKETING

Governments, museums, hospitals, charities, and many other organizations are becoming marketing organizations (see Table 1.1). The basic marketing concept of consumer orientation, goal orientation, and creation of systems to make it all happen apply just as much to a hospital or a museum as a stereo manufacturer. There are, however, some important differences between profit and nonprofit marketing.

Multiple publics. In profit-making firms, the customer pays for the good or service and receives the merchandise. Nonprofit organizations have two publics or target audiences. First is the donor group or taxpayers that provide funding for the operation. Although taxation may be thought of as involuntary, the recent tax revolts, such as Proposition 13 in California, prove otherwise. Also, hospitals, for example, are usually funded by religious groups and/or various branches of government. Beneficiaries of hospital services are the patients who

◄ **TABLE 1.1 Nonbusiness Organizations and Their Customer Groups**

Organization	Product	Customer group
Museum	Cultural appreciation	General public
National Safety Council	Safer driving	Driving public
Political candidate	Honest government	Voting public
Family planning foundation	Birth control	Fertile public
Police department	Safety	General public
Church	Religious experience	Church members
University	Education	Students
City	Sightseeing	Tourists

Source: Philip Kotler, "A Generic Concept of Marketing," *Journal of Marketing,* 36 (April 1972): 47. Reprinted by permission of the American Marketing Association.

require the care. Both target audiences must be satisfied if the organization is to continue to run smoothly. Private and governmental organizations differ primarily on the basis of the donor's responsibility. Taxpayers are required to meet their obligations, whereas gifts to private organizations are voluntary. If the March of Dimes is going to be effective, it must convince enough people that the fight against birth defects is worth their money.

Nonprofit objective. A second distinction between profit and nonprofit marketing is the lack of profit goals of the latter group. This does not mean, however, that a nonprofit firm can be financially irresponsible. If a museum is operating at a deficit, it usually means that costs must be controlled or more revenues will have to be generated. Moreover, there are social profits that can accrue from nonprofit organizations. **Social profits** are benefits that are available to the whole society and that enhance the quality of life. Better health care, fire and police protection, more opportunities to view fine works of art, religious institutions that are more responsive to the needs of the people, and better educational systems are examples of social profits.

In a profit-making organization success is measured at least in part by the firm's realization of financial goals. The ability to attract funds to meet expenses in a nonprofit organization is not a valid measure of the success of the total organization. Some television churches, for example, have been more adept at raising money than at satisfying the religious needs of their flocks. At one time Father Flanagan's Boys Town was considered by some to be considerably better at fund raising than at child raising.[14]

Public scrutiny and nonmarket pressures. Public agencies are always subject to public scrutiny because of the American form of government. Raising postal rates or reinstituting the draft results in public participation and influence over the actual policy decisions. In 1980, for example, strong public pressure led to simple draft registration rather than a draft registration and classification. Classification is a much more detailed procedure requiring tests and physical examinations. To help avoid the need for a draft, the U.S. Army began to rely on marketing techniques (see Figure 1.5).

Government institutions are not subject to competitive pressures in the same way as profit-making organizations. Government entities do not have competitive constraints and are often forced to serve groups that profit-making firms would avoid because of lack of profit potential. An example would be providing health care in low-income neighborhoods. Politics can also exert pressure on governmental units to engage in activities that are financially unsound or benefit only a few. Setting up Amtrak routes in sparsely populated areas and making rivers such as the Arkansas navigable from Tulsa, Oklahoma, to the Mississippi River are examples.

Recently, the U.S. Armed Forces had a hot sauce problem. The type they were serving to America's 2 million servicemen was getting more complaints than compliments.
The Defense Personnel Support Center (DPSC), the Philadelphia-

WHY SHOULD THE ARMY BE EASY? LIFE ISN'T.

In the modern Army, the Cavalry flies, the Infantry rides, and the Artillery can hit a fly in the eye 15 miles away. It's a printed-circuit, solid-state, computerized Army.

And this special kind of Army requires a special kind of soldier. The kind of young man or woman who's eager to learn tomorrow's technology, tomorrow's skills. The kind of young man or woman impatient for a challenge and hungry for responsibility.

Today's Army is a unique opportunity. To discover hidden talents, to develop special abilities, and to equip yourself with the skills you need.

If you'd like to serve your country as you serve yourself, call toll free 800-421-4422. In California, call 800-252-0011. Alaska and Hawaii, 800-423-2244. Better yet, visit your nearest Army Recruiter.

ARMY. BE ALL YOU CAN BE.

Source: Courtesy of U.S. Army.

based agency that supplies America's fighting men with hot sauce (as well as food, clothing, and medical supplies) might have ignored the problem in years past. The hot sauce was supplied under contract by companies which made it according to government-provided specifications.

The hot sauce specifications were reviewed, however—and relaxed. As a result, DPSC has begun purchasing part of its hot sauce from commercial producers.

This reflects a new military attitude, says DPSC public affairs officer James L. McKenna. "It used to be that a soldier in a chow line was expected to eat what was put in front of him," he explains. "Now, we view our servicemen as customers."[15]

SOCIAL MARKETING

The application of marketing theories and techniques to social situations is called **social marketing.** It may be viewed as consisting of three main elements:

1. Satisfaction of human needs. The key term is *human needs,* not those that are business- or product-oriented. An opportunity is seen for marketing techniques to be used to sell clean air, clean water, and adequate housing, for instance.
2. Expansion to social fields. Marketing is seen as an instrument that can be used to further all the goals of society. It is suggested that marketing techniques can be used to help achieve socially desirable goals such as population control, improved racial tolerance, and increased support of education.
3. Consideration of societal impact. A new imperative is presented: that business must assess not only the profitability of its actions, but also the overall effect those actions have on society.[16]

Satisfying human needs. For the marketing concept to be applied successfully, whether by a private enterprise or in a social context, the consumer's (society's) self-interest must be satisfied. The role of self-interest was recognized as far back as 1776, when the economist Adam Smith conceived the principle of the "invisible hand." His theory states that resources will be allocated efficiently in a free market system that appeals to individual self-interest.

From a company's viewpoint, the marketing manager must identify consumer self-interest and then determine how to react to it. But consider the following example:

The tobacco industry has certainly been consumer oriented in postwar years. The industry has adapted skillfully to changing consumer preferences as the major prewar brands have yielded to a proliferation of new shapes and styles. Industry sales and per capita cigarette consumption have gained steadily. Do we conclude that a consumer orientation is enabling this industry to adapt with perfect harmony to environmental change? Hardly. A powerful and growing array of forces are united in an effort to erase the industry altogether. These forces emanate from state and federal government, the medical profession, and concerned citizens at large. They are generated by persons whose most likely common bond is that they are *not* consumers of the product. These individuals have managed to create a steady stream of woe for the tobacco industry.

What had made the future of the industry in the coming decades a question-mark is not its failure to provide consumers with a pleasant, satisfying product but rather the product's vulnerability to society's deepening concern over human well-being.[17]

Changing social attitudes and values. In addition to satisfying human (society's) needs, marketing can be used to achieve social goals. Can marketing change people's attitudes toward such matters as littering, birth control, and law enforcement? Perhaps, but only by ultimately appealing to individual self-interest. The concept of appealing to self-interest is known as the **empirical-rational strategy.**[18]

Once people become rationally aware of their interests, they will pursue them. An attitude that stems from an individual's basic values (good or bad, right or wrong) and is strongly supported by his or her culture will be difficult to shift in a direction that is incongruent with those values.[19] Marketing strategy cannot in the short run change social values. One example is the inability to market birth control information in many parts of the world.

The problem of scarce resources. The third dimension of social marketing is marketing's impact. Marketing under conditions of limited resources has added new dimensions to the problem of societal impact. New questions are being raised, such as "Should it be sold?" and "What are the costs to society?" In response, the term **creative demarketing** has been coined, meaning a strategy designed to discourage consumption in general or to discourage a certain class of customers from consuming a particular product.[20] Oil marketers have used this strategy extensively during the recent petroleum crises.

In addition to management demand, marketers are examining their product mix and distribution channels more closely in order to identify waste and inefficiency. They are also bracing themselves for more regulation as the government tries to supervise the allocation and usage of scarce resources. Perhaps government involvement is most obvious in the automobile industry, where a spate of laws regulating efficiency of engines, pollution safety, and so on have recently been passed.

A preview of the book

With a basic understanding of marketing, the marketing concept, and the broadened marketing concept you are now prepared to venture ahead into the book. You will find that every chapter is written from the perspective of a marketing manager. Although some descriptive material is necessary (as in this chapter) to set the stage, the focus is on managerial decision making. The rest of Part One presents an expanded view of the marketing system and a discussion of the external environment with which the manager must cope. Problems related to inflation, shortages, changing values, and other contemporary challenges are woven through the text, as well as examples of nonprofit marketing.

Part Two describes the marketplace. You will learn how and why a market is often subdivided in order to develop a more effective marketing mix; you will also have a better understanding of consumer motivations and purchasing patterns. This portion of the book concludes with a description of marketing research and information systems, which provide the information on which marketing managers base their decisions. Parts Three through Six discuss the marketing mix outlined earlier in this chapter. Part Seven discusses the roles of managers in planning, organizing, and controlling the marketing operation. This section will help you understand how marketing strategies are developed and marketing problems defined and solved.

Part Eight focuses on three topics that are considered important by most marketing managers. The first topic is consumerism, which affects all of us, not just the business sector. The second is industrial marketing. Although industrial marketing examples are used throughout the text, the subject matter is important enough to warrant a separate chapter. The material covers industrial buyer behavior and how industrial marketing mixes differ from those of consumer goods companies. The third topic is international marketing. As American firms enter the international market, they find a vastly different operating environment. We will explore the opportunities and problems of doing business in a world made ever smaller by improvements in transportation and communication.

A career in marketing

Choosing a major field of study can be a hard decision. What are the chances of getting ahead if you major in marketing? Figure 1.6 presents the business backgrounds of key officers of major corporations. Many board chairpeople and company presidents come from marketing. The pay for top marketing executives is not bad either, as Table 1.2 shows. I have projected salaries for top marketing executives in a large corporation for 1982.[21] A senior marketing executive in a major organization will earn almost $150,000 in 1982. Entry level salaries of course are a very small proportion of a top executive's income. Yet this should give you an idea of what can be achieved during a person's career. (Marketing careers are discussed in more detail in the epilogue to the text.)

◢ **FIGURE 1.6 Primary career emphasis of chief executives.**

Financial	19.5%
Administrative/ General Management	16.4%
Marketing	13.7%
Legal	12.0%
Production/ Operations	10.7%
Banking	10.7%
Technical	9.4%
Founder	5.1%
Other	2.4%

Source: Data from "How Much Does *Your* Boss Make?" *Forbes,* June 11, 1979: 117–48.

▲ **TABLE 1.2   Estimated 1982 Salaries for Top Marketing Executives**

Position	Salary (in thousands of dollars)	Position	Salary (in thousands of dollars)
Top sales and marketing	146	Top public relations	67
Top divisional marketing	116	Top advertising	71
Top marketing	118	Distribution	74
Top sales	109	Marketing research	67
Top international marketing	103	International general sales	67
Top public relations/advertising	91	Product/brand sales	58
		Sales promotion	56

SUMMARY

Marketing may be defined as human activity directed at satisfying needs and wants through the exchange process. Exchange occurs when there are at least two parties, each having something of potential value to the other. In America this typically involves one party offering money and the other a good or service. Profit and nonprofit institutions strive to facilitate the exchange process. This is done through following the "right" principle: that is, the organization's attempt to get the right goods or services to the right people at the right place at the right time at the right price using the right promotional techniques. Without exchange, an organization will cease to exist.

Marketing is divided into two broad categories—macro and micro. Macro is concerned with the study of broad marketing systems. Macro systems are examined for getting goods and services from producer to consumer and in the comparison of one country's marketing system with that of another. We examine macro marketing systems by studying the transactional flows that deliver a standard of living to a society. Macro marketing, however, is not simply the study of distribution. On the contrary, it also involves an analysis of how a marketing system affects society. For example, how does a marketing system meet the social needs and quality of life demands of a society? When studying macro marketing, we also examine societal impacts upon marketing. For example, what role does government play in influencing marketing?

Micro marketing is the analysis and examination of individual consumers, business organizations, and industries. This text will focus basically on micro marketing. In order to accomplish the goals of an organization, many firms have adopted the marketing concept. The foundations of the marketing concept are consumer orientation, goal orientation, and the systems approach. The marketing concept has evolved from a production orientation to a sales orientation and finally to a marketing orientation. Effective implementation of the marketing concept requires a strong commitment from all levels of management.

The marketing concept can be implemented via the marketing mix: promotion, pricing, distribution, and the product itself. Without a successful marketing mix, the firm is ultimately doomed to failure. The specific functions carried out within a marketing department include tasks that generate demand or sales and those concerned with servicing demand after it has been created. In addition, several activities such as general marketing administration, financing, and marketing research support the marketing functions necessary to generate and service demand.

In recent years marketing has expanded beyond the profit-making organization. The basic marketing concept has been successfully applied to many non-business organizations. These organizations generally have multiple publics, a nonprofit orientation, and are subject to much more public scrutiny and non-market pressures than most profit-making entities. One aspect of the broad marketing concept is social marketing. Social marketing entails satisfaction of human needs, expansion into social fields, and consideration of the impact of marketing on society.

KEY TERMS

Marketing	Systems orientation
Exchange	Marketing mix
Barter	Broadened marketing concept
Macro marketing	Social profits
Micro marketing	Social marketing
Marketing concept	Empirical-rational strategy
Consumer orientation	Creative demarketing
Goal orientation	

REVIEW QUESTIONS

1. What are some reasons for studying marketing? Why would an accountant need to be acquainted with marketing?
2. What is marketing? How does micro marketing differ from the macro marketing perspective?
3. What is a firm's marketing mix? Why is it an important determinant of a firm's success?
4. Distinguish between obtaining demand and servicing demand. What are some means of fulfilling these functions?
5. What is social marketing? Why is it important?

DISCUSSION QUESTIONS

1. Define and discuss the basic elements of the marketing concept. Do you think most businesses have adopted this concept?
2. What problems are involved in implementing the marketing concept? Recommend steps by which a firm can make the transition smoothly.
3. How do you think nonprofit organizations can utilize the marketing concept? Give examples to illustrate your answer.
4. What is meant by creative demarketing? How should this strategy be applied in the context of the energy crisis?
5. Should marketing managers be concerned about social issues? Do you think they have the right or the responsibility to deal with social problems? Give reasons for your answer.

NOTES

1. Reavis Cox, *Distribution in a High Level Economy* (Englewood Cliffs, N.J.: Prentice-Hall, 1965), p. 149.

2. Charles C. Slater, "Marketing Process in Developing Latin-American Societies," *Journal of Marketing,* July 1968, p. 50.

3. Martin Kriesberg, "Marketing Food in Developing Nations—Second Phase of the War on Hunger," *Journal of Marketing,* October 1968, p. 58.

4. Ibid.

5. Philip Kotler, *Marketing Management Analysis, Planning, and Control,* 4th ed. (Englewood Cliffs, N.J.: Prentice-Hall), 1980, p. 21.

6. Shelby Hunt, "The Three Dichotomies of Marketing: An Elaboration of Issues." In *Macro Marketing Distributive Processes From A Societal Perspective,* ed. Charles C. Slater (Boulder: Graduate School of Business Administration, University of Colorado), 1976, p. 56.

7. Sam Harper, "Profits, Not Market Position, Keep Aim of PM." Reprinted with permission from the July 14, 1980 issue of *Advertising Age.* Copyright 1980 by Crain Communications, Inc.

8. "Munsingwear: A Belated Quest for Innovation and Marketing Pizazz," *Business Week,* May 12, 1980, p. 100.

9. The source for this vignette is Linda Synder Hayes, "Hush Puppies Roar Again," *Fortune,* July 14, 1980, pp. 143–144.

10. Charles Ames, "Trapping U.S. Substance in Industrial Marketing," *Harvard Business Review,* July–August 1970, p. 94. Copyright © 1970 by the President and Fellows of Harvard College; all rights reserved. See also "Marketing Concept under Fire and Other Big Problems for Marketers," *Marketing News,* July 1, 1977, p. 9.

11. Ames, p. 97.

12. Richard Lewis and Leo Erickson, "Marketing Functions and Marketing Systems: A Synthesis," *Journal of Marketing,* 33 (July 1969): 12.

13. Carlton McNamara, "How Marketing Is Practiced in 640 Companies," *Sales Management,* October 14, 1970, p. 60; see also Philip Kotler, "The Major Tasks of Marketing Management," *Journal of Marketing,* 37 (October 1973): 42–49. Reprinted by permission of Sales & Marketing Management magazine. Copyright 1970.

14. "Boys Town Bonanza," *Time,* April 10, 1972, pp. 17–18.

15. Cecelia Lentini, "DPSC: Supplying the Military's Human Needs." Reprinted with permission from the July 14, 1980, issue of *Advertising Age.* Copyright 1980 by Crain Communications, Inc.

16. Andres Takas, "Societal Marketing: A Businessman's Perspective," *Journal of Marketing,* 38 (October 1974): 2. Reprinted by permission of the American Marketing Association. Other recommended articles on social marketing include E. B. Weiss, "The Coming Change in Marketing," *Advertising Age,* February 3, 1971, pp. 33–34; Philip Kotler, "A Generic Concept of Marketing," *Journal of Marketing,* 36 (April 1972): 46–54; David Luck, "Social Marketing: Confusion Compounded," *Journal of Marketing,* 38 (October 1974): 70–72; and Ben Enis, "Deepening the Concept of Marketing," *Journal of Marketing,* 37 (October 1973): 57–62.

17. Leslie Dawson, "The Human Concept: New Philosophy for Business," *Business Horizons,* December 1969, p. 33.

18. Robert Chin and Kenneth D. Benne, "General Strategies for Effecting Change in Human Systems." In Warren G. Bennis, Kenneth D. Benne, and Robert Chin, *The Planning of Change,* 2nd ed. (New York: Holt, Rinehart and Winston, 1969), pp. 32–59.

19. David Krech, Richard S. Crutchfield, and Egerton L. Ballachey, *Individual in Society* (New York: McGraw-Hill, 1962).
20. Philip Kotler and Sidney J. Levy, "Demarketing, Yes, Demarketing," *Harvard Business Review,* December 1971, pp. 74–80; see also Nessim Hanna, A. H. Kizilbach, and Albert Smart, "Marketing Strategy under Conditions of Economic Scarcity," *Journal of Marketing,* 39 (January 1975): 63–80.
21. These salaries are projected using a 10 percent annual rate of inflation. The base data are from John A. Fischer, "Marketers Get a 10% Raise," *Sales and Marketing Management,* February 4, 1980, pp. 43–45.

◢ **CASES**

1.1 Mumford Toasters

In 1955 Ronald Mumford graduated from the University of Wisconsin with a degree in engineering. He went to work for General Electric in the Consumer Products Division. Over the years Ronald had many opportunities to participate in the development of product concepts for a variety of kitchen appliances. As he climbed the corporate ladder he began to feel that he would not be satisfied until he had his own business. Consequently in 1965 he resigned from General Electric and opened Mumford Toaster Products in Racine, Wisconsin.

Ronald took his engineering knowhow coupled with years of practical experience and designed an oven toaster that was basically very simple. The toaster was a square metal box with a heating element in the top that browned the toast. It had a pull-out tray and would hold four regular slices of bread.

At the time no comparable product existed. Sales of the Mumford Toaster rose dramatically from 1,400 units in the first year to 200,000 units in the second year. As the product began to "catch on" and distribution spread from Wisconsin to surrounding states, the giant competitors began to take an interest in it. Yet it was not until the end of the fourth year, when Mumford's sales were slightly over 1 million units, that the competition actually entered the marketplace.

Mumford Toasters has 47 employees. All production and design work is done by Mumford himself when he has time; all the company's new concepts are based on his ideas. Virtually all the employees are engaged in some form of production, either on the line or in packaging, shipping, or receiving. Other personnel include a sales manager, a bookkeeper, and an accountant. There are no salespeople in the company. The sales manager hires a battery of manufacturer's representatives, who work on a commission basis throughout the United States.

Mumford has examined his operation and decided that in order to effectively meet the competition he will have to adopt the marketing concept. He realizes that he needs someone to help him implement the concept.

1. As a consultant to Mr. Mumford, explain how he might implement the marketing concept.
2. What benefits may accrue to the firm from utilizing the concept?

1.2 The Bazaar

In Asian cities, there are a multitude of food shops and perhaps an inexhaustible supply of street vendors. Yet more than half of all food purchases are made within a bazaar. A bazaar is a food market in which many tiny and highly specialized retailers offer their wares. The markets are considered by many to be colorful, noisy, hectic, and often crowded. By Western standards, however, they may seem insanitary, dirty, and unattractive to the person who does not enjoy haggling over prices. Quality of the products is often virtually impossible to tell prior to purchase, and merchandise is not sorted or graded in any fashion.

The merchants operating in the bazaars start early in the morning with purchases at a central wholesale market. They usually carry their wares directly to their stalls. In tropical areas, mornings are devoted to sales, and the vendor seeks to minimize the amount of leftover goods from the previous day. In the afternoons, vendors clean their stalls and trash is removed by the market workers. The bazaars are often extremely hot. Coupled with rough handling and no packaging, these conditions shorten a product's life dramatically.

Bazaars vary from city to city and country to country. In their crudest form, bazaars are nothing more than an open-air display of merchandise placed on makeshift structures or directly on the street. At the other extreme, air-conditioned buildings house the stalls, refrigeration equipment is prevalent, and packaging is also evident.

1. Is a bazaar an example of macro marketing or micro marketing? Why?
2. Would you say that the individual vendors within the bazaar have adopted the marketing concept? Why or why not?
3. Do you feel bazaars should be replaced with modern American-type supermarkets in most of these countries? Defend your answer.

2

Marketing systems and marketing management

OBJECTIVES

To gain an in-depth understanding of marketing as a system.

To become acquainted with the marketing model.

To become aware of marketing's internal and external environments.

To learn about the external factors that affect marketing.

To understand the functions of and need for marketing management.

To become acquainted with strategic planning.

As early as 1972, Bell executives began to recognize the need for the marketing concept. A study found that AT&T lacked internal systems for addressing customer needs, ensuring that new products and services reflected those needs, and delivering individualized solutions to customers' problems.

The report recommended that AT&T set up a new marketing department at headquarters under a senior executive. From 1973 to 1978, the Bell System spent over $2.1 billion converting to a marketing organization.

Examples of Bell's new philosophy include its Design Line of decorator telephones (Mickey Mouse is one), many of which it buys from outside suppliers. The company also began to open retail stores for the new line and had about 1,800 locations by 1978. Special kiosks set up during the Christmas shopping season sell about 80,000 telephones.

Bell's manager of residential planning sees lots of opportunity for developing innovative services—for example, systems that would enable a customer who is not at home to turn off the stove, air conditioner, or hot-water heater simply by dialing a number. By 1990, the total market for residential products and services might be $55 billion, as opposed to a mere $5 or $6 billion in 1980. But the immediate future is limited. The advent of the "home of the future" will have to wait until AT&T's nascent consumer research determines what customers really want, and appliance manufacturers and builders tailor their products to the capabilities of the telephone system.

On the business customer side, market managers concentrate on anticipating customer needs rather than simply reacting to market developments, as AT&T too often has done in the past. For the first time, AT&T has performed classic market analyses segmenting business customers into more than fifty industry classifications and studying each segment to determine how communications affect profit and loss. The aim of the exercise is to increase the amount of money corporations spend with the Bell System by finding ways they can use communications to fatten their profits—for example, by cutting down on travel.[1]

The Bell System story raises some interesting questions. Why did a monopoly need to adopt the marketing concept? Was it only because of new competition, or were there other factors? How does change take place in an organization moving toward a marketing orientation? Perhaps most important, how can management plan for change, take advantage of market opportunities, and accomplish its objectives? The first half of this chapter presents a marketing model that will help you conceptualize the total marketing environment. It will help you understand why change was necessary at Bell Telephone. The second half of the chapter moves from the total environment to the individual firm. Specifically, it explains the nature and functions of marketing management in a marketing-oriented organization.

The marketing model: an integrated system

In order to understand the nature of a marketing-oriented firm in a competitive environment, we will examine it in a systems context. Recall that a **system** is an organized whole—or a group of diverse units that form an integrated whole—functioning or operating in unison. The units are interdependent and are continually interacting, usually in response to some type of control. The control in marketing is exercised by management, which manipulates the marketing mix (promotion, the product, pricing, and distribution) in order to meet the needs of a target group of customers.

Control of the marketing mix is important for two reasons. First, it enables the marketing manager to develop goods and services to meet opportunities uncovered in the marketplace. Second, control is needed to alter existing goods and services in response to user and potential user feedback. This feedback focuses on how well a good or service meets user needs.

In an examination of the gum and candy market, Squibb Corporation's Life Savers division uncovered the fact that children were not happy with existing bubble gum products. The primary source of dissatisfaction was that the bubble gums were too hard to chew. Life Savers had uncovered an opportunity! If a soft bubble gum could be developed, the firm felt it could penetrate a major share of the $460 million per year bubble gum market in the United States. Life Savers laboratory research produced such a gum. It was introduced in 1974 and known as Bubble Yum—the first soft bubble gum.

Marketing responsibilities did not end with the successful introduction of Bubble Yum. In fact, marketing responsibilities never end as long as a product or service is on the market. The product must be continually monitored and the mix must be adapted to the changing needs of the marketplace. Information feedback, for example, found that consumers were complaining Bubble Yum grew hard to chew over a period of time. Chewers also noted that Bubble Yum had a short taste life.

Marketing management then reformulated the product and promoted the product as "now yummier." The advertising theme emphasized "smoothness,

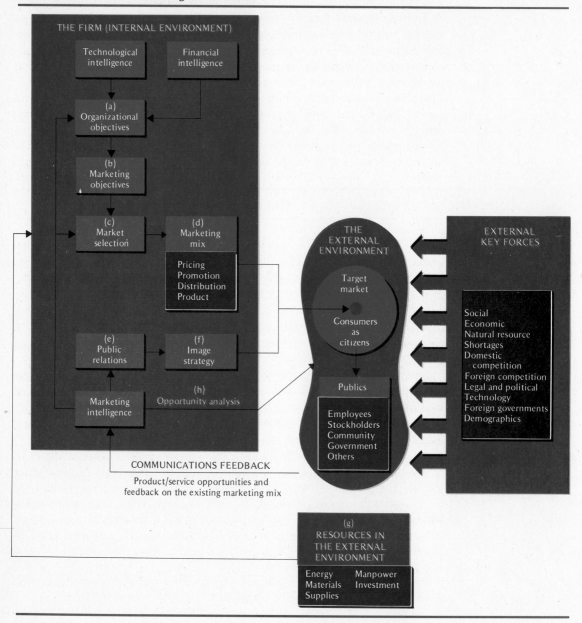

long-lasting flavor and better bubble-blowing characteristics." Bubble Yum packaging was also changed to include a "now yummier" slogan. The product is now the best-selling bubble gum in the United States. Estimated market share in 1981 was 35 percent.[2]

Life Savers' marketing managers were following the marketing model (Figure

2.1). This flow diagram is a visual illustration of the variables that interact, the sequence of their interaction, and their interdependence.

Transactions are created and stimulated by offering consumers what they want. Marketing information helps the firm develop the proper goods and services. Promotion, fair prices, and credit terms help stimulate exchanges and determine values (what things are worth). Credit and distribution also facilitate the exchange process. That is, getting the product or service to the consumer and offering terms that enable an individual to acquire the merchandise or service allows exchange to occur. All this activity takes place within an environment.

Marketing's environment may be divided into two major subsystems—the **internal subsystem** (within the organization) and the **external subsystem** (outside the organization). Each major subsystem can limit the success of the enterprise. For example, financial constraints may limit inventory levels or the size of the promotional budget. Externally, government regulations can limit package sizes, pricing plans, product names, and so on.

Conversely, the subsystems can also present opportunities for increasing the firm's marketing success. Internally, for example, analysis of credit information on existing customers may provide insights for new pricing strategies. Externally, changing social attitudes can offer many growth opportunities, such as the movement toward informality that spawned a dynamic increase in denim fabric sales.

THE INTERNAL SUBSYSTEM OF MARKETING

The importance of goals. Let us begin our examination of the marketing model by looking at the internal environment of the firm. A firm's goals provide the basis for intelligent organizational planning (Figure 2.1, box a). Without well-defined and realistic objectives, a firm is like a ship without a rudder. Control becomes impossible because there are no standards for measuring success or failure.

But goals must never be established in a vacuum. Rather, they must be based on relevant marketing, financial, and technological input. What is our borrowing capacity? What technology do we have available or can we acquire? What are the characteristics of the population we are trying to reach? These and similar questions must be answered before realistic objectives can be established.

Goals for a profit-oriented organization. Organizational goals are the necessary point of departure for developing a successful marketing mix. An obvious long-run objective for virtually all organizations is survival. In addition to survival, profit maximization is often mentioned as a major goal. Companies strive for at least a satisfactory level of profits—that is, a return perceived as adequate by the firm's owner/managers or stockholders. An adequate return is normally judged as a return commensurate with a perceived level of risk for the industry and for the organization. Often, goals are stated in terms of market share or target return on investment. General Electric, for example, strives for a 20 percent return on investment after taxes. This specific target figure provides management with a planning goal.

There's no business without show business.

When the curtain goes down for the evening, know what theatre-goers turn into?

Restaurant-goers. Taxi-riders. Shoppers.

Theatre-goers turn into consumers.

A lot of consumers. More people go to live theatre performances than to professional baseball, football, and basketball games combined.

Any smart businessman knows: the arts mean business.

Support That's where **The Arts** the people are.

National Endowment for the Arts

Ad A Public Service of this newspaper & The Advertising Council
Council

In addition to profit goals, many firms establish social goals. Examples of social goals include increasing the intrinsic value of the product or service, decreasing the resources needed for production, recycling old products and packages, and reducing pollution. As society has become more aware of pollution, of wasteful production processes, of poor product quality (such as lack of food value in cereals), and so forth, it has become necessary for firms to develop a social conscience. If a company or industry does not establish social goals on its own, it may find itself forced to do so by governmental regulations.

Goals for nonprofit organizations. Nonprofit institutions such as governmental units, civic organizations, and charities must also develop organizational goals. A charity may have as a goal the feeding and clothing of 5000 families during the next six months. A health organization may strive to provide 200 complete physical examinations each day. An objective of the National Endowment for the Arts is to improve the image of the arts among the general population and to increase public donations by X percent. Advertising helps nonprofit organizations achieve their objectives (see Figure 2.2).

Inputs from other departments. Cooperation among all departments is necessary for efficient accomplishment of company goals. Marketing is only one cog in the organizational machine and should not dominate the company. Marketing depends on production for basic information on what can be produced, how many pieces can be produced per unit of time, and so forth. By the same token, there are inherent conflicts between production and marketing goals. Production tends to be preoccupied with lowering costs. This normally translates into lack of variety because of long production runs, fewer product features (to avoid production problems), and lengthy intervals between model changes. These desires of the production department are anathema to marketing managers.

Financial management provides critical information on pricing strategies, inventory levels, and product development costs. Again, financial goals may easily conflict with marketing goals. Financial executives may lean toward limited inventories, fewer models, less money for promotion and basic research (owing to the difficulty of measuring returns), and "quick return" pricing policies.

Marketing objectives. Marketing objectives, derived from organization goals, are a logical extension of corporate objectives (see Figure 2.1, box b). The accomplishment of marketing goals should aid in the accomplishment of company goals. For example, if the company's main objective is to obtain a dominant share in a high-volume market, the main marketing objective should not be to develop a product with exclusive appeal and high price. This would not be a high-volume strategy.

THE TARGET MARKET

After marketing goals have been defined, the company determines its **target market** (Figure 2.1, box c); that is, it identifies the consumers or firms who are most likely to buy or use its product or service. Only when a clear and precise target has been established can a marketing mix be developed (Figure 2.1, box d).

Segmentation. In order to define a target market clearly, segmentation is normally required. **Market segmentation** is the process of identifying and evaluating various strata or layers of a market. Some potential customers will have a stronger need or desire for a product or service than others. Some groups will respond more quickly or favorably to a specific marketing mix than others. Adults, for example, may respond more favorably to a table-service restaurant than teenagers and young children. Children and teenagers are more receptive to the marketing mix of a fast-food chain.

One way to visualize market segmentation is through the use of a **market grid,** a two- or three-dimensional box subdivided by relevant market characteristics. As a marketing manager divides and redivides the total market, he or she is examining smaller, more precisely defined groups of potential buyers with relatively homogeneous characteristics. An industrial products manufacturer segments its market by product lines and type of potential customer (see Figure 2.3). Each of the submarkets can then be analyzed on the basis of whether or not the firm can effectively serve and compete in a given submarket and on the basis of its profit potential. If a submarket is still too large to be meaningfully analyzed, it may be further segmented.

Market gridding (and segmentation) are useful as long as the defined subsegments exhibit different consumption patterns for the product or service or respond differently to the marketing mix. Assume that both office and home furniture manufacturers had the same abrasives usage rate, used exactly the same type of abrasives, and had the same purchase rates for the industrial products manufacturer's marketing mix. Segmentation by office and home furniture manufacturers would be a useless exercise. (Segmentation will be treated in detail in Chapter 4.)

THE MARKETING MIX AND TRADEOFFS

The marketing mix is developed in order to achieve marketing and company goals by satisfying a target group of consumers. The components of the market-

FIGURE 2.3 Market grid for an industrial products manufacturer.

Product lines \ Customer groups	Machine shops	Food processors	Furniture manufacturers
Cutting tools			
Abrasives			
Portable air tools			

ing mix are the controllable elements of marketing. These four key variables (price, promotion, distribution, and the product itself) are the tools marketing managers have at their disposal. Public relations (Figure 2.1, box e), a component of promotion, plays an especially important part in presenting the corporate image to various publics—for example, stockholders and the community at large.

Different departments are often forced to compromise, and tradeoffs must be made among various pricing, product, distribution, and promotion strategies. One typical tradeoff is between product quality and price. The ideal situation is a low price and high quality, but this is rarely attainable. Instead, the manager must decide the tradeoff values, as perceived by the target market, between raising the quality and also raising the price. Other tradeoffs include personal selling versus advertising, intensive product distribution versus lower-quality dealers, and extensive service versus lower prices.

A second set of marketing tradeoff decisions has now evolved. It relates to the broader marketing concept and includes such considerations as the firm versus society and the firm versus the government. Assume, for instance, that a manufacturer can produce a central air-conditioning system for private homes at a relatively low price. Yet, because of the design, it is an inefficient user of energy. The tradeoff is between a low-priced product and high energy consumption.

Many fast-food restaurants do not hesitate to wrap a hamburger in paper and put it in a styrofoam box to retain heat before finally putting the burger in a sack, when in fact the patron will eat the burger in the restaurant! The tradeoff is a warm hamburger and the visual appeal of the package versus potential lower sales without the excess packaging. The packaging also means wasted paper, which uses up natural resources and produces litter. In the long run, this becomes a tradeoff between the firm and the government. The company must decide whether pleasing the consumer is worth the risk of government legislation against nonreturnable containers. In Oregon, for example, the state government, reacting to the litter problem, has outlawed disposable soft-drink bottles.

THE EXTERNAL SUBSYSTEM

Let us turn now to the external environment and the target market. Remember that tradeoff decisions within the marketing mix must ultimately satisfy the target market and society as a whole. For years, large, fast automobiles with rigid metal steering posts, sharp instrument knobs, and no seat belts were eagerly bought by consumers for their "flashy designs" and power. Society, acting through government, decided the basic automobile was unsafe and uneconomical for American consumers. New regulations require greater gas mileage, less pollution, and a host of safety features. In today's environment, a firm cannot produce a good or service for a target market and ignore its impact on society.

Society: consumers and publics. The target market is made up of potential consumers of the product. These consumers also play a role as part of a larger group—the general public. The public comprises not only potential consumers, but employees, stockholders, governmental units, and others. Marketing managers must consider the needs of the public as well as the target market. The firm, for example, is expected to be a good corporate citizen in the communities in which it conducts business. A company that ignores the public may develop a poor image.

The ''public'' an organization faces is a heterogeneous group including employees, stockholders, and the community. Each of these ''publics'' has unique needs that must be met to ensure the firm's long-run survival. Stockholders are looking for a certain return on investment; employees seek security and job satisfaction; the government passes legislation and informal guidelines; and the community requires that the firm be a good neighbor.

All organizations present several distinct images to their various publics and consumers. Part of a company's image may be developed by a public relations department (Figure 2.1, box e) or advertising (see Figure 2.4). Other aspects of a

---

◢◢ **FIGURE 2.4 Using promotion to create a positive company image.**

Why we take care of our trees.

If you were a farmer whose only crop had a 50 year growing cycle, you'd take very good care of it, right? Well, we are that farmer. Our crop takes 50 years, on average, to reach maturity.

That's why we plant up to six seedlings for every tree we harvest, why we nurture them, prune them, thin them, protect them from insects, disease and fire.

That's why we continually explore new forest management techniques that promise more trees per acre, and new manufacturing processes that promise more wood and paper per tree.

That's why we increasingly use what once was wasted, either to make products like yeast, chunk bark and particleboard, or to generate energy.

It's a matter of self-interest, finally. Only by managing our trees prudently can we provide the jobs, products and profits we all need and the forests we all love.

 **Boise Cascade Corporation**
Wood and paper for today, trees for tomorrow.

Source: Courtesy of Boise Cascade Corporation.

firm's image include its physical facilities, employee contact with the external environment, and the firm's marketing mix. The firm's image (Figure 2.1, box f) is the major determinant of how various publics and consumers interact with it.

Resource requirements. A second aspect of the external environment is the resources used by the organization (Figure 2.1, box g). Resources are acquired by producing a product or service that is desired by society. Without a desirable good or service, the firm will not make sales and thus will not receive the revenues needed to acquire resources. This basic truism is coming under increasing criticism, however. For example, even though consumers have shown that they are willing to pay a premium for disposable bottles and cans, is this an efficient use of resources? The Boise Cascade advertisement (Figure 2.4) focuses on the efficient use of resources as means of promoting the company image.

In periods of shortage, companies must vie with other organizations for scarce raw materials. When shortages arise among raw materials that have multiple uses, allocation decisions must be made. One decision rule marketing managers often follow is to produce goods or services in order of marginal profitability and resource requirements. Assume that the marginal profits and demand for an aluminum manufacturer are: Product A, $1, 10,000 units; product B, $0.75, 25,000 units; and product C, $1.50, 5,000 units. Also assume that equal amounts of inputs (aluminum) are required to produce one unit of A, B, or C. If the manufacturer can acquire only enough raw aluminum to produce 15,000 units of output, it would produce all of products A and C, and none of B. Other criteria besides profitability may alter the firm's production schedule. Product B may round out the product line and be necessary to complete a sale. Interstate highway signs, for example, have three basic signpost configurations. Usually, state governments need all three types. If only two were available, the manufacturer might be excluded from bidding on a signpost contract.

Monitoring change in the marketing system. The amoebalike shape of the external environment in Figure 2.1 is used to denote a state of flux or change. Marketing managers face an external environment that is continually evolving. Moreover, that environment is subject to a number of powerful forces that create and influence changes in consumer demand and in public needs and whims.

These external forces are not under the control of the marketing manager. The manager must understand and forecast how the key forces will affect the external environment and must alter the marketing mix and seek out new opportunities accordingly. The mechanism for monitoring change is the marketing intelligence system. A marketing intelligence system, as we will see in Chapter 7, is a device for communications feedback (see Figure 2.1). Government reports, private research reports, trade statistics, reports from field sales personnel, and market research studies are typical information conduits.

Marketing managers evaluate the information received through the marketing intelligence system and decide what changes, if any, should be made in the marketing mix. For example, deregulation of the airline industry has resulted in major changes in air routes and an increase in competition. Marketers also use the intelligence system to seek out and define new product and service opportunities, such as when Life Savers developed Bubble Yum (Figure 2.1, box h). The key forces for change in the external environment are social and economic factors, domestic and foreign competition, legal and political factors, technology, foreign governments, and demographic factors. We will look at these variables in detail in Chapter 3.

Marketing management

In order to utilize the marketing concept to respond to an ever-changing environment, an organization must have good management. **Marketing management** is the planning, organizing, and controlling of marketing activities to help the firm achieve its objectives. Specifically, marketing managers must develop both long-range and short-range plans. Next, they and others must organize the firm's resources to carry out the plans effectively and efficiently. Finally, a monitoring system must be created to correct deviations from the plans, or change the plans if necessary. The following example shows how plans must sometimes be modified to reach company goals.

Belco Pollution Controls is a well-established firm in the air and water treatment fields. In 1977, Belco's management developed a plan for expanding sales in the water treatment market. Good and bad features of competitors' products were analyzed, enabling Belco to develop a superior and patentable design. The original plan then called for aggressive sales efforts to market the new design. Unfortunately, the sales efforts were a flop: No customer wanted to be a guinea pig for a new installation that could cost $1 to $8 million.

Armed with this feedback from the marketplace, Belco revised the original plan. The strategy was to retrofit an existing installation. Not only did it cost the customer much less, but saved about two years lead time from the receipt of an order to final startup. The revised plan meant that Belco just broke even on the first installation. However, sales of the first unit quickly enabled the company to sell four more—at a nice profit.

STRATEGIC PLANNING

Marketing executives face two general types of decision making.[3] The first relates to routine day-to-day operations necessary to carry out short-range programs **(tactical planning).** The second relates to decisions that affect the long-run competitive position or perhaps the survival of the firm **(strategic planning).** A strategic decision guides the long-run use of the firm's resources based upon the firm's existing and projected internal capabilities, and long-range changes in the external environment. Examples of strategic decisions include:

1. Cessna's decision to produce executive jet aircraft.
2. RCA's entry in the computer industry (a strategic error).
3. Holiday Inn's acquisition of casinos and the building of new casinos.
4. Cado Systems Corporation's decision to build only minicomputers.
5. The sale by International Harvester of its Scout division.
6. The decision by the March of Dimes to fight birth defects instead of polio.

All these decisions affected the long-run course of the organizations, their resource allocation, and ultimately their financial success. An operating decision such as changing a package design or altering the sweetness of a salad dressing is probably not going to have a profound impact on the long-run profitability of the company. On the other hand, if the March of Dimes were still fighting polio, it would no longer exist, because most Americans view polio as a conquered disease. Strategic marketing management addresses not only the question of where the organization will be at a particular time (fighting crippling diseases), but how it will get there (focus first on polio, then on birth defects).

The strategic planning process involves four areas of decision making: determining the business mission; developing strategic alternatives; specifying oper-

---

◢ **FIGURE 2.5 The strategic planning process.**

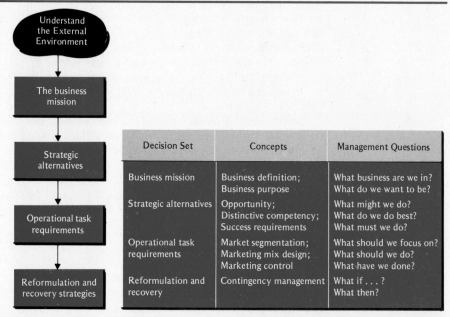

Decision Set	Concepts	Management Questions
Business mission	Business definition; Business purpose	What business are we in? What do we want to be?
Strategic alternatives	Opportunity; Distinctive competency; Success requirements	What might we do? What do we do best? What must we do?
Operational task requirements	Market segmentation; Marketing mix design; Marketing control	What should we focus on? What should we do? What have we done?
Reformulation and recovery	Contingency management	What if . . . ? What then?

Source: "The Strategic Marketing Management Process," in Roger A. Kerin and Robert A. Peterson, *Perspectives on Strategic Marketing Management* (Boston: Allyn and Bacon, 1980), p. 6. Reprinted by permission.

ational task requirements; and reformulation and recovery strategies (see Figure 2.5).[4] The starting point for strategic planning is a thorough understanding of the external environment as it relates to the firm.

Defining the business mission. Perhaps the single most important aspect of strategic planning is answering the question, "What business are we in?" The answer has a profound impact on long-run resource allocation, profitability, and survival. The classic example of defining the business mission too narrowly is the railroad industry. Most railroads defined their business as railroading rather than transportation. This led to significant inroads into their markets by trucking, pipelines, and airlines over a period of time. At one time, Gillette considered itself in the aerosol business because 80 percent of the antiperspirant buyers used aerosols. After the fluorocarbon propellant controversy, Gillette decided it was really in the "underarm business." This led to a reexamination of sticks, roll-ons, and alternative propellants to meet changing market demands. For years, Paper Mate was a lethargic firm bogged down in the consumer writing instrument business. In 1980, it redefined its mission as being in the office supply business. It now sells pens in volume to the commercial market. Paper Mate also began selling the products of Liquid Paper, a subsidiary of the same holding company as Paper Mate. Yet another example is Exxon. For years the firm has considered itself in the energy business, and not simply in petroleum. Thus, it has actively pursued geothermal, coal liquification, gas, solar, and even nuclear energy.

A related question to be asked when defining the business mission is "What do we want to be?" Answering it requires a thorough examination of the firm's technical capabilities, marketing expertise, and financial position. It also demands an understanding of trends in the external environment. The difference between what a firm is and what it wants to be is called its strategic gap.[5] This gap is the basis and impetus for examining strategic alternatives.

Developing strategic alternatives. The development of strategic alternatives requires an examination of opportunities created by new resources of the firm, such as a technological breakthrough, and changing needs in the external environment. One way to conceptualize the alternatives is through the use of a **strategic opportunity matrix** (see Figure 2.6). **Saturated markets** are those where total sales volume is not likely to increase much, regardless of marketing efforts. Examples might be soaps, black and white television, barbers and hairstylists, and soft drinks. A new product or service is going to gain market share only at the expense of an existing good or service. **Extensible markets** are those where marketing efforts can increase per capita consumption (fast food per capita consumption increased dramatically during the 1970s), or where there can be a significant increase in the number of consumers (the 1970s also saw a major increase in first-time visitors to theme parks).

If a firm decided to follow a market penetration alternative, it would try to increase market share through present product markets. If General Foods made a major push for Maxwell House coffee through aggressive advertising and cents-off coupons, it would be following a penetration strategy. In a broader

Market \ Product	EXISTING	NEW
SATURATED	Market penetration	Market development
EXTENSIBLE	Product development	Product/market diversification
NEW		Diversification

Source: Harry Henry, "Corporate Strategy, Marketing, and Diversification," in Stewart H. Britt and Harper W. Boyd, eds., *Marketing Management and Administrative Action,* 4th ed. (New York: McGraw-Hill, 1978), p. 67, Reprinted by permission.

sense, if General Foods tried to obtain a greater market share for its dry cereals or powdered drink mixes, it would be following a penetration alternative.

In market development, new missions are sought for existing products. The promotion of Arm and Hammer's baking soda as being good for deodorizing the refrigerator, healing sunburn, and cleaning the kitchen sink drain is an example. Another would be the railroads' long-term switch in emphasis from hauling people to hauling freight at low cost. In the nonprofit area, the growth of emphasis on continuing education and executive development by colleges and universities is a market development strategy.

A product development strategy in the context of the opportunity matrix is the creation of new products to replace existing ones. This is often a high-cost/low-return strategy, but there are, of course, exceptions. Such an exception may be the Bede Car. If its advertising claims are true (see Figure 2.7), it should definitely replace many existing cars.

Product/market diversification in extensible markets is one of the most common strategic alternatives. Tandem Computers defined its mission as being in the management information business. For a small company to try and compete head-on in the big computer market with IBM or the small computer market with firms such as Digital Equipment would be folly. Tandem did, however, develop a unique product that had no direct competition as of 1980. It is a "fail-safe" computer that will not lose data if any part of the system goes down. Other fail-safe computer systems require a redundant backup computer that lies idle unless the on-line system fails. Tandem's computer design allows dual central processors to share the data-processing workload and to take over the entire job should one break down. The Tandem product has been sold successfully to banks, airlines, and other types of firms where lost or interrupted data mean lost revenues. Thus, Tandem effectively offers a new product in a growing, yet highly competitive market.

The last strategy is entering a new market with a new product or service. This requires extensive planning and analysis. For example, a major manufacturer of pest control products for animals (flea collars, flea shampoos, chemicals to control diseases of tropical fish) is considering the manufacture of artificial fire logs. Most artificial logs are made of by-products and a paraffin by-product. The pesticide manufacturer's product would be coal-based, last twice as long as a product such as Duraflame, and cost about the same. As of this writing, research is still continuing and the firm has not made the final commitment.

Specifying operational task requirements. After strategic alternatives are evaluated and a course of action selected, operational task requirements must be

---

▲ **FIGURE 2.7 A new product created to replace present ones.**

Introducing the Bede Car. You could be in the driver's seat in a little more than 18 months.

Right this moment in Cleveland, there are 3 Bede Cars in the final stages of refinement. New generation cars designed to be totally energy efficient. In fact, our computer predicts you'll be able to get as much as 148 mpg at driving speeds of 55 mph. And you'll be able to buy the car for only about $8,000.

What's more, you won't sacrifice comfort or performance. The Bede Car is about the size of an intermediate automobile, but capable of luxury car performance.

How can it deliver high performance on minimum amounts of gasoline? By design. Bede Industries, the company that will produce the car, is in the business of creating and marketing energy efficient products.

By employing aerodynamic technology, principles of physics, heat recovery techniques, and the science of air-flow, we've been able to successfully launch a line of simple, yet efficient energy saving products for everyday use.

But then, innovating is the heart of our family owned company. *Bede and Avrea family members hold more than 160 U.S. patents.* And they include everything from a coolant recovery system used by automakers worldwide, to a heat and humidity transfer kit for the do-it-yourselfer.

For Bede, every problem involving energy is two-fold: reduce fuel consumption...but increase performance.

Bede uses aerodynamic design to maximize performance.

Part of the uniqueness contributing to the Bede Car's minimum fuel usage is a unique method of propulsion. A revolutionary ducted fan dramatically increases the performance of the 4-cylinder 75 H.P. engine powering the car. How! By eliminating transmission loss.

Aerodynamic design plays an important part in one of Bede's energy saving products for the home as well. The first patented device for recycling heat generated by a gas or electric clothes dryer. No one's been able to duplicate the efficiency of its design. The Bede Heat Saver has a 3-way valve that redirects warm air and moisture into your home in the winter. An average family of four can save up to $15.63 each month of the heating season. It has been proven as America's most successful energy saving product.

Bede uses the science of air flow to maximize efficiency.

To achieve a low coefficient of drag, or in layman's language, to reduce resistance, Bede engineers designed a totally innovative understructure for the car. With resistance all but eliminated, less fuel is needed for power.

In addition, a suspension system, unique to the Bede Car, dramatically reduces rolling friction, adding even more to fuel efficiency.

Two other products we've created for the home use our air flow knowledge to your advantage. The first is an easily installed reusable device that tells you when to replace the filter on your forced-air, heating/air conditioning system. When dirt builds up, it clogs the filter reducing air flow. That's when the Filter Alert™ activates—a 50% reduction of air flow makes it whistle a warning to alert you.

Our other product simply stops drafts cold. With Bede Draft Sealers,™ cold air won't enter and warm air won't escape through outlets or switchplates. They'll reduce heating and air conditioning costs $50 annually.

Saving energy can be simple, when you have the right ideas.

One of the simplest methods we've developed for recovering lost heat in your home is a small metal with a treated surface. It makes any size hot flue pipe behave like a radiator. These Bede Heat Fins can actually save you 5% of your heating dollar. You'll be able to recover 3200 BTU's of heat every hour your furnace is operating.

Energy is the source of our ideas. How to recover, redirect, re-use, and save energy can only come from understanding its basic principles. And that knowledge is what's given us the edge to make the products we do, to tool for the products on our drawing board, and to create the car.

Learn more about our car.

Come into any participating Ace or HWI dealer and get a free, detailed Bede Car brochure. You'll find it at the Bede products display. Take a serious look at our products too. You could save as much as $200 this heating season alone.

Available at fine stores nationally.

 bede industries, inc.
© Cleveland, Ohio 44144
The Bede Car is subject to further testing and development; design and performance may change as further development takes place.

Source: Courtesy of Bede Industries, Inc.

defined. This means using market segmentation to define a target market precisely. Next, a marketing mix must be created, with operational price, promotion, product/service, and distribution strategies. The marketing mix must be established in light of the company's resources and capabilities. It also must be (1) consistent—the various components must fit together to create an organized whole; and (2) properly timed—a hastily established marketing mix can be more costly than withholding the product from the market.

If a firm brings out a new line of power lawnmowers in the fall, competitors will have time to analyze the offering and counterattack when demand picks up in the spring. Moreover, dealers will be stuck with inventory through the winter months, thus creating ill-will within the distribution channel. Another example of a timing problem occurred when Kodak introduced its instant picture camera in the mid-1970s. Promotion created demand for the product, but a poor distribution strategy left dealers without inventory. Since demand for an instant camera had been created, many consumers purchased Polaroids, which were available. Kodak's advertising was selling Polaroid cameras.

Reformulation and recovery strategies. The last step in the strategic planning process is to create a set of contingency plans. **Contingency plans** take the form of "if-then" situations. If inflation increases to an annual rate of x percent, then we will do such and such. Contingency plans avoid panic decision making. Alternatives are well thought out over a period of time. United Parcel Service, for example, relies heavily on local delivery trucks as well as long distance trucks to meet its corporate mission. It has established elaborate contingency plans for a significant gasoline shortfall or gasoline rationing. The Associates, whose major business is consumer credit, has developed contingency plans to cope with growing inflation and the inflexibility of state usury laws.

In addition to basic contingency plans, management should periodically review strategies that are successful. Reasons for goal accomplishment should be delineated, and it should be determined that they still exist. If underlying success factors have changed, perhaps new success criteria have come into being, or the strategy may need to be altered.

We will return to the topic of planning in Chapter 21. Now we will look at organization, the second basic function of marketing managers.

ORGANIZATION

The organization structure provides the basis for putting plans into action. Organization helps make plans become reality. And because resources are always limited, they must be used in the most efficient manner possible. Structure can routinize activities, establish efficient work flows, and create lines of authority and responsibility. It also allows for specialization and direction. Perhaps most important, structure establishes systems such as market information that enable the firm to utilize the marketing concept effectively.

Functional structures. Unless a new company is being established, an existing structure must be modified to create a modern marketing organization. If a company had been production-oriented and organized along functional lines, its basic structure would be as shown in Figure 2.8. Note that sales and advertising are at lower levels in the corporate hierarchy than engineering, finance, and production. This type of firm produces a product based on its engineering and production knowhow and resources. It then hopes that the sales department can sell it.

Under a functional marketing-oriented structure, a marketing department is created and elevated to a status equal to that of the other functional areas. The marketing department is also organized according to its basic functions. **Functional structures** allow for specialization by areas of expertise. This structure is often used when a company first implements the marketing concept. As the firm grows, the personnel tend to become more specialized. A salesperson, for example, may call on only one type of customer. A new product development person may conduct research on only one type of product. At a major

◀ **FIGURE 2.8 Functional organization: production-oriented and marketing-oriented.**

Production-Oriented Functional Organization

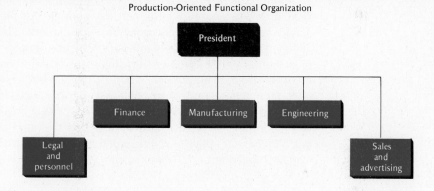

Marketing-Oriented Functional Organization

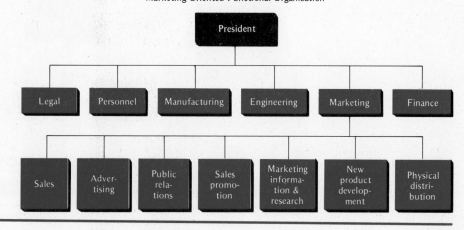

consumer goods manufacturer, one research team worked only on a soybean artificial bacon for six years.

But specialization requires coordination. Lack of coordination can result in inefficiencies and loss of market share and profits. A major copier manufacturer introduced a new line of machines in 1979. The product was thoroughly researched and based on what users said they wanted in a new line of equipment. Production lines were humming and distribution centers were stocked. The problem, however, was a lack of new product specifications for the sales training managers. In some regions, the product was available for delivery for two months before the sales force knew how to promote it. A recent study found that only 20 percent of the new products purchased by chain store buyers were on the store shelves one month later; 45 percent, two months later; and 57 percent, three months later.[6] This shows a major lack of coordination between sales and distribution departments. It wasted promotional dollars and slowed the time it took for the company to recover its new product development expenses.

Customer structure. An alternative to functional specialization is a **customer structure.** When types of customers have unique buying needs and respond in a different manner to the components of the marketing mix, a customer organization can be used, as shown in Figure 2.9. For example, a helicopter manufacturer such as Bell sells to two very different types of users. The military is interested in armor plating, guns, troop-carrying capacity, and so forth. Price is important, but secondary to battlefield performance. In the consumer area, television stations buy helicopters for rapid news coverage. Price is usually very important, as are methods of financing the purchase. The petroleum industry buys helicopters to shuttle workers back and forth to oil platforms and to explore rugged terrain. Dependability is usually the most important purchase

◢ **FIGURE 2.9 A customer marketing structure.**

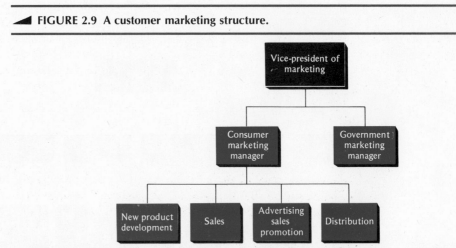

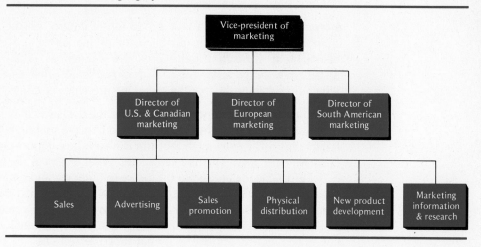

criterion for this group of buyers. If Bell's sales grow enough, the consumer group could be further segmented into petroleum and all other consumer purchasers.

Geographic organization. If a company sells on a worldwide or national basis, it may create a geographic structure. This form enables a marketing manager to react quickly to the unique needs of customers in a particular region. The geographic organization is usually used in combination with another type of structure (see Figure 2.10). A geographic structure is also commonly found within sales departments. Firms such as Procter and Gamble, R. J. Reynolds, T. J. Lipton, and Xerox employ several thousand salespersons. The geographic structure allows for a reasonable span of managerial control over the sales force. For example, a regional manager may have 10 zone managers reporting to him or her; the zone manager may be responsible for 15 district managers; and the district manager may be accountable for the work of 20 salespersons.

Several newer forms of organization such as product and venture management will be discussed in Chapters 8 and 9. We will also return to the topic in Chapter 22 to discuss organization and control.

CONTROL

The third major function of marketing management is control. The management tasks of planning and organizing cannot be effective without control, which provides the mechanism for correcting actions that are not efficient in aiding the organization to reach its objective. Without control, goal achievement becomes a hit-or-miss proposition. Even if a firm is fortunate enough to reach its goals without good controls, the chances are that some resources have been wasted. A good control system keeps marketing programs on track so that they can reach their goals within budget guidelines.

A broad perspective. In a very broad sense, control can be viewed as a restraint, curb, or regulation on behavior or marketing processes. **Marketing management control** is more precisely defined as relating to systematic measurement and revision of behavior or marketing processes. Using the broad definition, we may say that the following are types of control:

1. *Goals.* Goals influence managers and the decisions they make. Decisions are channeled into areas most likely to achieve corporate goals.
2. *Strategy.* The strategy of the firm is also a broad form of control. For example, the answer to the question "What business are we in?" defines decision-making areas, opportunity explorations, and organizational structures. If the railroads decide they are only in the railroad business, management will devote all its time and attention to "running a railroad." Individuals will not be exploring opportunities in trucking, pipelines, and so forth.
3. *Organization structure.* A formal structure restricts and guides the activities of people.
4. *Social controls.* Sometimes, informal norms and "ways of doing things" will serve as a means of informal control. At 3M Company, marketing managers traditionally never kill an idea without trying it out. The norm for a new product idea is to express the proposal in less than five pages.
5. *Financial controls.* Financial standards such as payback periods, return on investment, and desired profit margins serve as "accept-reject" controls for new projects and products.
6. *Budgets.* A key device for marketing control is budgets. Budgets limit the availability of resources to an operating unit. It is the most comprehensive device for marketing control.
7. *Schedules.* Schedules are used in sales, for example, to set the daily activities of the sales force. A schedule serves as a basis for controlling and guiding the sales force. Delivery schedules are used by distribution to determine when and how merchandise should be sent to a customer.
8. *Audits.* A traditional audit examines reported information to make certain that it was properly prepared and accurately portrays what was intended. The marketing audit is a systematic approach to appraising the overall performance of marketing management and the marketing function.

Control systems. The objective of controls and control systems is to make events conform to plans. A control system begins with marketing objectives. After plans are established, the organization structure must be created and the course of action dictated by the plan implemented. Next, performance is evaluated based on desired results. If the results are meeting the goal, the activities should be continued. If not, the degree of deviation from the standard should be examined. A large deviation necessitates a halt in the action until marketing managers can assess what is wrong. If the deviation is small, corrections can be made and activities can continue.

Montgomery Ward's strategic long-range plan called for it to fight its major competitors by entering major regional malls, carrying a wide variety of general merchandise, at prices comparable to Penney's and Sears. The overriding control standard was bottom-line profits of a certain percentage of sales. In 1979, Ward's profits fell 50 percent from the previous year. Various "minor actions" were taken to improve profitability. Yet by the end of the first half of 1980, Ward's was in the red. This called for a new strategic plan based on the major deviations from the control standard (profits).

By 1985, Ward's plans to convert about one-third of its stores into high-quality discount units. A Ward's executive vice-president notes: "We're going to be a cut above K-Mart in terms of price and service. Our closest competitor may be Target (a major discount chain)."[7] The new stores will feature fast-moving soft goods, such as clothes, towels, and sheets, and a central checkout system. In addition to the discount approach, Ward's will modernize its many old-line conventional stores to remain competitive.

The Ward's example shows how controls can signal the need for a new strategy. But a word of caution is in order. If control systems are not fully thought out by management, they can sometimes do more harm than good. Texas Instruments recently introduced a new home computer, the 99/4, that was a resounding flop in a $3 billion market. It has a full-color screen, programs that easily snap into a keyboard console, and a speech-synthesis chip that enables it to talk. The problem is that the 99/4 only plays games and helps manage household finances. The 1980 personal computer market was for machines that could solve serious problems. To do that, much more was needed than the 99/4 offered. The successful personal computer companies—Radio Shack, Apple Computer, and Commodore—have the businessperson and the professional as the target market. Texas Instruments is a classic case of failure to understand and properly segment the target market.

Where do controls come into the example? In tandem development with the 99/4 was a professional model 99/7, targeted to scientists and engineers. It was so powerful and inexpensive that it would probably have been an instant success. However, Texas Instruments is a rigidly controlled company with tight developmental budgets. There was not enough money (due to overcontrol) properly to produce and market the 99/4 and 99/7. Since the personal computer market potential in the 1980s is greater than that for professional models, funds were bled from the professional model to speed up introduction of the 99/4. The cannibalized budget of the 99/7 was not enough to bring the product to the marketplace.[8]

Another example of inflexible controls also relates to the computer industry. When IBM introduced its System 360 computer, it suffered service and maintenance problems that cost hundreds of millions of dollars to fix. The aftermath was a new and rigid control system of checks and balances for new product development. The system made IBM people so cautious that they quit taking risks. When a new president took over, one of the first actions he took to reverse that attitude was to loosen controls. He recognized that the control system would indeed prevent such an expensive problem as the System 360 from ever happening again, but its rigidity would also keep IBM from ever developing another major system.[9]

SUMMARY

Marketing can be viewed as an integrated system. A system may be defined as a set of interacting variables. It is an organized whole with units operating in unison and interacting in an interdependent manner, usually in response to some mechanism of control. The control in marketing is exercised through the marketing mix.

The marketing model consists of two major subsystems—the internal and the external. Each subsystem can limit the firm's success or provide opportunities for increased profitability. The internal system is created on the basis of the firm's marketing goals. Marketing goals, in turn, are derived from corporate objectives.

To achieve its marketing goals, the firm develops a marketing mix. The mix is constrained by both internal and external factors. Since resources are limited, they must be allocated in an optimal manner. Tradeoffs typically develop among various departments and various components of the marketing mix.

The external environment consists of two major groups—consumers and publics. Consumers are potential buyers of the company's products or service. The public (which is also a consumer) consists of employees, stockholders, governmental units, and others. Under the broadened marketing concept, the firm is expected to satisfy both its target market and the public in general.

The external environment is always changing. Several factors, most of which cannot be controlled by the firm, initiate and influence change. The firm must anticipate changes in these factors and determine what impacts these changes will have on it. If necessary, it should modify the marketing mix. The firm's long-run survival is predicated upon its successful adaptation of the marketing mix to meet continuing changes in the external environment.

Successful implementation of the marketing mix requires sound management. Marketing management is the planning, organizing, and controlling of marketing activities to help the firm achieve its objectives. Decision making takes place in two environments—short range and long range. Strategic decisions affect the long-run competitive position or perhaps the survival of the firm. A strategic decision guides the extended use of the firm's resources based upon existing and projected internal capabilities and long-range changes in the external environment. Strategic planning involves determining the business mission, developing strategic alternatives, specifying operational task requirements, and reformulation of recovery strategies.

A second basic function of marketing management is organization. Organization helps make planning become reality. Some common marketing organization structures are functional, customer, and geographic.

The third major function of marketing management is control. Control provides a mechanism for correcting actions that are not efficient in aiding the marketing organization reach its objective. Without control, goal achievement is uncertain. Effective control requires a good system. Such a system helps marketing managers spot major deviations from standards and aids in determining what corrective actions need to be taken.

KEY TERMS

System
Internal subsystem
External subsystem
Target market
Market segmentation
Market grid
Tradeoff
Marketing management
Tactical planning

Strategic planning
Strategic opportunity matrix
Saturated market
Extensible market
Contingency plans
Functional structure
Customer structure
Marketing management control

REVIEW QUESTIONS

1. Why is control of the marketing mix important?
2. What are the components of the marketing mix?
3. List and briefly define the external factors that affect marketing.
4. What is marketing management?
5. What is strategic planning?
6. Why is the organization function of the marketing manager so vital?
7. What is the objective of a system of controls?

DISCUSSION QUESTIONS

1. Explain the marketing model.
2. Give some examples of social goals for the following types of firms:
   a. Automobile manufacturer.
   b. Fast-food industry.
   c. Nonprofit hospital.
   d. Oil company.
   e. Television (broadcasting).
   f. University.
3. Why are tradeoffs in the marketing mix necessary?
4. Briefly explain the strategic marketing planning process.
5. Compare and contrast the functional marketing-oriented structure with the production-oriented structure.
6. Describe the role of the marketing mix in the marketing system. How does it help a firm implement the marketing concept?
7. Briefly discuss a firm's internal marketing environment. Explain the relationships that can develop between different departments in attempting to achieve company goals. Use examples to illustrate your answer.

NOTES

1. This excerpt is from Bow Uttal, "Selling Is No Longer Mickey Mouse at AT&T," *Fortune,* July 17, 1978, pp. 98–104.
2. The Bubble Yum story is from "Bubble Yum Not about to Gum Up Works," *Advertising Age,* July 28, 1980, p. 10.

3. The section on strategic planning is taken from "The Strategic Marketing Management Process," in Roger A. Kerin and Robert A. Peterson, *Perspectives on Strategic Marketing Management* (Boston: Allyn and Bacon, 1980), pp. 4–10.
4. Ibid.
5. Ibid.
6. "Marketing Newsletter," *Sales and Marketing Management,* June 18, 1979, p. 35.
7. "Mobil Helps an Ailing Ward into Discounting," *Business Week,* July 14, 1980, p. 39.
8. The 99/4 story is from Bro Uttal, "T.I.'s Home Computer Can't Get in the Door," *Fortune,* June 16, 1980, pp. 139–140.
9. Thomas J. Peters, "Putting Excellence into Management," *Business Week,* July 21, 1980, p. 205.

◢ CASES

2.1 American Home Products

American Home Products (AHP) produces some of the best-known consumer goods in the United States. Among them are Dristan, Anacin, Woolite, Easy-Off, Black Flag insecticides, Old English furniture polish, Preparation-H, Chef Boy-Ar-Dee, Sani Flush, and Wizard air fresheners. More important, during the past decade, its return on equity has topped 30 percent—a rate exceeded in the drug industry by only one firm.

American Home Products is unusual in that it is tightly controlled by a single individual, William LaPort, the chief executive officer. Mr. LaPort has placed very little emphasis on long-run strategic planning. Instead, his strategy focuses on current financial results. "We have no long-range strategy," LaPort says. "Our vision, our plan is for whatever period is necessary. We have nothing beyond a one-year budget but hope." In contrast, long-range planning, and particularly the constant updating of projections of investment spending, is a major consideration at firms like Procter and Gamble.

American Home Products seems to emphasize financial discipline and risk aversion. Mr. LaPort, for example, personally approves virtually all expenditures of more than $500, including such outlays as a typewriter and a secretarial pay raise. The only area in which American Home Products spends extensively is for advertising. The company prefers to spend primarily on established products with significant market shares. AHP believes it is easier to generate additional sales and earnings out of the advertising dollar that way than to invest big advertising dollars in new products. AHP appears willing to allow competitors to test and improve the viability of undeveloped markets before it enters. For example, AHP introduced a rug deodorizer in 1979 only after S. C. Johnson and Sterling Drug, along with Airwick, had done the innovating.

The future presents some interesting challenges. Foreign drug manufacturers are expanding aggressively in the United States. Important new scientific discoveries are dramatically increasing drug research productivity. New products are grabbing the market share away from Anacin and Dristan, American Home's two best-selling over-the-counter drugs. Also, the company seems to be suffering from a lack of successful new products.

1. Obviously, American Home Products has been very successful without formal strategic planning. Do you feel that AHP can continue with this course of action? Why or why not?
2. Does American Home Products have an informal strategic plan, perhaps carried strictly in the mind of the chief executive officer? Why? If you were going to help American Home Products implement a strategic plan, what steps would you recommend?

2.2 Shiner Brewery

Shiner is the third smallest brewery in the United States. It produces less than 75,000 barrels of beer a year. The company has actually doubled its production since 1968, but it isn't planning on getting big. Speedy Beale, the company's sales manager, explains that the brewery just can't manufacture much more and isn't interested in expansion. Most of Shiner's sales are in small towns in south-central Texas, although its beer is available in Dallas and at scattered locations such as Austin, Houston, and San Antonio.

The town of Shiner got its name from the rancher, H. B. Shiner, who donated 250 acres to the town in 1887 provided that it be named after him. The brewery was begun in 1909 and continues to operate much the way it did then. Its sales efforts consist of sending salespeople out on the road to spend a week with each beer distributor. Their sales pitch is a smile, a handshake, and a bottle of beer.

Shiner doesn't have an advertising agency. Nor does it have a consolidated advertising theme. It uses different approaches in different areas. The most often heard claim about Shiner is that it is a natural beer, brewed pure and simple with loving care that bigger breweries cannot put into their products. The brewery itself looks like a Spanish mission that has been turned into a factory. At one side there's a stand-up bar where visitors and a grateful group of locals can regularly sample the product for which the town is famous. Sometimes as many as 150 people take at least one draught here during an afternoon. The employees mix with the crowd from time to time, standing around with their plastic cups of Shiner like members of the family at a wedding reception.

Originally the beer was brewed darker and heavier than it is now. Then the brewmaster decided Americans wanted a lighter beer. Today he alone determines the nature of the product produced. Even during the changeover Shiner didn't lose all of the older drinkers who had grown up with its product. The brewmaster believes they are loyal to the label. Apparently a lot of Texans have more affection for the company than for heavier lager beer.

Shiner is made from artesian well water, barley malt, hops, and corn grits. This is a pretty standard list of ingredients. However, Shiner brews the beer for 30 days in contrast to the major breweries, which take only 7 to 10 days. Also, many larger breweries use substitutes such as fortified corn rather than real grits.

Seventy percent of Shiner's business is in returnable long-necked bottles, the kind that went out with pop-tops and came back in Texas in the 1970s. At Shiner long-necks never really went out.

1. Does Shiner have the marketing concept? If not, what advantages might accrue to the firm from adopting the concept? How might one establish the concept there?
2. Take each of the external variables that might affect a firm and discuss how each might affect Shiner.

3

The environment of marketing

OBJECTIVES

To gain further insight into the external environment of marketing.

To learn about the social factors that affect marketing.

To become aware of demographic trends.

To understand the relationship of law and politics to marketing.

To learn consumer and marketer responses to the state of the economy.

To become aware of trends in technology.

To gain an understanding of foreign and domestic competition.

Take a simple thing like breakfast. Not many years ago, millions of mothers felt duty-bound to cook a nourishing hot breakfast for their children. Today, they ask "Why suffer?" Increasingly, they find it morally acceptable to feed their children quickie breakfasts, or even to let them fend for themselves.

This may be ghastly news to America's nutritionists, but it is dandy news for companies that make instant breakfasts. Tracking the social changes that affect business demand keeps a staff of researchers busy at Yankelovich, Skelly & White, Inc., the Madison Avenue public opinion and market research concern. Working for 96 sponsoring companies, including General Electric and Procter & Gamble, Yankelovich puts numbers on seemingly nebulous trends ranging from "tolerance for chaos and disorder" to "social pluralism," "living for today," and "focus on self."

Yankelovich's Monitor project each year asks 2500 people nationwide about, say, how important they think it is to plan in advance and how much they enjoy doing things on the spur of the moment. To get the detailed data on such trends, Monitor sponsors pay about $15,000 per year. Another service, called Corporate Priorities, examines how much the public and a cross section of the leadership community really care about controlling air pollution, regulating business, and other public demands. One obvious value is to show its 30 sponsoring corporations which issues they must seriously address—and which they can safely ignore.

Yankelovich, Skelly & White provide a valuable service to many of America's largest corporations. They serve as one source of input into the firm's marketing intelligence system by monitoring social trends. This chapter will better acquaint you with each of the external environment factors introduced in Chapter 2 (see Figure 3.1).

◄ FIGURE 3.1 The external environment of marketing.

Understanding the environment

Before we examine individual factors, a few comments about the external environment are in order. First and foremost, the external environment must be understood. Unless it understands the external environment, the firm cannot plan because it does not know how it got in its present position and what forces will influence its future. Understanding the environment helps a firm not only to alter its present marketing mix, but to identify new opportunities as well. The makers of Sweet n Low artificial sweetener understood America's preoccupation with weight consciousness. This led to the development of Butter Buds, a butter substitute with no calories or fat. Texas Instruments was aware of the great value affluent young American families placed on educational toys for their children. TI utilized its technology to produce "Speak and Spell," a learning aid that helps children spell. In the early 1980s TI has had difficulty meeting the demand for the toy, despite a relatively high price.

The external environment is always changing. Think for a moment about how attitudes and values have changed since your childhood. Recall products that were really "in" that are shunned today. If the external environment were static, the need for an information system would be dramatically lessened. A one-time study could be undertaken, and a marketing mix could then be developed. But this is simply wishful thinking. A product that is in demand today may be ignored tomorrow due to technology, natural resource shortages, or changing economic conditions.

All these external factors cannot be controlled by marketing managers. Even so, they are extremely relevant to marketing planning and decision making. Strategic marketing planning for *The New York Times* requires an understanding of the technology of electronic newspaper production. The Yankelovich studies would help the *Times* better understand people's attitudes and values and thus determine the structure and format of the paper. For example, knowledge of attitudes toward leisure and the importance of self-development will aid in selecting the number and type of articles pertaining to these subjects.

But even though *The New York Times* is one of the nation's most widely read newspapers, it cannot significantly influence social or any other type of change in the external environment. No one business is large or powerful enough to create change. Marketing managers are basically adapters rather than fundamental agents of change. For example, the giants of the domestic automotive industry did not adapt quickly enough to changes in the late 1970s and paid a huge premium in lost sales and profits.

Social factors

Social change is perhaps the most difficult external variable for marketing managers to forecast and integrate into marketing plans. Whereas there are hundreds (perhaps thousands) of economic forecasters, there are very few firms analyzing and forecasting social trends. We have to depend largely on our knowledge of the past and on what we can see happening around us. Let us look at some of the more obvious trends and forces.

CHANGING VALUES

During America's first 150 years, four basic values strongly influenced attitudes and life styles.[1] The first was self-sufficiency: every person stood on his or her own two feet. The second was upward mobility: if you did the right thing, success would come. Next came the Protestant ethic: hard work, dedication to family, and frugality. The fourth value was conformity. No one wanted to stick out like a sore thumb; being different was not a desirable trait.

The last half-century, most noticeably after World War II, has been a period of upheaval in traditional values and attitudes. Economic growth, population growth, perceived abundant resources, and other factors resulted in a new social climate after World War II. This, in turn, led to new values. Advanced technology and widespread education resulted in antifunctionalism. Americans were beginning to question the emphasis on the material, the empirical, and the scientific in their society. Advanced technology and population growth, resultant crowding and urban decay led to a reaction against complexity. Some of the values that had their genesis after World War II have become pervasive. Two of the most important for marketing management are the continual decline of the Protestant ethic and an increase in self-orientation. Another key social change of the 1960s and 1970s has been in attitudes toward the family.

THE DYING PROTESTANT ETHIC

The Protestant ethic stresses self-sacrifice, self-denial, living for tomorrow as opposed to today, sacrificing today for future rewards, and service to others. The idea was to work long and hard and save for a rainy day. A person's job was supposed to be the major source of fulfillment, and leisure activities were viewed in a negative manner. George Bernard Shaw wrote: "Perpetual holiday is a good working definition of hell."

Today the old Protestant ethic is virtually dead. In 1979 only 13 percent of the adults polled in a nationwide survey found their work truly meaningful and more important to them than leisure pursuits.[2] Managers often say, "People aren't willing to work as hard as they used to." There are several reasons for this change.

1. The fear factor has declined in our society. The fear of unemployment, starvation, or not being able to keep one's family together has declined due to a host of social programs.
2. Automation and assembly lines tend to minimize the importance of worker motivation.
3. In periods of high inflation, it is difficult to use money as a motivator.[3]

What does this mean for the marketing manager? With the decline in work as a person's primary means of self-identification, new life styles began to emerge. In the 1950s, for example, if a person was a banker this defined his or her life style. Today a person can be a banker and also a gourmet, fitness buff, dedicated single parent, and conservationist. Each of these life styles has different goods and services associated with it. Each represents a target audience. For example, for the gourmet, marketers offer cooking utensils, wines, and exotic foods. This market is reached through *Bon Apetit, Gourmet,* and similar magazines. The banker-fitness buff also buys Adidas equipment, special jogging outfits, and reads *Runner* magazine.

As the importance of work has declined, attitudes toward leisure have also changed. In today's society, the pursuit of leisure is completely acceptable. It is all right to go skiing, play golf, bowl, or just stay home and relax. This has opened up countless opportunities for astute marketing firms. AMF's slogan is "We make weekends." The firm produces bowling equipment, motorcycles, sailboats, fishing gear, and other leisure products. Leisure does not have to be sold. The firm no longer has to convince the consumer that it is all right to have some spare time and then sell the leisure-oriented good or service. Today's marketer can concentrate on marketing the product or service.

THE SELF-ORIENTATION

Closely related to the decline of the Protestant ethic is the growth of a self-orientation, what is sometimes called "the age of me." It is the age of self-interest: "I want to be me," "I'll do it my way," "Looking out for number one." The drive for self-fulfillment puts service to self ahead of service to others. It says live for today instead of tomorrow.

One result of this orientation is the remarkable change of attitudes toward marriage and divorce. Nearly one out of two first marriages now end in divorce. This means more single-person households, with corresponding needs for shelter, durable goods, and even single-oriented entertainment. Changing attitudes toward marriage and divorce have also dramatically altered family decision making. There are more individual decisions rather than group decisions. Moreover, children are being given decision-making responsibilities at an earlier age. Marketing mixes for some children's foods, toys, clothing, and athletic equipment have been altered to appeal more directly to the young decision makers.

The "age of me" has also meant changes in the nonprofit sector. Charities now have a much harder time raising money, and there has been a decline in volunteerism. There has also been a decline in voter participation. These changes in people's attitudes have been major factors in the growing utilization of the marketing concept in the nonprofit sector. Americans have been less willing to donate their time, money, and energy to charitable causes, yet they expect more from society's institutions. This phenomenon is called the **psychology of entitlement.** Instead of saying "I should take care of my health," people are saying "*They* should take care of my health." This places new and additional burdens on institutions and shifts certain types of responsibilities to institutions and away from individuals. For example, the drive for a national health care plan would shift responsibility from you and me to a governmental body. This would have profound effects on private health care marketers.

The early 1980s also produced a decline in the perceived importance of some social issues. Concern about other people, the cities, minorities, the environment, and the poor is much less. In contrast, concern about things like pensions, benefits in the workplace, adequacy of social security, and national health insurance for me—not the poor—is rising.[4] Ultimately public attitudes and feelings are codified into government legislation that reallocates resources from the private sector to the public sector or within the public sector. As resources are shifted, the desirability of specific market targets also changes. A relaxation of environmental pollution standards, for example, would have a negative effect on sales and profits of manufacturers of pollution control equipment.

The "age of me" has other marketing implications:

1. The emphasis on individuality has produced less peer pressure to conform. Thus, promotions with the theme of "buy this product because everyone else does" will be less effective. But commercials exploiting the drive for personal success are quite acceptable.
2. The demand for customized products and a wider variety of merchandise has increased. This decreases the economies of mass production and can create major inventory problems. Sneakers and tennis shoes were either

white or blue for many years; today there are hundreds of styles and colors to choose from.

3. People will pay more for personal care products (goods that perform a personal service or make a personal statement). They will spend more time selecting them because value is being added in terms of their life styles.

4. Brands will be selected to fit the "me image" a person is attempting to project. A "macho cowboy" may drive a Ford pickup, smoke Marlboros, drink Miller beer, wear boot-cut Levis, and absolutely refuse to wear jewelry unless it is a small trinket in his cowboy hat. Even though a product performs satisfactorily, it still must answer the question, "Is this brand the most appropriate for me?"

5. Promises of convenience in product or service promotion are acceptable. There is nothing wrong with doing things the easy way.[5] Doing things the easy way also means that more products which used to be considered luxuries are now viewed as necessities (see Figure 3.2).

◀ **FIGURE 3.2 Percentage of men who believed a product/service was a necessity.**

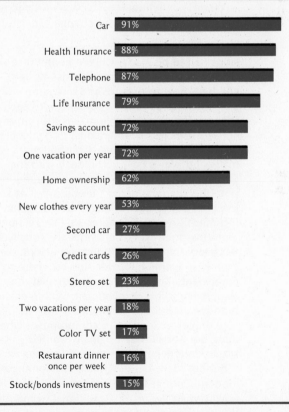

Results are from a nationwide Lou Harris survey commissioned by Playboy Enterprises.
Source: Bob Arnold, "MT Observer," *Marketing Times,* May–June, 1979, p. 3. MT, business update for the management professional, is published by Sales and Marketing Executives International.

THE CHANGING ROLE OF FAMILIES AND WORKING WOMEN

A third major social phenomenon that has had a profound effect on marketing is the changing role of families. The most important aspect from a marketing perspective is the huge growth in the number of working women. Part of this change is due to the decline of the Protestant ethic and the growing interest in self-fulfillment. Another factor, particularly in lower socioeconomic groups, is monetary need. In higher socioeconomic groups, money is also an important consideration so that the family can lead the kind of life style to which it aspires.

Today more than half of all women work. Compared with 1970, more women now have:

1. Moved into middle management in many companies that had no women there previously.
2. Moved further up the ladder in many companies where women had already achieved middle-management status.
3. Made the jump into at least the lower rungs of top management in some of America's largest companies.[6]

When women entered the workforce in mass, the "traditional family" began to change. Some of these changes are discussed below:

Within the traditional arrangement, there were areas where decisions had to be made. Chief among these were how to use the money the husband earned (consumption), when to stop having children, how to nurture and discipline children, and what leisure activities should be pursued with each other, children, kin, friends. The working wife makes those formerly long-standing consensuses less spontaneous, more problematic, and less common than they once were. Consequently, decisions have to be made and issues have to be dealt with that rarely had to be grappled with before. These newly emerging decisions exist at both the "general policy" level as well as at the more specific level of "policy outworking." At the "policy level," the issues include: Can a couple agree that she is now a coprovider with him—that their work behaviors are equally significant and interchangeable? At the "policy outworking level," take, for instance, so elemental a decision as where to live. In traditional arrangements, there was consensus that the couple lived as near as possible to his employment. Within egalitarian settings where both are employed, a complex set of negotiations (i.e., give and take processes leading to compromises where each gets something but not all they originally wanted); now it becomes requisite to determine if they should live nearer to his or her job.

Besides there being virtually no nonnegotiable issues among modern (younger) marriages, there is also the critical question of how women negotiate. Traditional women tend to negotiate with their husbands and try to persuade him to compromise on the basis of collective interests—what is best for the family group, for their marital relationship, for the children. Modern women tend to negotiate more in terms of their own individualistic interests — "my husband should change because it is best for me."[7]

The decline of commitment to the homemaker and mother roles as the only outlet for women has important marketing implications. Products that reduce time in handling routine household chores, new advertising themes, and new market segments, such as the young career woman, are suggested by this phenomenon. The whole concept of a woman as a homemaker is being reexamined. For example, a mail order consultant estimates that "11 billion hours of shopping time worth about $55 billion of retail value have been dislocated as a result of U.S. women entering the work force. Because more women are working instead of shopping, it is the greatest mail-order bonanza of all."[8]

Research has also shown very distinct consumption patterns among working females. They obviously enjoy garbage disposals, eating out, ready-to-wear clothes, and other goods and services that save time. Beyond this, however, is a whole different life style and the requisite goods and services utilized by many working women. In the grocery area, for example, consumption differences are much greater than just heavier use of convenience foods (see Table 3.1). These women entertain more, dress better, buy less children's food, and so forth.

Demographic factors

Although social variables are extremely important for marketing managers, they are no more significant than demographic factors. **Demography** is the study of vital statistics concerning such things as ages, births, deaths, and locations of people. The basis for any mass market is people. By 1984, there will be about 230 million consumers in the United States.[9] While this may be heartening to some marketers, it does not tell the entire story. The percentage increase in population has been falling since 1950. It is expected to rise slightly until 1985, and then begin to fall again. We are fast moving toward **zero population growth (ZPG).** This means that the average woman of childbearing age is expected to bear fewer than 2.1 children during her lifetime, and that this will not produce the two children required to replace herself and her husband, because some children will die before reaching adolescence.[10] And there have been other demographic changes as well.

ONE-PERSON HOUSEHOLDS

An interesting phenomenon discovered in the 1980 census was the dramatic increase in the number of one-person households. From 1970 to 1980 the total number of households increased by 26 percent, yet total population increased by only 8 percent. This helped reduce the average size of the household from 3.14 persons in 1970 to 2.78 persons in 1980.[11] One out of every four house-

TABLE 3.1 Product Profile for Full-Time Working Women (Incidence of Usage Compared to All Women)

	High usage		Low usage
Health & beauty aids			
Eye makeup	+55%	Buttermilk	−41%
Face makeup	+48%	Dry starch	−37%
Tampons	+44%	Disposable diapers	−32%
Lipstick and lipgloss	+34%	Infant foods	−31%
Nail polish	+32%	Soap/detergent for	
Hairspray	+30%	baby diapers	−26%
Deodorants and anti-		Instant powdered	
perspirants	+27%	puddings	−26%
Creme hair rinse	+21%	Scouring pads	−24%
Hair conditioners	+18%	Metal polish	−23%
Wine		Flavored gelatin	
Imported dinner table		desserts	−23%
wines	+41%	Cake mixes	−23%
Sangria	+41%	Strained or junior	
Champagne, cold duck,		baby food	−23%
sparkling burgundy	+36%	Bathroom cleaners	−22%
Pop/party wines	+19%	Window cleaners	−22%
Domestic table wines	+15%	Brown sugar	−21%
Other		Whipped topping	−21%
Cellophane tape	+56%	Meat extenders	−20%
Chewing gum	+46%	Scouring powder	−20%
Frozen vegetables		Tomato and	
(prepared with sauce)	+34%	vegetable juice	−19%
Canned cat food	+34%	Pretzels	−19%
Colas and other		Honey	−18%
carbonated drinks	+30%	All purpose	
Diet margarine	+25%	household cleaners	−18%
Packaged moist dog food	+19%	Snack/spread cheese	−18%
Frozen pastries	+18%	Flour	−17%
Fresh milk		Canned spaghetti	
(skimmed low fat)	+17%	and macaroni	−15%
Plastic sandwich		Dry milk	−15%
or food bags	+15%	Instant or freeze-	
Soap/detergent for		dried coffee	−15%
fine fabrics	+14%		
Boneless packaged ham	+14%		

Source: Target Group Index, 1977.

holds in 1980 consisted of persons living alone or with nonrelatives (a 66 percent increase since 1970).[12] This change is partly due to an increase in women 65 years or older living alone and young women remaining single longer.

A NEW POPULATION AGE MIX

As total population growth slows, some age categories will continue to increase in size (see Figure 3.3). In other words, the **population age mix** will

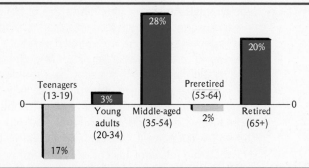

Source: U.S. Bureau of the Census, *Projections of the Population of the United States: 1977 to 2050,* Series P-25, No. 704, and Series P-20, No. 800.

change. A large number of women will reach their prime childbearing years by 1985, causing a dramatic increase in the number of children born. This is good news to marketing managers who cater to the infant segment of the population.

The new mass market. As the children born during the post-World War II "baby boom" get older, the largest single market will shift from teenagers to people in their late twenties. The average age in 1985 will be 32 years.[13] Unlike the huge teenage market of the 1960s and early 1970s, the mass market of the 1980s will consist of more mature, self-confident consumers. To the U.S. Forest Service, this older population means a decreasing emphasis on skiing and hunting. Half of all waterfowl hunters are under 25 years old, and two-thirds are under 35. With fewer teenagers in sight, Blue Bell, Inc., is putting more emphasis on jeans that are "cut for the more mature figure." Coca-Cola is another company that is changing in anticipation of a changing population mix.

Revlon, Inc., is pitching its formerly teenage-oriented Natural Wonder cosmetics line to a broader "13-to-40" audience and using older models to promote it. Procter and Gamble has decided the aged population is large enough to test-market disposable diapers for incontinent adults. The "heavy users" of soft drinks are teens and pre-teens, who comprise a shrinking market. Consequently, Coca-Cola decided to alter its product mix to follow the growing 25-to-35-year-old market. It purchased Taylor California Wines and is currently marketing wine as aggressively as soft drinks. Splashy advertisements featuring comparative taste tests and testimonials about the quality of Taylor wines were unheard of until Coke came on the scene.

The elderly market. A second major population group that continues to grow at a remarkable rate is older people. There are now 44 million Americans over 55 years old.[14] This figure will continue to grow through the end of this century and the early part of the next. The general rise in the number of births in the twentieth century largely accounts for the rapid increase in the number of elderly people. Moreover, as medical care continues to improve, the life span of the average American lengthens.

Elderly consumers are a special market. They require more medical attention and purchase many leisure-related products. The travel, entertainment, and recreation industries will be major beneficiaries of the growth of this market, and the demand for retirement homes should also increase. Many older people have relatively low current incomes but large amounts of acquired assets. Thus buying a home for retirement is not a problem for many retirees. It is also a commonly held misconception that most elderly people live below the poverty level. The Department of Commerce claims that only 9 percent of those over 55 years old fall into this category.[15] In other words, over 90 percent of the elderly are not poor.

The growth of the elderly market segment has not gone unnoticed by marketing managers. For example in the media area, there is a new magazine, *Prime Time,* targeted to persons over 45 years old; and a cable network, the Cineamerica Satellite Network, with programs to viewers over 50 years of age. As one marketer put it: "We've been ignoring a market almost twice as large as the total population of Canada. Some firms like Clairol have noticed the potential of the market. They promote Silk and Silver hair coloring with an attractive older model, using the theme 'Free, Grey, and 51.'"

POPULATION CONCENTRATIONS

From the young to the very old, America is a nation on the move. But before we look at migration patterns, let us examine the current situation. A **standard metropolitan statistical area (SMSA)** is a city or group of cities with a population of at least 50,000. The SMSA includes the county containing the city or cities and contiguous counties that are economically and socially integrated into the primary county. Today there are over 250 SMSAs containing about 70 percent of the nation's population.

SMSAs are essentially integrated trade areas. They were developed in order to more closely approximate the purchasing power and life styles of a geographic area. In a SMSA a central city, such as Chicago, is surrounded by bedroom communities that are still part of the greater Chicago market. Some SMSAs are losing large numbers of consumers while others are growing by leaps and bounds. Since 1970 the population of the booming Southeast and Southwest (the Sunbelt) has grown six times as fast as that of the Great Lakes regions and ten times as fast as that of the combined Mideast and New England regions (see Figure 3.4).[16]

During the 1960s the major movements were of middle-class whites to the South and low-income blacks to the North. The flows were approximately equal in each direction, with the South experiencing only a small increase. Since 1970, however, dramatic increases in economic activity have brought the outflow of people from the South and Southwest to a virtual halt and accelerated the flow of people into those regions.

Migration tends to shift income concentrations, and this creates new markets

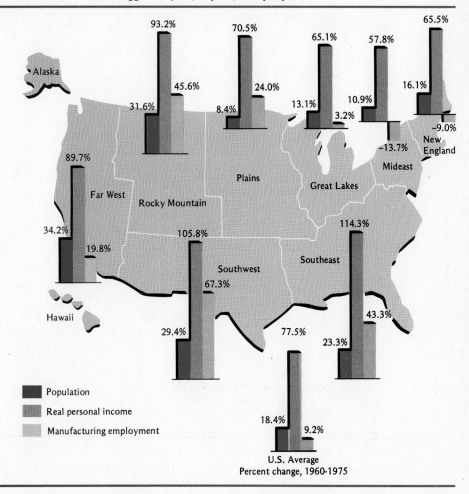

and destroys old ones. As new markets develop, retailers pour in to serve the region. Manufacturing also follows population flows, creating more new jobs and further stimulating immigration. A rapidly expanding tax base often means that tax rates can be stabilized, making the area even more attractive. The reverse is true in areas that are losing population.

THE ROLE OF MONEY

A population, regardless of its concentration, must have purchasing power to be attractive to the marketer. Americans' incomes are continually rising. More families and individuals can afford the "good life" as **disposable (after-tax) in-**

Type of product	1960	Percent	1970	Percent	1979	Percent
TSH total consumption	324.9		618.8		1,509.8	
Food, beverages, and tobacco	88.0	27.1	147.1	23.8	321.3	21.3
Purchased meals	17.2	5.3	31.5	5.1	76.0	5.0
Food (excl. alcoholic beverages)	20.5	21.7	118.6	19.2	267.9	17.7
Alcoholic beverages	10.6	3.3	17.7	2.9	34.2	2.3
Tobacco	6.9	2.1	10.8	1.7	19.2	1.3
Clothing, accessories, jewelry	32.2	9.9	55.6	9.0	117.5	7.8
Women's and children's	14.4	4.4	25.1	4.1	54.5	3.6
Men's and boys'	7.7	2.4	13.6	2.2	28.8	1.9
Jewelry and watches	1.9	0.6	4.1	0.7	10.3	0.7
Shoes, incl. cleaning, repair	4.7	1.4	8.0	1.3	16.1	1.1
Personal care	5.2	1.6	10.9	1.8	20.3	1.3
Housing	48.1	14.8	94.0	15.2	241.5	16.0
Household operations	46.1	14.2	87.8	14.2	219.5	14.5
Furniture, equip., and supplies	22.2	6.8	44.1	7.1	99.1	6.6
Electricity	5.1	1.6	9.9	1.6	32.2	2.1
Gas	3.3	1.0	5.6	0.9	16.6	1.1
Telephone and telegraph	4.5	1.4	10.1	1.6	25.5	1.7
Domestic service	3.8	1.2	5.1	0.8	8.3	0.6
Medical care expenses	20.0	6.1	49.9	8.1	146.8	9.7
Personal business	14.2	4.4	31.3	5.1	82.2	5.4
Transportation	42.4	13.1	78.0	12.6	212.2	14.1
User-operated transportation	39.1	12.0	72.5	11.7	200.5	13.3
Purchased transportation	3.3	1.0	5.5	0.9	11.7	0.8
Recreation	17.9	5.5	41.0	6.6	101.0	6.7
Private education and research	3.7	1.1	9.9	1.6	23.5	1.6
Religious and welfare activities	4.9	1.5	8.5	1.4	19.2	1.3
Foreign travel and other, net	2.1	0.6	4.7	0.8	4.8	0.3
Percent of total					**100.0**	

Source: U.S. Bureau of the Census, *Statistical Abstract of the United States, 1980* (Washington, D.C., 1980), p. 442.

comes rise. Most important, the number of poor families will continue to decline throughout the next decade (see Table 3.2). New consumption patterns will develop as people move from low incomes to moderate wealth and others from moderate incomes to even higher socioeconomic classes.

The upper middle income group ($25,000–$50,000) will grow faster than any other during the 1980s. The main reason is the growing number of households with more than one wage earner. The number of households with incomes of $25,000 or more, measured in constant dollars, will increase by 70 percent in this decade, or three and a half times as rapidly as total households.[17] By 1990 this group will account for roughly one-third of all U.S. households. But it is becoming increasingly difficult for families to achieve upper middle income status without both spouses working.

The ramifications of changing income groups are important for marketing managers. Retailers in New York City and Chicago detect a movement of affluent young couples back toward the center city. They attribute it to the energy crisis and to dual career, childless families. Each spouse, faced with a commute, wants to minimize travel time to have more time together. Mr. Seymour/Martinique, a manufacturer of high-fashion footwear, expects strong growth because of greater family incomes and increased need for status footwear. Pittsburgh-based Ryan Homes, Inc., one of the country's largest homebuilders, plans to build more luxury townhouses for the upper middle income market. The firm plans to build homes with more conveniences and a study or game room instead of an additional bedroom. Ryan Homes' research found that many of the two-income families have decided to have no children. Marketers must reexamine their market targets and their marketing mix as more families can afford "the good life" and the number of lower-income families declines.

Growing patterns of affluence are creating important changes in consumer spending patterns. The largest portion of an American income goes for food, beverages, and tobacco (see Table 3.2). Housing and household furnishings claim the next largest outlays, followed by transportation. As you can see, a large amount of money is spent on basics—food, shelter, and transportation. Did you realize, however, that Americans spend almost as much money on recreation as on clothing.

Trends in consumption expenditures are important for forecasting future levels of demand. They also help identify new growth opportunities and even markets that should be avoided. Clothing and personal care items and services have commanded a shrinking share of the consumer's dollar since 1960. This is also true for food, beverages, and tobacco. On the other hand, medical care and transportation expenses are taking a bigger portion of our budgets.

CHANGING MINORITY MARKETS

Minority markets are growing during the 1980s, but they are also becoming more diverse. Because of their higher birth rates, blacks will increase faster than the total population. By 1990 blacks will number 29.8 million and comprise 12.6 percent of the population.[18] As a market, blacks will become sharply divided into several groups. There is a relatively small but growing group that is educated, affluent, and leaving the central cities for the suburbs. The typical black executive is a 43-year-old male vice-president or manager who earns $40,000 or more annually and works 55 hours a week at a billion-dollar industrial corporation, probably in the East or Midwest. Black executives' jobs are likely to be in sales and marketing (20.6%), personnel (16.6%), finance, accounting, and auditing (14.2%), general management (13.9%), and manufacturing (9.1%).[19]

Blacks now constitute more than half of the population of five major cities and between 40 and 50 percent in eight other cities. This concentration creates a market that is physically accessible. There are some obvious advantages in marketing to a concentrated consumer group rather than one that is physically dispersed.

A few general differences between black and white consumption patterns are as follows:

Black families purchase substantially more of the following products than white: cooked cereals, corn meal, cream, rice, spaghetti, frozen vegetables, syrup, vinegar, and others.

Depending on the study read, blacks purchase more Scotch than any other market segment with one report stating the figure to be one-half of the total Scotch consumption.

Other products consumed more by blacks than by whites include floor waxes, household insecticides, toilet and laundry soap, and so on.

Whites spend more than blacks of similar income for such products as food, housing, medical care, auto transportation, and insurance, while blacks spend more for such products as clothing and home furnishings, while saving more. The spending for recreation and leisure of blacks and whites of similar incomes is mixed.[20]

Another major minority demographic change will be the continued growth of the Hispanic population, which will soon rival the size of the black market. As a result, Spanish-language media will continue to grow as effective means of reaching this market. There are three basic submarkets in the Spanish-speaking community. There is the Puerto Rican segment in the greater New York area, the Cuban community in Florida, and the Mexican-American population across the Southwest and in the Los Angeles area.

Like the black market, Spanish-speaking consumers require a unique marketing mix. In New York, for example, there are unique differences in retailing in Spanish neighborhoods. Grocery and personal care shopping is about equally divided between supermarkets and *bodegas*. A *bodega* is the small local store where only Spanish is spoken. It is a neighborhood institution that often provides such services as check cashing, credit extensions, loans, and the translation of documents into English and vice versa. The *bodega* is the communications center for the community. It is the proving ground for any new brand, whether sold in supermarkets or not. The bodega does not carry more than two brands of most items due to the size of the store, so competition for shelf space is keen.

A Pepsi Challenge is a Pepsi Challenge is a Pepsi Challenge — but only if it's in English. Selling the stuff to a widely diversified Hispanic population is another matter altogether.
In New York, the intention was to run the "Catch that Pepsi spirit" campaign, in Spanish, on Spanish TV. It would have been a disaster. "You can't use that slogan in the Spanish market," says an account manager involved in the Pepsi campaign, "because the spirit relates to something dead." ("The Pepsi ghost" might be a fair translation.)
Instead, the agency came up with "Pepsi Saluda," a series of TV spots featuring neighborhood "bodegas" (grocery stores) and "bodegeros" (bodega owners). "We put the bodegas on TV and tell a little bit about the bodegero, plus Pepsi," the executive explains. "We're giving the bodegeros a chance to see themselves on TV and to tell all their friends and customers to watch."

In Los Angeles, radio is in wide use, and not only for Pepsi-Cola, but for Mountain Dew, a great seller with the Mexican market. "Give me a Dew" has been literally translated into "Dame una Dew," and Pepsi Challenge spots have been made over to feature Hispanics. Radio is the key here because the market is younger—Mountain Dew drinkers falling between 12 and 24 years old—and they spend more time in front of radios (and TV) than behind books and newspapers. When Los Angeles Hispanics aren't hearing the Pepsi message on the radio, they're seeing it at Spanish parades and festivals.[21]

Political and legal factors

The third uncontrollable external variable is political and legal changes. Business needs government to establish the "rules of the game." In turn, government needs business because the marketplace generates funds (through taxation) that support public efforts to educate our youth, protect our shores, and so on. The private sector also serves as a counterweight to government. The decentralization of power inherent in a private enterprise system supplies the limitation on government essential for the survival of a democracy.

Let us look first at the laws that affect business in the United States, and then at the regulatory agencies of the federal government.

PRIMARY LAWS THAT AFFECT MARKETING

The Sherman Act of 1890. Historically, the first federal law of major importance to marketing focused on antitrust activities. The Sherman Act is at the heart of antimonopoly legislation. It reads as follows:

Section 1. Every contract, combination in the form of trust or otherwise, or conspiracy, in restraint of trade or commerce . . . is hereby declared to be illegal. . . .

Section 2. Every person who shall monopolize, or attempt to monopolize, or combine or conspire with any other person or persons, to monopolize . . . trade or commerce . . . shall be deemed guilty of a misdemeanor.

The language of this act is vague; it made no attempt to define in concrete terms what is meant by "combination" or "restraint" or "trade" or "monopolize." It thus left the way open for court rulings that have lessened its effectiveness. Yet it did declare in forthright language the two main targets of antitrust action: (1) "restraint of trade"—restraining others from competing, and (2) "monopolizing"—eliminating, or trying to eliminate, competitors.

The Clayton Act of 1914. In this law Congress tried to remedy the weaknesses of the Sherman Act by prohibiting three specific kinds of monopolizing behavior:

1. Discrimination in the prices charged to different buyers. (This prohibition was aimed at local price cutting and at the granting of favored treatment to particular buyers, which gave them an unfair advantage over rivals.)
2. Leasing or selling goods under "tying contracts." (A tying contract requires the lessee or buyer to refrain from using or dealing in the goods of any competitor.)
3. Combining two or more competing corporations by acquiring or pooling ownership of their stock. (This was aimed at the merger movement.)

The Federal Trade Commission Act of 1914. Enacted at the same time as the Clayton Act, this law did two things. First, it established a new independent agency, the **Federal Trade Commission (FTC),** to deal with antitrust matters. Second, it outlawed "unfair methods of competition." What methods were to be regarded as unfair? The law did not say. It left that decision to the new commission.

The Robinson-Patman Act. The Robinson-Patman Act of 1936 explicitly prohibits a seller from giving quantity discounts or charging different prices to different buyers, except to the extent that lower prices can be justified by lower costs. A firm can, however, lower a price to meet an equally low price of a competitor. The act also gave the FTC power to establish maximum limits on quantity discounts granted to any customer or class of customers, regardless of differences in the costs of serving them. It also prohibited the granting of brokerage allowances by a seller to a buyer or a brokerage firm owned by the buyer. Sellers must also make any supplementary services or allowances to all purchasers on a proportionately equal basis. Finally, Robinson-Patman makes it illegal for a buyer knowingly to induce a discriminatory price from a seller.

The Wheeler-Lea Act. The Wheeler-Lea Act of 1938 broadened the FTC's powers to include the prohibition of practices that might injure the public without affecting competition. It also extended the FTC's authority over the false advertising of food, drugs, cosmetics, and therapeutic devices.

Consumer protection laws. In addition to the major pieces of legislation outlined above, there have been many laws passed to protect the purchaser, user, and innocent third parties. A sampling of these laws is shown in Table 3.3.

◀ **TABLE 3.3 Legislation Designed to Protect the Consumer**

Mail Fraud Act of 1872
To make it a federal crime to defraud through the use of mail.

Food and Drug Act of 1906
To regulate interstate commerce in misbranded and adulterated foods, drinks, and drugs.

Federal Food, Drug, and Cosmetic Act of 1938
To strengthen the Food and Drug Act of 1906 by extending coverage to cosmetics and devices; requiring predistribution clearance of safety on new drugs, providing for tolerance

for unavoidable or required poisonous substances; and authorizing standards of identity, quality, and fill of container for foods.

Flammable Fabrics Act (1953)
To prohibit the shipment in interstate commerce of any wearing apparel or material which could be ignited easily (amended 1967 to include household products).

Automobile Information Disclosure Act (1958)
To require automobile manufacturers to post the suggested retail price on all new passenger vehicles.

Food Additives Amendment (1958)
To amend the Food and Drug Act by prohibiting use of new food additives until promoter establishes safety and FDA issues regulations specifying conditions of use.

Textile Fiber Products Identification Act (1959)
To cover the labeling of most textile products not covered by the earlier Wool or Fur Products Labeling Acts.

Kefauver-Harris Drug Amendments (1962)
To require drug manufacturers to file all new drugs with the Food and Drug Administration; to label all drugs by generic name; and to require pretesting of drugs for safety and efficacy.

Fair Packaging and Labeling Act (1965) (Truth-in-Packaging)
To regulate the packaging and labeling of consumer goods and to provide that voluntary uniform packaging standards be established by industry.

National Traffic and Motor Vehicle Safety Act (1966)
To authorize the Department of Transportation to establish compulsory safety standards for new and used tires and automobiles.

Child Safety Act (1966)
To strengthen the Hazardous Substances Labeling Act of 1960 by preventing the marketing of potentially harmful toys and permitting the Food and Drug Administration to remove inherently dangerous products from the market (amended 1969).

Cigarette Labeling Act (1966)
To require cigarette manufacturers to label cigarettes: "Caution: Cigarette smoking may be hazardous to your health."

Consumer Credit Protection (1968) (Truth-in-Lending)
To require full disclosure of annual interest rates and other finance charges on consumer loans and credit buying including revolving charge accounts.

Fair Credit Report Act (1970)
To regulate credit information reporting and use, provide consumer access to credit files, limit consumer liabilities from lost or stolen credit cards to $50.

Consumer Product Safety Act (1972)
Created the Consumer Product Safety Commission.

Consumer Goods Pricing Act (1975)
To prohibit the use of price maintenance agreements among manufacturers and resellers in interstate commerce.

Magnuson-Moss Warranty/FTC Improvement Act (1975)
To authorize the FTC to determine rules concerning consumer warranties and provide for consumer access to redress, such as the class action suit. Also expand FTC powers over unfair or deceptive acts and practices.

Source: Adapted from "Significant Consumer Protection Legislation Enacted, 1872–1972" in *Consumerism: Viewpoints from Business, Government, & the Public Interest* by Ralph M. Gaedeke and Warren W. Etcheson (Canfield Press Book). Copyright © 1972 by Ralph M. Gaedeke and Warren W. Etcheson. By permission of Harper & Row, Publishers, Inc.

State laws. State legislation that affects marketing varies from state to state. Oregon, for example, limits utility advertising to 0.5 percent of the company's net income. California has forced industry to improve consumer products and has also enacted legislation to lower the energy consumption of refrigerators, freezers, and air conditioners. In 1980, Massachusetts charged Bang and Olufsen of America and several retailers with conspiring to fix prices on top-quality audio equipment. In the same year, nine dairies in New Jersey agreed to pay the state more than $2 million to settle price-fixing charges.

THE REGULATORY AGENCIES

Although state regulatory bodies are more actively pursuing marketing violations of their statutes, it is the federal regulators that generally have the greatest clout. The two most directly and actively involved in marketing affairs are the Consumer Product Safety Commission and the Federal Trade Commission. Both agencies will be discussed throughout the text, but a brief introduction is in order at this point.

The Consumer Product Safety Commission (CPSC). The sole purpose of the **Consumer Product Safety Commission (CPSC)** is to protect the health and safety of consumers in and around their homes. It has the power to prescribe mandatory safety standards for almost all products consumers use (about 15,000 items). The CPSC consists of a five-member committee with approximately 1,100 staff members, which include technicians, lawyers, and administrative help. It can fine offending firms up to $500,000 and sentence its officers up to a year in prison. It can also ban dangerous products from the marketplace. We will discuss the CPSC further in Chapter 23.

The Federal Trade Commission (FTC). The Federal Trade Commission consists of five members each holding office for seven years. The main provision of the Federal Trade Commission Act is section 5, which gives the commission the power to prevent persons or corporations from using unfair methods of competition in commerce. It also has the power to investigate the practices of business combinations and to conduct hearings.

Antitrust activities. Two major antitrust cases filed by the FTC in recent years are those against IBM and the cereal industry. In the first instance IBM was accused of price discrimination, of "buying" scientists and engineers from its competitors, and of having entered into tying agreements. The case against IBM involves billions of dollars worth of capital investment and stock. The second major antitrust case was filed against Kellogg, General Foods, General Mills, and Quaker Oats, charging them with a variety of unfair methods of competition. The FTC does not claim that any conspiracy was involved, but that longstanding industry practices are anticompetitive and permit the companies to share monopoly power.

Advertising regulation. Since 1970, the FTC has shifted its emphasis to the advertising industry. In the past it had generally directed its efforts toward removal of deceptive advertising. In the landmark case of the *Federal Trade Commission* v. *Sperry & Hutchinson Company,* the Supreme Court ruled that the FTC did not have to prove that a practice was "deceptive," only that it is "unfair" to consumers.

Deception usually is related to a specific advertising claim. An advertisement does not have to deceive anyone, but simply have the "tendency or capacity" to deceive. Generally, deception falls into one of three categories: (1) unconscionable lie, (2) claim-fact discrepancy, and (3) claim-belief interaction. The first is the easiest to prove. If a bracelet is advertised as being able to cure cancer if worn for three consecutive days, it is an obvious misstatement of truth. In the second case, an ad may be judged deceptive if a qualification must be placed on the ad for it to be properly evaluated. "As recommended by three out of four doctors" is such an example. What kind of doctors? where? under what conditions? The third basis of deception occurs when an ad interacts with beliefs and attitudes to create a deceptive belief. For example, assume a soap manufacturer finds that adding blue crystals to a soap powder results in housewives attributing more cleaning power to the soap. An ad that states, "Now, brand XYZ with new blue crystals" does not really say it will get clothes cleaner, but is still deceptive.

Unfair advertising is much more difficult to pin down. The question is, "unfair to whom?" A person with a college degree is less likely to be misled than a grade school dropout. The commission has concentrated its efforts in several areas in attempting to enforce the "unfair" doctrine. Advertisers making a claim without adequate proof have come under increasing fire. Special audiences, such as children, ghetto dwellers, and the elderly, are being closely watched by the FTC.

FTC power curtailed. The FTC is not an agency without teeth; it has a vast array of regulatory powers (see Table 3.4). In fact, during the mid to late 1970s, the FTC began using its power to the hilt. Some claimed that the FTC had gone beyond enforcement to social engineering. It proposed such things as (1) banning all advertising to children under the age of 8, (2) banning all advertising of sugared products that are most likely to cause tooth decay to children under age of 12, and (3) requiring dental health and nutritional advertisements to be paid for by industry.[22] Finally, business decided it had "had enough" and lobbied for curtailment of FTC power. The result of a two-year struggle was the passage of the FTC Improvement Act of 1980. Its major provisions were these:

1. It removes the FTC's use of "unfairness" as a criterion for industrywide trade rules against advertising. This meant that all the children's advertising proposals mentioned above were suspended because they were based almost entirely on the unfairness standard.
2. Oversight hearings on the Federal Trade Commission must be conducted every six months. This basic tool of congressional review will serve to keep the commission accountable and keep Congress aware of one of the many regulatory agencies it created and is responsible for monitoring.

▲ **TABLE 3.4 Powers of the FTC**

Remedy	Procedure
Cease and desist order	A final order to cease an illegal practice—often challenged via the courts.
Consent decree	Business consents to stop the questionable practice without admitting illegality.
Affirmative disclosure	Requires advertiser to provide additional information about products in their advertisements.
Corrective advertising	Requires advertising to "correct" the past effects of misleading advertising (e.g., 25 percent of media budget to FTC approved advertisements or FTC specified advertising).
Restitution	Require refunds to consumers misled by deceptive advertising. According to 1975 Court of Appeals decision, cannot be used except for practices carried out *after* the issuance of a cease-and-desist order (still in appeal).
Counteradvertising	FTC proposed that FCC permit advertisements in broadcast media to counteract advertising claims (also proviso for free time under certain conditions).

Sources: Robert E. Wilkes and James B. Wilcox, "Recent FTC Actions: Implications for the Advertising Strategist," *Journal of Marketing,* vol. 38 (January 1974), pp. 58–60; Dorothy Cohen, "FTC Orders Corrective Ads: Restitution Waiting in Wings," Legal News Section, *Marketing News,* October 1, 1971; Dorothy Cohen, "Court Decisions Weaken FTC's Public Interest Power," Legal News and Views Section, *Marketing News,* February 14, 1975, p. 4, published by the American Marketing Association. Reprinted by permission.

THE IMPACT ON MARKETING MANAGEMENT

It is rare that businesses band together to create change in the external environment such as the FTC Improvement Act. Generally marketing managers only react to legislation, regulation, and edicts. Although most of this discussion has focused on regulation of product, price, and promotion, it should be noted that distribution is also heavily regulated. Tying contracts that require a customer to buy something he or she does not want in order to get a desired product are illegal. If a manufacturer requires a dealer to carry a full line of its products, it may be in violation of the Clayton and Sherman acts. If a franchise agreement allows the franchise holder to sell only to customers within an assigned sales territory, the agreement is illegal. A franchise agreement cannot prohibit a franchise holder from carrying competitor's products.

The point is that every aspect of the marketing mix is subject to legal rules and restrictions. It is the duty of marketing managers (or their legal assistants) to understand these laws and conform to them. It is easy for a marketing manager (or a lawyer) to say no to a marketing innovation. The challenge is not simply to keep the marketing department out of trouble, but to help it implement creative new programs to accomplish marketing objectives. Lawyers must "offer solutions their clients can live with," insists John Richman, the company lawyer who worked his way up to chairman of Kraft, Inc. "The lawyer is paid to get things done, not to say they can't be done," Richman argues.[23]

Throughout the text, we will refer to the laws covered in this section and others that affect marketing decision making. It is important to realize that failure to comply with regulations can have major consequences for the firm. Sometimes just sensing trends and taking corrective action before a government agency acts can help avoid regulation. For example, toning down hard-hitting advertisements to children might have avoided an FTC inquiry. The impact a ruling can have on a firm is illustrated below by the case of the Johnson Products Company.

Johnson Products Company has marketed a line of black personal grooming products for 26 years. These include hair relaxers, conditioners, shampoos, hair dressings, and cosmetics sold under the brand names Ultra Sheen, Afro Sheen, Ultra Wave, and Bantu. From 1954 to 1974 Johnson Products had a virtual monopoly in its market.

But in 1974, the FTC, acting on its own initiative, began a probe of advertising practices of hair relaxers to black consumers. The commission decided that sodium hydroxide, the active chemical in hair straighteners, could be dangerous to the skin, eyes, and scalp. Since Johnson Products was the most visible and dominant marketer of such products, it was ordered to put health warnings on its packaging and in its advertising.

In the meantime, cosmetics giants such as Revlon, Clairol, Alberto-Culver, and L'Oreal took note of the high profit rates in the black products industry and decided that if they were going to enter that market, they might as well strike while Johnson was at a disadvantage.

"Those were very frustrating times," recalls Grayson Mitchell, a Johnson Products executive. "Here we had spent a lifetime developing a reputation in the industry and the FTC in one fell swoop practically destroyed us."

"For nearly two years we had to put warnings on our products and our ads, which had a negative impact on the consumer's mind. Meanwhile, large competitors were copying our products and penetrating the marketplace."

"The difference was that these new competitors were exempt from the FTC ruling because the commission had singled out Johnson Products Co. So the competitors were able to play up in their advertising the fact that their products didn't contain health warnings. And the outrageous part of the whole situation is that all of the hair relaxers had about the same amount of sodium hydroxide in them. They were parity products."

Eventually, the FTC equalized its regulation of the black personal products industry.[24]

Economic factors

In addition to political and legal, demographic, and social factors, marketing managers must understand and react to the economic environment. The two areas of greatest concern to most marketers are inflation and recession.

INFLATION

During several periods in the 1970s and also in the early 1980s, marketers were caught in a vise: high inflation that squeezes profit margins and a recession that cuts buyer purchasing power. Marketers have also been faced with no real economic growth yet continued high rates of inflation—**stagflation.**

A number of pricing strategies to cope with inflation will be discussed in Chapter 11. But in general, marketers must be aware that inflation causes consumers to do two things:

1. Decrease their brand loyalty. In a recent research session, a panelist noted: "I used to use just Betty Crocker mixes, but now I think of either Betty Crocker or Duncan Hines, depending on which is on sale." Another participant said: "Pennies count now, and so I look at the whole shelf, and I read the ingredients. I don't really understand but I can tell if it's exactly the same. So now I use this cheaper brand, and honestly, it works just as well."[25]
2. Stock up. Many consumers take advantage of coupons and sales to stock up.

As inflation continues to pound the consumer, there is intense pressure to buy more economically. But consumers will resist as much as possible actually decreasing their standard of living.

In creating marketing strategies, managers must realize that no matter what happens to the seller's cost, the buyer is not going to pay more for a product than the value he or she places on it. No matter how compelling the justification might be for a 10 percent price increase, the marketer must always examine its impact on demand. The marketing manager should also develop an effective cost forecasting system and use anticipatory pricing. That is, use the expected cost at the time of shipment as input to fixed price quotes or to build in escalators.

New and higher rates of inflation have now caused significant changes in the marketing mix. These will be discussed in detail in later sections of the book.

RECESSION

The problems of inflation and recession go hand in hand, yet they require different strategies. Some suggested actions to counter the effects of reduced demand are these:

Improve existing products and introduce new ones that help customers reduce manufacturing hours, waste, and material costs. Recessions increase demand for products and services that (1) produce economy and efficiency, (2) offer value, (3) help organizations streamline practices and procedures, (4) improve customer service.

Maintain and expand such customer services as (1) sales of replacement parts and (2) line extension and modification. These address recession needs to postpone new equipment and materials purchases.

Hold the line on prices and continue emphasis on top-of-the line products. Emphasize value in promoting them by demonstrating their quality, durability, satisfaction, capacity to save time, and money. High-priced value items consistently fare better during recessions.[26]

In total dollars (millions)		In percent of sales		In dollars per employee	
1. General Motors	$1,950	1. Cray Research	14.0%	1. Cray Research	$11,399
2. Ford Motor	1,720	2. Amdahl	13.0	2. Amdahl	10,698
3. International Business		3. Applied Materials	12.9	3. Applied Materials	8,059
Machines	1,360	4. Cordis	11.2	4. International Flavors &	
4. General Electric	640	5. Teradyne	10.4	Fragrances	7,554
5. United Technologies	545	6. Systems Engineering		5. Eli Lilly	6,602
6. Boeing	525	Laboratories	10.3	6. Upjohn	6,137
7. Eastman Kodak	459	7. John Fluke Mfg.	10.1	7. Shared Medical	
8. International Telephone &		8. Intel	10.1	Systems	6,131
Telegraph	436	9. Data General	10.0	8. Merck	6,106
9. Du Pont	415	10. National		9. Polaroid	5,950
10. Exxon	381	Semiconductor	9.4	10. Lubrizol	5,800

Source: Data from Standard & Poor's Compustat Services, Inc.

Technology and resources

Inflation and recessions can sometimes be fought through new technology. New machines that offer significant reduction in the cost of production provide a powerful tool for fighting inflation. A firm's technology can be one of its most valuable assets (see Table 3.5). The Bell System, Texas Instruments, Boeing Corporation, IBM, General Electric, and others have technical capabilities that often make the marketing task relatively easy.

EXTERNAL TECHNOLOGY

Technology that is external to the firm (owned by other companies or governments) is an uncontrollable variable the marketing manager must monitor. An example of what can happen if technology is ignored is provided in the Sweda example below.

By 1970, Sweda had captured 13 percent of the U.S. cash register market, which as late as 1960 was 90 percent in the hands of NCR.

Yet because of previous Sweda management's fixation with the success of its mechanical registers, Sweda failed to make a timely switch to the electronic cash registers (ECRs) that now dominate the marketplace. By the mid-1970s, the company, by then relocated to Pine Brook, N.J., was losing money. It had dropped from second to fourth in the market with only an 8 percent share, and it was in clear danger of becoming a major casualty of the microprocessor revolution. By 1980, Sweda had not fully recovered its market share.

So marketing managers must be aware of how technology outside their industry can influence their firm. For example, one growth area of the 1980s will be the use of industrial robots. General Electric expects eventually to replace at least half of its 37,000 assembly workers with robots. Volume production of robots will reduce the cost of a typical robot from $50,000 to $10,000 by 1990 creating a demand of about 200,000 units per year (from 1960 to 1980, only 3,500 robots were installed).[27] This new technology is making it possible to replace skilled workers. The new generation of machines can "see," "feel," and even "think." Thus unemployment may rise and personal incomes could fall if the use of robots becomes common.

Cable television, electronic catalogs, and two-way interface systems may revolutionize the way people shop. Interface systems may also have a profound impact on our banking and transportation systems. If people shop at home, what happens to regional shopping malls? What are the implications for Sears, K-Mart, and their competitors? Will product testing become so refined that prototypes will be sent to a preselected sample of homes and then modified as respondents feed back data on their interactive systems? Will there be shrinking markets for "dumb" products that can no longer compete against more sophisticated computerized units?

In another area, biological or genetic engineering holds great promise for the 1980s. It is unlikely that biotechnology will create an industry of its own, like semiconductors. Instead, it will diffuse into such industries as chemicals, drugs, food, and energy.

NATURAL RESOURCE SHORTAGES

Part of America's research and development efforts are directed toward offsetting natural resource shortages. The synthetic fuels programs, development of solar and geothermal energies, creation of lighter weight yet stronger metals and plastics are a result of natural resource shortages. In the energy area, marketing managers may react to rising energy costs by taking the following actions:

Prices of all products will rise, especially of those that require a great deal of energy for their manufacture and transport.

To reduce costs, manufacturers will tend to standardize products. They will pay less attention to the needs and desires of individual market segments.

New products will be introduced that are more durable, require less service, and require less energy in their manufacture, distribution, and use (see Figure 3.5).[28]

Energy is only one area where shortages have occurred. Others include shortages of water, forest products, minerals, and clean air. In general shortages widen the gap between consumers' expectations for a better way of life and their ability to obtain such a life style. Like inflation, shortages may lead to more rational purchasing and less emotionalism in buying decisions. Consumers may emphasize high quality, long life, ease of use, enhancement of earnings, and dependability when buying goods and services. The consumer may become more concerned with durability of a product and service rather

One reason to buy:

This new Learjet 25D flies 16 passenger miles on one gallon of fuel

Here are four more reasons:

1. It costs less than $2 million.

Only one business jet carries eight passengers and has a price tag under $2 million. And you're looking at it.

2. You get nearly two million miles of engine warranty.

General Electric fully warrants its reliable engines, including 100 percent parts and labor, should one need removing for engine-caused repair during the first 4,000 hours of flight. That's equivalent to

eight years of normal flying — nearly two million miles.

3. We've made some great improvements to the airplane.

Most noticeably, the new Century III$_S$ (Softflite) wing makes the 25D even more docile in landings, while maintaining traditional Learjet high performance.

4. You can get one quicker than you think.

We've just increased production. That means a few more 25Ds are coming available in

the months ahead. For specifics, call either Phil Lovett, who's in charge of U.S. sales, or Finn Hedlund, who is responsible for international sales. They're both at (602) 294-4422.

Gates Learjet Corp., P.O. Box 11186, Tucson, AZ 85734. Telex: 666-408.

Now building our second 1,000.

Source: Courtesy of Gates Learjet Corporation, P.O. Box 11186, Tucson, Az. 85734.

than style. The drive toward rationalism will create a greater need for useful decision-making information. Advertisements and labels that inform rather than just persuade will be in vogue. Planned style obsolescence, where a firm deliberately brings out a new style without improving its functional quality, will be increasingly rejected by consumers in a shortage era.

Marketing managers should be aware that the era of shortages will last throughout the 1980s and probably into the next century. This may make us into a conserver society.[29] Such a society promotes a conserver ethic not so much from social desirability as from perceived ecological necessity. It promotes economy of design, and favors reuse and recycling.

Competition

DOMESTIC COMPETITION

Another uncontrollable variable to which we will refer throughout the text is domestic competition. It is wise to examine potential reactions by competitors to every contemplated change in the marketing mix. Defining markets and their potential must also be done in light of the competition. What is a competitor? Marketing managers generally define their competition as firms who are selling goods and services that customers and potential customers view as potential substitutes. The Miami Chamber of Commerce considers Las Vegas a competitor for the tourist and convention dollar. It probably would not consider a Smithsonian tour of Ireland as competition. Why? Those who would take the Smithsonian tour probably would not feel that lying in the sun at Miami Beach would be a reasonable substitute for an educational tour.

As population growth slows, as costs continue to rise, and as resource availability tightens, both larger and smaller firms find they must work harder to maintain their profits and market share. For years GAF Corporation ranked third behind Eastman Kodak and Polaroid in the photography market. In 1977 GAF threw in the towel because the amateur photography market had been dominated for so many years by Kodak that it was impossible for GAF to compete in the domestic market.

Some smaller firms are able to survive in highly competitive markets by producing a unique product. Steiger Tractor Company, founded in 1969, has become a viable competitor (sales over $100 million) in an old and stable market. It produces a big articulated tractor. Unlike most farm tractors, the articulated tractor bends in the middle to make turning easier and uses all four wheels for traction, thus enabling it to pull bigger loads. As a result, these tractors can cut labor costs by as much as 33 percent per acre.

The Steiger example illustrates that with good marketing strategies, it is still possible for small firms to compete effectively against the giants. Regardless of size, the marketing mix provides any management with the four tools of competition: price, promotion, distribution, and product/service offerings. Steiger developed a unique product in order to compete. Firms like K-Mart, Air California, Texas Instruments, and Radio Shack (home computers) use price as a primary means of competition. 7–Eleven stores use distribution to gain a competitive advantage. Their strategy is to provide shopping convenience by having over 5500 stores located close to where customers live and work. Some large firms like Procter & Gamble are superior competitors in every aspect of their marketing mix. They have an excellent research staff that enables them to bring out the "right" products, an efficient distribution system involving thousands of stores and institutions, aggressive pricing, and the largest promotion budget in the world.

FOREIGN COMPETITION

Procter & Gamble is a worthy competitor throughout the free world: It has penetrated markets in over a hundred countries. Many foreign competitors are doing the same in the United States. It is no longer satisfactory for the marketing manager to worry just about domestic competitors. In automobiles, textiles, watches, television, steel, and many other areas, foreign competition has been severe. Historically, foreign firms have been able to penetrate American markets by concentrating on price. Today the emphasis has switched to product quality. Datsun, Nikon, Sony, Rolls Royce, and Sandoz Pharmaceuticals are noted for quality, not cheap prices. (There will be more discussion of foreign competition in the chapter on international marketing.)

Actions of foreign governments

The final external variable with which marketers must contend is actions of foreign governments. Usually these actions affect most firms indirectly, through inflation and unemployment, rather than directly. The most obvious action of foreign governments that has affected American companies was the creation of OPEC. OPEC is a **cartel.** In a cartel the decision making with regard to pricing and output is made by the central association (governments). The quadrupling of oil prices in 1973 in addition to the large increase in 1979 created worldwide inflation and recession. Chances are that few raw material cartels will have the success of OPEC, with the possible exception of a bauxite (aluminum ore) cartel, as the analysis below shows. Of the 66 important raw materials in international trade, there are only 18 whose supply is dominated by developing countries.[30]

Imported oil accounts for about half of all energy consumed, so that importing nations are highly dependent on continuous supplies from OPEC. Unlike chromium, of which the United States warehouses a three-year supply, stocks of crude oil in consuming countries represent only about three months' consumption. The fact that oil users cannot change quickly to coal (as coffee drinkers switch to tea) is another factor in OPEC's favor.
Most commodities require considerable labor to produce, so that when they are withheld from the market and production stops, governments have to contend with large numbers of unemployed workers. Petroleum production, however, needs relatively little labor. By closing a valve, the oil can be kept in the ground. The production of agricultural products, once started, goes on; and if these commodities are stored, they are subject

to rot. Oil can be stockpiled without damage for as long as the producer wants.

None of the other 17 commodities whose supply is dominated by the developing countries has characteristics of petroleum which would enable them to be readily cartelized. Four are vegetable oils, for which there are many substitutes. Sisal, jute, and natural rubber already have been replaced in many uses by synthetics.

Exporters of coffee, tea, and cocoa are limited in the action they can take, first because there are readily available substitutes, and second, because there are so many producing nations that it is just about impossible for them to take any concerted action.[31]

Besides joining a cartel, a government can take action that severely limits or even prohibits imports (a **boycott**) of specific brands or types of goods. For the American exporter, important restrictions can severely limit market potential. A worse fate is **expropriation,** when American production facilities, products, and distribution equipment are confiscated by the foreign government. American firms that extract minerals and agricultural organizations have been the most common victims of expropriation.

Not all actions of foreign governments are against outside firms. Sometimes foreign investment is encouraged through special tax incentives. In other cases, a government will guarantee the training of the labor force for production lines. High-technology companies are often courted so that a country can further its economic growth. This courtship can take the form of product purchase, consulting, or the establishment of marketing and/or production facilities in the host country.

Many governments encourage importation of needed items but also aid their firms to become more proficient exporters. Nowhere is this more evident than in Japan, where government and the large trading companies are in a virtual partnership. Although the U.S. government helps American exporters, the relationship is not that close. In fact, it is often claimed that lack of support accounts for why only 25,000 out of 250,000 of United States manufacturers are exporters.

So the American marketer needs to understand the actions of foreign governments from several perspectives. First, the firm must understand the impact that cartels may have on the American economy and the availability of supplies. Second, the marketer should be on guard for important restrictions on the company's products or services. Third, the firm must also carefully examine incentives offered by foreign countries to American exporters. Many such offers can be very lucrative. Finally, the American firm needs to understand the types of aid available to it through the U.S. government.

SUMMARY

A successful marketing mix requires a thorough understanding of the external environment. The external environment is always changing and is not subject to control by marketing managers. One important uncontrollable factor in the external environment is social factors. For example, America's values have changed dramatically within the past 150 years. Today we see the death of the Protestant ethic, multiple life styles, changing attitudes toward leisure, a strong self orientation, and changing roles for families. More women have entered the workforce than ever before. This has led to increased family incomes and different consumption patterns.

The second uncontrollable variable is demographic factors. There are more one-person households than ever before; total population growth has slowed dramatically; and the average age during the middle of the 1980s will be approximately 32 years. The elderly market also continues to grow at a remarkable rate. Many marketers are now developing specific mixes to reach changing demographic target audiences. Another demographic trend is the movement toward the South and the Southwest from the Frostbelt.

Disposable after-tax incomes have been rising. This means that more families can afford "the good life" than ever before. The upper middle income group ($15,000 to $50,000) is growing faster than any other. Naturally growing patterns of affluence are creating important changes in consumer spending patterns. Yet another demographic trend that marketing managers must be aware of during the 1980s is changing minority markets. Among blacks, for example, there is a relatively small but growing group that is well educated, affluent, and leaving the central cities for the suburbs. The other extreme is the large group of blacks that lack college educations and are confined to blue collar or menial jobs. The continued growth of the Hispanic population is creating a market that rivals the size of the black market. New Spanish-language media have been developed to reach this market. Like the black market, the Spanish-speaking market often requires a unique marketing mix.

A third uncontrollable external variable is political and legal factors. The most important legislation affecting marketing includes the Sherman Act, the Clayton Act, the FTC Act, the Robinson-Patman Act, the Wheeler-Lea Amendment to the FTC Act, and various consumer protection laws. The two agencies that are most directly and actively involved in marketing affairs are the Consumer Product Safety Commission (CPSC) and the Federal Trade Commission (FTC). The FTC is concerned primarily with antitrust enforcement and advertising regulation. Because every aspect of the marketing mix is subject to legal rules and restrictions, it is imperative that marketing managers (or their legal assistants) understand these laws and work within them.

A fourth factor in the external environment is economic variables. The two areas of greatest concern are inflation and recession. In the late 1970s and the early 1980s, marketers were caught in a vise of high inflation, margins, high unemployment, and a lack of economic growth—stagflation. Inflation may cause consumers to decrease their brand loyalty and in some cases stock up on merchandise. Recession, on the other hand, results in different patterns of consumer behavior.

New technology is another external factor that can have a profound impact on the organization. Many firms such as the Bell System, Texas Instruments, and Boeing Corporation rely heavily on technology to compete. Yet marketing managers must be aware of how technology outside their own firm can influence their organization. Failure to adopt new technology can put an organization at an extreme competitive disadvantage.

Besides technology, marketing managers must also be concerned with natural resource shortages. Energy is one of the most obvious areas where shortages have occurred. Others include shortages of water, forest products, minerals, and clean air. In general, shortages widen the gap between consumer expectations for a better way of life and their ability to obtain such a life style.

Two other uncontrollable variables are domestic and foreign competition. It is wise to examine potential reactions of competitors to every contemplated change in the marketing mix. As population growth slows, costs continue to rise, and resource availability tightens, both larger and smaller firms find they have to work harder to maintain their profits and market share. Some smaller firms are able to survive in highly competitive markets by producing a unique product. Often sound marketing strategies make it possible for small firms to compete effectively against the giants.

The final external variable with which marketers must contend is actions of foreign governments. Often governmental activities affect firms indirectly (such as through inflation and unemployment) rather than directly. The most significant act of foreign governments that has affected American companies during the last decade was the creation of OPEC.

KEY TERMS

Psychology of entitlement
Demography
Zero population growth (ZPG)
Population age mix
Standard metropolitan statistical
  area (SMSA)
Disposable (after-tax) income

Federal Trade Commission (FTC)
Consumer Product Safety Commission
  (CPSC)
Stagflation
Cartel
Boycott
Expropriation

REVIEW QUESTIONS

1. Why is it vital to the firm to be aware of its external environment?
2. Give some examples of how changing family roles has affected the marketing mix.
3. Why should the marketing manager be aware of trends in consumption expenditures?
4. List the major pieces of legislation that affect marketing practices and tell what the objective of each act is.
5. How does the Consumer Product Safety Commission work to protect the consuming public?
6. What are some reactions of consumers to inflation?

DISCUSSION QUESTIONS

1. Briefly describe the impact of the Protestant work ethic on marketing. Is marketing "better off" because of the decline of this value? Why or why not? (Consider all aspects.)
2. Why is government regulation necessary? Who benefits—consumers or business? Why?

3. What gave rise to the FTC Improvement Act of 1980? What impact do you think it will have?
4. Why is research and development of concern to the marketing manager?
5. Which tools of the marketing mix do you think are the focus of the following concerns? Which external environmental factors do you feel have most greatly influenced them?
   a. McDonald's.
   b. Mail-order catalog businesses.
   c. General Motors.
   d. Oil companies in periods of shortages.
   e. Airline industry.
6. Why are American marketers welcomed by some foreign governments and victimized by others?

NOTES

1. This section is based on a speech by Florence Skelly of Yankelovich, Skelly, & White, a New York marketing and attitude research firm. The talk was given on January 30, 1976, before the Soap and Detergent Association Annual Convention. I have also drawn from "Changing Attitudes," an in-house document written by Florence Skelly.
2. Daniel Yankelovich, "We Need New Motivational Tools," *Industry Week,* August 6, 1979, pp. 2–7.
3. Ibid.
4. James B. Lindheim, "Focus on Self, Escapist Behavior, and a Spate of 'Me' Issues Have Rewritten the Rules of the Game for Our Nation's Institutions," *Public Relations Journal,* January 1980, p. 34.
5. These five factors are adapted from "Age of Me Poses New Problems for Marketers," *Marketing News,* June 30, 1978, p. 3.
6. "Women in Command: A Progress Report," *Marketing Times,* January–February 1979, pp. 20–21.
7. John Scanzoni, "Changing Sex Roles and Emerging Directions in Family Decision Making," *Journal of Consumer Research,* December 1977, pp. 185–189.
8. "Marketing Notes," *Marketing News,* April 23, 1976, p. 2.
9. U.S. Bureau of the Census, "Projections of the Population of the U.S.: 1977 to 2050," Series P-25, No. 704, p. 2.
10. James Foust and Al Southwood, "The Population Fizzle," *Business Horizons,* 16 (February 1973): 5–20.
11. Vincent P. Barabba, "How Demographics Will Shape the Decade," *The National Underwriter,* January 12, 1980, p. 32.
12. Ibid.
13. *Population Estimates and Projections* (Washington, D.C.: U.S. Bureau of the Census, October 1975), p. 11.
14. *Grey Matter,* 49, (1978). New York: Grey Advertising Company.
15. Ibid.
16. "The Second War between the States," *Business Week,* May 17, 1976, p. 92.
17. "Dual Incomes Will Lift More Families to Middle Class Affluence in the Decade," *The Wall Street Journal,* June 27, 1980, p. 23.
18. Thayer C. Taylor, "We the People: Older, Smarter, Liberated, Richer." In *The Marketer's Complete Guide to the 1980s* (New York: Sales and Marketing Management, 1980), p. 7.

19. Profiling the Typical Black Executive," *Business Week,* January 21, 1980, p. 32.

20. Thomas Barry and Michael Harvey, "Marketing to Heterogeneous Black Consumers," *California Management Review,* 17 (Winter 1974): 50. Copyright © 1974 by The Regents of the University of California. Reprinted by permission of The Regents.

21. Dylan Landis, "Flavors of Spanish," *Advertising Age,* April 6, 1981, pp. 5–18.

22. "Washington Issues and How They May Affect Advertising," *AAAA Washington Newsletter,* April 1980.

23. "When Lawyers Dictate the Limits of Marketing," *Business Week,* July 14, 1980, p. 80.

24. Bernard F. Whaler, "Beleaguered Johnson Products Company Plans War with Cosmetology Giants," *Marketing News,* February 22, 1980, p. 7.

25. "The Templeton Tapes," *Selling with Your Back to the Wall.* Special insert in *Sales and Marketing Management,* June 9, 1980.

26. Bob Arnold, "On Outfoxing Recessions," *Marketing Times,* January–February 1980, p. 11.

27. "Robots Join the Labor Force," *Business Week,* June 9, 1980, pp. 62–78.

28. Leon Winer and L. S. Schiff, "Rising Energy Costs Will Alter Marketing Patterns," *Marketing News,* May 6, 1977, p. 4. Reprinted by permission of the American Marketing Association.

29. See Stanley J. Shapiro, "Marketing in a Conserver Society," *Business Horizons,* April 1978, pp. 3–13.

30. Donald A. Ball, "It's Tough to Create Commodity Cartel; Only for Petroleum Where All Systems Go," *Marketing News,* November 4, 1977, p. 1.

31. Ibid.

◢ CASES

3.1 Hart, Schaffner & Marx

Hart, Schaffner & Marx (HSM) manufactures and retails top-of-the-line men's suits, including the Hickey-Freeman and Christian Dior brands that sell for at least $500. Although the firm has generally avoided competition over the years by appealing to the top-of-the-line market niche, there have been some limitations to this strategy. HSM's revenues during the past ten years have grown at an average rate of just about 6 percent per year, about half the rate of similar manufacturers. Profits similarly have suffered.

At this juncture, HSM is expanding its product line from the top-of-the-line merchandise to the mass markets. This is not HSM's first effort to produce and sell mass-marketed products. In 1974, the company entered the leisure suit business but subsequently withdrew. It recently introduced a Playboy brand line of men's suits that will retail for $125 to $200. It also acquired Country Miss, Inc., a New York maker of medium-priced women's sportswear, suits, and dresses, which is HSM's first venture in women's wear manufacturing.

HSM currently has 275 retail stores that sell the company's products and those of other manufacturers. It plans to acquire soon additional chains of retail outlets.

The company's traditional custom base is men, 35 to 50 years old, which will obviously have some impact on the new strategy. Also, Levi Strauss plans to introduce new lines of men's suits that will retail for about the same price as the

Playboy brand. Hagar Company, the nation's largest pants maker, has also made a new push in medium-priced separates that can be made into suits.

1. Discuss how each of the uncontrollable external variables will affect or can affect the new HSM strategy.
2. Would you recommend an even lower-priced line of men's and women's clothing? Why?

3.2 The American Cola Company

Bart Levy, president of American Cola, was quite disturbed by a market research report that crossed his desk recently. The report said that there have been two dramatic changes in the profile of the American population: a sharp increase in the median age and an even sharper rise in the number of people over 65. The so-called aging of America is a result of simultaneous declines in the birth and mortality rates.

Expecting that the trend will continue, the Census Bureau says that by the year 2030 the average age of Americans will be over 37, compared to just under 29 today. Perhaps more important, one in six Americans will be over 65. That's a total of almost 50 million senior citizens, a huge potential market.

Levy forwarded this information to the company's director of long-range planning, asking for comments and a plan. After six months Jim Bell, director of planning, reported the following: The 13–24 age group, which consumes one and one-half times as much cola per capita as the general public, will shrink by 8 percent in the next decade. Accordingly, the planning committee recommends the purchase of a winery and expansion of the company's food division, which manufactures such products as orange juice, coffee, and tea—beverages that are more popular with older consumers.

Levy is not sure this would be a wise decision. He believes there are two approaches to selling to the growing senior citizen market: (1) creating new products geared specifically to older people or (2) convincing these people that products already on the market are appropriate for them. Although the first approach might seem virtually foolproof, several things could go wrong. For one, the new product must satisfy real needs, because people will see through a gimmick. But even if older consumers can benefit from a product, they still may not buy it. Items that are intended especially for the elderly seem to carry a certain stigma, and the act of buying them can involve a painful reminder of the greater vulnerability that often accompanies aging. Thus Levy feels that the greatest potential of the growing senior citizen market may not be in products intended for the elderly, but rather in the elderly's willingness to spend more on goods and services that are now being sold mostly to younger customers. He uses blue jeans as an example of a product that was once sold almost exclusively to people under 25 but is now popular with people in their thirties and forties.

1. Levy has come to you for advice. Which approach would you recommend and why?
2. Are these the only two approaches to the problem? Can you think of others? Is it really critical for the company to tap this market? Does a firm have to be all things to all people?
3. What other uncontrollable variables must be considered before purchasing a winery or expanding orange juice, coffee, and tea production?

Keystone Company*

The Keystone Company, located in Portland, Maine, manufactured a variety of paper products, both consumer and industrial: corrugated and solid fiber shipping containers, corrugated and solid fiber packing materials, grocery bags and sacks, and folding cartons. Recently, Keystone has started to manufacture a line of folding paraffined cartons.

John Marsh, the firm's president, believed that existing markets and competition were changing. For example, many of Keystone's competitors had increased their product lines and were now manufacturing wrapping paper, asphalt laminated paper, and a line of industrial specialties, including insulating material and board and paper specialties. Most of Keystone's output was used for food packaging, but John Marsh believed that Keystone needed to achieve stability through product and industry diversification.

Keystone was really a regional manufacturer which had supplied the needs of its customers since the turn of the century. Its customers were loyal, but other competitors were beginning to carry more diversified lines. Moreover, a few national firms were beginning to penetrate its territory. Sales volume had been decreasing at the rate of from 2 to 5 percent for each of the past three years. John Marsh had spoken to his production and engineering personnel and arrangements had been made gradually to diversify the product line so that Keystone would be competitive with new products. The problem now was for Keystone to expand its sales territory and develop a competitive marketing program.

John Marsh had always maintained that the company's primary objective should be to sell its products. Due to changing competitive conditions, Roy Howard, a maketing consultant, had been engaged. After a careful study, Howard recommended that the firm implement the marketing concept. Marsh and many of his executives had read or heard of the marketing concept, but they were primarily concerned with manufacturing and accounting. The sales manager, Joe Gannon, had been with Keystone for 30 years, and believed that what was really needed was permission to hire five more salespeople. Gannon believed that the present number of salespeople could not call too frequently on accounts and that this resulted in mediocre service and follow-up.

The production manager, Larry Wise, maintained that his department could make more units if sales could only sell the units. In past years, Wise had not been able to produce enough units to keep up with customer demand, but now this situation had changed.

Figure 1 shows the present organization structure. According to Roy Howard, the sales function needed to be reassessed. The choice was not to hire more aggressive salespeople, but to make an effort to learn what customers really wanted. It was also necessary to resolve some disputes over lack of coordination between personal selling and warehouse management. Items that were sold were frequently out of stock, and this resulted in delivery delays.

Joe Gannon proposed that order administration should report to him. This would ensure coordination between direct selling and order administration. Warehouse management would report to staff services, and in this way coordination between production and sales management would be ensured. Since neither

---

* Case prepared by Professor Ronald D. Michman, Shippensburg State College, Shippensburg, Pennsylvania.

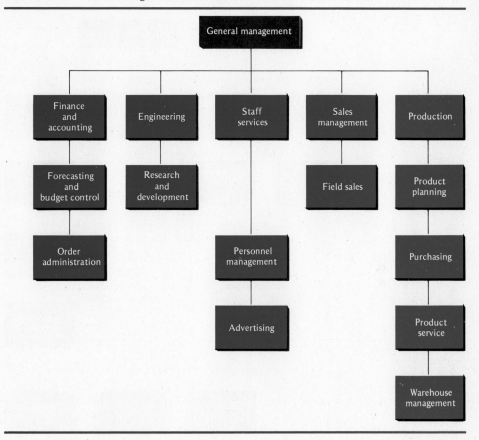

production nor sales management would be in charge of this function, this would be a reasonable compromise. Gannon believed that production had too much to do, and that that was the reason for the lack of coordination between sales and the knowledge of inventory levels in the warehouse. Figure 2 describes Gannon's proposal for reorganization.

John Marsh proposed that Joe Gannon might also supervise advertising, since one tended to pave the way for the other or to reinforce the other. Gannon did not really believe that advertising should be his responsibility, but after some minor objections, he agreed that he would be the logical one to do the job. Gannon was afraid not to agree with Marsh. It was at this point that Roy Howard, the marketing consultant, introduced Figure 3. According to Howard, it was the responsibility of the marketing manager to direct, coordinate, and control the marketing functions of Keystone. That would include pricing, distribution, forecasting, customer service, market research, advertising, and public relations. Roy Howard submitted a job description for the marketing manager position.

JOB DESCRIPTION: MARKETING MANAGER

I. Functions

Administer and coordinate Marketing Division activities. Responsible for

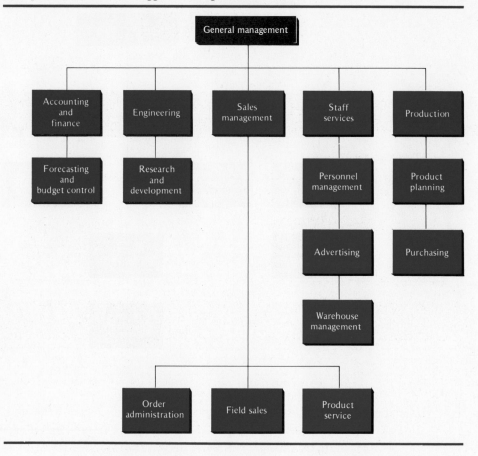

the efficient operation of the division and for achieving the maximum volume of profitable sales. Should carry out all policies and procedures established by the president and the board of directors.

II. Responsibilities and authority
   A. Formulate and direct overall sales policies and procedures necessary to ensure optimum sales of company products.
   B. Establish terms of sale for different products.
   C. Establish the price structure of company products.
   D. Initiate and conduct market research to determine market potential, penetration, and market share for all products.
   E. Provide division managers with detailed forecasts of anticipated sales.
   F. Initiate plans for modification of existing products, delete slow selling products from the product line, and develop new products.
   G. Recommend priority schedules to each division manager.
III. Relationships to others
   A. Accountable to the president for achievement of assigned functions and responsibilities.

Figure 3 organization chart:

General management

- Accounting and finance
  - Corporate budget and control
- Personnel
- Marketing manager
  - Assistant marketing manager
    - Purchasing
    - Marketing research
    - Sales budget and forecasting
    - Production marketing planning
    - Advertising
    - Warehouse management
  - Sales management
    - Field sales
    - Sales training
    - Product sales service
- Engineering and research
- Production

B. Maintain close liaison with division managers and control their tasks.

C. Supervise all those reporting directly to him.

D. Maintain close liaison with those in charge of accounting and finance, engineering and research, personnel, and production.

The reaction of Larry Wise to Figure 3 was that many of these marketing tasks could be combined and that two or three individuals could perform the functions satisfactorily. Wise believed that the product sold itself. Wise also wondered whether warehouse management, production-marketing planning, product sales service, and purchasing should be placed under the supervision of the marketing manager.

Gannon immediately seized the opportunity after seeing Figure 3 to declare his desire to assume the position of marketing manager. Gannon believed he had really been performing many of these functions through the years.

John Marsh reacted favorably to Figure 3. He asked that Gannon be considered for the position and that Howard and his consulting firm be in charge of selecting three candidates to be ultimately interviewed by Marsh. Marsh publicly praised the job description developed by Roy Howard.

1. Indicate the reasons why the Keystone organization has developed in this manner.
2. Comment on the viewpoints of John Marsh, Joe Gannon, Larry Wise, and Roy Howard. Do you agree or disagree with any of these people?
3. Point out the direction in which you believe the Keystone organization should develop.

PART Two

Understanding the marketplace

4

Market segmentation

OBJECTIVES

To understand the concept of market segmentation and its importance in marketing.

To examine the basic forms of segmentation.

To analyze the criteria for successful segmentation.

To understand the process of market segmentation.

To realize the shortcomings of market segmentation.

To become aware of the strategy of product differentiation.

To gain insights into product positioning.

Anheuser-Busch, the nation's No. 1 brewer, took a wait-and-see stance while the No. 2 and No. 3 brewers brought forth "light" beers, then came out of its corner with a one-two punch: Anheuser-Busch Natural Light and Michelob Light.

Market segmentation was the key to Anheuser's moves. Miller Lite was aimed at male, blue-collar drinkers. By the end of 1975 it had carved out a 2% share of the entire beer market and was growing. In 1980 it held 60% of all the light beer market. Schlitz sought a different segment; the Milwaukee brewer avoided Miller's macho approach and stressed Schlitz Light's taste. In doing so it won about 20% of the light beer category, which by the end of 1976 had doubled, comprising 4% of all beer sales.

Anheuser-Busch had been keeping a wary eye on all this and brought out its Natural Light in 1977, stressing its lack of synthetic ingredients—and appealing to the health-conscious. In six months, the brand caught up with Schlitz Light.

But Anheuser-Busch was not happy. The brewer felt it needed another market segment and this pointed to another brand. Miller Lite had been in the market for about two years and had thoroughly entrenched itself as the leader in the category. While Anheuser-Busch management was confident Natural Light would make significant inroads, the company also knew it would be extremely difficult to challenge Miller Lite for leadership in the short term because of that brand's immense head start. In addition, it seemed that the entire light beer category was posing a potential threat to another Anheuser-Busch brand, Michelob. Though Michelob sales in 1978 grew at the same phenomenal rate—over 20% per year—as in the past several years, it appeared that light beer was holding back the growth of Michelob. Michelob and the entire light beer category was attracting the same market segment. Both products were being used by the young, up-scale, white-collar beer drinker. Consumers began showing up with light beer in situations where they normally would have had a Michelob. Finally, Anheuser-Busch management saw a strategic opportunity to flank Miller Lite with a second light beer, thereby exerting competitive pressure on the category leader along two fronts.

Through 1977, 23 separate brands of light beer had been introduced. These brands were clustered on the basis of one characteristic—calories. All the light beers in the market late in 1977 had fewer than 100 calories. There was no brand of light beer providing a calorie and taste alternative between the light category and regular beer, which averages around 150 calories per 12 ounce can.

This was the opportunity Anheuser-Busch was looking for. So into the void between light beers and regular beers Anheuser-Busch introduced Michelob Light—"The one light beer with a few more calories but a lot more taste."

But Michelob Light offered one important additional ingredient that no other light beer offered: prestige. And because Michelob Light would be priced at parity with Michelob, Anheuser-Busch could support the brand image by establishing a price premium differential between Michelob Light and other light beers. By 1980 Anheuser-Busch had captured 23% of the total light beer market.[1]

The light beer story illustrates how market segmentation can be used successfully to gain market share and profit objectives. What is market segmentation? How can markets be segmented successfully? What are the steps involved in the segmentation process? Where do product differentiation and positioning fit into the picture?

What is market segmentation?

The market for virtually any product is not an amorphous mass of people or firms, but a set of subgroups with differing needs and desires. **Market segmentation** is the process of dividing a heterogeneous market into segments which are relatively homogeneous and identifiable for the purpose of designing a marketing mix to meet the needs of consumers in segments which are attractive to the firm. When Henry Ford began producing the Model T, he stated: "they [consumers] can have their car in any color they want as long as it is black." His was an undifferentiated strategy with no segmentation.

Today automobile manufacturers recognize a myriad of segments that, taken as a whole, constitute the market for automobiles. There are segments for hot rodders, mothers with children, young families, status seekers, and even states (for example, California has air quality regulations that require certain engine modifications).

Recall that marketing managers have as a primary function to define their target market after establishing marketing objectives. Segmentation aids managers in selecting market targets because it involves the examination of various potential customer profit and market share opportunities. Anheuser-Busch, for example, found a major opportunity with Michelob Light. Once an opportunity is identified, the marketing mix is created to satisfy the target audience. Segmentation is thus a first step in the planning process that ultimately determines how and where marketing resources (the marketing mix) will be allocated.

Segmentation enables marketing managers accurately to define target consumers and zero in on understanding the needs of a specific group. In the long run, segmentation helps management to identify its best profit opportunities and results in a more efficient allocation of resources.

UNDIFFERENTIATED MARKETING

Some firms do not segment their markets. Companies following this strategy are engaging in **undifferentiated marketing.** They use one product and one mix for all potential market segments. Undifferentiated marketing goes back to our Model T example, in which one product is produced for everyone who is willing to buy it. No attempt is made to cultivate various strata of the marketplace. Many small businesses and some large ones still follow this strategy. For example, some large bakeries adopt an undifferentiated approach to the selling of bread. The idea is to appeal to as many similar needs among the customers as possible. If the firm using undifferentiated marketing is a national company, it will use distribution to the mass market and national advertising media to reach "everyone." At one time Coca-Cola followed this policy with a single product and a single 8.5-ounce green bottle. The same is true for the Hershey Company, with one candy bar for everyone, and the Dentyne Company, which sold only one size package of Dentyne gum. One advantage of undifferentiated marketing is the potential for substantial production and marketing cost savings. Since only one item is being produced, the firm should achieve economies of mass production. Also, marketing cost may be lower, since there is only one product to promote and a single channel of distribution.

Approaches to segmentation

If a firm decides to follow a segmentation strategy, it may proceed in two ways. A marketing manager may analyze a general market target looking for segments that will afford profit opportunities. This technique was used when Anheuser-Busch explored the light beer market and then developed Michelob Light. Several years ago General Foods did a major segmentation study of the dog food market that ultimately resulted in the Cycle line of dog foods. Xerox and IBM also performed segmentation research prior to developing products for the small business.

A second approach to segmentation occurs when a firm already has a product and purchasers and potential buyers are examined to learn about consumption motives, rates of use, and so forth. These data are then used to develop a promotion, distribution, and pricing strategy to meet the firm's objectives. Abbott Laboratories successfully sold the prescription product Selsun for a number of years. Selsun contains a 2.5 percent selenium sulfide solution for the control of dandruff. Abbott recognized that this was too strong for the consumer market. A segmentation study identified a target group that was seeking more effective dandruff control than was being provided by the market leader, Head and Shoulders. From the research, a 1 percent selenium sulfide product was formulated and named Selsun Blue for the over-the-counter market. Today it is one of the most successful dandruff shampoos on the market. Another common example of where a product exists yet the market must be segmented is the airlines industry. New routes, fares, promotional themes, plane interiors and exteriors, and similar factors are based on segmentation studies. Braniff, for example, has long considered itself the businessperson's airline. Air Jamaica, by contrast, appeals and caters to an entirely different market segment.

Before we explore the various ways a market can be segmented, one point needs to be made. Segmentation does not always mean breaking down or disaggregating a total market. If a company takes its current customers and breaks them down by age or income it may find little, if any, useful information. Segmentation is often a multidimensional process involving many variables. Even more important is that segmentation is often an aggregation rather than a disaggregation process. The idea is to cluster groups of people or companies that will be most responsive to a certain product feature. The aggregation process continues until all potential buyers for a product are identified. The group is then analyzed to determine common characteristics and whether there are enough buyers to satisfy the firm's profit objectives. We will have more to say about the aggregation process later in the chapter. Let us turn now to the key means of segmentation.

THE FIVE BASIC SEGMENTATION FORMS

There are five basic forms of segmentation: (1) demographic—by age, sex, income; (2) geographic—by region, urban or rural; (3) psychographic—by life style or personality; (4) by benefit (tastes good, feels good); and (5) by volume (heavy user, light user).

Demographic and geographic. Perhaps the most common forms of segmentation are along demographic and geographic lines. Common forms of demographic and geographic segmentation for consumers, industrial markets, and government are shown in Table 4.1. (See Chapter 3 for a detailed discussion of demographic and geographic trends.)

◢ **TABLE 4.1   Forms of Demographic and Geographic Segmentation**

	Demographic	Geographic
Consumer	Age, family size, education level, family income, nationality, occupation, race, religion, residence, sex, social class	Region of country, city size, market density, climate
Industrial	Number of employees, size of sales, size of profit, type of product line	Region of country
Government	Type of agency, size of budget, amount of autonomy	Federal, state, local

TABLE 4.2   The Basis for Analyzing Life Styles

Activities	Interests	Opinions
Work	Family	Themselves
Hobbies	Home	Social issues
Social events	Job	Politics
Vacation	Community	Business
Entertainment	Recreation	Economics
Club membership	Fashion	Education
Community	Food	Products
Shopping	Media	Future
Sports	Achievements	Culture

Source: Joseph Plummer, "The Concept and Application of Life Style Segmentation," *Journal of Marketing,* 38 (January 1974): 34. Reprinted by permission of the American Marketing Association.

Psychographic. Race, income, occupation, and other demographic variables are usually helpful in developing segmentation strategies but often do not paint the entire picture. Demographics provides the skeleton, but psychographics adds meat to the bones. **Psychographics** is the development of psychological profiles of consumers and psychologically based measures (types) of life styles.

Life styles are usually analyzed on the basis of activities, interests, and opinions. Examples of each of these factors is shown in Table 4.2. A marketing manager conducts research and then clusters people with common activities, interests, and opinions. These in turn are given a "life style name" that relates to their behavior patterns. *Playboy,* for example, has a strong following among most men except for "the quiet family man," "the traditionalist," and "the discontented man."

The value of life style segmentation can best be illustrated by the following example. Heavy users of shotgun ammunition tend to be younger, lower in income and education, and concentrated in blue-collar occupations.[2] They are likely to reside in the South and to be from a rural area. Certainly this is helpful to any manufacturer of shotguns and ammunition, but is it enough?

Table 4.3, a psychographic study of the heavy ammunition buyer, reveals many additional facts. Hunting is not an isolated pastime, but is associated with other outdoor sports and activities. Thus joint promotion might be possible between camping gear and ammunition manufacturers. Since the heavy ammunition buyer probably enjoys fishing as well, the two products might be stocked close together in a retail store. The ammunition purchasers are likely to be do-it-yourselfers, suggesting that shells might sell where hardware and tools are sold. Since the heavy buyers are not strongly opposed to violence on television, detective stores, westerns, and war programs should reach the "right" market. Finally, this group's heavy newspaper readership may serve as a warning to ammunition manufacturers not to switch from this medium without good reason.

Life style segmentation begins with people and then categorizes them in such a way as to provide a broad, realistic, and lifelike view of the consumer—

Base	Percent who spend $11+ per year on shotgun ammunition (141)	Percent who don't buy (395)
I like hunting	88%	7%
I like fishing	68	26
I like to go camping	57	21
I love the out-of-doors	90	65
A cabin by a quiet lake is a great place to spend the summer	49	34
I like to work outdoors	67	40
I am good at fixing mechanical things	47	27
I often do a lot of repair work on my own car	36	12
I like war stories	50	32
I would do better than average in a fist fight	38	16
I would like to be a professional football player	28	18
I would like to be a policeman	22	8
There is too much violence on television	35	45
There should be a gun in every home	56	10
I like danger	19	8
I would like to own my own airplane	35	13
I like to play poker	50	26
I smoke too much	39	24
I love to eat	49	34
I spend money on myself that I should spend on the family	44	26
If given a chance, most men would cheat on their wives	33	14
I read the newspaper every day	51	72

Source: William Wells, "Psychographics: A Critical Review," *Journal of Marketing Research,* 12 (May 1975): 198. Reprinted by permission of the American Marketing Association.

a **user profile.** The life style data can be used to position a product on the basis of the user profile. In other words, the advertiser can show potential buyers how the product "fits" into their lives. An advertiser can learn what "tone of voice" should be used in advertising. Should it be serious or humorous, authoritative or cooperative, upbeat or traditional? Life style segmentation can also help marketers understand what rewards people are seeking in their activities and interests. In turn, this may suggest new product opportunities.

It should be pointed out, however, that demographic variables are almost always essential to a consumer goods market segmentation program. Assume that a psychographic profile reveals a certain attitude and that a marketer wishes to capitalize on that attitude through promotion. The attitude must be associated with a specific set of demographic statistics to enable the marketing manager to find the right media to reach that particular market segment.

Benefit. So far we have discussed segmenting markets by demographic, geographic, and psychographic factors. Now let us examine a fourth major segmentation basis—by benefit. The form of segmentation that has received the most attention in recent years is **benefit segmentation.** A segment is developed on the basis of what a product will do rather than consumer characteristics. One of the first uses of benefit segmentation was in the marketing of toothpaste. Based upon research, the toothpaste market was divided among (1) people who wanted a pleasant flavor, (2) people who wanted to avoid tooth decay, (3) active individuals who wanted brighter teeth, and (4) economy-minded purchasers.[3]

If a marketer knows what benefits are desired by consumers, the marketing mix for an existing product can be modified to reflect market desires. If this is not possible, perhaps a new product can be developed. It should be easier to develop a promotional program after benefit segmentation has been carried out, since this is how the marketer learns what product features the consumer is seeking.

The marketing manager can also determine what products come closest to meeting the desired benefits, and thus learn the strengths and weaknesses of the competition. By examining demographic information, the characteristics of persons seeking particular types of benefits can be analyzed. This information can be compared with media profiles to match media audiences and the target market. For example, people who go to Burger King are seeking a restaurant with a good community image, tasty food, and friendly employees. Many people who eat at McDonald's want a place popular with children, plus convenience; variety of foods was deemed of less importance. A marketing mix can be designed by Burger King and McDonald's to further enhance these desired benefits.

Perceptual mapping is often used to sharpen a product's perceived benefits picture. Several brands and product attributes are "mapped" using advanced statistical techniques. The closer together the brands are on the map, the greater the perceived similarity. Also, the closer a particular attribute is to a particular brand, the greater the likelihood that consumers believe the brand possesses that attribute.

Confusing? Not really. Look at Figure 4.1. This perceptual map shows the relationships among product attributes, brands of sports cars, and typical car owners.[4] For example, "high durability" and "high reliability" are in close proximity to "high resale," indicating that consumers view reliability and durability as important determinants of a high resale value. Also, note that none of the sports cars came close to these benefits—this may indicate a marketing opportunity. Similarly, the Opel was viewed as basically a city car, whereas the Corvette was perceived in terms of speed and racing—yet without the prestige of the Jaguar.

Perceptual mapping helps marketers distinguish among competing brands and find unfilled niches in the marketplace. By examining a brand on a perceptual map, the marketing manager can assess the brand's strengths and weaknesses. For example, returning to Figure 4.1, the Ghia is viewed as economical to drive and maintain but hardly beautiful, fast, or prestigious.

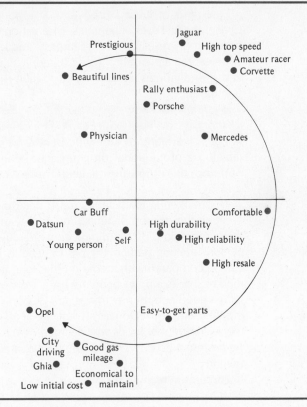

Source: Paul Green, "A Multidimensional Model of Product Features Association," *Journal of Business Research,* 2 (April 1974): 113. By permission.

Like virtually all other marketing research tools, perceptual mapping is not without problems. If the benefits and brands are clustered close together, distinctions among brands are not sharp enough for successful segmentation. Perceived benefits and relative costs do not always translate into easily predictable buying behavior. Sometimes consumers will tell a researcher how important a benefit is to them, but when the time comes to spend their own money it is a different story.[5]

Volume. The fifth major basis for segmentation is by volume of consumption. There are heavy, moderate, and light users for just about every form of product, as well as nonusers. Often "heavy users" account for a very large portion of a product that is consumed. Thus a firm might want to target its marketing mix to the heavy user segment. Miller did this when it changed Miller beer from the "Champagne of Bottled Beers" to a blue-collar orientation. Blue-collar workers are the "heavy users" of beer and could not identify with the "champagne" image. Now advertisements depict "exciting" blue-collar workers, such as tug-boat captains and oil-rig workers, drinking Miller beer (see Figure 4.2).

The heavy users of industrial helicopters are petroleum companies and pipelines. The Republican and Democratic parties closely guard their lists of heavy donors to state and national campaigns. Sometimes heavy users can be segmented geographically. It is obvious that snowmobiles sell better in the North and automobile air conditioners in the South. Some of the markets where rates of consumption are not so obvious for given products are shown in Table 4.4.

Criteria for successful segmentation

For segmentation to be successful, four basic criteria must be met:

1. *Substantiality.* The segments must be large enough to permit a viable market effort directed toward them.
2. *Measurability.* The segments must be identifiable and measurable.
3. *Response rates.* The segments must exhibit differences in responses to the marketing variables.
4. *Accessibility.* The segments must permit the firm to direct different marketing efforts toward the segments.

Substantiality. The first criterion, substantiality, simply makes the point that the segment or segments defined must be large enough to enable the firm to reach its profit objectives. If carried to a ridiculous extreme, one could say that every person in a market represents a segment. That is, we are all different in some unique manner. It obviously does not make sense to carry segmentation

◄ FIGURE 4.2 Advertisement showing glamorous blue-collar occupation.

Source: Courtesy of Miller Brewing Company.

	The best	The worst
Beer & ale (% of drinkers who consume)	Milwaukee (67.9)	Dallas/Fort Worth (44.2)
Bicycles (% adults who ever bought)	Minneapolis/St. Paul (30)	Atlanta (18.5)
Brief cases (% of adults who ever bought)	Los Angeles (12.9)	Cincinnati (6.2)
Canned chili (% of homemakers who use)	Dallas/Forth Worth (72.7)	Boston (6)
Deodorants & antiperspirants (% adults who use once a day)	Baltimore (88.1)	Minneapolis/St. Paul (78.3)
Foreign travel (% adults who traveled in past three years)	Seattle/Tacoma (38)	Cincinnati (10.8)
Fur coats (% adults who ever bought)	Detroit (11)	Cincinnati (6.4)
Insecticides (% of homemakers who use at least once a month)	Houston (61.9)	New York (26.4)
Life insurance (% adults who currently have)	Pittsburgh (80.3)	Miami (53.4)
Lipstick (% of women using at least twice a day)	Seattle/Tacoma (58.2)	Cincinnati (35.6)
Men's neckties (% men who bought one within 12 months)	Cleveland (18)	Pittsburgh (10.2)
Motor oil (% adults who buy)	Dallas/Fort Worth (64.8)	New York (40.8)
Panty hose (% women who bought in past month)	Houston (61.1)	Miami (39.7)
Paperback books (% adults who bought in last 30 days)	Seattle/Tacoma (53.2)	Dallas/Fort Worth (31.3)
Popcorn (% adults who buy for home use)	Minneapolis/St. Paul (54.3)	Miami (26.5)
Restaurants (% adults who visited past month)	Seattle/Tacoma (72.6)	Washington, D.C. (54.9)
Scotch whisky (% of drinkers who consume)	New York (35.9)	Cincinnati (9.6)

Source: "More Bang for the Dollar." Reprinted with the special permission of *Dun's Review,* October 1978, p. 107. Copyright 1978, Dun & Bradstreet Publications Corporation.

this far. If a marketing manager starts with a market of limited sales potential, segmentation may not be a viable option. The market for customized, personal 747 airplanes is so small that Boeing would be foolish to try to segment it. On the other hand, the total 747 market is segmented by commercial versus military, by airline, and by cargo versus passenger.

Measurability. The second criterion is measurability. The marketing manager must be able to measure and quantify a potential market segment to determine its variability. The Canadian Government Office of Tourism wanted to conduct a study of Americans who are potential vacation travelers to Canada. Since Canada hoped to expand the number of Canadian vacations taken by United States travelers, it was not enough to examine the 5 percent of the American population that had already been to Canada. Nor should everyone taking a vacation be considered part of the market. In this case, the study was based on persons who had taken a week's vacation within the past year and had traveled the requisite distance for a Canadian vacation (whether they had gone to Canada or not).[6]

Assume that a cosmetics company wanted to conduct a segmentation study to ascertain the market size and demographic characteristics of married women who were strongly desirous of a secret lover. Identifying and measuring the nature of this market would be difficult at best. Researchers have found it difficult to measure the success of Operation Crime-Stop because crime segmentation studies have found certain types of people much less likely to report crimes committed on them or their families. Also, some types of crime, such as shoplifting, are traditionally underreported.

Response rates. The third segmentation criterion implies that if various segments respond in similar ways to a marketing mix, there is no need to develop a separate mix for each segment. If, for example, all segments respond in identical fashion to price changes, there is no need for different prices for individual segments.

Accessibility. The final criterion requires that segmentation characteristics can be identified and then measured. Most important, the marketer must have access to segmented markets. Assume that a liquor company finds through market research that heavy users of a new brand of Scotch are extroverted female divorcees with a swinging life style. If the company cannot determine which media this group watches, reads, or listens to, or where its members live and shop, segmentation is useless. Of course, there may not be a medium that reaches such individuals.

How to segment a market

The most common forms of "real world" market segmentation studies are conducted in the following manner:

1. Select a market or product area for study.
2. Choose a form for segmenting the market (any one or a combination of the forms discussed above).
3. Pick segmentation descriptors within the form selected, such as benefit—benefits sought; demographic—age, income, race; geographic—region, state, county, SMSA.
4. Design and conduct research.
5. Analyze the size and nature of the segments as determined by the research.
6. Select market segments and design the marketing strategy (product development, promotional themes, pricing strategies, and distribution channels) to reach target consumers.

Select a market or product for study. The market or product area where the segmentation research will be undertaken should depend upon the firm's objectives—where it wants to be and who it wishes to serve, and its resources. Often the research will actually be conducted in subsegments of markets already served. For example, Anheuser-Busch's study of the light beer market is a segment of the total beer market. Sometimes market segmentation studies will be done in related fields, such as when Frito-Lay examined the snack spreads and dips markets.

In other cases, research will be done when a significant technological breakthrough occurs. For example, a major pesticide manufacturer developed a product to control flea reinfestation. Current products kill adult fleas but not eggs; therefore, when the eggs hatch the problem surfaces again. The manufacturer did a major segmentation study to examine various markets and delivery systems. Markets researched included pet shop owners, kennels, cat owners, and dog owners. Length of effectiveness (a benefit) was also studied for each segment. Delivery options included foggers, pump sprayers, aerosols, powders, and shampoos.

Choose a form of segmentation. After a general area of research has been selected, managers must then choose a form or forms of segmentation. It might be demographic, psychographic, benefit, geographic, or by volume. The basis selected is normally the result of managerial opinion and past experience. A manufacturer of hair-coloring preparations might want to examine markets segmented demographically and by life style. Bell Telephone might choose volume of long-distance calls as a form of segmenting its long-distance market.

Pick segmentation descriptors. After a form has been chosen, the marketer must select the **segmentation descriptors.** The descriptors are the units of analysis of the form of segmentation. For example, if a company decides to use demographics as a basis of segmentation, it may use age, occupation, and income as descriptors. A firm using geographic segmentation might select urban versus rural as the descriptors. In the flea control example mentioned above, there were several forms of segmentation:

Form	Descriptor
Benefit	Length of flea control
Life style	Hunters (with dogs) versus nonhunters
Demographic	Kennel owners, veterinarians, type of pet, size of pet
Geographic	Rural versus urban, state

Design a survey and conduct research. Survey design will be discussed in detail in Chapter 7. Obviously, the researcher must interview relevant consumers. It would do little good to conduct a study about flea products with people who do not have a pet. Also, the research must be representative of the target customers the firm is attempting to analyze.

Analyze the size and nature of the segments. At this point segments have been formed by sorting respondents into various categories. Profiles and benefits sought are examined and the size of the segments estimated. We found, for example, a segment of 1.5 million suburban owners of dogs that weigh more than 50 pounds who claim they "definitely will try the product." This group wanted to purchase the product in aerosol form and have it work for a five-month period. For such a product they are willing to pay $5.95. Further analysis of the segment uncovered the media they listen to, watch, and read, and the current flea control products they use. Similar information was also analyzed for other segments that would meet the profit goals of the pesticide manufacturer.

Select market segments and design marketing strategy. After examining the research findings for the flea product segmentation study, the firm identified seven segments that will satisfy its profit objectives. Unfortunately resource availability and short-run production capability will limit output to 900,000 units. At this point, the manufacturer rank-ordered its segments by profitability and selected segments (beginning with the most profitable) until it could no longer satisfy production requirements. It ended up with four segments: veterinarians that specialized in small animals located in the Sunbelt states, kennels located in the Sunbelt states, owners of dogs weighing over 50 pounds, and owners of dogs weighing 20 to 50 pounds.

Next, a marketing mix was developed to reach each segment effectively. Every one required a different product and delivery method. Products were sold through different channels, such as direct mail to kennels and pet stores for dog owners, and each product was promoted differently. The veterinarians were reached through advertising in professional journals. *Better Homes and Gardens, Outdoor Life,* and *Good Housekeeping,* plus other magazines, were used to inform dog owners about the product. Different price strategies were also applied for each market segment.

Problems, fallacies, and countersegmentation

Segmentation is not a cureall and it is not for all companies. In fact, some costs may be increased by segmentation. For example, differentiated products mean fewer economies of scale and higher production and inventory costs. Greater variety often means greater product complexity and perhaps more "bugs." Different promotional strategies for various segments may mean higher promotional expenditures. If different distribution channels are required, these costs too will be higher.

In addition to cost considerations, some markets may be too small to be segmented in an economical way. A market may not have enough distinguishing characteristics to be segmented. Or a marketing manager may discover a basis for segmentation but may not be able to identify and reach the target consumers. In some cases, heavy users make up such a large proportion of the sales volume that they are the only relevant target. If a limited group accounts for most of the sales, marketing efforts must be directed at this group.

THE MAJORITY FALLACY

Another point to remember in segmentation research is that the marketing manager should avoid the **majority fallacy.** A firm should enter a market only if it is large enough to meet profit goals. This does not mean that an organization should always target its efforts to the biggest, most easily accessible market segment. The reason is that competitors are probably following the same logic, so everyone is fighting for the same group of customers.

For years companies like Procter & Gamble, Colgate Palmolive, and Bristol Meyers have been vying for sales in the bar hand soap market. It has been segmented and resegmented by bar size, institutional versus home-use, scent, deodorant ingredients, color, mildness, price, and other factors. Yet a small Minnesota company, Minnetonka, avoided the majority fallacy and brought out a liquid hand soap called Softsoap. Sales have been dramatic since introduction. By the time you read this, the giant firms such as Chesebrough-Pond's (maker of Vaseline Intensive Care products) will probably have their "me too" liquid hand soap on the market.

COUNTERSEGMENTATION

It has sometimes been said by economists and others that many markets are oversegmented. In the automobile industry, for example, there is something for everyone. There are big cars, little cars, fast cars, station wagons, convertibles, and so on. However, in 1979 the total number of models available from United States manufacturers dropped to its lowest in nineteen years. The trend continued in 1980. What does this mean? Recession, shortages, and rapid inflation in the early 1980s have made customers more sensitive to the relationship between price and satisfaction in purchase decisions. In some markets people are increasingly willing to accept products less tailored to their individual needs if substitutes are available at a lower cost.[7]

This new strategy of reducing the number of market segments is called **countersegmentation.** It can be implemented by eliminating products that serve specific segments, and therefore dropping the segment, or clustering existing segments together. In the late 1970s, for example, Sears produced over a dozen different lawnmowers to reach as many market segments. By 1980 the number was cut almost in half. The key to successful countersegmentation is to be able to reduce production costs (fewer designs, longer production runs, smaller total inventory, fewer production setups, and a smaller amount of specialized production tooling expense) and pass part of the savings on to the consumer. This will enable the firm to reach consumers who are now placing more emphasis on price and value rather than convenience more effectively. Westinghouse has lowered its number of refrigerator models from 40 to 30, resulting in longer production runs, lower warehousing costs, and less downtime. Both sales and profits are up, in part due to a new aggressive pricing strategy.

The concept of countersegmentation does not mean that market segmentation is dead—far from it. There will always be many consumers who will not sacrifice convenience for lower price. Furthermore, many markets are not oversegmented. Others that are highly segmented such as custom houses, clothing, furniture, and toys reach consumers who demand certain products and are not satisfied with compromise.

Product differentiation and market segmentation

Segmentation is predicated upon examining a market on one or several criteria and then designing a marketing mix to reach the target segment. It is a market-oriented strategy. **Product differentiation** has a different conceptual basis. The objective is to distinguish one firm's goods from another's. The differences can be either real or superficial.

When Xerox introduced the plain-paper copier it had a number of very real advantages over electrostatic models. Yet the Xerox copiers were new products; they use regular paper and dry toner and produce a sharper image. At the other extreme, bleaches, aspirin, regular gasolines, and some soaps are differentiated by trivial means such as brand names, packaging, color, or smell. The marketer is attempting to convince consumers that a particular product is different and that they should therefore demand it over similar items. If a substantial number of people can be persuaded to demand the product, the seller can usually raise its price above the general market level.

BASES OF PRODUCT DIFFERENTIATION

The bases for product differentiation are usually brand name, minor ingredients or product feature variations, and packaging. Thus the manufacturers of one aspirin will tell you "doctors recommend it most"; another says it "gets into the bloodstream faster"; and yet another "it won't upset your stomach." Promotion is the vehicle that makes product differentiation work. It tells you over and over again that brand A is different from brand B.

A good quality bath towel is just that . . . a bath towel. That is, until it is emblazoned with the YSL symbol. These, of course, are the initials of the famous designer Yves Saint Laurent. Now it is no longer "just a bath towel." We have created a designer bath towel to be sold through finer stores and, naturally, commanding a premium price. Every time you see a designer product advertisement for Yves Saint Laurent it exudes quality and prestige. Thus people will buy our towel not only for what it will do (dry you off), but for what it means (look at me, I have good taste). The purchaser may even put the towel away until company comes!

Another very successful example of product differentiation was based upon packaging and a brand name. Pantyhose were a fairly homogeneous product until L'Eggs came along with its name and egg-shaped package and rack. Promotion was also effectively used to inform and persuade the consumer to purchase L'Eggs. Many forest product firms such as Georgia Pacific and Weyerhaeuser wrap cut lumber in polyethylene sheets with their brand on it to differentiate their timber from that of other firms. Acme Brick stamps its name on every brick and then warns consumers about purchasing inferior quality bricks.

In summary, product differentiation begins with the product and asks, "How can we make this one different from all the rest?" Market segmentation begins with the total market and asks, "What are the characteristics of the overall market and how can meaningful segments be reached?"

PRODUCT POSITIONING AND REPOSITIONING

It is hard to find a marketing manager who can discuss new or old products without mentioning **product positioning** in the same breath. Newton Frank, vice-president of Data Development, says that positioning is the finding of a niche in the marketplace for a new product.[8] Positioning, for our purposes, refers to the way a consumer views a product or service in relation to all other products or services the potential buyer perceives as possible substitutes: The company positions its product or services so that it has a certain image among potential customers.

From a strategy perspective, positioning is creating a product or service consumers will view in a certain manner relative to other products. The focus is on promotion, end uses, and creating the right product. In other words, positioning is creating a product's place in the market. That place depends on how the consumer perceives the product. If you and I were going to create a new cigarette and position it as a manly smoke, then it would have characteristics and packaging more like Marlboro and less like Eve or Virginia Slims. The U.S. Army positions itself as a place to learn a trade and meet new friends. The Marines are positioned as an elite group with superior training: they are "only looking for a few good men." Disneyland is positioned as a place with fun rides and fantasy; and Marineland of the Pacific has a position of being education-oriented and a place to observe a variety of sea life.

Kraft produces two premium ice creams, both aimed at the quality-oriented consumer. The first, Breyers, is positioned as the "all-natural ice cream." The second brand, Sealtest, benefited from a consumer taste test against parlor ice creams. It is positioned as "the supermarket ice cream with that ice cream parlor taste." Both brands have done extremely well. Another example of successful positioning is when S. C. Johnson brought out the aerosol furniture polish Pledge. The story is told below. The Pledge case illustrates again the point that positioning is how consumers see the product relative to all others. Pledge was seen as a dusting aid, not as an aerosol rubbing polish. Why did consumers see it as a dusting aid? Because that's what Johnson's promotion told them it was.

Johnson's competitors predicted failure. They believed the housewife would not pay a premium price for a polish in the new package, particularly since the product was not as good as Johnson's Old English and other bottled creams. Besides, furniture polish lasted so long that the size of market would not sustain the costly introduction needed.

Pledge was an instant success. The competition swallowed its predictions and rushed out with an aerosol cream polish that did not succeed in challenging Pledge. Why? Because S. C. Johnson had positioned its product not as a furniture polish, but as a dusting aid ("Waxed beauty instantly as you dust"). The competitor positioned its product as an old-fashioned rubbing polish in an aerosol can. The dusting positioning added a convenience benefit and made the product itself "new." And, not incidentally, it induced the housewife to use it regularly, not occasionally.[9]

Positioning for the same market. **Head-on positioning** is becoming a popular marketing strategy after years of unpopularity. When two products are competing directly, as very similar or identical products, they are engaged in head-on positioning. Tylenol was positioned head-on against Datril, and Gillette put Earth Born shampoo directly against Clairol's Herbal Essence. Armour's Dial deodorant is competing in the same perceptual space as Procter & Gamble's Sure.

It is possible for a manufacturer to influence or change the positioning of a brand by manipulating various factors that affect a person's attitude toward the brand. Through the right promotion the manufacturer can adjust the position of the brand in the mind of the consumer. One success story in this area is the repositioning of Johnson's Baby Shampoo from a product strictly for infants to one "gentle enough to use every day." Johnson's Baby Shampoo is now the world's best-selling shampoo. Similarly, Marlboro was just another lackluster cigarette until it was repositioned with a masculine, outdoor image. In 1976 it

PRODUCT DIFFERENTIATION AND MARKET SEGMENTATION

moved into the number one position in the filter tip market, a position long held by Winston.

Service positioning. Services may be positioned in the same manner as products. This is known as **service positioning.** Avis positioned itself as the aggressive underdog in its battle with Hertz for dominance of the huge automobile rental market. The Massachusetts state lottery positioned its new daily numbers game directly against "the mob." The introductory lottery promotion noted that "our system is parimutuel betting, so our payoffs are better than the mob's; the profits go back to your city or town, not to organized crime."

POSITIONING AND PRODUCT DIFFERENTIATION

The relationship between positioning and product differentiation needs to be clarified. Positioning is psychological in nature; it results in certain attitudes toward a product or service. In defining a target market, positioning often plays a key role. When Johnson and Johnson redefined its target market for its baby shampoo from mothers with babies to all adults who shampoo every day (or quite often), the product had to be repositioned. Promotion had to create a different mind-set about the product. Product differentiation is a strategy to create distinctions among similar products. Therefore, product differentiation is a tool to achieve positioning objectives. Bayer Aspirin uses product differentiation (brand name, promotion, packaging) to create a quality positioning. After all, "it's the one doctors recommend most." Bayer is positioned in approximately the same space as St. Josephs and above (in terms of price and quality) store brands like Safeway Aspirin or Rexall Aspirin. Basically superficial product differences have been used to reach positioning objectives.

Returning to our cigarette example, Eve is viewed as a very feminine cigarette because of its packaging, shape, and promotional themes. It is perceived as being on the other end of the continuum from Marlboro. Few men will smoke Eves—not because an Eve isn't a good smoke but because it is positioned as a feminine cigarette. Again, product differentiation (package, brand name, promotion themes) have been used to achieve positioning objectives.

PRODUCT DIFFERENTIATION AND MARKET SEGMENTATION

Whereas product differentiation begins with the product, market segmentation begins with the market and consumers' similarities and differences. With market segmentation, new products are often created to reach a desired segment. With product differentiation, the product typically already exists and may be changed with a new package or brand name. In many cases, a new product differentiation strategy is nothing more than a new promotional theme. Dr. Pepper was a lackluster soft drink until promotion positioned it as a unique type of soft drink.

Digital Equipment Corporation successfully segmented the computer market and targeted its products to the small business computer user. On a positioning scale, it is seen by computer buyers as:

Products for the Large Computer Market	IBM x	Control Data x		DEC x	Wang x	Radio Shack x	Products for the Small Computer Market

Of course, IBM and DEC produce a much broader range of equipment than their position on the scale. Yet in the purchasers' minds the manufacturers are perceived in the above relationships. Positioning is relating one product or company to another. If there are no competing products, no substitutes, no complementary items, there is no positioning.

There are a number of segments in the toy industry, such as age, benefits sought, sex of child, theme of toy. One large market segment is benefits sought (benefit segmentation), and a major portion of this market is "good value for the money." Tonka Industries serves part of this segment by producing durable metal cars, trucks, and construction equipment. It has positioned itself in the minds of consumers as a maker of quality toy vehicles.

Can product differentiation be used in conjunction with market segmentation? Sure. Coke saw how large the cherry-prune flavor of the soft drink market was growing. Coke could not penetrate this market with another product called Dr. Pepper. It emulated the taste of Dr. Pepper, came up with a different package, and called it Mr. Pibb. Coke wanted to call it Dr. Pibb but was afraid of a lawsuit. Thus product differentiation was used to move into the cherry-prune flavor segment of the soft drink market. Dr. Pepper and Mr. Pibb are positioned in the same perceptual space.

SUMMARY

Market segmentation is the process of dividing a heterogeneous market into segments that are relatively homogeneous and identifiable for the purpose of designing a marketing mix to meet the needs of a segment. Segmentation aids marketers in selecting targets because it involves the examination of various potential customer profit and market share opportunities. However, all firms do not engage in segmentation. Companies that do not segment their markets are said to be using an undifferentiated marketing strategy. The goal of this strategy is to appeal to as many similar needs among customers as possible with a single product or service.

If a firm decides to follow a segmentation strategy, it can (1) analyze a general market target, looking for segments that will afford profit opportunities, or (2) if the firm already has a product, examine purchasers and potential buyers and use these data to develop a marketing mix for a segment that best meets the firm's objectives.

There are five basic forms of segmentation: demographic, geographic, psychographic, benefit, and volume. The most common forms of segmentation are demographic and geographic. Life style or psychographic segmentation can help marketers understand what rewards people are seeking in their activities, interests, and opinions. Benefit segmentation is developed on the basis of what a product will do for the user. The marketing manager can then determine what products come closest to meeting the desired benefits, thus learning the strengths and weaknesses of the competition and suggesting new product development opportunities. Volume segmentation is usually done on the basis of heavy, moderate, and light users. Although heavy users may be a small percentage of a market, they may account for a major portion of total consumption.

In order to segment a market successfully, four criteria must be met: (1) the segments must be large enough to permit a viable market effort; (2) the segments must be identifiable and measurable; (3) the segments must exhibit differences in response rates to the marketing variables; and (4) the segments must permit the firm to direct different marketing efforts toward the segments.

To segment a market, a product or market area has to be selected for study. Second, a form of segmentation must be chosen. Next, segmentation descriptors are selected. A survey is then designed and conducted. The marketing manager must then analyze the size and nature of the segments as determined by the research. Finally, market segments must be selected and a marketing strategy designed to appeal to those segments.

Segmentation is not a cureall that should be followed by all companies. In fact, some costs are higher due to segmentation. Segmentation creates demands for greater variety, and therefore results in fewer economies of scale. Firms also must be careful to avoid the majority fallacy. In some cases, markets can be considered oversegmented. The strategy of reducing the number of market segments is called countersegmentation. This often results in significant cost savings.

Product differentiation begins with the product and asks, "How can we make this one different from all the rest?" Market segmentation begins with the total market and asks, "What are the characteristics of the overall market and how can meaningful segments be reached?" Positioning refers to the way a consumer views a product or service in relation to all other products or services the potential buyer perceives as possible substitutes. A product is positioned so that it has a certain image among potential buyers. Positioning can be used to implement either a product differentiation or a market segmentation strategy.

KEY TERMS

Market segmentation
Undifferentiated marketing
Psychographics
User profile
Benefit segmentation
Perceptual mapping
Segmentation descriptors

Majority fallacy
Countersegmentation
Product differentiation
Product positioning
Head-on positioning
Service positioning

REVIEW QUESTIONS

1. What is market segmentation? Why is it important to marketers?
2. Given that a market can be successfully segmented, what approaches may be used in marketing the firm's products?

3. What is a perceptual map? How and for what reasons is it used?
4. Describe the characteristics that form the basis of life style segmentation.
5. Briefly describe the sequence of steps taken to segment a market.
6. Evaluate the concept of product positioning and repositioning. Why would a marketer want to reposition a product?
7. What is positioning? How is it accomplished?
8. What is product differentiation? Give several examples.

DISCUSSION QUESTIONS

1. Comment on the benefits derived from following a differentiation strategy. What are the most common methods employed in differentiating one's product?
2. Discuss the usefulness of psychographics and life style analysis to market segmentation. Why are demographic and geographic market characteristics not usually enough to define a particular market accurately?
3. What is meant by volume segmentation? Why is the heavy user of interest to the marketer? Along what characteristics might heavy users of laundry detergents differ from light users?
4. Discuss the relationship among product differentiation, market segmentation, and product positioning.
5. State the four basic criteria for successful segmentation. How does the marketer evaluate the size and worth of various segments?
6. What do customers gain and lose when a firm follows a countersegmentation policy and reduces product offerings?
7. What are the problems associated with market segmentation? Can it be used at all times? If not, explain situations in which segmentation may not be desirable or feasible.

NOTES

1. "A-B" Aims to Win by Segmenting Light Beer," *Marketing News,* December 19, 1978, pp. 5–8. Reprinted by permission of the American Marketing Association.
2. William Wells, "Psychographics: A Critical Review," *Journal of Marketing Research,* 12 (May 1975): 196–213.
3. Segmentation benefits are taken from Joseph Plummer, "The Concept and Application of Life Style Segmentation," *Journal of Marketing,* 38 (January 1974): 33–37.
4. Paul Green, "A Multidimensional Model of Product-Features Association," *Journal of Business Research,* 2 (April 1974): 107–118.
5. For an excellent summary of the advantages and disadvantages of perceptual mapping, see Nariman Dhalla and Winston Mahatoo, "Expanding the Scope of Segmentation Research," *Journal of Marketing,* 40 (April 1976): 34–41.
6. See Shirley Young, Leland Ott, and Barbara Feigin, "Some Practical Considerations in Market Segmentation," *Journal of Marketing Research,* 15 (August 1978): 405–412.
7. See Allen T. Resnik, Peter Turney, and Barry Mason, "Marketeers Turn to Counter-Segmentation," *Harvard Business Review,* 57 (September–October 1979): 100–106.
8. "Determine Appeal of Concept, Positioning, Use Several Measures," *Marketing News* April 23, 1976, p. 8.
9. "Marketing Tales," *Product Marketing,* April 1977, p. 43. Reprinted by permission.

4.1 Fingerhut Corporation

The Fingerhut Corporation is a direct mail marketer that sells to middle- or low-income families throughout the United States. It is considered one of the most successful mail order retailers in the United States. The entire operation runs on credit because all products are first sent for approval. If a customer decides to keep what is ordered, Fingerhut sends a book of monthly payment stubs. In turn, the customer is charged the going rate of interest.

Once Fingerhut identifies a steady customer, it never lets the person go. When someone moves from one city to another, Fingerhut makes certain that it has the new address. This is simply part of Fingerhut's overall data base. The data bank is a major tool at Fingerhut.

To obtain new customers, Fingerhut rents mailing lists and sends out catalogs and fliers. When the initial order comes in, Fingerhut begins to draw a profile of the buyer. As the company says, "We open a personal store for each customer." Along with the first product ordered, the company sends a questionnaire asking how many children the customer has, how old they are, their birthdays, what sort of dwelling the family lives in, and so on. Thereafter, instead of sending out the same catalogs and fliers to all 5 million customers, Fingerhut sends colorful envelopes containing from one to twenty single-page fliers promoting specific products the firm's marketing executives think that particular customer is likely to buy. For example, a month before a young couple's son turns 10, the parents receive a packet that includes a letter from a Fingerhut executive promising that if they will agree to try any of the products offered, Fingerhut will send a free birthday gift suitable for a 10-year-old boy. The more orders you place, the more packets arrive in the mail. Some customers hear from Fingerhut as often as once a week.

1. Is this the ultimate form of segmentation? That is, is each customer treated as a separate market?
2. How does Fingerhut position itself in relation to other mail order firms such as Speigel's, Montgomery Ward, and Eddie Bauer?
3. What forms of market segmentation would you say Fingerhut is employing? Explain your answer.

4.2 The U.S. Army Reserve

In the late 1970s and early 1980s, the U.S. Army Reserve became concerned about the lack of new volunteers joining up. It also voiced concern over the lack of reenlistments of current reserve members. The Reserve decided to commission a market research study to examine potential benefits consumers are seeking and to determine those most likely to find those benefits by joining the U.S. Army Reserve.

The goal is to attract as many high-quality recruits as possible and to encourage current reservists and guardsmen to remain in the service beyond their initial six-year term. However, alternative programs might entail substantial differences in cost or difficulty in implementation. Most people would like to follow career paths that involve high salaries without responsibility, excitement without risk, and security without boredom.

In the real world such possibilities rarely exist; in making a career choice, it is necessary to consider the tradeoffs among a number of career attributes. The following factors were examined in the survey: starting pay; initial term of service (four years, six years, eight years); enlistment bonus; educational assistance; federal income tax deduction for military pay; post exchange and commissary privileges; hair regulations; hours of meetings each month (twelve hours per month or sixteen hours per month); content of unit meetings (50 percent military training and 50 percent community service, or 75 percent military training and 25 percent community service, or all military training); period until retirement; and whether or not the employer will make up the pay difference for the annual two-week training.

The survey found that various types of financial benefits were the most important factors in making the decision to join the reserve. Educational assistance, enlistment bonuses, and increased starting pay were found to have the greatest impact on increasing enlistments. Life style considerations such as frequency of meetings, length of meetings per month, and hair regulations were not as likely to have a strong impact on enlistments. Those most apt to enlist were (1) still in high school, (2) most likely to have had a vocational curriculum, (3) most likely to be currently unemployed, and (4) less likely to be from a large urban area.

1. Did the Army Reserve conduct a segmentation study? Why or why not?
2. What kind of segmentation is the Army Reserve attempting to utilize?
3. What other forms of segmentation could it use?
4. Given the information provided in the research, what would be the next step you would recommend? Why?

5

The decision-making process in consumer buying

OBJECTIVES

To gain an overview of consumer behavior.

To examine a model of consumer behavior and analyze its components.

To identify and understand the internal and external factors that affect buyer behavior.

To evaluate the consumer decision-making process.

To become aware of the consumer's post purchase evaluation process.

To integrate the concepts of consumer behavior and marketing strategy.

In the early 1970s, consumers began switching from heavier liquors such as scotch and bourbon to lighter drinks, including vodka and gin. Even the sales of the stronger blended whiskeys were in a state of decline. It seemed so logical in the face of this trend to stop sales declines of whiskey by introducing a new, lighter-flavored product. This feeling was not confined to one distiller; the entire industry was rushing to be the first with a new light whiskey.

Extensive research was used to back the creation of the "right" product. Product characteristics such as "separate," "clear," "light," "dry," and "white" were introduced to several thousand survey respondents. When asked to choose which best described the new product, the words "dry" and "white" were big winners. Survey participants also felt that it should be priced with upper-medium brands currently on the market. Also, the survey indicated that people were very curious to try the new dry-white whiskey. This was encouraging, since curiosity usually plays a big part in the successful introduction of a new liquor product. It was also targeted to a growing market segment—the well-educated professional person 25 to 35 years old.

The name Frost was selected from over 700 potential trademarks. It was perceived as upbeat, modern, and clean. The latter part of the name, 8/80, referred to the eight steps in the distillation process and the fact that it was 80 proof. The label was designed to create a quality image through the use of silver and black colors. Several drinks were concocted that required the new Frost 8/80, including the "Diamond Lil" and "Moby Dick." Full-page four color ads were used in eight major magazines to build brand awareness. Brown-Forman forecasted sales of 100,000 cases the first year. In reality they sold only one-third of their projected volume. Two years after the introduction of Frost 8/80, it was withdrawn from the market. Brown-Forman lost about $2 million on the product.

Brown-Forman was not the only loser. Every other distiller that brought out a light whiskey experienced disappointing sales. Light Old Crow, for example, was another major disaster. What went wrong? Marketing people are still "sifting through the ashes" to find the answer. Although research showed the product to be unique, this alone does not mean consumers will try it. Also, it looked like vodka and tasted like whiskey, which violated people's preconditioned feelings and beliefs about liquors. Many consumers also did not seem to understand what the product was. Is it like vodka, gin, or what? Another possibility is that consumer preferences for light liquors were being satisfied by existing items such as gin and vodka. Perhaps the true reason will never come to light.[1]

The Frost 8/80 story illustrates some important aspects of this chapter. Despite the elaborate research and already existing trends away from heavy liquors, the light whiskeys were a failure. Understanding consumer decision processes is not easy. In fact, the way you and I process information could have created part of the problem. What were the distillers telling us this product really was? One retailer placed Light Old Crow next to the regular Old Crow and created a sign that read "Now you can have Old Crow light or dark." This seemed to run counter to the "positioning" the distillers were trying to establish.

What types of decisions do consumers make? More important, how are these decisions made? How does buyer behavior interact with marketing strategy? Let us take a closer look.

Consumer buying decisions

Buyer behavior is the process and act of decision making of people involved in buying and using products. When buyers make decisions, they are engaging in a problem-solving task. When you purchase a good or service, you suppose you have acquired something that will alleviate a perceived need. There are various degrees of problem solving, including these:

1. Routinized response behavior
2. Limited problem solving
3. Extensive problem solving

ROUTINIZED RESPONSE BEHAVIOR

Much consumer behavior is **routinized response behavior.** For example, you select a Coke because you want a soft drink. You are familiar with existing brands; there are no or few social attitudes associated with the product; you have tried all major brands and know their taste; and you have also learned that a Coke will quench your thirst. The problem-solving task is fairly simple. There is little need for new information, so the decision is quickly made.

Routinized response behavior is often habitual consumer behavior. That is, we purchase the same brand over and over with little forethought. People who engage in such behavior are said to be **brand loyal.** Perhaps you have brand loyalty to an after-shave or perfume, an ice cream, or a type of suit or dress. Brand loyalty simplifies the purchase/decision-making process. However, even brand-loyal buyers sometimes switch brands. We may try a new product out of curiosity. Sometimes dealers are out of our favorite brand, or perhaps a special price discount will cause us to try a different product. It is the task of the marketing manager with a brand-loyal target audience to maintain the quality of the product or service, make certain that distribution is sufficient, and continue to promote the item to reinforce a positive product image.

LIMITED PROBLEM SOLVING

Limited problem solving involves a more detailed decision-making process than habitual behavior. It typically occurs when the buyer is attempting to choose from among two or more brands in a familiar product class. At this point the decision maker has already decided to buy a particular type of product but has not decided on a brand. For example, if a person in Los Angeles has decided to go to New York for a vacation and has decided to fly, the problem boils down to selecting an airline. Assuming that our traveler does not frequently fly the Los Angeles–New York route and therefore does not prefer one airline over another, he or she is faced with limited problem solving. Our vacationer has flown and traveled enough to know the criteria by which he or she will make the decision, such as convenient departure times, whether or not it will be a dinner flight, movies scheduled for the flight, ticket price, and so forth. These criteria are based on past trips to other cities.

Since there is more information to be processed by the decision maker than in the Coke purchase, decision-making time will be longer. It is the function of the marketing manager faced with a limited problem-solving target audience to convince consumers to buy the firm's product or service. Research must be used to make sure that the firm's product or service mix effectively meshes with the needs of the target audience. Special price deals, trial offers, or trial sizes should be considered by the marketing manager to get people to try the company's brand. American Airlines, for example, offers a variety of promotional air fares to get consumers to fly American. It is hoped by American's management that a good flight and courteous service will create a brand preference for American over competing carriers.

EXTENSIVE PROBLEM SOLVING

Extensive problem solving is the most complex form of purchase decision. The consumer is not familiar with the product class or the brands available and must often engage in an extensive information search. The product may or may not involve social risk; it may also have major economic consequences. Home video recorders represent an extensive problem-solving situation for many potential buyers. Should I buy one? What advantages will I receive? Are the benefits worth the cost? What are the characteristics of the various brands? Which of these characteristics are important to me?

The marketing manager has several responsibilities when faced with this type of target consumer. First, promotion to the target audience should be extensive and informative. A good advertisement will tell consumers what they need to know to make the purchase decision. For example, an advertisement for RCA video recorders should not stop at promoting the quality image of

RCA. It must also stress the benefits of owning *any* video recorder and discuss the unique advantages of the RCA brand.

The purchase process

Figure 5.1 shows some of the more important considerations in buying a product. With routinized response behavior, the consideration is simple. If, for example, you routinely purchase Exxon Unleaded gasoline, your decision is limited to picking an Exxon station that is reasonably close and has fair prices. On the other hand, extensive problem solving requires a number of buying decisions. What is a fair price? Should I buy a product that will not pollute the environment? Is it safe? Where can I get service? Will I get good service?

Let us assume that a college student concerned about the price of gasoline and his or her distance from campus decides to search for an alternative to using an automobile. He or she might consider taking a commuter train, riding a bus, or purchasing a motorcycle. Numerous bits of information must be processed before a decision can be reached. Questions such as safety, convenience, and cost must be resolved before a mode of transportation (product class) can be selected. Let us assume that after an extended search, the student selects a motorcycle. A motorcycle is economical and will give him or her additional flexibility besides going to and from school. For many people, safety considerations and concern for his or her self-image would rule out a motorcycle. Our student, however, has been able to overcome these objections in his or her own mind. At this point, the extended decision-making process continues with an evaluation of brands. Which cycles give the best value for the

◢ **FIGURE 5.1 Purchase considerations.**

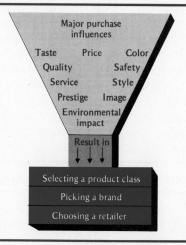

money? Which brands have the best resale value and the most safety features? Which dealer gives the best price discounts and quality service? Which is better — an American brand or a foreign make?

These levels of problem solving are not limited to a single individual; actually, up to five different people could be involved in the purchase decision:

1. The instigator
2. The influencer
3. The decision maker
4. The purchaser
5. The consumer

To illustrate, let us use the Green family, which lives in a suburb of St. Louis. Mr. Green plays golf at the municipal course once a week with several friends. A member of the foursome mentions that his son, a friend of Mr. Green's boy Tom, will be attending camp this summer. The friend of Mr. Green's has played the role of instigator. He is the one who suggested, initiated, or planted the seed. Mr. Green returns home and mentions to his wife Nancy that one of Tom's friends is going to camp this summer.

Nancy likes the idea of Tom experiencing the great outdoors and decides to call a school counselor for possible recommendations. The school counselor provides Nancy with data and suggestions regarding several Missouri summer camps for boys. The counselor in this situation is an influencer — someone whose opinion is valued in the decision-making process. Nancy finally selects Camp Run-A-Muk for a two-week stay. She has played the role of decision maker. She has made the decision of product or service class (going to summer camp) and chosen a service retailer (Camp Run-A-Muk). If a product had been involved, Nancy would have selected a brand as well as the retailer. Mr. Green sends in the reservation form and the check. He is the purchaser of the service. Young Tom Green gets to experience the wonders of outdoor living. Tom is the consumer.

This illustration points out how important it is for marketing managers to understand who plays what role in the decision process. The director of the summer camp, for example, needs to promote the nature of the camp and its advantages over competing facilities to both the decision maker and the influencer. He or she must also understand the importance of various attributes of a summer camp for both influencer and decision maker. A school counselor may value educational opportunities and variety of activities in making a recommendation. The decision maker, Nancy Green, may place more emphasis on finding a camp fairly close to home that offers the most activities for the money. The promotion appeals used by the camp for each of these people should vary and should be strongly influenced by knowledge of consumer attitudes and preferences.

A model of consumer behavior

In order to put the consumer decision-making process in perspective, we will look first at a simplified information-processing model. A model is a represen-

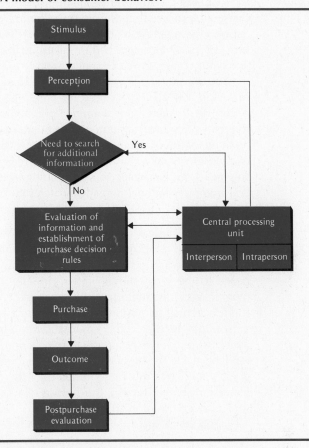

tation of reality usually reduced in scale and simplified. A good model provides a systematic and rational means for understanding a phenomenon. Figure 5.2 shows a model of consumer buying behavior. Let us begin with a brief overview of the model before examining each component.

STIMULUS, PERCEPTION, SEARCH

A **stimulus** is any unit of input into any of our senses—sight, smell, touch, hearing. A stimulus might be the feel of a sweater you are examining, the color of an automobile, the design on a package, a brand name mentioned by a friend, an advertisement on television, the perfume worn by a stranger. Response to a stimulus depends upon how the consumer processes the content, form, complexity, and amount of information presented by a stimulus or stimuli.

Attention. As consumers, we can be considered information-processing systems. We acquire data, store it, manipulate it, and give out information. Information processing begins with acquiring information. In order to accomplish this task, the consumer must first devote attention, or some of the capacity of our central processing unit, to the stimulus.

One characteristic of attention is that it is selective. You may, for example, have as a goal finding a can of baked beans in a supermarket. Thus you scan and ignore many rows of canned goods until you see the baked beans. Or you may be considering the purchase of a new suit. As you read a newspaper, you may stop and glance at an ad for a new sports car but then quickly turn the page. The car data is not stored in your memory. When your eye catches a picture of a suit advertisement, you stop and read it carefully. This information is retained for future use. Attention also has levels of intensity. We often pay close attention to certain information when we are involved in extensive problem solving. If, for example, you were going to purchase a boat for the first time, you would pay attention to ads by Starcraft, Wolverine, Ranger, and other boat manufacturers.

Perception. **Perception** is the process by which we select, organize, and interpret stimuli into a meaningful and coherent picture. In essence, it is how we see the world around us. It is important to realize that two people can be exposed to the same stimuli under virtually identical conditions but perceive them in very different ways. For example, three people might be sitting in a room watching television when an advertisement flashes on the screen. One person may be thoroughly engrossed in the message and become highly motivated to purchase the product. The second individual may find the message repugnant. He or she may lose any previous desire for the product. The third person may have mentally "tuned-out" the commercial. Thirty seconds after the advertisement is over, this person cannot tell you the content of the message or even the product advertised.

Perception is also an organizational process. You do not perceive sheet metal, paint, and four tires—you perceive an automobile. We not only organize our perceptions, we also generalize them. We perceive new stimuli in the same manner as a stimulus with which we are familiar. In other words, we perceive and evaluate new things in light of past experiences. New products are perceived in a fashion similar to the closest possible substitutes; so, as the following example shows, are new experiences.

A savage who has never seen a civilized man or any of the paraphernalia of advanced civilization sees an Army airplane descend from the skies and make a three point landing and sees Second Lieutenant Arbuthnot come out of the plane. Obviously, our savage will see the airplane and Arbuthnot as organized objects but will they, because he has never seen their like before, be completely meaningless to him? Again, the meaning he experiences may be wrong, but there will be meaning. He may experience the meaning of a "bird" as part of his purely visual precept of the airplane; he may ascribe the meaning of "God" or its equivalent to Arbuthnot, 2nd Lieutenant AUS. He will not have to wait until he has had further and extended experiences with these strange objects before his perceptual field is organized into a meaningful one.[2]

Search. After stimuli are perceived, it is possible that more information will be needed. Additional search is unnecessary for many purchases: You walk past a candy machine, remember your many past pleasant consumption experiences with a Milky Way, and so you buy one. But assume you are going to purchase a new car. The decision becomes more complicated, and you are motivated to search for more information. The decision to search is based upon the perceived value of the new information in relation to the costs of obtaining it. Most people buying a new car would probably like information on various models, options, gas mileage, durability, passenger capacity, and so forth. The trouble and time it takes to get this data are less than the cost of buying the "wrong" car.

Whether or not you search for information also depends somewhat on what you already know. Generally speaking, the more you know about a potential purchase, the less you search. John's hobby is fishing, and he is an ardent reader of fishing magazines and catalogs. He has no hesitation about purchasing an expensive new reel without gaining further information. A second closely related factor in this instance is confidence in your decision-making ability. Not only did John have plenty of stored information, but he had confidence in his ability to make the "right" decision. People who lack this confidence will continue an information search even when they have large amounts of stored data.[3]

Once a decision to search has been reached, it can take place internally or externally or both. If the search is internal, the person strives to recall past information stored within his or her memory. Perhaps you encounter a brand of cake mix in the supermarket that you tried some time ago. You begin to search your memory . . . did it taste good? did the guests enjoy it? was it easy to prepare?

On the other hand, you may engage in an external search. If you decide an external search is necessary, there are six ways to get information:

1. *Impersonal advocate.*   Mass media advertising, including reading magazine ads, listening to radio commercials, reading newspaper ads, viewing TV commercials, or looking at point-of-purchase displays.
2. *Impersonal independent.*   Checking with *Consumer Reports* or finding a technical report on the product.
3. *Personal advocate.*   Asking sales clerk's or store manager's opinion.
4. *Personal independent.*   Trying to remember what brand a friend or neighbor uses, asking opinions of family members or close friends, asking the opinion of a neighbor or co-worker.
5. *Direct observation/experience.*   Asking for a product demonstration, relying on past personal experience, trying the product before buying, or reading the information on the package.
6. *Pick a brand.*   Picking a brand and trying it out.[4]

INTRAPERSONAL COMPONENTS OF THE CENTRAL PROCESSING UNIT

The **central processing unit (CPU)** "oversees" the decision-making process and strongly affects the information acquisition function (see Figure 5.3). We will begin by examining the intrapersonal aspects of the CPU: needs and wants, learning and memory, attitudes and personality. The CPU is virtually synonymous with the central nervous system and includes both conscious and subconscious processes. Its two major functions are to react (via perception) to stimuli and to "oversee" the decision-making process.

Needs. A major component of the human psyche is needs. A **need** is anything an individual depends on to function efficiently. Needs are said to be at the root of all human behavior. Without needs, there would be no behavior patterns. The most popular scheme for categorizing needs was conceived by the psychologist A. H. Maslow.[5]

Physiological needs—food, water, and shelter—are basic to survival and must be satisfied first. Safety needs include freedom from pain and discomfort. Safety is also related to fear of change. Research has shown that most people prefer an orderly and continuous pattern in their day-to-day activities.

According to Maslow, after our physiological and safety needs have been fulfilled, love becomes the dominant need. Love is defined to include acceptance by one's peers as well as sex and romantic love. The need for esteem, the fourth need, is subdivided into two categories. One form of esteem is self-respect and a feeling of accomplishment. The second category is the esteem of others. Prestige, fame, and recognition of one's accomplishments are manifestations of this form of esteem. Note that love is acceptance without regard to contribution; esteem is acceptance based on contribution to the group.

Self actualization is our highest need. It refers to self-fulfillment and self-expression—reaching the point in life at which "you are what you feel you should be." Maslow felt that very few people ever reach this level.

According to Maslow, as a person obtains increasing fulfillment of one need, a higher-level need becomes more important. Also, some people have stronger needs at one level than at another. For example, safety and the fear of change may be very important to one person and relatively unimportant to another.

◀ **FIGURE 5.3 Components of the central processing unit.**

Central Processing Unit	
Interperson	Intraperson
Reference group	Needs and wants
Family	Learning
Culture	Beliefs and attitudes
Social class	Personality
Life cycle	

Learning. **Learning** is the process that results in changes in behavior, immediate or expected, which come about from experience and practice or the conceptualization of that experience and practice in response to stimuli or situations.[6] We cannot directly observe learning. If Judy sees an advertisement for a new radio and then goes to the store the next day and buys that radio, we infer that learning has taken place. The definition also points out that experience can alter our behavior. If Judy tries the new radio when she gets home and does not like it, she may not purchase that brand again. **Conceptual learning** (nonexperiential learning) is also important. Assume, for example, that you are standing at a soft drink machine and notice a new flavor, Rondo, that is labeled "lightly carbonated." Since lightly carbonated beverages have tasted flat to you in the past, you choose a different drink. You have learned that you do not like Rondo without ever trying one.

We learn faster and retain or store the information longer the more important the material to be learned, the more reinforcement received while learning, and the greater the stimulus repetition. If you are seeking information on new living room furniture, any furniture ads you see promoting living room pieces will be more readily learned by you. Why? Because you feel this information is important in making a purchase decision.

If you see a package of Doublemint gum (stimulus) in a supermarket, purchase it (response), and find the gum to be quite refreshing, your behavior has been positively reinforced. On the other hand, assume that you see a new soap product and purchase it. If the soap does not do a decent job of cleaning your clothes (negative reinforcement), you will not buy the product again. When there is no reinforcement, positive or negative, there is no strong incentive to engage in the same behavior pattern again or to avoid it. There was little learning. Thus if a new brand evokes neutral feelings, some marketing activity such as a price change or an increase in promotion may be required to induce further consumption.

In general, learning tends to increase:

1. As the number of reinforcements increase.
2. When there are rest periods between responses.
3. As the size of the reward increases.
4. When rewards are intermittent or varied.
5. When there is little time lapse between response and reward.

Repetition is a key strategy in promotional campaigns because different schedules of repetition can lead to different patterns of learning. Dr. Pepper uses repetitious advertising so you will learn that it is a unique soft drink. In general, advertising messages should be spread over time rather than being clustered at one time. There are, however, many other factors, such as seasons and holidays, that can affect promotion schedules.

Stimulus generalization occurs when one response is extended to a second similar stimulus. When marketers have a successful, well-known brand name, they often use it for a family of products (see Figure 5.4). Such brand families aid in the introduction of new products and facilitate the sale of existing items.

Old Faithful.

Good Old Faithful. Always got you where you were going. Always did it economically. A whole generation of Americans grew up with Old Faithful. And now, 27 years and 33 million cars later, it's still a symbol of dependability and economy.

Now there's a car that's just as reliable and economical as Old Faithful ever was. It's New Faithful. The 1977 VW Rabbit. With engineering so advanced that automotive experts have

hailed it as the kind of car Detroit will be building in the 1980's.

The Rabbit has a new fuel injection system, so it starts up quick as a bunny. Springs like one, too. 0 to 50 in just 7.7 seconds. The Rabbit also has advanced engineering features like negative steering roll radius to help maintain directional stability in the event of a front-tire blowout; rack-and-pinion steering for more direct maneuvering and better road feel; and

©VOLKSWAGEN OF AMERICA, INC.

New Faithful.

an independent stabilizer rear axle, low in unsprung weight, for better road holding.

New Faithful lives up to Old Faithful's reputation for economy, too. Because it has fuel injection, you can use the most economical grade of gas.* But you won't have to use it very often. Rabbit gets 37 mpg on the highway, 24 in the city. (That's EPA's estimate for manual transmission. Actual mileage may vary, depending on driving

habits, car's condition and optional equipment.)

Dependability and economy. That's what Old Faithful gave a whole generation of Americans. And that's what New Faithful is giving a whole new generation of Americans.

New Faithful. The 1977 VW Rabbit.

VW Rabbit

More Volkswagen from Volkswagen

*California excluded.

Source: Courtesy of Volkswagen of America.

Some examples include Kraft, Pepperidge Farm, Checkerboard Square, Betty Crocker, Craftsman, and Penncrest. We also have **stimulus discrimination,** the ability to select the correct stimulus from others similar to it. Product differentiation strategy seeks to create stimulus discrimination. For example, advertising is used to teach us that all aspirin is not alike. Some other aspects of stimulus discrimination as they relate to marketing are these:

1. A new product has the greatest chance of success if it is noticeably better than established products on some dimension that is important to consumers.
2. If the new product is not better, but is distinguishably different from competing brands in some way, it has a reasonable chance for success.
3. If the new product is virtually identical with competitive products, it has little chance of marketing success.[7]

Beliefs and attitudes. Learning, beliefs, and attitudes are closely linked. An **attitude** is a learned predisposition to respond in a consistently favorable or unfavorable manner with respect to a given object, such as a brand.[8] A **belief** is what you think about an item such as strawberry Jello. Attitudes tend to be longer lasting and more complex than beliefs, and consist of clusters of interrelated beliefs. Attitudes also encompass our value system, which represents our standards of good and bad, right and wrong, and so forth. Thus you may have a specific attitude toward Disneyworld. It is based upon beliefs about need for entertainment, cartoon characters, fantasy, crowds of people, waiting in lines, and many other things. Disneyworld may also be highly valued by you as good, clean, wholesome fun.

A multifaceted object (like a brand) can be viewed as a bundle of attributes leading to costs and benefits of different desirability to potential buyers or segments of the market. The chances or probability that you will buy a certain brand depends upon several things:

1. That buying a brand will lead to a specific outcome; for example, buying a Coke and drinking it will give you a cola taste.
2. The negative or positive feeling toward that outcome; for example, the cola flavor will taste good.
3. All-important outcomes associated with the product; for example, when drinking a Coke there will be a good taste, your thirst will be quenched, and you will feel refreshed.

Every product or service has attributes. A person buys an item that he or she feels possesses positive attributes that are important to him or her. A professional person may desire the following in a new watch: accuracy, day and date, a prestige brand name, and good value for the money. The buyer will evaluate watches considered to have a prestige name, such as Rolex, Pulsar, and Seiko. The watch finally selected will be the one perceived to have certain attributes which the person wants in a watch. It also will be the watch that offers the greatest amount of the most desirable outcomes. For example, after accurate time, the professional person may be seeking prestige; he or she would then select the Rolex.

In some instances, several other factors can influence what we buy:[9]

1. A person with influence over us (influencer) may expect us to buy or not to buy a specific type of product or brand. An influencer can be a parent, spouse, friend, boss, doctor, and so on.
2. An individual's motivation to comply with the expectations of the influencer.

Returning to our watch example, assume that the professional person's spouse already owns a Rolex and would like our purchaser to buy the same brand. If it is important for the professional person to meet the expectations of his or her spouse when buying a watch, this would reinforce the decision to buy a Rolex. Now let us assume a second relevant influencer enters the picture. This is the professional person's boss, who does not like subordinates to wear the same status symbols as he or she does. The superior's attitude is, "if I own a Rolex, my employees should wear something less showy and expensive." In order to avoid alienating the boss, our watch purchaser may buy a Seiko. In other words, maintaining a good relationship with a superior outweighed all other factors in buying the watch.

Changing attitudes. If a marketing manager's product or service is meeting its profit goals, positive attitudes merely need to be reinforced. However, if the brand is not doing well, the manager must strive to change the attitudes of the target audience. This can be accomplished in three ways:

1. Changing the belief(s) about the attributes of the brand.
2. Changing the relative importance of these beliefs.
3. Adding new beliefs.[10]

The first technique involves taking neutral or negative product attribute beliefs and trying to make them positive. Curtis Mathis, a southern manufacturer, produces the highest priced television sets in America. Many people view the price attribute very negatively. Curtis Mathis has attempted to overcome this by advertising its products as "the most expensive televisions in America and darn well worth it." The advertisements then explain the additional value the consumer receives from a Curtis Mathis set.

The second approach to attitude modification is to change the relative importance of a person's beliefs toward an attribute. Mercedes-Benz manufactures relatively expensive automobiles. Although they cost as much or more than Cadillacs, the Mercedes vehicles did not have electric seats until 1981. Other attributes of the car, such as high resale value, quality of workmanship, and leather interiors, were always featured. The sales approach was "if you can get all these other features, electric seats are really immaterial." Strangely enough Mercedes did offer *heated* seats, but not the type of electric seats American consumers know.

The third approach is to add new beliefs. This technique relies upon repositioning, which we have already discussed. In the mid-1970s Ford repositioned its Thunderbird from a classic car with prestige and luxury for only a few to a prestige and luxury car for middle-class Americans. Sales results proved that Ford had created a very successful repositioning strategy. In another example, Blue Nun has promoted the idea that its white wine goes with just about anything—that it is not limited to fowl and fish.

Does attitude change actually result in different consumption patterns? Studies have found that:

1. The more favorable the attitude, the higher the incidence of product usage.
2. The less favorable the attitude, the lower the incidence of usage.
3. The more unfavorable people's attitudes are toward a product, the more likely they are to stop using it.
4. The attitudes of people who have never tried a product tend to be distributed around the mean in the shape of a normal distribution.[11]

Personality. The final intrapersonal component of the central processing unit is personality. **Personality** is a broad term; it is a way of organizing and categorizing the consistencies of an individual's reactions to situations. Thus, personality is a composite of psychological makeup and environmental forces.

A major theory of personality has been developed from the thought of Sigmund Freud. He postulated that the personality has three basic dimensions, the id, the ego, and the superego. The id is the mechanism that leads to strong drives and releases large quantities of energy. It is dedicated to finding pleasure and releasing tension. It is not influenced by ethics or morality but compulsively seeks pleasure and satisfaction.

The ego is the mechanism that helps an individual cope with reality. It is the equilibrating device that leads to socially acceptable behavior. It imposes rationality on the id. The ego weighs the consequences of an act rather than rushing blindly into pleasurable activity. The superego is a person's conscience. It tries to keep behavior in line with what is morally right or wrong. In essence, the id urges an enjoyable act; the superego presents the moral issues involved; and the ego acts as the arbitrator in determining whether to proceed or not.

According to Freud, the mechanism that leads to behavior is largely unconscious. Freud felt that a person's life is centered on sexual gratification. Therefore much of an individual's behavior is triggered by the id, with its strong sexual drive (see Figure 5.5). Over the years psychoanalytic theory has been broadened to include the need for power and personality development as behavior triggers.

◄ **FIGURE 5.5 Appealing to sex drives.**

Source: Courtesy of Faberge Inc.

An individual's personality is manifested in a consistent pattern of responses to the environment. These consistent behavior patterns or tendencies are called **personality traits.** Marketing experts have used both standard personality tests and customized measures in an attempt to relate personality traits and buyer behavior. Most research has failed to establish a strong relationship between the two. However, low correlations between specific traits and particular products suggest that other factors within the buyer's psyche also influence the purchase decision. And some studies have found significant relationships between personality factors and brand purchases. Some examples are shown in Table 5.1.

◀ **TABLE 5.1   Selected Personality Traits and Significantly Related Consumer Behavior**

Personality trait	Consumer behavior
Aggressiveness	Men prefer a brand of dress shirt whose advertising emphasizes masculinity, a manual razor over an electric razor, and a brand of beer associated with taverns that cater to "an outspokenly masculine group of students"; they also use more cologne and after-shave lotion.
Conservatism (cautiousness)	More favorable attitude toward buying a small car.
Intellectual efficiency	Early adoption of cable television.
Interest in people	Preference for common stocks over savings accounts, convertibles over sedans.
Need for order	Men smoke more cigarettes per day; men prefer one unspecified magazine to another.
	Husband: More loyal to favorite brand of one-ply and two-ply toilet tissues; less loyal to first-choice brand of tea; less loyal to second- and third-choice brands of beer; fewer coffee units purchased.
	Wife: More loyal to first-choice brand of tea; more loyal to second- and third-choice brands of tea; fewer consecutive purchases of the same brand of beer at the same store; less loyal to store for tea purchases: more consecutive purchases of tea in a given store; more shopping trips to purchase tea; higher average number of beer units purchased per shopping trip.
Self-acceptance	Housewives more innovative in appliance purchases; early adoption of cable television.
Self-confidence, self-esteem	More difficult to persuade male college students. The higher *or* lower, the more difficult to persuade; the more moderate, the easier to persuade: generalized self-confidence; self-confidence specific to car-buying ability.
	New car buyers high *or* low in generalized self-confidence, but low in self-confidence specific to buying a car, take friends to the showroom to help them in the purchase.

Source: Adapted from: William Wells and Arthur Beard, "Personality and Consumer Behavior," in *Consumer Behavior: Theoretical Sources,* eds. Scott Ward and Thomas Robertson, © 1973, pp. 180–189. Reprinted by permission of Prentice-Hall, Inc., Englewood Cliffs, N.J.

Personality does affect the evaluation and information processing function. For example, an efficient person tends to engage in a less lengthy information search. An experimenting individual tends to analyze a brand differently from a conservative person. A tender-minded person would not respond in the same manner as a tough-minded person to a life insurance advertisement "to protect your family when you are gone."

INTERPERSONAL COMPONENTS OF THE CENTRAL PROCESSING UNIT

Let us turn our attention now to the interpersonal aspects of the central processing unit. These include reference groups, family, culture, social class, and the life cycle.

Reference groups. **Reference groups** are groups that influence our behavior and attitudes. They are the people we rely on in forming our own beliefs and attitudes. In essence, people are psychological participants in their reference groups. They believe in the group's goals, values, and activities.

You do not have to belong to a group in order for it to qualify as your reference group. If you are a member, it is called an **affiliative group;** if not, it is called an **aspiratory group.** The most important affiliative group for most of us is our family. Others include our co-workers, church members, club members, and so forth. Many affiliative groups are also primary reference groups. The latter are characterized by significant personal interaction and cooperation among members. Secondary reference groups are selected on the basis of interests and often do not have much face-to-face interaction. A good example would be the Republican or Democratic party.

In contrast to affiliative groups, aspiratory reference groups are those that individuals would like to join. You may wish to be invited to join a fraternity or sorority. A young executive might like to join the country club. To gain membership in an aspiratory reference group, one must conform to the norms of the group. **Norms** are the values and attitudes deemed acceptable by the group. Thus a student who wants to join a particular fraternity dresses like its members. He may go to many of the restaurants, clubs, and so on that fraternity members patronize. He tries to play a role that is acceptable to the fraternity members. Group roles are behavior patterns based on the group's norms.

Reference groups have three important marketing implications: (1) They serve as information sources and influences of quality perceptions; (2) they affect individuals' aspiration levels; and (3) their norms serve as constraints or influences on consumption.

Self-concept. Reference groups are an aid in a person's development of a self-concept. We all have several different self-concepts. First, there is the real self-image. It refers to how a person really views himself or herself. Next is the ideal self. It represents the way an individual would like to be. Generally speaking, we try to raise our real self-concept toward our ideal self (or at least narrow the gap). For example, a consumer does not often buy products that would jeopardize his or her self-image. If you consider yourself a contemporary dresser, you will avoid clothing that doesn't project a "with-it" image.

A third form of self-concept is the reference group self, sometimes called the real other self. This may be defined as the way an individual thinks other people view him or her. If you think a particular group views you as a leader, for example, you may assume a leadership role. An important aspect of the reference group self is the fact that a person's perception of how others view him or her may or may not be realistic. You have probably seen someone play the role of a "big shot" because he or she believes everyone else will be impressed.

A person's behavior depends largely on his or her self-concept. Consumers tend to see the environment in a way that is compatible with their self-image. Their identity as individuals is something they want to protect. Thus the products and services we purchase, the stores we patronize, and the credit cards we carry support our self-images. Marketing managers often try to market their product by appealing to self-image. For example, the Marlboro smoker reinforces a rugged, free-spirit self-image, while the Cadillac driver reinforces a "big shot" self-concept.

Family. A person's self-concept is also influenced by his or her primary affiliative reference group—the family. Our parents influence our consumption and behavior patterns, standards, and values from infancy through the teenage years and beyond. Marriage brings forth a new set of roles and purchasing patterns for both partners.

Four types of family role structures have been identified: (1) autonomous—equal number of decisions by each spouse, but each decision is made by one spouse or another; (2) husband dominant; (3) wife dominant; and (4) syncratic joint decision making. Role structures vary significantly depending upon the type of item purchased.

Culture. Purchase roles within the family are influenced by culture. **Culture** may be defined as the set of values, ideas, attitudes, and other meaningful symbols created to shape human behavior and the artifacts of that behavior as they are transmitted from one generation to the next.[12] Culture is environmentally oriented. The nomads of Finland have developed a culture for Arctic survival. Similarly, the natives of the Brazilian jungle have created a culture suitable for jungle living.

Culture by definition is social in nature. It is human interaction that creates values and prescribes acceptable behavior. Thus culture gives order to society by creating common expectations. Sometimes these expectations are codified into law; for example, if you come to a red light, you stop the car. As long as a value or belief meets the needs of society, it will remain part of the culture; if it is no longer functional, the value or belief recedes. The value that large families are "good" is no longer held by a majority of Americans. Since Americans live in an urban rather than a rural environment, children are no longer needed to perform farm chores. Children in today's society are an economic liability rather than an asset.

Culture is not static. It adapts to changing societal needs and evolving environmental factors. The rapid growth of technology in this century has accelerated the rate of cultural change. Inventions such as the elevator made possible modern high-rise cities. Television changed entertainment patterns and family communication flows, and heightened public awareness of political and other news events. Automation has increased the amount of leisure time available and adversely affected the Protestant work ethic. Many cultural norms evolve because of a societal need for solutions to recurring problems. The process of learning a culture is called **socialization.** If a person leaves one society to live in another and learns its culture, the process is called **acculturation.** In our early years, the family is the basic source of socialization. After we enter school, other reference groups transmit cultural norms.

Social class. Another interpersonal factor that influences the central processing unit is a consumer's **social class,** his or her status rank within society. A number of different techniques and criteria have been developed for measuring and defining social class. Some of the more popular rankings are shown in Table 5.2. Depending on whose scheme one is using, the portion of the population in any given rank can vary substantially. For instance, the number of people in the upper class varies from 0.4 percent (Carman) to 10.5 percent (Mathews and Slocum).

Each social class has a number of separate life styles, although individual life styles exhibit greater differences between classes than within a given class. The most critical separation between the classes is the one between the middle and the lower class. It is here that the major shift in life styles appears.

William Wells, a noted marketing scholar, explains the interrelationships of life styles as follows:

The lower class person typically prefers discipline, structure, order, and directive leadership. He is family-centered with an extended family having many cooperative relationships. He is person-centered; he sees the locus of cause for events and actions in persons rather than in events and the environment.

A basic characteristic of his life is an orientation toward security. This derives from an occupational requirement that allows little room for anything but following directives of others. The important thing then becomes adopting a "low profile" and building up seniority so as to gain job protection in an industrial society in which he is considered to be an object rather than a person. Obviously, then, this results in "getting by" rather

◀ TABLE 5.2 Social Class Distribution Percentages

Level	Carman[a]	McCann	Warner	Mathews & Slocum	Rich & Jain	Hollingshead[b]
I Upper	0.4%	3.0%	0.9%	10.5%	4.2%	3.0%
II U-Middle	10.8	12.0	7.3	20.6	23.6	8.0
III Middle	30.8	29.5	28.7	27.5	37.2	22.0
IV L-Middle	50.0	34.1	43.4	35.3	13.6	46.0
V Lower	8.0	21.4	19.7	6.1	21.4	18.0

[a] Carman's classes are referred to as: Upper; U-Middle; L-Middle; U-Lower; L-Lower.
[b] Hollingshead's distribution allows for 3% unknown.
Source: William Wells, *Life Style and Psychographics* (Chicago: American Marketing Association, 1974), p. 241. Reprinted by permission of the American Marketing Association.

than "getting ahead"—the latter being characteristic of the middle class. Therefore, while interested in a good standard of living, the lower or working class person is not attracted to the middle class life style with its concern for status and prestige. . . .

Manipulating one's life style so as to gain status and prestige is basically a phenomenon of the middle classes. This involves a more outward orientation toward society in general, and one's peers in particular, than is true of the lower classes. It presupposes that a person has some particular goal to attain. This can be likened to a "becoming process," although not perhaps in the healthiest sense of the word. It does seem as if the middle class life style is more dynamic and changing as opposed to the more static life style of the lower class.

Upper social class individuals also seem more likely to think of themselves as "nice looking people" and to be more confident of their own abilities. All of the findings in this paragraph would seem to support the contentions of earlier writers on social class. Apparently, people of upper social class are more confident, outgoing, culturally oriented, and concerned with their own personal vanity than are people of just high income alone. They also seem to be a bit more "permissive" than higher income people, in the sense of being willing to tolerate all the protests that are going on. . . .

It appears that the upper social classes are more likely to try to contribute something to society, in the sense of writing something that has been published, doing volunteer work for charitable organizations, and taking an active part in local civic issues. On the other hand, they seem to have less interest in the home in general, and in children in particular, than do the upper income (and corresponding lower class) individuals.[13]

Given these distinctions in life styles, marketing managers can target their appeals by class, as the following discussion of the blue-collar market shows.

The blue collar market has several major attractions for marketers:

1. Blue collar occupations—craftsman-foreman, machine operatives, service workers and laborers—earn better wages now than ever before.
2. The blue collar grocery shopper has strong brand allegiance. And food takes up more of the household budget. Blue collar households tend to be heavier users than their white collar counterparts of instant mashed potatoes, packaged dinner mixes, packaged cold cuts, TV dinners, wrapped bread, and peanut butter. The blue collar market seems to favor pop wines and beer over spirits such as scotch and bourbon.

Most often it is the blue collar woman who travels down the supermarket aisles. If this type of woman is married to someone who holds a blue collar job, she is likely to work blue collar too. But women's lib has affected her. She's more likely to seek work once her children are of age. And she's more likely to have outside contacts and friends than she was a decade ago, when her social circle was limited to the family.

How large is the blue collar market? There is some dispute over the definition of the market, with those eager to promote the market increasing its size to include clerical workers. Measured this way, 66 percent of America's working population is blue collar. And of blue collar women, 46 percent work.[14]

Life cycle. Life styles are distinctive modes of living. The **life cycle** describes the ways in which attitudes, and behavioral tendencies, change over time. These changes occur because of developing maturity, experience, income, and status.

Life styles can be strongly influenced by age-related stages of the life cycle. Teenage life styles are quite different from those of middle-aged people who, in turn, have life styles that are different from those of the elderly.

All of us pass through the orderly series of stages shown in Figure 5.6. The current decline in family size means that less time is now spent in the dependent children stages of the cycle. The tendency for delaying the first marriage has also meant that people stay in the young single stage for a longer period. Marital events in the life cycle are being compressed into a shorter span of years. From 1965 to 1976, the divorce rate doubled in the United States.[15] Yet four out of five divorced persons remarry by middle age, thereby reentering the traditional life cycle.[16]

The lower portion of Figure 5.6 gives some of the characteristics of the traditional life cycle and purchase patterns. It is not uncommon for young marrieds to move into the young divorced stage. At this point, their consumption patterns often revert back to those of the young single stage of the cycle. This may be true even though they are psychologically unprepared to begin playing the "mating game" again. And this is especially true if the young couple had children (almost 60 percent of all divorces involve young children).[17] The cost of maintaining two households after a divorce often drastically reduces the discretionary income of the father. If the wife was not in the workforce, she must often enter it. This creates more expenses, such as child care, new clothes, transportation, and so forth.

Middle-aged families are those whose head is 35 to 64 years old. A growing segment of this age group is the middle-aged married without children. Urban, highly educated women show the greatest tendency to remain childless.[18] People in this group are said to be in the "carefree stage" of life. Financial worries are at a minimum, health is usually good, and they are not involved in the complexities and demands of child rearing. Divorce is less common among middle-aged couples. The middle-aged divorced with children experience many of the same problems as the young divorced with children. Financial burdens are usually less because the spouses are further along in their careers (assuming both have been working). The latter stage of the traditional life cycle (middle-aged without dependent children) has been described as the period of the "empty nest." This is the "carefree" stage in the traditional cycle when couples with lessened financial burdens can try new life styles.

The last major segment is the older stage (65 years and above). It begins when the head of the household retires. Older unmarrieds are either divorced or widowed. Older consumers have fewer time commitments, but usually also less current income and a lower standard of living. If they have sufficient savings, persons in this stage can lead an active life of travel and recreation. If their savings are minimal and/or their health is poor, the final stage may be one of struggle.

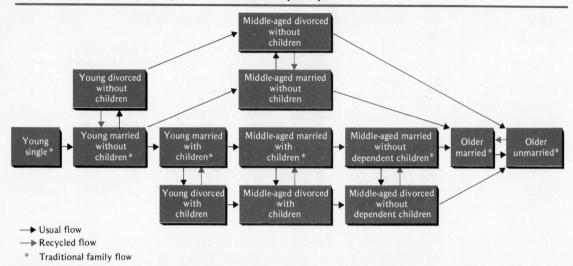

→ Usual flow
→ Recycled flow
*   Traditional family flow

Young single	Young married without children	Young married with children	Middle-aged married with children	Middle-aged married without dependent children	Older married	Older unmarried
Few financial burdens. Fashion opinion leaders. Recreation-oriented. Buy; Basic kitchen equipment, basic furniture, cars, equipment for the mating game, vacations.	Better off financially than they will be in near future. Highest purchase rate and highest average purchase of durables. Buy: Cars, refrigerators, stoves, sensible, and durable furniture, vacations.	Home purchasing at peak. Liquid assets low. Dissatisfied with financial position and amount of money saved. Interested in new products. Like advertised products. Buy: Washers, dryers, TV, baby food, chest rubs and cough medicine, vitamins, dolls, wagons, sleds, skates.	Financial position still better. More wives work. Some children get jobs. Hard to influence with advertising. High average purchase of durables. Buy: New, more tasteful furniture, auto travel, unnecessary appliances, boats, dental services, magazines.	Home ownership at peak. Most satisfied with financial position and money saved. Interested in travel, recreation, self-education. Make gifts and contributions. Not interested in new products. Buy: Vacations, luxuries, home improvements.	Drastic cut in income. Keep home. Buy: Medical appliances, medical care, products which aid health, sleep, and digestion.	Same medical and product needs as other retired group; drastic cut in income. Special need for attention, affection, and security.

Sources: Patrick E. Murphy and William A. Staples, ''A Modernized Family Life Cycle,'' *Journal of Consumer Research* 6 (June 1979): 17, 67; William Wells and George Gubar, ''Life Cycle Concept in Marketing Research,'' *Journal of Marketing Research* 3 (November 1966): 362. Reprinted by permission of the American Marketing Association.

Consumer decision making — the evaluation process

Let us return to our model of consumer behavior; a portion of the model is reproduced here (see Figure 5.7 on p. 138). At this point we have acquired our information and are ready to make a decision. Information can be combined in various ways to make a decision, and different decision rules can be used under different conditions. It is important to understand how a consumer finally decides to buy or not to buy the firm's product or service. If the marketing manager understands the decision strategy, he or she can adapt to it or try to get the consumer to use a strategy more favorable to the seller. Consumers use five basic decision rules; affect-referral, linear compensatory, conjunctive, disjunctive, and lexicographic.[19]

THE AFFECT-REFERRAL RULE

This rule depends upon previously formed attitudes or feelings about each purchase alternative (brand). The decision is based on a single overall impression, and the alternative that provides the best choice is selected. If you were going to purchase a new car, you would buy the one that overall seems just right for you. Following the affect-referral rule does not involve evaluating specific alternatives.

LINEAR COMPENSATORY RULE

A consumer using this rule would develop a mental matrix based on several attributes that were weighted by their importance to the buyer. The weighted evaluations of each car, for example, are then added to obtain an overall rating. The car with the highest overall score is selected. For example, assume that the most important attributes to you are these:

Gas mileage   .5
Style   .3
Maintenance-free .2

You must now evaluate three cars:

	Datsun	Toyota	Ford
Gas mileage	5	4	3
Style	4	3	4
Maintenance-free	3	5	3

where rating 5 is excellent, 4 is good, 3 is average, 2 is below average, and 1 is poor. Your overall ratings would be as follows:

Datsun = .5(5) + .3(4) + .2(3) = 4.3
Toyota = .5(4) + .3(3) + .2(5) = 3.9
Ford   = .5(3) + .3(4) + .2(3) = 3.3

Following the linear compensatory rule, this consumer would purchase the Datsun.

THE CONJUNCTIVE RULE

A consumer who used the conjunctive rule would also develop a mental ma-

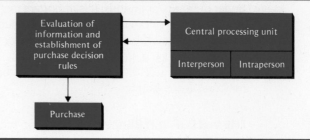

trix. Within this rule, however, there are predetermined cutoff points for each attribute. So any car not meeting the cutoff point is excluded. For example, any car not achieving 20 miles per gallon would be excluded and any car rated by *Consumer Reports* as having above-average maintenance problems would be dropped from consideration. The car that rates the highest and meets all the cutoffs would be selected. This is a noncompensatory model in that low ratings below the cutoff on one attribute cannot be offset (compensated for) by high ratings on another attribute. For example, a car getting 50 miles to the gallon yet with above-average maintenance problems would be excluded.

THE DISJUNCTIVE RULE

The disjunctive rule also involves cutoff points. However, it is used when only a single criterion is utilized in selecting a brand. If a product possesses the minimum standard on the selected criterion, it is included in the set of acceptable alternatives. Thus the car with great gas mileage and a poor service record still would be considered if good gas mileage was the single evaluative criterion. The disjunctive rule allows for more than one alternative to be chosen. So a second rule, such as the linear compensatory rule, would be used to make the final selection. The disjunctive rule is often used to narrow the field to a smaller range of alternatives.

THE LEXICOGRAPHIC RULE

This rule begins with a ranking of attributes in order of importance: gas mileage, most important; style, second in importance; maintenance, least important. The product or service alternatives are compared on the most important attribute. The one most preferred is then selected. In our automobile example, Datsun got the best gas mileage; therefore, it would be the one purchased. If there had been a tie between two or more cars on the most important attribute, then the decision would be based on the second most important attribute. This is a noncompensatory rule. If Datsun had horrible styling (the second most important attribute), it would still be chosen under the lexicographic rule.

Postpurchase evaluation

After a decision is made and the consumer buys a good or service, he or she is expecting certain outcomes. These outcomes may or may not become reality. The car you bought may turn out to be a lemon. Or it may be the finest vehicle you have ever owned. Positive (or negative) reinforcement is then channeled back into the central processing unit for storage.

The degree of satisfaction or dissatisfaction with an identical product will vary from person to person. We all have different values, expectations, and needs. But in general people who feel they are competent in their everyday lives tend to be more satisfied with their major purchases than those who feel less competent.[20] Also, the more a consumer searches, the more satisfied he or she tends to be with a purchase.[21]

One important element of any postpurchase evaluation is the reduction of any lingering doubt that the decision was the right one. I feel sure that you have made a major purchase at one time or another and then asked yourself, "did I do the right thing?" When people are aware of a lack of consistency among their attitudes, values, and opinions, they tend to feel an inner tension. This phenomenon is called **cognitive dissonance.** If a student decides to cut class in order to visit a friend, he or she may feel somewhat apprehensive about this action. The student's behavior is inconsistent with his or her beliefs about attending class. The theory of cognitive dissonance holds that

when a person chooses between two or more alternatives, discomfort or dissonance will almost inevitably arise because of the person's knowledge that while the decision he has made has certain advantages, it also has some disadvantages. That dissonance arises after almost every decision, and further, that the individual will invariably take steps to reduce this dissonance.[22]

The magnitude of dissonance is a function of the following factors:

1. The more attractive the rejected alternative, the greater will be the magnitude of the dissonance.
2. The more important the decision, the stronger will be the dissonance.
3. The intensity of dissonance becomes greater as the number of negative characteristics increase.
4. As the number of rejected alternatives increases, the greater will be the dissonance.
5. The greater the perceived similarity of alternatives (cognitive overlap), the greater the dissonance.
6. The more recent the decision between alternatives, the greater will be the magnitude of dissonance because of the phenomenon of forgetting.
7. A decision that violates a strongly held attitude produces greater dissonance than a decision that rebuts a weaker belief.[23]

Consumers can reduce dissonance in several ways. Obtaining new information through search can help reduce dissonance. Naturally, the new data should be consistent with previous decisions. Also, information can be avoided that would contradict those decisions. It has been shown, for example, that new car owners read significantly more advertisements for the car they have just purchased than for other cars.[24] Another study found that after a specific phonograph record had been selected, the unchosen alternative was downgraded.[25] In some instances people will deliberately seek out discrepant facts in order to refute them and reduce dissonance.[26] If a decision maker can find weak arguments against a particular decision, they will build the decision maker's confidence.

Marketing managers can aid in reducing dissonance by communicating effectively with purchasers. A note inside the package congratulating the purchaser on making a wise decision may aid in dissonance reduction. Research has shown that postpurchase letters sent by manufacturers and dissonance-reducing statements in instruction booklets result in fewer product returns and future-order cancellations.[27]

Consumer behavior and marketing strategy

Now that we have reviewed a model of consumer behavior and its many facets, we need to stress again that the heart of the marketing concept is the consumer. Without an understanding of how a person processes information and ultimately makes buying decisions, no manager can effectively implement the marketing concept. If consumer behavior is understood, a better marketing mix can be developed. The ability to create a product or service and persuade the target audience to buy these offerings over all competitors has its genesis in insight into the consumer purchase process.

By understanding decision rules, for example, a marketer may alter a product design to meet a lexicographic rule being used by the target audience. In the case of cars, if gas mileage is the most important, then more resources can be devoted to that feature, perhaps at the expense of styling. Moreover, good gas mileage can be the dominant theme in the manufacturer's advertising. If most consumers are utilizing a compensatory model, gas mileage increases may not be stressed as much. This is because the new gas mileage technology will mean that "bugs" have yet to be worked out, therefore giving the car a poor service history that will offset the better gas mileage. Every attribute of the marketing mix may have to be altered depending upon how the consumer acquires, processes, and uses decision-making information.

SUMMARY

Buyer behavior is the decisions and acts of people involved in buying and using products and services. When buyers make decisions, they engage in a problem-solving task. There are three degrees of problem solving: (1) routinized response behavior, (2) limited problem solving, and (3) extensive problem solving. Extensive problem solving often requires a myriad of buying considerations.

Up to five different people can be involved in the purchase decision. The instigator suggests, initiates, or plants the seed for the purchase process to begin. The influencer is someone whose opinion is valued in the decision-making process. The decision maker actually selects from among alternatives. The purchaser is the person who pays for the good or service. Finally, the consumer is the user of the good or service.

A model of consumer behavior begins with a stimulus, any unit of input into our senses. Perception is the process by which we select, organize, and interpret stimuli into a meaningful and coherent picture. The third step in the consumer behavior model is to determine whether or not additional information is needed to make the decision. If information is required, a search can take place either internally or externally. After the additional information is gathered, it is evaluated and purchase decision rules are established.

The evaluation and establishment of purchase decision rules as well as the perception process are dependent upon our central processing unit. The central processing unit oversees the decision-making process and strongly affects the information acquisition function. The central processing unit may be divided into two major components: intrapersonal factors and interpersonal factors. Intrapersonal factors are needs and wants, learning, beliefs and attitudes, and personality. Interpersonal factors include reference groups, family, culture, social class, and stage of the life cycle.

After decision rules have been established and the information evaluated, the purchase is made. The outcome will be positive, negative, or neutral. This information is then returned to the central processing unit for storage and possible future use. An important element of any postpurchase evaluation is the reduction of cognitive dissonance.

By understanding the role of cognitive dissonance in consumer decision making as well as how consumers make decisions, marketing managers can effectively implement the marketing concept. An effective and efficient marketing mix can be established only when buyer behavior is thoroughly understood.

KEY TERMS

Buyer behavior
Routinized response behavior
Brand loyal
Stimulus
Perception
Central processing unit (CPU)
Need
Learning
Conceptual learning
Stimulus generalization
Stimulus discrimination
Attitude
Belief

Personality
Personality traits
Reference group
Affiliative group
Aspiratory group
Norm
Culture
Socialization
Acculturation
Social class
Life cycle
Cognitive dissonance

REVIEW QUESTIONS

1. What is meant by attention and perception? How might a marketer improve his or her chances of being paid attention to and perceived?
2. Define learning in the context of consumer decision making. What factors influence rate of learning and subsequent retention?
3. What is the difference between attitude and perception? How are they related? What functions do they perform?
4. Define social class and discuss class differences in purchase decision processes and products sought.
5. How does an individual's personality affect the purchase decision?
6. Define reference groups and state their importance to marketers.
7. Explain cognitive dissonance and identify the ways marketers attempt to reduce this factor in the buying decision.

DISCUSSION QUESTIONS

1. Why is it important for the marketer to understand who plays what role in the decision process?
2. Is it possible for a marketer to create a new set of consumer needs and wants? How would this task be accomplished? Would it be profitable to do so?
3. Describe situations in which stimulus generalization is sought by marketers. Why should this be so? Are there cases in which stimulus discrimination is more appropriate?
4. What objectives are being sought by consumers in their purchase decisions? Discuss the importance of the hidden motivators of buying behavior.
5. How does importance of purchase, financial status, and time pressure affect consumer decision making? Evaluate each separately.
6. Discuss the importance of culture in marketing strategy and in understanding consumers.
7. Analyze the life cycle concept and review the types of products purchased in each stage. How would an astute marketer use this knowledge in understanding the basic motivators of customer decision making?

NOTES

1. This story is derived from "Light Whiskeys," *Forbes,* July 15, 1972, p. 40; and "How a New Product Was Brought to Market Only to Flop Miserably," *The Wall Street Journal,* January 5, 1973, pp. 1, 11.
2. D. Krech and R. S. Crutchfield, "Perceiving the World." Reprinted in *Behavioral Sciences Foundations of Consumer Behavior,* ed. J. B. Cohen (New York: Free Press, 1972), pp. 148–149. Copyright © 1972. Used by permission of McGraw-Hill Book Company.
3. Peter D. Bennett and Gilbert Harrell, "The Role of Confidence in Understanding and Predicting Buyers' Attitudes and Purchase Intentions," *The Journal of Consumer Research* (September 1975), pp. 110–117.
4. William B. Lowden and Peter W. Hermann, "The Effect of Self-Confidence and Anxiety on Information Seeking in Consumer Risk Reduction," *Journal of Marketing Research* 14 (May 1979): 268–274.
5. The discussion of needs is largely adapted from Joe Kent Kerby, *Consumer Behavior —Conceptual Foundations* (New York: Dun-Donnelley, 1975), pp. 42–64.

6. Del I. Hawkins, Kenneth A. Coney, and Roger J. Best, *Consumer Behavior: Implications for Marketing Strategy* (Dallas: Business Publications, 1980), p. 271.

7. Kenneth E. Runyon, *Consumer Behavior,* 2nd ed. (Columbus, Ohio: Charles E. Merrill, 1980), p. 234.

8. Martin Fishbein and Icek Ajzen, *Belief, Attitude Intention and Behavior* (Reading, Mass.: Addison-Wesley, 1975), p. 6.

9. For a more in-depth reading of the Fishbein model, see Joel B. Cohen, Martin Fishbein, and Allie Ahtola, "The Nature and Uses of Expectancy-Value Models in Consumer Attitude Research," *Journal of Marketing Research* 9 (November 1972): 455–460.

10. Hawkins et al., *Consumer Behavior,* p. 343. Reprinted by permission.

11. Rom J. Markin, Jr., *Consumer Behavior — A Cognitive Orientation* (New York: Macmillan, 1974), p. 204. Reprinted with permission of Macmillan Publishing Co., Inc. Copyright © 1974, Rom J. Markin, Jr.

12. The definition of culture and much of the discussion that follows is adapted from James Engel, David Kollat, and Roger Blackwell, *Consumer Behavior,* 3rd ed. (New York: Holt, Rinehart and Winston, 1978), pp. 65–74.

13. William Wells, *Life Style and Psychographics* (Chicago: American Marketing Association, 1974), pp. 242, 249, 251. Reprinted by permission of the American Marketing Association.

14. "Are Blue Collar Buyers Different?" *Media Decisions,* May 1977, pp. 72–73. Reprinted by permission.

15. Patrick E. Murphy and William A. Staples, "A Modernized Family Life Cycle," *Journal of Consumer Research,* 6 (June 1979): 12–22.

16. Ibid.

17. Ibid.

18. Ibid.

19. These rules are taken from Gerald Zaltman and Melanie Wallendorf, *Consumer Behavior: Basic Findings and Management Implications* (New York: Wiley, 1979), pp. 310–312.

20. F. Andrews and S. Withey, "Developing Measures of Perceived Life Quality: Results from Several National Surveys," *Social Indicators Research,* 1974, pp. 1–26.

21. R. Cardozo, "An Experimental Study of Consumer Effort, Expectations, and Satisfaction," *Journal of Marketing Research,* August 1965, pp. 244–249.

22. Leon Festinger and Dana Bramel, "The Reactions of Humans to Cognitive Dissonance," in Arthur J. Bachrach, ed., *Experimental Foundations of Clinical Psychology* (New York: Basic Books, 1962), pp. 251–262.

23. Markin, *Consumer Behavior: A Cognitive Orientation,* pp. 145–147. Copyright 1974, Rom J. Markin, Jr. Reprinted by permission of Macmillan Publishing Co., Inc.

24. D. Ehrlich, S. Guttman, P. Schonbach, and J. Milles, "Post-Decision Exposure to Relevant Information," *Journal of Abnormal and Social Psychology* 54 (May 1957): 98–102.

25. L. A. LoScuito and R. Perloff, "Influences of Product Preferences on Dissonance Reduction," *Journal of Marketing Research* 4 (August 1967): 286–290.

26. J. L. Freedman, "Preference for Dissonant Information," *Journal of Personality and Social Psychology* 8 (August 1968): 172–179.

27. J. H. Donnelly, Jr., and J. M. Ivancevich, "Post-Purchase Reinforcement and Back-Out Behavior," *Journal of Marketing Research* 7 (May 1970): 399–400.

5.1 The Creamoline Corporation

The Creamoline Corporation was founded in 1894 in Philadelphia. Its basic product, a clear, jelly-like petroleum-derivative substance, was the only product manufactured by Creamoline until 1955. Creamoline petroleum jelly can be used for minor cuts and abrasions, preventing diaper rash, soothing chapped lips, and the like.

The company's second product is Creamoline high-care hand lotion. Like the petroleum jelly, it became a huge success. Women use the product to soothe chapped hands and to keep their skin feeling creamy and moist. Buoyed by their success, Creamoline's executives decided to enter the male cosmetics market with an after-shave lotion.

Care was taken to ensure that the new product would succeed. The laboratory spent nine months formulating and testing a number of different compounds designed to quickly soothe burning skin after shaving and to have a pleasant fragrance. At last the lab narrowed the choice to two formulas: A and B. A blind test (no label) was used in six major test markets throughout the United States to compare not only A and B but also the two best-selling brands currently on the market. All the products were in white packages with the label "After-Shave Lotion" followed by the letter A, B, C, or D. Consumers were asked to use each of the four products over an eight-week period, using one product for a week and then switching to another until each of the four brands had been used for a total of two weeks. Strict sampling instructions and usage procedures were set up to assure a reliable test.

When the results were in, the survey showed that test product B was similar in virtually all major attributes with the two leading national brands, C and D. Test product A, however, was viewed superior in almost all product-attribute categories to both test product B and the two national brands. Thus the company decided to roll out the new product (test brand A) nationally.

The new brand was called Creamoline High-Care After-Shave Lotion. After it had been on the market for four months it became apparent to the firm that it had a real loser. Subsequent interviews with people who had purchased the product revealed a very interesting phenomenon. Almost all claimed that the product was greasy, oily, and seemed to have a petroleum jelly base. These claims had not been made during the blind test, and in fact the product did not contain any greasy or oily ingredients. Marketing executives could not figure out the cause of this phenomenon.

1. Using the material that you have learned in this chapter, explain why these results may have occurred.
2. How could the company have avoided this costly mistake?
3. If you were called upon as director of marketing research to explain to the marketing manager what happened, what explanation would you offer?

5.2 Kitchen Pride Foods

Kitchen Pride Foods was founded in 1948 in St. Louis, Missouri. Kitchen Pride became one of the first chicken broiler processors to operate its own sales and distribution network in 1960. By the mid-1960s, the company was firmly established in the poultry processing business through its functions of live production, hatchery operation, and feed mills. Kitchen Pride uses a quality product as the cornerstone of its marketing strategy. Through its modern processing plants, Kitchen Pride produces millions of pounds of branded poultry each week.

Prepackaged chicken offers three unique advantages for the producer of poultry products. When poultry comes to market prepackaged, cut and wrapped, the meat market manager saves time and money. Second, packaging extends the life of the product. Finally, profits from poultry increase because of brand name marketing. Prepackaging does, however, have one important drawback. Certain parts of the chicken which are not prepackaged are unsellable to consumers. The question then was what to do with the residual elements.

The immediate answer was to develop the product into pet food. But the profits gained from the sale of residual parts to the pet food industry were relatively low. Seeking more profitable avenues, Kitchen Pride began to experiment with processing the parts into simulated pork products such as ham, luncheon meats, and frankfurters. Another producer successfully marketed a product called turkey ham, which is a cured turkey by-product that tastes like ham. Kitchen Pride successfully developed a frankfurter that was made out of the chicken by-products.

The chicken franks were marketed in the company's familiar red and white package using the Kitchen Pride logo. After several months of test marketing, the chicken franks results were dismal. The marketing manager knew that in taste tests of unlabeled products, consumers could not tell the difference between chicken franks and beef or pork franks. He remarked to the company president that he wished he had a better understanding of consumer behavior.

1. How might a more thorough understanding of consumer behavior help the marketing manager more effectively market the product?
2. A number of different individuals may be involved in the purchase decision for chicken franks. What roles might those be in a "typical" family?
3. Trace the decision to buy or not buy the chicken franks through the consumer behavior model when a potential purchaser encounters the product in the supermarket.
4. What factors in the central processing unit may be influencing a person's decision not to buy the chicken franks?

6

Industrial organization: behavior and management

OBJECTIVES

To understand the nature and importance of industrial marketing.

To describe industrial buying practices and situations.

To introduce various roles in the industrial purchasing process.

To become aware of the industrial purchase environment.

To present a model of industrial buyer behavior.

To understand the development of industrial marketing strategy.

Marketing managers in the steel industry can no longer decide what to sell, then expect somebody to buy it, according to John B. Judkins, Jr., general manager of sales, Inland Steel, Chicago.

"First and foremost, we must continue to work on developing new steel which we can produce with less weight and greater strength. The classic example of this crying need is in the automobile, but in no way is it restricted to that.

"Another need," said Judkins, "is to develop the ability to produce a more finished product which can be readily used by our customers. With continuing high labor rates, anything we can do to save our customers labor-intensified operations will obviously be an economic saving.

"An example of this is the prepainting of large steel coils which saves the paint spraying or dipping of each steel fabricated part. This not only saves labor costs but the capital investment in painting capability.

"In this total environment, marketing managers need to know more about our customers' products and their requirements," Judkins said. "We have to develop a larger cadre of people who can live with their customers and translate their needs to our marketing plans.

"It is no longer possible for us to make the products we want to make and expect our customers to use them. It is no longer possible for us to spend a major share of our research dollars on internal processing materials. We must direct more, if not most, of our research capabilities to new steel products.

"This puts a new dimension of responsibility on marketing managers," said Judkins. "We must know what's going on and what will probably happen, then have the courage of our convictions to motivate our companies down the proper road."

Good selling practices are still necessary, Judkins said, but they are no longer enough. "The need is to develop the kind of people who can go well beyond the purchasing offices, indeed into our customers' plants, engineering departments and, most important, production design areas, to try and understand and get a jump on the future," he said.[1]

The Inland Steel marketing executive's discussion of meeting customer needs and new product development exemplifies the acceptance and utilization of the marketing concept by an ever-growing number of industrial goods organizations. Yet steel marketing is not identical to marketing toothpaste or any other consumer good. True, there are many similarities—but there are numerous differences as well. How are industrial firms different from consumer good companies? How do they buy? What is their purchasing environment like? How does an industrial model of buyer behavior differ from a consumer model? What is different about industrial research and planning? How does the marketing mix vary as compared to a consumer marketing mix? These are the kinds of questions we will explore in this chapter.

The industrial market

Industrial marketing may be defined as the marketing of goods and services to industrial and institutional customers. One technique for examining what institutions are involved in industrial marketing is to examine the federal government's **standard industrial classification (SIC)** system. The SIC meeting categorizes all United States businesses by product or market segment. It begins with the ten basic industries that encompass industrial marketing:

Agriculture, forestry, and fisheries

Mining

Construction

Manufacturing

Transportation; communication, electric, gas, and sanitary devices

Wholesale trade

Retail trade

Finance, insurance, and real estate

Services

Public administration

The basic reporting units in the SIC system are firms and products. Based upon primary activity, they are classified into four-digit groups. The four-digit groups are classified into three and ultimately two digits. Table 6.1 shows an example of two-, three-, four-, and five-digit codes. The fifth and subsequent digits are product classifications.

Industrial customers (1) purchase goods and services for production of their own goods and services or (2) buy for resale to others. Here we will look only at the first category of industrial customer; wholesalers and retailers will be discussed in Part Five.

CHARACTERISTICS OF INDUSTRIAL MARKETS

There are approximately 321,000 manufacturing establishments in the United States, employing over 20 million people.[2] Despite the large number of pro-

TABLE 6.1 Major Industrial Good Classifications and the SIC System

Division	Major groups (2 digits)	Groups (3 digits)
A. Agriculture		
B. Mining		
C. Construction		
D. Manufacturing	20. Food	
E. Transportation	21. Tobacco	
F. Wholesale trade	22. Textile mill	
G. Retail trade	23. Apparel	
H. Finance	24. Lumber and wood	
I. Services	25. Furniture	
J. Public administration	26. Paper	
K. Nonclassifiable	27. Printing	
	28. Chemicals	
	29. Petroleum	
	30. Rubber	
	31. Leather	
	32. Stone, clay, glass	
	33. Primary metal	
	34. Fabricated metal	341. Metal cans
	35. Machinery	342. Cutlery, hand tools
	36. Electrical machinery	343. Heating equipment
	37. Transportation equipment	344. Fabricated structural metal
	38. Instruments, etc.	345. Screw machine products
	39. Miscellaneous	346. Metal forgings and stampings
		347. Coating, engraving
		348. Ordinance
		349. Miscellaneous

Groups (3 digits)	Industries (4 digits)	Products (5 or more digits)
342. Cutlery, hand tools	3421. Cutlery	34231. Mechanics' hand service tools
	3423. Hand and edge tools	34231 11. Pliers
	3425. Handsaws and saw blades	34231 21. Ball peen hammers, etc.
		34232. Edge tools, hand operated
		34232 11. Agricultural edged hand tools
		34232 31. Axes, adzes, hatchets, etc.
		34233. Files, rasps, and file accessories and other hand tools
		34233 11. Shovels, spades, scoops, telegraph spoons, and scrapers
		34233 21. Light-forged hammers (under 4 pounds), excluding ball peen hammers, etc.

Source: Executive Office of the President, *Standard Industrial Classification Manual* (Washington, D.C.: U.S. Government Printing Office, 1972).

ducers, a few firms account for most of the manufacturing employment and the value added by manufacturing. For example, approximately 2000 firms (each with over 1000 employees) employed over 5 million people, creating $123 billion in value added. In contrast, slightly more than 200,000 manufacturers (each with fewer than 20 employees) employed 1 million people, for a value added of only $19 billion. Many industries are dominated by a small number of companies. This often means similar sales prices, huge organizations with tremendous purchasing power, and similar marketing policies. Some of our more concentrated industries are shown in Table 6.2. In the automotive and telephone industries, two of America's most important, four firms account for over 90 percent of all production.

But regardless of the degree of economic concentration or the size of the firm, demand in the industrial sector is based on final consumer desires. That is, demand for industrial goods is derived from demand for consumer goods. The demand for shoe manufacturing equipment depends on consumer demand for shoes. Demand for lumber is based on consumer housing needs, the demand for offices, and so forth. **Derived demand** is actually based on expectations of future demand for consumer products. A firm that manufactures racquet ball racquets is not going to wait until sales are much greater than production capacity before ordering new assembly machines. If the company expects sales of racquets to rise, then the equipment will be purchased. Sometimes an industrial manufacturer can influence the demand for consumer goods and subsequently the demand for its products and services through promotion of the consumer goods. One example is shown in Figure 6.1.

Price is often a secondary factor in the industrial marketplace. If the demand for shoes is surging, relatively large price increases for shoe manufacturing equipment often will not halt manufacturers' orders for new machines. Dura-

◢ **TABLE 6.2   Percentage of Shipments Accounted for by Large Manufacturing Companies, Selected Industries, 1980**

Industry	4 largest firms	8 largest firms
Motor vehicles	93%	99%
Aircraft	66	86
Petroleum refining	31	56
Computing equipment	51	63
Telephone and telegraph	D	D
Iron foundries	34	45
Farm machinery and equipment	47	61
Cigarettes	84	D
Organic fibers, noncellulosic	74	91
Soap and other detergents	62	74
Radio and television communications equipment	19	33

D = Withheld to avoid disclosure.

Source: U.S. Department of Commerce, *Statistical Abstract of the United States, 1980* (Washington, D.C., 1980), pp. 821–822.

149

THE INDUSTRIAL MARKET

*DuPont certification mark for fabrics meeting its standards.
DuPont makes fibers, not fabrics or fashions.

Qiana* excites

Jerry Silverman's dots terrific. So luxurious you'd never suspect it's practical.

Fashion of Qiana
fabric shown available at
Bergdorf Goodman, Younkers.
Gus Mayer-New Orleans.

DU PONT

Source: Courtesy of Du Pont Company, Public Affairs Department, Wilmington, Delaware 19898.

bility, quality, and ability to deliver may easily take precedence over price. Often the price of a component, such as a car battery, is an insignificant part of a product's total cost. Yet it is a necessary part of the final product, so the manufacturer may be forced to accept large battery price increases. Or a manufacturer may seek help on value engineering, the substitution of materials that are less costly.

Marketing executives also can expect to face increasingly urgent requests for in-plant assistance in value engineering as well as the latest word on short- and long-run product substitution possibilities. The objective of value engineering is to identify materials and products which perform a given function at lower total cost than those currently in use. The vendor who can respond with significant value engineering studies will enjoy an advantage in the negotiation process that he would not have without them. To the buyer with a 5% net profit, a savings of $50 on purchased materials equals the profit on a $1,000 sale!

Although value engineering teams are commonplace in purchasing, there is a growing tendency to expect more of this analysis from vendors. Sales presentations that don't incorporate at least the assurance of this kind of assistance aren't likely to arouse much interest on the part of buyers or receive a positive response from them.[3]

When demand for consumer products rises, it is usually followed by a short spurt of investment in new machinery. A small change in consumer demand may lead to large increases in industrial demand—the **accelerator principle.** Table 6.3 presents a simple example of the accelerator principle in action. Assume that our shoe manufacturer currently has ten machines with a normal capacity of 100,000 pairs of shoes per year. Also assume that at the end of each year one machine reaches the end of its useful life of ten years. As long as demand remains constant at 1 million pairs of shoes, XYZ Manufacturing will buy one machine a year. In 1980 demand for XYZ shoes rises to 1.2 million pairs, yet only one machine is bought. Why? If management thinks the increase in shoe demand is only temporary, an increase in capacity cannot be justified. Part of the 200,000 units may be produced by working overtime and/or adding another work shift. Profit margins per unit will fall, however, because of overutilization of equipment and overtime payments. By 1982 management has decided that the 200,000 additional pairs of shoes is a true long-run change. One machine is needed for replacement, plus two others to meet the new level of demand. Thus a 20 percent increase in consumer demand has caused a 300 percent increase in industrial demand. The principle also works in reverse. A large drop in consumer demand may cut industrial orders to zero.

◀ **TABLE 6.3   The Accelerator Principle**

	XYZ shoe demand	Number of machines	Required	New machines purchased
1980	1,000,000	10	10	1
1981	1,200,000	10	12	1
1982	1,200,000	12	12	3

INDUSTRIAL BUYING PRACTICES

Fluctuations in demand require careful buying practices. The industrial purchaser must avoid having raw material inventories which are too high during slack periods, yet the firm must be able to meet demand when it accelerates. Industrial buyers rely on the following methods for purchasing products: sampling, inspection, negotiated contracts, and description.

Sampling. Buying by **sampling** occurs when products (usually raw materials or agricultural items) have been graded into standardized lots. A sample is taken and analyzed to determine the exact quality. At this point, price is negotiated or based on a predetermined price-quality schedule. Sampling is used to purchase items like bauxite or wheat, where examining each individual unit is not technically or economically feasible.

Inspection. **Inspection purchasing** is used when the items to be bought are not standardized. Since each product or item is different, inspection requires the evaluation of every unit. Industrial and livestock auctions are one example of this purchasing process. Bidders are invited to look over each item — machines, desks, vehicles, livestock — and then make bids based upon perceived values.

Negotiated contracts. A third buying practice is through **negotiated bidding.** When product or service specifications can be precisely described by the purchaser, suppliers are invited to submit bids. Bidding is common at all levels of government and in many industries. Often the bid that is accepted is not the one that offers the lowest price; other factors, such as past performance, technical competence, understanding of the problem, qualifications of the personnel, and similar factors may be weighted more heavily. This is particularly true when research and development or consulting work is being placed out for bid.

If the branch of government (or the industrial firm) cannot define the problem precisely or is not certain of the effort and materials necessary to fulfill the objective, a **cost-plus contract** may be negotiated. This procedure guarantees the supplier a percentage profit or fee upon completion of the contract. Government contracts for advanced weapons systems and industrial contracts for the construction of dams, steel mills, petroleum refineries, and large manufacturing plants are often on a cost-plus basis.

Description purchasing. In situations where a long relationship has resulted in mutual trust between parties, purchase may be by **description.** The purchaser simply describes the color, shape, strength, and size of the item or type of service needed, and the supplier provides the item or service. Catalog buying is a common form of description purchasing. A buyer examines the specifications and orders items that best meet the organization's needs.

INDUSTRIAL BUYING SITUATIONS

The type of buying practice often depends on the buying situation. There are three fundamental buying situations: new task, modified rebuy, and straight rebuy.

New task buying. **New task buying** means purchasing a product or service when a new need or demand has arisen. This situation represents the greatest opportunity for new vendors to sell to an industrial purchaser. No long-term relationship (at least for this product) has been established; specifications may be somewhat fluid; and buyers are generally more amenable to new sellers. If the new item is a raw material or critical component part, the buyer cannot afford to run out of a supply. The seller must be able to convince the purchaser that his or her firm can deliver a quality product on time. This need has become even more critical in the 1980s, with the many threats of shortages.

Modified rebuy. **Modified rebuy** is normally less critical and time consuming than new task purchasing. In this situation the purchaser wants something different from the original good or service. It may be a new color, greater tensile strength in a part, more respondents in a marketing research study, or washing windows in addition to the floors in a janitorial contract. Since the two parties are familiar with each other and credibility has more than likely been established, buyer and seller can concentrate on the specifics of the modification. In some cases, modified rebuys are opened up to outside bidders. This strategy is used by the purchaser to make sure that the new terms are competitive. If Boeing, for example, decides that it needs additional tensile strength in an airfoil for a cargo jet, it may open the bidding to examine the price-quality offerings of a number of metal fabricators.

Straight rebuy. The **straight rebuy** is the situation suppliers relish. The purchaser is not looking for new information or at other suppliers. An order is placed, and the goods and services are provided just as in previous orders. Straight rebuys are usually made routinely by a purchasing agent, since the terms of the purchase have been hammered out in earlier negotiations. This type of industrial purchasing is the most common for standardized products. It is also used for some custom goods when a buyer simply duplicates the original specifications. The longer a straight rebuy relationship exists, the greater the interdependence between the two organizations becomes. To break this cycle, a new supplier must usually have a significant competitive advantage, such as better design or lower cost. Otherwise a very creative marketing program is necessary to get the purchaser to consider a new vendor.

ROLES IN THE INDUSTRIAL PURCHASING PROCESS

As in consumer purchasing, different people play roles in the purchasing process. The basic roles are these:

- *Users.* Although he or she does not make the decision in many cases, a **user** will often initiate the buying process and play an important role in defining the specifications. A forklift truck driver may request a new lift truck and have a major voice in specifications for the new equipment.
- *Influencer.* A wide variety of people acting in response to many different motivations fall into the category of **user.** An influencer's judgment or per-

ception of a specific product or company could affect a decision, even though he or she has no direct connection with it. A division manager, for example, may have major input into the brand of forklift trucks to be considered.

◄ *Buyer.*   Depending on the importance of the decision, the **buyer,** the individual who negotiates the purchase, could range from the president of the company to the purchasing agent.

◄ *Decision maker.*   In complex situations, it is often very difficult to say who makes the actual decision. It is important to differentiate the formal from the informal **decision maker.** A formal decision maker may be a purchasing agent, while the real (informal) decision maker is the forklift truck driver.

◄ *Gatekeeper.*   Any member of the group who regulates the flow of information is the **gatekeeper.** Frequently, it is the purchasing agent who views the gatekeeping process as a source of power.

In viewing a decision-making unit, a marketer must ask four basic questions:

1. Who is in the decision-making unit?
2. What is each member's relative influence in the decision?
3. What are each member's evaluation criteria and how does he or she rate each prospective supplier on these criteria?
4. How do I communicate with the members of the unit?[4]

The example that follows shows how marketers in the metals industry approach the decision makers.

For the metals customer, cost is paramount and delivery a close second only at the simplest end of metal working. In firms making things like washers and brackets, the buying influence rests with the purchasing agent, especially one with a cost or delivery problem.

For these firms, salespeople are hired for their "following" among buyers, especially in secondary steel. These salesmen know the local steel users intimately and are often alumni of their production floors. They know exactly which coil or bundle of sheets in inventory will product a part at the lowest metal price, yet not fail in service or cause the scrap metal rate to jump.

But even in such simple items as bolts, nuts and appliance parts, metal quality has a lot to do with production rates and finished part acceptability. From this point on up the scale of sophistication in metal working, design engineers wield the key buying influence. Both distributors and mills know that their best marketing effort now becomes their sales engineer sitting down with a customer's designer, preferably one with a new-part problem to solve.

Mills and distributors both add that their pitch is best delivered in weekly plant visits by salespeople armed with industry gossip about competitors or customers.

The mills and distributors focus on design engineers because they specify changes in raw materials. If there are metallurgical innovations to sell, or a cheaper but better alternative, design engineers must be convinced.

An Alcoa spokesman noted that its sales engineers are in "hourly" contact with key design engineers and managers in Detroit and in the aerospace business. That effort has led to aluminum's inroads in recent years in steel markets for car parts.[5]

THE INDUSTRIAL PURCHASING ENVIRONMENT

All those involved in the industrial purchase make decisions in an environment that is distinctly different from that for consumer goods. Industrial purchasers are influenced by emotional factors, yet the emphasis in industrial goods is decidedly more rational than in consumer products. For example, industrial buyers demand good price-value relationships, exact tensile strength of metals, assurances of supplies, technical assistance, and similar factors. But industrial buyers are also strongly influenced by emotional motives. They like to be considered "shrewd buyers" and seek recognition for making the "right" decisions. Desire for advancement, deference to group leaders, and the importance of friendships and favors can also affect the industrial purchase decision.

Professionalism. Another feature of the industrial purchase environment is professional purchasing. The purchasing agent or other industrial buyer is often a prime buying influence. Even if they are not the formal decision makers, they usually have some input into the purchase process. The professional buyer has a thorough understanding of sources of supply, vendor characteristics, product/ service knowledge, and the needs of the organization. Even if the purchasing professional does not pick the brand or detail the product specifications, he or she typically selects the sources of supply. When new vendors approach an industrial organization, their first contact is usually with the purchasing professional.

The tremendous power wielded by the purchasing professional often makes the industrial salesperson shudder when contact is first made. A profile of a professional purchaser as seen by one salesperson is presented in the box below.

The typical buyer is a man past middle-life, sparse, wrinkled, intelligent, cold, passive, noncommittal with eyes like a codfish, polite in contact, but at the same time, unresponsive, cool, calm, and damnably composed as a concrete post or a plaster of paris cat; a human petrification with a heart of feldspar and without charm; or the friendly germ, minus bowels, passions, or a sense of humor. Happily, they never reproduce, and all of them finally go to hell.[6]

Reciprocity. Another unique aspect of the industrial purchasing environment is reciprocity. In essence, it means "you buy from me and I'll buy from you." The practice exists in most areas of industrial purchasing but seems to be particularly the custom in paints, transportation, and chemicals. Generally speaking, reciprocity is found in industries where products are homogeneous and/or there is not a high degree of price sensitivity.

In theory, reciprocity tends to make sense. Why not buy from your customers if prices and all other things are equal? Indeed, this seems only fair and helps maintain goodwill between the organizations. Yet what may seem "only right" often can become **coercive reciprocity.** Firm A, for example, purchases $2 million worth of goods and services from firm B. It then tells B that if it wants to maintain A's business, it must purchase certain products from A at prices that are not competitive. In this example, A is using reciprocity to avoid price competition. In some industries, coercive reciprocity has extended beyond price competition to forcing subordinate companies to purchase inferior products.

Since large firms such as General Motors, Du Pont, and others have literally thousands of suppliers, it is almost impossible to avoid dealing with vendors who are also customers. Therefore, reciprocity itself will probably never be declared illegal. Price fixing, of course, is illegal under various statutes. And reciprocity that suppresses competition violates antitrust legislation. Formal systems that track purchases by customers and pass this information on to sales management to be used as leverage to gain purchasing concessions is also considered evidence of reciprocal dealing.[7]

A model of industrial buyer behavior

One way to place industrial purchasing in perspective is to use a model of the process. The model here, developed by Jagdish Sheth, is the one most often used to explain industrial buyer behavior (Figure 6.2).

PURCHASER EXPECTATIONS

We begin by looking at item 1, expectations. The decision may be made or initiated by purchasing agents, engineers, end users, service management, and others. Their expectations refer to the perceived potential of alternative suppliers to satisfy company objectives. Expectations are derived from the buyers' personal backgrounds. For example, a purchasing agent may at one time have been an end user. Getting a price break, providing extra supplies on short notice, maintaining delivery schedules during periods of shortage, and having a product exceed specifications all have a positive impact on the purchaser.

In complex purchase decisions, such as machinery for a new production line, a buying center may engage in an active search for information. Several possible sources of information are shown in the model (see 1b). Since percep-

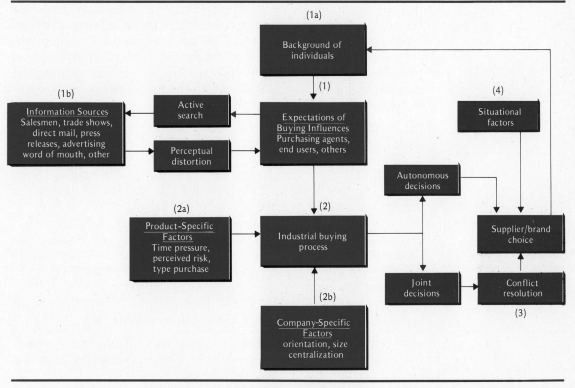

Source: Jagdish N. Sheth, ''A Model of Industrial Buyer Behavior,'' *Journal of Marketing* 37 (October 1973): 51. By permission of the American Marketing Association.

tion is selective and information is analyzed based upon a person's unique central processing unit, perceptual distortion will occur. Perceptual distortion is the extent to which each participant modifies information to make it consistent with his or her existing beliefs and previous experience. For example, a purchasing agent has always received on-time delivery from American Office Equipment. A secretary calls the purchasing agent and complains that American Office Equipment has not delivered ten filing cabinets as specified in a recent purchase order. Because of the positive image of American Office Equipment held by the purchasing agent, he or she may perceive this information as being due to slow delivery by a truck line or rationalize the situations in some other manner.

THE BUYING PROCESS

The second major component of the model is the industrial buying process. Product-specific factors refer to the perceived amount of risk in the decision, how critical time pressure is to obtain the product, and whether it is an installation, component part, supply item, and so on. An installation, for example, will generally be a more complex decision and involve a greater number of buying influences than the routine purchase of supply items. If a critical component part is in short supply, time constraints may force the firm to bypass a detailed purchase evaluation procedure. Instead, the buyer may turn to the vendor who can provide the item quickly and meet minimum standards of quality. Price will be a secondary consideration.

Risk plays an important part in the Sheth model. Perceived risk can be one or all of the following:

1. *Functional risk.* The risk that the product will not perform as expected; for example, that the new batteries for a forklift truck will not hold up under extensive use.
2. *Physical risk.* The risk of physical harm; for example, the increased possibility of cancer when exposed to polyvinyl chlorides in the production of plastic products.
3. *Financial risk.* The risk that the product will not meet its financial goals or that it will not be cost effective; for example, a new lightweight aluminum structural component for a cargo jetliner creates additional drag over the airframe, and extensive redesign work and retooling negates the cost savings of the new part.
4. *Psychological risk.* The fear of not being accepted by other purchasing agents, the fear of failure or lack of recognition or promotion.

If perceived risks are low, the probability of an autonomous decision increases, and vice versa. In situations where one person holds an extensive amount of power, the decision may also be autonomous.

Company-specific factors refer to the general reference system of the personnel, such as engineering orientation or centralization or decentralization. It has been determined that

The relative importance of the influence of the central purchasing department on the buying decision increases as:

1. Market variables become more important relative to product variables
2. The size of the firm and the spatial separation of its activities increases
3. The organization assigns specific responsibility to the purchasing department, in a formal sense.[8]

CONFLICT RESOLUTION

If several people are involved in the purchase decision, each will evaluate vendor offerings from a personal viewpoint. As a result, conflict may arise, and must be resolved before a vendor and brand can be selected.

Conflict resolution can take one of several forms. In the problem-solving approach, information is acquired and assessed, decision rules are established, and a solution is agreed upon. A second approach for resolving conflict is through persuasion. A user, manager, or other influential group member attempts to influence dissenting members by getting them to alter their decision criteria or reassess the product or service being evaluated.

If conflict cannot be resolved by rational problem solving or persuasion, the buying center may resort to bargaining (I'll go along with vendor A, but only if you will agree to change the product specifications). When bargaining fails (or sometimes before any rational technique is used), the group members may engage in politicking. Group members may side with the formal leader in the hope of pay increases or promotions. In other cases, the marketing or engineering buying center members may vote together as a bloc.

SITUATIONAL FACTORS

Regardless of the method used, a decision is finally reached. Specifications are established, suppliers chosen, and brands are determined. One final factor that Sheth notes is unique situational variables. These variables can run the gamut from the president's brother owning a major vendor organization to extremely high demand for the firm's output. Although the model recognizes situational variables, it does not try to explain their impact on industrial decision making. So many things could affect the decision process either positively or negatively that it would be impossible to list or categorize them all.

With our understanding of buyer behavior increased by the model, let us turn now to the development of marketing strategies.

Industrial marketing strategy

The starting point in industrial marketing is having clear, well-defined, and measurable goals. These should be grounded in input from research and development, finance, production, and marketing managers. Once objectives are established, the firm can begin developing a target market and designing a marketing mix to reach the target. A marketing information system is just as important for feedback purposes in industrial marketing as in consumer marketing. The industrial firm must monitor environmental change and alter its marketing mix to meet the changing needs of the target audience.

DEFINING A MARKET TARGET

The firm must define its target audience on two levels: macro and micro.[9]

Macrosegmentation. **Macrosegmentation** establishes general areas of market potential. Bases for macrosegmentation include such variables as SIC codes (three- or four-digit), size of firms, location, and product applications. If these factors are sufficient to explain differences in industrial buyer behavior, further segmentation is not necessary and a marketing strategy should be developed. For example, the automotive and surgical tool industries have profoundly different product applications for steel. Accordingly, the purchase behavior of steel-buying centers in the two industries is quite different. In this case, product application can be used as a basis for segmentation.

Microsegmentation. **Microsegments** are groups of industrial purchasers with similar buyer behaviors within a macrosegment. Table 6.4 indicates three major ways to segment markets: (1) characteristics of the buying organization, (2) characteristics of the buying center, and (3) characteristics of individual decision participants. Group I factors are basically macrosegmentation variables; II and III factors are micro in nature. Microsegments tend to be more behaviorally oriented and thus often more difficult to identify and classify. Yet research has shown that microsegmentation is a viable and worthwhile endeavor.[10] According to Frederick Webster:

◢ TABLE 6.4   Variables for Industrial Segmentation

I. Characteristics of the buying organization:
   A. Type of organization—manufacturing firm, educational institution, transportation authority, hospital, governmental agency, public utility.
   B. Organization "demographics"—number of employees, annual sales volume, industry affiliation (SIC group), geographic location, number of plants.
   C. Product application—end use.
   D. Type of buying situation.
   E. Degree of source loyalty, and whether the supplier is "in" or "out."
   F. The existence of purchasing contracts of various kinds, such as annual requirement suppliers, stockless purchasing, and so on.
   G. Presence or absence of reciprocity.

II. Characteristics of the buying center:
   A. Composition—buying roles.
   B. Stage in buying decision process.
   C. Type of uncertainty perceived in the buying center—need, market, or transaction uncertainty.
   D. Degree of decentralization—locus of buying responsibility within the organization.
   E. The task assigned to the buying center—the specific type of problem being solved.
   F. Amount of time pressure felt by members of the buying center.
   G. Type of conflict resolution characteristically used in the buying center—persuasion, compromise, bargaining, negotiation.
   H. Decision rules and characteristic types of purchasing strategies used.

III. Characteristics of individual decision participants:
   A. Demographics—age, occupation, education, industry experience.
   B. Organizational role—position in organization and within buying center.
   C. Professional affiliations outside of organization.
   D. Psychographics—attitudes toward and preferences for suppliers and brands; degree of self-confidence.
   E. Perceptions of rewards or punishments for risk taking.
   F. The individual's "loyalty domain," interactions with and sentiments toward other members of the buying center.
   G. Buying criteria—reliability, price, product quality.

Source: Frederick E. Webster, Jr., *Industrial Marketing Strategy* (New York: Wiley, 1979), pp. 78–79.

Data for macrosegmentation are available from secondary sources such as the Census of Business for minimal expenditures of time and money.

Obtaining data for developing microsegmentation strategy is more complex than for macrosegments. The company's sales force is an obvious place to begin, since salesmen are usually good sources of information about customer characteristics and buying behavior. For sophisticated measures of organizational buying behavior, such as buyer's self-confidence and degree of perceived risk, professionally conducted market research studies may be necessary.

The strategic implications of microsegmentation lie primarily in promotional strategy and to a lesser extent in product, price, or distribution refinements. Decisions influenced by segment differences at the micro level include selecting individuals in the buying organization upon whom to make sales calls, design of sales presentations to stress specific product features relevant for the decision criteria used by these individuals, selection of advertising media to reach decision influences, budgeting the total amount of selling effort required as a function of degree of perceived risk, and so on.[11]

Effective segmentation enables the marketing manager to define the greatest sales and profit opportunities. Not only must potential revenues be examined, but potential competitors' actions as well. High-profit potential market segments with heavy competition may be less attractive than segments with moderate profit potential and no competition. Highly competitive markets should be avoided unless the firm has a significant competitive advantage.

Capitalizing on competitors' flaws becomes an important tactic for Nalco Chemical, Oak Brook, Ill. Dick Hertz, marketing manager, power generation chemicals, builds a pool of information on competitors' strengths and weaknesses, including their capabilities in local markets. Nalco product managers use the data to put together local marketing programs that stress Nalco's comparative strengths—without mentioning competitors by name.[12]

The marketing mix

After the market target has been identified, a marketing mix can be developed. This process normally begins with the creation of product strategies.

PRODUCT STRATEGIES

New product development. By capitalizing on competitive products' weaknesses and a firm's own unique technology, a firm can develop successful new products. The basic process for developing new products is the same for both consumer and industrial goods. New product goals are established; opportunity explorations develop new concepts and ideas; the screening phase eliminates the concepts that are poor product line fits, or economically or technically unsound; and a preliminary profit plan is created. If a concept meets the

INTERVIEW GUIDE—INMONT CORPORATION
NEW ADHESIVE SYSTEMS

Name of Company: _____ Date: _____

Address: _____ City: _____ State: _____

Individuals Interviewed: _____ Title: _____

_____   _____

_____   _____

Industry: _____ Description of Company: _____

_____

- -

A. **Products used**
   1. Adhesives used and where used. (Satisfied–Dissatisfied)
   2. Do you prefer multipart systems or single part systems? Would you consider using a more extensive two-part system in a one-part package to replace cheaper systems presently used? (Explore!)

B. **Present application system used**
   1. Describe the present delivery system(s) used for applying adhesives, etc.

Diagram

_____

Desciption of system in operation (cartridge vs. gun, power source, etc.)

   2. Cost factors regarding present system.
      Number of unit setups
      Initial cost
      Labor cost
      Space expenses
      Raw material cost
      Maintenance cost
      Product wastage
      Unacceptable product
      Rate of delivery
      Time equipment run
   3. Explore problems in use of existing systems.
   4. Does the system you described represent general industry practice?

C. **New adhesive system**
   1. What was the respondent's reaction to the proposed new adhesive system in regard to:
      Applicability to present operations
      Cost of equipment

Cost of raw materials
Decreasing wastage
Lower capital cost
Maintenance
Product reliability
Application rate
Space
Labor

2. Other advantages/disadvantages of new adhesive system.
3. Do you think this system offers enough overall advantages over your present system to be considered as a replacement? Yes__No__Why?
4. How many units would you consider purchasing? Would they be used in addition to or to replace present equipment? (Determine lead time) (Obsolescence)

Source: E. Patrick McGuire, *Evaluating New Product Proposals* (New York: The Conference Board, 1979), pp. 68–69.

financial criteria in the preliminary profit plan, actual development begins. Concurrently communications, pricing, and distribution strategies are created. The product is test marketed, refined, and (if it passes the test market) introduced to the marketplace. (This process will be discussed in greater detail in Chapter 9.)

In industrial product development it is the usual practice to screen product concepts first with marketing and sales personnel. Often production and purchasing also provide insights into the merits of new products. Purchasing often is a procurer of the company's own products and is therefore in a position to evaluate them. For example, a major producer of machine tools is a large user of its own products, and it tests and evaluates new concepts in its own shops. Some manufacturers have a close working relationship with a relatively small number of customers. In these instances, the customers provide an excellent sounding board for screening new ideas.

Industrial market researchers rely very heavily on personal interviews of customers and potential customers for new product ideas and prototype testing (see Table 6.5). The personal interview is necessary for lengthy questionnaires that may take several hours to complete and deal with complex product concepts. Mail and telephone surveys are used to broaden the base of the survey and verify key points in the personal interviews. Not all interviews are with customers and potential customers. A steel manufacturer, for example, maintains a panel of machine designers who are contacted by mail on a regular basis and asked for their opinions on new alloys, extrusions, and so on. Samples of a proposed new product, along with descriptive literature, are sent to the designers months before the product is to be introduced. Often commentary from the panelists is valuable in suggesting worthwhile modifications of a product before its introduction.

Most industrial companies feel it is desirable to test prototypes.[13] The process is usually expensive, time consuming, and often provides competitors with a glimpse of the firm's product strategy. Moreover, in high-technology industries such as semiconductors and computers, the prototype may become dated before the "bugs" can be worked out. Then why test prototypes? Because the cost of failure after national introduction is too great. The costs of new assembly lines, raw material acquisitions, filling the distribution channels, and training the sales force are too great to be left to chance, as the example of what happened to the Skil Corporation shows.

The Skil Corporation, like most of its competitors in the tool industry, used to pay little attention to market testing possibilities for its industrial products. Most new entries in this field were modifications or extensions of existing lines. The producers could usually make such products on existing production equipment and distribute them fairly routinely through their regular channels.

Increasing costs and competition combined to make market testing a necessity in order to confirm that the market for a new item would justify its development.

Skil initiated its market testing program with the introduction of a new type of concrete hammer. Concrete hammers are portable, pneumatically operated devices used to break up concrete. Skil engineers, in analyzing the operation of conventional concrete hammers, found that these hammers did only about 60% of the work. The tools hammered up and down, using conventional low-cost star drills, but the workmen still had to rotate the hammer back and forth, in order to break through the concrete. Among other things, this made the task very tiring for workmen, and Skil engineers theorized that concrete hammers could be improved if they would be designed so that the drill would not only move up and down but also rotate. Product prototypes embodying this approach were designed.

Initial field testing had convinced the company that the product concept was very salable. But Skil marketers remained somewhat worried about obtaining satisfactory distribution, particularly since most distributors were already well stocked with conventional-type hammers and steel drill bits.

It was decided to try a limited or trial introduction of the product and yet continue to test the market at the same time. . . . Skil began with a relatively small position in the concrete hammer market. With this new entry, its sales climbed to the point where the company captured more than half of the market, and competitors were eventually forced to emulate the new product's design to keep pace.[14]

Managing existing products. After a product is introduced to the market, it usually becomes part of a product line. Product line development is based upon customer needs, competitive offerings, a manufacturer's capabilities, and marketing strategy. Such strategies might be to meet competition head-on, to serve a particular type of customer with a full line of products, or to be the low-price producer in an industry. We will return to product line strategies in Chapter 8.

PRICING STRATEGIES

Industrial pricing strategies are derived from pricing objectives. The most effective strategies take both demand and costs into account. Although strategies for consumer and industrial products both begin with goals and then are based upon demand and/or costs, there are some essential differences. In the industrial goods market, there is greater use of bidding, negotiations, and leasing.

Competitive bidding. Selling in the industrial goods market may require pricing on a bid basis. Bid pricing is unique because the quantity demanded is specified in the bidding prospectus or specifications. The bid price therefore becomes a function of cost and competitors' actions. Price is usually the most important determinant of the winning bid, but other factors may enter into consideration. For example, industrial purchasers may also evaluate the bidder's past experience (particularly in the area of research and development), and the technical competence of its employees.

Let us look at a strategy to determine whether or not the firm should bid at all. A number of considerations enter into the analysis of a bidding opportunity: plant capacity, competition, follow-up, quantity, delivery, and profit.[15] The possibility of gaining future business as a result of a successful initial bid will affect plant capacity. Also, if a firm is operating at 50 percent capacity, it may be more anxious to acquire a large job than a firm operating at 95 percent capacity.

Highly competitive bids are generally less attractive for each bidder than bidding situations where there is little if any competition. Follow-up bidding opportunities are another important factor. In the case of a federal government contract, a winning bid receives a federal stock number and a high probability of repeat orders from the agency.[16] Winning a bid also often makes other users aware of the firm's offerings. The quantity desired in the bid proposal may be large enough to enable the firm to achieve economies of scale. This would make the bidding proposition more attractive.

Delivery is also an important consideration. A firm must be able to provide the merchandise on time if it expects future business from the purchaser. Many companies will omit a bid if the contracting officer believes that the firm cannot deliver according to specifications. This is true even if the firm is the low bidder. Another delivery consideration is that if the purchaser requires delivery of all the goods at one time, it may tax the bidder's distribution system, and other regular customers may receive poor service during this period.

After the firm delineates the basic factors in bid determination, it should weight each according to its importance to the firm. Table 6.6 shows the weightings for a hypothetical organization. Quantity and delivery are given the lowest priority and profit the highest. The next step is to evaluate each factor either high, medium, or low according to potential benefit to the company. These factors are then assigned some quantitative value. In this example, high is 10; medium, 5; and low, 0.

◀ TABLE 6.6   Analysis of Bidding Opportunities

Ideal bid opportunity

Prebid factors	Weight	×	Rating High (10)	Rating Medium (5)	Rating Low (0)	Value
Plant capacity	20		10			200
Competition	20		10			200
Follow-up	15		10			150
Quantity	10		10			100
Delivery	10		10			100
Profit	25		10			250
Total	100					1,000

Case 1

Prebid factors	Weight	×	Rating High (10)	Rating Medium (5)	Rating Low (0)	Value
Plant capacity	20		10			200
Competition	20		10			200
Follow-up	15		10			150
Quantity	10		10			100
Delivery	10		10			100
Profit	25			5		125
Total	100					875

Case 2

Prebid factors	Weight	×	Rating High (10)	Rating Medium (5)	Rating Low (0)	Value
Plant capacity	20				0	0
Competition	20			5		100
Follow-up	15				0	0
Quantity	10		10			100
Delivery	10		10			100
Profit	25				0	0
Total	100					300

Source: Stephen Paranka, "Question: To Bid or Not to Bid: Strategic Prebid Analysis," *Marketing News,* April 4, 1980, p. 16.

The product of the weight and the rating can be used to compare the bid opportunities of various projects over a period of time. The higher the total value, the more the company should consider bidding on the project. Table 6.6 shows an ideal bidding opportunity and two others that are not. In case 1, the profit opportunity was lower than the firm's average rate of return. Yet other factors still make the request for bid attractive. Case 2 was based on the following circumstances:

Bids were sought for Item Y representing the equivalent of a normal two-month sales volume for this particular product. The bid set was received at a time of high business activity, sales of Company A being about 110% of the established quota. Item Y was a standard product which had been produced for many years.

Bid histories showed the bid price required to win the contract was about 34% discounted from the posted list price. Delivery requirements presented no problem to Company A. Existing facilities and equipment easily could meet the contractor's desired delivery date.

Potential follow-up for additional contracts on this particular product was low, since the customer was trying to upgrade operations with products more up-to-date than Item Y. The large discounts offered in previous bids meant the anticipated profit on this contract was low.

Plant capacity was ranked zero because the company was already operating at a high level of production. There wasn't a follow-up benefit, so this factor was also rated zero. Finally, the need to grant a high discount from the posted list price minimized potential profit, so this factor was rated zero as well.

Computation of the weight factors times the ratings resulted in the low total of 300. As a result of this value weighting, Company A did not develop a bid for this contract. Company B received the contract with a bid price of 35% discount off list price.[17]

Negotiation. A second unique aspect of industrial pricing is the importance of negotiation. Even when a company bids on a project, the purchaser may not reject the bid but instead bargain with the supplier for a better price. This is very common among buying centers trying to obtain the best contract possible for their companies.

Leasing. As an alternative to actual purchase, many firms are now turning to leasing. In fact, the 1970s and early 1980s represented a boom period in industrial equipment rentals. Leases account for the acquisition of 20 percent of all capital goods in the United States.[18] A large distributor of earth-moving equipment uses leasing plans to meet price-oriented foreign competition. Medical equipment manufacturers found that leasing appealed to both profit and nonprofit hospitals. It enabled the institutions to minimize rate increases and provided an alternative means of financing expensive equipment.

Today just about anything can be leased, from complex satellite communication systems to oil supertankers. The main reasons for the growth of leasing may be summarized as follows:

1. Leasing provides 100 percent financing.
2. Leasing frees working capital.
3. Leasing preserves credit capacity.
4. Leasing helps avoid equipment disposal problems.
5. Leasing allows for the acquisition of equipment when other financing sources are not available.
6. Leasing protects against the risks of equipment obsolescence.
7. Leasing allows for piecemeal financing of small acquisitions.

8. The after-tax cost of leasing is less than the after-tax cost of equity.

9. Lease payments provide a greater tax shield than depreciation or interest.[19]

PROMOTION STRATEGIES

Personal selling. Personal selling is much more pervasive in the industrial market than in the consumer market. This is because of the greater complexity of many industrial products, the higher costs, and the need for customization of many items. Industrial salespeople often have technical and business backgrounds that enable them to speak the language of business while selling chemicals, buildings, communications equipment, computerized machine tools, and so forth. Sometimes a team is developed that combines people with business and technical expertise.

One reason for this approach is that in many cases the industrial buyer is an information seeker, so one role of the salesperson is information provider. Often the salesperson is challenged to show how his or her product or service will meet the needs of the potential buyer better than a competitor's offerings. This requires very high levels of technical expertise, coupled with a thorough understanding of the buyer's operations.

Salespersons also have more responsibility for detailed order preparation, installation, and follow-up than consumer products salespersons. Selling a pair of shoes to a consumer is usually a simple task: There is no order preparation because the shoes are not custom designed; there is no installation, and usually there is little follow-up. In contrast, consider a Bell Telephone sales engineer's order for a new communications system for a large plant or hospital. It is not uncommon for such orders to be over 100 pages in length. Often the sales engineer will take a unique customer request back to plant engineers for the creation of a custom switchboard or other communication hardware to meet the customer's need. After the sale, the sales engineer continues to monitor the creation of the system prior to installation. When the new system is installed, the sales engineer works as a liaison between the installers and the customer to make certain that there are no problems and that the equipment is installed exactly as ordered. Routine follow-up continues long after the system is in operation.

Advertising. Industrial selling and advertising go hand-in-hand. Eighty-eight percent of all industrial companies advertise, and virtually all sales managers believe that advertising supports their field sales efforts.[20] Advertising themes are often used to tie in sales presentations to prospects and customers. The major media for industrial advertising are trade journals and general business magazines, direct mail, and industrial directories. Business publications account for about 65 percent of industrial advertising budgets; direct mail, 13 percent; and industrial directories, only 5 percent.[21]

Historically, industrial advertising has been considered cold, factual, and boring. It was assumed that buying centers simply wanted advertisements crammed with facts — and no frills. Astute marketers soon realized that often their message simply was not getting through. Dull and unexciting ads were not capturing the buying centers' attention. The 1980s is seeing a blurring of what is clearly industrial advertising and what is clearly consumer advertising in creative approach, appearance, use of media, and audience needs.

Comments such as these have led to a growth of "capabilities advertising" — showing how a vendor can meet a purchaser's needs. The capabilities message respond to the buyers' needs for systems solutions to problems and for reassurance about corporate reputation and stability, and make pledges of on-time delivery of quality goods and services.

Because potential buyers for many types of industrial goods are difficult to locate, some sellers use coupons and toll-free phone numbers to identify prospects. Figure 6.3 shows one type, and the example following another.

◢ **FIGURE 6.3 Using coupons to encourage inquiries from potential customers.**

Source: Courtesy of Ryder Truck Rental Inc.

Marketers such as Eaton's Engineered Fasteners Div., Cleveland, Associated Spring's Barnes Group, Bristol, Conn., and Clayton Manufacturing, El Monte, Cal., help to qualify prospects by including a bounceback response card in the initial packet of literature they send to inquirers. The card may ask several qualifying questions or just one vital one—Do you want a salesperson to call? In either case, if the reply is favorable, the company notifies the salesperson and expects him to follow up.

Indeed, Clayton, whose ads generated over 10,000 inquiries last year, has its follow-up system down to a fine art. When leads come in, they're first screened to eliminate obvious dead ends. They are then coded for later computer interpretation and sent to an outside fulfillment house. The fulfillment house sends out a predetermined package of literature to the prospect and mails a notice of the inquiry to the appropriate field salesperson or independent rep.

The package sent to the prospect contains a cover letter, literature, and the bounceback card, asking 10 questions, among them, Do you intend to purchase this type of equipment? and Do you want to see a salesperson? If the card signals an imminent intent to buy, it's photocopied at once and mailed to the salesperson or independent sales rep.

Next, the salesperson or rep is asked to call on the prospect, evaluate the lead, and tell the company when he expects the prospect to buy.[22]

Sales promotion and publicity. Another excellent source of sales leads is trade shows. These are the oldest form of promotion and quite different from all others, since the potential buyer goes to see the seller's wares. Many shows are based on product type—computers, office machines, refrigeration equipment. In other cases they are organized around industries—health care, road construction, publishing. The keys to a successful trade show are a large percentage of attendees having specific buying plans, buying influencers and decision makers, plenty of time for each visitor to see all the exhibits, and high traffic density (about four visitors per 100 square feet of exhibit space—anything less is too light and anything much higher is too congested).[23]

Other common forms of industrial sales promotion are catalogs and specialty items such as calendars and business gifts. Catalogs are the most important form of sales promotion after trade shows. Buying centers use catalogs to find potential suppliers and compare prices, terms, and specifications. If a manufacturer's product is not listed in a catalog, the form is often not even considered. If the manufacturer produces a catalog that does not reach the proper buying centers, the firm's products will not be considered. Generally, firms will use a mailing list compiled by the salesforce, buy additional mailing lists, and also use advertising with coupons to reach as many potential customers as possible.

To reinforce advertising, sales promotion, and personal selling, the firm relies on public relations. Public relations helps create the proper image to key publics such as government, stockholders, and buying centers. The tools of public relations will be discussed in Chapter 18. Public relations help generate free publicity through speeches by executives, press releases, and so forth. It also can create third-party credibility about the products and services a firm offers when stories appear in trade magazines and other publications.

DISTRIBUTION STRATEGIES

Industrial distribution channels are shorter than those for consumer goods. This is because buying centers are often purchasing complex, customized, and expensive goods from a vendor. To go through a wholesaler or a retailer would be senseless. For supply items, most industrial wholesalers specialize by industry and are the supermarkets of industrial distribution. These organizations are called industrial distributors.

When a manufacturer sells supply items through an industrial distributor, it is expected that the distributor will supply technical assistance and service to the end user. Some other reasons for using industrial distributors are these: (1) The distributor can provide the necessary sales effort. (2) The distributor can provide local market coverage. (3) The distributor can provide warehousing for the manufacturer. (4) The distributor can perform a credit function for the manufacturer. (5) The distributor is often a good source of local market information. (6) The distributor can lower the cost of distribution for the manufacturer.[24]

If a manufacturer does not "go direct" with its own salesforce or use industrial distributors, it may rely on manufacturers' representatives. Manufacturers' representatives are agents of the manufacturer and usually have little say in pricing or delivery policy. They are, in essence, independent salespersons who work on a direct commission. They must be effective at the art of selling, since their livelihood depends upon closing the deal. Manufacturers' representatives usually have well-established contacts in their territory and, because they work for several manufacturers of complementary products, have a wide product line to offer potential buyers. Since they are paid only when a sale is made, the manufacturer avoids fixed selling costs. Manufacturers' representatives are often found in territories where the sales potential is not enough to pay for a company salesperson.

The major disadvantage of using manufacturers' representatives is that they may not devote the attention to a manufacturer's products that the firm feels it deserves. Since they work strictly on commission, the manufacturer can expect little account service from the representatives. Moreover, reps cannot be expected to fill out marketing intelligence reports or do other paperwork not directly associated with sales. Since manufacturers' reps are independent businesspersons, they are difficult for the manufacturer to control. If the rep does not want to work on a certain day, there is little that the manufacturer can do about it.

SUMMARY

Industrial marketing is the marketing of goods and services to industrial and institutional customers. Industrial customers purchase goods and services for production of their own goods and services or buy for resale to others. The industrial market has several unique characteristics. For example, it is dominated by large firms, and many industries are highly concentrated. Demand in the industrial sector is derived from demand for final consumer goods. Demand may be relatively insensitive to price and possibly characterized by rather large fluctuations. These fluctuations in demand are due to the accelerator principle.

Industrial buyers rely on several methods for purchasing products: sampling, description, negotiated contracts, and inspection. The type of buying practice applied depends on the buying situation. There are three fundamental buying situations: new task, modified rebuy, and straight rebuy. New task buying means purchasing a product or service when a new need or demand has arisen. A modified rebuy is normally less critical and time consuming than new task buying. In this situation, the purchaser wants something different from the original goods or services yet usually deals with a familiar vendor. In some cases, modified rebuys are opened up to outside bidders. The straight rebuy is the situation suppliers enjoy: the purchaser simply places an order with the same vendor and the goods or services are provided just as in previous orders.

Many different people can play roles in the industrial purchasing process. The basic roles are these: user, influencer, buyer, decider, and gatekeeper. The gatekeeper regulates the flow of information. The decider is the person who makes the actual decision. The buyer does the physical purchasing; an influencer acts as an opinion leader; and users may not make the decision, but they often initiate the buying process.

The industrial purchase environment is characterized by both emotional and rational factors, yet the emphasis in industrial goods is decidedly more rational than for consumer products. Industrial buyers place more emphasis on price-value relationships, assurances of continuity of supply during periods of shortage, and similar factors. Yet they are also influenced by emotional motives, such as being considered "shrewd buyers" and seeking recognition for making the "right" decisions. The industrial purchase environment is also characterized by professional purchasing. The professional buyer has a thorough understanding of sources of supply, vendor characteristics, product service knowledge, and the unique needs of the organization. Another unique factor in the industrial purchase environment is reciprocity.

The major components of a model of industrial buyer behavior are purchase expectations, information search, the industrial buying process, conflict resolution, and situational factors.

In many respects an industrial marketing strategy is similar to a consumer marketing strategy. First, there must be a well-defined target market. This can be accomplished through a combination of macro and micro segmentation. Macrosegmentation establishes general areas of market potential; microsegments are groups of industrial purchasers with similar purchasing characteristics within a macrosegment. Next, a marketing mix must be developed. The industrial marketing mix has many unique characteristics as compared with a consumer marketing mix. Yet it still requires the development of product, price, promotion, and distribution strategies.

KEY TERMS

Industrial marketing
Standard industrial classification system (SIC)
Derived demand
Accelerator principle
Sampling
Inspection purchasing
Negotiated bidding
Cost-plus contract
Description purchasing
New task buying
Modified rebuy

Straight rebuy
User
Influencer
Buyer
Decision maker
Gatekeeper
Coercive reciprocity
Macrosegmentation
Microsegments

REVIEW QUESTIONS

1. What is industrial marketing? For what purposes are industrial purchases made?
2. Which buying method would industrial purchasers use for the following product types:
   a. Office supplies.
   b. Leather.
   c. General contractor for building site.
   d. Computer.
   e. Coal.
3. How can new product ideas and prototypes be evaluated in the industrial market?
4. What differentiates the industrial segment from the consumer market with respect to pricing?
5. How does the selling of industrial goods differ from the selling of consumer goods?
6. When should industrial distributors be used? When should manufacturers' representatives be used?

DISCUSSION QUESTIONS

1. What distinguishes the industrial purchase decision from the consumer purchase decision?
2. Why do you think the gatekeeper has such power in the industrial purchase decision?
3. How does the industrial firm segment its markets?
4. What problems may be encountered by a bidding firm that is awarded a contract?
5. Why would more intensive training be expected of the industrial salesperson?
6. When is leasing a superior alternative to the purchase of industrial goods?

NOTES

1. "Steel Marketers Must Learn Customers' Special Needs," *Marketing News,* May 30, 1980, p. 8.

2. U.S. Department of Commerce, *Statistical Abstract of the United States, 1976* (Washington, D.C., 1976), p. 757.
3. Richard M. Hill, "Suppliers Need to Supply Reliably, in Volume, with Value Engineering Analysis, Market Data," *Marketing News,* April 4, 1980, p. 7.
4. This material is from Rowland T. Moriarty and Morton Galper, *Organizational Buying Behavior: A State-of-the-Art Review and Conceptualization* (Cambridge, Mass.: Marketing Science Institute, March 1978), pp. 24–25.
5. Jack Thornton, "Honing Sales Techniques," *Industrial Marketing,* June 1980, p. 68.
6. Charles A. Koepke, *Plant Production Control,* 3rd ed. (New York: Wiley, 1961), p. 60.
7. Frederick E. Webster, Jr., *Industrial Marketing Strategy* (New York: Wiley, 1979), p. 65.
8. Kjell Gronhaug, "Exploring Environmental Influences in Organizational Buying," *Journal of Marketing Research* 12 (August 1976): 225–229.
9. See Yoram Wind and Richard Carelozo, "Industrial Market Segmentation," *Industrial Marketing Management,* April 1974, pp. 153–166.
10. Webster, *Industrial Marketing Strategy,* p. 82.
11. Ibid., pp. 80, 82.
12. "Industrial Newsletter," *Sales and Marketing Management,* February 4, 1980, p. 28.
13. E. Patrick McGuire, *Evaluating New Product Proposals* (New York: The Conference Board, 1979), p. 72.
14. Ibid., pp. 81–82.
15. This section is taken from Stephen Paranka, "Question: To Bid or Not to Bid? Answer: Strategic Prebid Analysis," *Marketing News,* April 4, 1980, p. 16.
16. Ibid.
17. Ibid.
18. Paul Anderson, "Industrial Equipment Leasing Offers Economic and Competitive Edge," *Marketing News,* April 4, 1980, p. 20.
19. Ibid.
20. Sally Scanlon, "How Industrial Sales Executives Use — And View — Advertising," *Sales and Marketing Management,* May 19, 1980, p. 56.
21. Robert W. Haas, *Industrial Marketing Management* (New York: Van Nostrand Reinhold, 1976), p. 201.
22. Sally Scanlon, "Striking It Rich with Industrial Ads," *Sales and Marketing Management,* June 18, 1979, p. 43.
23. Haas, *Industrial Marketing Management,* p. 218.
24. Ibid., p. 155.

◢ **CASES**

6.1 Vining Labs

Mr. Bob Vining is manager of Field Evaluation and Sales Demonstrations for American Chemical Corporation. Throughout his career, he has been critical of the purchasing decisions of the industrial buyer. This is because he feels that despite the magnitude of the business conducted, most purchasing agents rely on limited and questionable information on which to base their decisions. This contention is particularly true in the area of plant and sanitary maintenance products.

Not long ago, Mr. Vining began looking into the possibility of providing these same purchasing agents with a product evaluation service that would detail product effectiveness and make recommended purchase decisions.

His initial research uncovered the fact that there were already two such testing services in existence. One, Buyers' Laboratory, was established in 1961 and currently has a client base of over 2000 subscribers. The other competitor is the U.S. Testing Laboratory, which is also widely known. Their evaluations, particularly those of Buyers' Laboratory, are based on a performance rating of each of the important factors within the product and also include pertinent additional information. A ranking is then established based on this data, and reported in a format similar to that used by *Consumer's Report*.

Mr. Vining is of the opinion that this information is limited in scope and does not take into account product costs, or more important, the labor requirements associated with the product's use. Since labor costs constitute a disproportionate share of maintenance expense, information identifying the product's labor requirements would be of paramount value. For example, a floor polish durable enough to forego frequent applications would warrant a relatively high rating because it would eliminate a portion of the labor costs and thus lower the total maintenance expense. Mr. Vining also feels that climate conditions also affect product performance. Mr. Vining lives in Phoenix, Arizona, where summer temperatures often soar above 110 degrees. Products that perform well in other parts of the country may not reach the same standards in the torrid Southwest.

Mr. Vining believes that his primary advantages would be a more detailed cost-benefit analysis and the product's evaluation in an environment which would approximate that of the ultimate user. In an effort to limit himself, he has tentatively decided to concentrate on the category he knows best — floor care products. This is the largest category of plant and sanitary maintenance products, with an approximate southwestern regional sales volume of $160 to $200 million. This category was also chosen because of its relative ease of laboratory evaluation and the low overhead involved. Mr. Vining realizes that in order to enter the business, he must quit his job, which currently pays him $45,000 per year. However, he is not certain how he should proceed.

1. What steps would you recommend that Mr. Vining take to analyze the market potential?
2. Discuss the factors in the external environment that Mr. Vining should evaluate before reaching a final decision.

6.2   Northrop Corporation

Northrop Corporation is one of the smaller American aerospace corporations. It is unique in that it relies primarily on its own salesmanship. Northrop, which does more business abroad than at home, tends to go it alone rather than using Washington's active assistance. It tends to specialize in relatively cheap and simple aircraft.

Northrop claims it is not just peddling military hardware, but also offering to help solve a customer nation's broader problems. "A customer's economic and political needs are just as important and interesting to us as the airplane itself," notes a senior company executive. For example, the Spanish government, which sought employment opportunities and knowhow with its fighter planes, got the chance to assemble the airplane it bought.

Aircraft designers, not salespeople, are the first to call on potential customers. Then the engineers develop planes to meet a cost target. By limiting its technical risk from the start, Northrop has always delivered on time and at the promised price. An example is the F-5 Tiger, the most widely deployed American supersonic fighter. Northrop has sold over 2000 of the lightweight jets to 25 nations. The plane has a limited combat range—about 300 miles—and firepower, but it is ideal for countries like Egypt and Indonesia. The economy model fighter, priced at about $3 million, suits many nations that cannot afford to pay five times as much for top of the line American tactical fighters.

To obtain a Swiss contract for 72 F-5s, Northrop made a unique commitment. The company promised to find new business for Swiss manufacturers amounting to at least one-third ($150 million) of the fighters' cost over an eight-year period. Most of the Swiss companies that need help are relatively small and lack international experience outside Europe, which Northrop can provide. The company's Swiss Offset Program is so named because it seeks to offset the order with benefits to the purchaser.

1. Do you feel that Northrop has the marketing concept? Defend your position.
2. If you feel that Northrop does not have the marketing concept, how would you implement it?
3. What information would be needed to establish a marketing intelligence system for Northrop?
4. Discuss the potential subdepartments within an overall marketing organization at Northrop.

7

Marketing information systems and marketing research

OBJECTIVES

To learn the meaning and importance of marketing research.

To gain insight into the scope of marketing research activity.

To learn the steps involved in a research project.

To convey the importance of properly evaluating market research studies.

To discover what is meant by a marketing information system and its role in the marketing function.

Procter & Gamble Company is the nation's 23rd largest industrial concern, and it does business more frequently with American consumers—about 17 million transactions a day, it estimates—than any other corporation.

In 1980, it received and answered upward of 250,000 calls and letters from customers. Half of these communications were requests for information, a sixth were expressions of praise, and a third were complaints of all kinds, including those about products, ads and even the plots of soap operas that the company sponsors on TV.

Also, P&G phoned or visited some 1.5 million people during 1980 in connection with about 1,000 research projects; that's up from 250,000 such interviews six years ago. These people are questioned extensively on their likes and dislikes about P&G products including their names, packaging and hundreds of other details. In addition, P&G does an unusual amount of continuing "basic" research into how people go about washing clothes, preparing meals, doing the dishes and other household tasks.

Generating this mountain of information is only half the process. It's what P&G does with it that really sets the company apart from the corporate pack. The data is funneled monthly to every major segment of the company—including the executive suite—where it is sifted and resifted for implications for P&G's marketing, advertising, manufacturing and research and development operations.

"In our business, we are forever trying to see what lies around the corner," says Edward G. Harness, P&G's chairman. "We study the ever-changing consumer and try to identify new trends in tastes, needs, environment and living habits. We study changes in the marketplace and try to assess their likely impact on our brands. We study our competition. Competitive brands are continually offering new benefits and new ideas to the consumer, and we must stay ahead of this."

At least once a year, P&G conducts market research on each of its brands. Frequently, these surveys turn up consumer attitudes that prompt the company to tinker even with its best-selling products—perhaps because consumers don't like something specific about the P&G brand or prefer a rival product. Tide detergent, one of P&G's biggest sellers, has been changed significantly 57 times since it was introduced in 1947, Mr. Harness, the chairman, says.

Sometimes a consumer gripe about one product can't be solved

177

directly, but instead leads to another product. In its Downy fabric-softener research, P&G learned that people disliked having to run down to their washing machine on every rinse cycle to pour in Downy. P&G couldn't solve the problem by changing Downy, but it instead came up with Bounce, a nonwoven rayon sheet impregnated with softener that is tossed into the dryer with the clothes.[1]

Think of it, 1.5 million people interviewed every year by a single company. Why is this necessary? What does it accomplish? How is it done? Let us take a closer look at how companies gather information for marketing decisions.

What is marketing research?

There are as many definitions of marketing research as there are books on the subject. However, most of them have certain characteristics in common. First, most definitions describe it as a systematic search for information. Second, nearly all suggest that marketing research involves data analysis and interpretation in addition to data collection. The third characteristic most of these definitions have in common is the recognition that marketing research exists for the purpose of providing decision-making data for management. So we can define **marketing research** as the planning for, collection, and analysis of data relevant to marketing decision making, and the communication of the results of this analysis to management.

Who does marketing research?

Three types of organizations actually design and implement marketing research studies: advertising agencies, independent marketing research firms, and corporate marketing research departments. Corporate marketing research departments include those of manufacturers such as Procter & Gamble, General Foods, and General Mills; retailers such as Sears, K-Mart, and Southland (7-Eleven stores); and service businesses such as American Airlines, Hertz, and Merrill Lynch. Examples of advertising agencies that conduct a significant amount of research are J. Walter Thompson, Grey Advertising, Doyle Dane Bernbach, Foote, Cone and Belding, Leo Burnett, and Needham, Harper and Steers, Inc.

ADVERTISING AGENCIES

Although advertising agencies conduct numerous studies, they are always directed toward a client's needs and usually initiated by the client. For example, if General Foods is concerned about how it should position Country

Time lemonade relative to competing products, the company may commission its advertising agency to do a study. The advertising agency may attempt to pick the "right grandpa" to be a Country Time spokesperson in an advertisement. The agency may film the same commercial using three different "grandpas." Consumers would then be asked which one they liked the best, which one seemed most believable, which one seemed like a "real" grandfather.

RESEARCH FIRMS

An independent marketing research firm is a company whose primary business is the sale of marketing research services. Such firms can be classified in two groups on the basis of the nature of the information they provide — custom or ad hoc research firms and syndicated-service research firms.

Syndicated services. These firms compile a standardized set of data on a continuing basis — every month, every six months, once a year — and distribute it to anyone who subscribes to the service. Examples include the Nielsen and American Research Bureau (ARB) TV audience reports, the ARB radio audience reports, the Target Group Index (TGI) magazine audience and readership reports, the Selling Areas Marketing (SAMI) warehouse movement reports, and the Nielsen retail shelf audits (see Figure 7.1). A company subscribes to a syndicated service much the way a consumer subscribes to a magazine. All subscribers to a given service get the same or similar information in the same or similar form.

Data from syndicated services are an important input to the marketing information systems of many firms. These data are usually used for control purposes — that is, to monitor the effectiveness, on an ongoing basis, of the firm's marketing strategies. For example, Nielsen store audit data that show the movement of products off the retail shelf might be used to monitor the retail sales of a particular product. Because many subscribers share the expense of collecting and processing the data, the cost to individual subscribers is low. For this reason syndicated services are often good buys on a cost-versus-value-of-information basis.

The following is an excerpt from an A. C. Nielsen sales brochure for its Retail Index System.

The key to being useful to such a broad range of management functions lies in the breadth and relationship of data types available. The Nielsen Retail Index System provides continuous information on a wide range of marketing variables, which give the marketer an accurate and complete picture of what is happening at the retail level, both nationally and regionally; for his own brands as well as those of his competitors. The data are normally provided on a monthly basis but with an option for weekly data, if the additional investment is warranted by the client risk or need.

To Measure Your Consumer Sales Relation to Competition
Sales in units (or equivalents) and dollars for the total product
class, client brands and competing brands; all specified sizes,
flavors, etc.

To Measure Your Sell-in to the Retailer
Total merchandise purchased by retailers is shown by brand,
product class and store type.

To Evaluate Your In-store Position
Inventories are reported like sales, but volume and share totals
refer to the amount of unsold merchandise on hand at the retail
store.

To Evaluate Pricing Strategies
Average prices recorded on the date of audit (weighted by sales
volume) are shown for each brand, by size, type and area for
chains and large independents.

To Track Advertising Efforts
A compilation from outside sources—of network and spot television, magazine and newspaper expenditures—is reported on a
monthly basis with each shown separately by media type and on
a brand basis.

To Analyze Sales and Marketing Efforts by Sales Areas
As an option, clients can obtain data according to their own sales
regions providing a means of analyzing sales performance.

To Monitor Competitive Marketing Efforts
Promotional efforts (advertising, deals, displays, etc.) are reported for competitive brands allowing analysis of a variety of
marketing strategies and their success or lack of success.

Sampling
The 1300 store sample of retail food outlets reflects the unpro-
jected purchases of an equivalent 1,600,000 households—or
4,600,000 people, who spend about $3.5 billion annually in these
sample stores.

The Audit Work
Assuring the accuracy and reliability of the raw data gathered
from the sample stores is the responsibility of the Nielsen field
representative. For that reason, the men and women who perform the detailed store audit tasks are full-time, college-educated
and well-trained professionals with an average of over eight
years in-field experience.[2]

Custom research firms. These firms do one-of-a-kind research projects, usually for the purpose of providing data that are relevant to current decision
making—where to locate a new store, what creative strategy to use in next
year's advertising, and the like. These studies are ordinarily designed and con-

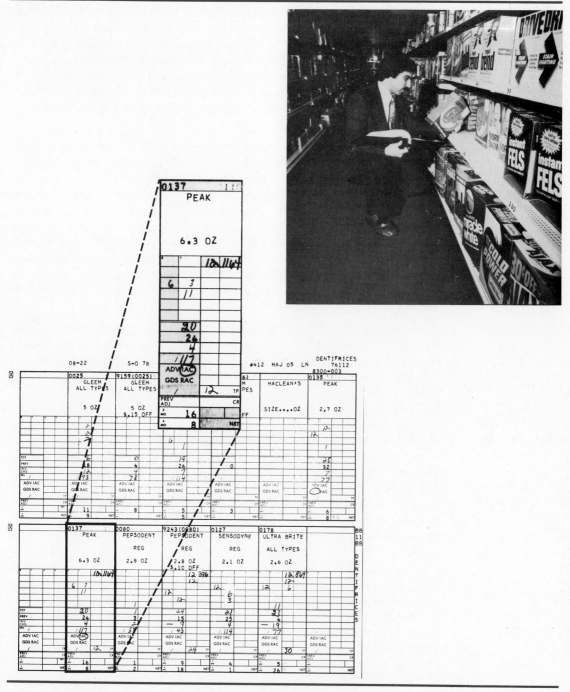

Source: Courtesy of A. C. Nielsen Company.

ducted for a single client, with all the data generated by the study becoming the property of that client.

A variation of custom research performed by some firms is the **omnibus survey.** In an omnibus survey, any company can buy a single question or ask several questions. For example, if a research director only needs to know how many people have bought Blue Nun wine in the past three months and how it compared with other white wines purchased during the past three months, he or she could add these questions to an omnibus survey. Omnibus surveys are carried out on a regular schedule—monthly, quarterly, or biannually (see Figure 7.2).

Field service. In addition to these two general types of marketing research firms, a number of organizations provide specialized services. Most significant among these is the field service firm. These organizations provide interviewing and other field services to custom research firms, syndicated service firms, and corporate marketing research departments on a subcontract basis. Besides interviewing, field service firms provide focus group facilities, mall intercept locations, test product storage, and kitchen facilities to prepare test food products. They also conduct retail audits. After an in-home interview has been completed, field service supervisors validate the survey by recontacting the respondent to make sure certain responses were recorded properly and the person was actually interviewed.

America's major research organizations. Table 7.1 (p. 184) provides a ranking by actual or estimated 1979 sales or expenditures for both profit and nonprofit research organizations. The profit-making organizations are numbered 1 through 23. Nonprofit firms are inserted where appropriate in the table. The Bureau of the Census is the largest nonprofit research organization in America. A number of corporations have in-house research capabilities and do a considerable amount of work directly without the help of outside suppliers (except for field services). Examples include Procter & Gamble, General Foods, General Mills, Quaker Oats, and Pillsbury. A dozen or more American universities are affiliated with nonprofit survey organizations whose main purpose is to serve the needs of academicians, but some also do work for commercial organizations. These include the Research Triangle Institute (supported by Duke, North Carolina State, North Carolina, and North Carolina Central), the National Opinion Research Center (University of Chicago), and the Institute for Social Research (University of Michigan).

Among the profit-oriented institutions, the top four are all syndicated service firms. Number one, Nielsen, relies heavily on its well-known TV audience reports (which account for 11 percent of its business) and its less well-known retail shelf audit data (65 percent).[3] Number two, IMS, provides a number of services that are similar to Nielsen's except that it specializes in the pharmaceutical-medical area. Half of IMS's sales come from pharmaceutical-medical audits, while the rest come from other syndicated services. Third-ranked Selling Areas–Marketing (SAMI) compiles and sells data on the movement of products, while Arbitron provides TV and radio audience data. The

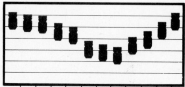

Source: Courtesy of Consumer Response Corporation.

next eight firms are all custom research firms.

In addition to this group of large firms, there are a large number of small firms in the industry, and new firms are constantly being formed. Research in Perspective, Research 100, Benson & Benson, Newman-Stein, and Custom

Rank	Organization	Revenue (in millions)
1.	A. C. Nielsen Co.	$302.1
2.	IMS International	88.8
	Demographic Survey Division, Bureau of the Census	70.0
3.	SAMI	54.4
4.	The Arbitron Co.	44.1
5.	Burke Int'l Research	42.6
6.	Market Facts	19.2
7.	Westat Inc.	14.4
8.	Audits & Surveys	14.0
9.	Marketing & Research Counselors	13.1
10.	ASI Market Research	12.3
11.	Chilton Research	12.0
12.	Yankelovich, Skelly & White	11.8
	Research Triangle Institute	11.5
13.	Ehrhart-Babic Associates	10.4
14.	National Family Opinion	10.0
	National Opinion Research Center (University of Chicago)	9.9
15.	NPD Research	9.7
	Procter & Gamble	9.7
16.	Data Development Corporation	9.6
17.	Louis Harris & Associates	9.3
18.	National Analysts	8.7
19.	Opinion Research Corporation	8.2
	The Institute for Social Research (University of Michigan)	8.0
20.	Elrick & Lavidge	7.1
21.	Walker Research	7.0
	General Mills	6.0
22.	Starch INRA Hooper	5.5
	General Foods Corporation	5.0+
	Quaker Oats	5.0+
23.	Decisions Center	5.1

Nonprofit organizations and in-house facilities are shown in italics.
Source: Jack Honomichl, "Adding Nonprofit Researchers to Top 23 List," *Advertising Age* (June 16, 1980), p. 60. Reprinted with permission. Copyright 1980 by Crain Communications, Inc.

Research are examples of successful firms founded in recent years by former officers or employees of other marketing research organizations.

CORPORATE MARKETING RESEARCH DEPARTMENTS

As Table 7.1 shows, corporate market research departments directly account for a substantial amount of total research expenditures. Indirectly, of course, they account for all the profit-oriented research expenditures. A 1978 survey of corporations by the American Marketing Association found that 74 percent

◀ TABLE 7.2 Market Research Activities of American Companies

Kind of research	Percentage doing	Percentage done by market research department	Percentage done by another department	Percentage done by outside firm
Advertising research				
A. Motivation research	48%	28%	3%	17%
B. Copy research	49	22	6	21
C. Media research	61	24	11	26
D. Studies of ad effectiveness	67	38	5	24
Business economics and corporate research				
A. Short-range forecasting (up to 1 year)	85	52	31	2
B. Long-range forecasting (over 1 year)	82	50	30	2
C. Studies of business trends	86	61	21	4
D. Pricing studies	81	36	44	1
E. Plant and warehouse location studies	71	30	38	3
F. Acquisition studies	69	29	38	2
G. Export and international studies	51	24	25	2
H. MIS (management information system)	72	26	44	2
I. Operations research	60	17	42	1
J. Internal company employees	65	18	41	6
Corporate responsibility research				
A. Consumers' "right to know" studies	26	11	12	3
B. Ecological impact studies	33	5	25	3
C. Studies of legal constraints on advertising and promotion	51	12	34	5
D. Social values and policies studies	40	18	17	5
Product research				
A. New product acceptance and potential	84	71	7	6
B. Competitive product studies	85	71	9	5
C. Testing of existing products	75	49	20	6
D. Packaging research: design or physical characteristics	60	36	16	8
Sales and market research				
A. Measurement of market potentials	93	82	7	4
B. Market share analysis	92	80	9	3
C. Determination of market characteristics	93	83	6	4
D. Sales analysis	89	64	24	1
E. Establishment of sales quotas, territories	75	27	48	—
F. Distribution channel studies	69	31	37	1
G. Test markets, store audits	54	38	9	7
H. Consumer panel operations	50	32	5	13
I. Sales compensation studies	60	14	43	3
J. Promotional studies of premiums, coupons, sampling, deals, etc.	52	34	15	3

Source: Dik Warren Twedt, *1978 Survey of Marketing Research* (Chicago: American Marketing Association, 1978), p. 41. Reprinted by permission.

have a formal marketing research department.[4] Generally speaking, the larger the company the more likely it is to have a research department. For example, 87 percent of the firms with sales over $500 million reported having formal research departments. Such departments tend to be rather small; the average size was seven employees, and industrial organization departments averaged only three people. Other survey results indicate that marketing research was considered a staff function reporting to a general marketing manager. Research departments spend most of their money for outside services (except among the very largest departments).

The activities engaged in by most departments are shown in Table 7.2. Note that the most common activities center around forecasting, measuring market potential, and new product research. But these departments vary greatly in form and in the jobs they perform. General Foods has a highly developed research group with more than 300 employees and can do all types of marketing research and all phases of a project in house. Anderson-Clayton Foods, located in Dallas, has fewer than ten people working in marketing research and relies heavily on outside suppliers to design and conduct research studies. However, these two companies have something in common: they both work largely with primary data (new data). This is in contrast to the marketing research departments of companies like Braniff Airlines, which not only are relatively small but deal primarily with secondary data (data that has already been gathered from company operations, such as traffic on various routes, and data from library sources such as the *U.S. Census of Population*). So marketing research departments come in all shapes and sizes and are structured to suit the information needs of the firms they serve.

Preparing a research project: preliminary analysis

When confronted with a situation that may require marketing research, the researcher has two questions to deal with. First, is formal research really called for in this case? Second, if it is called for, what form should the research take? The answer to the first question is developed in a **preliminary analysis,** as follows:[5]

1. Reach an agreement on the nature of the problems and the research objectives—this provides focus for the research effort.
2. Perform a background investigation—check existing data for anything relevant to the research problem.
3. Perform an informal investigation—conduct a mini-study.

Problem statement. The first step in the research process must be the development of a problem statement and a statement of research objectives on which the decision maker and the researcher can agree. This is not as easy as it sounds, but it is important because these statements will provide direction for the remainder of the study. Some situations may require only a problem statement; others lend themselves more readily to the specification of research objectives. In some cases identifying and structuring the problem may itself turn out to be the objective of a major research effort.

Situation analysis. The background investigation, sometimes referred to as the **situation analysis,** is particularly important to the outside consultant or to any researcher dealing with a particular type of problem for the first time. The purpose of this step is to permit the researcher to become immersed in the problem. It is necessary to become familiar with the company, its products, its markets, its marketing history, the competition, and so forth. On the basis of this background investigation it may become necessary to go back and respecify the problem statement and research objectives developed in the first step.

Informal investigation. The informal investigation is the final step in the preliminary analysis. It can be looked upon as a miniresearch study. In this stage data may be collected from people outside the company—consumers, retailers who handle the product, and others. The purpose is to determine, on the basis of a cursory and relatively inexpensive survey, whether to proceed with a formal study. As in the background investigation, information may be uncovered that suggests a need to respecify the problem. Study of this problem will end here if the solution is clear or if it appears that the cost of obtaining the information required to solve it will outweigh the expected value of the information. If the answer is not clear and if the projected value of the required information exceeds its cost, the next step is to design and carry out a formal study.

Designing and conducting a formal study

The steps involved in designing and conducting a formal study are as follows:

1. Specify the data required to meet the research objectives.
2. Determine the most efficient and accurate means for gathering the data.
3. Design the data collection forms.
4. Specify the sampling procedures to be used.
5. Specify the data collection procedures.
6. Develop a plan for processing the data.
7. Develop a plan for analyzing the data.
8. Prepare a report on the results.

SPECIFYING DATA NEEDS AND SELECTING SOURCES

At this point it is necessary to develop a complete list of all the data required to meet the research objective. Then the researcher should determine the sources for each type of data. There are really only two general types of data used in marketing research—primary data and secondary data. Let us look first at secondary data and its uses.

Secondary data. **Secondary data** are data collected for any purpose other than the one at hand. Major sources of secondary data are outlined in Table 7.3. Most research efforts rely at least in part on secondary data because it can ordinarily be obtained quickly and at relatively low cost. The problem is locating the relevant data. There are firms, such as the Information Source in Los Angeles, that specialize in obtaining secondary data for a fee.

The advantages of using secondary data are the savings in time and money if they solve the researcher's problem. Even if the problem is not solved, secondary data can aid in the formulation of the problem definition, suggest research methods and other types of data needed for solving the problem, pinpoint the types of persons who should be approached and their locations, and serve as a source of comparative data by which primary data can be analyzed and evaluated.

The disadvantages of secondary data are due primarily to a lack of fit between the researcher's unique problem and information that has already been gathered. A major consumer products manufacturer was interested in determining the market potential for a fireplace log made of coal rather than compressed wood by-products. There were plenty of secondary data about total wood consumed as fuel, quantities consumed by state, and types of wood burned. There were also secondary data available about consumer attitudes and purchase

◀ **TABLE 7.3   Sources and Descriptions of Secondary Data**

Source	Description
1. Internal information	Any internal company information that may be helpful in solving a particular marketing problem. Examples include sales invoices, other accounting records, data from previous marketing research studies, and historical sales data.
2. Government agencies	The Bureau of the Census and many other federal agencies provide perhaps the largest single source of secondary data for marketing researchers. In particular, the *Censuses of Population, Housing, Business, Agriculture, Manufacturing,* and *Transportation* are widely used.
3. Syndicated research services	Companies such as A. C. Nielsen, Arbitron, IMS International, and SAMI are major sources of secondary data.
4. Trade associations	Many trade associations, such as the National Industrial Conference Board and the National Retail Merchants Association, collect data that are of interest to members.
5. Custom research firms	Custom research firms can provide data from old studies of related problems.
6. Research bureaus, professional associations, foundations	A variety of nonprofit organizations collect and disseminate data that are of interest to marketing researchers.
7. Commercial publications	*Advertising Age, Sales Management, Product Marketing, Merchandising Week,* and many other commercial publications provide useful research data.

patterns of wood by-product fireplace logs. These data were panel information gathered by a syndicated service. As you can imagine, the wealth of secondary information provided the researcher with many insights into the artificial log market. Yet nowhere was there any information that would tell the firm if consumers would buy such a product made of coal.

A second problem relates to the quality of secondary information. Often secondary data sources do not give detailed information that would enable a researcher to assess their quality or relevance. Where possible, it is important to know: (1) who gathered the data, (2) why it was obtained, (3) what methodology was used, (4) how classifications, such as heavy users vs. light users, were developed and defined, and (5) how old the information is.

Part of the quality dilemma will be answered during the 1980s with the growth of huge secondary data banks kept by some of America's largest corporations. Some examples of major data base systems are shown in Table 7.4. J. Walter Thompson and *The New York Times* have developed a system called AMI (Advertising/Marketing Intelligence) which is a data bank focusing on people, products, organizations, and promotional activities for more than 60 trade and professional publications. Examples of output from the AMI system are shown in Figure 7.3 (p. 192). A good data bank, such as AMI, can save countless hours of manual search time.

Primary data. Recall that step one in the research process is specifying the type of data needed. In addition to the use of secondary data, researchers often rely on **primary data,** data that are collected for the first time for the purpose of solving the particular problem under investigation. There are four ways of generating primary data—survey, observation, experiment, and simulation. **Survey** and **observation** are assembly procedures in which the researcher takes a passive attitude toward the phenomenon under investigation. This is in contrast to the **experiment,** which is distinguished by the researcher's manipulation of one or more independent variables (price, shelf space, advertising expenditures, and package design) for the purpose of measuring the impact of different levels of the independent variable on the dependent variable (market share, unit sales, dollar sales). **Simulation** in this context typically involves the development of mathematical models of marketing phenomena. The idea is that once this is done, various parameters of the model can be adjusted to reflect changes in the firm's marketing program and the impact on sales or profits estimated.

Although no exact figures are available, it is acknowledged that in commercial marketing research the survey is by far the most widely used method of obtaining data. Surveys involve asking people questions, while observation means watching people or phenomena such as traffic flows or the movement of products from a retail shelf. There are good reasons for the dominance of the survey in marketing research. Observation has the advantage of permitting you to see what people actually do rather than what they say they do. However, it has the serious disadvantage of providing no information about who they are or about why they do what they do. In most marketing research the "why" of consumer behavior is important.

▲ **TABLE 7.4 Major Data Base Services and Their Offerings**

Data base	Description	Producer	Vendor	Price
Enviroline	Abstracts of literature on the environment from special reports, conference proceedings, and 3000 international journals.	Environment Information Center, Inc.	Lockheed Corporation, System Development Corporation	$90 per hour.
New York Times Information Bank	Abstracts of *The New York Times*, 13 other newspapers, and over 40 magazines.	*The New York Times*	*The New York Times*	$80 to $110 per hour.
Japanese Economic Information Service	Data on the Japanese economy, including a macroeconomic model and forecasts.	Data Resources, Inc. (McGraw-Hill)	Data Resources, Inc. (McGraw-Hill)	$6400 annual subscription plus charges for computer time.
Petroleum Data System	Geological and production data on every gas and oil field or reservoir in the U.S., Canada, and the outer continental shelf.	University of Oklahoma, under contract to the U.S. Geological Survey	General Electric Information Services	Determined by complexity of search; $30 minimum for data on one field.
Philosopher's Index	Citations and abstracts of the literature on philosophy, esthetics epistemology.	Philosophy Documentation Center, Bowling Green State University	Lockheed Corporation	$55 per hour.
NTIS	Citations and abstracts of unrestricted technical reports from federally sponsored R&D projects.	U.S. National Technical Information Service (Commerce Department)	Lockheed Corporation, System Development Corporation Bibliographic Retrieval Services, Inc.	$35 per hour from Lockheed and SDC; $27 to $44 from BRS.

PROMT	Citations and abstracts on new products, technology, markets, etc., from over 2000 U.S. and foreign publications.	Predicasts, Inc.	Lockheed Corporation, System Development Corporation	$90 per hour.
Dow Jones News/Retrieval Service	Complete and abridged articles from *The Wall St. Journal*, *Barron's*, and the *Dow Jones News Service*; price quotations on stocks, bonds, options and mutual funds.	Dow Jones & Co.	Dow Jones, Bunker Ramo Corporation, Telerate Systems, Inc., General Telephone & Electronics	$50 per user location and $40 per hour from Dow Jones; other vendor prices vary.
LEXIS	The full text of state and federal court decisions, statutes, regulations, etc.	Mead Corporation	Mead Corporation	Minimum $500 monthly charge for one terminal; additional hourly fee (averaging $60 to $90) for computer time.
Disclosure Online	Extracts from SEC filings of over 12,000 publicly held companies.	Disclosure, Inc.	Lockheed Corporation, Mead Corporation	$90 per hour from Lockheed; Mead's use charges same as for LEXIS.

Source: Walter Kiechel, "Everything You Always Wanted to Know May Soon Be On-Line," *Fortune*, May 5, 1980, p. 228. Used by permission. FORTUNE Art Department.

Q. What new brands of beer have recently been introduced in the U.S.?

```
NYT-JWT            ADVERTISING/MARKETING INTELLIGENCE
                   NEW PRODUCTS AND BEER

NEW PRODUCTS       CENTURY IMPORTERS, NOTING GROWTH OF IMPORTED    ANNY
BEER AND ALE       BEER SALES OVER PAST YEAR, IS RELAUNCHING       OCT 29 1979
CENTURY IMPORTERS  CARLSBERG LINE, NOW IN SIX-PACKS AND WITH       P:6 C:2
OGILVY & MATHER    NEW LABEL; O&M HANDLES AD CAMPAIGN

AD CAMPAIGNS       JOSEPH GEORGE DISTRIBUTORS WILL INTRODUCE       MAC
BEER AND ALE       MONTEJO, MEXICAN BEER FROM THE YUCATAN;         NOV 05 1979
JOSEPH GEORGE      CARTER, CALLAHAN & ASSOCIATES SUPPORTS VIA      P:32 C:3
CARTER CALLAHAN    PRINT, BROADCAST AND P-O-P CAMPAIGN
```

Q. Is the life insurance industry running into any regulatory problems?

```
NYT-JWT            ADVERTISING/MARKETING INTELLIGENCE
11-05-79 TO        INSURANCE
12-06-79

ACCOUNT CHANGES    CUNA MUTUAL INSURANCE SOCIETY AWARDS ITS        ADVERTISING AGE
INSURANCE          $1,500,000 ACCOUNT TO GREY-NORTH, ITS FIRST     NOV 05 1979
CUNA MUTUAL        AGENCY                                          P:8 C:3
GREY-NORTH

INSURANCE          LIFE INSURANCE INDUSTRY FACES HEAVY PRESSURE    PR NEWSLETTER
PUBLIC RELATIONS   FROM FTC TO CURB ABUSES IN SALES TACTICS;       NOV 07 1979
TOBIAS, A SERBER   INDUSTRY'S PR PROBLEMS NOTED; GERBER'S          P:3 C:1
                   RESPONSE TO TOBIAS ARTICLE IN NYT NOTED
```

Q. What is the demographic outlook for household detergents and soaps in the 1980's?

```
NYT-JWT            ADVERTISING/MARKETING INTELLIGENCE
11-05-79 TO        DETERGENTS AND DEMOGRAPHICS
12-06-79

DETERGENTS         FROST & SULLIVAN STUDY EXPECTS SALES OF         DRUGSTORE NEWS
RESEARCH           HOUSEHOLD DETERGENTS AND SOAPS TO FLATTEN       NOV 12 1979
FROST & SULLIVAN   DURING 1980'S DUE TO SHRINKING FAMILIES AND     P:24 C:1
                   MORE CASUAL HOUSEKEEPING STANDARDS
```

Q. What were the details of the most recent Nielsen study on cable TV reach?

```
NYT-JWT            ADVERTISING/MARKETING INTELLIGENCE
                   NIELSEN AND CABLE

CABLE TELEVISION   A C NIELSEN'S FIRST NATIONAL PAY CABLE AUDI-    ADVERTISING AGE
COMMUNICATIONS     ENCE REPORT FINDS MOVIES OUTRANK COMPETING      SEPT 24 1979
A C NIELSEN        PRIME TIME FARE; ALSO FINDS SUPERSTATION        P:1 C:1
                   SIGNALS OUTRATE LOCAL INDEPENDENTS; STUDY
                   DETAILED

AUDIENCE RESEARCH  A C NIELSEN STUDY SHOWS CABLE PENETRATION OF    TV-RADIO AGE
CABLE TELEVISION   HOUSEHOLDS REACHED 18.8% IN MAY 1979, COM-      SEPT 24 1979
A C NIELSEN        PARED TO 16.6% IN 1978; LEVEL IN TOP 25 DESIG-  P:31 C:1
                   NATED MARKET AREAS WAS 13.2%
```

Source: Courtesy of AMI, The Advertising and Marketing Intelligence Service from The New York Times Information Service and J. Walter Thompson Company.

Experiments also suffer from this problem. Experiments are particularly difficult in the marketing field because so many factors (competitors' advertising, weather, economic conditions) are encountered in actual situations that may affect the dependent variable but are beyond the experimenter's control.

Each procedure has its natural place in marketing research. Observation is the natural way to monitor things like the movement of a product off the retail shelf (store audits) or traffic levels (car counters). Experimental designs are widely used in the test marketing of new products and new advertising campaigns and for testing things like the optimal amount of shelf space to devote to a product. Surveys prevail in studies intended to find out what people think or feel or why they like or dislike a particular product, store, price, or the like. The researcher's job is to select the data collection method that will provide the desired data most accurately and efficiently.

Surveys. A number of different survey methods are used in marketing research. The choice of a particular method should be a function of the type of information required and the funds available for the study. Type of information required should be the overriding consideration. Individuals can be interviewed in person, over the telephone, via mail, or by means of computer terminals.

There are four possible personal interview situations—door to door, mall intercept, focus group, and executive interview. In the door-to-door interview, the respondent is interviewed at home. This is the most costly survey method and is typically regarded as generating the most complete and reliable data.[6] The **mall intercept interview** involves interviewing people in the common areas of shopping malls. It is the economy version of the door-to-door interview. This approach provides personal contact between interviewer and respondent without interviewer travel time and mileage costs. To obtain the right to do this type of interviewing, the research firm may rent office space in the mall or pay so much per day. Mall intercept interviews must be brief, and it is sometimes difficult to obtain a representative sample of the area in question. Only the shortest of mall interviews are done "standing-up" in the mall. Usually the respondent is asked to go to the researcher's office at the mall. There the researcher can conduct the interview (rarely over 15 minutes in length), show the respondent concepts of products or a test commercial, or have the person taste a new food product (see Figure 7.4).

The **focus group** is a third type of personal interview. Seven to ten people with the desired characteristics are recruited by random telephone screening or in some other way. Qualified consumers are usually offered an incentive ($15–$20 is common) to participate in a group discussion. The place where this discussion is held will probably have a conference table (some are set up like home livingrooms) and audio taping equipment. It is likely to have a viewing room with a one-way mirror so that clients may watch the session, and it may be equipped with videotaping equipment. During the session a moderator will lead the group through a discussion of a series of topics. In a study of dog food, for example, the moderator might lead a group of product users into a discussion concerning their awareness of existing brands, usage rates, words used to describe dog food, and so forth. This technique is used primarily as an exploratory tool—as a prelude to a formal study.

The **executive interview** is the fourth type of personal interview and can be viewed as the industrial counterpart of the door-to-door interview. Businesspeople are interviewed at their offices concerning their usage, preferences, and perceptions of business products and services. These interviews are usually quite expensive because the interviewers must set up appointments, often have to wait to see the appropriate person, and frequently encounter canceled appointments.

Source: Courtesy of Roger Gates.

Compared to the personal interview, the **telephone interview** offers the advantage of lower cost and the potential for the best sample of any of the survey procedures. It is frequently criticized for providing poorer-quality data than the personal interview. However, recent studies have shown that these fears may be exaggerated.[7] There are at least two types of telephone interviewing—from-home interviewing and central-location interviewing. The former, as the term implies, is done from home. Central-location telephone interviewing is done from a "phone room" set up for this purpose. A phone room has a number of phone lines, individual interviewing stations, possibly monitoring equipment, and headsets so that the interviewers can have their hands free.

The principal advantage of the central-location telephone interview lies in the ability to control interview quality and productivity. Its principal disadvantage compared to the from-home interview is the added cost—supervision, facilities, and interviewer travel time and mileage. The use of Wide Area Telephone Service (WATS) lines in conjunction with central-location telephone facilities permits the research firm to interview people across the country from a single location.

Mail surveys have a number of apparent benefits—low cost, elimination of interviewers and their biases, elimination of field supervisors, centralized control, actual or promised anonymity for respondents (which may elicit more candid responses), and so forth. Some researchers feel that mail questionnaires give the respondent an opportunity to make more thoughtful replies and to check records, talk to family members, take stock of certain items, and the like.[8] The big problem with mail questionnaires is low response rates.[9] And the problem with low response rates is that certain elements of the population may be more likely to respond than others.[10] This means that the resulting sample may not be representative of the population being surveyed. For example, the sample may have too many retired people and too few working people. In this case answers to a question about attitudes toward social security might indicate a much more favorable view of the system than is actually the case. A second serious problem with mail surveys is that there is no one to prod respondents to clarify or elaborate on their answers.

Mail panels such as those operated by Market Facts, National Family Opinion Research, and NPD Research offer an alternative to the one-shot mail survey. A mail panel consists of a national sample of households recruited to participate for a given period. Panel members often receive gifts in return for their participation. The panel is in essence a sample that is used several times. The panel's composition can be checked to make sure it is a true cross section of the total population. The response rates from mail panels are high compared to those achieved in one-time mail surveys. Rates of 70 percent (of those who agree to participate) are not uncommon.[11]

A recent development in marketing research technology is the **computer interview,** in which interactive computer terminals are used to interview people directly. Questions are printed out on the terminal and the respondent types in replies. At this point questions are limited to the multiple-choice variety. This approach is currently being used in a mall north of Chicago by A. C. Nielsen. Little is known about the advantages and disadvantages of this type of interviewing, but it may have a bright future in that it eliminates the interviewer and simplifies data processing. A variation of this procedure is computer-assisted interviews used primarily in telephone interviewing. The interviewer conducts a phone interview while being fed questions in varying sequences by a computer. Replies are typed directly into the computer, so totals are being continually updated. This technique is a variation of the central-location telephone interview.

Observation. Observation in marketing research takes four forms: people watching people, people watching physical phenomena, machines watching people, and machines watching physical phenomena. "People watching people" is illustrated by the use of observers to trace the traffic patterns of customers in order to determine the effects of different merchandise arrangements on those patterns. "People watching physical phenomena" includes the use of human observers to count vehicular traffic flow past a proposed site for a retail store or to keep track of the actual movement of products off a retail shelf. In the two other types of observation, machines—movie cameras, videotape equipment, traffic counters—are substituted for the human observer.

Experiment and simulation. In an experiment the researcher manipulates one factor, called the **independent variable** (price), and attempts to measure its effect on another factor, called the **dependent variable** (sales). For example, management may be divided over how to price a new product. One group feels it should be priced 20 percent above competing products. The other group feels that its price should be equal to that of competing products. An experiment might be set up in which the product is introduced in two very similar cities on a test basis. Everything would be done exactly the same way in both cities except that the higher price would be charged in one and the lower price in the other. Most experiments are much more complicated than this example, but they follow this general pattern.

A simulation is the creation of a complex model to resemble a real process or system, and experimenting with the model in the hope of learning something about the real system. Because of the complexity of simulations, they are almost always carried out on a computer. Simulations have been used most successfully in distribution, followed by promotion and pricing.

DESIGNING THE DATA-GATHERING FORMS

Most marketing research projects require some type of data-gathering form. The supermarket auditor needs a form for recording counts; the observer of frozen-food purchasers needs a form for recording observations; the interviewer needs a form from which to read questions and on which to record responses; and experiments may benefit from the use of forms for recording experimental results. Forms ensure that the same observations, questions, or measurements are made in every case. They reach their highest levels of sophistication in the survey questionnaire.

Types of information solicited. Four basic types of information can be solicited from a respondent—state of mind, state of being, behavior, and intention information. Examples of the various types of information are provided in Table 7.5. It is generally agreed that it is easier to obtain accurate state of being and behavior information than accurate state of mind and intentions information. For this reason behavior information is often obtained as a substitute for preference or intention information. For example, instead of asking people which fast-food restaurant they prefer, ask them which fast-food restaurant they pa-

◀ TABLE 7.5   Types of Information Solicited by Marketing Researchers

Type of information	Example
State of being	Age, income, sex, and other demographic characteristics
State of mind	Attitudes, images, opinions, brand preferences, and the like
Behavior	Actions—brands purchased, frequency of purchase, all facets of consumption behavior
Intention	Planned actions in regard to consumption behavior—intention to purchase a new car next year

Source: Ben Enis and Keith Cox, *The Marketing Research Process* (Pacific Palisades, Calif.: Goodyear, 1972), pp. 173–174. Copyright © 1972 by Goodyear Publishing Co. By permission.

tronize most frequently. Instead of asking a beer drinker which brand of beer he or she intends to purchase next, ask about past purchasing behavior and project it forward. The idea is that the behavior reporting will often provide a better idea of state of mind or intentions than a direct question on the subject. In many cases both the relevant behavior information and state of mind or intention information are sought so they can be compared. One might say that the trick of questionnaire design is to obtain the desired information by asking the respondent a question that he or she can reasonably be expected to answer accurately.

Qualities of good data-gathering forms. It is extremely important that a question be asked in a clear and concise manner. Ambiguous terminology should be avoided—for example, "Do you live within ten minutes of here?" or "Where do you usually shop for clothes?" The first example depends upon mode of transportation (maybe the person walks), driving speed, perceived elapsed time, and other factors. It would normally be prudent to show the respondent a map with certain areas delineated and ask if he or she lives within the area. The second question depends on the type of clothing, the occasion, the member of the family, and so on.

Clarity also implies the use of reasonable terminology. A questionnaire is not a vocabulary test; jargon should be avoided, and language should be geared to the target audience. A question such as "State the level of efficacy of your preponderate dishwasher powder" would probably be greeted by a lot of blank stares. It would be much simpler to say "Are you (1) very satisfied, (2) somewhat satisfied, or (3) not satisfied with your current brand of dishwasher powder?" Clarity can also be improved at the beginning of the interview by stating the purpose of the survey. The respondent should understand the nature of the study and what is expected of him or her. Sometimes, of course, the true purpose of the study must be disguised in order to obtain an unbiased response. A major food processor developed a package that would enable liquids, such as milk, to be kept without refrigeration for several weeks as long as the carton was unopened. This new process could save untold millions in refrigeration expenses, yet it goes against everything Americans have been taught about food sanitation and storage. So the study was disguised as an orange juice taste test. Half of the consumers were given cartons of the product to take home and told that refrigeration was not necessary; the other half were told to refrigerate the product. Subsequent call-back interviews revealed a significant difference in the perceived quality of the identical product. And the manufacturer decided that cultural taboos were too strong to overcome. A final aspect of clarity is the avoidance of two questions in one—for example, "How did you like the taste and texture of the coffee cake?" This should be broken into two questions— one concerning taste and the other texture.

Not only should a question be clear, it also should not bias a respondent. A question such as "Have you purchased any quality Black and Decker tools in the past six months?" biases respondents. Questions can also be leading: "Weren't you pleased with the good service you received last night at the Holiday Inn?'' These examples are quite obvious; unfortunately, bias is often much more subtle.

Steps in questionnaire design. Designing a questionnaire is a tedious and time-consuming process. The first step is the development of a list of topics that must be covered in the questionnaire. This list should be developed with the research objectives in mind. Topics that are not directly related to these objectives should be dropped unless there is some strong reason for including them. The second step is to write specific questions to deal with each topic. Finally, the preliminary version of the questionnaire should be pretested in a pilot study in order to identify unforeseen problems.

Most questionnaires are designed for data processing from the survey instrument. For example, Table 7.6 shows a page from an actual survey. Along the right-hand column are computer card column numbers. The interviewee response (either 1 or 2 for column 57) is entered on a card, tape, or computer disc. Rather than looking all over the questionnaire for the response to a ques-

---

◢ **TABLE 7.6   Excerpt from a Questionnaire Designed for Simplified Data Processing**

Now I have just a few more questions for classification purposes.

16. Are you employed outside your home?

CONTINUE WITH Q.17 ⟵ Yes 1

SKIP to Q. 21 ⟵ No 2

17. If you were to purchase this new communications service where would you be most likely to use it, in your home, office or both?

Home 1
Office 2
Both   3

18. What is your occupation? (TYPE OF WORK, NOT PLACE OF EMPLOYMENT)

---

19. Are you in a management related position?

CONTINUE WITH Q. 20 ⟵ Yes 1

SKIP TO Q. 21 ⟵ No 2

20. Is that upper, middle, or lower management?

Upper 1
Middle 2
Lower 3

21. What was the last grade of school you completed? (HAND CARD C TO RESPONDENT)

A. Some high school or less 1
B. Completed high school 2
C. Some college 3
D. Completed college 4
E. Graduate school 5
F. Other education beyond high school
(business, nursing, etc.) 6

---

tion, the data entry operator can simply look down the right side of the questionnaire.

SELECTING SAMPLING PROCEDURES

The selection and development of sampling procedures is an important part of most primary data collection efforts. Seldom can you take a census of all the possible users of a new product, nor can you interview them all. This being the case, procedures must be developed for selecting or **sampling** the group to be interviewed. Several questions must be answered before a sampling plan is selected. First, the population or universe of interest must be defined. This is the group from which the sample will be drawn. It should include all the people whose opinions, behavior, preferences, attitudes, and so on are of interest to the marketer. For example, in a study whose purpose is to determine the market for a new canned dog food the universe might be defined to include all current purchasers of canned dog food.

After the universe has been defined, the next question is, Must the sample be representative of the population? The answer to this question determines which of the two broad types of sampling procedures — probability or nonprobability — should be used. If the answer to this question is yes, a probability sample is called for. Otherwise, a nonprobability sample might be considered.

Probability samples. **Probability samples** have the desirable characteristic of permitting the researcher to estimate how much sampling error is present in a given study. Three types of probability samples are commonly used in marketing research: simple random samples, cluster or area samples, and stratified samples.

The **simple random sample** must be set up in such a way that every element of the population has an equal chance of being selected as part of the sample. An example would be a situation in which a university is interested in obtaining a cross section of student opinion on a proposed sports complex to be built using student activity fees. If an up-to-date list of all the students enrolled at the university can be obtained, a sample that meets all the requirements of a simple random sample can be drawn by using random numbers from a table (most statistics books have such tables) to select students from the list.

A solution for a number of the problems — lack of up-to-date lists, high cost, the expense of making callbacks — associated with simple random samples can be found in the use of area or **cluster samples.** In this approach the researcher randomly selects a number of geographic starting points. For example, a grid overlay might be superimposed on a map of the area to be surveyed. Then row and column coordinates can be selected at random. Next, the nearest street intersections to these coordinates are located. Finally, the interviewer is given a route to follow from the starting point. This route will typically consist of a particular city block or blocks. Interviewers are often given additional instructions that include a procedure for selecting respondents. Rather than sampling a single unit, every household on the block (or every *n*th household) is interviewed. The cluster is the city block.

The third type of probability sample is the **stratified sample.** A stratum is a segment of the population having one or more common characteristics. It might be a sex stratum (male), an age stratum (age 20–35), or some other characteristic of interest. A stratified sample is appropriate in cases in which the reseacher knows that the population to be investigated is composed of subgroups that are heterogeneous with regard to the variable(s) of interest. For example, assume that previous studies of fast-food restaurant patronage found that adults under 35 eat in fast-food restaurants an average of four times a week, while those 35 or over eat in fast-food restaurants only once a week on the average. People under 35 make up 45 percent of the population, and people 35 or over make up 55 percent of the population. Age would therefore provide a basis for stratification. This means that when the sample is actually selected (simple random sample or cluster sampling procedures will be used to locate prospective respondents), the people interviewed must be tallied by age groups. If the total sample size is 1000, interviewing of people under 35 would cease when 450 had been interviewed. Interviewing of people 35 or over would continue until 550 had been interviewed. More detailed strata might be discovered based on sex, income, occupation, or other factors. The key is that the behavior of people in different strata must be significantly different with regard to the variables that are of interest to the marketer.

Nonprobability samples. **Nonprobability samples** include all samples that cannot be considered probability samples. Specifically, any sample in which there is little or no attempt to ensure that a representative cross section of the population is obtained can be considered a nonprobability sample. The researchers cannot statistically calculate the reliability of the sample — that is, the degree of sampling error that can be expected. Examples of nonprobability samples include the quota sample and the convenience sample. The convenience sample is based on the use of respondents that are "convenient" or readily accessible to the researcher — employees, friends, relatives, and the like. Quota samples are based on the practice of interviewing a certain number of people who meet certain qualifications regardless of how they are located.

There is nothing wrong with nonprobability samples as long as the researcher understands the nature of this type of sample. The problem is that there is no way of knowing how much sampling error has been accumulated. Much marketing research is based on nonprobability samples because of their lower cost.

Types of errors. Any time a sample is used in marketing research, there will be two major types of errors: (1) **Measurement error** occurs from the difference between the information desired by the researcher and the information provided by the measurement process. (People may tell an interviewer that they purchase Coors beer when they do not.) (2) **Sampling error** results from a sample not being representative of the target population in certain respects.

Sampling error can be broken down into several components. Nonresponse error is created when the sample actually interviewed differs from the sample drawn because the original persons selected to be interviewed either refused to cooperate or were inaccessible. (Some persons may be embarrassed to discuss their drinking habits and refuse to be interviewed.) Frame error arises if the sample is drawn from a population (or "frame") that differs from the target population. For example, if a telephone survey is taken to ascertain Chicago beer drinkers' attitude toward Coors and a Chicago telephone directory is used as the frame (device or list from which the respondents are selected), the survey will contain frame error. Not all Chicago beer drinkers have a telephone. Many who do have a phone have an unlisted number. An ideal sample is identical in all important characteristics to the target population to be surveyed. Random error is created through the sample being different from the frame from which it was drawn because of sampling fluctuations. For example, we might take a random sample of beer drinkers in Chicago and find that 16 percent regularly drink Coors beer. The next day we might go through the exact sampling procedure again and find that 14 percent regularly drink Coors beer. The difference is due to random error.

DATA COLLECTION PROCEDURES

Whether the study is being administered by a marketing research firm or a corporate marketing research department, the field work or interviewing will most likely be conducted by a subcontractor—a field service firm. Most studies will involve data collection in several cities and require working with a comparable number of field service firms. It is therefore crucial that all these subcontractors do everything exactly the same way. This requires that detailed field instructions be developed for every job. Nothing should be left to chance; no interpretations of procedures should be left to the subcontractors.

PROCESSING THE DATA

When the completed data forms or questionnaires have been returned to the local field service firm, data processing begins. The first step in this process is editing the completed questionnaires. This involves checking to see that the respondent is qualified, that all the questions that should have been asked were asked, that questions that should not have been asked were not asked, and that other interviewing standards and procedures were followed.

Next, a certain percentage of each interviewer's work is validated. This involves calling the listed respondents and asking them whether they were interviewed, where they were interviewed, and whether certain questions were asked. The interviews that pass these tests are sent on to the client firm.

When the interviews arrive at the client firm, they typically are revalidated to ensure data was recorded accurately and the proper person was interviewed. Next, codes must be developed for the answers to questions such as "Why do you use brand X?" The answers to such a question must be placed in a smaller number of categories. After this process has been completed, the data will be converted into some computer-readable medium—computer card, magnetic tape, or disk.

▲ TABLE 7.7   A One-way Frequency Count

Brand	Frequency	Percentage
Budweiser	38	19.0%
Miller	41	20.5
Schlitz	36	18.0
Coors	71	35.5
Others	14	7.0
Total respondents	200	100.0

DATA ANALYSIS

The next step in the process is analysis of the data. The purpose of this analysis is to interpret and draw conclusions from the mass of data that have been collected. The marketing researcher attempts to impose some order on those data. Three types of analysis are commonly used in marketing research: one-way frequency counts, cross tabulations, and statistical analysis. Of these, statistical analysis is the most sophisticated, one-way frequency counts the simplest.

One-way tabulations.   One-way frequency tables provide counts of the various responses to a question. The answers to the question "What brand of beer do you drink most often?" are shown in Table 7.7. One-way frequency tables are nearly always done, at least as a first step, in data analysis. They provide the researcher with a general picture of the results of the study.

Cross tabulations.   Cross tabulations, or "cross tabs," permit the analyst to look at the responses to one question in relation to the responses to one or more other questions. For example, cross tabbing the answers to the questions summarized in Table 7.7 by age of respondent provides the information shown in Table 7.8. This table provides all the information in the previous table; in addition, it shows the relationship between age and brand usage. It indicates that Coors is much more popular among the younger group, while brand prefer-

◢ TABLE 7.8   A Cross Tabulation Based on Table 7.7

	Age of respondent					
	Under 35		Over 35		Total	
Brand	No.	%	No.	%	No.	%
Budweiser	15	15	23	23	38	19
Miller	12	12	29	29	41	20.5
Schlitz	13	13	23	23	36	18
Coors	51	51	20	20	71	35.5
Others	9	9	5	5	14	7
Total respondents	100	100	100	100	200	100

ence is much more evenly divided among older beer drinkers. A number of strategy implications for the various brands are suggested.

Data analysis involves the use of powerful statistical techniques to analyze the relationships between variables and between respondents. A discussion of these techniques is beyond the scope of this text; the interested reader should consult a text devoted to statistical techniques for more detailed information.

Communicating the results to management

The final step in a formal study is to communicate the findings and conclusions of the study to management. This is a key step in the process because if the marketing researcher wants those conclusions acted upon, he or she must convince the manager that the results are credible and justified by the data collected. The researcher will ordinarily be required to present both written and oral reports regarding the project. The nature of the audience must be kept in mind when these reports are being prepared and presented. In either case the reports should begin with a clear, concise statement of the research objectives. This should be followed by a complete, but brief and simple, explanation of the research design or methodology employed. A summary of major findings should come next. The report should end with a presentation of conclusions and recommendations for management.

Since most of you who enter marketing will become research users rather than research suppliers, it is important to know what to look for in a report. Evaluating research will be a much greater portion of your job than other aspects of marketing research. Like many other items we purchase, quality is not always readily apparent. Nor does a high price for the project necessarily guarantee superior quality. The basis for measuring quality is to return to the research proposal. Did the report meet the objectives established in the proposal? Was the methodology outlined in the proposal followed? Are the conclusions based on logical deductions from the data analysis? Do the recommendations seem prudent, given the conclusions?

Is the writing style crisp and lucid? It has been said that if the reader is offered the slightest opportunity to misunderstand, he or she probably will. The report should also be as concise as possible. It should follow the format outlined earlier so that salient findings and recommendations can quickly and easily be determined.

The following is an example of using marketing research to solve a specific problem.

When Flicker, American Safety Razor's (ASR) top-selling women's shaver, was revamped, the changes included new colors for both product and packaging. The long-standing pink-and-white combination was changed to mauve, a distinctive designer color that

203

ASR was certain would stimulate sales. Personal interviews with women across the country had indicated that mauve was the most popular color among the more than two dozen casings shown.

However, four other colors had been closely bunched immediately behind mauve in consumer preference. There surely had to be a way to take advantage of the other color preferences and stimulate sales even more. But how? They couldn't replace mauve; that would be self-defeating. And, it didn't make too much sense to distribute other colors at random. Flicker, in a choice of colors, was tested in Boise; Tucson; Portland, Maine; and Green Bay, Wisconsin. The tests were conducted in both food chains and drug chains, ranging from one to four outlets per chain, plus major independents. The retailers included Albertson's, Walgreen's, Revco, C.V.C., Skaggs, Food Giant, Kohl's, and Piggly-Wiggly. A total of 140 stores participated, 35 in each community.

Flicker displays were placed at either the front end, near the blade rack, or in the health and beauty aid aisle. Throughout the test, pricing was maintained at the everyday level established by the retail outlet. All product color variations tested were equally represented in each of the four test markets. A group of stores with mauve-only displays was set up as the control against which the sales in the stores with multicolored Flicker would be measured.

The movement of product was measured weekly by the testing organization, which verified results over an eight-week period. The overall results showed that the existence of Flicker in multiple colors increased consumer takeaway by 65 percent.

With such strong test market results, ASR management decided to include Flicker in the four additional colors—light blue, light green, burgundy, and peach—in all floor and counter displays during the spring and summer promotions. Meanwhile, the first-choice mauve package will continue to appear on the blade rack and in the health and beauty aid section. ASR officials are certain that this decision will help fortify Flicker's No. 1 position in the female shaving category and actually put more distance between Flicker and all other women's shavers.[12]

Marketing information systems

In order to react to a changing environment, the marketing manager must have information. The mechanism for providing decision-making data is the **marketing information system (MIS),** sometimes called a decision support system. It may be defined as a set of procedures and methods for the regular and planned collection, analysis, and presentation of information for use in marketing decisions. The MIS is the lifeline that enables intelligent decisions to be made regarding the marketing mix. As noted above, it is a continuous process that gathers data from a variety of sources, synthesizes it, and funnels it to those responsible for meeting the needs of the marketplace.

MARKETING RESEARCH AND AN MIS

How does marketing research differ from an MIS? Marketing research is problem-oriented. It comes into use when managers need guidance to solve a specific problem. Marketing research, for example, has been used to find out what features consumers want in a new microprocessor. It also has aided product development managers in deciding how much milk to add in a new cream sauce for frozen peas. The Army has used marketing research to develop a profile of the young person most likely to be positively influenced by recruiting ads.

In contrast, an MIS *continually* channels information about environmental changes into the organization. One of the best descriptions of the difference between marketing research and marketing information systems is provided by Robert Williams, the originator of marketing information systems:

The difference between marketing research and marketing intelligence is like the difference between a flash bulb and a candle. Let's say you are dancing in the dark. Every 90 seconds you are allowed to set off a flash bulb. You can use those brief intervals of light to chart a course, but remember everybody is moving, too. Hopefully, they'll accommodate themselves roughly to your predictions. You might get bumped and you may stumble ever so often, but you can dance along.

On the other hand, you can light a candle. It doesn't yield as much light but it's a steady light. You are continually aware of the movements of other bodies. You can adjust your own course to the courses of others. The intelligence system is a kind of candle. It's no great flash on the immediate state of things, but it provides continuous light as situations shift and change.[13]

FUNCTIONS OF AN MIS

Let us examine in more detail the functions of a marketing information system. These include classification, measurement, analysis, reporting systems, information retrieval systems, and decision models (see Figure 7.5).[14]

Input into the system can come from a variety of internal and external sources. Written reports from salespersons, credit information regarding customers, sales data, marketing research reports, economic forecasts, consultant reports on social trends, detailed marketing expenditure data from the accounting department, government reports, information published by competitors, trade reports, and data from members of the distribution channel can serve as inputs into the information system. Some authors, in fact, include data collection techniques as part of the basic information system.

Classification. The first requirement for an MIS is to develop a classification scheme for the raw data. Without a classification scheme, raw data is for the most part virtually useless. Sometimes data that enter a system, such as an eco-

▲ **FIGURE 7.5 The MIS system.**

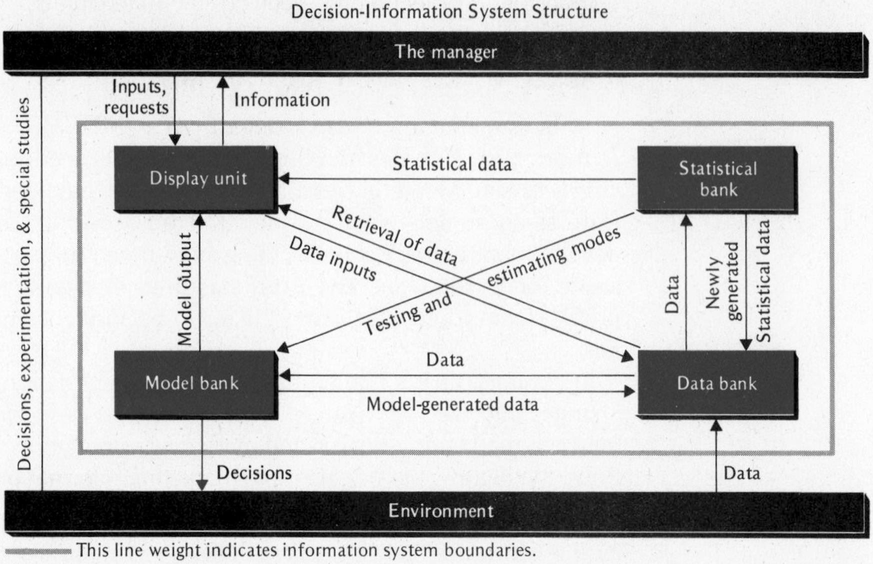

Decision-Information System Structure

Source: David B. Montgomery, "The Outlook for MIS," *Journal of Advertising Research* 13 (June 1973): 17. Reprinted from the *Journal of Advertising Research*. © Copyright 1973 by the Advertising Research Foundation.

nomic report, has been classified. In other situations, such as sales data classification, codes must be prepared. For example, a classification system will contain a number of mutually exclusive dimensions, $c_1, c_2, c_3, \ldots c_n$, such that:

c_n = customer description

c_1 = SIC code

c_2 = corporation/partnership sole proprietorship

c_3 = region headquarters

c_4 = type of product purchased

c_5 = credit terms

Such a basic classification taxonomy will enable marketing managers to examine their customer base.

Measurement and analysis. One common form of measurement is monitoring, as in the Nielsen Retail Index. It also includes advertising awareness tracking studies, number of complaint reports per week, and so forth. Analysis often relies on the traditional techniques of marketing research.

Decision models. Measurement is a standard tool used to solve marketing problems. A second form of problem solving that offers potential for substantial payoffs is the use of models. Every person examining a table of numbers has a set of constructs in his or her mind that tells the person when a number may have meaning and deserve further consideration. This is because in the person's head is an implicit model.

An MIS generally relies on two types of formal models. The first is a **simulation model,** which is a quantitative representation of a dynamic system used to evaluate decision alternatives. ASSESSOR, for example, is used by marketers of package goods and pharmaceuticals to pretest new product alternatives.[15] Another model, NOMAD, delineates the new product acceptance process.[16]

The second type of model is an **allocation model** (normally linear programming models) used to allocate marketing resources. Coca-Cola, for example, has developed a model to allocate funds to advertising. Other allocation models allocate product development funds, establishment of sales territories, and determination of sales quotas.

Reporting systems. Perhaps the most common use of an MIS is in reporting systems. In fact, some companies that claim ownership of an MIS in reality have nothing more than a reporting system for such items as costs, shipments, sales, and inquiries received. In essence, this is a form of scorekeeping.

Information retrieval systems. A final function of an MIS is information retrieval. The computer data bank provides the basis for an information retrieval system, which must accept isolated, significant items of information from many sources; organize, index, and store these data; and disseminate logical sets of information later upon request. The data bank may, for example, include the collection and maintenance of competitors' actions, customer purchases, test market activity, and government regulations.

Good data banks can lead to the development of more effective and realistic models. This, in turn, means better decision making. Data banks can also provide insights into past product activity and customer reactions that will help researchers design better test market strategies. By examining promotion allocations and sales activity, media planners gain insight into whether and where media dollars should be spent.

THE POPULARITY AND UTILIZATION OF MARKET INFORMATION SYSTEMS

Advantages. Many large corporations have eagerly embraced the MIS concept (see Table 7.9). As they have discovered, the advantages of an effective MIS are immense. Some of these advantages include the following:

1. Substantial cost savings are realized. One direct mail insurance company developed a simple computer program to compare past response rates of various market segments and thereby saved $40,000 that would have otherwise been wasted by mailing to households with a low probability of response. The cost to the company in computer time and other variable costs approximated $3000; the net profit contribution was $37,000.
2. Marketer's understanding of their decision environment is increased. One advantage, often associated with building mathematical models, is explication. The decision maker is forced to view the decision and information environment within

which he or she operates. This perception often leads to facing decision areas too often shoved under the carpet, as well as recognizing relationships between decisions and information flows that have never been noticed before.

3. Decision-making effectiveness is upgraded. Many companies can now retrieve and utilize information they never before had access to. This addition of facts to replace intuition in decision making has led to more effective and less "seat-of-the-pants" decision making than in the past.

4. Information value is improved. Tied to decision-making effectiveness but worthy of its own note is the improved quantity and quality of information provided to the marketing manager. Managers, in many cases, have been given relevant, reliable, and timely information that never before has been available.[17]

Why don't more firms have an MIS? It would be a disservice to leave the impression that virtually all or even most firms have an effective MIS. In reality, they do not. What we have described is what should be, not what in fact typically exists.

The reasons most firms do not have an MIS are people and money. Much of the value of providing accurate, relevant, and timely information to marketing decision makers comes from more effective decision making — decisions based on fact rather than on intuition. But all too often if a top corporate executive cannot see profit results directly attributable to the MIS, he or she is not impressed. Second, marketing practitioners and system designers have had great difficulty communicating. This has led to sizable gaps in information needed and information offered. The end result has been an emphasis by system designers on data warehousing instead of on matching user needs.

A third reason for the slow growth of the use of MIS is that the training of marketing managers and system users has fallen below an acceptable level.

◀ **TABLE 7.9   Firms with Successful Marketing Information Systems**

American Airlines	Johnson & Johnson
AT&T	Lever Bros.
Chemical Bank (N.Y.)	Mead Corporation
Coca-Cola	Monsanto
Deering Milliken	Olin Corporation
Du Pont	Pillsbury
First National City Bank (N.Y.)	Pittsburgh Steel
Ford Motor Company	RCA
General Electric	Schenley
General Mills	Singer
General Motors	Standard Oil (N.J.)
Grumman	Union Bank (L.A.)
Hallmark Cards	U.S. Rubber
Honeywell	U.S. Steel
IBM	Westinghouse
International Paper	Weyerhaeuser

Source: Richard H. Brien, "Marketing Information Systems: The State of the Art," *1972 Combined Proceedings, American Marketing Association*, p. 137.

Decision makers can hardly be expected to use an information system if they do not understand what it can and cannot do.

SUMMARY

Marketing research is the planning for, collection, and analysis of data relevant to marketing decision making, and the communication of the results of this analysis to management. Marketing research exists to serve the marketing decision maker.

Three types of organizations actually design and implement marketing research studies: advertising agencies, independent marketing research firms, and corporate marketing research departments. Advertising agencies typically conduct research initiated by the client. Research firms may be categorized two ways. First, there are the syndicated services, which compile a standardized set of data on a continuing basis. Second are the custom research firms that do one-of-a-kind research projects. A variation of custom research is the omnibus survey. In an omnibus survey, any company can buy a single question or ask several questions. Omnibus surveys are carried out on a regular schedule—monthly, quarterly or biannually. Field service firms are the production line of marketing research. They are the organizations that provide interviewing for marketing research departments, advertising agencies, and research firms.

The larger the company, the more likely it is to have a research department. However, research departments tend to be rather small because most of the actual work is farmed out to custom or syndicated services. The research department initiates the project, analyzes the outside report, and makes recommendations to management.

When a firm decides to conduct marketing research, it should first develop a preliminary analysis. This includes agreeing on the nature of the problem, a background investigation, and an informal investigation. After a preliminary analysis has been completed, the firm can design a formal study. The steps are these: (1) specify the data required; (2) determine the most efficient means of gathering the data; (3) design the data collection forms; (4) specify the sampling procedures; (5) specify the data collection procedures; (6) develop a plan for processing the data; (7) develop a plan for analyzing the data; and (8) prepare a report to present to management.

A marketing information system (MIS) is a set of procedures and methods for the regular and planned collection, analysis, and presentation of information for use in marketing decisions. Marketing research is problem-oriented. It is used when the need arises to have certain data. An MIS continually channels information about environmental changes into the organization. The functions of an MIS include classification, measurement, analysis, reporting systems, information retrieval systems, and decision models. Although an MIS can offer an organization many benefits, firms have been slow to adopt the idea. This is primarily due to lack of understanding and appreciation by the people involved, as well as the cost factor.

KEY TERMS

Marketing research
Omnibus survey
Preliminary analysis
Situation analysis
Secondary data
Primary data
Survey
Observation
Experiment
Simulation
Mall intercept interview
Focus group interview
Executive interview
Telephone interview
Mail survey
Mail panel

Computer interview
Independent variable
Dependent variable
Sampling
Probability sample
Simple random sample
Cluster sample
Stratified sample
Nonprobability sample
Measurement error
Sampling error
Marketing information
   system (MIS)
Simulation model
Allocation model

REVIEW QUESTIONS

1. What are three types of organizations that do marketing research? What function does each perform?
2. How is the data provided by syndicated service research used by the subscribing firm? What types of information are provided?
3. Name some activities carried on by corporate market research departments.
4. What are secondary data? Where could one find the following information?
   a. The population of Ontario, Canada.
   b. Average per capita income in Wyoming.
   c. The number of new housing units started in California.
   d. The number of banks in the Minneapolis-St. Paul area.
   e. The number of refrigerators imported into the United States in the past year.
5. What are the advantages and disadvantages of using secondary data?
6. Discuss the ways of obtaining primary data. Note the disadvantages and advantages of each.
7. List and discuss the functions of a market information system.

DISCUSSION QUESTIONS

1. What is marketing research? Why is it important to the firm?
2. Why is situation analysis so important in the marketing research process?
3. In analyzing research findings, why is it important to know the methodology used?
4. What could cause a new product failure even if the firm conducts marketing research?
5. Do you think manufacturers of consumer products are more involved in marketing research activities than wholesalers or retailers? Give reasons for your answer.
6. What are some possible reasons that marketing research is not undertaken?
7. Explain in your own words how a marketing information system differs from marketing research.
8. How can the marketing manager justify the expense of an MIS?

NOTES

1. "At Procter and Gamble Success Is Largely due to Heeding Consumer," *The Wall Street Journal,* April 19, 1980, p. 1. Reprinted by permission of *The Wall Street Journal,* © Dow Jones & Company, Inc., 1980. All rights reserved.
2. A. C. Nielsen Company, "Nielsen Retail Index Brochure."
3. Jack J. Honomichl, "For Top Ten Researchers, A Good '75," *Advertising Age,* March 15, 1976, pp. 1, 53–54.
4. Dik Warren Twedt, *1978 Survey of Marketing Research* (Chicago: American Marketing Association, 1978).
5. Harper W. Boyd, Ralph Westfall, and Stanley F. Stasch, *Marketing Research* (Homewood, Ill.: Irwin, 1977), pp. 117–122.
6. Ibid., pp. 206–211.
7. "Phone vs. Personal Interviews," *Marketing News,* September 10, 1976, pp. 6–7; Theresa Rogers, "Interviews by Telephone and in Person: Quality of Response and Field Performance," *Public Opinion Quarterly* 50 (spring 1976): 51–65.
8. Leslie Kanuk and Conrad Berenson, "Mail Surveys and Response Rates: A Literature Review," *Journal of Marketing Research* 12 (November 1975): 440–453.
9. Michael S. Goodstadt, Linda Chung, Reena Kronitz, and Gaynoll Cook, "Mail Survey Response Rates: Their Manipulation and Impact," *Journal of Marketing Research* 14 (August 1977): 391–395.
10. Ibid.
11. "Consumer Mail Panels" (Chicago: Market Facts, 1976), pp. 1–17.
12. Alan D. Goldberg, "Testing Helps Flicker Look Sharper," *Sales and Marketing Management* (March 17, 1980), pp. 78–80.
13. Robert J. Williams, "Marketing Intelligence Systems: A DEW Line for Marketing Men," *Business Management,* January 1966, p. 32. Reprinted by permission.
14. Much of this section is taken from Malcolm McNiven and Bob D. Hilton, "Reassessing Marketing Information Systems," *Journal of Advertising Research* 10 (February 1970): 3–12. Reprinted from the Journal of Advertising Research, © copyright 1970 by the Advertising Research Foundation.
15. John D. C. Little, "Decision Support Systems for Marketing Managers," *Journal of Marketing* 43 (summer 1979): 9–26.
16. David B. Montgomery and Glen L. Urban, "Marketing Decision Information Systems: An Emerging View," *Journal of Marketing Research,* May 1970, p. 26.
17. Charles D. Scherve, "Management Information Systems in Marketing—A Promise Not Yet Realized," *Management Informatics* 3 (May 1974): 184–185.

◀ **CASES**

7.1 Cessna Aircraft

Cessna Aircraft is one of the largest manufacturers of small, private business airplanes in the United States. It is always looking for new market opportunities, which may involve cultivating existing segments or developing and exploiting new ones. Recent research by Cessna uncovered that a very small percentage of the total adult population enrolls in private pilot-training programs. However, the number of people with pilots' licenses is increasing. About half of the individuals who enter a training program complete it. Eventually about one out of five people with a private pilot's license owns a private airplane. So pilot training is an important part of the total market for Cessna and its competitors.

A small percentage of pilots are women. Similarly, a small percentage of the students in training programs are women. This figure has shown only a slight increase in recent years; moreover, there are very few women instructors in pilot-training programs. A substantial number of women have the necessary skills, time, and income to enroll and complete the basic training program. Cessna would like to know why more women don't enter the program and how the program and/or promotional materials could appeal to and motivate more women to consider or inquire about such programs.

There may be several specific market segments worthy of examination. These include wives of pilots, businesswomen, women who could benefit from the use of business aircraft, women who have the income and desire to travel for pleasure, and young women who seek future employment as corporate aircraft pilots. Cessna realizes that the limiting factor may be low levels of interest or motivation and perhaps attitudes toward the desirability of women pilots. But opportunities for women are increasing in many different fields. Cessna therefore believes that a vital market may exist that is not being fully exploited.

1. Develop a marketing research project that will help Cessna evaluate the importance of the women's market.
2. Suggest research that will determine not only the size of the market segment, but also why women are not currently enrolling in training programs.

7.2 Pizza Heaven

Pizza Heaven is a small, west coast independent chain of pizza restaurants that cater primarily to college students. Accordingly, they are usually located near a campus and promote their offerings extensively in college newspapers. In the last year, Pizza Heaven sales have slipped, and management feels that the national chains such as Pizza Hut and Pizza Inn are making inroads into its market, along with single-store, independent pizza restaurants.

Pizza Heaven decided to conduct marketing research to determine its image among its customers and to see if the company needs to reposition itself. The first step was to conduct focus groups in three cities in California and in one college town in Oregon and in Washington.

According to the focus groups, the college students expected to find a dark, informal fun atmosphere in a pizza restaurant. They did not want to see noisy games or movies at the restaurant. College students claimed they used coupons extensively. The respondents particularly liked the two-for-one coupons offered by Pizza Inn. Pizza was considered an intermediate food — something between a fast hamburger and a formal restaurant. Group participants thought of pizza primarily as a group activity rather than a dating situation. They noted that pizza was also a mood or an impulse food because of its distinct taste. They enjoyed eating other foods at pizza restaurants. College students usually eat pizza with more than one person, and not everyone may want pizza. Submarine sandwiches came up quite frequently as food that many ordered. Convenience plays a big part in where the students choose to eat pizza.

Naturally, the most important feature in a pizza restaurant was the quality of the pizza. A good pizza was defined as hot, with a lot of fresh ingredients. It should have a large quantity of cheese, sauce, and meat. Some students claimed they would drive farther to get a favorite pizza (which was usually produced by an independent pizza restaurant). They said the independent's pizza was typically thicker and had more ingredients for the same amount of money than the average chain pizza.

The college students were generally negative toward luncheon specials. They said the pizzas were usually cold and dry. Also, they noted that the selection was often poor. Many of them did not think of pizza for lunch.

The group participants were asked to make some general recommendations. These were as follows: (1) make the atmosphere lighter, at least until eight P.M.; (2) provide frosty beer mugs and make sure the beer is served cold; (3) divide one area of the restaurant for just drinking and talking; (4) provide larger napkins; (5) change the type of music to tapes or piped-in; (6) post the nutritional value of the pizza; (7) have some form of self-service for drinks; and (8) serve higher quality pizzas.

1. Now that Pizza Heaven is armed with the information from the focus groups, should it begin implementing the findings? Why or why not?
2. If additional research should be undertaken, what topics should be covered? Why?
3. Outline the procedure for implementing additional market research.

◀ CASE FOR PART TWO

Herman's Supermarket*

Joe Herman had worked for a number of supermarket chains, including Safeway, Acme, and Food Fair. Herman had been a supermarket manager and an area personnel supervisor. One summer, while vacationing with his family in a resort area, Herman happened to notice an empty store site that had been abandoned by A & P some five years earlier. The resort city had a population of 18,000, and for shopping purposes served between 100,000 and 400,000 people during the summer. The major industry was tourism. A number of hotels and boarding houses were located within the city, but only a few were near the projected site.

Herman thought the site had potential for a supermarket and employed the services of a local college marketing professor to conduct a neighborhood customer analysis. Joe Herman and the marketing consultant discussed the possibilities of analyzing four factors:

1. Product assortment. This would be considered by the number and types of like and unlike stores surrounding the proposed site.
2. Population density. This would be considered by population per square mile within 3 miles of the potential site location.
3. Traffic configuration. This would be considered by the distance of major traffic arteries and traffic control devices.
4. Planned or unplanned development. This would be considered based on planned development in the surrounding area.

The consultant's report compared changing neighborhood population patterns with a national study (see Table 1). The 65 age group and over increased in the

---

*Case prepared by Professor Ronald D. Michman, Shippensburg State College, Shippensburg, Pennsylvania.

◀ TABLE 1 Population Shifts in the United States, 1960–2000

Age	Population (in millions)					Percentage change			
	1960	1970	1980	1990	2000	1960–1970	1970–1980	1980–1990	1990–2000
Under 20	9	77	73	77	81	+11.1%	− 5.2%	+ 5.7%	+ 4.3%
20–24	11	17	21	18	19	+54.3	+22.6	−15.4	+ 7.8
25–34	23	26	37	42	36	+10.4	+46.1	+13.1	−14.6
35–44	24	23	26	37	41	− 4.5	+ 9.6	+45.5	+13.0
45–54	21	23	22	25	36	+13.3	− 3.9	+ 9.9	+45.1
55–64	16	19	21	20	22	+19.4	+13.0	− 3.4	+10.6
65 and over	17	20	24	28	29	+20.4	+19.8	+15.4	+ 3.9
	181	205	224	247	264	+13.4%	+ 9.4%	−10.0%	+ 7.2%

Source: Based on data from Bureau of the Census, *Current Population Reports,* Series P-25, using Series E for projection purposes. Reported in William Lazer, "The 1980's and Beyond: A Perspective," *MSU Business Topics,* spring 1977, p. 24.

▲ **TABLE 2   Families by Income and Age** (all figures in 1975 dollars)

	Total families	Annual family income before taxes							
		Under $5,000	$5,000–10,000	$10,000–15,000	$15,000–20,000	$20,000–25,000	$25,000–35,000	$35,000–50,000	$50,000 and over
1975									
Families: Millions	56.7	6.6	12.0	12.8	10.5	6.8	5.1	2.1	0.8
Distribution	100.0%	11.7%	21.1%	22.6%	18.5%	12.1%	9.0%	3.7%	1.4%
Percent of total family income	100.0%	2.2%	10.2%	18.0%	20.7%	17.4%	16.1%	9.5%	6.0%
Distribution: Families by age of head	100.0%	100.0%	100.0%	100.0%	100.0%	100.0%	100.0%	100.0%	100.0%
Under 25	7.8	14.6	12.6	9.6	5.1	1.9	0.9	*	*
25–34	23.3	18.9	20.4	28.8	29.0	24.1	16.8	9.5	8.6
35–44	19.1	11.4	14.0	18.1	22.7	26.1	24.3	23.4	21.1
45–54	19.8	11.0	12.7	16.7	21.4	26.3	34.1	37.8	36.5
55–64	15.7	13.4	13.8	15.6	15.3	16.2	19.2	23.5	23.1
65 and over	14.4	30.7	26.6	11.1	6.6	5.4	4.8	5.9	10.7
1980									
Families: Millions	61.2	5.2	9.9	11.6	11.0	8.8	9.2	3.8	1.7
Distribution	100.0%	8.5%	16.2%	18.9%	18.0%	14.4%	15.0%	6.2%	2.8%
Percent of total family income	100.0%	1.3%	6.4%	12.3%	16.4%	16.9%	22.7%	13.1%	10.9%
Distribution: Families by age of head	100.0%	100.0%	100.0%	100.0%	100.0%	100.0%	100.0%	100.0%	100.0%
Under 25	7.7	15.5	11.9	11.9	7.8	3.8	1.8	0.6	
25–34	25.1	20.7	20.1	26.6	31.4	32.2	23.4	16.3	8.9
35–44	19.8	12.9	13.4	16.2	20.4	24.1	27.7	24.2	24.6
45–54	17.7	10.5	9.8	14.0	16.2	19.0	25.9	33.1	34.5
55–64	15.4	12.8	12.8	15.9	15.5	15.0	15.9	20.1	24.6
65 and over	14.2	27.6	31.9	15.4	8.7	5.9	5.2	5.8	7.5
1985									
Families: Millions	66.3	4.5	9.8	10.8	11.2	10.0	12.2	5.3	2.5
Distribution	100.0%	6.8%	14.7%	16.3%	17.0%	15.1%	18.4%	8.0%	3.8%
Percent of total family income	100.0%	1.0%	5.2%	9.6%	14.0%	16.0%	25.8%	15.3%	13.2%
Distribution: Families by age of head	100.0%	100.0%	100.0%	100.0%	100.0%	100.0%	100.0%	100.0%	100.0%
Under 25	7.0	15.3	10.7	11.6	8.0	4.6	1.9	0.9	
25–34	25.8	20.8	21.0	26.2	31.2	32.5	26.7	19.4	10.3
35–44	22.4	14.8	14.5	17.9	22.5	26.7	29.3	26.7	26.8
45–54	16.2	10.7	8.8	12.0	14.3	15.6	21.2	29.5	32.3
55–64	14.6	12.9	12.4	14.0	13.8	14.1	15.6	18.3	23.2
65 and over	13.9	25.5	32.6	18.4	10.2	6.5	5.3	5.2	7.4

Source: Fabian Linden, "Family Income—1985," *The Conference Board Record,* May 1976, p. 26.

neighborhood approximately 23 percent from 1970 to 1980. The marketing professor estimated that this same group would increase by approximately 18 percent from 1980 to 1990. The report noted that about 60 percent of the senior citizens in the neighborhood lived in a middle-income municipal housing project constructed three years ago. These senior citizens maintained their own apartments and did their own shopping. Many of them shopped together in car pools. However, the new supermarket would be within walking distance of the housing complex. Senior citizens currently totaled about 35 percent of the neighborhood population.

Another group living within the neighborhood was a number of singles from

Measure	1965	1970	1975	1980
Gross national product	$1,142.9	$1,336.8	$1,475.0	$1,930.0
Disposable personal income	$ 762.6	$ 937.5	$1,085.0	$1,390.0
Per capita disposable income[a]	$3,925.0	$4,575.0	$5,080.0	$6,240.0
Supernumerary income (after taxes)	$ 45.5	$ 77.0	$ 90.0	$ 170.5
Supernumerary as % of DPI	6.0%	8.0%	8.5%	12.5%
U.S. population	194.3	204.9	213.6	222.8
Persons by age				
Under 18	69.7	69.7	66.3	63.3
18–24	20.3	24.7	27.6	29.4
25–34	22.5	25.3	30.9	36.2
35–44	24.4	23.1	22.8	25.7
45–54	21.8	23.3	23.8	22.6
55–64	17.1	18.7	19.8	21.0
65 and over	18.5	20.1	22.3	24.5
Marriages	1.8	2.2	2.3	2.5
Births	3.8	3.7	3.2	3.9
Families	48.0	51.6	55.7	61.1
Households	57.4	63.4	71.1	78.2
Educational attainment[b]				
Elementary or less	34.0	30.3	27.0	23.5
Some high school	18.6	18.7	19.9	20.9
High school graduate	31.7	37.1	42.8	48.7
Some college	9.1	11.2	13.3	16.1
College graduates	9.7	12.1	15.1	19.3
Total employment[c]	71.1	78.6	84.9	96.1
White-collar workers	31.9	37.2	42.1	49.2
Blue-collar workers	26.2	28.0	28.2	31.7
Service workers	8.9	10.4	11.6	12.7
Other	4.1	3.1	2.9	2.5
Working women				
As % of women 16 years and over	38.8%	42.8%	46.2%	48.5%
Place of residence[d]				
Metropolitan area	128.6	137.1	143.3	150.4
Central city	61.8	62.9	61.4	59.8
Outside central city	66.9	74.2	81.9	90.6
Nonmetropolitan area	61.0	62.8	66.6	70.8
Families by income class				
Under $5,000	8.6	7.5	7.8	7.3
$5,000–10,000	13.4	12.4	12.5	12.5
10,000–15,000	12.9	13.2	14.2	14.5
15,000 and over	12.9	18.6	21.2	26.9

Note: Dollar figures in billions; all other figures in millions, unless otherwise indicated, in 1975 prices.

[a] Figures are in actual dollars.

[b] Based on persons 25 and over.

[c] 1965 figures not strictly comparable with figures for later years.

[d] Based on the civilian noninstitutional population.

Source: Fabian Linden, "The Second Half of the Seventies," *The Conference Board Record,* December 1975, p. 14.

the ages of 20 to 44, with the majority falling between the ages of 28 to 34. This group lived in luxurious garden apartments and comprised about 20 percent of the neighborhood population. The report noted that a great many of the married couples had relocated to the suburbs in the past five years. Because of changing conditions in the neighborhood, the consultant hesitated to forecast the growth or decline of the singles market. The singles were a relatively well-educated group. They averaged about two years of completed college work, and their incomes were between $12,000 and $25,000.

Another market segment comprised of young married couples amounted to about 25 percent of the neighborhood population from 1970 to 1980. The consultant, however, forecasted the decline of this market segment to approximately 15 percent of the population by 1990. Many of this age segment from 25 to 34 lived in rented two- or three-family homes or were owners of these dwellings. Although many of this age group were of Italian and Polish extraction, they did not subscribe to foreign-language newspapers. Other age groups lived in this neighborhood, but none was really significant in size. The majority of the young marrieds commuted to a nearby city where there was a government installation; others were employed by a division of General Electric. Incomes were generally between $15,000 and $30,000 a year. A number of the wives, as the children reached school age, were employed in clerical capacities part time during the winter and full time over the summer.

Tables 2 and 3 show families by income and age and selected measures of growth. These tables should provide deeper insights into this market.

In all probability, public transportation would matter much more to the senior citizen market or to housewives without cars than to the singles market. Public bus transportation was available, with a bus stop located on the corner of the empty store site. The bus made a stop every twenty minutes between the hours of 8 A.M. and 6 P.M. In the evening the bus ran on the hour until 12 midnight. There was no service on Sunday. The empty store site did have a parking lot with space for about 50 automobiles. Other stores were located across the street and approximately one city block away.

The consultant pointed out in his report that the proposed supermarket should serve the needs of the senior citizens market, a singles market, and a young married market, most of whom were in rental housing. Another market would be tourists who might reside nearby over the summer months. The supermarket would be the only one within walking distance of the senior citizen housing. However, there was a K-Mart and a Rite-Aid drug store nearby. Moreover, there was a branch of the public library and a post office located within walking distance of the supermarket site.

The municipality had plans to construct a civic center for conventions. Most of the other plans centered around trying to increase the number of tourists.

1. What information should be ascertained about the senior citizen, singles, and young marrieds market?
2. What other information about the resort area should Herman ascertain?
3. What additional information should Joe Herman try to obtain before making a decision?
4. Should Joe Herman occupy the abandoned site and serve available neighborhood markets?

PART Three

Product concepts

8

Product and service management

OBJECTIVES

To examine the nature of products and the role products and services play in our society.

To develop a product classification scheme.

To understand the role of product manager.

To gain an appreciation of the product life cycle concept.

To analyze the product adoption process.

To examine techniques for managing a product line.

To understand the distinctions between product and service management.

Lever Brothers Company lost money in 1978 through 1980 and was only marginally profitable before that. Over the past two decades, many of Lever's new products have been costly flops (among them, Drive detergent and Twice as Nice shampoo). In the same period, several of its once-thriving brands—Lux toilet soap and Pepsodent toothpaste, for example—have suffered from inattention. Currently, Lever's laundry detergents (its top brands are All and Wisk), dishwashing soaps (Dove and Lux), toothpastes (Aim, Close-up, and Pepsodent) and toilet soaps (Dove, Caress, Lux, and Lifebuoy) have shares of the market that are, at best, half those of Procter & Gamble's competing products.

Lever's big problems began in the mid-1940s when rival P&G introduced Tide. Touted as a "revolutionary washday miracle," it was the first laundry product manufactured by chemical synthesis, instead of by processing animal fats and lye, and was a superior cleaner. By 1949, one-fourth of the nation's households were using the P&G detergent.

At first, Lever mistook the new product as a fad; realizing its mistake, it hurried to catch up with its own new laundry products, Surf and Rinso Blue. But the company was outmuscled by P&G. Once, as Lever crews went door-to-door in Philadelphia and Baltimore handing out free Rinso Blue samples, P&G representatives moved up the other side of the same streets distributing Tide coupons. After eight years Lever had lost $31 million trying to beat Tide.

In 1960, P&G's Crest toothpaste won an unprecedented seal of approval from the American Dental Association. Lever's assessment: The endorsement and Crest's "Look Ma, no cavities" ads would do little to improve the 10% market share the brand had earned since its 1955 introduction. But Crest went on to capture more than one-third of the toothpaste market, taking sales away from Lever's Pepsodent and Stripe.

For consumers, the most tangible sign of Lever's comeback attempts in 1981 were the company's national introduction—including free samples mailed to millions of homes—of Shield deodorant soap. Lever also had a bevy of other new products rolling into test markets or national distribution: Sunlight dishwashing liquid, DX toothbrushes, Mrs. Butterworth's pancake mix, Mr. Marinade marinating mix, Autumn margarine and Body by the Numbers shampoo.[1]

The Lever Brothers story illustrates the point that some products, like Lifebuoy, have a very long life, whereas others in the same category have a very short life span. Do you remember Drive detergent? If products like soap have such a long life, why is Lever Brothers on a crash product development program? Do you market a new product just like a mature one in the same product class? How does a marketing manager know when to drop a product from the line? Let us take a closer look at product management and the product life cycle.

This chapter begins with the definition of a product and the role products and services play in our society. Next, a product taxonomy (classification system) will be developed to help you understand why different products require unique marketing mixes. As in the soap example, sales of a $150 million-a-year product simply cannot be left to chance. The person who is accountable, who directs marketing strategies and tactics, is a product or brand manager. We will take a look at the evolving role of this critical individual. We will also see why strategies must be altered as a product moves through its life cycle. Sometimes, for example, products must be modified or eliminated.

Product managers do not always manage products; sometimes they supervise services—for example, manager of freight services or manager of term life insurance. There are real differences between service and product marketing, as we will see later in the chapter.

What is a product?

Planning and development of the marketing mix normally begins with a clear definition of the firm's product or service and proceeds with distribution, promotion, and pricing strategies. For example, King Candy developed a new line of sugarless candy bars with none of the bitter aftertaste that accompanies similar products. The marketing manager could not develop his strategy until he knew how the consumer saw the product. Was it viewed as medicinal, to be consumed by diabetics and others on sugar-free diets, or was it just another candy for weight-conscious consumers?

A product is not just a physical object, but what consumers perceive it to be. Many products are symbolic; they help us play our roles in society. A man's tie helps identify him as a white-collar worker. A pin-striped suit is often associated with conservatism. People consume products and services not only for what they do, but also for what those products and services mean to other members of society. We may define a **product** as any want-satisfying good or service and its perceived tangible and intangible attributes. Packaging, style, color, warranties, options, and size are among the features a product may have. Just as important are intangibles such as service, the retailer's image, the manufacturer's reputation, and the way you believe others will view the product.

The heart of a product is the physical unit or basic service. A label or brand name adds a new dimension. Two physically identical coats, one with a Penney's label and the other a Saks Fifth Avenue label, are not the same product.

They have different levels of prestige and status, not to mention price. A person wearing the Saks coat to a restaurant may carefully hang it on the back of the chair to expose the label; the person wearing the Penney coat may fold it to hide the label.

A product taxonomy

Products can be divided into two general groups—consumer goods and industrial goods. **Consumer goods** are purchased by the ultimate buyer. **Industrial goods** are used in making other products. The same market strategies are not appropriate for both, because they are distributed, sold, and purchased differently.

CONSUMER GOODS

Consumer goods run the gamut from ice cream and magazines to new homes and expensive cars. Classifying such a diversified array is not easy, and no classification system is perfect.[2] However, we will divide consumer products into four categories: convenience, shopping, specialty, and unsought goods (see Figure 8.1). This system is based on the way people view and subsequently buy various products.

▄◣ **FIGURE 8.1 A comprehensive classification for consumer goods.**

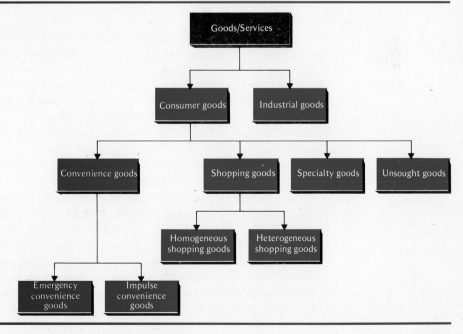

Convenience goods. **Convenience goods** are relatively inexpensive items that require little shopping effort. Many food products, candy, soft drinks, combs, aspirin, small hardware items, and countless other things fall into the convenience goods category. They are bought routinely day in and day out, usually without significant planning. This does not mean that the consumer is unaware of convenience good brand names. Some, such as Coke, Bayer Aspirin, and Right Guard deodorant, are very well known. Convenience goods normally require wide distribution in order to sell in sufficient quantities to meet profit goals.

Convenience goods may be further divided into staple, emergency, and impulse items. Any convenience good can become an emergency good if there is a sudden, strong, compelling desire to buy a product. Assume you are visiting a distant city and suddenly find yourself caught in a heavy rain. An umbrella may become an emergency good for you. If you wake up in the morning and suddenly find yourself out of coffee, it becomes an emergency good. Because the need is urgent, prices are usually higher than in competing stores in a store that specializes in emergency convenience goods, such as 7-Eleven, Circle K, Wag-A-Bag, or U-Totem.

Impulse or unplanned items are purchased without planning. Often these items are placed near supermarket checkout counters to encourage sales. Razor blades, some magazines, candy, flashlight batteries, pens, and other knickknacks are often impulse items. Some shoppers do not plan grocery purchases but enter the store and buy on impulse. This raises an important point: the purchaser may be aware of general needs, such as meats, drinks, and so on, and yet purchase in specific product categories like ham and beer on impulse. Brand names may also be bought on impulse—Armour ham and Budweiser beer, for example.

Shopping goods. **Shopping goods** are more expensive than convenience goods and are found in fewer stores. Consumers usually buy these items only after comparing style, suitability, price, and life style compatibility in several stores. People actively seek out shopping good stores for comparison purposes—they are willing to put some effort into this process. Brands are compared as well as stores; service and warranty work are often important considerations as well. Major appliances, automobiles, furniture, and most clothing are typical shopping goods.

A shopping good may not be purchased for a considerable period after the decision to buy the product is made. For example, you may decide to purchase a new home several years before you can save enough money for the down payment. During that period you may actively seek information about the housing options available. Unlike convenience goods, shopping goods may offer substantial monetary savings in return for time expended. Also, since convenience goods are bought frequently, we have more knowledge about these products than we do about shopping goods, which are purchased less often.

Shopping goods can be further divided into homogeneous and heterogeneous merchandise. Homogeneous products have essentially the same features. Refrigerators, ranges, dishwashers, and television sets are examples of this type of product. Brand names are very important, since consumers view them as assurances of quality. Heavy advertising by firms like Zenith, Whirlpool, and General Electric contributes to heightened brand awareness and consumer preference for the products of these firms over very similar merchandise. This is a classic case of product differentiation, and as a result substantial price decreases may lead to large increases in demand.

Heterogeneous merchandise is nonstandardized and stylistic in nature. Better clothing, most furniture, and some automobiles fall into this category. Retail salespeople often play a role in helping the consumer select heterogeneous shopping goods. They perform an informational function by explaining product features and benefits that are not readily apparent to prospective buyers. Price is usually secondary to life style and self-image compatibility. Single swingers want racy, flashy cars to fit their image. The executive demands a Cadillac or Continental, and the suburban homemaker wants a station wagon. These are, of course, stereotypes which may not typify most people today.

Specialty goods. When consumers will search extensively for an item and are extremely reluctant to accept substitutes for it, it is a **specialty good.** Fine watches, Rolls Royce automobiles, expensive stereo equipment, very fine clothing, and gourmet food products are generally considered specialty merchandise. Because of the diligent searching effort of specialty goods buyers, only one store in a city or region may carry the item.

Specialty goods represent a near-perfect fit between the consumer's physical and/or psychological needs and the product's benefits. Brand names are very important, as well as quality of service. Selective, ego-oriented advertising is used by a number of specialty good sellers to maintain their products' exclusive image.

Unsought goods. Products that the consumer does not know about or knows about but does not actively seek out are referred to as **unsought goods.** New products fall into this category until advertising and distribution increase consumer awareness of them.

Some goods are perennially marketed as unsought items. Insurance, cosmetics and housewares sold door to door, encyclopedias, and similar items necessitate aggressive personal selling and highly persuasive advertising. Leads to potential buyers are aggressively sought by salespeople. The company must go directly to the consumer through a salesperson, direct mail or direct-response advertising in magazines, or newspapers and other media, since the consumer usually does not seek out the item.

What is relevant for the marketing manager is how a majority of the target consumers perceive a product. For example, to most adults a Baby Ruth candy bar is a convenience good. I, however, crave them. A Baby Ruth is a specialty good for me. I have been known to leave my home after the 10 o'clock news and search for a half hour (several stores were closed) until I found one. A young child with only 50 cents to spend may act as if candy bars are a shopping good. The point is, product classes depend on consumer perceptions and not just the physical attributes of the product. If most view it as a convenience good, then a convenience good strategy of competitive prices, many retail sellers, and perhaps heavy advertising and promotion are called for. Other types of products, of course, need different strategies.

INDUSTRIAL GOODS

Industrial products are primarily those items used in producing other goods. These goods are classified by function performed or by accounting treatment. Functional classification is based on whether the goods become part of the final product or are used to produce other goods. A third functional designation is farm products, which the federal government classifies with industrial goods. The accounting breakdown is done on the basis of the tax treatment of the product. Expense items have a relatively short life span and are continually consumed in the company's operations; capital goods typically last for a number of years and are depreciated over several years. (Depreciation is the deduction from accounting income for the possible loss in value of a property due to wear and tear, time, and obsolescence.)

Industrial goods can be broken down into six major categories: installations, accessory items, component parts and materials, raw materials, supplies, and services (see Figure 8.2). Our discussion will begin with the capital goods — installations and accessories — and then continue with the remaining industrial goods, which are considered expense items.

Expense items are used and paid for within a single accounting period. Because of their relatively short life span, purchases of expense items involve less risk than purchases of capital goods. **Capital goods,** such as buildings and plants, represent a major commitment against future earnings and profitability. Their long life span is amortized over a longer period to reflect the gradually declining utility of the capital good. Longer negotiation periods, more exhaus-

---

◣ **FIGURE 8.2 A classification system for industrial goods.**

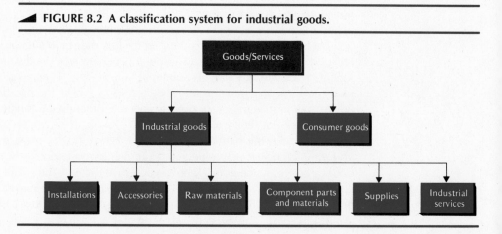

tive planning, and the judgments of many individuals may be needed before the decision to purchase a major capital good is made.

Installations. **Installations** are large, expensive capital items that determine the nature, scope, and efficiency of a company. Buildings and major production equipment, such as presses, metal stamping equipment, vats, and overhead cranes, are considered installations. Mineral rights and timber holdings, the primary assets of some companies, are also classified as installations.

When a company like Anaconda finds and procures a major new source of copper, this changes the scope and capacity of the organization. In another example, the demise of the large car caught Detroit napping in 1980. It will take from 1980 to 1985 for U.S. auto makers to raise their four-cylinder engine capacity from 22 to 40 percent of capacity. In the meantime, Detroit continues to lose market share to imports that are virtually all four-cylinder vehicles. The U.S. auto industry's failure to acquire the "right" installations may mean a permanent loss in market share.

Accessories. **Accessories** do not have the same long-run impact on the firm as installations, but they are still capital goods. They are less expensive and more highly standardized than installations. Copy machines, electric typewriters, and smaller machines such as table drills and saws and desks are typical accessories. If a company buys one too many desks, this will have almost no impact on profitability. If it builds one too many plants, the results could be disastrous.

The smaller impact of accessories usually means that fewer individuals are involved in the purchase decision. It is quite common for accessories to be bought by a purchasing agent. Since many accessories are standardized rather than custom built, they can be sold through industrial distributors and office equipment retailers.

Raw materials. In contrast to the first two categories, **raw materials** do become part of the final product. They can be defined as items that have undergone no more processing than is required for economy or protection before being incorporated in the final product. Raw materials can be further subdivided into natural products and farm products.

Because of limited total supplies, natural products are subject to extensive regulation in many nations. Price fixing and collusion among exporting countries have resulted in artificially high prices for petroleum, bauxite, and other natural products. America's raw materials industries tend to be dominated by a small number of large firms.

The second category of raw materials—farm products—has a much different industry structure. In the United States, there are approximately 2.5 million farms employing a total of over 3.9 million people.[3] Price and crop production is strongly influenced by governmental policy rather than by free-market actions. Virtually all farm products are grown seasonally, so storage plays a large part in total price. Specialization by region often requires extensive transportation to distant markets, and long hauls typically mean higher distribution costs.

Component parts and materials. Like raw materials, **component parts and materials** are incorporated into the end product. They may be custom-made items such as a drive shaft for an automobile, a cabinet for a computer, or a special pigment for painting U.S. Navy harbor buoys. In other situations component parts may be standardized for sale to numerous industrial users. Integrated circuits for minicomputers, cement for the construction trade, and steel for various applications are common examples of standardized component parts and materials.

Availability of supply and consistency of quality are two critical considerations in component parts and materials purchases. Lack of parts can shut down an assembly line. Lack of uniform quality can result in product failures, which cause bad will and costly warranty repairs. In some cases, extensive replacement markets develop. Tires and batteries for cars and trucks, paper for a computer printer, oil rig drill bits, and batteries for electric watches are excellent examples of part replacement markets. Sometimes companies make more money from component parts in the long run than they make from the primary product. Inexpensive "instant cameras" vastly stimulated the demand for costly instant color film. Mr. Coffee II's are designed to appeal to the cost-conscious consumer, yet they create additional demand for Mr. Coffee filters. Brand names become very important in these and similar replacement markets.

Supplies. The fifth category of industrial goods is **supplies,** which are purchased routinely and in fairly large quantities by lower-echelon personnel. Supplies are expense items and do not become part of the final product. Thus they have less impact on the firm's long-run profits.

Supply items run the gamut from pencils and paper to paint and machine oil. Usually these items are purchased from office supply stores or industrial distributors. Distribution of such items is extensive, since industrial buyers will rarely search for supply items. Competition, however, may be intense. Bic and Paper Mate, for example, compete heavily in the inexpensive ballpoint pen market.

Services. The last category of industrial products is **services.** Companies employ service organizations to plan, facilitate, or support their operations. The selling of a service, whether it is a janitorial cleaning service or management consulting, is usually done on a personal basis. Purchasers must be convinced of their need for the special skills of outside firms and/or the cost effectiveness of hiring them.

Although a company can usually afford to hire its own maintenance personnel, it may find it less expensive to enter into a maintenance contract with repair personnel who agree to be "on call." Sometimes, consultants in fields such as marketing, engineering, and production can bring unique talents to bear on a specific problem that does not occur frequently enough to warrant the hiring of full-time professionals. Hiring an advertising agency is a common practice to avoid the expense of having high-priced advertising professionals on the staff.

The product manager concept

Regardless of whether it is an industrial good or consumer good, a convenience item or an installation, in a large corporation there will usually be a **product manager** for the item. We will use the terms "product manager" and "brand manager" interchangeably. Technically, a brand manager is responsible for a brand, whereas a product manager has authority for several brands within a product group.

Procter & Gamble, Schlitz Brewing, Pillsbury, General Mills, and Lever Brothers all use the product manager form of organization. In the industrial good area, Union Carbide, Bell Helicopter, Texas Instruments, Uniroyal, and General Dynamics have embraced the product manager concept. Even the U.S. Postal Service has product managers. Yet many organizations are not happy with the product manager concept. Hunt Foods, Heinz, Kimberly Clark, and Sterling Drug have drastically altered their use of the product manager concept. Pepsi, Levi Strauss, Purex, and Eastman Kodak have dropped it altogether. In order to understand the controversy, we must first examine its brief history.

THE ORIGINAL PRODUCT MANAGER CONCEPT

As major consumer goods companies grew in sales, number of product lines, and organizational complexity during the 1950s and 1960s, new organizational arrangements for marketing were developed to better cope with the dynamic nature of the marketing environment. In its original form, the product manager's position was to consist of

1. Creation and conceptualization of strategies for improving and marketing the assigned product lines or brands.
2. Projection and determination of financial and operating plans for such products.
3. Monitoring execution and results of plans, with possible adaptation of tactics to evolving conditions.[4]

Operationalization of the product manager concept has varied, with occupants of these positions being referred to as a little marketing manager, entrepreneur, information center, influence agent, integrator, little general manager, product planning and development analyst, boundary spanner, and marketing brain center.

The areas of controversy in product management center on what decision areas product managers should be responsible for, with whom they should interact, and how much responsibility they should have. Key points of discussion are these:

> Should product managers be responsible for the profit achieved by their products?
> Should product managers act only as a source of information for their products?

Should advertising decisions be outside the scope of the product manager's responsibilities?

Should product managers have responsibility for marketing research decisions?[5]

THE CONTEMPORARY PRODUCT MANAGER

The product manager of the 1980s, while not a "little marketing manager," does seem to have more authority than ever before. The role of planner and coordinator has also expanded. Today the product manager engages in planning product objectives and strategy, monitoring progress, coordinating budget development and control, and working with other departments on product cost and quality.[6] But the product manager still often lacks authority over critical functions such as pricing and advertising. As the executive vice-president of a drugs product company has noted:

We give much authority to the product manager other than the copy side — sales promotion, for example. But we let him know he is not to be the final authority on advertising. We say the person who knows the most about advertising should make the ultimate decision.[7]

Not only must management obtain decisions from the executives who are most competent to make these decisions, but it must also control the allocation of resources among products. The president of a liquor company comments as follows: "Our brand managers make many decisions but they don't make the key ones. Someone at a higher level must look at the broad allocation of expenditures."[8]

The future of the product manager, however, seems bright. By 1985, he or she should have more authority and responsibility than ever before. The greatest expansion of responsibility will occur in long-range product planning, achieving profit objectives, and general product decisions. William D. Smithburg, executive vice-president, U.S. grocery products, Quaker Oats, Chicago, recently discussed the product manager of the 1980s:

There has been a premium on sophisticated and meticulous training. The result has been a highly trained and capable force of brand managers, but all this discipline and sophistication runs the risk of creating a sameness in both marketing strategy and execution.

Now the emphasis is shifting to stimulating originality. The manager has to have alternate courses to take if the FTC rules against one course, or the FCC prohibits one kind of broadcast advertising, or a nutrition group launches a drive against some ingredient. . . .

The evolving brand manager will have to be more aware of the outside forces in our world. The day is over when product people couldn't believe that someone could question their right to offer any product that consumers would buy. . . . Now brand managers have to know how new attitudes are formed and new groups rally around causes. They must be more broadly trained to understand the human climate.

They must understand the nature of these external problems, be able to anticipate them, and be innovative enough to find ways to turn them into opportunities.

[In addition,] because of the growing pressure for profitability that we're seeing now — and that is sure to continue through the '80s — there will be changes in the bottom-up planning process.

Before the brand manager works out his plans, senior management will set tighter guidelines. The use of capital will be considered at the start. The return expected on investment will help determine priorities and investments in advertising and promotion.

We face a much more disciplined market — and that calls for the disciplines of a management that understands both the marketing and financial dynamics of a product.[9]

The product life cycle

Once a product or service reaches the market, it enters the **product life cycle.** The life cycle is nothing more than the pattern of demand for a product over time. Generally speaking, it is the responsibility of the product manager to guide a product through its life cycle. This usually means altering marketing strategies and tactics as the product matures. The product life cycle is a theoretical concept, just as pure competition is a theoretical concept in microeconomics. But it can serve as a conceptual base for examining product growth and development (see Figure 8.3).

When a new product is brought out, sales are usually low. This may be because of a lack of distribution, consumer awareness, or consumer unwillingness to try new items. With consumer recognition and acceptance plus more dealers handling the product, sales should increase at an ascending rate.

◀ **FIGURE 8.3 Stages in the product life cycle.**

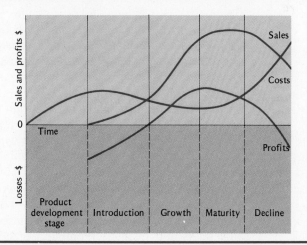

Sales, however, are predicated on company actions, competitors' aggressiveness, the "newness of the product," and a host of other external variables. At some point, the rate of growth will subside as competition becomes more effective and more people acquire the product. Eventually sales reach a plateau and begin a permanent decline. The mass market has been saturated, new technology has been developed, and channel members are no longer willing to carry the item. Products, however, do not always cooperate with textbook theory.

LIFE CYCLE STAGES

A basic product life cycle consists of four stages: (1) introduction, (2) growth, (3) maturity, and (4) decline. In the first stage costs of development are rather high and can represent a considerable investment before a single penny of sales is made. It is even a longer period before revenues are greater than costs and the product returns a profit. This usually occurs around the end of the introductory phase of the cycle.

Before we examine these stages, several additional points need to be made. First, not every product goes through every stage. In fact many goods never get past the introduction stage. Second, the length of time a product spends in any one stage may vary dramatically. Third, some products, such as fad items, move through the entire cycle in weeks. Others, such as Scotch whiskey and filter cigarettes, have been in the maturity stage for years. And changes in a product can change its life cycle. **Repositioning** a product can lead to a new growth cycle. Repositioning is basically changing the perceived image on uses of the product. Arm and Hammer repositioned its 130-year-old baking soda as a multipurpose product useful for everything from brushing teeth to eliminating refrigerator odors.

Introduction. Erasable pens, information data banks for personal use, room deodorizing air conditioning filters, and wind-powered home electric generators have recently entered the product life cycle. They face many obstacles. A high failure rate, little competition, frequent product modification, and limited distribution typify the introduction stage of the life cycle. Demand comes from the **core market,** in which there is an almost perfect match between the product offering and consumer needs. The consumers in the core market are most likely to buy the product.

Both production and marketing costs are high because of the lack of mass production economics. Often this leads to high retail sales prices in an attempt to recover costs quickly. High dealer margins, often necessary to obtain adequate distribution, may also necessitate a strategy of high prices. Profits, if any, are small in this phase of the life cycle.

Promotion strategy is centered on developing product awareness and informing consumers about how the product or service can benefit them. Intensive personal selling is required to gain acceptance for the product among wholesalers and retailers. Promotion of convenience goods often requires heavy consumer sampling and couponing. Shopping and specialty goods demand educational advertising and personal selling to the final consumer.

Growth. If a product survives the introductory stage, it moves into the growth stage of the life cycle. Sales are now growing at an increasing rate; many competitors are entering the market; large companies are beginning to acquire the small pioneering firms; and profits are healthy. Emphasis begins to switch from promotion of a product category (e.g., home video cassette recorders) to aggressive brand advertising (e.g., Sony vs. Panasonic and RCA) and the differences between the products.

Distribution becomes a major key to success during the growth stage, and in later stages as well. Manufacturers scramble to acquire dealers and distributors. Without adequate distribution it is impossible to establish a strong market position.

Toward the end of the growth phase prices normally fall and profits begin to peak out (reach maximum levels). Price reductions result from increasing economies of scale and increased direct competition. Also, development costs have been recovered. Demand is no longer limited to high-income consumers as the product reaches the vast middle-income market. Products currently in the growth stage include minicomputers, small cars, wide-body fuel efficient medium range jets, and designer jeans.

Maturity. A period during which sales continue to increase, but at a decreasing rate, signals the beginning of the maturity stage of the life cycle. Most products that exist today are in the maturity stage, and therefore most marketing strategies are for mature products. Normally this is the longest stage of the cycle.

During the maturity stage annual models begin to appear for shopping goods and many specialty goods. Product lines are widened to appeal to many market segments, and service and repair take on a more important role as manufacturers strive to distinguish their products from others. Product design tends to become stylistic (how can the product be made different?) rather than functional (how can the product be made better?). Powdered drink mixes, electric drip coffee pots, and high-meat-content dog foods are good examples of products that are in the maturity stage of the life cycle.

As prices and profits continue to fall, marginal competitors begin dropping out of the market. Dealer margins also shrink, resulting in less shelf space for the mature product, lower dealer inventories, and a general reluctance to push the product.

Promotion to the dealer is often intensified during this stage in order to retain loyalty. Heavy consumer promotion by the manufacturer is also required if market share is to be maintained. Long product usage and intensive promotion lead to strong brand loyalties. Coca-Cola, Winston, Smucker Jellies, Visine, and Ford Motor all have millions of loyal customers who will search for these brands and accept few or no substitutes.

Decline. A permanent drop in sales signals the beginning of the decline stage. The rate of decline is governed by how rapidly consumer tastes change and/or substitute products are adopted. Many convenience goods and fad items lose their markets overnight, leaving large inventories of items such as pet rocks that cannot be sold. Others die more slowly, like the convertible automobile, black and white console television sets, and nonelectric watches. In the late 1970s, more than 16,000 skilled Swiss watchmakers lost their jobs because of the shift in demand to digital watches.

Falling demand forces many competitors from the market. Often a small specialty firm will buy manufacturing rights for a product and sell it to the original core market. Ipana toothpaste was acquired by two Minnesota businessmen after being dropped by a major packaged-goods company. Within five years the new firm had over 1.5 million loyal Ipana users. Promotion becomes very selective as the market continues to shrink. Exposure of the product to the consumer declines in importance. Mass retailers may drop the product, thereby requiring the manufacturer to distribute through specialty outlets.

Not all products face an inevitable death as they move through the life cycle. Sometimes they can be given new life through repositioning or product modification. Johnson and Johnson's success with baby shampoo repositioning has given management the confidence to try the same tactic again. Recent ads tout Johnson's baby lotion as being not only for the baby, but also for cheek protection, leg shaving, face washing, all-over body massaging, and after-sun moisturizing. This is called **innovative maturity.** Tactics to achieve innovative maturity include these:

1. Promoting more frequent use of the product by current consumers.
2. Developing more varied use of the product by current consumers.
3. Creating new consumers for the product by expanding the market.
4. Finding new uses for the product.

Ralston Purina excels at innovative maturity, as the following example shows.

The only thing worse than a stagnating product is deciding what to do with it, says William P. Stirlitz, vice-president of the grocery products division at Ralston Purina. Perhaps it would be wise to kill off the product, but Stirlitz feels a better approach is to keep an open mind toward revitalizing a doddering brand. In fact, Ralston has derived a better return from recycling efforts on mature products or even declining ones than on almost all its other business projects. In the 1960s and 1970s, Ralston was earning minimal profit from its Hot Ralston cereal. The product was kept around mostly for nostalgic reasons until a new manager took the brand elements apart. He updated packaging, advertising and promotion and made pricing more competitive. A sharp improvement followed, producing a profit yield which has grown each of the last 10 years. In another instance, management took a dismal view of the 40-year-old Ry Krisp business in the early 1960s. Ralston even made efforts to sell the brand, but it drew no takers. Finally, under a new manager and after several reintroductions and line face lifts, profits are up 1000 percent. While recognizing a product's life stages is crucial, Stirlitz concludes, it is also important to consider committing resources to rebuilding an old product with the same dedication and creativity as you would with a new one.[10]

The life cycle as a managerial tool

In addition to providing a theoretical framework, the product life cycle concept may be used as a managerial planning tool. Marketing strategies must change as the product goes through the life cycle. If managers understand the cycle concept, they are in a better position to forecast future sales activities and plan marketing strategies.

A brief summary of strategic considerations at various stages of the product life cycle is presented in Table 8.1. Care must be taken to make certain that a product has moved from one stage to the next before altering the marketing strategy. A temporary sales decline could be misinterpreted as a sign that the product is going "down the tubes" and stimulate a pull-back of marketing support. This can then become a self-fulfilling prophecy.

Determining when a product is in transition from one stage to the next can be quite difficult. Researchers have developed models that forecast the growth and maturity phases of a new product on the basis of test market data, but most of the models have difficulty forecasting sales decline.[11] Marketing managers can use leading indicators to forecast when a product is entering the maturity phase. These include the proportion of new triers of a product versus replacement sales; declining profits; overcapacity in industry; appearance of replacement products; increasing price elasticity; present users' consumption rate; and style changes.

Economic factors can also play a critical role in life cycle management. A significant economic downturn in the introductory phase may kill a good product. On the other hand, a mediocre item may succeed (at least through the introductory stage) during a boom period. A product in the growth stage stands a better chance of surviving an economic downturn. Management may be required to alter the product form (use less costly components), reduce the price, or increase advertising expenditures. Products in the maturity phase are mostly likely to rise and fall in sales with changes in level of economic activity. This is particularly true for shopping goods, which consumers can postpone buying until times are better. Finally, a product in the decline phase will have its exit hastened by a major downturn.

TABLE 8.1 Strategic Considerations in the Product Life Cycle

Effects and responses	Stages of the product life cycle			
	Introduction	Growth	Maturity	Decline
Competition	None of importance.	Some emulators.	Many rivals competing for a small piece of the pie.	Few in number with a rapid shakeout of weak members.
Overall strategy	Market establishment; persuade early adopters to try the product.	Market penetration; persuade mass market to prefer the brand.	Defense of brand position; check the inroads of competition.	Preparations for removal; milk the brand dry of all possible benefits.
Profits	Negligible because of high production and marketing costs.	Reach peak levels as a result of high prices and growing demand.	Increasing competition cuts into profit margins and ultimately into total profits.	Declining volume pushes costs up to levels that eliminate profits entirely.
Retail prices	High, to recover some of the excessive costs of launching.	High, to take advantage of heavy consumer demand.	What the traffic will bear; need to avoid price wars.	Low enough to permit quick liquidation of inventory.
Distribution	Selective, as distribution is slowly built up.	Intensive, employ small trade discounts since dealers are eager to store.	Intensive; heavy trade allowances to retain shelf space.	Selective; unprofitable outlets slowly phased out.
Advertising strategy	Aim at the needs of early adopters.	Make the mass market aware of brand benefits.	Use advertising as a vehicle for differentiation among otherwise similar brands.	Emphasize low price to reduce stock.
Advertising emphasis	High, to generate awareness and interest among early adopters and persuade dealers to stock the brand.	Moderate, to let sales rise on the sheer momentum of word-of-mouth recommendations.	Moderate, since most buyers are aware of brand characteristics.	Minimum expenditures required to phase out the product.
Consumer sales and promotion expenditures	Heavy, to entice target groups with samples, coupons, and other inducements to try the brand.	Moderate, to create brand preference (advertising is better suited to do this job).	Heavy, to encourage brand switching, hoping to convert some buyers into loyal users.	Minimal, to let the brand coast by itself.

Source: Nariman K. Dhalla and Sonia Yuspeh, "Forget the Product Life Cycle Concept," *Harvard Business Review,* January–February 1976, p. 104. Copyright © 1975 by the President and Fellows of Harvard College; all rights reserved.

USING THE PRODUCT LIFE CYCLE FOR ENTRY STRATEGIES

Product life cycles can be for a single product, such as Coors, or for an industry, such as beer. The industry life cycle is an aggregation of individual product life cycles. When entering a market, management can pursue one of several entry strategies based on the product life cycle.

Blanket coverage tactics. If a company decides to enter the industry product life cycle at the growth stage, it may follow a heavy user or blanket coverage tactic. **Blanket coverage** refers to a mass media blitz and intensive product distribution. In 1979, Airwick introduced Carpet Fresh deodorizer. It spent $16 million in advertising to reach virtually all American women between 21 and 60 years of age. The product was heavily promoted to wholesalers and retailers to load the channels. By 1980, Carpet Fresh had an estimated 80 percent market share of a $100 million a year market. But although blanket coverage was successful for Airwick, it can sometimes be expensive and wasteful. Often, blanket coverage reaches many people who are not candidates for a good or service.

Heavy user tactics. A second technique for product introduction is to classify heavy users both psychographically and demographically and then employ the media and distribution channels with heavy user profiles. This method is not foolproof either, because heavy users are not necessarily early adopters. The latter group is composed of individuals who are the most receptive to trying new products and services. Thus a heavy user strategy is usually more successful in the growth or early maturity phase of the industry life cycle rather than the introductory phase. When Quaker Oats began adding line extensions to its basic grits, such as grits and bacon bits, and grits and cheese, it promoted the product heavily to blue-collar southern adults without college educations. This group constitutes the heavy grits eaters.

Early adopter tactics. A third approach is targeting the introductory marketing mix toward early adopters. If a sufficient number of early triers can be successfully reached, they will provide an early source of revenue, serve as word-of-mouth advertisers, and most important, legitimize the new product. **Legitimization** means that the innovators psychologically pave the way for noninnovators to try the product. Naturally, it helps if innovators are opinion leaders. Most research has shown that there is considerable overlap between the two.[12] RCA's SelectaVision passed Sony's Betamax in 1978 by using a consumer magazine campaign designed to reach early triers (in this case, young professionals). RCA also offered a $100 rebate on the $1000 player-recorders and gave away two free VCR movies. By using a strategy to reach innovators, RCA successfully overcame the early market leader.

PRODUCT ADOPTION

In order to appreciate the tactics just discussed and see how a product moves through the life cycle, let us examine the product adoption process (see Figure

235

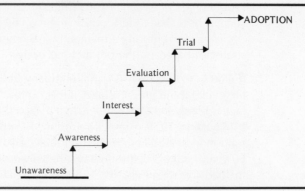

8.4). Regardless of when a firm enters the industry product life cycle, a marketing manager should understand the product adoption process in order to increase the chances that a new item will be successful. This involves, first of all, knowing what is meant by innovation and diffusion. An **innovation** is any product or service that we perceive as new (such as a once-a-day pill that would take the place of eating). Note that a product may have been around for a long time, yet still be seen as new—for example, yogurt. The **diffusion process** is the sales rate of a new product in an economic system over time. The **adoption process** consists of the decision-making steps consumers go through before buying a good or service.

During the awareness stage, an individual becomes aware of the innovation but lacks information about it. During the interest stage, need is aroused and the individual seeks information. During the evaluation stage, the individual mentally compares the product's attributes to his or her needs. The trial stage consists of an initial purchase to determine how well the product satisfies those needs. Adoption follows a satisfactory trial, and the product is used regularly thereafter.

Factors that affect adoption. The trial stage of the adoption process is basically an exercise in attempted risk reduction by the consumer. One obvious way to lower perceived risk is to offer the new products in small quantities. This is not much consolation to a manufacturer of videocassette recorders. Its only strategic move may be to offer a "free home trial," an effective guarantee, or something of a similar nature. Many producers of consumer goods, however, can market trial sizes to gain consumer acceptance. Hidden Valley Salad Dressings offers ten-cent miniature bottles of its new flavors to induce trial.

Several other determinants of trial are relative advantage, communicability, and complexity. **Relative advantage** is the degree to which an innovation is perceived as being better than any possible substitute. The microwave oven has a strong relative advantage over a conventional oven for rapid cooking. **Communicability** is the ability to verbalize product attributes. Much more can be said about a new car than about a new salt shaker. If a product is complex, extra promotional effort on the part of the marketing manager may be required because some people are more likely than others to buy a new product.

Adopter categories. Everett Rogers has classified product adopters into five groups, as shown in Figure 8.5. Before we discuss these categories, however, it should be noted that they were forced into a normal statistical distribution quite arbitrarily. A product with a high relative advantage will tend to display a positively skewed distribution.[13] In other words, more than 16 percent of the market for such a product will be innovators and early adopters and a smaller percentage will be in the late majority of adopters and laggards. The reverse is true of a new product with a relatively low comparative advantage. An example of a product with high relative advantage is microwave ovens, which had many early purchasers because of the advantages of microwave cooking over conventional cooking.

For many products, early adopters are relatively young, have more disposable income than their peers, and are better educated. Studies show that early users read more magazines, particularly ones that relate to potential purchases. These consumers belong to more organizations and are more mobile than other consumers. They also exhibit strong needs for achievement, change, and exploration. While they do not actively seek risk, early users are more likely to take risks than other consumers. Also, different groups of individuals may be early adopters for different products. An early purchaser of new soaps may not be an early purchaser of new appliances. Generally speaking, early triers are often heavy users of a product category. For example, heavy users of ready-to-eat cereals tend to be early triers of new cereal products.

Early majority buyers (34 percent) are much more cautious and thoughtful in making purchase decisions. They do not consider buying a good or service until they have communicated with early triers. Most early majority buyers are of above-average socioeconomic status. This group is generally willing to as-

---

FIGURE 8.5 Adopter categorization on the basis of relative time of adoption of innovations.

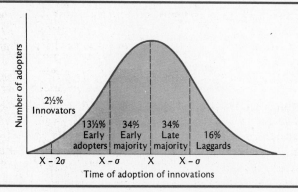

Source: Everett M. Rogers, *Diffusion of Innovations* (New York: Free Press, 1962), p. 162. By permission.

sume some risks, but will not engage in extensive risk taking. The next 34 percent of consumers are referred to as the late majority. They are below average in socioeconomic status and tend to have a higher average age than the other groups. These consumers are strongly oriented toward their reference groups and do not depend on advertising or personal selling for information. In this category adoption normally results from economic need rather than from the influence of an opinion leader. Laggards represent the bottom rung of the social and economic ladder. By the time this group adopts a product, the early adopters have switched to something new. This group strongly resists change. Its members cling to the past and tend to associate with people who hold viewpoints similar to their own. Advertising to this group is virtually a waste of time and money.

PRODUCT MIX STRATEGY

The marketing or product manager must determine the product mix that will most effectively reach his or her target market — early adopters, the majority, or even laggards. A **product mix** is the total list of products offered for sale by the company. A **product line** refers to a group of products intended for essentially the same uses and often possessing similar physical characteristics. Three important variables must be examined in developing a product strategy. First, management must decide the proper depth of each product line. **Product depth** is the average number of goods or services offered by a company within each product line. General Foods, for example, offers a large number of different types and flavors of cereals, thereby creating a deep product line (see Figure 8.6). Xerox offers twenty-two copiers, also creating a deep product line.

Polaroid, Maytag, and Xerox have deep product lines but little **product width.** The width of a product mix may be defined as the number of different product lines found within the company. It is the second variable that must be examined in developing a product strategy. Allegheny Ludlum Industries utilizes a very wide product mix, including Allegheny Steel, Special Metals, Jacobsen mowers, True Temper tools and sporting goods, Carmet and IPM audio products, and Arnold magnetic tapes.

Product lines that are closely related in end use, production requirements, or distribution channels are characterized by **product line consistency** — the third element of the product mix. Allegheny Ludlum obviously lacks consistency in its product lines. General Foods, on the other hand, has a very wide product mix with a high level of consistency.

A firm with a wide product line attempts to reach many, if not all, segments of its present market. It is relying on a well-defined image in the marketplace to help sell its products. If a company develops an inconsistent product line mix, it tacitly implies that the firm's best profit opportunities lie in widely diverse markets. An organization with a highly consistent product mix attempts to reap greater economies of scale from current production lines, channels of distribution, media mix, and so forth. A depth strategy is an attempt to reach virtually all consumers by giving them a plethora of product choices.

Coffees	Desserts	Cereals	Household products	Pet foods	Other grocery products

Width of Product Mix

Depth of Product Mix

Coffees	Desserts	Cereals	Household products	Pet foods	Other grocery products
Maxim Freeze-Dried Coffee Maxwell House Coffee (Regular) Ihstant Maxwell House Coffee Instant Sanka Coffee Sanka Coffee—97% Caffein Free	Jell-O Gelatin Desert Jell-O Pudding and Pie Filling Jell-O Instant Pudding Dream Whip Dream Whip Whipped Topping Mix	Grape-Nuts, 40% Bran Flakes Raisin Bran, Sugar Crisp Corn Flakes, Fruit Cereal Honeycomb, Oat Flakes	SOS Soap Pads Satina Ironing Aid Tuffy Plastic Mesh Ball (dishwashing aid)	Gaines Meal Gaines Biscuits Gaines Bits Gaines Variety	Kool-Aid Soft Drink Mix Log Cabin Syrup Tang Instant Breakfast Drink Baker's Cocoa Baker's Instant Chocolate Flavor Mix Good Seasons Salad Dressing Mixes Good Seasons Open-Pit Barbecue Sauce Good Seasons Shake'n Bake seasoned coating mixes for chicken and fish

Managing the product line: the portfolio approach

Regardless of whether a firm used a width or depth strategy, it can improve the management of the product line by following a **portfolio approach.** With the portfolio approach each product in the line is classified by its present and/or forecasted growth and measure of market share dominance. The product life cycle that has been described provides the foundation for forecasting growth and analyzing the cost of gaining or holding market share. The portfolio approach also assumes that market share is strongly and positively correlated with product profitability.[14] The market share used by the product portfolio approach is **relative market share**—the ratio of the company's share of the market to the share of the largest competitor. If, for example, your firm has a 50 percent share and the competitor has 5 percent, the ratio is 10 to 1. On the other hand, if your firm has 10 percent and the largest competitor has 20 percent, the ratio is .5 to 1.

It is also assumed that during the growth phase of the life cycle market share can be increased at a relatively low cost by obtaining a disproportionate share of incremental sales. This is particularly true when incremental industry sales are coming from new users rather than heavier usage by existing users. Assume, for example, that microwave crunchy crust pizza is in the industry growth stage. It will be easier for General Foods to gain market share by selling to more new triers than Totino than by slugging it out with Totino in a mature market. In the maturity phase of the life cycle, gains in market share usually come only at the expense of a competitor, and such gains are often time consuming and costly.

Figure 8.7 shows the four most commonly used share/growth categories for product portfolio management: the star, the cash cow, the dog, and the problem children.

Stars. **Stars** are market leaders and growing fast. For example, in electronic toys Simon was the market leader in a growth market for several years. Star products usually have large reported profits, but require a lot of cash to finance the rate of growth. The tactic for marketing management is to protect existing market share. This is done by reinvesting earnings in product improvement, better distribution, more promotion, and production efficiency. Management must strive to obtain a majority of the new users as they enter the market.

Cash cows. A **cash cow** product usually generates more cash than is required to maintain its market share. It is a low growth market, but the product has a dominant market share. The Clorox Corporation owns Kingsford Charcoal,

▲ **FIGURE 8.7 The product portfolio.**

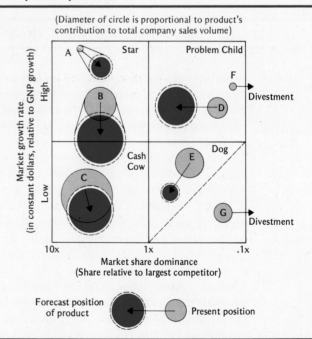

Source: George S. Day, "Diagnosing the Product Portfolio," *Journal of Marketing* 41 (April 1977): 34.

Match Charcoal Lighter, Prime Choice steak sauce, Cooking Ease spray lubricant for frying foods, and a chain of restaurants. Yet its cash cow is Clorox bleach, with a 60 percent market share in a slow growth market. Anheuser-Busch expects beer to be a cash cow for the organization by the mid-1980s, and the brewery is actively seeking outlets for the anticipated cash.

The basic strategy for a cash cow is to maintain market dominance. This includes price leadership and making technological improvements on the product. Pressure to extend the basic line should be resisted unless primary demand for the product category can be dramatically increased. Instead, excess cash should be allocated to other product areas where growth prospects are the greatest. It should be noted that Clorox has been highly successful by stretching the Clorox line to the liquid formula from the original dry bleach.

Dogs. **Dogs** have low growth potential and a subordinate market share. Most of these eventually leave the marketplace. Examples include Gillette's Nine Flags aftershave lotion, Warner-Lambert's Reef mouthwash, Frost 8-80 white whiskey, Campbell's Red Kettle soups, Xerox computers, and the Convair 880.

In mature markets like aftershave, jet airplanes, soups, and mouthwash, there is usually one leader. There are rarely opportunities for growth at a reasonable cost without a dramatic technological breakthrough. Because there is little growth, there are very few new users. Attempts to obtain greater market share usually meet with stiff competition. Sometimes dogs can be made into successful products by focusing on narrow subsegments of the market, or repositioning the product. In other situations, dogs can be successfully harvested. That is, consciously cutting back on all support costs to the bare minimum will often bring in a trickle of positive cash flow until the product dies. But not all dogs die quickly even when harvested: Lever has sold Lifebuoy soap for years with little promotional backing.

Problem children. **Problem children** exhibit rapid growth but poor profit margins. They create a tremendous demand for cash. If cash support is not forthcoming, they eventually become a dog. The strategy options are to invest heavily to obtain better market share, acquire competitors to get the necessary market share, or drop the product. Sometimes the product can be repositioned to move it into the star category.

OVERALL PRODUCT PORTFOLIO STRATEGY

The basic strategy of product portfolio management is to have some products generate cash and other items use that cash to create growth. The long-run viability of the product mix depends upon the size and vulnerability of the cash cows and star prospects. Of course, the dogs and problem children must also be accounted for. If resources are spread too thin, the entire product mix will consist of mediocre products.

In Figure 8.7, the present position of each product is defined by relative share and market growth rate. The blue circle represents the forecast for the various products. Tactics for each product are as follows:

Aggressively support the newly introduced product A to ensure dominance (but anticipate share declines due to new competitive entries).

Continue present strategies for products B and C to ensure maintenance of market share.

Gain share of market for product D by investing in acquisitions.

Narrow and modify the range of models of product E to focus on one segment.

Divest products F and G.[15]

Product modification. Sometimes products require modification. This decision is often less drastic than dropping an item and usually has less impact on long-run profits. Many times the change may be a subtle modification in quality or style that may not even be perceived by consumers. For example, a few years ago many liquor distillers dropped the proof of their whiskeys from 86 to 80 with scarcely a gurgle from the drinkers. The Tide soap sold in 1982 is quite different from the Tide detergent sold in 1947 when it was first introduced. It is different in cleaning performance, appearance, physical properties, sudsing characteristics, and packaging. In total, there have been 55 significant modifications in Tide's lifetime.

Sometimes modifications consist of nothing more than redesigning a logo or package. Morton Salt has changed the hair style and skirt length of its "when it rains, it pours" girl several times in the past 75 years in order to give the product a contemporary image (see Figure 8.8). Another common practice is to modify components—plastic radiator fans on automobiles instead of metal ones, for example.

Product deletion. The decision to drop a product is usually a critical one and is far more serious than product recall. Dying products often take an undue portion of management's time as they attempt to breathe new life into dogs. There is also the question of whether or not the resources used to produce and market the product can be used more effectively elsewhere.

In line with our discussion of product portfolios, most products are eliminated because of low profits, low sales, and/or poor future prospects. Dropping a product affects not only the company but its customers as well. Retailers may lose large profits if the dropped item sold well in their stores. Consumers who used the product may have to make major changes in their consumption patterns and/or life styles. Discontinuation of the Studebaker automobile drastically changed the purchase patterns of loyal Studebaker owners.

Questions of an ethical nature may also arise in a product deletion decision. Does the company have an obligation to provide spare parts for goods previously purchased? Must the company give notice to present customers that it will drop the product or the line in the near future? Most of us would agree that replacement parts should be produced, but more difficult questions then arise regarding "how long" and "how many." If replacement demand is five units per year for an obscure part, how many should the company produce before permanently closing the production line? To avoid sticky questions, some firms simply leave the product in the line. It seems that managers get attached to products and "hate to see them go." Tradition is also hard to overcome in getting management to drop an old product. In a more practical vein,

Source: Courtesy of Morton Salt Division of Morton-Norwich.

if the product is a good "fit" in the line or would leave a gaping hole in the product line, management may decide to retain it even at a loss. For example, if a firm produces three typewriters—a portable, manual standard, and electric standard—it may retain the manual standard even if it is sold at a loss to avoid creating a large hole in its product line.

Managing services

Our discussion throughout this chapter has focused on products. Yet in most cases the word *services* could easily have been interchanged with the word *products*. There are important distinctions between them, however.

THE IMPORTANCE OF SERVICES

Today more than half of our personal consumption expenditures go for services. Rising affluence, fulfillment of basic needs (food, clothing, shelter), the complexity of society (your income tax), more leisure time, the dying Protestant work ethic, and the complexity of products have led to ever-increasing demand for services.

Services generally fall into two categories: personal and business. Personal services include financial services, transportation, health and beauty, lodging, advising and counseling, amusements, maintenance and repair, real estate, and insurance. Of course this is not an exhaustive list, nor are all these services intended strictly for the final consumer. Business firms, for example, utilize all the services just mentioned plus others that are strictly business-oriented, such as advertising agencies, market research firms, and economic counselors.

Many large manufacturers have recognized the movement toward services and have jumped on the bandwagon. Coca-Cola has developed a multimedia learning system for schools. G. D. Searle, a pharmaceuticals manufacturer, has a new service entitled Project Health that will sell preventive medicine programs to industry. Singer is moving into preschool education. Upjohn, another pharmaceuticals maker, has a subsidiary that performs paramedical and housekeeping chores for newly discharged hospital patients. Gerber Products is moving into nursery schools and insurance.

HOW SERVICES DIFFER

A good image is even more important to a service firm than to a company that sells tangible products. There are very few objective standards for measuring service quality. Products can be examined on the basis of ingredients, tensile strength, weight, size, and so on, but services are often judged subjectively. Not only is a service usually complete before a buyer can evaluate its quality, but defective services cannot be returned. Another reason for the importance of image to service firms is that many people utilize certain services, such as plumbing, carpentry, and television repair, rather infrequently and therefore choose a company on the basis of perceived reputation.

Price competition such as that found in car rental companies, figure studios, the airlines and other standardized services is quite severe, since each company offers essentially the same thing. Another reason for price cutting is the difficulty of demonstrating dependability, skill, and creativity. Some firms have attempted to overcome this problem by offering low introductory rates to new customers.

Another unique aspect of service marketing is the difficulty of standardizing output. One ball game is very exciting; the next one is an exercise in boredom. Similarly, flying Delta today will not guarantee on-time arrival even though you flew Delta last week and arrived 15 minutes early. It is therefore incumbent on marketing managers to pay particular attention to quality control in an attempt to achieve a satisfactory level of service.

Services cannot be saved. Once the game is over, that's it! This is particularly important for promoters of amusements, transportation services, hotels, and the like. An empty room or seat brings in no revenue. Sometimes a variable pricing strategy (charging different prices to different purchasers for the same service) may induce the low-price buyer into the market even though the incremental revenue is below total cost.

DEVELOPING SERVICE MANAGEMENT STRATEGIES

One way to conceptualize service management is to examine the level of customer contact required to give the service. Customer contact refers to the physical presence of the customer in the system. Creation of the service is the work required in providing the actual service. The greater the amount of time a customer is in the service system, the greater the interaction between the system and the customer. Usually it is more difficult to control and gain economies of scale in high-contact services.

Let us take two examples. A hair salon is a high-contact system. The customer is greeted by the receptionist; the shampoo person washes the customer's hair; and a stylist creates the hair fashion. On the other hand, a car wash may have little, if any, contact with the customer. If it is a self-service system, the customer provides the labor and the service operator offers location, water, soaps, perhaps waxes, and sells towels through a vending machine. In a full-service car wash, customer contact is confined to the cashier and final inspection before driving away. Computer time-sharing services also have virtually no customer contact.

Marketing strategies vary dramatically depending on level of customer contact (see Table 8.2). In a low-contact service like credit reporting, the facility does not have to be near the customer's home or work. If there is little customer contact, the facility layout should be designed to enhance production. On the other hand, a high-contact service such as a physician's office must meet the psychological needs of the customer. A patient who walks into a doctor's office and finds a dirty floor, cheap furniture with holes in it, and overflowing ashtrays with stale cigarette butts may turn around and walk out. Process design can also be very important in high-contact situations. Layout of a styling salon, for example, begins with a reception desk, then an adjacent room for hair washing, and a third station for styling.

In many high-contact industries, the customer sets the production schedule by showing up. Also, worker skills must include public relations. Quality control in high-contact services is basically doing a good job and maintaining an image. If a worker does a good job but displays a poor attitude, the service may lose the customer.

Some services combine high- and low-contact characteristics. For example, airlines are high contact at ticket counters and within the planes. They are also quasimanufacturers in their approach to baggage handling, billing, and airplane maintenance. Thus, some aspects of airlines should follow the high-contact strategies and others the low-contact strategies. Usually it is most economical to shift as much of the operation into low-contact duties as possible. This

Decision	High-contact system	Low-contact system
Facility location	Operations must be near the customer.	Operations may be placed near supply, transportation, or labor.
Facility layout	Facility should accommodate the customer's physical and psychological needs and expectations.	Facility should enhance production.
Product design	Environment as well as the physical product define the nature of the service.	Customer is not in the service environment, so the product can be defined by fewer attributes.
Scheduling	Customer is in the production schedule and must be accommodated.	Customer is concerned mainly with completion dates.
Production planning	Orders cannot be stored, so smoothing production flow will result in loss of business.	Both backlogging and production smoothing are possible.
Worker skills	Direct workforce comprises a major part of the service product and so must be able to interact well with the public.	Direct workforce need only have technical skills.
Quality control	Quality standards are often in the eye of the beholder and hence variable.	Quality standards are generally measurable and hence fixed.
Time standards	Service time depends on customer needs, and therefore time standards are inherently loose.	Work is performed on customer surrogates (e.g., forms), and time standards can be tight.
Wage payment	Variable output requires time-based wage systems.	"Fixable" output permits output-based wage systems.
Capacity planning	To avoid lost sales, capacity must be set to match peak demand.	Storable output permits setting capacity at some average demand level.
Forecasting	Forecasts are short-term, time-oriented.	Forecasts are long-term, output-oriented.

Source: Richard B. Chase, "Where Does the Customer Fit in a Service Operation?" *Harvard Business Review* 56 (November–December 1979): 137–142. Reprinted by permission of the *Harvard Business Review*. Copyright © 1978 by the President and Fellows of Harvard College; all rights reserved.

allows the service to be run more like a production operation, using work measurement techniques, batch scheduling, and inventory control.

MANAGING SERVICE DEMAND AND SUPPLY

Modifying service demand, particularly in high-contact businesses, can be very difficult. The most obvious tool for control is price. Off-season motel rates, happy hours at bars, weekend discounts on long distance telephone calls, and early bird movies are examples. Another management strategy is to develop demand during slack periods. A classic example would be McDonalds' Egg McMuffin and its entire breakfast line. Universities sometimes rent their facilities during the summer to corporations for seminars or to consultants conducting training programs. Another technique is the development of complementary services that help to avoid bottlenecks or provide supplemental services. A good example is the use of a lounge in restaurants to shuttle customers in for a drink during rush hours. Not only does it make the wait more palatable, it also generates additional funds for the restaurant. Reservation systems are also a common technique used to manage demand.

Controlling the supply of services is usually easier than managing demand. Many restaurants, theme parks, hotels, and others use part-time employees. Also, during rush periods employees perform only the services necessary to meet demand. During off periods they engage in recordkeeping, counting inventory, cleaning equipment, and other supporting tasks. Supply can also be controlled by minimizing contact or letting customers do more for themselves. Examples include self-service stations, salad bars, and mark and bag your own groceries. A final technique for controlling supply of services is sharing capacity. Airlines often share baggage systems and ramps, credit unions share files, and doctors who are overloaded make referrals.

THE MARKETING CONCEPT IN SERVICE ORGANIZATIONS

Because of the unique problems facing service firms, many have been slow to adopt the marketing concept. Where the concept has been utilized, the company is less likely to have all its marketing mix activities carried out in the marketing department. Responsibility for new service offerings and evaluation of present offerings are often handled by other departments.[16] Such fragmentation of the marketing function makes control more difficult and probably reduces the effectiveness of the marketing strategy.

Service firms also tend to spend less on marketing activities than product manufacturers.[17] The lack of financial support for marketing may also partially explain why service companies do more advertising development "in house" and use marketing research and consulting firms less frequently. It is difficult to develop an effective marketing program without a strong financial, as well as philosophical, commitment to the function. Perhaps as the service industries mature, there will be a shift in their commitment to marketing.

SUMMARY

A product is any want-satisfying good or service and its perceived tangible and intangible attributes. Many products are purchased not for the function they perform, but for what they mean psychologically.

Products and services can be divided into two broad groups: consumer goods and industrial goods. Consumer goods, in turn, may be divided into four major categories: convenience, shopping, specialty, and unsought goods. The criteria for categorizing consumer goods is based on the way people view products and subsequently purchase them. The industrial goods market is broken down into six categories: installations, accessory items, component parts and materials, raw materials, supplies, and services.

Regardless of whether a product is an industrial or consumer good, there will usually be a product manager for the item in a large-scale corporation. In its original form, the product manager's position was similar to that of a mini marketing manager. The product manager of the 1980s is more of a planner and coordinator.

It is usually the responsibility of the product manager to manage the product through its life cycle. The life cycle is a measurement of sales and profits over time. The four stages of the life cycle are introduction, growth, maturity, and decline. Changing consumer attitudes, competition, the number of dealers carrying a product, and other factors normally necessitate a different marketing mix for each stage of the cycle. Sometimes, products can be repositioned to enter a new growth stage.

Not everyone is equally likely to adopt a new product. Individuals who purchase a good or service before most others are called early adopters. Other categories of adopters are early majority, late majority, and laggards.

As a product moves through its life cycle, it is often part of a product line. The product manager may employ a portfolio approach to managing the product line. Each product is classified by present and forecasted growth and measure of market share dominance. The basic strategy of portfolio management is to have some products generate cash and other items use that cash to create growth.

As a product enters the latter stages of the product life cycle, it may be necessary to eliminate it from the product line. This decision is usually based on future sales and profit expectations. Product deletion is usually far more serious and important to the long-run success of the firm than product modification.

Services are an extremely important segment of the American economy, accounting for over half of our personal consumption. Very few objective standards exist for measuring the quality of services. Price competition is normally rigorous in this area because of the homogeneity of service offerings within an industry. Because services are labor-intensive, it is difficult to standardize service output. The intangible nature of service marketing has resulted in slower adoption of the marketing concept by service firms than by product organizations.

KEY TERMS

Product	Innovative maturity
Consumer goods	Blanket coverage
Industrial goods	Legitimization
Convenience goods	Innovation
Shopping goods	Diffusion process
Specialty goods	Adoption process

Unsought goods
Expense items
Capital goods
Installations
Accessories
Raw materials
Component parts and materials
Supplies
Services
Product manager
Product life cycle
Repositioning
Core market

Relative advantage
Communicability
Product mix
Product line
Product depth
Product width
Product line consistency
Portfolio approach
Relative market share
Stars
Cash cows
Dogs
Problem children

REVIEW QUESTIONS

1. What are consumer goods? How are they classified? In what ways do they differ from industrial goods?
2. What products are classified as unsought goods? How are they marketed? Do they ever become sought?
3. List the four stages of the product life cycle. What factors account for the shape of the sales curve?
4. Describe the competitive situation and overall strategy throughout each stage of the product's life cycle.
5. Describe the product adoption process. What factors influence the diffusion rate?
6. Discuss the similarities and differences between the marketing of products and the marketing of services.

DISCUSSION QUESTIONS

1. Why is classification of the product an important factor in determining the marketing mix?
2. Why are some consumers willing to undertake an extensive search for specialty goods?
3. Identify the tangible and intangible attributes of the following products. How do they affect the value of the product? What benefits are derived from its use?
   a. Perrier.
   b. Chevy Citation.
   c. Designer clothes.
   d. IBM 360 computer.
   e. Tide.
4. The product manager concept has gained in popularity in recent years. Why? What advantage does it offer?
5. What is the general relationship between market share and profitability? Provide reasons supporting this correlation.
6. What does the product life cycle concept tell us about the firm's future cash flows? What might a firm do to close a projected profit gap?
7. How would you describe the kinds of individuals who respond to innovations? What impact would this have on the marketing of the product?

NOTES

1. "New and Improved," *The Wall Street Journal,* February 5, 1981, pp. 1, 21. Reprinted by permission. © Dow Jones & Company, Inc. 1981. All rights reserved.

2. The original classification system was suggested by Melvin T. Copeland in "Relation of Consumer's Buying Habits to Marketing Methods," *Harvard Business Review,* April 1923, pp. 282–289.

3. U.S. Department of Commerce, *Statistical Abstract of the United States, 1980* (Washington, D.C.: Government Printing Office, 1980), p. 420.

4. David J. Luck, "Interfaces of a Product Manager," *Journal of Marketing* 33 (October 1969): 32–36. Reprinted by permission of the American Marketing Association. See also David J. Luck, *Product Policy and Strategy* (Englewood Cliffs, N.J.: Prentice-Hall, 1972).

5. Richard T. Hise and T. Patrick Kelly, "Product Management on Trial," *Journal of Marketing* 42 (October 1978): 28–33.

6. Victor P. Buell, "The Changing Role of Product Management in Consumer Goods Companies," *Journal of Marketing* 39 (July 1975): 3–11; Richard M. Clewett and Stanley F. Stasch, "Shifting Role of the Product Manager," *Harvard Business Review,* January–February 1975, pp. 65–73.

7. Buell, "Changing Role of Product Management," p. 7.

8. Ibid., p. 10.

9. "Brand Manager Role Evolving in Tougher Market: Smithburg," *Marketing News,* November 17, 1978, p. 6.

10. Marketing Reporter, *Product Marketing,* April 1977, p. 14.

11. David R. Rink and John E. Swan, "Product Life Cycle Research: A Literature Review," *Journal of Business Research,* September 1979, pp. 219–243.

12. See James R. Meyers and Thomas S. Robertson, "Dimensions of Opinion Leadership," *Journal of Marketing Research* 9 (February 1972): 41–46.

13. Robert A. Peterson, "A Note on Optimal Adopter Category Determination," *Journal of Marketing Research* 10 (August 1973): 325–329.

14. Sidney Schoeffler, Robert D. Buzzell, and Donald F. Heany, "Impact of Strategic Planning on Profit Performance," *Harvard Business Review* 52 (March–April 1974): 137–145; and Robert O. Buzzell, Bradley T. Gale, and Ralph G. M. Sultan, "Market Share—A Key to Profitability," *Harvard Business Review* 53 (January–February 1975): 97–106.

15. George S. Day, "Diagnosing the Product Portfolio," *Journal of Marketing* 41 (April 1977), p. 35.

16. William R. George and Hiram C. Barksdale, "Marketing Activities in the Service Industries," *Journal of Marketing* 38 (October 1974): 65–70.

17. Ibid.

◢ CASES

8.1 The Condor Kite Company

Since the dawn of humanity people have wanted to fly like the birds. They have tried to launch themselves from any available precipice using all imaginable contraptions. Leonardo da Vinci designed a hang glider but never flew it. The first true hang gliders emerged in the late nineteenth century. In fact the Wright brothers' first effort was a hang glider. Their aircraft was simply a hang glider with an engine.

In the 1950s a NASA scientist designed a glider for possible space capsule reentry, but funds for the project were cut from the budget. In the late 1960s sports enthusiasts in California picked up his design and used it to glide from the sand dunes to the beach. Since then the sport has mushroomed in the United States. There are approximately 45,000 fliers and 30,000 hang gliders active today. Hang gliding has been declared the fastest-growing sport in America.

Eight to ten manufacturers account for 75 to 80 percent of all hang glider sales. Fifteen smaller companies account for the remaining market share. Hang gliders come in many designs and range in price from $400 to $2500. Most of the companies are in California.

Condor Kite Company was founded in August 1973 in Missouri. During its first year sales were quite low, since few people in that part of the country knew what a hang glider was and those who did thought that anyone who would engage in the sport was insane. Gradually, however, sales increased and dealers were acquired across the state and the nation. Condor now has 12 dealers in the United States and Brazil. The product is as good as or better than those of the industry leaders. Performance is way above the industry norm, but the price of Condor gliders is 15 percent below that of the industry leaders.

Condor has regular promotional tours of its facilities and sends out literature to all its dealers. It enters meets throughout the country and often wins. Condor advertises only during the seasonal months and in major hang-gliding publications. Little is actually known about the individuals who buy hang gliders, why they buy them, or what types of gliders they prefer. Identifying potential customers is extremely difficult. Also, the company's sporadic advertising has not kept the name Condor in the minds of many potential buyers. There are not enough Condors flying to create the word-of-mouth advertising needed to sell them.

1. How would you classify the Condor product?
2. Where are hang gliders in the product life cycle?
3. Where are Condor Kites in the product life cycle?

8.2 Ovaltine

Ovaltine is a product that has been around for many years. During the Depression, it attracted mothers who, when well-rounded, nutritious meals were hard to come by, found Ovaltine supplied added nutrients and was "good" for their children. It also attracted children because they could send in their labels and get their very own Little Orphan Annie dog whistles and secret decoder rings.

The problem, however, was that the mothers were buying it, but the children were not voluntarily drinking it or liking it. The taste was flat, and children, then as now, were not much inclined to drink something because it was good for them. Nevertheless, the product kept selling during the 1930s and 1940s. However, when the children of those nonpermissive times grew up and became parents, they did not force their children to drink Ovaltine. The marketing philosophy at Ovaltine seemed to be "a good product will succeed on its own."

Management was quite complacent until Nestle introduced Quik, a milk additive. "Quik just adds a chocolate flavor to milk, without any of Ovaltine's nutritive value," management stated. Then they decided it wouldn't fly. It flew. Quik and later Hershey's Instant and others created a new milk additive category, and Ovaltine watched in dismay as the sales of these new products caught up and went right past good old Ovaltine. Why? Better marketing; better taste; changing life styles; and price. Ovaltine estimates Quik has up to 50 percent of the market; Hershey's, 20 percent; and Ovaltine, 15 percent. Ovaltine, unlike the others, speaks of itself as a "meal supplement" nutritively head and shoulders above the other milk additives, and resents being categorized with them.

New management was brought in and immediately uncovered two major problems. One, it needed a new flavor for Ovaltine (more chocolatey chocolate — less malty malt) to attract new users, especially children, but it needed to change the flavor in such a way that old users were not alienated. It also needed a newer, more efficient manufacturing process. A new flavor was developed using blind taste tests and in-home product placements that resulted in much higher consumption with the new Ovaltine. The new Ovaltine was brought into the marketplace with one simple labeling change. It said "Now concentrated improved flavor, same nutrition." There was no other indication that the product was new.

1. Where was Ovaltine in the product life cycle before the reformulation? Why?
2. Has management created a "new" product with the reformulated Ovaltine?
3. If it is a new product, should there be more promotion to make the consumers aware of it?
4. Is Ovaltine simply being repositioned? What does that mean in terms of product life cycle?

9

New product/service planning and development

OBJECTIVES

To determine the strategic considerations in new product development.

To understand the risk and importance of new product development.

To review the various forms of organization for new product development.

To learn the steps involved in the new product development process.

Heublein, Inc., sees gold in consumers' changing life styles and values, and in America's changing demographics. These changes are vital to the Hartford, Conn.-based company in the development of its strategies for the 1980s.

Heublein is committed to new product development as "the lifeblood of its marketing orientation," according to Stuart D. Watson, chairman and chief executive officer.

Heublein introduced 17 new products and line extensions—both in the U.S. and abroad—in 1979. During this period, Heublein sold over $4,000,000 of products that didn't exist at the company five years ago. Heublein is developing products at such a fast rate that there were 20 ideas ready and near entry into the marketplace, either as test products or for rollout, in 1980.

Concerning the changing life styles and demographics, some shifts seem to favor continued consumption of fast foods, premium wine, and specialty grocery products. . . . The number of consumers in Heublein's target category—primarily age 25 to 44—will be increasing. The number of consumers in the 45 to 60 age group also will be increasing. . . . These people are important to Heublein because there are more of them than ever, they have more disposable income than the average consumer, and they are adapting to the life styles and value structures of the younger generations. A new category, the "new old," or people over 60, Heublein believes will be an active group for the firm in the '80s.[1]

Strategic considerations in new product development

New products, as noted by the Heublein Company, are the life blood of many companies. How do companies like Heublein plan and organize for new product development? More important, what steps do they take to increase their chances of having a winner? Without new products, many firms simply cease to grow. A recent study showed that firms obtain an average of 15 percent of their current sales volume on products introduced within the past five years.[2] When firms do not change their product mix to meet the requirements of changing consumer desires, government regulation, competition, and a host of other factors, market share and profits usually decline. Generally, a firm must be in a long-run growth market or suffer a declining return on investment without new products.

Often, new products are introduced in response to a consumer need rather than in response to a new scientific or technological discovery. In this case, the product manager must understand the need. For a number of years, it has been technically feasible for a computer to read printed characters through pattern recognition. At first glance, this seems to be a natural market. Rather than keypunching cards from typewritten documents and then feeding the cards into computers, the typewritten documents could be fed directly into computers. Why has this market not developed? Because the real need is for low-cost original data entry. The best way to accomplish this is to create the data and simultaneously enter them in the computer. Even the typewritten document is not necessary.

So new product development needs careful planning and evaluation if it is to be successful. Risks must be assessed, and a balance struck between innovation and conservatism.

THE RISK OF DEVELOPMENT

In the past, even the recent past, new product development managers often had a better chance of success by gambling in Las Vegas. Failure ratios in the mid-1970s averaged 40 to 50 percent, and in some industries as high as 84 percent.[3] A classic failure was Ford's $50 million loss on the Edsel, but lists of new-product failures are virtually endless. A few additional examples include Dupont's Corfam leather substitute, Listerol disinfectant (produced by Warner-Lambert, the manufacturer of Listerine), and Post's breakfast cereals with freeze-dried fruits. Remember that product failure does not mean the product did not sell at all. It means that the good or service did not meet management's expectations.

Things are looking up, however. The 1980 survey by the Conference Board found only one in three new products failing in the past five years.[4] It should be noted that these were products new to the firm, not line extensions. When Heublein brings out a new blend Jacare wine, it is a line extension. If Anderson Clayton markets a new Seven Seas salad dressing, this too is a line extension. A **line extension** is a similar product (often with the same overall brand name) to

TABLE 9.1 Success Rates for Major New Products

Percentage of successful new products	Percentage of companies selling primarily to	
	Industrial markets	Consumer markets
All succeeded	9%	18%
90 to 99%	7	4
80 to 89	16	9
70 to 79	11	11
60 to 69	16	12
50 to 59	15	15
40 to 49	4	2
30 to 39	9	9
1 to 29	5	4
None succeeded	8	16
	100%	100%

Note: The success rate reported by each company represents the percentage of all major new products introduced to the market by the company during the previous five years which subsequently met management's expectations in all important respects.
Source: New Product Winners and Losers. (New York: The Conference Board, 1980). Reprinted by permission.

that currently being sold by a company. The Conference Board survey also found that 62 percent of the firms surveyed expected their new product success rate to be higher during the next five years than the previous five. Several factors seem to account for the better batting average. First, there is a sharper pinpointing of responsibility for new products and finer coordination among all units involved in the new product process—in other words, better management. Second, there are new tools of prediction and more highly trained individuals in new product development. Two-thirds of the surveyed firms reported significant improvements in the accuracy of their first-year sales forecasts.

Very few firms achieve a 100 percent success rate (see Table 9.1). To strive for 100 percent success may mean you are so conservative that many good opportunities will be passed by. It has been said that if Procter & Gamble's current standards for new products had been applied to Pringles potato chips, the product would never have reached the market. Some other highlights of the Conference Board's research were these:

- Firms selling mainly to industrial markets launched an average of eight major new products during the last five years, compared with six for consumer-oriented firms.

- Among those with perfect batting records over the last five years were a metal components and equipment company, which had more than 100 successful new products; an electric components firm, 25 successes; and a petroleum products company, 9 winners. Those with 100 percent failure rates included a chemical firm with 20 new product losers; a manufacturer of heating equipment, 11 failures; and a producer of sports equipment, 6 strikeouts.

Insufficient and poor market research is the leading cause of new product failure. Cited next most often as reasons for failure are technical problems in design or production, and errors in timing the product's introduction.

Sometimes, a product that looks like it "can't fail" succumbs to the whims of the marketplace. Pillsbury found this to be true with its Appleasy desert.

Appleasy looked like a winner when it was whipped up in Pillsbury Co.'s test kitchen. The new dessert—apples in cinnamon sauce with a crunchy streusel topping—was the product of three years of exhaustive research. It was cheap, easy to fix and fast.

There was just one problem: Not very many people liked it. There weren't enough apples, the cinnamon was overpowering and the topping was too sweet. "It was a magnificent flop," says one Pillsbury executive.

Pillsbury began looking for an easy-to-prepare dessert in June 1975. Initial ideas ranged from instant yogurt to Boston cream pie to fudge sauce with a brownie topping. But a fruit dessert emerged as the favorite in "focus group" discussions with consumers.

Pillsbury chose apple because "the majority of consumers eat and perceive apples to be good; you know, 'An apple a day keeps the doctor away,' " explains Allen A. McClusker, a marketing executive who joined Pillsbury after Appleasy was developed. Pillsbury's test kitchen, which is a cross between a laboratory and a kitchen, came up with a recipe using freeze-dried apples. All you had to do was add boiling water, stir, wait five minutes and eat.

Consumer panels were interviewed to help pick a name. The early choice, Hot Apple 'n Crunch, was dropped because Appleasy conveyed the convenience image better. After consumer taste tests had been completed, however, Pillsbury began skimping on apples because the price of apples more than doubled. Appleasy was introduced in April 1978 and failed.

"The product became less Appleasy and more starch and sugar," Mr. McClusker says. He adds, "A lot of people tried it but didn't come back for seconds. There was no problem with convenience, but lots of problems with quality." Pillsbury won't say exactly how much it lost on Appleasy, but the figure was well over $1 million.

Because of high advertising costs, Pillsbury is trying harder than ever to weed out new products that show little promise in the grocery market. "Market research and product research is the cheapest part of the ritual," explains Mr. McClusker. Advertising is the most expensive. Pillsbury recently dropped plans to market a high-quality frozen croissant even though it got high scores in consumer taste tests.

"The problem was that people didn't know when to eat it," says Thomas R. McBurney, a Pillsbury vice president. "The reaction was, 'It sure tastes good, but I don't know what it is. Do I eat it for dinner or breakfast?' " Pillsbury decided not to undertake the expense of trying to educate the public about croissant consumption.[5]

CONSERVATISM IN NEW PRODUCT DEVELOPMENT

To avoid disasters like Appleasy, Corfam, Oven Crock baked beans, and similar products, new product development has become more conservative. Soaring costs, government regulation, and lack of governmental support for basic research have added to the conservatism. Performance demands are higher; products stay in research and testing longer; and products must pay back their investments much earlier than in the 1970s—sometimes in only one-third to one-half the time. Roger R. Robins, executive vice-president of Purex, says: "In the last year, on the basis of high capital risk, I turned down new products at least twice as often as I did a year ago. But in every case, I tell my people to go back and bring me some new product ideas."[6] RCA stopped designing and manufacturing its own videotape recorder because of the risks involved, and now sells Matsushita's product. Rockwell International Corporation found that its newly acquired Admiral Group Division could not compete in price with Japanese television manufacturers because the Admiral plant was full of outdated manufacturing and testing equipment. They got out of the television business, despite the fact that Rockwell executives thought that they had a superior product.

The risk is usually much less in a line extension than with a new product, so many new product managers take the conservative approach rather than risk a completely new product. If a product has strong brand identification, a large market share, and a substantial advertising budget, a line extension will have a better than average chance for success. In 1976 there were 10 items under the Tylenol brand; by 1979, the list had grown to 19. There were several liquid forms, tablets, extra strength liquids and tablets, and five Co-Tylenol products.

THE SUCCESS OF INDUSTRIAL GOODS

Table 9.1 shows that 42 percent of both industrial and consumer product firms had success ratios of 70 percent or better. Yet industrial firms had fewer replies in the "no success" category. A study of industrial goods organizations found 11 key factors that determined success. In order of importance, these were

> Introducing a unique but superior product
> Having market knowledge and marketing proficiency
> Having technical and production synergy and proficiency
> Avoiding dynamic markets with many new product introductions
> Being in a large, high-need growth market
> Avoiding introducing a high-priced product with no economic advantage

Having a good "product/company fit" with respect to managerial and marketing resources

Avoiding a competitive market with satisfied customers

Avoiding products "new to the firm"

Having a strong marketing communications and launch effort

Having a market-derived idea with considerable investment involved.[7]

The keys to successful new product development may seem obvious: bring out a superior product and understand the marketplace. Yet many companies ignore these fundamental tenets. Failure usually results from the lack of, or poor, marketing research. Other common reasons are technical problems in the design of products and mistakes in timing the product's introduction. For example, a cough drop manufacturer recently brought out a new "ice-blue" line extension cough drop of a well-known brand. The product met with only moderate success, partially because of poor timing. It was introduced in the Midwest and on the East Coast in mid-May, after the "cold and flu" season.

Management of new product development

To increase the chances of success, a sound new product development structure must be created within the company. There are several approaches management can take. One is to create a department or committee to manage the development process. Or, new product ideas may be the responsibility of a single individual—the new products manager. In some organizations it is the new products manager who develops new concepts, tests the ideas, and, if new products result, turns them over to a product manager after they have been introduced into the market. This format is common in medium-size and larger companies. In other companies, such as Texas Instruments and Westinghouse, product managers are responsible for developing line extensions and items related to their basic product responsibilities. Product managers are typically required to obtain the approval of top management or a group product manager before turning an idea over to research and development or marketing research. It is usually the function of the product manager to monitor the concept through the development process.

NEW PRODUCT COMMITTEES

Often product managers or a new product manager cannot handle the product development load as the organization grows. Ideally, information should be obtained from the marketing, engineering, production, and finance areas before making product decisions. Although committees provide more of this information, they may also obscure individual responsibility, take a long time to reach decisions, and include people with interests that are too far removed from company operations to be effective. So committees have both advantages and disadvantages for new product development.

Some advantages of the new product committee structure may be summarized as follows:

1. Ideas and expertise of key executives may be pooled.
2. Decisions are likely to be accepted by the firm, since they were made by individuals from various departments.
3. The committee may be organized and used when needed.
4. The members may be recruited for special purposes—that is, brainstorming for new product ideas or for the entire new product development process.

Some disadvantages of this structure are these:

1. Committee activity takes valuable executive time; members may avoid involvement so they can return to regular responsibilities.
2. This type of committee structure lacks clear lines of authority and responsibility that may result in "buck passing."
3. New product planning and development in many instances should be a full-time job and not occur only when there is a need.
4. Members of the committee tend to concern themselves only with their departmental objectives, rather than with the firm's goals, resulting in a narrow view of the committee's purpose.
5. If the committee exists only on a part-time or as-needed basis, the members are not fully knowledgeable about the new product decision-making process.[8]

NEW PRODUCT DEPARTMENTS

To overcome the problems inherent in committees, some firms have established product development departments that include members from the key functional areas listed earlier. One study revealed that of 2000 large firms in several industries, 869 had formal new product departments.[9] Ideally, people selected for the new department can still communicate effectively with their peers in the operating departments. Also, a formal department means that authority and responsibilities are well defined and given to specific individuals.

Typical of the major responsibilities of a department are recommending new product objectives and programs, planning explorative studies, evaluating concepts and ideas for new products, coordinating testing, and directing interdepartmental teams. The new product department can be situated in one of several places within the organization (see Figure 9.1). It can be a separate line department with functional authority to develop new products. This structure frees the development department from undue influence from production, marketing, and other groups. It also vests the department with the authority to "get things done" in the development structure. The new product development manager relies less on people outside his or her sphere of influence. As a high-level staff activity, new product development usually has the strong support of top management. As a staff function, however, it must go through other functional areas to carry out various activities. For example, the department must rely on marketing to conduct the marketing research, production to build the prototypes, and finance to develop financial statements. These activities must be carried out without direct control by new product development in the staff structure.

◢ FIGURE 9.1 Alternative methods of organizing a new product department in a nondivisionalized company.

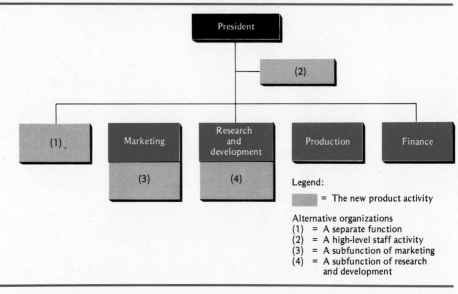

Legend:

▨ = The new product activity

Alternative organizations
(1) = A separate function
(2) = A high-level staff activity
(3) = A subfunction of marketing
(4) = A subfunction of research and development

Source: Edgar A. Pessemier, *Product Management: Strategy and Organization* (New York: Wiley), p. 417. Used by permission.

If a company is highly consumer-oriented, it may elect to place new product development within the marketing function. This organizational form may result in products highly attuned to the customers' needs. On the other hand, production and financial considerations may not receive the attention they deserve. Production management, for example, may feel left out of the planning process and may be less than enthusiastic about estimating production runs, developing prototypes, and so forth. The final alternative is to make the new product development department part of research and development. This is quite common in the chemicals, pharmaceuticals, and electronics industries, where basic research is a well-funded and vital part of the organization. Having new product development and basic research grouped together can provide significant advantages. When the two groups work and communicate in close proximity, new product development can suggest areas where basic research can provide the potential for major commercial successes. Sandoz Pharmaceuticals has done very well with this form of organization.

NEW PRODUCT VENTURE MANAGEMENT

A relatively new form of organization that is easily adapted to committee or department organization is **venture management.** A venture group is an entrepreneurial, market-oriented, multidisciplinary group comprising a small number of representatives from marketing, technology, and finance, focused on a

▲ **FIGURE 9.2 The venture team concept: a conceptual diagram.**

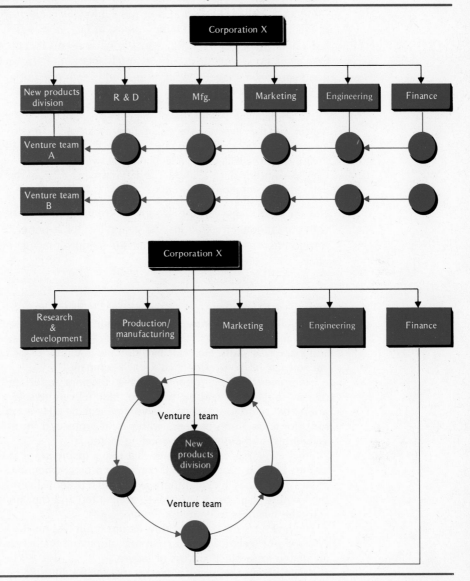

Source: Adapted from Richard M. Hill and James D. Hlavacek, ''The Venture Team: A New Concept in Marketing Organization,'' *Journal of Marketing* 36 (July 1972): 47. By permission of the American Marketing Association.

single objective—planning their company's profitable entry into a new business (see Figure 9.2).

Venture groups are most frequently used to handle important business and product tasks that (1) do not fit neatly into the existing organization, (2) demand more financial resources and longer times to mature than existing organiza-

261

MANAGEMENT OF NEW PRODUCT DEVELOPMENT

tional units can typically provide, and (3) require imaginative entrepreneurship that is neither sheltered nor inhibited by large organizations.

General Mills, Du Pont, 3M, and Union Carbide have achieved mixed results from venture group experiments. In fact, corporate venturing generally has a poor track record. What went wrong? It seems that good product or brand managers, good engineers, or top-notch accountants do not necessarily make good venture managers. What is needed is entrepreneurial talent. As one corporate president says:

I have an unfailing test for identifying entrepreneurial types. I throw every candidate right in with the alligators. The establishment man complains he can't farm alligators in a swamp. The entrepreneur farms 60% of the alligators, markets another 30% for everything but their squeal, drains their part of the swamp, and leases the land for an amusement park overlooking "Alligatorland." The other 10% of the alligators? That's his delayed compensation.[10]

Not only do many venture groups lack entrepreneurs; they are also saddled with bureaucratic frustrations and generally lack experience with new product development. An example of successful venture management is the 3M Company.

At 3M, assuming there is a worthwhile basis for initiating a new business venture, an entrepreneur is named to prove the business concept. He "hires" the people he needs from the technical and marketing staffs. He finds facilities. He is Venture Manager, counterpart of the president of a small company.

He proves that his products (a) have customer appeal and utility, (b) can be made by feasible processes, and (c) can be sold at prices that build future profits as volume expands. He establishes roots for a long-term business with patent protection, technical know-how, and pioneering marketing methods.

Small new product companies that thrive (many never make it) assume the status of an official corporate project when management has satisfied itself (a) there is desirable potential and (b) the Venture Manager is sufficiently committed and capable to carry the business to its full potential.

The new product manager now assumes full responsibility and authority for technical, manufacturing, and marketing. He is accountable for project success or failure.

At 3M, we house technical and marketing people side by side. We send scientists and engineers into the market. We involve marketers in testing and using products. We do all we can to get each to appreciate the other's viewpoint.[11]

NEW PRODUCT DEVELOPMENT ORGANIZATION

Critical factors for new product organization are (1) freedom from bureaucratic constraints, (2) an entrepreneurial atmosphere, (3) input from all functional areas, and (4) extensive top-management involvement and commitment. The firms that are most successful in new product activities are generally those in which top management is involved in both the formulation and implementation of new product strategy. Conversely, in less successful firms top management is only nominally involved or limits its interest to financial targets, the approval of overall new product budgets, and formal financial performance review.[12]

The new product development process

OBJECTIVES

Management's objective in formalizing the product development process is to maximize potential return from the total product mix in light of the firm's resources. In a study of new product objectives of 35 high-technology firms in the United States, researchers found that most companies expressed them in a financial context. Gillette's chairman and president, Colman M. Mockler, Jr., told stockholders that "in considering new products [we] are applying stringent criteria on investment, profit margins and potential size of market. These factors are carefully weighed against the degree of risk involved."[13] Several common techniques are used to rank investment alternatives financially. Perhaps the one used most often after simple sales and profit estimates is payback.

Payback. The **payback** period is the number of years it takes the firm to recover its original investment in a new product by net returns before depreciation but after taxes. Assume that a company is considering two new products and that each has a developmental cost of $300,000. Net returns forecasted for each product are as follows:

Year	Product A	Product B
1	$150,000	$ 40,000
2	105,000	60,000
3	55,000	80,000
4	25,000	120,000
5	5,000	200,000

As you can see, product A has the quickest payback—three years. It pays back half the original investment the first year, another $105,000 the second year, and the remainder in year 3. The shorter the payback period, the quicker the firm recovers its original investment. Product B has a payback of four years, taking a year longer to recoup the original new product investment. If payback were the only criteria, the firm would choose product A. As you can see, however, this could be a mistake.

Payback ignores the cash flows after the breakeven point is reached. Product A, a faddish item, has a very short life cycle. Product B, on the other hand, reveals continued growth from year 1. Projects with longer payback periods traditionally are part of long-range planning, for many new products do not yield their highest returns for a number of years. Payback also ignores the magnitude of the original cost. In our example, both products had developmental expenses of $300,000. But what if product A's development cost had been $25,000 and product B's $4 million? The firm may have selected product A simply because of lack of funds or unwillingness to risk $4 million.

Payback does have some good points. It can be argued that paybacks of three or four years or longer are so uncertain that it is better not to consider them at all. In our simple example, we assumed that each year's cash flow was equally likely to materialize. Also, a company that has limited development funds must necessarily concentrate on products that offer a quick return.

Return on investment. **Return on investment (ROI)** is another tool commonly used to evaluate new product alternatives. It can be used as a yardstick to discover which products offer the highest returns. These are then compared with the cost of capital for the firm. **Cost of capital** is the weighted average of the various types of funds the company uses, such as bonds and common stock. The ROI formula is as follows:

$$\text{Percentage return on investment} = \frac{\text{Average earnings after taxes and depreciation}}{\text{Average investment}}$$

If product X has average earnings of $15,000 per year and an average investment of $105,000, then estimated ROI would be $15,000/$105,000 or 14.3 percent. Return on investment calculations can vary substantially depending upon the depreciation and tax criteria used. Obviously the same policies must be in force when comparing two new product alternatives, or the comparison will be "apples and oranges" instead of "two apples."

Return on investment requires that costs and revenues be projected for the estimated life of the product. To avoid too much long-range guessing, some marketing managers calculate ROI for fixed time periods—for example, at the end of the first, third, and fifth years. The major problem with this simple formula is that it does not account for the time value of money. Two products may have identical rates of return, but different investment and cash flow periods. One product may have a high initial investment and become profitable eight years after introduction; a second product with the same ROI may have a moderate initial investment and profitability the first year. The latter product would certainly be more desirable because of the lower initial outlay and faster dollar returns because these dollars can then be reinvested or used in the business again.

Net present value. Let us carry the evaluation of new products one step further using the net present value approach. **Net present value** accounts for the time value of money. Assume one product would return $1 million tomorrow and another product would return $1 million five years from now. If everything else is the same, the first product is more desirable. Would you rather have $1000 today or 20 years from now? If you took that $1000 today and invested it at 18 percent per year, the compounded value would be $27,393 at the end of 20 years! The longer it takes to receive money in the future, the less it is worth today. This is the notion of present value, usually called discounting.

	Product M			Product N		
Year	Net cash flow	If (14%)	PV of cash flow	Net cash flow	If (14%)	PV of cash flow
1	$ 50,000	.88	$ 44,000	$ 10,000	.88	$ 8,800
2	40,000	.77	30,800	20,000	.77	15,400
3	30,000	.71	21,300	30,000	.71	21,300
4	10,000	.64	6,400	40,000	.64	25,600
5	5,000	.57	2,850	50,000	.57	28,500
	$135,000			$150,000		
PV of inflows			$105,350			$ 99,600
Less cost			−10,000			−10,000
Net present value			$ 95,350			$ 89,600

Assume that we have two products, M and N, and each has a five-year life span. The cost of both projects is $10,000, and the cost of capital to the firm is 14 percent. The expected cash flows and present values are shown in Table 9.2. The actual dollar cash flows for products M and N are $135,000 and $150,000, respectively. Without considering the time value of money, the firm should go with product N. However, Table 9.2 shows that M's largest cash flows occur soon after the product is launched, and N's major cash flows occur later in the life cycle. The net present value of M is $5750 greater than N. Why? Again, because $1 received and reinvested today is worth more than $1 received and reinvested tomorrow.

STEPS IN THE NEW PRODUCT DEVELOPMENT PROCESS

Now that you are familiar with the common financial tools used to rank new product alternatives, we can examine the actual steps in the **product development process.** After financial and other objectives are established, the formal evaluation process begins. The specific stages may be referred to as opportunity exploration; screening; developing a preliminary profit plan; product, strategy, and communications development; test marketing; and market introduction. Figure 9.3 depicts the product development process.

The importance of input from many areas cannot be overemphasized. Figure 9.3 shows key information input levels for production, engineering, and finance. It is assumed that marketing has primary responsibility for new product activity. For example, at the goal-setting level, financial success criteria, marketing segmentation objectives, and product efficiency requirements all serve as inputs into the development of new product objectives. When ideas are first evaluated, finance officers provide rough screening criteria, such as maximum investment demands. Engineering will give an estimate of technical feasibility. Similar types of inputs will continue throughout development. Marketing often serves as the focus for new product development, but it requires an integrated team to achieve long-run success.

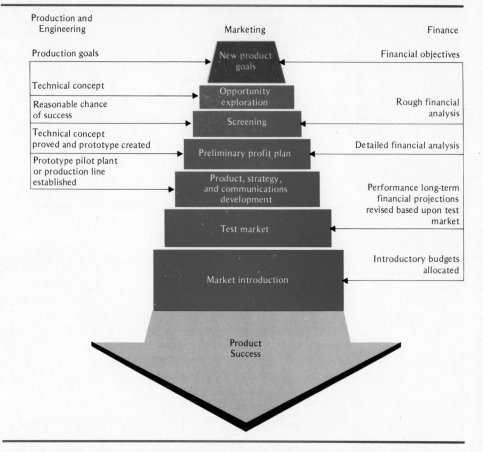

Opportunity exploration. The first task, after establishing objectives, is opportunity exploration. This is the process of obtaining new ideas or concepts for products. Smaller firms usually depend on employees, customers, investors, and distributors for new ideas. But the sporadic nature of informal idea gathering has led most major companies and many of the progressive smaller firms to use brainstorming and focus groups.

Perhaps you have participated in a brainstorming session at one time or another. The goal of **brainstorming** is to have the group think of as many ways to vary a product or solve a problem as possible. Criticism is avoided, no matter how ridiculous the idea seems at the time. The emphasis is on sheer quantity of ideas, with objective evaluation postponed to later steps of development. Approximately 25 years ago, one of the product attributes a brainstorming session conceived for carpet sweepers was "color." Until that time all sweepers had been black or dull gray. By introducing a line of pastel "decorator" colors, Bissell was able to reverse a declining sales trend.

Focus groups are a widely accepted tool for generating concepts. A manufacturer of small electrical appliances used focus groups composed of homemakers to find out what appliances were most helpful in the kitchen, what functions still had to be done by hand, what tasks they would like to see handled by new appliances, and what existing products were least efficient. Similarly, a baby food manufacturer found that its market was stabilizing and decided to determine the feasibility of producing individual servings of food for the elderly. Focus groups were used to explore the eating habits and food preferences of senior citizens. New product strategies were conceived on the basis of the information supplied by the focus groups.

Screening. As ideas emerge, they are checked against the firm's new product goals and long-range strategies, a procedure called **screening.** Many product concepts are rejected because of poor product fit, unavailable technology, lack of company resources, and low market potential. (There is considerable market potential for a safe, fast-acting weight-reducing product. Much less potential exists for a dog collar with a built-in radio.)

Most ideas are eliminated at this stage as obvious misfits. Frito-Lay considered developing a powdered soft drink but dropped the idea because it didn't fit their snack food product mix. A judicious job of screening is very important, since concepts that go beyond this stage receive careful scrutiny and a considerable investment of time and company resources.

Concept tests are often used at the screening stage to evaluate concept alternatives. Focus groups not only aid in concept development, but are also used to screen ideas. Concept and blind product tests have been fairly good predictors of early trial and repeat purchases for line extensions. They have also been fairly accurate for new products that are not "me-too" items but are not easily classified into existing product categories and do not require major changes in consumer behavior, such as Betty Crocker Tuna Helper, Cycle dog food, and Libby Fruit Float.[14] Concept and early product tests have not been accurate in predicting the success of new products that create new consumption patterns and require major changes in consumer behavior, such as microwave ovens, videocassette recorders, computers, and word processors.

The preliminary profit plan. If a product concept makes it through the screening stage, a preliminary profit plan is developed (see Table 9.3.). Rough performance statements are drawn up, and ROI, net present value, and payback are calculated, along with other financial measures. This requires not only general sales estimates, but production costs, financing charges, developmental expenses, and so forth.

Technical development can often be an expensive proposition. Bayer, for example, in pursuing a concept for an active new pharmaceutical ingredient, estimates that it must synthesize and test 10,000 compounds.

Product, strategy, and communications development. If the concept passes the preliminary profit plan stage, it is ready for the main part of the developmental process. Product, strategy, and communications development begin simultaneously, not in sequence. Promotion, for example, does not wait until the

PROJECT ___X___   Page 1 of 2

PROPOSAL _____ TITLE _____ Connector _____

PROJECT, PROPOSAL NO.: __1234__ EVALUATED BY: _____HHH_____ ON: __March 11, 1981__

CUSTOMER: _____ MARKET: __Commercial__ PRODUCT: __Electronic__

(1) Projections
(a) Sales

	1st YEAR 19 __82__	2nd YEAR 19 __83__	3rd YEAR 19 __84__	4th YEAR 19 ___	5th YEAR 19 ___
Sales of new product	$ 200,000	$ 300,000	$ 100,000	$	$
Lost sales of replaced product	40,000	29,000	—		
Net added sales	$ 160,000	$ 280,000	$ 100,000	$	$
Average sales per year (1)	$ 180,000	$	$	$	$

(b) Gross Profit Margin

Estimated product cost	$ 3.50 / Ea.	Source	Product Estimate 8775
Predicted selling price	$ 9.00 / Ea.	Source	Sales Forecast by J.D.
Added sales of exist. prod.	$ — /	Source	

Gross margin $(MG) = \dfrac{(9.00 - 8.50)}{9.00} = .61$

(c) Derating Factors

Probability of marketing success	.80	Source	Sales Forecast by J.D.
Prob'y. of Eng. success	.70	Source	Eng'g. Estimate 6789
Life expectancy—years 3	.75	Source	Forecast—Std. Derating
Combined derating factor (Sc)	.42		

(d) Project Costs

	High Estimate	Low Estimate		
Engineering development	$ 10,000	4,000	Source	Eng'g. Estimate 6789
Production tooling	$ 14,000	8,000	Source	Product Estimate 8775
Inventory	$ 3,000	3,000	Source	
	$ —	—	Source	
Total project costs (C)	$ 27,000	15,000		

(2) Management Control Factors

Sales volume	.9	Less than preferred volume
Engineering capability	1.0	
Marketing capability	1.0	
Facilities capability	.9	Need Special Molding Press
Market direction	.8	Special Application
Combined mgt. control factor	.65	

TABLE 9.3 (*continued*)

Explanatory Notes for Evaluation Form

PROJECTIONS

Sales

Sales of new product. Four years is considered to be the "norm."

Lost sales of replaced product. This is a factor in cases where an existing product is to be replaced by the new product.

Average sales per year. Summation of total net added sales divided by the number of years for which these sales are estimated (1, 2, 3, or 4 years).

Gross Profit Margin

Estimated product cost. A "target" cost is obtained from the marketing organization.

Predicted selling price. This is obtained from the marketing organization.

Added sales of existing products. In some cases, the sale of a new product will cause the additional sales of one or more existing products.

Derating Factors

(1) *Probability of marketing success.* Rating scale in which 1.00 is perfect. Factor is an expression of confidence in the estimate of average sales per year.

(2) *Probability of engineering success.* Rating scale in which 1.00 is perfect. Factor is an expression of confidence in the ability to produce the item at the specified cost or lower, and to meet or exceed technical requirements.

(3) *Life expectancy—years.* Four rating factors as follows:

4 years life expectancy = 1.00
3 years life expectancy = .75
2 years life expectancy = .50
1 year life expectancy = .25

Combined derating factor. (1) $\times$ (2) $\times$ (3).

MANAGEMENT CONTROL FACTORS

The following factors are each rated on a scale in which 1.00 has been assumed as the norm for purpose of illustration only.

(1) *Sales volume.* Reduced if estimated sales volume of the new product appears to be outside a predetermined, optimum range. This optimum sales volume varies from product to product.

(2) *Engineering capability.* Reduced if the new product should for some reason fall outside the company's current engineering capabilities.

(3) *Marketing capability.* Reduced if the new product could not be marketed through the company's existing marketing organization.

(4) *Facilities capability.* Reduced if the proposed product should require additional capital facilities.

(5) *Market direction.* A rating expressing the relative desirability of the market in which the proposed product would be sold. The company sells to a number of major markets, each of which is rated according to its relative attractiveness. The relative attractiveness of a particular market may change from time to time, and this change is reflected in the assigned rating factor.

Combined management control factor. (1) $\times$ (2) $\times$ (3) $\times$ (4) $\times$ (5).

Source: The Conference Board, *Evaluating New Product Proposals* (New York: The Conference Board, 1973), pp. 30–31.

product is fully developed. An ideal new product development flow chart is shown in Figure 9.4.

The type and amount of additional product testing will vary, depending on how easy it is to manufacture the item and its impact upon consumer usage patterns. If Seven Seas is testing a new salad dressing flavor, it will go directly into advanced taste tests and perhaps extended home use tests. However, if Seven Seas decided to develop a new line of soft drinks requiring new production facilities, it would most likely engage in extensive product concept testing, examining numerous attributes of the product before actually making it.

The marketing strategy is being refined as product concept testing and use testing take place. Channels of distribution are selected. Pricing policies are developed and tested. Target market characteristics and demand estimates are de-

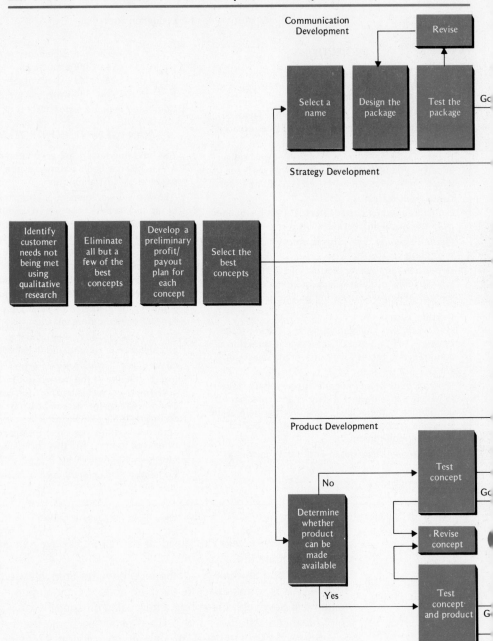

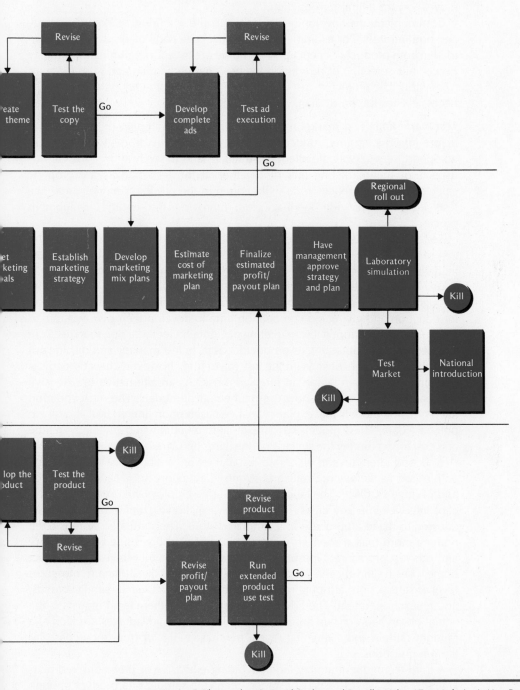

Source: Jay E. Klompmaker, G. David Hughes, and Russell J. Haley, "Test Marketing in New Product Development," *Harvard Business Review,* May–June 1976, pp. 132–133. Copyright © 1976 by the President and Fellows of Harvard College; all rights reserved.

termined. Management also continually updates the profit plan as the product moves toward actual introduction.

Communications development feeds into the maturing marketing strategy and product tests. For example, logo and package copy themes can be examined in both product concept tests and home use tests. Communication strategy also entails selection of promotion themes, the media mix, and sales force introduction. The projected cost of the communication strategy is then revised, if necessary, for the profit plan.

Test marketing. **Test marketing** is the final chance to "tie up the loose ends" before introducing the product nationally or regionally. It gives management an opportunity to evaluate alternate strategies and to see how well the various aspects of the marketing mix fit together. If the test markets are properly selected, they will reflect what will happen in the product's market area. The tests can also provide feedback for improving the entire development process.

Test marketing is not cheap. Other problems besides costs include (1) the loss of the surprise element, (2) the difficulty of selecting "representative" test markets, (3) the possibility of having the company name associated with a "dud," (4) the chance that a test market will be sabotaged by competitors through increased promotion or lower prices, (5) the need to delay production introduction and giving the competition time to develop their own version. In 1980, Carnation skipped test marketing of Come'n Get It dry dog food because competitors were obtaining its product ideas from test markets and rushing out with their own versions. Without test marketing, however, the company is gambling rather than taking an intelligent risk. As an alternative to extensive test marketing, some firms now use mathematical models. The most common are regression models that explain variance based upon limited trial and repeat purchase data. These models have the greatest reliability and efficiency in time and cost for predicting the success of line items and "me-too" type products.[15]

A second alternative to elaborate test marketing is laboratory tests. Two examples are Yankelovich, Skelly and Whites' Laboratory Test Market and Elrick and Lavidge's COMP. The laboratory technique employs the use of mall intercept interviews in key cities. Respondents are shown commercials and then allowed to make a purchase in a simulated store. The simulated store is often nothing more than a room in the mall with metal shelves lined with grocery and other supermarket-type products. The consumer then takes the product home, uses it, and receives a callback interview. The questionnaire measures level of satisfaction, attribute ratings of the test product versus similar brands, and repurchase intent. The advantage over some mathematical models is the actual observation of purchase behavior. The two disadvantages are lack of a random sample and estimating repeat purchase behavior from repurchase intention questions.

A third technique that may aid in avoiding extensive or premature test marketing is **sales waves tests.** Consumers receive a sample of a product through an in-home placement. Over a period of time, they are offered an opportunity to purchase additional units of the product. By requiring actual purchase of the concept/product, it is assumed that consumer usage will approximate adoption and retrial rates. One major drawback of sales waves research is the extended time sometimes required for repurchase. An excellent example of product development and the use of sales waves is presented below.

Heinz, despite its successes in the marketing of tomato products (its ketchup holds a 40 percent share and keeps growing), had rung up a "singularly undistinguished" record in the new products field in recent years. Great American soup, Happy soup, Heinz salad dressings, and Help fruit drink were all aimed at large, well developed, highly competitive categories where consumer satisfaction with existing products was rather high. The company steered away from this type of product on its latest try.

This was a significant move, because large, growing markets are an irresistible temptation for most companies. They are dynamic, they are visible, and they are talked about in advertising circles.

With this kind of logic, Heinz began analyzing some dull, static, relatively uncompetitive categories because it was their hypothesis that poor category trends were symptomatic of either weak competition or basic consumer dissatisfaction with existing products. They felt that the dullest category in the eyes of most marketers was perhaps the ripest for innovation. Their search led to chili and gravy products. The steps Heinz took were as follows:

1. Competing products were taste tested with consumers.
2. Consumer focus group sessions were held which revealed high levels of dissatisfaction with existing products. In both categories, there were large percentages of consumers who were still preparing gravy and chili from scratch.
3. Following further study by the market research department, the company defined the gravy (packed in resealable glass jars) and chili (all ingredients except the meat) product concepts.
4. Small and then large concept tests were conducted.
5. Tests of various recipes were done, again, as in the previous steps, with company marketing, market research, and R&D people working in close cooperation.
6. Examination was made of a number of market forecasting research techniques, and Data Development Corp.'s Sales Waves was chosen (the Yankelovich Laboratory Test Market, the company felt, would be more appropriate at a later stage of the effort).
7. Sales waves were generated at intervals. Heinz felt that at the end of the third wave a reasonably stable core group of loyal purchasers began to emerge.

Interestingly, Heinz's later test market results paralleled Sales Waves numbers perfectly. This information was key in minimizing factory production and inventory costs for test market.

Second, they learned specifically how the product was used.

Heinz learned what percent of volume is used as is, versus in recipes; they learned the time of day the product was used; they learned what recipes the product was used with, and they even learned what percentage of volume was served hot versus cold.

Third, they learned about package size and the number of units consumed per usage occasion. They also found, too, whether an additional size might be appropriate.

Finally, Heinz discovered the demographics of their hard-core loyal user. Keep in mind that by the end of the test, the number of respondents was relatively small, but Heinz did get pretty clear direction in terms of their target user. The ultimate result? Heinz Homestyle gravies, Chili Fixins, and Heinz basic white sauce.[16]

Market introduction. The final step, as in the Heinz chili and gravies, is market introduction. New product development is a long, costly process. One study revealed that 58 ideas are required to yield one new product (see Figure 9.5).[17] Is it worth it? The answer is yes. It definitely pays to develop a good, sound program for new product development. Firms with relatively unsophisticated approaches to new product decision making have lower average profitability than those with more sophisticated approaches.[18]

The expense at this point of development is minimal compared to introduction costs. Salespeople must be trained; complete promotion campaigns have to be developed; production facilities must be built; distribution channels have to be supplied with inventory; and sometimes parts must be produced and distributed. Gillette's Good News razor was launched with a $6 million promotion campaign, not counting free samples.

◢ **FIGURE 9.5 Mortality of new product ideas (by stage of evolution — 51 companies).**

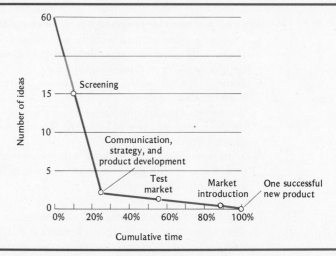

Source: Booz, Allen and Hamilton, Inc., Management Research Department, modified by author. By permission.

Often products are "rolled out" regionally rather than nationally. Production and inventory requirements are simply beyond the capacity of smaller companies. Logistics and capital requirements occasionally force even the largest firms to follow this strategy. In large firms, a national roll out may require a significant amount of logistical coordination. Various divisions, for example, must be encouraged to give the new item the attention it deserves. If it is to be sold internationally, the new product may have to be altered to meet the power and design requirements of other countries. Different packaging and labeling may also be required. Sales training sessions must be scheduled, spare parts inventoried, service personnel trained, advertising and promotion campaigns readied, and wholesalers and retailers informed of the new item. As you can see, roll out is not a quiet and simple task after a long and trying development period.

A FINAL NOTE ON NEW PRODUCT DEVELOPMENT

In today's marketplace, economic criteria are necessary but not totally sufficient factors for new product decision making. The social dimensions of new product strategy must also be considered. Among the factors to be examined are these: (1) environmental and production compatibility, (2) environmental and user compatibility, (3) recycling potential, and (4) social and moral impact. If corporations do not consider social criteria, they may find themselves with a declining market—the product legislated off the market (unsafe children's toys and ineffective products), or restricted marketing mix options. For example, cigarette manufacturers cannot advertise on television or radio. (We will return to this topic in much greater detail in Chapter 23.)

SUMMARY

Without new products, many firms simply cease to grow. Often, new products are introduced in response to consumer need rather than in response to a new scientific or technological discovery. Failure ratios in the mid-1970s averaged 40 to 50 percent, and in some industries as high as 84 percent. However, a 1980 survey found only one in three new products failing in the past five years. This is due to sharper pinpointing of responsibility for new products and a better coordination among all business units involved in the new product process. Also, there are new tools for success prediction and more highly trained individuals in new product development.

Because new product failures can be very expensive, and in some cases destroy the firm, new product development has become quite conservative. Soaring costs, government regulation, and lack of governmental support for basic research have added to this conservatism. New product development tends to be more successful in the industrial area than in the consumer area. The keys to successful new product development are bringing out a superior product and a thorough understanding of the marketplace.

Management of new product development in small companies is handled by one individual or by a new product committee. In larger organizations, companies may utilize new product departments. Typical responsibilities include recommending objectives and programs, planning exploratory studies, evaluating concepts and ideas for new products, coordinating testing, and directing interdepartmental teams. Other organizations have created formal new product development organizations called venture groups that are responsible for the new product development process.

Management's objective in formalizing the product development process is to maximize potential return from the total product mix in light of the firm's resources. Common financial tools used as new product measures include payback, return on investment, and net present value. After financial and other objectives are established, the formal evaluation process begins. The specific stages are opportunity exploration, screening, developing a preliminary profit plan, product strategy and communications development, test marketing, and market introduction. Although marketing may have primary responsibility for new product activity, it is actually an integrated management team that creates successful new products.

KEY TERMS

Line extension
Venture management
Payback
Return on investment (ROI)
Cost of capital
Net present value

Product development process
Brainstorming
Focus group
Screening
Test marketing
Sales waves tests

REVIEW QUESTIONS

1. Why is the continued development of new products important to the firm? What stimulates the quest for new products?
2. Why has the new product success rate improved in recent years?
3. List the various approaches to new product development and assess the merits and shortcomings of each.
4. Discuss the stages of product evolution and the role of production, engineering, and finance in the development and commercialization of new products.
5. Identify the various methods used by most companies to generate new product ideas.
6. Why is the estimation of future sales, costs, and profits the crucial determinant of new product development and commercialization? How does the firm go about approximating these key variables?
7. How does degree of risk influence product innovation and the required financial return?

DISCUSSION QUESTIONS

1. Explain the role and importance of market research to new product development and successful commercialization of the item.
2. How can ROI analysis and the net present value concept aid in the selection of new product candidates?
3. Discuss the sunk costs associated with the various stages of new product evolution.
4. Several recent studies among large manufacturers of consumer products have shown companies reporting new product success rates over the last five to ten years as high as 100 percent and seldom lower than 30 to 40 percent. In comparing these rates to

the results from more general studies, how would you explain the apparent discrepancy?

5. Discuss the role of research in the new product development process. What types of studies might be done at different points in the process, and what are the objectives of these studies?

6. What are the reasons for test marketing? Can you name any infamous product failures that resulted from lack of test marketing?

7. Due to the overnight appearance of product imitators, many innovative firms are becoming increasingly hesitant about introducing new products. Do you agree or disagree? What should the innovative firm do to discourage imitators?

NOTES

1. Henry R. Berstein, "Heublein: New Product for New Demographics," *Advertising Age,* March 31, 1980, pp. 62–65. Reprinted with permission. Copyright 1980 by Crain Communications, Inc.

2. "Survey Finds 67% of New Products Succeed," *Marketing News,* February 8, 1980, p. 1.

3. "Disastrous Debuts—Despite High Hopes, Many New Products Flop in the Market," *The Wall Street Journal,* March 23, 1976.

4. "Survey Finds," p. 1.

5. Lawrence Ingrassia, "There's No Way to Tell If a New Food Product Will Please the Public," *The Wall Street Journal,* February 26, 1980, p. 1. Reprinted by permission of *The Wall Street Journal,* © Dow Jones & Company, Inc. 1980. All rights reserved.

6. "The Breakdown of U.S. Innovation," *Business Week,* February 16, 1976, p. 59.

7. R. G. Cooper, "The Dimensions of Industrial New Product Success and Failure," *Journal of Marketing* 43 (summer 1979): 93–103.

8. Advantages and disadvantages from Robert D. Hisrich and Michael P. Peters, *Marketing a New Product: Its Planning, Development and Control* (Menlo Park, Calif.: The Benjamin/Cummings Publishing Company, 1979), p. 422. Reprinted by permission.

9. Booz, Allen and Hamilton, *Management of New Products* (Chicago, 1968), p. 20.

10. Mack Hanan, "Venturing Corporations—Think Small to Stay Strong," *Harvard Business Review,* May–June 1976, pp. 139–148. Reprinted by permission. Copyright © 1976 by the President and Fellows of Harvard College; all rights reserved.

11. Robert M. Adams, "How 3M Builds Idea-Nurturing Work Climate," *Marketing Times* 15 (March–April 1978): 13–14. Reprinted from *Marketing Times,* business update for the management professional, published by Sales and Marketing Executives International.

12. Hanan, "Venturing Corporations," p. 140.

13. "Gillette Will Keep Up Its Cost-Conscious Marketing," *Advertising Age,* April 26, 1976, p. 10. Reprinted by permission. Copyright © 1976 by Crain Communications, Inc.

14. E. M. Tauber, "Forecasting New Product Sales Prior to Test Market," *Food Product Development,* April 1977, pp. 68–78.

15. Ibid., p. 77.

16. "Heinz Eyed Orphan Areas, Did Homework on Gravies, Chili Mix," *Marketing News,* November 19, 1976, p. 1.

17. Booz, Allen and Hamilton, p. 9.

18. Albert V. Bruno, "New Product Decision Making in High Technology Firms," *Research Management,* September 1973, pp. 28–31.

9.1 Pampers

Pampers, the disposable diapers, were not thought up overnight. A Procter & Gamble engineer, who also happened to be a grandfather, was babysitting for his first grandchild, a job that included changing diapers. He decided there must be a better way than using cloth diapers. He took his concern back to the corporation and was asked three questions: (1) Was there real consumer need for an alternative method of diapering? (2) Did Procter & Gamble have the scientific and technological ability to develop the product? and (3) Was the potential market of such a product large enough to offer some promise of making a profit?

To confirm that other consumers shared the engineer's need for an alternative diapering method, P&G used consumer research. Thousands of mothers were asked how they diapered their babies and how they felt about their current diapering methods and products. The consumer research showed that mothers found cloth diapers were uncomfortable for their babies. The cloth diapers bunched up, did not keep the babies dry enough, and required plastic pants that could irritate the baby's tender skin.

Procter & Gamble calculated that there were more than 15 billion diaper changes a year in the United States. This was certainly an impressive market—if an effective and efficient alternative method of diapering could be invented. After nine months of research, the product development team came up with a diaper pad for insertion in plastic pants. The pad, which used a special pleat for better fit, was absorbent and flushable. The test market, however, was a disaster. It was test marketed in the South, and while 80 to 90 percent of the babies were wearing elasticized plastic pants, southern parents weren't about to subject their babies to a Turkish bath.

After six months of additional research, another product was created. The plastic pants were replaced by a newly invented thin sheet of plastic across the back that kept the moisture in but allowed some circulation to alleviate the hothouse effect of plastic pants. Another invention allowed fluid to pass through the absorbent material, but prevented most of it from coming back through. This kept babies drier and more comfortable. The new product seemed to solve all the problems consumers had with cloth diapers.

1. What step would you recommend P&G take next?
2. Who should be involved at this point besides marketing? What should their functions be?
3. Would a national roll out be advisable at this time? Why or why not?

9.2 General Pet Products, Inc.

A perennial problem of dog and cat owners is ticks and fleas. General Pet Products manufactures a wide array of pet-grooming nonprescription pet drug items. Sargents and Hartz dominate the pet product market with a 58 percent share, followed by General with a 16 percent share.

General's marketing manager, Wayne Lucas, believed that the time was ripe for increased product diversification in the tick and flea collar market. General, Sargents, Hartz, and several other manufacturers offer a clear or black 90-day dog and cat collar designed to fit all breeds, including Great Danes. Excess collar is simply trimmed off and thrown away. Aside from Sargents' flea tag collar, which contains the pesticide in the tag rather than in the collar itself, there is little product differentiation in this market.

Lucas contracted with Qualitative Dimensions, Inc., to explore dog and cat owners' perceptions and needs in the flea and tick collar market, using focus groups in four cities. A summary of the behavior research follows:

1. Approximately 25 percent of all pets have ticks as well as fleas. Most respondents believe that current products are ineffective for controlling ticks, particularly if they have been in use for more than a month.
2. Buckles on the leading brands are cumbersome.
3. Pet owners have little fear that handling the collars is a health hazard. The directions simply remind people to wash their hands after touching the collar.
4. Flea tags are generally viewed in a mixed light. Owners comment that (1) the tag is more permanent than the collar, (2) little children might grab the disk and put it in their mouths, and (3) the dog might chew it off.
5. Most owners feel that $2 is a reasonable price to pay for an effective 90-day collar.
6. Owners' design ideas include the following: (1) Make a regular collar with a slit so that the flea protection can be put into it when needed; (2) increase the number of sizes.

Respondents were shown three prototype collars that General is considering. The first is the Dry Thermoset, which releases the chemical slowly as the animal's body temperature increases. This collar will last 120 days and only releases the chemical when the pet is active. Owner comments include the following: (1) It's not gummy, but it's heavy and stiff; (2) if it stayed dry it might work better; (3) it's a very masculine collar; (4) it looks scruffy, not neat and petite.

The second prototype is a leather-lined flea collar. Comments include: (1) It must be expensive; (2) why make it permanent unless it is refillable; (3) it must be stronger than the rest; (4) when leather gets wet it will shrink; (5) the plastic chemical strip looks as if it might come off too easily when children play with the dog.

The final prototype is a perforated tag containing a colored pellet. Comments include: (1) I like seeing the pellet in there; (2) I'm impressed with the idea of replacing it when it melts away; (3) it must have a childproof holder; (4) you can probably save money by buying just pellets rather than the whole collar; (5) flea tags are practical — they should not be overly decorative.

1. Should Lucas introduce any of the prototype products in test markets?
2. Do you feel that General is following a logical sequence for new product development? Why or why not?

10

Branding, product responsibility, and packaging

OBJECTIVES

To review the terms associated with branding and examine its legal aspects.

To judge the advantages of branding and gain insight into the "battle of the brands."

To examine brand loyalty and brand switching.

To gain a better understanding of the issues of warranties, product safety, and product liability.

To highlight the strategic importance of packaging and labeling.

A success at R. J. Reynolds Industries, Inc., has created a little problem: Smokers of Camel Lights and Camel Filters are so happy to have Ol' Joe, the one-humped camel, adorning new packs of their cigarettes that they won't buy the old packs.

For 68 years, packs of stubby, unfiltered regular Camels have pictured Ol' Joe, a dromedary who used to travel with the Barnum & Bailey Circus. To exploit the familiarity of Ol' Joe's image, Reynolds decided to expand its use, substituting it for the modern, multi-toned designs with small, stylized camels on packs of Lights and Filters.

Reaction to the change was stronger than the company anticipated. Since the new packs were introduced in early 1981, the old packs have been piling up in supermarkets, and Reynolds is having to take them back.

The change has resulted in a ten percent growth in market share for Camels. The increase in market share is worth millions to R. J. Reynolds.[1]

The Camel's cigarette story shows the tremendous impact a successful brand can have on market share, competition, and profits. It also shows how valuable a brand name or a trademark can be to a firm. In this chapter, we will examine brand names and trademarks and their role in marketing. We begin with the difference between a brand name, a trademark, and a patent, then examine some of the legal aspects of branding and the concept of brand loyalty. We will see how warranties and guarantees add a further dimension to perceived product quality and may aid in developing brand loyalty. For even when formal warranties are not issued with a product, companies face growing responsibility for product liability.

In the final section, we will look at the roles of packaging and labeling in developing a total product. Because the government has recently stepped into the packaging and labeling area, marketing decisions have become even more complicated.

Brands, trademarks, patents

SOME DEFINITIONS

Brand is a broad term used to describe product identification by word, name, symbol, or design, or a combination of these. Manufacturers and middlepeople use brands to identify their goods and distinguish them from others. **Trademark** is a legal term meaning the words, names, or symbols (logotypes) that the law designates as trademarks. A **brand name** is the part of the brand that can be vocalized, such as McDonald's; the golden arches symbol, as well as the name, is the McDonald's trademark. **Service marks** are used to indentify services—an example is H&R Block. **Certification marks** are used to identify goods and services as having met certain qualifications. The Good Housekeeping seal and the UL mark of Underwriters Laboratories signify that a product has met the testing standards of those organizations.

Two other useful terms are copyrights and patents. **Copyrights** concern literary and artistic expression, an original song or a new dress design can be copyrighted. **Patents,** on the other hand, concern inventions that have to do with function or design. A new device for making milk, for example, could be patented. Specifically, the works or the design of the machine would be patented. Figure 10.1 illustrates the major differences between copyrights and patents.

LEGAL ASPECTS OF TRADEMARKS

One of the most important aspects of trademark law is that the mark need not be registered to be protected. According to common law, trademark rights can be acquired by using the mark in marketing a good or service. The Lanham Act of 1946 provides for the registration of marks with the U.S. Patent Office but does not require such registration. (Perhaps one reason people confuse trade-

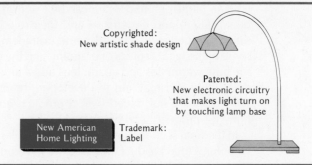

Copyrighted:
New artistic shade design

Patented:
New electronic circuitry
that makes light turn on
by touching lamp base

New American
Home Lighting

Trademark:
Label

marks and patents is that both operations are handled by the Patent Office.) In addition to providing a way of registering trademarks, the Lanham Act specifies what types of marks can be protected and the various remedies available for trademark violations.

Advantages of registration. Any good or service shipped in interstate commerce can have its mark registered as a trademark. The process of registration takes about one year after the application is filed. Once a person or corporation has received federal registration, it has the following advantages:

1. It is constructive notice of the registrant's claim of ownership, applicable nationwide to everyone subsequently adopting marks (a trademark search report should always be obtained before adopting a new mark).
2. It will be listed on search reports obtained by others.
3. It is evidence, although rebuttable, of the registrant's exclusive ownership rights, shifting the burden of proof to anyone challenging those rights, and in some circumstances it can be conclusive evidence of those rights.
4. It gives federal courts jurisdiction to hear infringement and related claims of unfair competition under state law.
5. It can be used as a basis for registration in some foreign countries.
6. It can be recorded with the U.S. Customs Service to prevent importation of infringing foreign goods.

Also, registration allows the use of "Registered U.S. Patent Office," "Reg. U.S. Pat. Off.," or ® as notification to others that the trademark is registered.

The life span of trademarks. Rights to trademarks continue as long as the mark is used. Normally the mark is considered to have been abandoned if the firm does not use it for two years. If a new user picks up the mark after owner abandonment, the new user can claim exclusive ownership of the mark.

Infringement remedies. If two firms happen to be using the same trademark, the first user is considered the rightful owner. This holds true even if the second company registered the mark first. When an organization is convicted of trademark infringement, it faces severe penalties. For example, the injured party can sue for (1) triple the amount of damages actually suffered and (2) any profits the offending firm made from the mark. Federal law also allows for the destruction of all materials bearing the infringing mark. This could be costly if a company has a warehouse full of merchandise bearing the illegal mark.

SELECTING A TRADEMARK

One of the first questions a marketing manager must answer in selecting a name or logo (symbol) for a trademark is whether it will be an arbitrary symbol or name, or something related to product attributes. An example of an arbitrary name that meant nothing is Exxon. Since the original meaning was neutral, Exxon could create the image it wanted. A name or logo associated with petroleum would have limited the use of the name Exxon. On the other hand, a trademark can often help sell a product, such as Lip Quencher lipstick. This trademark promotes a product attribute—its moisturizing ingredients. Examples of other arbitrary trademarks that have been successful are Log Cabin syrup, Yuban Coffee, and Reeds Mints.

Unless a firm wants to create an image, it is usually better to use a trademark suggestive of the product. Most markets are so competitive that products and services need all the help they can get. Close-up toothpaste effectively suggests cleanlinesss and fresh breath. Kool-Aid tells mothers that the product is refreshing and thirst-quenching. Trav-L-File suggests that the product is a lightweight portable filing cabinet. A mark should be easy to spell and pronounce, such as Tide, Milk-Bone, and Now cigarettes. In 1980 Paulan chain saws ran an extensive advertising campaign to explain how to pronounce the brand name. Many consumers have difficulty pronouncing the name of fashion designer (also a brand name) Yves St. Laurent.

A brand name generally should not be associated with a geographic region unless it will enhance the image of the product. Old El Paso Mexican goods uses a geographic identity to further its image. Western Airlines, although still primarily a western carrier, now serves a much broader territory. Perhaps it has outgrown or is outgrowing its name.

Surnames should be avoided when selecting a trademark. As a general rule, anyone having that surname is free to use it in connection with his or her products or services. Lays potato chips and Wilson sporting goods are two examples that violate this rule. Trademarks that are confusingly similar to those of existing products should also be avoided. Wyler's Country Prize lemonade mix was sued for trademark infringement by General Foods. Research revealed that customers were confusing the Wyler product with General Food's Country Time lemonade. Wyler lost and now calls its lemonade Borden Prize. Faberge, determined to use the trademark Macho for its new men's cologne, purchased a small California cosmetic company for $200,000 just to get the brand name.

PROTECTING A TRADEMARK

Despite the severe penalties for violating someone else's trademark, many companies seem to be in a constant battle to protect their mark. Not only must companies fight "me-too" brand names, but also the problem of becoming generic. Some better known trademarks that have fought the "me-too" problem recently include Playboy, Ocean Spray, Ultra-Brite, Tylenol, Scrabble, Prime Choice, Chanel No. 5, Tic Tac candy, and Lysol. Sometimes the problem goes beyond similar-sounding names to actual counterfeiting. Walt Disney estimates that it loses about $10 million a year from unauthorized use of the Disney name and characters. Levi Strauss recently won a $500,000 cash settlement from London-based Nolton Management, Ltd., which had been accused of conspiring to sell as many as 3 million bogus pairs of Levis a year. The court ordered Nolton not to produce or sell any more fakes.

The generic problem is more difficult to defend against. A **generic name** consists of a word or words used to identify a class or type of products. Generic terms that were once brand names include aspirin, cellophane, nylon, lanolin, shredded wheat, milk of magnesia, and kerosene. The public must recognize a trademark as a trademark and not a product class. If it becomes generic, the trademark is declared public property. Imagine the field day other manufacturers would have if Coke, Kleenex, Xerox, Jello, Fritos, Jeep, and Scotch Tape were declared generic. In fact, all these brands have had to defend themselves in court as not being generic. To avoid the generic problem, firms should always use a trademark as a capitalized proper adjective — Fritos corn chips or Scotch brand cellophane tape. "Band Aids" will foster a generic lawsuit; instead, the name should be Band Aid bandages.

It is the owner's responsibility to protect a brand name. To use a similar or even the same brand name is not a criminal act per se. Neither the Federal Trade Commission nor any other branch of government protects the trademark owner; the firm itself must bring a lawsuit against the infringing firm. For example, Pepsico sued a discotheque that opened with the name Pepsi. The soft drink company did not want the public to think that it had gone into the entertainment business. When the *Pittsburgh Press* newspaper repeatedly failed to capitalize the trademark Frisbee, Wham-O Manufacturing Company sent the editors 100 flying saucers, each imprinted "pittsburgh press."

THE ROLE OF GOVERNMENT IN TRADEMARKS AND PATENTS

The Lanham Act has successfully brought order to the American trademark system. Without the act and the U.S. Patent Office, invention and brand ownership determination would be chaotic. But government intervention in the trademark and patent system has not been without controversy. In 1978, the Federal Trade Commission said that it wanted the Commerce Department's Trademark Trial and Appeal Board to cancel Cyanamid Corporation's exclusive use of the trademark Formica. The FTC claimed that the term was generic. A little-known provision of the Lanham Act authorizes the FTC to seek cancellation of generic marks, and the Formica case was the first time the agency had used the generic provision. In another case, the FTC accused Borden's ReaLemon of predatory trade practices. It cited as evidence a 90 percent market share of the reconstituted lemon-juice market. An FTC judge ruled that although the ReaLemon trademark was not generic, it had become such a powerful marketing weapon that Borden should be forced to license the trademark to any competitor that wanted to use it. The license fee would be one-half of one percent of sales. To date, neither the ReaLemon nor Formica cases have been resolved.

Effective lobbying by powerful business groups and election of a conservative president have reduced the activist role of the FTC. The remainder of the 1980s should see a slightly greater pro-business slant in FTC decision making.

Types of brands

When several different products have the same brand name, it is referred to as a **family brand.** Nabisco markets a number of different cookies and crackers using the familiar Nabisco name and shield. Sony puts its family brand on radios, television sets, stereos, and other electronic products.

It is usually to the manufacturer's advantage to use a family brand name when possible because it facilitates the introduction of new products. You would probably be more likely to buy a new frozen dessert with the Sara Lee family brand name rather than one with Joe's Frozen Desserts on it. Since consumers are already familiar with the Sara Lee name, less money is required to promote the new product.

The brand of a manufacturer, such as Kodak, La-Z-Boy, Fruit-of-the-Loom, and Harley Davidson, is called a national brand or a **manufacturer's brand.** The term *national brand* obviously is not always accurate, since many manufacturers serve only a regional market. I use the term *manufacturer's brand* because it more precisely defines the brand's owner.

Historically, the brands of wholesalers and retailers have been labeled *private brands*. Again, this term is not always an accurate description. The connotation of the word *private* is that items bearing this brand are distributed only in the retailer's or wholesaler's own stores, whereas most manufacturers' brands are marketed through a variety of wholesalers (see Figure 10.2). Definitional problems arise here, because some manufacturers restrict their retail distribution to a particular geographic area. Oldsmobile, Magnavox, Hart Shaffner and Marx, and Rolex products are just as privately distributed as most wholesaler brands. That is, only certain stores are allowed to carry the product, yet they are sold throughout the United States. To avoid this problem, we will use the term **dealer brand** for all brands of wholesalers or retailers. Penncrest (a J. C. Penney's brand), Craftsman and Kenmore (Sears brands), Signature and Airline (Montgomery Ward brands), and IGA (Independent Grocers' Association) are all dealer brands. Sears' own brands now account for over 90 percent of the company's volume.

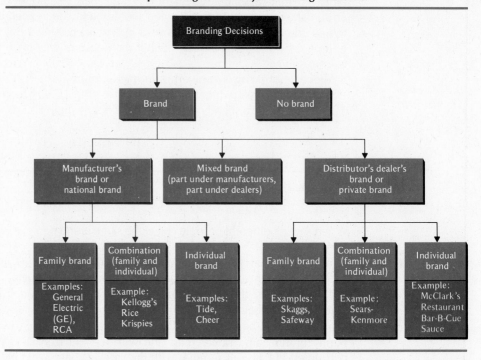

USING MANUFACTURERS' BRANDS

Most wholesalers are too small to develop their own brands and rely instead on manufacturers' brands. As retailers and wholesalers grow, they ultimately have to decide whether to establish their own dealer brands or continue to sell only manufacturers' brands.

There are several good reasons for managers' staying with the manufacturers' brands and not developing dealer brands. Heavy advertising to the consumer helps "presell" the buyer and develop strong consumer loyalties. All the dealer has to do is store the merchandise and display it, since the consumer already has a strong desire to buy it. It is not uncommon for Procter & Gamble, Colgate-Palmolive, or Gillette to spend over $10 million a year promoting a single product.

Well-known manufacturers' brands can help bring in new customers and enhance the dealer's prestige. For example, a small lawn mower and bicycle repair shop in a midwestern college town was fortunate enough to acquire the right to distribute Lawnboy lawn mowers. Sales grew rapidly; the shop was remodeled for a higher-quality clientele; and the entire operation acquired a more professional and businesslike image.

Intensive promotion by the manufacturer also encourages rapid turnover, which aids in lowering the dealer's selling costs. Most manufacturers offer rapid delivery to dealers, thus enabling them to carry less inventory. Lower inventory requirements mean that less working capital is required.

A final factor that is quite important to many retailers and wholesalers is varying product quality. If, for example, a retailer sells a manufacturer's brand that happens to be of poor quality, the customer may simply switch manufacturer's brands but continue to trade with the retailer. If it had been the retailer's own brand, it might have lost a customer.

USING DEALER BRANDS

Why have dealer brands? Again, there are several good reasons. Manufacturers' brands typically offer a lower gross margin than the dealer can earn on its own brand. Moreover, the manufacturer retains control over the brand and may decide to drop the product or remove the dealer as a distributor. Dealers that spend substantial sums of money developing a consumer franchise dislike the uncertainty of future supply associated with some manufacturers' brands.

Dealer brands offer higher gross margins and tie the customer to the dealer. If a person likes Lucerne cottage cheese, he or she may purchase it only at Safeway, thus stimulating store loyalty. Since dealer brands do not identify the manufacturer, the retailer or wholesaler can switch producers without the consumer ever knowing it. A dealer might find it advantageous to convert to a new manufacturer if the firm can produce the dealer brand more cheaply, offer faster and more dependable delivery, or offer higher quality at the same cost.

But dealer brands also have several drawbacks that can cut deeply into their larger gross margin. For example, the dealer must promote its own brands; no one else will do it. Promotion can be expensive. Sears and Penney's spend many millions on promotions every year.

In order to sell merchandise at a competitive price, dealers must buy their brands in fairly large quantities. Not only do large inventories tie up working capital, they also entail risks such as fire, theft, obsolescence, and deterioration. Even though a dealer can change sources of supply without the consumer knowing it, it still has to find the right suppliers. It is often a headache to locate good, reliable manufacturers to produce dealer brands. Some manufacturers refuse to produce dealer-brand goods because they believe they are cutting into their own market.

A final disadvantage of dealer brands is that if the product is not good, the consumer has only the dealer to blame. Poor-quality dealer brands can result in loss of customers and the creation of a negative image for the dealer. If you buy an Airline color television from Montgomery Ward that proves to be unsatisfactory, you may decide that the television set is indicative of the quality of all Ward's products and simply stop shopping at Ward's.

THE BATTLE OF THE BRANDS

As dealer brands continue to grow in sales, distribution, and promotion, consumer brand awareness also increases. The fight for distribution and shelf space between manufacturers' and dealer brands has been called "the battle of the brands."

Dealer brands currently account for 40 percent of auto tire volume and 30 percent of all grocery volume. The thrust of dealer brand growth has been the giant retailers. Most of these organizations hope to have at least one-third of their sales in their own brands. In one emerging technique for stimulating wider distribution, retailers' brands are placed in noncompetitive outlets such as service stations.

Giant retailers, because of their extensive retail distribution systems and close contact with the ultimate consumer, are finding that they can supply product services more efficiently than the manufacturer. Ultimately this will result in further erosion of manufacturer's brands and perhaps lower prices for the consumer.

Manufacturers are not sitting idly by while dealer brands are growing in importance. Many manufacturers are encouraging the growth! Net profit of manufacturers on dealer brands is satisfactory and often more predictable than the profit on their own brands because of long-term contracts with dealers. Some manufacturers are realizing much greater economies of scale by obtaining additional dealer-brand volume. The economies gained enable the manufacturer to be price-competitive and also raise total profits. Finally, a manufacturer that produces for a dealer may achieve a "favored status" position with that retailer for the manufacturer's own brand. Obtaining a solid distribution position with Penney's, Montgomery Ward, or Western Auto Supply can be a significant competitive advantage.

The battle of the brands does not imply the ultimate demise of manufacturers' brands. It simply means that the competition between dealer brands and manufacturers' brands for shelf space will continue to intensify. Dealers are not without problems. Severe supply problems, shrinking shelf price differentials between manufacturers' and dealer brands, and consumer dissatisfaction with the quality of some dealer brands assure the long-run viability of manufacturers' brands.

Brand loyalty

Brand loyalty is consistent repeat purchasing of a brand over time. Achieving consumer loyalty for a specific brand is important for marketing managers. Loyalty ensures future sales and usually gives the brand good word-of-mouth advertising.

But brand loyalty has proved to be a very complex phenomenon. It is likely, based upon current knowledge, that personality is an important factor in developing brand loyalty for some products.[2] For example, personality variables were used to discriminate correctly 86 percent of the time between Chase and Sanborn versus Folgers coffee purchasers.[3] The relevance of personality to brand loyalty depends upon the nature of the product and the target market. It is easy to get ego involved with cars, cosmetics, furniture, and clothes. On the other hand, most of us are probably not ego involved with toothpicks, umbrellas, and wallboard.

The importance of reducing consumer risk is an important dimension of brand loyalty. As consumers develop more information and experience about a brand or product group, these help reduce risks for future purchases. The correctness of our decision to buy brand A is continually reinforced as we keep using brand A and find the results satisfactory. As long as a product meets preconceived expectations, actual performance is often ignored. In a recent study of purchases of women's clothing, one respondent said, "I am satisfied because it did not rip, shrink, or fade." Overt search for a new brand would have begun only if one of the negatives had occurred.[4]

BRAND SWITCHING

We change brands for many reasons, not just because we are dissatisfied with our present brand. Perhaps an effective promotion has convinced you that Mrs. Paul's fish sticks are crunchy and delicious without a strong fishy aftertaste. Therefore, you experiment by purchasing Mrs. Paul's rather than your present brand. Once your curiosity is satisfied, you will probably return to your own brand. For two products A and B, purchase behavior might be this: AAAA-BAAA.

Brand switching may result from chance or random encounters with a new brand. You see a neighbor with a new television and you buy the same brand. Perhaps you pick up a package of swiss cheese from the dairy case and decide that it is the best you have ever tasted. If you like a new or untried brand, it might be diagramed as AAABBBBB; if your chance encounter was negative, it would be AAABAAAA. Sometimes we change brands to reinforce our original purchase decision. In other words, we prove to ourselves that our first choice was correct by trying another product that is probably inferior. People who switch for reassurance usually return to the old brands quickly. These consumers may know or strongly suspect in advance that the new brand will prove unsatisfactory.

Probably the most common reason for changing brands is promotion. You see an advertisement for a new product and you give it a try. Coupons, money-back offers, free samples, sweepstakes, and other forms of sales promotion also create brand switching. The key to brand switching is for the marketing manager to maintain a high level of product quality. Getting consumers to switch brands is only half of the battle. If the product is of lower quality than the buyers had expected, they will switch again. Price is usually a factor in promotional brand switching. If, for example, a consumer is using brand A, the lower the price of brand B relative to A, the greater the probability of a switch to B. In other words, if product B is being promoted heavily and is a lot cheaper than A, chances are greater for a switch than if B costs much more than A.

Brand switching is rarely based upon the consumer acquiring huge amounts of information about all product alternatives and then rationally sifting through each one and selecting a new brand. Consumers base their purchase decisions on their most important product attribute dimensions rather than on all available information.[5] As more information is gathered, the consumer will regard the situation as hopelessly complex. At this point, there may be a tendency to give up and make the choice impulsively.

GENERIC PRODUCTS

Generic products are no-frills, no brand name, low-cost products that became quite popular in the late 1970s. (A generic product and a brand name that becomes generic, such as cellophane, are not the same thing.) As of 1980 there were approximately 63 different generic items available in consumer markets (see Figure 10.3). One-third of the nation's grocery stores stock generics. In food products, generic sales tend to peak in the month following introduction. Then comes a steady decline, with a sales plateau reached after eight months. This strange life cycle may be due to introductory publicity and lack of follow-up promotion. Consumers may be finding that generic quality is below that of other brands. Consumers are not willing to sacrifice if quality is below that of other brands. And consumers are not willing to sacrifice quality despite the fact that generic prices are substantially lower on most items.

◢ **FIGURE 10.3 Generic products distributed by Jewel Food Stores.**

Source: Jewel Food Stores, a division of Jewel Companies, Inc.

Generic products are not limited to consumer items. In the industrial area many accessories, raw materials, and component parts are sold on a generic basis. For example, in the refrigeration industry copper, capacitors, refrigerant, and driers are available as generic items. Generics are used in industry for the same reasons as they are in consumer goods. The sameness of certain products, general lack of brand preference, and the opportunity to stock one brand instead of three or more have created generic demand in industry.

Product warranties

Whether or not a product is generic or a well-known branded item, it is important to know if it is covered by some type of warranty. Unfortunately, when many people try a different product and find it defective, they often switch brands rather than complain to the manufacturer.[6] Manufacturers may try to discourage brand switching through the offer of an expressed product warranty. A **warranty** is intended to be a confirmation of the quality or performance of a good or service. An express warranty is made in writing, while an implied warranty is an unwritten guarantee that the good or service is fit for the purpose for which it was sold. All sales have an implied warranty under the Uniform Commercial Code.

Express warranties range from simple statements such as "100 percent cotton" (a guarantee of quality) and "complete satisfaction guaranteed" (a statement of performance) to extensive documents written in obscure language. Warranties are important marketing tools because the consumer views them as a dimension of product quality. According to a study by Kelly Shuptrine, the more expensive the product, the greater the difficulty of understanding the warranty. Ultimately this means that many customers are at the mercy of the dealer or perhaps the manufacturer for a proper interpretation of the warranty. Shuptrine also noted that 40 percent of the American people did not have the educational background to interpret the average warranty on products priced under $100.

WARRANTY LEGISLATION

Congress passed the Magnuson-Moss Warranty-Federal Trade Commission Improvement Act on January 4, 1975, to aid consumers in understanding warranties and to get action from manufacturers and dealers. If a manufacturer promises a **full warranty,** it must meet certain minimum standards, including repair "within a reasonable time and without charge" of any defects and replacement of the merchandise or a full refund if the product does not work "after a reasonable number of attempts" at repair. And the law demands that any warranty that does not live up to this tough prescription must be "conspicuously" promoted as a **limited warranty.**

General Motors, Goodyear, Zenith, and Bulova have all switched to limited warranties as a result of this law. Wright and McGill, the manufacturer of Eagle Claw hooks, rods, and reels, dropped the "lifetime guarantee" from its products. Others have shed their warranties altogether, including Fisher-Price toys, Kroehler furniture, and Levi Strauss. "They [warranties] don't sell pants anyway," explains Levi Strauss' lawyer, Willard Ellis.[7] Thus in several cases the law has resulted in less protection (at least explicit protection) in the consumer goods market than there was before.

But the government has also been active. Recently, the FTC issued a complaint against Korvettes, the New York City discount chain. Citing its authority under the Magnuson-Moss Act, it claimed that Korvettes had not properly displayed warranties to shoppers prior to purchase. It called for the chain to keep actual warranties mounted in binders for easy inspection by customers and to post in stores 8½" × 11" signs reading "Compare Warranties Before You Buy!" Korvettes also had to conduct warranty awareness training programs for its salespeople. In addition to monitoring warranties, the government has now become active in the area of product safety.

Product safety and product liability

The National Commission on Product Safety reported to Congress that each year 30,000 Americans are killed in accidents involving products, 110,000 are permanently disabled, and 20 million are injured.[8] On the basis of these data 2 Americans will be killed, 7 permanently disabled, and 114,000 injured by products in approximately the time it will take you to read this chapter. The poor safety record of American products led Congress to pass the Consumer Product Safety Act in 1972. Briefly, this act

1. Establishes a 5-member Consumer Product Safety Commission (CPSC) whose purpose is to reduce the risks faced by customers in their use of consumer products.
2. Gives the commission a variety of remedies for dealing with hazardous products, depending on the severity of the hazard. Ban and seizure are appropriate for "imminently hazardous" products.
3. Provides for rather severe civil and criminal penalties for violation of the law or commission rules.

PRODUCT LIABILITY SUITS

If you are injured by a product, you can sue the manufacturer or the dealer. Specifically, the purchaser of the product can sue regardless of whether or not he or she bought the product from the manufacturer. The nonpurchasing user or consumer can sue, and the bystander can sue (see Table 10.1). A bystander, for example, would be an individual who is hit by an automobile that goes out of control because of a defect in the steering mechanism. Awards of $250,000 to $500,000 are not uncommon in **product liability** cases, with claims now occurring at a rate of over 1 million per year.[9]

Case	Decision
MacPherson vs. *Buick Motor Co.*, New York, 1916	A manufacturer is liable for negligently built products that are "reasonably certain to place life and limb in peril," even though consumers do not buy directly from the manufacturer.
Greenman vs. *Yuba Power Products, Inc.*, California, 1963	A manufacturer is strictly liable when he sells a product that proves to have a defect that causes injury.
Larson vs. *General Motors Corp.*, U.S. Court of Appeals, 8th Circuit, 1968	When faulty design of a product worsens an injury, a plaintiff may recover damages for the worsened part of the injury, even if the design defect did not cause the injury in the first place.
Cunningham vs. *MacNeal Memorial Hospital*, Illinois, 1970	It is not a defense to claim that a product (in this case, blood infected by hepatitis) could not be made safer by any known technology. This ruling of the Illinois Supreme Court, the only case in which judges squarely refused to consider "state of the art," was reversed by a state statute defining the selling of blood as a service.
Cronin vs. *J. B. E. Olson Corp.*, California, 1972	A product need not be "unreasonably dangerous" to make its manufacturer strictly liable for defective design.
Bexiga vs. *Havir Mfg. Co.*, New Jersey, 1972	If an injury is attributable to the lack of any safety device on a product, the manufacturer cannot base a defense on the contributory negligence of the plaintiff.
Berkebile vs. *Brantly Helicopter Corp.*, Pennsylvania, 1975	Whether the seller could have foreseen a particular injury is irrelevant in a case of strict liability for design defect.
Ault vs. *International Harvester Co.*, California, 1975	Evidence that a manufacturer changed or improved his product line after the manufacture and sale of the particular product that caused an injury may be used to prove design defect.
Miscallef vs. *Miehle Co.*, New York, 1976	Evidence that an injured plaintiff obviously knew of a danger inherent in using a product will not defeat his claim if the manufacturer could reasonably have guarded against the danger in designing the product.
Barker vs. *Lull Engineering Co.*, California, 1978	A manufacturer must show that the usefulness of a product involved in an accident outweighs the risks inherent in its design. In this radical ruling, the court shifted the burden of proof in design defect from plaintiff to defendant.

Source: "The Devils in the Product Liability Laws." Reprinted from the February 12, 1979 issue of *Business Week* by special permission, © 1979 by McGraw-Hill, Inc., New York, NY 10020. All rights reserved.

In one example, the six manufacturers that produce football helmets had annual sales approximating $25 million in 1978. They were faced with $150 million in product liability suits at that time: the lawsuits were six times the size of the industry and 150 times expected profits.[10] Situations like this have caused product liability insurance to skyrocket. The Knapheid Corporation was founded in 1848 to produce wagons. Today it manufactures specialty truck bodies and hoists and has never had a product liability suit filed against it. Yet in a recent three-year period the firm's product liability insurance premiums soared nearly 3000 percent. The president felt fortunate because other small business owners he knew were not able to get insurance at all, at any price.

A manufacturer or dealer has three basic defenses against a product liability lawsuit. First, if the user discovers a product defect and continues to use the item, knowing the risks he or she is taking, the manufacturer is relieved of responsibility. Second, the manufacturer or dealer is absolved of liability if the consumer misuses the product. If, for example, a person falls off a chair while standing on one of its arms and trying to reach an object on a high shelf, the chair manufacturer would not be held liable in a product lawsuit. The last defense is that the product is not defective. For example, a man trying to reach his car keys through a side vent window inadvertently hit his eye on the point of the window and put it out. The jury held that the window was not defective and that its design was adequate for normal use.

PRODUCT LIABILITY RISKS AND PRODUCT RECALL

To prevent liability suits, marketing managers must engage in liability prevenion planning.[11] This entails:

1. Setting up the product safety committee
2. Periodic safety audits and tests
3. Contingency planning for product recall.

A product safety committee will centralize authority and responsibility and eliminate departmental biases. The committee should consist of high-ranking managers from engineering, design, purchasing, manufacturing, quality control, marketing, legal affairs, and insurance. The committee's basic responsibilities are these:

1. To establish safety policies and procedures
2. To arrange seminars and training sessions on product liability prevention
3. To inform top management of all product evaluations and developments
4. To conduct safety audits and tests.

A product safety audit should follow the system proposed in Figure 10.4. The product is described, the environment in which it is used is analyzed, users' characteristics are examined, and sources of failure are determined. For example, could the product fail because the hazards are not sufficiently explained in the owner's manual? Could substandard materials create failure? Next, a composite list of sources of failure is created. By varying the number

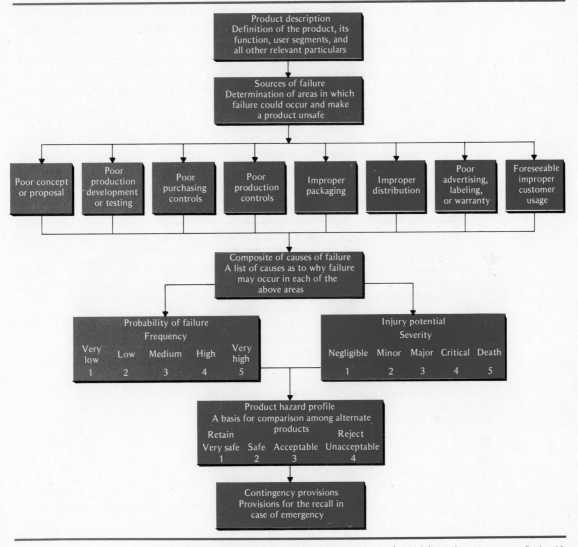

Source: R. Chandran and R. Linneman, "Planning to Minimize Product Liability," *Sloan Management Review* 20, 1 (fall 1978): 37. By permission of the publisher. Copyright © 1978 by the Sloan Management Review.

and type of sources of failure, the firm can see how various combinations of factors could lead to product failure. The product is then rated to determine overall failure and injury potential. Based upon these data, product modifications can be made if necessary, and in severe cases products can be recalled.

Regardless of whether or not a firm initiates a product recall, it should have a contingency plan to prevent confusion if recall is ever required. The Consumer

Product Safety Commission was involved in recalls of over 15 million product units during its first twenty months of operation. Approximately 25 percent of all consumer goods firms listed in *Fortune's* 500 were involved in such recalls in one year, and the Conference Board estimates that more than 25 million product units are recalled every year.[12]

Product recall can be very costly for the company. General Motors spent $3.5 million on postage alone when a problem with motor mounts was detected in 6.5 million of its cars. Bon Vivant, a soup manufacturer, went bankrupt when botulism was discovered in its canned vichyssoise.

Product recall contingency planning requires a task force composed of managers from the same areas as the safety committee. In fact, the product safety committee often assumes responsibility for recalls. The basic process is reverse distribution created by dissemination of information (see Table 10.2). Informa-

◢ **TABLE 10.2 Source, Type, and Flow of Information Necessary for Product Recall**

Source	Type	Flow
Quality control/ engineering	1. Nature of defect 2. Production facility/materials/ design causing defect ⟶ 3. Remedial action	Production/ inventory control
Production/ inventory	1. Product/codes/names/batches 2. Amount manufactured 3. Work-in-process, in-plant finished goods inventories	Distribution
Distribution	1. Quality of product shipped 2. Location/name of resellers 3. Product-in-transit 4. Reseller inventory quantity 5. Off-plant warehouse inventory quality	Customer service
Customer	1. Invoice data (price, discounts, and so forth) 2. Instructions for recall procedure 3. Names of customers if available 4. Summary of data collected from quality control, production/ inventory control, distribution	Public relations
Public relations	1. Formal notification of recall publics containing information collected above	Regional district sales and services managers, government agencies, resellers, customers

Source: Roger A. Kerin and Michael Harvey, "Contingency Planning for Product Recall," *MSU Business Topics,* summer 1975, p. 7. Reprinted by permission of the publisher, Division of Research, Graduate School of Business Administration, Michigan State University.

tion about the defect must flow to the customer, and the defective item must be physically returned for repair or replacement. Wholesalers and retailers must be told to freeze inventories of questionable goods and return them to the manufacturer. The case of the San Francisco Shirt Works is illustrative of the voluntary product recall action.

After learning that it had sold shirts which failed to meet the federal standard for flammability of clothing textiles, the company voluntarily notified the Consumer Product Safety Commission (CPSC) of this fact. Letters were then sent to 420 retailers who had purchased these shirts informing them of the potential hazard and asking that the garments be returned for the full purchase price. Provisions were made to make refunds to consumers as well. . . .

Bassett Furniture Industries and the CPSC recently launched a voluntary notification program to inform 1,654 purchasers of certain Bassett cribs that modification kits are available free of charge. The CPSC believes that infants may be entrapped and strangled in the cribs because it has received and investigated two reports of such occurrences.

Some firms have used their advertising programs to educate consumers on product safety. Shell Oil Co., in conjunction with the CPSC, has published 35 million safety booklets titled "The Unexpected Dangers Book," warning of the hazards of misusing gasoline, batteries, and other products. The booklets are featured in Shell TV advertisements and distributed through participating Shell service stations and national magazines.

A company's sales force may also be employed to enhance product safety. Travelers Insurance Co. has reprinted and distributed several thousand copies of CPSC material on bicycle safety through Travelers Insurance agents throughout the United States.[13]

Packaging

Traditionally, packages have been viewed in a very utilitarian fashion, that is, as a means of holding contents together or as a way of protecting the product as it moves through the distribution channel. Today, however, the package plays a much greater role in marketing-oriented firms. Packaging is a big business, with sales of $46 billion in 1979. In 1980 packaging products consumed an estimated 68 million tons of materials, including 75 percent of paperboard, 60 percent of glass, 25 percent of plastics, 22 percent of paper, 19 percent of aluminum, 15 percent of wood, and 7 percent of all steel produced during the year.[14]

PACKAGING AND MARKETING

The package is strongly linked to strategic marketing decisions and has critical implications for each of the major components of the marketing mix. The product and its package are often inseparable from the consumer's perspective. Sophisticated packaged goods companies have known for many years that subtle changes in packaging can dramatically alter the consumer's perception of the product and thus the product's acceptance. A study by the author, for example, found significantly different perceptions of potato chips in terms of freshness and crispiness depending upon the type of bag. The chips in both purchases were identical and less than a week old![15]

The package should communicate an image to the consumer that will obtain positioning objectives for the firm. A package design communicates product attributes such as gender identification, natural or artificial, modern or old-fashioned, as well as the social-symbolic meanings of presitge and quality.

The consumer is almost appallingly literal in the expectation that the product will be exactly as pictured on the illustration. In one instance, a manufacturer of frosting mix "improved" the package by changing the illustration of the frosted cake to what was thought to be a much more realistic, more appetizing version—only to find that the brand's market share was cut in half! Interviews with consumers who had switched away from the brand revealed that although they thought the new package "looked just fine," the color of the frosting had changed just enough to signal a difference in the type of chocolate flavor. Although the product was unchanged, there was enough difference in the two photographic renditions to result in a 50% sales decline. Both packages were carefully designed by professionals, but the subtle visual difference (which resulted in a not-at-all subtle share difference) was not detected prior to actual sales tests and subsequent interviews with consumers.[16]

PACKAGING STRATEGIES

Packaging can often be used to segment markets. Different size packages, for example, can and do appeal to heavy users versus light users. Salt is sold in a variety of package sizes, ranging from single serving to picnic size to giant economy size. Campbell's soup is now packaged in single-serving cans aimed at the elderly and singles market segments. This package complements their other sizes. Beer and soft drinks are similarly now marketed in a variety of package sizes and types. Packaging convenience can increase a product's utility and therefore increase market share and profits:

The consumer's convenience requirements have many dimensions: consumers are constantly seeking items that offer ease of handling, easy opening and reclosing, reusability, and disposability. Surveys conducted by *Sales and Marketing Management* magazine have revealed that housewives dislike—and avoid buying—ice cream boxes that leak, vinegar bottles that are too heavy or too fat, immovable pry-up lids on glass bottles, key-opener sardine cans, and cereal boxes that are hard to pour. Such packaging innovations as zipper tear strips, hinged lids, tab slots, screw-on tops, and pour spouts were introduced to solve these and other problems. Similarly, catsup bottles now have wide necks, perishable medicine tablets are individually packaged in foil, cheese slices are individually packaged in cellophane, brown sugar is nonlumping and pourable from spouts, and potato chips are now stacked in space-saving, air-tight, recappable, crushproof canisters.[17]

Price/package interaction. A good package that increases consumer satisfaction will mean that consumers may be willing to pay more for the product. Package sizes can also be a factor in reaching target retail sales prices. When trying to convey a prestige image, packaging can play an important role (see Figure 10.5). For example, the use of foil coatings and unusual designs can denote a quality image. On a more mundane basis, the use of inexpensive packaging materials in both consumer and industrial goods can increase dam-

◀ **FIGURE 10.5 Using prestige packaging to position a product.**

The ultimate men's fragrance in an elegant new spray

Source: Courtesy of Shaller-Rubin Assoc. for Royal Copenhagen Porcelain Manufactory Ltd., Copenhagen, Denmark; Swank Inc., Sole Dist.

age and breakage. Thus there is a tradeoff between the quality of packaging materials versus claims for unusable and damaged products.

Promotion/package interaction. In today's self-service world, the package represents the last chance to communicate a sales message to the prospective buyer. The package is the "silent salesperson" at the point of purchase. An effective package can communicate with the consumer and influence purchase behavior. Unattractive packages can lose a sale when a person had been presold through advertising. One study revealed that one-third of the consumers presold by advertising switched products when confronted with more attractive alternatives.[18]

The first promotional task of the package is to attract attention. Since perception is selective, the package should be designed to attract attention in a visually cluttered environment. After it has gained the prospective buyer's attention, it should inform the buyer about the product and persuade him or her to buy it. The package must convey the right emotional qualities about the product so that it fills the consumer's needs. Let us look at the example of Fresh Start.

In 1977 Colgate-Palmolive test-marketed Fresh Start, a new granular detergent. . . . In a category noted for me-too products and "shouting" packages, the challenge was to create a package that would establish a strong brand identification and be visually compelling, both singly and in mass display. It was equally important that the package immediately herald the fact that the product was a highly concentrated powder and thus represented a formula breakthrough in laundry detergents.

As a first step, important questions had to be answered about the physical package. Should the plastic bottle be opaque with vivid color to heighten shelf impact or should it be clear to show the product and dramatize the blue granules? Both concepts were tested, and the appeal of the clear bottle won hands down. Two key functional features were incorporated into the bottle: an easy-grip handle and a plastic closure that doubled as a measuring device.

As for graphic needs, the decision was made to apply brand identification directly to the bottle with no background color or shape to obscure product visibility. After extensive design exploration, the main graphic element was conceived—a strong blue, orange, to yellow, to white-hot symbol connoting energy and cleaning power and used to underscore the brand logotype.

The marriage of this brand-identifying graphic with the see-through plastic bottle resulted in a package distinct in this product category—one that is particularly effective when displayed in multiples. Sent to test-market with print and television backing, Fresh Start did so well that Colgate began plans for a national rollout almost immediately.[19]

Packaging/physical distribution interactions. The objective of physical distribution is to get the merchandise to the purchaser in good shape at the least cost and in a timely fashion. Once a product leaves its place of origin, the typical package is exposed to multiple hazards:

> Damage from shocks and vibrations during normal handling, storage and transportation.
>
> Deterioration or contamination with foreign matter such as fungi, insects, bacteria, dirt, chemicals, water, and corrosive gases.
>
> Losses from pilferage or unauthorized package openings.
>
> Contamination from unanticipated chemical interactions between packaging materials and product ingredients.
>
> Damage from environmental factors such as high temperature, freezing, high altitude, excessive humidity, and sunlight.
>
> Creation of surface imperfections such as mars, dents, scratches, finish discoloration, and loss of gloss or shine.[20]

A good package must protect the product from these hazards at a reasonable cost.

PACKAGING RESPONSIBILITY

As top management has become aware of the importance of packaging in the marketing mix, responsibility for the function has been escalated up the corporate hierarchy. George Weissman, president of Philip Morris, has stated:

> If there is a single concept underlying the success of Philip Morris packaging, it is that we don't regard packaging as a disjointed or low-echelon endeavor. To us, excellence in our packaging is virtually indistinguishable from excellence of product. Both are absolutely top priority items.
>
> And so our packaging operations involve executives representing production, quality control, sales, marketing, advertising, purchasing, and accounting—all the way to senior management: our chairman, our president, and others. All regularly review every contemplated innovation or change in packaging. For many years, Philip Morris has been most keenly aware of its vital importance, and that's an understatement.[21]

LABELING STRATEGIES

An integral part of any package is its label. The Food and Drug Act of 1906 signaled the beginning of congressional concern with labeling information. This act prohibited false labeling of foods and drugs. As the economy continued to grow and develop, Congress realized that the 1906 legislation was too vague and general to provide adequate consumer protection.

In 1967 the Fair Packaging and Labeling Act was passed. It sought regulations requiring labels and packages to disclose sufficient information regarding product ingredients and composition to establish or preserve fair competition between competitive products by enabling consumers to make rational comparisons with respect to price and other factors or to prevent consumer deception.

Labeling strategy generally takes one of two forms: informational and persuasive. A **persuasive label** focuses on a promotional theme or logo with information for the consumer of secondary importance. Standard promotional claims include "new," "improved," and "super." Research has shown that this terminology has no significant effect on evaluations of most convenience goods and shopping goods.[22] Consumers have been satiated with "newness" and hence discount these claims.

Information labeling, on the other hand, is designed to help consumers in making proper product selections and to offer lower cognitive dissonance after the purchase. Sears attached a "label of confidence" tag to all its floor covering products. This new label gives such product information as wearability, color, features, cleanability, and care and construction standards. Most major furniture manufacturers affix labels to their wares that explain construction features such as steam bent frames, number of coils, and fabric characteristics. The labels also usually inform the potential buyer of what effort, if any, is required to maintain the furniture's finish. This type of information labeling enhances the quality image of the product and contributes to the sale.

Convenience good labeling, on the other hand, is often ignored or is not an image-enhancing factor. With food products, for example, research found that the vast majority of consumers neither use nor comprehend nutrition in arriving at food purchase decisions.[23] This is rather ironic, since in early 1980 the Food and Drug Administration decided to push for complete ingredient labeling, more open dating, and more nutritional labeling.[24]

All these factors, then, affect the marketing manager's decisions about labeling: he or she (and all those involved in the packaging decision) must consider government regulations, target markets, sales objectives, the firm's image, and so on each time a product must be labeled.

SUMMARY

A brand is a word, name, symbol, or device, or combination of these, used by a manufacturer or wholesaler to identify its goods or services and distinguish them from others. A trademark is a legal term that includes only the words, names, or symbols the law designates as trademarks. Copyrights concern literary and artistic expression; patents are inventions related to function and design.

The Lanham Act of 1946 provided for the registration of trademarks with the U.S. Patent Office. Although a mark does not have to be registered, many advantages accrue to firms that register their marks.

Marketing managers must guard against well-known brand names becoming generic. A generic name consists of a word or words used to identify a class or type of product. To avoid the generic problem, firms should always use a trademark as a capitalized proper adjective. It is the owner's responsibility to protect a brand name, and it is not a criminal act, per se, to use a similar or even the same brand name. The firm must bring a lawsuit against the infringing organization.

Brands and trademarks help consumers identify products and services they wish to purchase and those they wish to avoid. The manufacturer's brand is sometimes referred to as a national brand. Dealer brands, those of a wholesaler or retailer, have historically been called "private brands." Because both types of brands offer unique advantages and disadvantages to the dealer, the situation has led to a battle of the brands. In recent years, the battle has resulted in significant dealer brand growth.

Brand loyalty is consistent, repeat purchasing of a brand over a time. Loyalty ensures future sales and usually gives the brand good word-of-mouth advertising. People sometimes switch brands because of curiosity, chance, reinforcement of the original brand image, or promotion.

Generic products are no-frill, no-brand-name, low-cost products that became quite popular in the late 1970s. Generic sales tend to peak shortly following introduction; then comes a steady decline, with a sales plateau reached within a year. Generic prices are usually substantially lower than their branded counterparts.

One factor often lacking in generic products is an expressed warranty. An expressed warranty is made in writing; an implied warranty is an unwritten guarantee. The Magnuson-Moss Warranty-Federal Trade Commission Improvement Act was designed to aid consumers in understanding warranties and to eliminate slow warranty action by manufacturers and dealers.

Congress passed the Consumer Product Safety Act in 1972 to help reduce the number of product accidents that kill or injure many consumers each year. Growing rates of product-related injuries and deaths have led to an increasing number of product liability suits. The possibility of incurring a product liability suit, coupled with the impact of the Product Safety Act, has led to a growing number of product recalls. To prevent liability suits, marketing managers must engage in liability prevention planning. This entails setting up a product safety committee, periodic safety audits and tests, and contingency planning for product recall.

Packing has become an increasingly important element of the product mix in many corporations. It represents the manufacturer's last chance to "sell" the product before the consumer makes the purchase/no-purchase decision. The label is also an integral part of the package. Labels are done in one of two forms: informational or persuasive.

KEY TERMS

Brand
Trademark
Brand name
Service mark
Certification mark
Copyright
Patent
Generic name
Family brand
Manufacturer's brand

Dealer brand
Brand loyalty
Generic product
Warranty
Full warranty
Limited warranty
Product liability
Persuasive label
Informational label

REVIEW QUESTIONS

1. What is the difference between the terms "brand," "trademark," and "brand name"? In what ways are they similar?
2. Identify the general guidelines used in selecting a trademark.
3. How does a manufacturer go about protecting its trademark? What criteria are applied in deciding trademark infringement cases?
4. Evaluate the advantages of branding from the firm's viewpoint. In what ways does the consumer benefit from branding?
5. What are the advantages and disadvantages of manufacturers' brands?
6. What factors lead to brand switching?
7. What is the distinction between expressed and implied warranties?
8. Why is packaging of such importance to marketing managers? What factors need to be considered in the design of the package?

DISCUSSION QUESTIONS

1. Why do many firms use a family brand? What are the risks associated with this strategy if a new product is substandard?
2. What does the future hold for manufacturers' brands? How will they be able to maintain their share of the market?
3. Why has there been increased litigation concerning product liability? What social changes have accelerated the public's demand for safer products?
4. How does the manufacturer use package sizes and types as a segmentation tool? Provide examples to support your answer.
5. What effect do you feel informational labeling has had on product choice? How does your analysis vary across product categories?

NOTES

1. Janet Guyon, "Camel Maker's Problem: Smokers Who Just Can't Get Over the Hump," *The Wall Street Journal,* May 4, 1981, p. 29.
2. Robert P. Brody and Scott M. Cunningham, "Personality Variables and the Consumer Decision Process," *Journal of Marketing Research* 5 (February 1968): 50–57; see also Joseph N. Fry, "Personality Variables and Cigarette Brand Choice," *Journal of Marketing Research* 8 (August 1971): 298–304.
3. Brody and Cunningham, "Personality Variables," p. 55.
4. John E. Swan and Linda Jones Combs, "Product Performance and Consumer Satisfaction: A New Concept," *Journal of Marketing* 40 (April 1976): 25–33.
5. Fleming Hanson, "Consumer Choice Behavior: An Experimental Approach," *Journal of Marketing Research* 6 (November 1969): 436–443; Jerry Olson and Jacob Jacoby, "Cue Utilization in the Quality Perception Process," in M. Venkatesan, *Proceedings Third Annual Conference of the Association for Consumer Research* 2 (1971): 167–179.
6. C. L. Kendall and Frederick A. Russ, "Warranty and Complaint Policies: An Opportunity for Marketing Management," *Journal of Marketing* 39 (April 1975): 42.
7. "The Guesswork on Warranties," *Business Week,* July 14, 1975, p. 51. See also "Ads Not Part of Final Warranty Rules," *Advertising Age,* January 5, 1976, p. 2; "New Warranty Law under Attack by Business," *Advertising Age,* July 7, 1975, p. 1; and "Initial FTC Guides for Warranty Law Out; Ad Rules Still Coming," *Advertising Age,* July 21, 1975, pp. 2ff.

8. Arnold A. Bennigson, "Product Liability—Producers and Manufacturers Beware," *Research Management* 18 (March 1975): 16.

9. Howard C. Sorenson, "Product Liability: The Consumer's Revolt," *Best's Review* 75 (September 1974): 48; see also Conrad Berenson, "The Product Liability Revolution," *Business Horizons* 15 (October 1972): 71–80.

10. Norman Polsky, "Product Liability—How Does It Affect You?" *Management World,* March 1978, p. 33.

11. The liability prevention planning material is from Rajan Chandran and Robert Linneman, "Planning to Minimize Product Liability," *Sloan Management Review* 20, 1 (fall 1978): 33–45.

12. E. P. McGuire, "Product Recall and the Facts of Business Life," *The Conference Board Record,* February 1975, pp. 13–15; see also "Managing the Product Recall," *Business Week,* January 1975, pp. 46–48.

13. Paul Busch, "Some Marketers Aid Product Safety Effort," *Marketing News,* August 11, 1978, p. 4. Reprinted by permission of the American Marketing Association.

14. "Consumer Winning Improvements in Packaging, Industry Is Advised," *Marketing News,* November 17, 1978, p. 7.

15. Carl McDaniel and R. C. Baker, "Convenience Food Packaging and the Perception of Product Quality," *Journal of Marketing* 41 (October 1977): 57–58.

16. D. K. Warren Twedt, "How Much Value Can Be Added through Packaging?" *Journal of Marketing* 32 (January 1968): 58.

17. William G. Nickles and Marvin A. Jolson, "Packaging—The Fifth 'P' in the Marketing Mix?" *S.A.M. Advanced Management Journal* 41 (winter 1976): 13.

18. Harold S. Gorschman, "New Dimensions in Unhidden Persuasion," in *Marketing Update,* ed. Harold W. Berkman (Dubuque, Ia.: Kendall Hunt Publishing Company, The Academy of Marketing Science, 1977), p. 331.

19. Robert E. Lee, "Packaging: Is Yours Doing The Right Job for Your Product," *Management Review,* November 1978, pp. 51–55.

20. Allan Easton, "Purposes and Analysis of Industrial Package Design," *Industrial Marketing Management,* July 1978, p. 316.

21. Dale Brubaker, "Five Reasons Why Brand Managers Should Get Out of Packaging," *Marketing News,* July 1, 1974, p. 5. Reprinted by permission of the American Marketing Association.

22. Michael L. Dean, James J. Engle, and W. Wayne Talarzyk, "The Influence of Package Copy Claims on Consumer Product Evaluations," *Journal of Marketing* 36 (April 1972): 34–39.

23. Jacob Jacoby, Robert W. Chestnut, and William Silberman, "Consumer Use and Comprehension of Nutrition Information," *Journal of Consumer Research* 4 (September 1977): 119–127.

24. "FDA, USDA, FTC Urge More Stringent Food Labeling Regulations," *Marketing News,* January 25, 1980, p. 1.

◢ CASES

10.1 The Sure-Grip Corporation

Sure-Grip was founded in 1937 to manufacture skates for roller rinks. The company established its reputation in the business by introducing wheels made of gear fiber—a durable hardened canvas material—with a rubber center strip. The wheels wore longer and provided better traction than the maplewood wheels then in use. Through the years sales growth was steady. In 1977 the outdoor skating craze was just getting under way, and the president's son decided to make himself some skates. He brought an old pair of Adidas jogging shoes to the factory and fastened them to a set of wheels. The skates worked, and they looked like a good idea to the president. No one else had yet put skate wheels on a jogging shoe.

The president went down to a local shoe store, bought a load of tennis shoes, mounted them on skate wheels, and handed out the skates to workers. They were well received. "Joggers" were born. The company made a deal with a northeastern manufacturer to manufacture jogging shoes specially modified to hold skate rivets, and Joggers came to market in November 1977. For almost a year, the company had no direct competition in the outdoor skate market.

The Jogger is a quality product from the aluminum plate to the angle of the cushions to the axles and precision-ground bearings. The company backs its quality claim with a one-year replacement warranty against wear and tear and a lifetime guarantee against manufacturing defects.

Recently Sure-Grip has seen less expensive models of jogging-shoe skates enter the market from Taiwan. The import sells for approximately $50 at retail versus $70 for Joggers. The company president has voiced several concerns. First, he does not want the term Joggers to become generic. Second, he is worried that the importers may use names very similar to Joggers in order to increase their sales. Third, the company has developed a new product which is a skate designed to be fastened to ski boots, and the firm wonders whether or not there can be a tie-in with the successful Jogger brand name.

1. You have been hired as a consultant to react to the president's concerns with a specific course of action. List your recommendations and defend them.

10.2   American Pacemaker

A pacemaker is a cluster of transistors, circuit boards, and a battery sealed in a stainless steel case the size of a cigarette lighter. Each year pacemakers are implanted in the chests of more than 150,000 people, all of whom suffer from some form of cardiac irregularity. The electronic pulsors of the pacemakers regulate the life-giving beats of the human heart.

Early in 1979, some of the cardiac patients American Pacemaker served found that their 18-month-old pacemakers had strayed from their prescribed settings and were beating either too fast or too slow. At the same time, the company examined test samples that hung in its own laboratory testing tanks in a saline solution, an environment approximating that of the chest cavity. Several more defective pacemakers were discovered.

An independent laboratory test found that a small number of transistors, supplied to American Pacemaker by an outside vendor and worth about $2.25 each, had been contaminated with enough moisture to affect the performance of pacemakers worth $2,295 each. The defect could not be detected by visual or electronic means. The transistors had been used in the assembly of 589 pacemakers, 552 of which had already been implanted in patients.

Roughly 90 percent of all pacemaker wearers have adequate heart function to survive even total failure of their pacemakers, and although the initial installation of a pacemaker involves hospitalization, replacement of a defective pacemaker is a comparatively minor procedure.

At this point a single-paragraph press release revealed only that American Pacemaker had notified physicians about the transistor problem, that removal was recommended at the physician's office at the physician's discretion, and that the Food and Drug Administration was reviewing the matter.

Concerned pacemaker patients called, saying: "I have a pacemaker. Is it yours?" Physicians the company had not been able to reach called, chagrined at having learned about the recall from their newspaper-reading patients rather than from the company. At this point, the company president asked, "What do we do now?"

1. You are a consultant to American Pacemaker. Outline a recall strategy to follow from this point forward.
2. If you had been in charge of the recall originally, what steps would you have followed to make certain that it proceeded more smoothly?

Trim Products*

Mr. Harvey J. Shapiro, vice-president of new product development for Trim Products, had just received a preliminary report from his staff. Jubilant at the overwhelming success of its diet products, the company was giving serious consideration to expanding the product line to include Trim Eggs, a ready-to-use cholesterol-free product that could be sold alongside fresh eggs. Trim Eggs would be sold in supermarkets and grocery stores in six-pack or single containers. Mr. Shapiro needed to analyze the business situation and evaluate this expansion possibility and make a recommendation to the president of the company.

HISTORY

Trim Products was a division of one of the giants in the food processing industry, with sales in excess of $400 million. The Trim Products division was developed only fifteen years ago and was oriented toward growth through new product development. Generally the product development process went through five stages: (1) targeting the market, (2) determining uses and motives, (3) search for product ideas, (4) screening, and (5) business analysis. Each of the diet products had undergone such monitoring, and Trim Products was proud of its success record: four out of five of its new products did better than break even.

Some of the most successful products were Trim Bread, Trim Cheese, Trim Yogurt, Trim Salad Dressing, and Trim Jams and Jellies. According to analysis, this diet market was estimated at $500 million and still growing. From 1964 to 1970 the percentage of families using low calorie products increased from 47 to 70 percent, and this percentage had maintained itself. Trim Products had estimated that over 65 million adults were overweight and that the typical dieter was under 54 years of age, the household head had some college training, and families with dieters had incomes of more than $15,000 yearly and generally resided in a metropolitan area or its suburbs. A survey of Trim Bread users revealed that 51 percent were motivated to purchase for weight-reducing reasons, 47 percent to maintain their current weight, 20 percent on a doctor's recommendation, and 16 percent because they were diabetic.

The new strategy for the 1980s was to penetrate the large potential market of working wives. Working wives would seem to be good customers for frozen and prepared foods. There also seemed to be a relationship between membership in Weight Watchers and the purchase of frozen foods and diet products. Naturally, many of the members of Weight Watchers would use its products.

PRODUCT BACKGROUND

The dietary program to reduce serum cholesterol usually includes the use of skim milk, lean meats such as chicken and turkey, and fewer eggs. A large number of medical authorities believe that upset in the body's capacity to cope with choles-

---

* Case prepared by Professor Ronald D. Michman, Shippensburg State College, Shippensburg, Pennsylvania.

terol and saturated fats in the normal manner is the cause of arteriosclerosis. Arteriosclerosis (hardening of the arteries) is a condition in which arteries become so lined with deposits of cholesterol compounds and fatty materials that blood flow is restricted. A number of studies have reported a link between high cholesterol and the incidence of heart attack. Therefore, many doctors have advocated a reduction of foods high in cholesterol, such as egg yolks, bacon, and a number of dairy products.

Egg substitute products generally included the same basic ingredients: egg white (82 percent), liquid corn oil (10 percent), and nonfat dry milk (7 percent). These ingredients were frozen, and the leading brand, Egg Beaters, packaged the product in an 8.5 ounce container which was advertised as the equivalent of four large eggs. In order to defrost it, the package must be taken out of the freezer and placed in the refrigerator for at least 12 hours prior to use. Another method would be to immerse the product in a large bowl of hot water for at least 30 minutes. However, it would be possible to defrost the product in a few minutes with a microwave oven. The substitute egg generally has about 40 calories, compared to 80 calories for whole eggs. Egg substitutes were sold in the frozen foods section of most supermarkets, usually in the same cabinet with frozen waffles and other frozen breakfast foods.

COMPETITION

The egg substitute market was estimated by Harvey Shapiro as a $20 million national market. All the competitive offerings were similar in terms of price, calories, and ingredients. The major distinction was that Trim Eggs offered convenience. Competitive brands had to be thawed before use. Trim Eggs had another competitive advantage; this product could be sold alongside fresh eggs.

Shapiro did not know how many customers of other Trim products would have a cholesterol problem or would desire to purchase Trim Eggs for the purpose of reducing calorie intake. However, it was believed that there would be some overlap.

The principal competition would be from Fleishmann's Egg Beaters and Morningstar Farms' Scramblers. Fleishmann's would have a strong identification with low-cholesterol products due to success with its margarine product. Fleishmann's is a division of Standard Brands, and Morningstar Farms is a division of Miles Laboratories.

TEST MARKET RESULTS

Test market results were mixed. Professional and managerial people and those with higher educational attainment purchased Trim Eggs. However, white-collar and especially blue-collar workers did not purchase the product in satisfactory numbers. Some younger couples purchased the product, believing in the prevention of cholesterol buildup before they became older. Shapiro believed that white-collar workers who live sedentary lives would be a good potential market. Several of those interviewed reported that they had looked for the product in the frozen food section. Purchasers of Egg Beaters and Scramblers would need to be reoriented. Advertising had been focused mainly on the over-35 age market. The advertising/sales ratio was 3 percent of anticipated sales to be allocated to advertising. In retrospect, this was viewed as a mistake, since most food companies reported advertising/sales ratios of from 5 to 7 percent. This was carefully verified from *Advertising Age* figures. Shapiro estimated that 50 percent of the advertising budget would be allocated to the introductory stage, and 25 percent to the growth stage. Twenty percent would be allocated to the maturity stage, and the final 5 percent to the decline stage.

THE MARKETING PLAN

Trim Products subscribed to a consumer-panel reporting service. In its data it was noticed that there was impressive growth in panel members using cholesterol-free food. Existing surveys taken by Trim Products revealed that users of cholesterol-free eggs found that defrosting the eggs was very inconvenient. A high percentage of purchasers were housewives.

Since Trim Products had other successful products, coupons would be inserted into the packages of Trim Cheese, Trim Yogurt, and Trim Salad Dressing permitting the consumer to purchase Trim Eggs at half price in a single or a six-pack container.

The company would allocate funds for advertising in such high-fashion magazines as *Vogue* and in newsmagazines. The theory was that the better-educated working wife would be an important market. Spot radio and television commercials would be used during the 6 P.M. and 11 P.M. news programs. Trim Products salespeople would receive instructions on how to sell the complete product line. Supermarket managers and store employees would be offered free samples.

As a result of these plans, a planned profit per unit schedule was developed.

◣ **Schedule I.** Sale in Six-Pack Containers: *Planned Profit per Unit*

Retail price per unit		$2.50
Less allowances and expenses:		
40% allowance to outlets	$1.00	
20% allowance for advertising	0.30	
Cost of manufacturing	0.50	
Cost of shipping	0.17	
Sales expense	0.20	
Administrative expense	0.15	$2.32
Planned profit per unit		$0.18

Shapiro believed that a profit margin of 18 cents per six-pack unit was low but would increase as costs of manufacturing and shipping were reduced when the product was sold in larger volume. Moreover, sales expense is generally lowered as the product enters the growth stage of the life cycle. The planned profit per unit would be approximately in the same proportion for Trim Eggs sold in the single container. Shapiro planned that the product would not be offered in the single container in the maturity stage of the life cycle. The unit of sale would be changed so that a six-pack and a three-pack would be offered. Each package would contain 8.5 ounces and be the equivalent of four large eggs. This would be similar to Fleishmann's Egg Beater brand.

Shapiro believed that the product was competitive, but that the market had to be broadened. However, the competition was formidable and initial costs were high. Consequently, Trim Products was indecisive about entering this competitive market.

1. What would you recommend Trim Eggs do to appeal to different consumer markets?
2. Do you believe the Trim Eggs strategy could have been improved in the market test stage?
3. What is your opinion of the profit potential of this product?
4. Do you believe that Trim Products should market this product? if yes, would you suggest any changes in the marketing plan?

PART Four

The nature of pricing

11

Demand and cost in price determination

OBJECTIVES

To realize the importance of pricing and the impact of demand and costs.

To understand the variety of pricing objectives.

To examine the determinants of price.

To review several cost-oriented pricing strategies.

To gain an awareness of the external factors affecting price.

In the late 1970s, Gillette began marketing Eraser Mate, an erasable pen. Scripto possessed the technology to develop a similar product so it decided to conduct preliminary marketing research. It found that a full 42 percent of the Eraser Mate purchases fell in the 11–14 age bracket. For a product retailing at almost $2, that was considered astounding. This indicated to Scripto that more than any other group, students have a need that erasable pens fulfill. It was precisely this group that Scripto had identified as the primary target, so the fit with the company's objectives was becoming tighter.

Stick pens are the largest segment of the writing instrument market with more than one billion units in yearly sales. So, Scripto decided to produce the world's first disposable, erasable pen.

Students were interviewed in focus groups, and researchers learned that they felt 98¢ would be a reasonable price for an erasable, disposable pen. They also said they would rather pay that amount for an erasable than 25¢ for a disposable Bic.

The price was verified in subsequent product placement tests using the actual product. Most importantly, a price of 98¢ gave Scripto the profit margins and projected sales volumes they were looking for. The Scripto disposable, erasable pen has been a major commercial success.[1]

The Scripto example illustrates several important points. First, the price must be perceived as fair by the target audience. Second, demand must be sufficient at the proposed price to meet sales projections. Third, the projected sales volume and profit margins must meet the firm's pricing goals.

We begin with a discussion of the importance of price and pricing objectives. The remainder of the chapter is devoted to the determinants of price: demand, cost, and other significant factors.

The importance of price

We live in a mixed free-enterprise society that depends primarily on a complex system of prices to allocate goods and services among consumers, governments, and businesses. A **mixed economy** is one in which both the government and the private sector exercise economic control. **Free enterprise** refers to the right to engage in virtually any economic enterprise. You can be a doctor or a salesperson or almost anything else provided you have the necessary qualifications. The American government plays a minor role in guiding business endeavors compared to the governments of most countries.

Since the government plays a minor role in resource allocation, something else must fulfill the role of allocator in our society. Consumers play this role quite nicely through the exercise of dollar votes. If people believe that a merchant has established a fair price for a good or service, they vote for (purchase) that product. For example, if you use Gleem toothpaste, you are in effect saying: "keep producing Gleem; it meets my price needs." Business firms that do a good job in satisfying the needs of the consumer receive more dollar votes (sales). The earned revenue may then be used by the firm to purchase additional resources to produce more goods and services. Companies that do not satisfy the consumer (and thus lack dollar votes) cannot effectively compete for resources and eventually switch their production to another product or go out of business.

Why is price so important? For several reasons. Executives are aware of the necessity to charge a price that will earn their company a fair return on its investment. The price strategy must produce a price that is not too high or low to achieve this goal. Stepping over either boundary could put the firm out of business in the long run. It is also important that customers perceive the price to be fair. Sometimes, the determination of what is too high, too low, or "fair" is very difficult.

In the field of industrial marketing, the McGraw-Hill Laboratory of Advertising Performance found that high price turns off more prospects than any other single thing.[2] It found that 60 percent of 1,423 marketing executives it surveyed cited the cost of the product as the major reason why they might not agree to the sale. So pricing is a vital component of the marketing mix.

Pricing objectives

Companies need pricing objectives that are specific, attainable, and measurable. Realistic pricing goals require periodic monitoring in order to determine the effectiveness of the company's strategy. Although profit maximization is often advocated by economists, it does not provide managers with all the criteria necessary for evaluating performance. Many firms do not have adequate accounting data for maximizing profits. It sounds simple to say that a company should keep producing and selling products or services as long as revenues are greater than costs. But developing accounting systems to tell management in a timely manner when that point has been reached can be very complex.

Sometimes, managers will say that their company is attempting to maximize profits; in other words, the goal is to make as much money as possible. Although this may sound impressive to stockholders, it does not provide an adequate basis for planning. Instead, it gives management license to do just about anything it wants to do. Assume that a marketing manager establishes a marketing plan that provides the firm with a return of 5 percent on investment at the end of a year. A stockholder might ask, "Why did management follow that particular plan?" The answer? It was trying to maximize profits. Did management maximize profits? Probably not, but proving it is very difficult. To avoid this problem, competent managers set realistic and measurable pricing goals. These include target return on investment, market share, and meeting competition.

TARGET RETURN ON INVESTMENT

Alcoa, Du Pont, General Electric, General Motors, International Harvester, Union Carbide, and Johns-Manville have a **target return on investment** as their principal pricing goal. This is a cost-based strategy. In the large corporations studied by the economist John Lanzillotti, the average target return was about 14 percent of invested capital after taxes.

A target return enables a company to establish the level of profits it feels will yield a satisfactory return. The marketing executive can use the standard to determine whether a particular price and marketing mix combination is feasible. Any given mix and price will attain the target return, or it will not. In addition, the manager must weigh the risk of a given strategy even if the return is in the acceptable range, as the following example shows.

During June 1977, Wolverine Brass Works introduced a line of faucets designed to appeal to builders of low-priced apartments and homes. They were priced competitively, says Kenneth Case, but not *too* competitively. Case, president of Citation Companies, Grand Rapids, Wolverine's parent, has strong views on that subject.

"I was brought up in the sales field and my first job with Wolverine Brass was sales manager," he says. "I am acutely aware that nobody can damage your profits more than a fainthearted sales manager who does not accept the discipline of pricing. We put it this way: You have a line of products, and this is the minimum profit you must make. If you are not making it, you have to either raise the selling price, lower the cost, or a combination of both. Or else drop the product because we can't afford to sell it."[3]

MARKET SHARE

Many companies believe that maintaining or increasing their market share is a key to the effectiveness of their marketing mix. As contrasted with a target return strategy, market share is a demand-oriented concept. Research organizations such as A. C. Nielson and Ehrhart-Babic provide excellent market share reports for many different industries.

Market share and return on investment are strongly related. On the average, a difference of 10 percentage points in market share is accompanied by a difference of about 5 points in pretax return on investment (ROI). A larger market share probably increases profitability because of greater economies of scale, market power, and ability to compensate top-quality management. American Can, Kroger, Sears, Swift, and Exxon have all made maintaining or increasing market share their primary pricing objective.

Sometimes, firms can "buy" market share, yet it is usually at the expense of profits. Chrysler Corporation in the mid-1970s and early 1980s offered substantial consumer rebates (effectively lowering its retail prices) to sell off high inventories and attempt to maintain market share. In 1980, the firm had the largest loss ever experienced by a major corporation. Price cuts alone will not enable a firm to maintain long-run market share. The product must meet the needs of the marketplace. When Miller Beer attacked the traditional market leaders in the late 1970s it bought market share through extremely large advertising expenditures. For several years Miller's profits were low to nonexistent, but economies of scale and a large market share have now made Miller beer very profitable.

The Miller strategy was to increase market share, whereas Chrysler was simply trying to hold its own. In other situations it may be better to give up market share. These three managerial strategies and when to use them are summarized in Table 11.1.

MEETING COMPETITION

A less aggressive pricing strategy than target return or market shares, followed by many companies such as Goodyear, Gulf, and National Steel, is to meet competition.[4] Usually this goal is easier to accomplish than those just mentioned and requires relatively little planning. Often firms competing in an in-

▲ TABLE 11.1   Market Share Price Strategies

Option	When to use it	Pricing strategy	Financial implications
1. Significantly increase market share	Growth market Have or can get equal or superior competitive strength No. 1 in market or good position to take it	Pricing at or below market, depending on competitive strength	Low profit now High profit later Low cash flow now
2. Hold share	No. 1 in market Nongrowth market Very strong competition	Maintain or increase price	Profits/cash flow now
3. Divest share	Dying market Inordinately high competitors' strength	High price premium	Maximum profit/cash flow in near term

Source: C. Davis Fogg and Kent H. Kohnken, "Price-Cost Planning," *Journal of Marketing* 42 (April 1978): 104. Reprinted by permission of the American Marketing Association.

dustry in which there is an established price leader follow the passive policy of meeting the competition. As a result, these industries typically have fewer price wars than those in which firms engage in direct price competition.

The determinants of price

After a marketing manager establishes pricing goals, a specific price must be set to reach these objectives. The price established depends primarily on (1) demand for the good or service and (2) the cost to the seller for that good or service. In addition, other factors such as distribution and promotion strategies, perceived quality, and stage of the product life cycle can influence price (see Figure 11.1).

DEMAND

When pricing goals are primarily sales-oriented, cost considerations are usually subordinated to demand considerations. **Demand** refers to the quantity of a company's product that will be purchased during a specific period and at various prices.

Elasticity of demand. To appreciate demand analysis, you should understand the concept of elasticity. **Elasticity of demand** refers to the responsiveness or the sensitivity of consumers to changes in price. If they are sensitive, demand is elastic; if they are insensitive, demand is inelastic. Elasticity over a range of a demand curve can be measured by a formula or by observing changes in total revenue. If total revenue rises as price declines, demand is elastic. If total revenue rises as prices are increased, demand is inelastic. The formula for elasticity is:

$$\text{Elasticity } (\Sigma) = \frac{\text{Percentage change in quantity demanded of good A}}{\text{Percentage change in price of good A}}$$

If Σ is greater than 1, demand is elastic.
If Σ is less than 1, demand is inelastic.
If Σ is equal to 1, demand is unitary.

Assume that demand for Pillsbury's frozen microwave pizza is as shown in Figure 11.2. Demand for Pillsbury's pizza is found to be elastic from $2 through $1 because as the price decreases, total revenue increases. We can just as easily use the formula to measure elasticity. For example, if the price drops from $2 to $1, elasticity of demand is as follows:

$$\Sigma = \frac{\% \Delta Q}{\% \Delta P}$$

$$\Sigma = \frac{1 \Delta Q1 / AvQ}{1 \Delta P1 / AvP}$$

$$\Sigma = \frac{(4785 - 1825)/[(1825 + 4785)/2]}{(2 - 1)/[(2 + 1)/2]}$$

$$\Sigma = \frac{2960/3305}{1.00/1.50}$$

$$\Sigma = \frac{.896}{.666}$$

$\Sigma = 1.35$ Demand is elastic.

Let us look at why demand was inelastic when the price fell from $1 to $0.75. Remember, of course, that the company's demand schedule does not allow it to sell 4785 units for $1 and then sell an additional 6375 units at $0.75 — instead, it's an "either–or" proposition. Therefore, in order to sell 6375, we are sacrificing $0.25 on 4785 units that could have been sold at $1 instead of

FIGURE 11.1 The determinants of price.

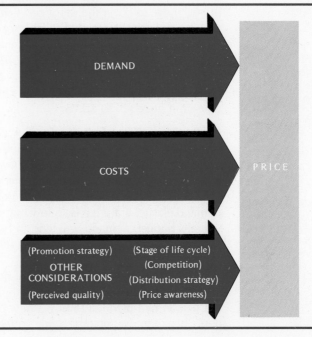

FIGURE 11.2 Demand schedule and demand curve for frozen microwave pizza.

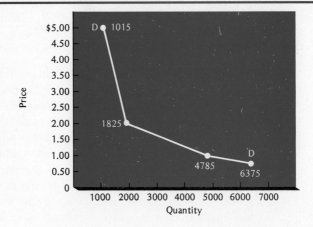

Price	Quantity demanded
$5.00	1015
2.00	1825
1.00	4785
.75	6375

the new price of $0.75. The total sacrifice when the price is dropped from $1 to $0.75 is $1196.25 (4785 × $0.25). Demand must be sensitive enough to the price change to cover the sacrificed revenue or total revenue will fall (demand will be inelastic). Note that Pillsbury sold an additional 1590 units when it dropped the price to $0.75. Thus the gross revenue gain from the price cut was $1192.50 ($0.75 × 1590). The gain of $1192.50 was not enough to offset the $0.25 per unit loss ($1196.25) on the 4785 units that could have been sold for $1. Demand was inelastic because not enough additional sales were made when the price fell to $0.75.

Factors that affect elasticity. Elasticity of demand is affected by a number of factors such as (1) the availability of substitute goods and services, (2) the price relative to a consumer's purchasing power, (3) the durability of a product, and (4) the other uses of a product. When a large number of substitute products are available, the consumer can easily switch from one product to another, making demand elastic. If a price is so low that it is an inconsequential part of an individual's budget, demand will tend to be inelastic. For example, if the price of salt doubles, you will not stop putting salt and pepper on your eggs because salt is cheap anyway.

Durable products such as automobiles often give consumers the option of repairing the old product rather than replacing it, thus prolonging its useful life. If a person had planned to buy a new car and the prices of automobiles suddenly began to rise, he or she might elect to fix the old one and drive it for another year. In other words, people are sensitive to the price increase, and demand is elastic. Finally, the greater the number of product uses, the more elastic demand will tend to be. If a product has only one use, as may be true of a new medicine, there is not much chance that quantity purchased will vary as price varies. A person will consume only the prescribed quantity, regardless of price. On the other hand, a product like steel has many possible applications. As the price of steel falls it becomes more economically feasible to use it in a wide variety of applications, thus making demand relatively elastic.

Estimating demand. Demand-oriented pricing policies are difficult or impossible to implement unless the firm has a reasonable estimate of demand. The use of demand estimation is not as widespread as the theoretical treatment of price might lead one to believe. One study found that slightly more than 50 percent of the responding companies engaged in some form of demand estimation. Often the estimation is limited to choosing among two or three potential prices.

Two reasons why many firms do not attempt to estimate demand are (1) the sheer difficulty of the process and (2) the fact that the potential cost may be greater than the payout. Economists know that the law of demand—as prices fall, quantity demand increases, and vice versa—holds in general. For example, from January 1975 to January 1976 retail coffee prices rose almost 19 percent and consumption declined 5 percent, to 31.6 gallons per capita.[5] Yet empirical research indicates that many demand curves are not smooth and negatively sloped. Studies show many unusual demand functions with positive slopes, kinks, and sudden backward bends.[6]

Experience can be carried a step further by using statistical analysis to examine past sales and prices. Simple regression analysis may show that for every $1 increase in price, sales will decline by 412 units.* If the variation in quantity sold may be largely "explained" by price variations (a high coefficient of determination), then merchants may use the information as a reliable basis for building a demand curve. Simple regression can be further extended by using multiple regression to examine a number of factors besides sales price that might influence demand. Factors such as inflation, competitors' prices, advertising volume, and retail stores selling the product may be included in the analysis to further refine the determinants of demand.

Laboratory experiments in which consumers pretend they are purchasing products have also been used to estimate demand. Often, however, they are just that—pretending. Although the methodology of laboratory experimentation seems to be sound, unrealistic purchase conditions taint the usefulness of this technique. Often, marketing research is called upon to estimate price and quantity relationships. The techniques used vary from simple to elaborate quantitative simulation models. (We will discuss demand estimation in more detail in Chapter 21.)

COST

Sometimes companies minimize or ignore the importance of demand and price their products largely or solely on the basis of costs. These companies are not following the marketing concept. Prices determined strictly on the basis of costs may be too high for the target market, thereby reducing or eliminating sales. On the other hand, cost-based prices may be too low, causing the firm to earn a lower return than it should. For example, Texas Instruments marketed its "Speak and Spell" toy for about half of what consumers were willing to pay for it. The firm was selling all it could produce but initially refused to raise the price because that would violate the corporate philosophy of lowering prices throughout the product life cycle. Economists use a variety of cost concepts in determining profitability and optimal output levels; see the appendix to this chapter for the cost schedules commonly used in price theory.

Markup pricing. **Markup pricing** is the most popular method used by wholesalers and retailers in establishing a sales price. When the merchandise is received, the retailer adds a certain percentage to the figure to arrive at the retail price. An item that costs $1.80 and is sold for $2.20 carries a markup of $0.40, or 18 percent of the retail price. The initial markup is also referred to as the "mark-on." If the retailer had to cut the price to $2 before the product could be sold, the difference between the cost and the selling price would be only $0.20, or 10 percent of the actual selling price. The latter figure is called gross

---

* The idea of least-squares regression analysis is to fit a straight line to the points of a two-variable scatter diagram so as to minimize the sum of the squared vertical deviations between the points and the line, thus giving a "best fit."

margin or **maintained markup.** The maintained markup reflects actual demand and is much more important than the mark-on.

Assume that a retailer determines from past records that operating costs are 32 percent of sales and profit is 7 percent. It can mark up its merchandise by 39 percent and both cover costs and earn a profit. However, if 7 percent is considered an unsatisfactory profit, the merchant will have to add more than 39 percent to the merchandise costs. There will be some markdowns, pilferage, and employee discounts. If these three factors amount to an additional 5 percent of sales, the retailer will have to use a mark-on of 41.90 percent to earn a 7 percent profit. The formula is

$$\text{Mark-on} = \frac{\text{Gross margin (39\%)} + \text{retail reduction (5\%)}}{100\% + \text{retail reductions (5\%)}}$$

$$= \frac{44\%}{105\%}$$

$$= 41.90\%$$

Thus to achieve a maintained margin of 39 percent, we must use an initial markup of 41.90 percent.

Sometimes retailers must establish a retail price based on a predetermined maintained margin and the unit cost. Suppose a merchant wants a gross margin of 42 percent (on retail) and an item costs $3.46. The formula for determining the retail price is

$$\text{Retail price} = \frac{\text{cost (3.46)}}{100 - \text{mark-on (42\%)}} \times 100$$

$$= \frac{3.46}{58} \times 100$$

$$= \$5.97$$

If no markdowns are experienced, a selling price of $5.97 will provide the merchant with the desired gross margin on retail.

Markups are often based on experience, yet this does not necessarily mean they are established without forethought. Among the factors that often influence markups are the appeal of the merchandise to the customer, past response to the markup (an implicit demand consideration), the promotional value of the item, the seasonality of the goods, fashion appeal, the traditional selling price of the product, and competition. The majority of retailers find it important to deviate widely from any set markup because of considerations like those just mentioned.

Formula pricing. A similar type of pricing to the use of markups is **formula pricing.** One simple formula used by a marketing research firm (that should know better than to ignore demand) is to charge five times the cost of the field work. Since field work is normally the most expensive part of a research project, this approach hopes to cover all costs and make a profit. More elaborate formulas are also used. For example, one manufacturer uses direct labor times 150 percent plus material costs times 200 percent plus actual shipping costs. The primary advantage of this technique is its simplicity. But like all basic cost-pricing strategies, it ignores demand.

Costs, stock turnover, and profits. There is a very important relationship between costs, (sales) stock turnover, and profit. **Stock turnover** refers to the number of times during a given period (usually a year) that the average amount of goods on hand are sold. Following are two common techniques for calculating inventory turnover:

1. Opening inventory at retail $18,000
   Closing inventory at retail 4,200
   2) 22,200
   Average inventory at retail $11,100
   Net sales $48,200
   $$\frac{\$48,200}{\$11,100} = 4.34 = \text{stock turnover}$$

2. Opening inventory at cost $ 9,000
   Closing inventory at cost 2,100
   2) 11,100
   Average inventory at cost $ 5,550
   Cost of goods sold $24,087
   $$\frac{\$24,087}{\$ 5,550} = 4.34 = \text{stock turnover}$$

Rapid stock turnover may mean limited investment in inventory, less need for storage space, fresher merchandise, or fewer markdowns. Generally speaking, high stock turnovers lead to higher profits. There are exceptions to this rule, however. Assume, for example, that a dealer reduces its stock and holds sales constant (an increase in turnover). Purchasing in small quantities may mean the loss of quantity discounts; higher expenditures for receiving, checking, and marking merchandise; and greater correspondence and clerical costs. In this situation, profits would fall.

The breakeven concept. Let us take a closer look at the relationship between sales and cost. **Breakeven theory** determines what sales volume must be reached for a product before the company "breaks even" (total costs equals total revenue).

The typical breakeven model assumes a given fixed cost and a constant average variable cost (variable cost per product). American Products (a hypothetical firm) has fixed costs of $2000, and the cost of labor and materials for each unit produced is $0.50. Assume that it can sell up to 7000 units of its product at $1 without having to lower its price. Table 11.2 and Figure 11.3 illustrate AP's breakeven point.

Output	Total fixed costs	Average variable costs	Total variable costs	Average revenue (price)	Total revenue	Total costs	Profit or loss
500	$2000	$0.50	$ 250	$1.00	$ 500	$2250	($1750)
1000	2000	0.50	500	1.00	1000	2500	($1500)
1500	2000	0.50	750	1.00	1500	2750	($1250)
2000	2000	0.50	1000	1.00	2000	3000	($1000)
2500	2000	0.50	1250	1.00	2500	3250	($ 750)
3000	2000	0.50	1500	1.00	3000	3500	($ 500)
3500	2000	0.50	1750	1.00	3500	3750	($ 250)
4000	2000	0.50	2000	1.00	4000	4000	(0)[a]
4500	2000	0.50	2250	1.00	4500	4250	$ 250
5000	2000	0.50	2500	1.00	5000	4500	$ 500
5500	2000	0.50	2750	1.00	5500	4750	$ 750
6000	2000	0.50	3000	1.00	6000	5000	$1000

[a] Breakeven point.

▲ FIGURE 11.3 Breakeven chart for American Products.

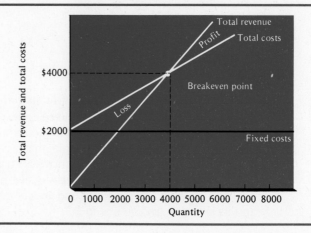

Average variable costs increase by $0.50 every time a new unit is produced, and total fixed costs remain constant at $2000 regardless of the level of output. Therefore 4000 units of output give AP $2000 in fixed costs and $2000 in total variable costs (4000 units × $0.50), or $4000 in total costs. Revenue is also $4000 at 4000 units (4000 units × $1), giving a net profit of zero dollars at breakeven. Notice that once the firm gets past the breakeven point, the gap between TR and TC gets wider and wider, since both functions are assumed to be linear.

A simple formula for calculating breakeven quantities is as follows:

Fixed cost contribution (FCC) = price − AVC (average variable costs)

$$= \$1.50$$
$$= \$\ .50$$

$$\text{Breakeven quantity} = \frac{\text{Total fixed costs (TFC)}}{\text{Fixed cost contribution (FCC)}}$$

$$= \frac{\$2000}{\$.50}$$

$$= 4000 \text{ units}$$

Advantages and disadvantages of breakeven analysis. The advantage of breakeven theory is that it provides a quick glance at how much the firm must sell to break even and how much profit can be earned if higher sales volume is obtained. If a firm is operating close to the breakeven point, it may want to see what can be done to reduce costs or find out whether any reasonable measures can be taken to increase sales. A final advantage is the fact that it is not necessary to compute marginal costs and marginal revenues in simple breakeven analysis. This is because price and average cost per unit are assumed to be constant. Since marginality accounting data are frequently unavailable, it is convenient not to have to depend on that information.

Breakeven theory is not without several important limitations. Sometimes it is difficult to ascertain whether a cost is fixed or variable. For example, if labor wins a tough guaranteed-employment contract, are the resulting expenses a fixed cost? What about middle-echelon executives — are their costs fixed? More important than cost determination is the fact that simple breakeven theory ignores demand. How does American Products know it can sell 4000 units at $1? Could it sell the same 4000 units at $2 or even $5? Obviously this would have profound effects on the firm's breakeven point.

The modified breakeven concept. The usefulness of breakeven analysis can be increased with the addition of demand considerations. Figure 11.4 shows various revenue functions for American Products at different sales prices. Letters A through D represent the "best estimates" of actual demand (a demand curve) at various prices. If AP charges a price of $5, sales are estimated at 400 units and $2000 total revenue. Total costs will be $2000 fixed costs plus $200 variable costs (400 × $0.50), or $2200. Thus if AP charges $5 a unit, it will end up losing $200. Using the same procedure, you can see that a price of $2 will be the most profitable for the company ($1000 total profit). Point C also represents the point farthest from the TC line, indicating the largest total profit. At a price of $1, sales will be 5050 units, resulting in $525 profit.

Notice also that the breakeven point varies as the price fluctuates. Breakeven quantities are as follows: $5 = 444 units, $2 = 1333 units; $1 = 4000 units, and $0.75 = 8000 units. The lower the selling price, given constant average variable costs and constant fixed costs, the higher the breakeven sales volume.

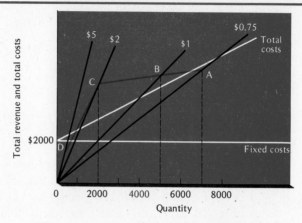

Price	Forecasted quantity demanded
$5.00	400
2.00	2000
1.00	5050
.75	7000

TARGET RETURN PRICING

Target return pricing is the most popular method of choosing a selling price. Merchants can easily figure a target return price by treating the desired profit as an addition to fixed cost. Desired profit, of course, is established by managerial judgment. If American Products has a desired profit of $900, and a price of $2.00 with an AVC of $.50, it can be plugged into the basic formula as follows:

$$FCC = \$2.00 - \$.50 = \$1.50$$

$$\text{Breakeven point} = \frac{\text{Total fixed cost} + \text{total desired profit}}{\text{Fixed cost contribution per unit}}$$

$$= \frac{\$2000 + \$900}{\$1.50}$$

$$= 1933.33 \text{ units}$$

American Products can easily achieve its target return on investment, assuming that its expected value of output forecast is correct. Since AP requires only 1933 units to achieve its target return and expects to sell 2130 units at $2, the firm will exceed its target return.

Large firms that use target return pricing usually come quite close to their goals. Our example of target return pricing is simplified owing to space considerations. Many companies use much more sophisticated and detailed approaches to the calculation of target return.

HOW INFLATION-BASED PRICING FEEDS UPON ITSELF

A target return objective and inflation psychology often create a **ratchet effect.**[7] This is the term used by economists to explain the tendency for prices to rise higher and higher, resisting the downward pressure of the marketplace even when demand is low. The problem seems to be particularly acute in large corporations.

Assume that the brake shoe division of U.S. Industries just had a normal year ending in 1982. It met its target return goal of $1 million profit. The corporate forecast for 1983 expects the brake shoe market to have an off-year. Bill Smith, recently promoted to division manager, studies Table 11.3 and realizes that his career is getting ready to receive a black mark. Since Bill has risen rapidly in the corporate ranks, he takes action to save his career (and division profits). He first raises prices 10 percent to $11 per unit. Bill then directs all subordinates to reduce fixed costs by 10 percent and orders the plant to sell unneeded machines and trim inventories to reduce the asset base. Bill justifies the price increase by asserting that unit costs have risen to an unprofitable level. He ignores the fact that lower projected volume, not higher costs, accounts for the change in cost per unit. Most of his customers will take the price hike in stride due to today's inflationary psychology. U.S. Industries' customers have already built in an expected 8 percent increase in prices, so another 2 percent will not be hard to swallow.

The year 1983 goes as Bill planned, and he is now one of the up and coming stars at U.S. Industries. Remember he did increase profits in a bad year (see Table 11.4). Headquarters of U.S. Industries ignores the effects of a 10 percent reduction in the salesforce, advertising, control expenses, manufacturing expense, and so on. These are the division manager's responsibilities. Headquarters is more concerned with strategic planning. Bill is not going to have to worry either; he is scheduled for a promotion in six months. This example points out how marketing managers (and higher management) have let inflation affect their price strategies. It also shows how American business can get caught in its own inflationary pricing trap.

◄ **TABLE 11.3   Brake Shoe Division Income Statement for 1982 and Forecast for 1983**

	1982 (Sales: 1 million units at $10 each)	1983 (Sales: 800,000 units at $10 each)
Sales	$10,000,000	$ 8,000,000
Variable costs ($5/unit)	$ 5,000,000	$ 4,000,000
Contribution margin	$ 5,000,000	$ 4,000,000
Fixed costs	$ 4,000,000	$ 4,000,000
Operating profit	$ 1,000,000	-0-

▲ TABLE 11.4 Income Statement for 1983

	1983 (Sales: 780,000 units at $11 each)
Sales	$8,580,000
Variable costs ($5/unit)	$3,900,000
Contribution margin	$4,680,000
Fixed costs	$3,600,000
Operating profit	$1,080,000

OTHER FACTORS THAT AFFECT PRICE

Other factors beside demand, costs, and inflationary psychology can affect price. The stage of the product's life cycle, the competition, product distribution, promotion strategy, and perceived product quality can have an important impact on pricing strategy.

The stage of the product's life cycle. As a product moves through its life cycle, its demand and competitive conditions tend to change. Prices are usually high during the introduction stage (but not always, as we will see in the next chapter) because demand originates in the core of the market and management hopes to cover developmental production costs.

The pricing strategy followed during introduction often depends on elasticity of demand. If demand is relatively inelastic, management may introduce the good or service at a fairly high price—for example, pocket calculators. If the target audience is highly price sensitive, it is often better to price the product at the market level or lower. When General Foods brought out Country Time Lemonade, it was priced like similar products in the highly competitive beverage market.

Prices generally begin to stabilize as the product enters the growth stage. Competitors enter the market, increasing the available supply. The product begins to appeal to broader, and often lower, income groups. Finally, economies of scale enable lower costs to be passed on to the consumer in the form of lower prices.

Maturity usually brings further price declines as competition increases and inefficient, high-cost firms are eliminated. Distribution channels are a significant cost factor owing to wide product lines for highly segmented markets, extensive service requirements, and the sheer number of dealers necessary for high-volume production. The manufacturers that remain in the market toward the end of the maturity stage typically offer similar prices. Only the most efficient usually remain, and they have comparable costs. Price increases at this stage are usually cost-initiated not due to greater demand. Nor do price reductions in the late phase of maturity usually stimulate demand a great deal.

Demand is limited, and similar cost structures mean that the remaining competitors will probably match price reductions.

The final stage of the life cycle, product decline, may bring on price declines as the few remaining competitors attempt to salvage the last vestiges of demand. When only one firm is left in the market prices begin to stabilize; in fact, they may eventually rise as the product moves into the specialty good category.

The competition. Competition, of course, varies during the product life cycle and at times may strongly influence pricing decisions. For example, although a firm may not have any competition, high prices can eventually influence another firm to enter the market. Tylenol, the nonaspirin pain reliever, had a stranglehold on its $60 million market for ten years. Johnson and Johnson's profit margin on this product was approximately 40 percent of sales. This plum looked so appealing to Bristol Myers that it jumped into the market in 1974 with an almost identical product, Datril.

Bristol Myers' marketing managers decided that the best way to obtain a significant market share quickly was through intensive price competition. Datril entered the market promoting its 100-tablet bottle at $1.85, claiming that this price averaged $1 lower than that of a comparable bottle of Tylenol. Johnson and Johnson quickly countered with a lower price, but it was too late. Datril was established as a viable competitor.

A recent study of 356 items that originally had no direct competition and then began to experience competition showed that this change resulted in a reduction of the unit selling price of between 10.8 and 17.5 percent, depending upon the size of the order.[8]

Distribution strategy. Adequate distribution for a new product can often be attained by offering a larger-than-customary profit margin on the item. A variation on this strategy is to give dealers a large promotional allowance to help offset the costs of promotion and further stimulate demand at the retail level. An effective distribution network can often overcome other minor flaws in a marketing mix. Perhaps a price is perceived by consumers as being slightly higher than normal, but if the good is located in a convenient retail outlet they may purchase it anyway. The case of Perrier is a good example of this phenomenon.

Perrier naturally carbonated mineral water has been distributed in the United States since the turn of the century, but until the late 1970s sales were flat and the product an obscure specialty good. It was available only in specialty food outlets and "better" restaurants. During 1977 management embarked upon an aggressive marketing program to make Perrier a mass market beverage. Naturally this called for an entirely different distribution strategy, and for going into grocery stores and convenience food markets. To obtain the necessary distribution, Perrier offered major price discounts to wholesalers and retailers on a market by market basis. By 1979, it was selling over 100 million bottles a year.

Promotion strategy. Price is often used as a promotional tool in order to increase consumer interest. Pick up your Thursday newspaper and turn to the grocery section. You will see ads for a number of products with special low prices designed to induce consumers to shop in a particular store. Manufacturers also place discount coupons in this section in the hope of influencing consumers to purchase their brand.

Manufacturers typically promote introductory price offers in order to help a product get through the introductory stage of the life cycle. Perrier, for example, used a massive "cents-off" campaign to acquaint consumers with the taste of Perrier. Salespeople will discount list prices in order to close deals that might otherwise go to competitors. Manufacturers may also bring out a "fighting brand" at a low price in the hope of reaching a lower-income market segment.

Price-quality relationships. A fighting brand is often viewed as a relatively low-quality product in the absence of additional product information. Conversely, consumers tend to rely on a high price as a predictor of good quality when there is a substantial degree of uncertainty involved in the purchase decision. A number of studies have shown this tendency for products such as coffee, stockings, aspirin, salt, floor wax, shampoo, clothing, furniture, perfume, and whiskey.[9] Reliance on price as an indicator of quality seems to exist for all products, but it manifests itself more strongly for some items than for others.[10] The assumption people make is that prices are higher because the products contain better-grade materials and more careful workmanship. That is, "you get what you pay for."

Research has also shown that if it is difficult for consumers to judge relative quality based upon a product's ingredients, they will continue to use price as a quality indicator.[11] In other words, price is not used as a quality indicator just for initial purchases, but for a series of repeat purchases. Therefore price has more than a transitory effect on the way consumers view products and services. A recent study, however, has shown that dealer brands (usually priced lower than manufacturers' brands) are a better buy.[12]

It follows that marketing managers can utilize high prices to enhance the image of their product. The Cadillac Seville is a moderate-sized car, yet it carries an $18,000-plus average price tag. Joy perfume breathlessly claims to be the most expensive in the world. This tactic is sometimes used for rather mundane products, as is illustrated by the Fuji bicycle ad in Figure 11.5. Marketing managers who attempt to raise the quality image of their product by selling at relatively high prices are following a **prestige pricing** strategy.

This strategy can be used to appeal to socially conscious buyers. A Cadillac Seville would probably lose its appeal for many people if it sold for $10,000. Designer jeans are sold for several times the price of similar jeans without the designer label. The prestige strategy is successful when the selling price is consistent with the consumer's attitude toward expected costs. You do not go into a Gucci shop in New York and expect to pay $9.95 for a pair of loafers. In fact, demand would fall drastically at the lower price. Bayer aspirin would probably

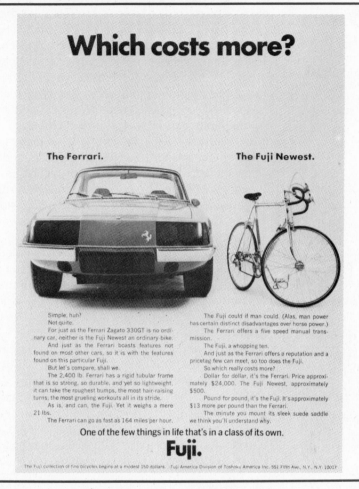

Source: Courtesy of Fuji America, Division of Toshoku America, Inc.

lose market share over the long run if it lowered its prices. A new mustard was recently packaged in a crockery jar. It was not successful until the price was increased from $0.49 to $1 a jar.[13]

SUMMARY

Price serves as an allocator of goods and services in our economic system. It is important to marketing executives because the price charged must earn the company a fair or target return on its investment. In order to do so, specific, attainable, realistic, and measurable pricing objectives must be established. These include target return on investment, market share, and meeting the competition.

The price established for a product depends primarily on demand for the good or service and the cost to the seller for that good or service. Demand refers to the quantity of a company's products that will be purchased during a specific period and at various prices. Elasticity of demand is the responsiveness or the sensitivity of consumers to changes in price. It is important to understand elasticity in order to estimate demand accurately. Elasticity is affected by the availability of substitute goods and services, the price of the product, durability, and other uses of the product.

Sometimes companies minimize or ignore the importance of demand and price their products largely or solely on the basis of costs. Pricing strictly on the basis of cost may cause the firm to lose potential profit. Markup pricing is the most popular method used by wholesalers and retailers to establish selling prices. Markup pricing is a cost-plus technique. The difference between the cost and the selling price is the maintained markup. Markups can be figured on the basis of cost or retail price. Markup and stock turnover determine gross profits. Generally speaking, higher stock turnovers will lead to higher profits.

Breakeven analysis determines the sales volume that must be obtained before total cost equals total revenue. A simple breakeven model assumes a given fixed cost and a constant average variable cost. Breakeven analysis provides a quick look at how many units the firm must sell before it starts earning a profit. The technique also reveals how much profit can be earned with higher sales volumes. A more advanced form of breakeven analysis considers estimated demand at various prices.

Target return pricing is the most popular pricing strategy in American business. It involves establishing a price that will earn the firm a predetermined level of profits. Many large firms that use target return pricing come very close to their profit goals. A target return objective and inflation psychology often create a ratchet effect. This is the tendency for prices to rise higher and higher, resisting the downward pressure of the marketplace when demand is low.

In addition, other factors such as distribution and promotion strategies, perceived quality, and stage of the product life cycle influence price.

KEY TERMS

Mixed economy	Formula pricing
Free enterprise	Stock turnover
Target return on investment	Breakeven theory
Demand	Target return pricing
Elasticity of demand	Ratchet effect
Markup pricing	Prestige pricing
Maintained markup	

REVIEW QUESTIONS

1. Explain how the consumer is involved in the allocation of resources in our society.
2. What are some criticisms of the profit maximization concept?
3. Cost data on Bio, a new antibacterial soap, indicates a fixed cost of $100,000 and a contribution margin of 80 percent. Management has suggested a selling price of 50 cents per unit. What is the unit sales volume required to break even?

4. What is markup pricing? What are some of the factors that influence a markup?
5. Spices of the Indies incurs average operating costs of 29 percent of sales and further incurs pilferage and markdowns running to 6 percent of sales. What mark-on should it put on its products to earn a profit of 8 percent?
6. Under what circumstances is price most often used as an indicator of product quality? Give specific examples..

DISCUSSION QUESTIONS

1. Discuss the various ways by which realistic pricing goals can be set.
2. Why should the marketing concept be a consideration in price determination?
3. Explain briefly the concept of the breakeven point. What are some of the limitations of this theory?
4. Explain the modified breakeven concept. How does it improve on traditional breakeven theory?
5. Briefly explain the basic elements of target return pricing. Use an example to illustrate your answer.
6. Analyze product pricing in terms of price sensitivity and the product's life cycle.
7. In your opinion, has the role of price increased or decreased in importance relative to the other marketing mix variables? What developments influenced your decision?

NOTES

1. This example is taken from "Success of Scripto Erasable Pen Due to Marketing Research," *Marketing News,* January 23, 1981, p. 8.
2. "That Old Devil Price," *Sales and Marketing Management,* September 17, 1979, p. 28.
3. "Wolverine: Down to Brass Tacks," *Sales and Marketing Management,* September 1977, p. 16. Reprinted by permission from Sales & Marketing Management Magazine. Copyright 1977.
4. Robert F. Lanzillotti, "Pricing Objectives in Large Companies," *American Economic Review* (December 1958): 921–940.
5. John C. Maxwell, "Price Boosts Hurt Coffee Consumption, Maxwell Says," *Advertising Age,* April 12, 1976, p. 8.
6. Edgar A. Pessemier, "An Experimental Method for Estimating Demand," *Journal of Business* 33 (October 1960): 373–383.
7. This material is adapted from Duncan C. McDougall, "The Corporate Ratchet Effect on Spiraling Inflation," *Harvard Business Review* 56 (November–December 1978): 12–20.
8. David N. Burt and Joseph E. Boyett, Jr., "Reduction in Selling Price after the Introduction of Competition," *Journal of Marketing Research* 16 (May 1979): 275–279.
9. A number of excellent studies have been conducted on the price-quality relationship. See, for example, Arthur G. Bedeian, "Consumer Perception of Price as an Indicator of Product Quality," *MSU Business Topics,* summer 1971, pp. 59–65; Alfred R. Oxenfeldt, "Developing a Favorable Price-Quality Image," *Journal of Retailing* 50 (winter 1974–1975): 8–17; Benson P. Shapiro, "Price Reliance: Existence and Sources," *Journal of Marketing Research* 10 (August 1973): 286–294.
10. Shapiro, "Price Reliance," p. 294.
11. Steven M. Cox, "The Relationship between Price and Quantity in Situations of Repeated Trial," *University of Michigan Business Review* 31 (May 1979): 24–29.

12. John E. Swan, "Price-Product Performance Competition between Retailer and Manufacturer Brands," *Journal of Marketing* 38 (July 1974): 52–59.
13. Kent B. Monroe, *Pricing: Making Profitable Decisions* (New York: McGraw-Hill,
1979), p. 38.

▲ **APPENDIX**

Types of Economic Costs

A variable cost is one that varies with changes in the level of output; an example is
materials costs. Fixed costs do not vary or change as output is increased or decreased; examples are rent and executive salaries.

In order to compare the cost of production to the sales price of the goods or
services, it is helpful to calculate costs per unit or average costs. Average variable
cost (AVC) equals total variable costs divided by output. Average total cost (ATC)
equals total costs divided by output. You will note in Table 11A.1 that AVC and ATC
are basically U shaped. Average fixed costs decline continually as output increases because total fixed costs are constant. Marginal cost (MC) is the change in
total costs associated with a one-unit change in output. For example, when
production rises from 37 to 39 units, the change in total cost is $10. This figure,
however, is for two units; therefore marginal cost is $5.

All the curves illustrated in Figure 11A.1 have a definite relationship. For example, AVC plus AFC equals ATC. Also, MC falls for a while and then turns
upward with the twenty-fifth unit. This means that diminishing returns have set in,
causing less output to be produced for every additional dollar spent on variable
input. MC intersects both AVC and ATC at their lowest possible points. When MC
is less than AVC or ATC, the incremental cost will continue to pull the averages
down. Conversely, when MC is greater than AVC or ATC, it pulls the average up

▲ **TABLE 11A.1   Basic Cost Schedules**

Output	Total fixed costs	Total variable costs	Total costs	Average variable costs	Average fixed costs	Average total costs	Marginal costs
0	$15	0	$ 15	0	—	—	—
2	15	$ 10	25	$5.00	$7.50	$12.50	$ 5.00
6	15	20	35	3.33	2.50	5.83	2.50
12	15	30	45	2.50	1.25	3.75	1.66
19	15	40	55	2.11	0.79	2.89	1.43
25	15	50	65	2.00	0.60	2.60	1.66
30	15	60	75	2.00	0.50	2.50	2.00
34	15	70	85	2.06	0.44	2.50	2.50
37	15	80	95	2.16	0.41	2.57	3.33
39	15	90	105	2.31	0.38	2.69	5.00
40	15	100	115	2.50	0.38	2.88	10.00
40.5	15	110	125	2.72	0.37	3.09	20.00

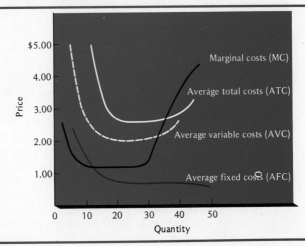

and ATC and AVC begin to rise. The minimum point on the ATC curve is the least-cost point for a fixed-capacity firm; it is not necessarily the most profitable point.

▲ CASES

11.1 Midcontinent Perfume Company

Midcontinent Perfume of Milwaukee, Wisconsin, distributes a wide line of quality women's perfumes to intermediate and high-priced department and specialty stores. It has recently decided to add a new lower-priced line to its product mix in order to capture a slightly different segment of the market. The new product is called "Passion Flower."

A recent market test revealed the following estimated total demand for the product at the quoted prices.

Price	Quantity
$15.00	25,000 units
$20.00	20,000 units
$22.50	19,000 units
$25.00	11,000 units
$27.50	10,000 units

The accounting department figured that the average variable cost for the new perfume would be $13 per unit. Fixed costs are estimated at $40,000.

1. Assuming that the market research studies are accurate, what price should be charged for the perfume?
2. What kind of market research study could have been done to determine the demand schedule for the perfume? Assume that fixed costs are $140,000 rather than $40,000. Should the company have produced in the short run? in the long run?
3. Discuss the advantages and disadvantages of breakeven analysis.
4. What is the breakeven point for this perfume? Of what significance is that point?

11.2 New Mexico Trailmaker Bus Line

New Mexico Trailmaker is a relatively small intrastate bus line headquartered in Albuquerque, New Mexico. The company was founded in 1949 by Al Goode. Goode received his basic training in Arizona during World War II and subsequently decided to move from his native state of Pennsylvania to the sunny Southwest. One driver was hired in 1949 to share the driving load with Goode on the line's only route, Albuquerque to Santa Fe. Over the years the line has prospered under good management; it now employs 187 people, who drive and maintain 41 buses.

John Zigler, vice-president for accounting, came to Goode in July 1980 with a proposal that he felt would partially offset the decline in revenue-passenger miles experienced by Trailmaker during the past twelve months. Zigler suggested that Trailmaker take advantage of the natural growth in tourist traffic that occurred every summer. Specifically, he recommended that an excursion fare be offered between Albuquerque and four major tourist destinations. Goode, a rather cautious man, reluctantly agreed to the rate decreases. He believed that this was an odd thing to do when total revenues were already declining, but he had trusted Zigler's advice for many years. The result of the excursion fare experiment are shown in the table below.

In February 1981 Zigler proposed to Goode that Trailmaker petition the New Mexico Transportation Authority for permanent excursion fares between Albuquerque and Gallup, Sante Fe, and Carlsbad. El Paso was excluded because Trailmaker could not use the main bus terminal, since that would require crossing the Texas border and would put the firm in interstate competition. Instead, Trailmaker used a satellite station in suburban El Paso that was located just inside the New Mexico border. Zigler believed that the company's El Paso market consisted of people living or visiting in areas near the satellite station. These consumers liked the convenience of the suburban terminal and were less price sensitive than those in the other markets.

1. Should Goode go along with Zigler's recommendation?
2. Did the study reveal elastic or inelastic demand for bus service?
3. Does additional research need to be done? If so, what kind?

◢ Results of Trailmaker's Excursion Fare Experiment

Destination	One-way fare from Albuquerque	Special excursion fare June 1– August 30, 1980	Number of passengers Average weekday, month before June 1, 1980	Number of passengers Average weekday, June 1– August 30, 1980	Number of passengers Average weekday, 3 months after August 30 1980
Gallup	$15.00	$12.00	312	401	341
Sante Fe	13.00	10.50	390	560	385
El Paso	19.00	14.00	30	75	70
Carlsbad	23.00	16.00	114	502	161

12 Pricing strategies and tactics

OBJECTIVES

To review the basic price-setting procedure.

To learn about new product pricing strategies.

To analyze special pricing tactics.

To examine bid pricing practices.

To understand pricing in a changing economy.

Competition increased in the northeast market in December, 1980, when a new low-fare carrier, New York Air, began flights between LaGuardia and Washington (D.C.) National Airport.

To attract the traveling public and to generate new travelers, New York Air offered unrestricted low fares, frequent flights and good service. During the first year of operation, New York Air saved the public more than $40 million with its low fares.

Ticket prices for flights between Boston and Washington, for example, are from 20 percent to 50 percent below those charged by other carriers. New York Air's low fares are unrestricted and available to all passengers on every seat on every flight. The carrier's fares have none of the typical airline discount fare requirements for round-trip purchase, minimum-maximum stays, or cancellation penalties.

New York Air features reserved and assigned seats, a clearly designated no-smoking section, "quick" cash register ticketing, complimentary cocktails on weekday flights, and "definite" departure and arrival times.[1]

New York Air has developed successful pricing strategies. What are the advantages and disadvantages of these strategies? What other strategies could they have followed? What steps are involved in setting a price? How have shortages and inflation affected price strategies? These are some of the broader questions we will consider in this chapter. We will also look at bidding strategies, which are very important in industrial and government pricing.

How to set a price

When a company develops a new product or service, one of the most important variables is setting the price. The basic price-setting procedure is shown in Figure 12.1.

Price strategies emerge from pricing objectives. The manager must understand what is to be accomplished with the price before setting up a pricing strategy. In Chapter 11, it was revealed that target return on investment, market share, and meeting competition are three common pricing goals. Another is maximization of cash flow, if a product has a short life or if the firm has experienced large developmental costs.

Understanding the target market. The next step in pricing is understanding the nature of the market as it bears on price. Is the target audience young or old? Wealthy or poor? What do they expect to pay for the product? What goals or services are perceived as substitutes? In the industrial market, most of the same questions should be asked. In addition, the seller should understand the importance of price relative to quality as well as price sensitivity.

By understanding the potential buyer, the marketer can develop a sound positioning plan and better estimate demand. For example, through marketing research the Steak and Ale restaurant chain found it was serving businesspeople at lunch and the over-30 set in the evenings. It decided to develop a new chain and position it to serve the middle-class and above young adult market.

◢ **FIGURE 12.1 How to set a price.**

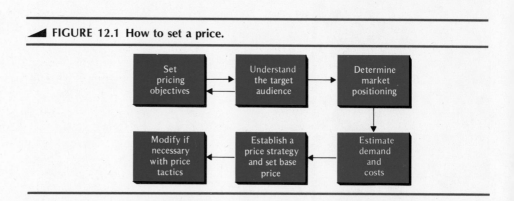

The result was Bennigans restaurants, characterized by plenty of brass fixtures and plants and aimed to appeal to a young, status-oriented group. The menu is limited to quiche, hamburgers, and a few other sandwiches. The decor, ambience, and music help establish the positioning of Bennigans and ultimately its prices. A Bennigans' hamburger costs about three times as much as a Big Mac from McDonald's. It is, however, a bit larger and has a few more embellishments.

Determining market positioning. It has been said in marketing that positioning is everything. While this is probably carrying things a bit too far, positioning does strongly influence the entire marketing mix. Both Hewlett-Packard and Texas Instruments have continued the positioning strategy for minicomputers in the 1980s they used for calculators in the 1970s. Hewlett-Packard markets special applications minicomputers for hospitals, the petroleum industry, and special engineering applications. Prices are usually above the market average. TI sells general purpose minicomputers that are viewed by the market as "good values for the money." As can be seen, positioning often determines the ultimate price strategy for the product. Can you imagine a new men's aftershave lotion by Oleg Cassini selling for $1 a bottle (regardless of how small the bottle is)?

Estimating demand and cost. After a general positioning strategy has been determined, the marketing manager should estimate demand and costs at several different price levels (demand and costs were covered in the previous chapter). It is important to remember that a strictly cost-oriented price policy which ignores demand violates the marketing concept. It also can have serious long-run consequences for the firm. For years U.S. Steel followed a cost-plus strategy: it tried to predict costs and pass them on to the consumer no matter how high they went. U.S. Steel kept prices high enough to allow ten to twelve smaller companies to take a substantial share of the market. As a result, U.S. Steel's market share has dwindled from 48 percent in 1910 to 34 percent in the mid-1950s to 23 percent in the early 1980s.

Establishing price strategy. A strategy establishes the basic long-term pricing framework for the product or service. The strategy should be a logical extension of the pricing objectives. A price strategy not only defines the initial price, it also gives direction for price movements over the product life cycle.

The degree of freedom a company has in pricing a new product or service (and setting a strategy) depends on the nature of the market and the other elements of the marketing mix. If, for example, a firm brings out a new item similar to a number of others already on the market, its pricing freedom will be restricted. The company will probably have to charge a price that is relatively close to the average market price if it is to be successful. On the other hand, a firm that is introducing a totally new product with no close substitutes will have considerable freedom.

Three basic strategies

There are three basic price strategies: price skimming, penetration pricing, and meeting the competition. We will look at each below.

PRICE SKIMMING

A firm with pricing freedom can select a penetration pricing strategy or a skimming pricing strategy for its new offering. **Price skimming** means charging a high introductory price, often coupled with heavy promotion.[2] As the product moves through its life cycle, the firm lowers its price to reach successively larger market segments. Price skimming has been described by some economists as "sliding down the demand curve." Examples of this strategy include the pricing of minicomputers, Concorde tickets, home videocassette player/recorders, and package tours to China. Two classic cases of skimming during the 1970s were digital watches and CB radios. Both were initially priced at several hundred dollars. By the maturity phase of the life cycle, the watches could be purchased for as little as $10, and the CB radios could be purchased for around $30.

When is skimming successful? Price skimming is successful when demand is relatively inelastic in the upper ranges of the curve. If, for example, people will pay $800 for a videocassette player/recorder, some individuals will probably pay $1200 for one with a twelve-hour recorder. When a product is well protected legally or represents a technological breakthrough or has in some other way blocked entry to competitors, price skimming can be utilized effectively. A third situation in which managers may follow a skimming strategy occurs when production cannot be expanded rapidly because of technological difficulties, shortages, or the time demands of skilled craftspeople.

The advantages of skimming. A successful skimming strategy enables management to recover its product development or educational costs quickly. Often, we must be "taught" the advantages of a radically new item such as home videorecorders. Even if an introductory price is perceived as "too high" by the market, managers can easily correct the problem by lowering the price. Thus, firms often feel it is better to "test the market" at a high price and then lower it if sales are not forthcoming. They are tacitly saying: "If there are any premium price buyers in the market, let's reach them first and maximize our revenue per unit." Naturally, a skimming strategy will encourage potential competition.

Du Pont has long been a classic price skimmer, as shown in the example below. Over the years, as Du Pont builds volume and competition rushes into the market, prices drop rapidly. Du Pont's Dacron, a polyester fiber, has slipped from $2.25 per lb. when it was introduced in 1953 to the 40¢ range. The price of

Qiana, a five-year-old synthetic fiber with the look and feel of silk, has dipped 35% since it was introduced.

"We were using ingredients we never used before," says a Du Pont spokesman of the Qiana introduction. "And there was no point putting it into men's underwear." Instead, Du Pont launched Qiana in the high-fashion prestige market—with an initial price to match: $5.95 to $8.95 per lb., compared with $8 to $10 per lb. for silk.

PENETRATION PRICING

Penetration pricing represents the other end of the continuum from skimming strategy. Penetration, for example, tends to discourage competition. When a firm introduces a new product at a relatively low price, hoping to reach the mass market in the early stages of the product life cycle, it is following a penetration pricing strategy. The low price is designed to capture a large share of the market, resulting in lower production costs.

Penetration pricing requires more accurate planning and forecasting than skimming because the firm must "gear up" for mass production and mass marketing. If the product does not reach its sales goals, the firm may experience heavy losses. Thus penetration is usually a much riskier strategy than skimming.

Effects of penetration pricing. Penetration pricing is predicated upon an elastic demand curve and the low unit costs resulting from economies of mass production. A successful penetration strategy can effectively block entry into the industry. Assume that Dynamic Dynamo, a hypothetical firm, has as its goal a 12 percent return on investment. Dynamic Dynamo will reach this goal at a sales level of 80,000 units. Also assume that total market demand for the product is only 100,000 units and that any firm that entered the industry would have a cost structure similar to DD's. Thus when DD achieves its maximization goal by selling 80,000 units at $3 each, only 20,000 units of demand remain for any potential competitor. If a competitor entered and sold 20,000 units at $3 each, its average cost would be $6.25, for a total loss of $65,000. The lack of economies of mass production makes profitable entry impossible for almost any new competitor. A well-financed organization would have to be willing to sustain substantial short-run losses to obtain penetration.

Sometimes competitors in an oligopoly situation will be following a skimming policy only to find a new firm entering with a penetration price. In 1975, for example, digital-watch manufacturers were slowly and profitably sliding down the demand curve. Texas Instruments pricked their pricing balloon by announcing a $20 watch in January 1976. As Robert J. Holtcamp, vice president of Litronix, a California digital watch producer, put it, "Our buyers stopped buying."[3] Just fifteen months earlier, the lowest-priced digital watch had been selling for $125. The only way Texas Instruments could profitably initiate a $20 penetration price was through huge economies of mass production and distribution. The firm shipped 4 million watches during 1976—more than the total of digital watches shipped by all the world's digital-watch manufacturers in 1975.

Another firm using penetration pricing is BSR, a British manufacturer of record changers. BSR sells record changers for virtually all the well-known phonograph brands except Magnavox. It produced and marketed 70 percent of the changers used on the 5.1 million phonographs sold in the United States in 1975. BSR's management believes that penetration pricing is the key to the firm's success.

The following example shows how another airline saved itself with this strategy.

In 1972, Texas International Airlines (TIA) was on the verge of bankruptcy. In 1978, the Civil Aeronautics Board (CAB) recommended that it be removed from the list of airlines eligible for subsidy because its "phenomenal growth had made it self-sufficient." A major reason for the change in its fortunes: Peanut Fares, discounts of 50% and more on routes that had a low percentage of seat occupancy. "We were laughed at when we proposed our first fare cuts," O'Donnell says. "But with no advertising—only the publicity of the CAB approval—we doubled our volume overnight." Since then, TIA has publicized its discounts heavily. Its Dallas/Fort Worth–Las Vegas flight, at $39 vs. the usual $114, was offered for $39 to the first person to show up with such items as $39 in Monopoly money or a résumé showing 39 jobs. Within three weeks after the $39 Las Vegas fare was announced, 89.9% of the first month's total space was sold out. At year-end, TIA was strong enough to be fighting two of the industry giants, Pan Am and Eastern Airlines, for control of National Airlines, itself a much larger carrier than TIA.[4]

Extinction pricing. Penetration pricing may be viewed as a long-run strategy. **Extinction pricing,** a derivative of that strategy, is basically short run in nature and is used as a way of eliminating competition. It involves pricing the product way below cost (often below variable costs) in order to drive independent or underfinanced competitors from the market. After the marginal competitors have been driven from the market, the firm raises its prices back to normal levels. Several national chains were guilty of extinction pricing during their early years. More recently, independent retail petroleum marketeers have claimed that the multinational firms are using extinction pricing to force small independents from the market.

MEETING COMPETITION

In addition to penetration or skimming strategies, there is a third basic strategy, meeting competition. If the firm has meeting competition as its pricing goal, the strategy is quite simple. The price charged is identical or very close to that of the competition. J. C. Penney, for example, shops Sears stores to make certain that it is charging comparable prices. Its advantage is simplicity. The disadvantage is that the strategy may ignore demand or cost or both.

Price tactics

After a price strategy has been selected (usually either skimming or penetration) for a new good or service, the next step is to set a base price. The base price takes into account the pricing objectives, positioning, demand, cost, and the price strategy. The **base price** represents the general price level at which the company expects to sell the good or service. The strategy determines the base price, which is then refined through tactics.

Price tactics are usually shorter run in nature than the price strategy and do not establish the general price level (above the market, skimming; at the market, meeting competition; or below the market, penetration). Price tactics allow the firm to adjust for competition in certain markets, meet ever-changing government regulations, take advantage of unique demand situations, and meet promotional and positioning goals. Examples of price tactics include discounts, geographic pricing, price flexibility, psychological pricing, unit pricing, and product line pricing. Each of these will be examined below.

DISCOUNTS AND ALLOWANCES

A base price may be altered (lowered) through the use of discounts and allowances. Discounts take a variety of forms and have several different objectives.

Quantity discounts. Probably the most common form of discount is the quantity discount. When a purchaser receives a lower price for purchasing in multiple units or above a specified dollar amount, he or she is receiving a **quantity discount.** In theory, the discount is based on the savings in transportation and other costs realized by the seller.

Quantity discounts can be placed on slow-moving items in order to increase their sales potential. Temporary quantity discounts may be established to help bolster sales during off periods. These discounts can also be used by wholesalers to discourage retailers from attempting to purchase directly from the manufacturer. If the discount is comparable to what the retailer might receive by going directly to the manufacturer, the retailer may continue to utilize the wholesaler.

Functional discounts. A second common form of discount is the functional discount. When a middleperson performs a service or function within a channel of distribution, it must be compensated. This compensation is typically a percentage discount from the base price and is called a **functional or trade discount.** Functional discounts vary substantially from channel to channel, depending on the tasks performed by the middlepeople.

A typical discount schedule results when a manufacturer quotes a retail list price of $500 and discounts of 45 percent and 8 percent. The retailer's cost will be $275 ($500 minus 45 percent). The wholesaler will pay $253 ($275 minus 8 percent). You will note that the total discount is not 53 percent off the list price ($500 × 0.53 = $265; $500 − $265 = $235). At 53 percent off the list price, the cost to the wholesaler would have been $235 instead of $253. Instead, discounts are figured on a chain basis from one level of the distribution channel to the next.

The complicated nature of today's physical distribution networks sometimes results in institutions receiving discounts that do not accurately reflect the services performed. Although the Robinson-Patman Act specifies that functional discounts must be justified on a service-cost basis, the FTC has shown little enthusiasm for delving into the functional discount question.

Seasonal discounts. A **seasonal discount** is a price reduction for buying merchandise out of season. It shifts the storage function forward to the purchaser. Seasonal discounts also enable manufacturers to maintain a steady production schedule year round. For example, a bathing suit manufacturer offers seasonal discounts in the fall and winter in order to keep its sewing crew employed full time. One of the most familiar examples of a seasonal discount is the half-price sales on Christmas decorations that begin December 26. Other examples are off-season rates at motels and resorts and discount air fares during off seasons.

Promotional allowances. A **promotional allowance** plays a dual role: it is a pricing tool and a promotional device. As a pricing tool, a promotional allowance is similar to a functional discount. If, for example, a retailer runs an ad for a manufacturer's product, the manufacturer may pay half of the cost. If a retailer sets up a special display, the manufacturer may include a certain quantity of "free goods" in the retailer's next order. General Foods regularly gives Safeway and other supermarket chains "free" cases of food products for performing specified services. Promotional allowances, like other forms of discount, must be made available to all purchasers on essentially the same terms. The Robinson-Patman Act prohibits differences in advertising allowances to similar purchasers.

GEOGRAPHIC PRICING TACTICS

Since many sellers ship their wares to a nationwide or even a worldwide market, the cost of freight can have a significant impact on the total cost of a product. Several different geographic pricing tactics may be utilized to moderate the impact of freight costs on distant customers.

FOB origin. If a product is priced **FOB origin,** the buyer pays the cost of transportation from the selling point. The term means that the goods are placed free on board a carrier and that at that point title passes to the buyer and transportation charges are paid by the buyer. Any damage claim beyond the point of origin must be filed by the purchaser against the common carrier.

FOB pricing treats all purchasers alike (there is no geographic price discrimi-

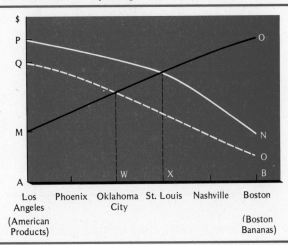

nation—the farther a buyer is from a seller, the more he or she pays because transportation costs generally increase as the distance merchandise is shipped increases). As a result of FOB origin pricing, natural market monopolies tend to develop, such as the one shown in Figure 12.2. American Products, located in Los Angeles, is selling FOB origin at a price of AM. As potential buyers are located farther from Los Angeles, we find delivered prices (origin plus freight) rising along path MO. Boston Bananas (BB), marketing a similar product to American Products, sells FOB origin at a price of BN, with total cost rising along path NP.

American Products has a freight advantage territory extending from slightly east of Oklahoma City back to the West Coast (market segment AX). Boston Bananas' freight advantage territory is segment BX. Assuming that both firms follow the FOB pricing policy strictly, each will be blocked from the other's market. The only way BB can increase its geographic market (assuming it is unwilling to alter its pricing tactic) is to cut the selling price at the origin. If BB follows this strategy, its new market segment would be BW at a price of OB.

Uniform delivered pricing. The opposite of FOB pricing is **uniform delivered pricing** or "postage stamp pricing." Under this tactic the seller pays the actual freight charges and bills every purchaser an identical flat freight charge. This policy equalizes the total cost for all buyers, regardless of where they are located. Naturally, uniform delivered pricing discriminates in favor of purchasers located far away from the seller, but price competition among buyers is eliminated. All buyers pay the same total price for the product.

This policy may be used when a firm is trying to maintain a nationally advertised price. Postage stamp pricing is also common when transportation charges are a minor part of total costs. The uniform delivered pricing policy is relatively easy to administer and, according to the FTC, is not illegal.

Zone pricing. **Zone pricing** is a modification of uniform delivered pricing. Rather than placing the entire United States (or its total market) under a uniform freight rate, the firm divides it into segments or zones (see Figure 12.3). A flat freight rate is charged to all customers in a given zone. For example, customers of Boston Bananas located in zone 1 might pay $5.00 per unit freight; those in zone 2, $10.00; and those in zone 3, $20.00.

Zone pricing eliminates price advantage among purchasers within large geographic areas. The policy discriminates against the buyers located closest to the seller within any given zone. A buyer located in Indianapolis pays the same rate as a purchaser in Amarillo, yet the Amarillo buyer is over 900 miles farther from Boston than the Indianapolis purchaser. Thus the Indianapolis buyer may seek another seller. Another problem of zone pricing is determining where to place the zone boundaries. A Cleveland buyer pays $5 freight, whereas the Indianapolis purchaser must pay $10—a 100 percent increase. The U.S. Postal Service's parcel post rate structure is probably the best-known zone pricing system in the country.

Freight absorption pricing. In **freight absorption pricing** the seller absorbs all or part of the actual freight charges. This tactic may be used in areas where competition is extremely intense, or it can be used to break into new market areas. A seller may follow this policy to achieve greater economies of scale. If the economies of scale are greater than the absorbed freight costs, the firm's total profits will increase. Sometimes a seller will offer all buyers the same price (uniform delivered pricing), but it will absorb all or part of the freight fee.

Basing-point pricing. Basing-point pricing is not as popular as it once was as a result of a number of adverse court rulings. A **basing-point price** tactic requires the seller to designate a location (say, Louisville) as a basing point and charge all purchasers the freight cost from Louisville regardless of the city from which the goods are shipped. If Boston Bananas used Louisville as its basing point and sold merchandise to another firm located in Boston, the buyer would pay freight charges from Louisville. This would be true even though the merchandise was shipped from BB's Boston warehouse. Freight fees charged when none were actually incurred are called **phantom freight.**

Basing-point pricing has been prevalent in the steel, cement, lead, corn oil, linseed oil, wood pulp, automobile, sugar, gypsum board, and plywood industries, as well as many others.[5] The basing-point system is used most often by firms that sell relatively homogeneous products and for which transportation costs are an important component of total costs.

SPECIAL PRICING TACTICS

Special pricing tactics, unlike geographic price tactics, are unique and defy neat categorization. Special tactics may be established to promote certain types of merchandise, to increase store patronage, to offer the consumer greater choice, and for a variety of other reasons.

Price variability. In the United States most prices are fixed without negotiation between purchaser and seller. Indeed, the foundation of mass self-service policies is a one-price policy. Can you imagine going into Kroger, Safeway, or A&P and bargaining for your groceries? A one-price or fixed price tactic is easier on sellers because it does not require personnel to spend their time negotiating prices. Also, it provides the dealer with a consistent profit margin. Many consumers feel more comfortable with a one-price tactic because they do not enjoy haggling over prices. Similarly, the merchant will not incur the ill will of customers who find out they have paid a higher price than someone else because they are not as good at bargaining.

Flexible or variable pricing is sometimes found in the sale of shopping goods and specialty merchandise as well as many industrial goods. Different customers pay different prices for essentially the same merchandise bought in equal quantities. Automobile dealers and many appliance retailers commonly follow this practice. It allows the retailer to adjust for competition by meeting another dealer's price. Also, flexible pricing enables the seller to "close a sale" with price-conscious consumers. If a buyer shows promise of becoming a large-volume shopper, variable pricing can be used to procure his or her business. The obvious disadvantages of variable pricing are (1) the lack of consistent profit margins, (2) the potential ill will of high-price purchasers, (3) the tendency for salespeople to "automatically" lower the price in order to make a sale, and (4) the possibility of a price war among sellers.

Single-price tactic. A single-price tactic is as much a promotional tool as a variable-price tactic. A merchant using this policy offers all goods and services at the same price (or perhaps two or three prices). Thus a retailer specializing in men's ties sells every tie for $10. The retailer also carries belts for $15, but that is the extent of its product line.

Single-price selling removes price comparisons from the buyer's decision-making process. The consumer simply looks for suitability and for the highest perceived quality. The retailer enjoys the benefits of a simplified pricing system and the minimization of clerical error. Continually rising costs are a constant headache for retailers following this strategy, often leading to frequent upward revisions of the selling price.

Multiple-unit package pricing. Multiple-unit package pricing attempts to increase the quantity sold in each individual transaction. A familiar example is the six-pack of soft drinks, beer, or even outboard-motor oil. Sometimes discounts are given for purchasing more than one item at a time. Recently, however, many retailers have moved toward not reducing the per-unit prices of multiple-unit packages. In fact, some retailers charge a premium for the convenience of buying a number of items in one package!

In an early study on multiple-unit pricing, "two for" and "three for" pricing boosted sales an average of 115 percent over single-unit pricing.[6] A 1970 study showed similar yet less dramatic results.[7] Recent tests have found definite limits on the advantages of multiple-unit pricing. Tests on which "two for" pricing was extended to three, four, five, and six for prices found a drop in sales for some of the higher multiples.[8] Other limitations on multiple pricing are that it is relatively ineffective for new products, for those with high prices, and for those that are consumed or used slowly.[9]

Price lining. When a retailer establishes a series of prices for a type of merchandise, it has created a **price line.** For example, a dress shop may offer women's dresses at $40, $70, and $100 with no merchandise marked at prices between those figures. Thus instead of a normal demand curve running from $40 to $100, the retailer has three demand points (prices)—the "curve" exists in a theoretical sense because people would buy goods at the in-between prices if it were possible to do so. For example, a number of dresses could be sold at $60, but no sales will take place at that price because it is not part of the price line.

Price lines reduce confusion for both the sales clerk and the consumer. The consumer may be offered a wider variety of merchandise at each established price. Price lines may also enable a merchant to reach several market segments. For consumers the question of price may be quite simple: all they have to do is find a suitable product at the predetermined price. The retailer may be able to carry a smaller total inventory than it could without price lines. This may mean fewer markdowns, simplified purchasing, and lower inventory carrying charges.

But price lines are not without disadvantages. If costs are continually rising, the retailer must begin placing lower-quality merchandise in stock at each established price or change the prices. Frequent price line changes create consumer confusion. A third alternative to rising costs is to accept lower profit margins and hold quality and prices constant: While this is admirable in the short run, in the long run it may put the retailer out of business. Another major problem is attempting to determine where to place the prices within a line. If the prices are too close together, the consumer may wonder why the price of one article is higher than that of another. If the price lines are too far apart, the dealer may lose a customer who is looking for a price (and quality) somewhere between the existing prices. Also, a salesperson will find it difficult to "trade up" customers (persuade them to buy higher-priced merchandise) if the price lines are too far apart.

Leader pricing. **Leader pricing** is an attempt by a seller to induce store patronage through pricing. It involves selling a product near cost or even below cost to attract customers. You see this type of pricing every week in the newspaper advertising of supermarkets, specialty stores, and department stores. Leader pricing is normally used on well-known items that consumers can easily recognize as bargains at the special price.

Cents-off promotion. **Cents-off promotion** is a common pricing tactic similar to leader pricing. However, rather than being initiated by the retailer, cents-off promotions are used by the manufacturer to increase the sale of a specific brand. With the exception of trade deals (discounts to wholesalers and retailers) and advertising, cents-off advertising is the most heavily used form of convenience goods promotion.

Occasionally a retailer promotes a cents-off item yet does not actually lower retail prices. One study of 3357 cents-off promotions showed that 19 percent of the retailers never passed the savings along to the consumer.[10] These stores were generally small, independent retailers rather than large chains.

Bait pricing. In contrast to cents-off campaigns and leader pricing, which are genuine attempts to give the consumer a reduced price, **bait pricing** is deceptive. The idea is to get the consumer into a store through false or misleading advertising and then use high-pressure selling to persuade the consumer to buy more expensive merchandise.

You may have seen this ad or a similar one:

REPOSSESSED . . . Singer slant-needle sewing machine . . . take over 8 payments of $5.10 per month . . . ABC Sewing Center.

This is "bait." When a customer goes in to see the machine, it has "just been sold," or else a salesperson shows the prospective buyer a piece of junk no one would buy. Then the salesperson says, "But I've got a really good deal on this fine, new model." This is the "switch" that may cause a susceptible consumer to walk out with a $400 machine.

Psychological pricing. **Psychological pricing** means pricing at odd prices to denote bargains and even pricing to imply quality. For years many retailers have used this pricing tactic by pricing their products at odd prices ($99.95, $49.95) to make consumers feel they are paying a "lower" price for the product. Does it work? Research has shown that such pricing has mixed results.[11] In fact, the effectiveness of psychological pricing may depend upon the type of product.

If odd pricing is effective, it will have a curious effect on demand. Since people will buy more at odd prices, demand will be relatively elastic and then inelastic for even prices as you move down the demand curve. Such a situation will create a "sawtoothed" demand curve. Odd prices will stimulate demand and even prices will curtail demand.

A study of pricing in the food industry revealed that retail food prices ending in 9 are most popular, and that prices ending in 5 are second most popular. Over 80 percent of the retail prices ended in 9 or 5.[12] Even pricing is sometimes used to denote quality, as in the case of a fine perfume at $100 per bottle, a good watch at $250, or a mink coat for $3000. It is assumed in these cases that more will be sold at even prices than at odd prices. The demand curve for such items would also be "sawtoothed," except that the outside edges would represent even prices (and, hence, elastic demand).

Unit pricing. **Unit pricing** is designed — at least theoretically — to aid the economy-minded purchaser in getting the most product per unit without regard to quality. For example, if two jars of peanut butter weigh 14 ounces and 18 ounces and their respective prices are $1.82 and $2.25, their costs per ounce (or per unit) are 13 cents and 12½ cents. The numerous manufacturers' and dealers' brands are easier to compare where unit pricing is available. This policy seems to be most applicable to grocery pricing.

Naturally, unit pricing is an additional expense to the store. The A. T. Kearney Company estimated that initial installation expenses ranged from 0.0088 percent to 0.04 percent of sales, and system maintenance costs ranged from 0.0074 percent to 0.095 percent of sales.[13] However, since dealer brands are usually cheaper than manufacturer brands, customers are expected to switch to dealer brands (because prices are cheaper per unit), enabling the store to earn a high total profit. Do consumers switch brands to lower-cost alternatives? Research has not provided conclusive evidence. For example, a study by Kroger revealed no tendency to switch brands.[14] Yet studies by Stop and Shop, Safeway, and King Soopers indicated that consumers were switching brands and purchasing different package sizes.[15] Academic research has also shown mixed results.[16]

One trend in unit price information during the 1980s will be the use of posted price lists in stores. In one study where unit prices were posted on separate shelf tags in a supermarket, consumer expenditures dropped 1 percent. When unit prices were displayed on an organized list like the one shown in Table 12.1, consumer savings were 3 percent.[17] The lists also resulted in a 5 percent increase in the market shares of the store brands.

PRODUCT LINE PRICING

Product line pricing differs from single-unit pricing because the marketing manager attempts to achieve maximum profits (or other goals) for the entire line. The emphasis is on the entire line rather than on any single component of the line.

Relationships among products. The manager must first determine the type of relationship that exists among the various products in the line. Items may, for example, be complementary, meaning that an increase in the sale of one good causes an increase in demand for the complementary product, and vice versa. The sale of Xerox paper and Xerox toner is predicated upon the demand for Xerox machines; thus the items are complementary.

A second possibility is for two products in a line to be substitutes for each other. If a buyer purchases one item in the line, he or she is less likely to purchase a second item in the line. If you go to an automotive supply store and buy

TABLE 12.1 Organized Unit Price Shopping List
(In order of Increasing Price per Quart)

Item	Size	Unit price	Price per quart
Par	48 oz.	54¢	36.0¢
Par	32 oz.	38¢	38.0¢
Sweetheart	32 oz.	55¢	55.0¢
Brocade	48 oz.	85¢	56.7¢
Sweetheart	22 oz.	39¢	56.7¢
Supurb	32 oz.	59¢	59.0¢
White Magic	32 oz.	59¢	59.0¢
Brocade	32 oz.	63¢	63.0¢
Brocade	22 oz.	45¢	65.5¢
Supurb	22 oz.	45¢	65.5¢
White Magic	32 oz.	45¢	65.5¢
Brocade	12 oz.	27¢	72.0¢
Supurb	12 oz.	29¢	77.3¢
Ivory	32 oz.	80¢	80.0¢
Dove	22 oz.	56¢	81.5¢
Ivory	22 oz.	56¢	81.5¢
Lux	22 oz.	56¢	81.5¢
Palmolive	32 oz.	85¢	85.0¢
Ivory	12 oz.	32¢	85.3¢
Palmolive	22 oz.	60¢	87.3¢
Palmolive	12 oz.	34¢	90.7¢

Source: J. Edward Russo, "The Value of Unit Pricing Information," *Journal of Marketing Research* 14 (May 1977): 194.

a certain type of car wax for your car, it is very unlikely that you will buy another car wax made by the same manufacturer (or by any other manufacturer) in the near future.

The third possible relationship among two products is a neutral one; that is, demand for one of the products is not related to demand for the others. Ralston Purina sells chicken feed and Wheat Chex, but the sale of one of these products has no known impact on demand for the other.

Joint costs. **Joint costs**—costs that are shared in the manufacturing and marketing of a product line—pose a unique problem when it comes to product pricing.[18] In oil refining, for example, fuel oil, gasoline, kerosene, naphtha, paraffin, and lubricating oils are all derived from a common production process. Any assignment of joint costs must of necessity be somewhat subjective.

Suppose a company produces two products, X and Y, with joint costs where costs are allocated on a weight basis; product X weighs 1000 pounds and product Y weighs 500 pounds based on a common production process. Gross margins (sales less cost of goods sold) might be as follows:

	Product X	Product Y	Total
Sales	$20,000	$ 6,000	$26,000
Less: cost of goods sold	15,000	7,500	22,500
Gross margin	$ 5,000	($ 1,500)	$ 3,500

This statement reveals a loss of $1,500 on product Y. Is that important? Yes, any loss is important. However, the firm must realize that on an overall basis, a $3,500 profit was earned on the two items in the line. Also, weight may not be the "right" way to allocate the joint costs. Other bases that might have been used include market value or quantity sold.

Bidding: a different approach to pricing

In addition to the pricing procedure I outlined above, you should also be familiar with bidding. The topic of competitive bidding and a strategy to determine whether or not to bid were introduced in Chapter 6. Here we will look at the usefulness of a bidding model.

The higher a firm bids on a contract, the larger its returns on costs will be. Also, the higher the bid, normally the lower the probability of obtaining a contract. Bidding therefore easily lends itself to application of probability theory. By examining past success ratios and previous winning competitive bids for a given type of product or service, a firm can construct a bidding model. For example, Table 12.2 shows various expected returns given alternative bids on a project with expected costs of $48,000.

Assuming that a firm desires to maximize its expected profits, it should bid $55,000. A lower bid, of course, has a greater chance, but at a lower profit. An expected profit criterion is useful for a firm making a large number of bids, with no single bid being a "life or death" situation for the firm. The expected profit criterion will be insufficient for decision making if factors such as excess capacity, need to keep the assembly line running, or possible alternative uses of a new technology that will be developed under a bid must be considered.

Does use of a bidding model mean more successful bids? One researcher compared bids at RCA without a model against model bidding for the same contract.[19] The results are shown in Table 12.3. As you can see, the model proved to be a significant improvement over conventional bidding procedures. A formal probability approach, with accurate probability estimates, is an effective managerial tool.

◀ **TABLE 12.2   Expected Returns in Competitive Bidding**

Our bid	Profit	Probability of success	Expected profit[a]
$48,500	$ 500	.96	$ 480
51,000	3,000	.82	2,460
55,000	7,000	.61	4,270
58,000	10,000	.24	2,400
62,000	14,000	.04	560
65,000	17,000	.01	170

[a] Expected profit equals profit × probability of success.

Test	Bid without model	Bid with model	Lowest competitive bid	Bid without model: percent under (over) lowest competitive bid	Bid with model: percent under lowest competitive bid
1	$44.53	$46.00	$46.49	4.2%	1.1%
2	47.36	42.68	42.93	(10.3)	0.6
3	62.73	59.04	60.76	(3.2)	2.8
4	47.72	51.05	53.38	10.6	4.4
5	50.18	42.80	44.16	(13.7)	3.1
6	60.39	54.61	55.10	(9.6)	0.9
7	39.73˙	39.73	40.47	1.8	1.8

Source: Franz Edelman, "Art and Science of Competitive Bidding," *Harvard Business Review* 43 (July–August 1965): 58.

Pricing in a changing economy

Rising consumer demand, demands for higher wages and unemployment benefits, governmental actions, policies of cartels, shortages, and archaic pricing policies have stimulated relatively high rates of inflation in the 1980s. To meet the continuing challenge of inflation, marketing managers are adopting new pricing tactics. These tactics can be conveniently categorized as based on either cost or demand.

COST-ORIENTED TACTICS

One popular cost-oriented tactic is culling low-margin products from the product line. This tactic may backfire because of (1) the high volume and, thus, high profitability of a low-margin item, or (2) a loss of economies of scale as certain products are eliminated, which lowers the margins on other items. Also, the entire price/quality image of the line may be affected.

Delayed-quotation bidding is very popular for industrial installations and many accessory items. Price is not set on the product until the item is either finished or delivered. Long production lead times and continual inflation have forced this policy on many firms. When Bechtel began building a new electrolytic copper refinery for ASARCO in Amarillo, Texas, in early 1973, the total price tag was estimated at $111 million. By the summer of 1974, with the plant 85 percent finished, the cost had moved up to $190 million.

Escalator pricing is similar to delayed-quotation pricing in that the final selling price will reflect cost increases incurred between the times when the order is placed and delivery is made. An **escalator clause** allows for price increases (usually across the board) based on the cost-of-living index or some other formula. As with any price increase, the ability to implement such a policy is based on an inelastic demand curve for the purchase involved. About one-third of all industrial products manufacturers now use escalator clauses. However, many companies do not apply the clause in every sale. Often it is utilized only for extremely complex projects of long duration and/or with new customers.

Any cost-oriented pricing policy that attempts to maintain a fixed gross margin under all conditions can lead to a vicious circle. For example, a price increase will result in decreased demand, which in turn increases production costs (due to lost economies of scale). Increased production costs require a further price increase, leading to further diminished demand, and so forth.

DEMAND-ORIENTED TACTICS

Demand-oriented pricing tactics concentrate on using price to reflect changing patterns of demand caused by inflation. Naturally, cost changes are considered, but primarily in the context of how increased prices will affect demand.

Price shading involves the use of discounts by salespeople to increase demand for one or more products in a line. Often shading has become habitual and is done routinely without much forethought. Ducommun is among the major companies that have succeeded in eliminating the practice. Ducommun sales managers have given salesmen the rule, "that we want no deviation from book price," unless authorized by management.[20]

When a firm determines that demand for its product is highly inelastic, it can increase prices after the merchandise is shipped with prior purchaser notification. Obviously, this is not a very popular practice among buyers:

"You get the stuff," grumbles one maker of logging equipment, "and you find the price is higher than was quoted." Adds a leading gear manufacturer, "Everybody we see is breaking every rule in the book. The price quoted to you when you place the order no longer means a thing."[21]

Another technique for controlling price increases is to provide "extra" services only if they are demanded. Repair services, peripheral equipment, and replacement parts are now priced separately rather than being included in a total package. Although it is not a new concept, **unbundling** has become increasingly popular in the industrial goods market, where there is considerable pressure to hold down price increases.

A natural tendency during inflationary periods is to reduce both cash and quantity discounts. The more progressive firms are maintaining their discounts on high-margin items and reducing or eliminating discounts on low-margin merchandise. Thus discounting is used to alter demand, rather than being arbitrarily eliminated.

SHORTAGE PRICING

Marketing managers are acutely aware of the scarcity of many productive resources. Most forms of energy, many metals and alloys, advanced electronic devices, and numerous other items will be difficult to obtain in ample supply and at reasonable prices throughout the 1980s. Marketing managers are having to assume new responsibilities and alternative marketing approaches to cope with the economic realities of long-run shortages.

Buyers' reactions to the shortage environment varied from hoarding and stockpiling to long-range purchase contract demands and increased price awareness. Competition for market share has also tended to decline in some industries. Several new competitive trends have begun to emerge: (1) less reliance on price competition, (2) some sharing of marketing resources, (3) increased efforts to integrate vertically to ensure a larger share of supplies, (4) a search for new ways to reduce marketing costs, (5) a reactivation of bartering arrangements, and (6) less reliance on demand stimulation activities.[22]

Some marketers have raised prices on low-margin items during shortage periods in order to (1) kill off demand and (2) still keep the products available for consumers who simply must have them, even at a higher price. Also, many firms forgo penetration pricing during times of shortage, since they are unable to produce and deliver the volume of merchandise required to make such a strategy feasible. Demand may also become more inelastic as firms struggle for existing supply. As a result sellers are in a position to raise prices even further. The ever-present threat of governmental price controls during periods of shortage may dampen enthusiasm for significant increases.

Other shortage-related price strategies include (1) tightening credit to minimize risk, (2) less reliance on discounts as a means of generating sales, (3) instituting more flexible price policies, (4) frequent price increments to maintain or improve margins, (5) reduction of freight absorption and delivered-price practices, (6) greater use of flexible sales contracts to incorporate frequent price increases, and (7) more centralized management of price adjustments.

When raw materials are scarce and a firm cannot raise its prices due to heavy competition or a government price freeze, the firm's ability to respond is severely limited. To offset this limitation a simple pricing model has been developed to take account of limited resources.[23] The model is explained in the appendix to this chapter.

SUMMARY

Pricing strategies are based on pricing objectives. Setting objectives is the first step in the price-setting procedure. The second step is to define the target market. By understanding the potential buyer, the marketer can develop a sound positioning plan and better estimate demand. The next step is to determine market positioning, for the positioning of a product often determines the ultimate price strategy. After a general positioning strategy is determined, the marketing manager should estimate demand and cost at several different price levels. Next, a price strategy must be established.

A price strategy establishes the basic long-term pricing framework for the product or service. There are three basic price strategies: price skimming, penetration pricing, and meeting the competition. Price skimming means charting a high introductory price and then, as the product moves through the life cycle, lowering price to reach successively larger market segments. Penetration pricing is the introduction of a new product at a relatively low price to reach the mass market in the early stages of the product life cycle. The low price is designed to capture a large share of the market, resulting in lower production costs. Meeting competition is defined as charging identical or very similar prices to that of major competitors. Its advantage is simplicity. The disadvantage is that the strategy may ignore demand or cost, or both.

After the basic price strategy has been established, the next step is to modify the base price with pricing tactics. The base price represents the general price level at which the company expects to sell the good or service. Price tactics are shorter run in nature than price strategy and are used to refine the base price. Price tactics allow the firm to adjust for competition, meet government regulations, take advantage of unique situations, and meet promotional and positioning goals. Examples of price tactics include discounts, geographic pricing, price flexibility, psychological pricing, unit pricing, and product line pricing.

Marketers need to be familiar with competitive bidding. Selling in the industrial goods market or to various levels of government often requires bid pricing. Bid pricing is unique in that the quantity demanded is specified in the bidding specifications. The bid price therefore becomes a function of cost and competitors' actions. The higher a firm bids on a contract, the larger returns on costs will be—and the lower the probability of obtaining the contract. Using bidding models based upon probability theory can increase the chance of obtaining a successful bid.

Inflation poses a unique problem for marketing managers. Some companies have eliminated low-margin products. Others have adopted delayed quotation pricing and escalator clauses. Still others have increased prices without notifying the purchaser. One common technique is unbundling of services. This involves charging extra for services when they are demanded, and not providing them otherwise. When shortages occur, some marketers have raised prices on low-margin items to (1) kill off demand and (2) still keep the products available for consumers who simply must have them, even at a higher price.

KEY TERMS

Price skimming
Penetration pricing
Extinction pricing
Base price
Quantity discount
Functional or trade discount
Seasonal discount
Promotional allowance
FOB origin
Uniform delivered pricing
Zone pricing
Freight absorption pricing
Basing-point pricing
Phantom freight

Flexible or variable pricing
Price line
Leader pricing
Cents-off promotion
Bait pricing
Psychological pricing
Unit pricing
Product line pricing
Joint costs
Delayed-quotation bidding
Escalator clause
Price shading
Unbundling

REVIEW QUESTIONS

1. What steps would a firm follow in setting the price of a new product?
2. Review the distinctions among skimming, penetration, and extinction pricing. Give special attention to the legality, time frame, and objective of each.

3. Why do manufacturers offer the trade multiple discounts and allowances?
4. What is the price lining approach to pricing? What are the advantages and disadvantages of this tactic?
5. What is the difference between leader pricing and bait pricing?
6. What relationships are important to the astute marketer in determining the correct prices for an entire product line, specifically with regard to competition?

DISCUSSION QUESTIONS

1. What factors would a firm analyze before initiating a price change for an established product?
2. What are the risks involved in pursuing a skimming strategy? What types of products are commonly associated with this pricing strategy? When is it not advisable to follow a skimming policy?
3. Due to the multiple channels of distribution employed by many firms, the manufacturer has little authority over the final selling price of a product; therefore, the importance of price as a marketing variable is reduced. Evaluate.
4. With so much emphasis on price, competitive bidding may overlook product quality. Discuss.
5. In periods of price guidelines, the list price may remain the same, but the buyer will probably be paying more for the item. Why?
6. The marketer determining price in a period of long-term inflation can employ a number of cost- and demand-oriented tactics. If you were presented with this problem, what tactics would you suggest?

NOTES

1. "New York Air to Compete 'Vigorously' in Low-Service, High-Fare Northeast Market," *Marketing News,* November 28, 1980, p. 12.
2. For an example of skimming in monopolies, see Alan Reynolds, "A Kind Word for Cream Skimming," *Harvard Business Review* 52 (November 1974): 113–120.
3. "How TI Beat the Clock on Its $20 Digital Watch," *Business Week,* May 31, 1976, pp. 62–64.
4. "Pricing," *Sales and Marketing Management,* January 1979, p. 44. Reprinted by permission from Sales & Marketing Management magazine. Copyright 1979.
5. F. M. Sherer, *Industrial Pricing Theory and Evidence* (New York: Rand McNally, 1970), p. 137.
6. M. Alexander (ed.), *Display Ideas for Supermarkets* (New York: Progressive Grocer, 1958), p. 73.
7. "How Multiple Unit Pricing Helps and Hurts," *Progressive Grocer,* June 1971, pp. 52–58.
8. Kenneth Runyon, *Consumer Behavior and the Practice of Marketing* (Columbus, Ohio: Charles E. Merrill, 1977), p. 363.
9. Alexander, *Display Ideas,* p. 73.
10. F. Robert Shoaf and Edward L. Melnick, "Retail Grocer Pricing Responses to Manufacturer-Initiated Cents-Off Package Promotions," *Journal of Consumer Affairs* 8 (summer 1974): 76–85; see also Craig L. Thrasher, "Price Leader Error Manipulation: Some Preliminary Views," *Journal of Consumer Affairs* 7 (summer 1973): 77–83.
11. Kent B. Monroe, "Buyers' Subjective Perceptions of Price," *Journal of Marketing Research* 10 (February 1973): 70–80; Jan Stapel, " 'Fair' or 'Psychological' Pricing?" *Journal of Marketing Research* 9 (February 1972): 109–110; Peter Cooper,

"Subjective Economics: Factors in a Psychology of Spending," in Bernard Taylor and Gordon Wills (eds.), *Pricing Strategy* (Princeton, N.J.: Brandon Systems Press, 1970), pp. 112–121.

12. Lawrence Friedman, "Psychological Pricing in the Food Industry," in Almarin Phillips and Oliver E. Williamson (eds.), *Prices: Issues in Theory, Practice, and Public Policy* (Philadelphia: University of Pennsylvania Press, 1967), pp. 187–201.

13. Kent B. Monroe and Peter J. LaPlaca, "What Are the Benefits of Unit Pricing?" *Journal of Marketing* 36 (July 1972): 16–22.

14. T. David McCullough and Daniel I. Padberg, "Unit Pricing in Supermarkets: Alternatives, Costs and Consumer Reactions," *Search, Agriculture* 1 (January 1971): 1–25.

15. Martin Cohen, "Report #1-203: Unit Pricing Study," Internal Report to Stop and Shop, Inc., June 29, 1970; Monroe Friedman, *Dual-Price Labels: Usage Patterns and Potential Benefits for Shoppers in Inner-City and Suburban Supermarkets* (Ypsilanti: Eastern Michigan University Center for the Study of Contemporary Issues, 1971); Lawrence M. Lamont and James T. Rothe, "The Impact of Unit Pricing on Channel Systems," in Fred C. Auvine (ed.), *Combined Proceedings 1971 Spring and Fall Conferences* (Chicago: American Marketing Association, 1972), pp. 653–658.

16. William E. Kilbourne, "A Factorial Experiment on the Impact of Unit Pricing on Low Income Consumers," *Journal of Marketing Research* 11 (November 1971): 453–455.

17. J. Edward Russo, "The Value of Unit Price Information," *Journal of Marketing Research* 14 (May 1977): 193–201.

18. See Arthur V. Corr, "The Role of Cost in Pricing," *Management Accounting* 56 (November 1974): 15–32; Alfred R. Oxenfeldt, "Product Line Pricing," *Harvard Business Review* 44 (July–August 1966): 137–144; for an interesting study on internal transfer pricing, see David Granick, "National Differences in the Use of Internal Transfer Prices," *California Management Review* 17 (summer 1975): 28–40.

19. Franz Edelman, "Art and Science of Competitive Bidding," *Harvard Business Review* 43 (July–August 1965): 53–66.

20. "Pricing Strategy in an Inflation Economy," p. 45.

21. Ibid., p. 48.

22. Nessim Hanna, A. H. Kizilbash, and Albert Smart, "Marketing Strategy under Conditions of Economic Scarcity," *Journal of Marketing* 39 (January 1975): 63–80.

23. See Kent B. Monroe and Andris A. Zoltners, "Pricing the Product Line during Periods of Scarcity," *Journal of Marketing* 43 (summer 1979): 49–59.

◀ **APPENDIX**

Pricing under Shortage Conditions*

In Table 12A.1, part A, $1 per unit sold of product C is used to cover fixed expenses and contribute to profits (fixed cost contribution = FCC). The FCC of product C is $1, B is 76 cents, and A is 59 cents. Yet in part B you can see that total

---

* This appendix is taken from Kent B. Monroe and Andris A. Zoltners, "Pricing the Product Line during Periods of Scarcity," *Journal of Marketing* 43 (summer 1979): 49–59.

	Product			
	A	B	C	Totals
A. Unit data				
1. Price	$2.20	$3.00	$4.00	
Variable costs:				
2. Direct labor	$1.20	$0.70	$0.60	
3. Direct materials	0.41	1.54	2.40	
4. Total	$1.61	$2.24	$3.00	
5. Contribution (1 − 4)	$0.59	$0.76	$1.00	
B. Data for planning period				
6. Demand (units)	6,200	8,100	5,000	—
7. Revenue (1 × 6)	$13,640	$24,300	$20,000	$57,940
8. Direct labor (2 × 6)	$ 7,440	$ 5,670	$ 3,000	$16,110
9. Direct materials (3 × 6)	2,542	12,474	12,000	27,016
10. Contribution (5 × 6)	$ 3,658	$ 6,156	$ 5,000	$14,814
11. Tons of material required	500	2,500	2,400	5,400
12. Units per ton (6/11)	12.4	3.24	2.083	—
13. Tons per unit (11/6)	.081	.309	.480	—
14. CPRU (10/11)	$7.32	$2.46	$2.08	—

demand (line 6) and resulting variable costs give the largest total dollar contribution to product B, with product C ranked second and product A, third.

Two common resources—labor and material—are required to produce the three products. The quantities of the resources necessary to produce one unit of output vary substantially from one product to the other. Product A is relatively labor-intensive since 74.5 percent of its direct variable costs can be attributed to labor (lines 2 and 4 in part A; $1.20/$1.61). Only 32.3 percent and 20 percent of the direct cost for products B and C is labor. Thus products B and C require much more material input.

Now suppose this common material resource becomes scarce and the firm has been advised that it can acquire no more than 3000 tons during the planning period. Furthermore, the world supply of this material is expected to be well below demand for at least several years. The firm must now consider the alternatives of reducing production of each product, eliminating a product and reducing production of the other products, or some reasonable combination of these choices.

There are a number of criteria available for making the allocation decision: (1) The firm could allocate the common resource using *unit product contributions* (gross margin). (2) The allocation could be made by using *total contributions per product over the planning period*. (3) The scarce material could be rationed in *proportion to the resource requirements* given in the plan of Table 12A.2, part B. (4) The firm could allocate the resource utilizing both the information on each product's unit contribution and how each product consumes scarce resources— *contribution per resource unit*.

As Table 12A.2 shows, the effect of a resource constraint on prices is a reduc-

Resource allocation criteria	Resource units	Units produced	Total contribution	Reduction in contribution due to resource constraint
A. Contribution per unit				
A	0	0	0	$3,658
B	600	1,944	$1,477	4,679
C	2,400	5,000	5,000	0
			$6,477	$8,337
B. Total product contribution per period				
A	0	0	0	$3,658
B	2,500	8,100	$6,156	0
C	500	1,041	1,041	3,959
			$7,197	$7,617
C. Proportion of resources required				
A	270	3,348	$1,975	$1,683
B	1,410	4,568	3,472	2,684
C	1,320	2,750	2,750	2,250
			$8,197	$6,617
D. Contribution per resource unit				
A	500	6,200	$3,658	0
B	2,500	8,100	6,156	0
C	0	0	0	$5,000
			$9,814	$5,000

tion in total contributions for the period. Moreover, if either criterion (1) or (2) were adopted, it would be necessary to eliminate product A from the line. For example, on a contribution per unit basis, product C has a FCC of $1, so 5000 units would be produced (see Table 12A.1, line 6). This would require 2400 resource units (see Table 12A.1, line 11). Since B has the second highest FCC, the firm would like to produce 8100 product units (total demand for B) but only has unit resources (3000 − 2400 = 600) to produce 1944 product units of B (600 × 3.24). Total profits using the FCC criteria given the availability of only 3000 resource units would be $6,477.

Using FCC or gross contribution (part B, Table 12A.2) may result in the exhaustion of available resources without maximizing the firm's return on investment. Neither approach accounts for the amount of scarce resource consumed per unit of output.

As shown in Table 12A.1, part B, a ton of the resource material will produce 12.4 units of A, 3.24 units of B, and 2.083 units of C. The contribution per ton of material is greatest for product A and least for product C. Consequently, when a resource is scarce, a method that allocates less resources to C and B and more to A improves contribution. Therefore, it is necessary to establish an allocation criterion that utilizes the information on each product's unit contribution and how each product consumes scarce resources.

By shifting emphasis from product contribution to contribution per resource unit, it is possible to determine the resource allocation that maximizes contribution subject to the resource constraints. For the example product line, the calculations are shown in Table 12A.1, part B. Thus, it is apparent that product A has the highest CPRU ton (line 14—$7.32). When the resource is in limited supply, the decision rule should be to allocate resources to the profit segments with the highest CPRU. Using the CPRU criterion, Table 12A.2 shows that product C, the highest-priced, largest-unit margin product, is a candidate for elimination.

This material illustrates a fundamental principle: *When the volume of products that could be sold is greater than the resource capacity to produce these products, the largest contribution (and profit) results from producing those products that generate the greatest contribution per resource unit used.*

◢ CASES

12.1 Mayfield Chemical Corporation

Mayfield Chemical has held the largest share of the suntan products market for the past sixteen years. Brown Body, Mayfield's suntan product brand, comes as a lotion, cream, or oil. It is packaged in both spray and squeeze bottle containers and is available in virtually every major drugstore in the United States.

Marjorie Helm, director of new product development, has been experimenting with an extract of the prickly-pear cactus referred to in the lab as MC-5. This substance has proved to be an extremely effective sunscreen—it blocks ultraviolet rays yet does not prevent tanning. Tests on paid volunteers revealed that when MC-5 was formulated into a cream-based product, it was 50 percent more effective than any comparable product now on the market. That is, a person could stay in the sun approximately twice as long without getting sunburned or blistered. By the same token, it took much longer to get a tan with the new product.

A 6-ounce container of Brown Body Cream costs Mayfield $0.68 to manufacture and distribute. This figure includes a fixed-cost allocation based on sales volume for the past year. The product has a suggested retail price of $1.40, and most retailers adhere to this price.

Brown Body Sunscreen has been selected as the name for the new product containing MC-5. Ken Price, the marketing manager, has received first-year demand estimates from the marketing research department as follows: retail price $1.10—1,400,000; retail price $1.40—1,000,000; retail price $1.80—800,000. Total unit costs will be approximately $0.73 for 1,000,000 to 2,000,000 units and $0.77 for 800,000 to 1,000,000 units.

Mayfield's pricing strategy for new products has always been to start with a relatively high price and then gradually lower it as production capacity increases or when it meets with significant sales resistance at the high prices. Several factors have caused Price to question whether this strategy should be followed in introducing Brown Body Sunscreen. First, the new Jacksonville, Florida, production facility has approximately 200,000 units per month of unused production capacity. Second, Goldtone, Mayfield's leading competitor, has developed a habit of emulating Mayfield's new products and then offering the merchandise at a price approximately 15 percent below Mayfield's. Third, Mayfield's excellent physical distribution system allows it to obtain intensive distribution of any new product within a short period. Finally, Brown Body Sunscreen has obvious and easily demonstrable advantages that will require little educational effort.

1. Should Mayfield change its pricing strategy?
2. How might the factors listed by Price affect the pricing strategy?

12.2 Pampers II

Pampers were first test-marketed in Peoria, Illinois. They were offered for sale at a price of about 10 cents a diaper. This price was based on the cost to produce about 400 million diapers annually. The Peoria test market was a major disappointment. Instead of the projected national sales level of 400 million diapers, the test indicated that the most P&G could hope to sell was less than half this amount.

The company could not afford to invest any more capital in the equipment and machinery needed to mass-produce Pampers if this was the best it could expect. At this point P&G had spent millions of dollars on a product that looked like a failure. Additional research soon uncovered the trouble: price. Consumers liked the disposable diaper idea, but they decided that 10 cents a diaper was too much to pay.

Although P&G found some additional ways to reduce the long-run cost of raw materials, production, and delivery, the savings were nowhere near enough to enable the company to lower the price of Pampers. There was only one way to achieve the necessary savings while maintaining quality: increase volume. If, instead of 400 million diapers a year, Pampers could sell a billion diapers, they could be sold at 6 cents each. This was because fixed costs would be spread over a greater number of units and additional economies of scale could be achieved at that higher diaper volume.

The product was introduced in Sacramento, California, at the new price. Consumer response was immediate. At the new price, consumers began using Pampers regularly and not just for trips or under special circumstances. They began to make repeat purchases of Pampers. Additional test markets were opened, and the success story continued. As the company rolled the product out nationally, new manufacturing facilities had to be completed to meet demand. Strong demand and limited supply—a combination that generally pushes prices up—did not faze P&G. The price of Pampers was relatively constant. By 1976, almost half the babies in the United States were wearing Pampers.

1. Describe the initial price strategy that P&G had planned to follow and its advantages and disadvantages.
2. What factors led P&G to move to a different price strategy? What are the advantages and disadvantages of that strategy?
3. How can P&G modify its new strategy with price tactics?

◢ CASE FOR PART FOUR

Marshall Chemical Company*

The Marshall Chemical Company had developed rapidly in the chemical industry after World War II and by 1965 had assumed a position of industry leadership in certain fields. The company, in the process of growth, had followed an aggressive policy of product research and product line diversification. As a result, Marshall Chemical was highly respected in the industry as a small, high-quality firm.

Marshall Chemical was especially known for its research program in chemical, pharmacological, and medical research. About two hundred of its products were responsible for 70 to 80 percent of its sales volume. Since leadership in the firm was primarily research-oriented, pricing was secondary in importance. Management had maintained that some fundamental pricing principles could be applied to all product groups. However, management was beginning to believe that this was not the most advisable policy to follow.

Marshall had developed such products as antibiotics, medicinal chemicals, vitamins, and hormones. The products were sold to pharmaceutical manufacturers who used them in developing preparations sold under their own brands on a retail basis. Some of these preparations might be sold only on a doctor's prescription. There are about a dozen large firms in this industry. Veterinary houses used Marshall products to compound medicines under their own brands for the treatment of animals. There are a few hundred such firms scattered throughout the country. Cosmetic manufacturers used Marshall products for preparations sold under their own brands through a wide variety of retail outlets. Marshall tended to sell only to a few small manufacturers that had achieved a reputation of quality in the industry.

Marshall sold their products to industrial buyers for use in vitamin enrichment of feeds for animals and poultry. In most instances, industrial distributors were used, except where large-scale orders were placed directly. However, most purchasers bought in small quantities. Government units were also buyers of Marshall products and made purchases mostly on bids. Marshall was not especially successful in this market, which it regarded as minor at best.

Although gross profits would vary widely on individual items, about 45 percent on sales was considered average. Selling and other distribution expenses were generally about 8 percent of sales. Net profit before taxes usually averaged about 15 percent of sales, and after taxes about 8 percent. Selling expenses and net profit percentages fluctuated among the different products as percentage of sales.

The launching of a new product is generally an expensive process. Only about half of Marshall's new products broke even. Pricing policies were generally inconsistent because research costs for new product development would vary. Generally the marketing department would try to develop the following information:

---

* Case prepared by Professor Ronald D. Michman, Shippensburg State College, Shippensburg, Pennsylvania.

1. Five-year unit sales forecast.
2. Selling and distribution expenses.
3. Costs to educate field personnel.
4. Guarantee policy.
5. The standard manufacturing cost to produce and provide a weighted five-year average cost.
6. All other manufacturing costs not included in the standard cost and relative to the product.
7. Development and future research expenses.

There was some dissatisfaction over the development of pricing policies for new products. Even though half of the new products were successful, which was the industry average, profitability was not that great on many of the products. Management was not certain of the reason but believed that pricing objectives and policies on new products should be reevaluated. Management was especially concerned over a few products that sold well, but whose costs were so high that Marshall did not break even on them for a few years.

Recently, Marshall had developed a new product that could be used by the cosmetic industry. The general manager believed that breakeven volume should be ascertained first, and then a target return pricing strategy of 15 percent utilized. Fixed costs were estimated at about $400,000. Sales were estimated to be about $1.2 million in the first year. At this sales point, variable costs would be about $720,000.

A conference was held, and among those present were the general manager, the marketing manager, the assistant marketing manager, the sales manager, and the product manager. A number of possibilities were suggested by these executives. The product manager cited the fact that in the chemical industry a firm has a virtual monopoly on a new product for anywhere from a few months to two years. Consequently, the product manager believed that a new product should be introduced at the highest possible price and then the price should be lowered once the breakeven point has been achieved. The price could then be computed on a 15 percent target return basis.

The sales manager tended to disagree with this policy. She maintained that this policy would tend to invite other firms to enter the market with similar products, and that Marshall would be in an awkward position later since deep price cuts would be made once competition developed. The sales manager also felt that the policy might generate customer ill will, since many buyers would believe they were charged unreasonably high prices in the early stages of product marketing. The product manager countered that in the early stages of the product life cycle, price reductions were to be expected. The sales manager, on the other hand, believed that if the price was fixed at the lowest possible level, other firms might hesitate to enter the market. Since a rival firm would have a heavy investment in research and development, this low-price policy of Marshall's would serve to deter other firms.

The marketing manager pointed out that a few rival firms prefer to estimate the price at which the product would settle after its introduction and charge this price at the onset. In this way a consistent price policy could be followed throughout the product life cycle, and the company would gain a reputation for uniformity. Moreover, he pointed out the following sales volume schedule:

Product group	Percentage of total company sales			
	1965	1970	1975	1980
Antibiotics	21%	18%	19%	18%
Medicinal chemicals	19	19	20	25
Vitamins	17	16	18	20
Hormones	15	12	11	10
Other	28	35	32	27

The marketing manager, however, believed that each product group should be treated separately and that different pricing strategies should be developed for each.

The general manager indicated that he had been associated with Marshall for thirty years and was displeased with the discussion. This executive referred to the great prestige Marshall had maintained in the industry. He felt that it was beneath the dignity of Marshall to engage in active price competition. His viewpoint was that since Marshall prepared quality products, prices should be established accordingly. Marshall observed a guarantee policy that was unequaled in the industry, and customers not only valued it, but should be willing to pay for it. Therefore, the general manager strongly favored cost-plus pricing or target return pricing. He was very much afraid of vertical integration. The trend toward vertical integration in the pharmaceutical industry was cited.

Finally, the assistant marketing manager believed that the establishment of pricing policies should be placed under a director of new products, a position he would perform for the company. The director of new products would be responsible for developing studies of different facets of a new product's potential, cost, and problems that might be encountered in developing the product and final marketing to the user. The studies should point out alternative ways of proceeding with development and implementation through research and development, acquisition, or subcontracting. Feasibility studies would have top priority. Since pricing is a comprehensive function, the new product manager would be responsible for gathering data from production, purchasing, research and development, and other departments within the firm that maintain data on costs of materials.

1. Compute the breakeven point on the new product that could be used by the cosmetic industry.
2. Discuss the viewpoints of the various executives. Do you agree or disagree with their thinking?
3. Suggest an approach Marshall could use in formulating pricing policies.

PART Five

Distribution structure

13 Basic channel theory and channel management

OBJECTIVES

To appreciate the importance of middlemen in the distribution function.

To identify the variety of channel functions and flows.

To review the basic channel systems.

To learn about the behavioral dimensions that affect distribution channels.

To become aware of the different factors that influence channel selection.

When G. Heileman Brewing Co. acquired troubled Carling National Breweries, Baltimore, in 1979 for $33 million, it passed two milestones. First, it gained an entrée to new markets in the Southwest, Southeast, and Northeast, thereby gaining national distribution overnight. Second, it took on its biggest acquisition challenge ever: a national brewer that had slid from an all-time high market share of 6% in 1963 to 3% recently, lost money in six of the past eight years, and floundered under a series of owners in the 1970s.

But in a matter of months, less time than management expected, Heileman turned Carling around and effectively integrated it into Heileman. "We're still more a multi-regional than a national," says chairman and President Russell G. Cleary. . . .

Heileman developed its scrappy marketing style in the process of expanding from being a tiny regional selling two brands in four midwestern states as recently as 20 years ago. In quick succession, it acquired faltering regional brewers such as Blatz, Wiedemann, Falls City, and Rainier at bargain-basement prices. In each case, the company beefed up advertising and promotion, added the brewer's distributors to the Heileman "family," continued the brands, and absorbed management personnel into Heileman. Heileman has become the king of beer market segmentation as a result: from the Northwest to the Midwest, some 30 different labels are available in different price categories. Separate Heileman brands are now No. 1 in Washington, Illinois, and Minnesota and No. 2 in Kentucky and Wisconsin.

Carling's size—and thus the size of its problems—made it a big gulp for Heileman to swallow. Nonetheless, the job was done with the usual style. One of Heileman's first moves was to call three meetings around the country with the 700-odd Carling distributors, only 200 of whom had previously sold any Heileman products. Both Cleary and the executive marketing vice president believe in maintaining close relations with distributors and they both attended the meetings. "Our message," says Cleary, "was that we were there to build sales and distribution, not to milk Carling. Right away the distributors' morale improved." Soon thereafter Heileman began adding Carling products to those of Heileman's 1,300 distributors in weak Carling areas. Moreover, some Carling distributors began to sell a few Heileman products.[1]

Why would Heileman Brewing Company pay $33 million for a company that had lost half of its market share in the past fifteen years and lost money in six of the eight years prior to acquisition? Primarily because of distribution. Beer in cans or bottles is very expensive to transport over long distances. Thus, the location of the breweries generally places constraints on the physical size of the firm's market. Second, Heileman acquired 700 new distributors when it purchased Carling. Without a distributor network to sell the beer, Heileman was boxed into its old markets. In the Northeast, for example, Heileman can brew its Heileman products in the old Carling Baltimore Brewery and use the old Carling distributors to sell Heileman beers.

The point of this example is very important. A company can have the best products in the world: yet without a good distribution system, sales will be mediocre or nonexistent. More small businesses fail due to poor distribution than any other factor. A **channel of distribution** is a system of relationships among institutions involved in the process of facilitating exchange and consumption transactions. The system focuses on the process of ownership and the physical transfer of goods and services. The success of any channel depends on how well it meets the shopping needs and habits of the target consumers and the cost constraints of the seller.

Since channel institutions, such as manufacturers, wholesalers, and retailers, tend to form buying and selling relations among themselves, they may be viewed as a system. We will look first at the structure and functions of channel systems. The nature of these systems and their behavioral dimensions, such as power, control, and institutional conflict, will be described later in the chapter. We will conclude with a discussion of the factors influencing channel selection.

Common channel systems

Figure 13.1 depicts common channels of distribution. Some of the channel members are described in the following list.

- *Agents and brokers.*   Agents and brokers do not take title to the merchandise and rarely handle the merchandise itself. A broker brings the buyer and seller together. Brokers are common in markets where it is hard to find potential buyers and sellers. An agent is a representative of a manufacturer or wholesaler. Agents do not take title and have little, if any, authority over the terms of a sale.
- *Industrial distributors.*   These are independent wholesaler organizations that purchase related product lines from many manufacturers and sell to industrial users. An industrial distributor often maintains a salesforce to call on account executives, make deliveries, extend credit, and provide information.
- *Industrial users.*   Industrial users buy products for internal use or for further

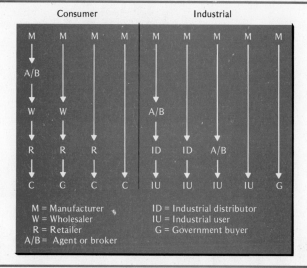

processing as part of the production process. They include manufacturers, utilities, airlines, railroads, and service institutions such as hotels, hospitals, and schools.

◢ *Government buyers.* State, local, and federal government purchasing agents buy virtually every good and service imaginable. Because of the quantities and specifications involved, these transactions are usually between the government and the manufacturer. Manufacturers are invited to submit proposals and prices for specific goods and services.

◢ *Wholesalers.* Wholesalers sell finished goods to institutions such as schools and hospitals. They also sell products to retailers and manufacturers. The historical function of a wholesaler has been to purchase from the manufacturer and sell to the retailer (see Chapter 14).

◢ *Retailers.* Retailers sell to the ultimate consumer and industrial end users. (This function will be discussed in detail in Chapter 15.)

Channel participants

Some institutions participate in channel functions but are not channel members (see Figure 13.2). A channel member engages in negotiating functions—buying, selling, and transferring title. Participants who engage in these functions are linked together by a "thread" of negotiation and are therefore members of the contractual organization (the marketing channel). Facilitating agencies do not perform negotiating functions and are therefore not members of the channel.

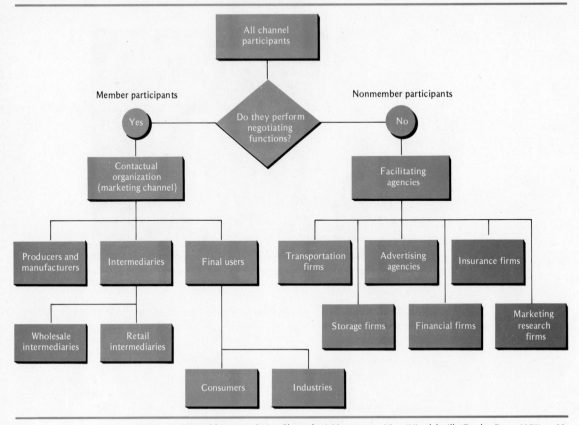

Source: Bert Rosenbloom, *Marketing Channels: A Management View* (Hinsdale, Ill.: Dryden Press, 1978), p. 22. Copyright © 1978 by Bert Rosenbloom. Reprinted by permission of Holt, Rinehart and Winston.

They do, however, facilitate the smooth functioning of the channel. A bank, for example, facilitates the buying and selling process throughout the channel by extending credit where needed. Truck lines physically move goods from the manufacturer to a wholesaler. Marketing research firms help determine the nature of the product to be produced and the type and location of retail outlets (channel structures). Research firms are also facilitating agencies, but not channel members.

Why are middlemen used?

We begin our study of distribution channels by examining why they exist and their various flows. The fundamental task of any channel is to move merchandise in an efficient manner. Efficiency is enhanced by reducing the number of individual transactions, and removing and overcoming discrepancies of quantity and assortment. Channels also help to bring buyers and sellers together. In addition, they perform a number of flow functions.

TO FACILITATE THE FLOW OF GOODS

Reducing the number of transactions. Assume for a moment that there are only four students in your class. Also assume that your professor requires five textbooks, each from a different publisher. If there were no bookstore (or middleman), twenty transactions would be necessary for each student to obtain the necessary books (see Figure 13.3). If a middleman is inserted between the publishers and the students, the number of transactions is reduced to nine. Each publisher sells to one bookstore rather than to four students. Each student buys from one bookstore instead of from five publishers.

Reducing and eliminating discrepancies. Perhaps the easiest way to understand the idea of a discrepancy of quantity is to relate it to our mass production economy. Economies of scale are achieved in industry through the use of efficient equipment capable of tremendous outputs of homogeneous products. Economies of scale, specialization of labor, and the use of professional management normally result in a lower average cost of production per unit.

Economies of scale require the development of distribution channels capable of overcoming barriers to exchange. Assume that Betty Crocker Instant Pancake Mix is produced at a rate of 5000 units in a typical day. Not even the most ardent pancake fan could consume that much mix in a year, much less in a day. The quantity produced to achieve low unit costs has created a **discrepancy of quantity**—the discrepancy between the amount of product supplied and the amount a final user wants to buy.

Mass production creates not only discrepancies of quantity, but also **discrepancies of assortment.** Firms achieve economies of scale by producing a homogeneous product or a base product with minor variations. In order for pancakes to have maximum utility, several other products are required to complete the assortment. At the very least, most people want a knife, fork, plate, butter, and syrup. Others might add orange juice, coffee, cream, sugar, bacon, sausage, eggs, and perhaps even a glass of champagne. Pillsbury, although a large consumer products company, does not come close to providing the optimum assortment we just described.

Other discrepancies exist in the marketplace based upon time, space, and perceived values. A temporal discrepancy is created when a product is produced and a consumer is not ready to purchase it. This is offset by storage by channel intermediaries and proper timing of production runs. Mass production requires a large number of potential purchasers, so markets are usually scattered over large geographic regions, creating a spatial discrepancy. Often international, or at least nationwide, markets are needed to absorb the outputs of mass producers. This makes local consumption (at the marketing site)

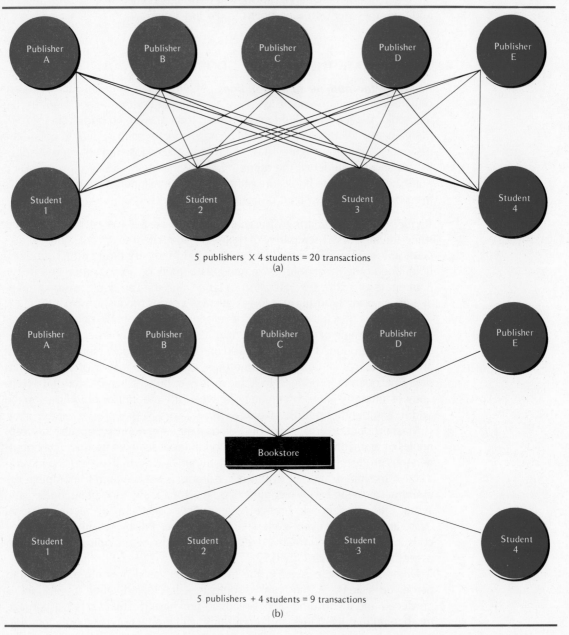

▲ FIGURE 13.3 Channel middlemen reduce the number of required transactions: (a) without a middleman; and (b) with a middleman.

5 publishers × 4 students = 20 transactions

(a)

5 publishers + 4 students = 9 transactions

(b)

inefficient if not impossible. Imagine the absurdity of all of us making a pilgrimage to Minneapolis to purchase Betty Crocker Pancake Mix.

A third discrepancy is of perceived values between what the producer and the potential buyer think the product is worth. This can be offset by channel intermediaries adjusting prices of the product to meet needs of the buyer. A wholesaler, for example, may add an accessory item to a basic product to meet local needs.

Sorting. In order to overcome discrepancies of quantity, assortment, and so on, channel members perform a **sorting function.** Sorting consists of the following activities:

1. *Sorting out.* Breaking down a heterogeneous supply into separate stocks that are relatively homogeneous. (Sorting out is typified by the grading of agricultural products.)
2. *Accumulation.* Bringing similar stocks together into a larger homogeneous supply.
3. *Allocation.* Breaking a homogeneous supply down into smaller and smaller lots. Allocating at the wholesale level is called "breaking bulk." Goods received in carloads are sold in case lots. A buyer of case lots in turn sells individual units. The allocation processes generally coincide with geographical dispersal and successive changes in ownership.
4. *Assorting.* Building up the assortment of products for use in association with each other. Wholesalers build assortments of goods for retailers, and retailers build assortments for their customers.

Without the sorting process, modern society, as we know it, would not exist today. We would have cottage industries serving local markets on a custom or semi-custom order basis. In short, we would return to a much lower level of consumption.

Locating buyers. In addition to the primary channel functions discussed above, channels provide several auxiliary functions. Channel members must locate buyers for their merchandise. A wholesaler seeks "the right" retailers in order to sell a profitable volume of merchandise. A sporting-goods wholesaler, for example, must find the retailers that are most likely to reach sporting-goods consumers. Retailers have to understand the buying habits of the final consumer and locate stores where the consumer wants and expects to find the merchandise. Every member of a channel of distribution must locate buyers for the products it is attempting to sell.

Storage. Merchandise must be stored within the channel in order for goods to be available when the consumer wants to purchase them. The high cost of retail space often means that storage is done by the wholesaler or the manufacturer.

Manufacturers serve wide markets covering large geographic areas. Often prompt delivery at reasonable cost can best be provided by strategically located warehouses close to the manufacturer's major markets. Thus wholesalers are usually responsible for finished-goods storage. It should be noted, however, that some manufacturers and retailers establish their own wholesaling operations.

TO MANAGE CHANNEL FLOWS

The sorting process is a function of distribution channels. A **channel flow** is movement within a channel. One of the most obvious flows is that of a product, which moves physically from the producer to the ultimate user. Other flows are title to the goods (ownership), promotion, communication, payment, and negotiation (see Figure 13.4). The flows shown in Figure 13.4 are the most common ones.

Physical flow. The physical flow results from the movement of supplies and finished products by various means of transportation. In the making and selling of carpets, for example, yarns are shipped to the mills, carpets are trucked to wholesalers or retailers, and an individual item is finally delivered to the end user or consumer. In some cases a retailer may take a special carpet order, and the product will be produced and shipped directly to the end user for installation. This is often true in new office buildings, churches, restaurants, hotels, and other institutions.

Title flow. The title to the good often takes a different route from the physical flow. For example, if your organization was building a restaurant, the carpet might be financed by a bank. If the carpet was obtained from a retail dealer (and the dealer had title), title would flow to the financial institution and, after payment by the restaurant, to the restaurant. When you purchase a car from a Chevrolet or other General Motors dealer, chances are that the title flow went from General Motors to General Motors Acceptance Corporation (it finances dealer inventories) to you. If you finance the car through GMAC, it will retain the title until you finish paying for the vehicle.

Promotion flow. After a manufacturer or retailer selects an advertising agency, the agency working with the client usually develops a promotional campaign. Note that the flow is basically downward to the target audience. Manufacturers, for example, promote carpets not only to the end user, but to the channel members as well. If wholesalers are not enthusiastic about the product, it will not be "pushed" to the retailer. The same is true at the retail level. Promotion is used not only to persuade other members to stock and sell an item, but to inform them as well. Informational promotion may explain the quality of a carpet in terms of materials used, tightness of the weave, colorfastness, stain resistance, and durability.

Communications flow. The longer the length of a channel—the more middlemen involved—the greater the likelihood of communications distortion. Channels are basically a communications conduit. Information about products and services flows down the channel to the end user. Communications also flow upward in a channel. Retailers often receive comments (or have their own thoughts) and complaints about products. This information is passed directly to the manufacturer or relayed to the wholesaler, who then tells the manufacturer what consumers are thinking. Ideas for product modification and different packaging or price strategies result from this upward communications flow.

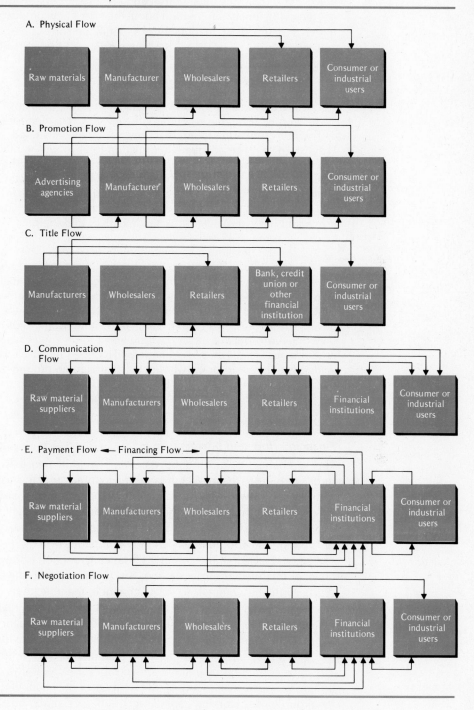

▲ **FIGURE 13.4 Key channel flows.**

A. Physical Flow

| Raw materials | Manufacturer | Wholesalers | Retailers | Consumer or industrial users |

B. Promotion Flow

| Advertising agencies | Manufacturer | Wholesalers | Retailers | Consumer or industrial users |

C. Title Flow

| Manufacturers | Wholesalers | Retailers | Bank, credit union or other financial institution | Consumer or industrial users |

D. Communication Flow

| Raw material suppliers | Manufacturers | Wholesalers | Retailers | Financial institutions | Consumer or industrial users |

E. Payment Flow ◄─ Financing Flow ─►

| Raw material suppliers | Manufacturers | Wholesalers | Retailers | Financial institutions | Consumer or industrial users |

F. Negotiation Flow

| Raw material suppliers | Manufacturers | Wholesalers | Retailers | Financial institutions | Consumer or industrial users |

Sometimes communications do not reach the intended audience. A pharmacist for a major hospital complained to a large drug wholesaler that he was not receiving timely information about the firm's new products. The pharmacist noted that the drug manufacturer's detail persons (salespersons) were not calling on him, nor was he receiving printed brochures about new ethical drugs.

The wholesaler agreed that the manufacturers were "falling down on their job," but when he interviewed detail men for several manufacturers, he found that they, too, were frustrated. They had more than adequate information to give out—written and oral. To them, the pharmacist himself was the villain. They were fed up with waiting as much as four hours to conduct a detail call. "That pharmacist thinks he is God," one salesman said. "He couldn't care less about how long he makes the salesman wait." The wholesaler took the initiative, told the pharmacist what the real problem was, and made appointments for him to see the detail men at given hours. But note that it is the manufacturer's communication line that has broken down, not the wholesaler's. The manufacturer has depended upon detail men to tell the potential pharmacist buyer about his products, which could then be sold and delivered by wholesalers to the buyer. The wholesaler's responsibility in communication was only to tell prospective buyers that they had the manufacturer's products available. Obviously, the manufacturer's feedback was inadequate in that it took a wholesaler to straighten out the manufacturer's communication problem.[2]

Financing flow and payment flow. Channels also have a financial function. First, a channel of distribution consists of middlemen that get the manufacturer's product to the market. It saves the manufacturer the cost of providing the distribution network (buildings, equipment, inventory, and parking space). Coke is sold in hundreds of thousands of locations throughout the world. Can you imagine the expense that would be involved if Coca-Cola had to set up a distribution network that was entirely company owned?

A second aspect of the channel's financing function is the credit provided to channel intermediaries. Inventories are financed as products flow through or are held in the channel. In most channels manufacturers provide credit to wholesalers and to retailers that buy directly from the manufacturer. Many wholesalers also grant credit terms to retailers. Thus a channel may provide a source of financing for its middlemen. The retailer may provide credit directly to the final purchaser, or credit may be obtained through a financial institution. The payment flow is essentially a reversal of the credit flow. Financial institutions may issue credit to any or all members of the channel to finance raw material purchases, working capital, accounts receivable, or even major capital items. A department store, for example, may go to an insurance company to finance construction of a new outlet.

Negotiation flows. The final major flow is that of negotiation. It is essentially a two-way flow where channel members bargain over prices, delivery terms, products, and delivery dates. Sometimes negotiation results in a conflict, and the eventual winner is determined by its power within the channel. (We will discuss behavior of channel participants later in the chapter.)

Types of channels

The number and types of middlemen in a channel depend on a variety of factors, to be covered later in the chapter. First, however, several important channel concepts need to be understood. These are the inability to eliminate channel functions, service channels, dual channels, nonprofit channels, and the systems concept of distribution.

Regardless of whether or not middlemen are present in the channel, the functions must still be performed. If there is no wholesaler, someone must physically store and move the merchandise, locate suitable retailers, promote the product, and so forth. Similarly, if a manufacturer decides to be its own retailer because of cost, promotion, or other considerations, it must decide on the number of stores, their locations, their layout, promotions and displays, and all the other retail and wholesale functions. Sometimes the reallocation of functions causes severe disruptions within a channel. If a manufacturer decides to perform the duties of the wholesaler and sell directly to the retailer, the wholesaler will resist strenuously. The ability to shift functions sometimes depends upon the relative power of various channel members.

SERVICE CHANNELS

Our discussion so far has centered on the distribution of goods rather than services. Most services have a very short channel: from the producer (the provider of the service) to the consumer. Unlike goods, services cannot be stockpiled, transported, or inventoried. They must be created and distributed simultaneously. Examples include barber shops, medical services, banking, legal services, hotel accommodations, and movies.

Location. An important key to the success of service channels is location. Since services cannot be stored, they will not be used if there is no place utility (or they will be used less frequently). A hair stylist, real estate firm, motel, or similar service organization will not be effective without a convenient location for potential users. A poorly located automobile repair shop may encourage some people to do the work themselves rather than drive to a distant location. Poorly located services may have to lower their prices below competitive levels in order to encourage business.

Service channel middlemen. Service channels are not limited strictly to the producer/creator of the service and the user. In a narrow sense, longer service channels can evolve. This phenomenon occurs when intermediaries other than the producer are utilized to make the service available and/or more convenient. An example is group insurance written through intermediaries, such as labor unions or employers. Retailers who accept VISA or Master Card are intermediaries for a bank's credit services.

Agents and brokers also lengthen the service channel. Their essential function is to bring performer and consumer or user together. They represent either of the primary channel components, and the longest service channel results where agents and brokers representing both seller and buyer intervene. Examples include the following: Artistic performers are represented by agents; rental agents represent the owners of rental housing and office space; travel agents represent all types of travel services; insurance agents and brokers are probably the most widely known service intermediaries.[3]

NONPROFIT CHANNELS

Nonprofit organizations are typically service-oriented, and location is important for these organizations also. A health care clinic to serve the needy must be located in a low-income area. Many target consumers lack the funds for public transportation and/or would feel psychologically uncomfortable in other parts of their community. Volunteers act as collection agents in strategic locations for many nonprofit organizations. The Jerry Lewis MD Telethon has hundreds of collection agents at the local level. These, in turn, report collections to regional facilities that report directly to the national level. Many universities are now offering courses in downtown hotels, on trains, at resort areas, on cruise ships, and in public parks. The service (continuing education) is being offered where and when the target market wants (or has the time) to acquire it.

Recycling of disposable bottles and cans is conducted on a profit and a nonprofit basis. It requires both a forward and a reverse distribution process. A soft drink can originally has the following flow: can manufacturer ⟶ beverage bottler ⟶ retailer ⟶ consumer. In recycling, the flow reverses back up the channel: consumer discards the can ⟶ independent can gatherer ⟶ reclamation center ⟶ aluminum smelter ⟶ can manufacturer.

MULTIPLE-CHANNEL SYSTEMS

So far our discussion of channels has centered upon a manufacturer having a single channel of distribution. Many companies have dual or multiple channels of distribution to reach different target audiences. A manufacturer of electrical wire and cable, for example, sells to electrical distributors, hardware wholesalers, or directly to repair and service shops.

Although multiple channels usually reach a larger potential market than single channels, they are not without problems. Conflict often develops between the intermediaries and the manufacturer. Disagreements on pricing, delivery dates, protected markets, and favoritism often arise. If the manufacturer uses different pricing tactics in different markets, it may be in violation of the Robinson-Patman Act.

VERTICAL CHANNEL SYSTEMS

Today, channels for both services and merchandise tend to be integrated into a system. Historically, this was not the case. Conventional distribution channels were fragmented, potentially unstable networks in which firms bargained with each other at arm's length, terminated relationships with impunity, and otherwise behaved autonomously. There was no coordination, no overall goals, lack of interdependence, and an absence of routinization. These conventional channels were high-cost and undependable operations. To overcome the deficiencies of conventional marketing channels, vertical systems developed. These can be described as

. . . professionally managed and centrally programmed networks, preengineered to achieve operating economies and maximum market impact. Stated alternatively, these vertical marketing systems are rationalized and capital-intensive networks designed to achieve technological, managerial, and promotional economies through the integration, coordination, and synchronization of marketing flows from points of production to points of ultimate use.[4]

In a **vertical channel system** firms are aligned in a hierarchy of levels (manufacturer-wholesaler-retailer). A **horizontal channel system,** in contrast, contains firms that are all on the same level (a system of wholesalers or a system of retailers).

Competition between different vertical channels, together with the need for more effective control by dominant channel members, has led to a closer relationship among channel participants. Efficient accomplishment of channel functions requires coordination among the various intermediaries and fulfillment of certain role expectations. A manufacturer, for example, expects wholesalers in the channel to promote its products to retailers and to perform several other functions as well.

Allocation of functions, operation of the system, and control are achieved through centrally positioned firms that manage the entire system. Sometimes the managing institution is referred to as the **channel captain** or **system leader.** Not all channels are coordinated, nor do they always have a leader. But all channels have members that rely on each other. This has led to the evolution of three basic types of vertically coordinated systems: corporate, administered, and contractual.

Corporate systems. A **corporate distribution system** represents the ultimate in channel control. When a single firm owns the entire channel, there is no need to worry about middlemen. A corporate system ensures a channel leader of supplies of raw materials and long-term contact with customers. It ensures adequate distribution and product exposure in the marketplace. Decision making by channel members is not independent or subject to major change without agreement by the channel leader (owner). Moreover, policies regarding different price levels and product mixes for separate markets or heavier promotion in certain geographic regions can easily be implemented.

Examples of corporate vertical systems abound. Evans Products Company (a manufacturer of plywood) integrated forward when it decided to establish its own sales branches and wholesalers. It bought the wholesale lumber distributors in order to market its products to retail dealers more aggressively. Forward integration occurs when a manufacturer acquires an intermediary closer to the target market, such as a wholesaler or retailer. A wholesaler could integrate forward by purchasing a retailer. Other examples of forward integration include Sherwin Williams, which operates over 2000 paint stores; Hart Schaffner and Marx, a long-established manufacturer in the menswear field, which owns over 100 clothing outlets.

Backward integration is just the opposite. It is exemplified by many large retail organizations. Sears has an ownership equity in production facilities that supply over 30 percent of the company's inventory requirements. Large food chains obtain almost 10 percent of their requirements from captive manufacturing facilities, many of which were acquired in the 1950s.

Corporate systems are no panacea. When a corporation assumes the entire channel responsibility, the need to perform channel functions is not eliminated. Singer has learned this the hard way, because lack of marketing know-how at the retail level is partly responsible for its recent poor financial performance.

Administrative systems. An **administrative system** is established when a strong organization assumes a leadership position. The strength and power of the firm may consist of sheer economic domination of other channel members. It can also stem from a well-known brand name. Companies like Gillette, Hanes, Campbell, and Westinghouse are administrative-system leaders. An administrative leader can often influence or control the policies of other channel members without the costs and expertise required in a corporate system. This may be accomplished by threatening to withdraw well-known brand names, advertising rebates, or planning aids. Yet the vertically aligned companies can work as an integrated unit to achieve information, transportation, warehousing, promotion, and other economies. The net result, compared to a conventional system, is usually lower overall cost, a better assortment of merchandise, faster turnover, and the ability to adjust to changing consumer preferences.

In an administrative system authority still rests with individual channel members. Yet to accomplish their goals, they must conform to the leadership of the channel captain. The channel thus develops a system-type orientation. Informal authority can flow down the channel from the manufacturer or up the channel from the retailer. Kraft Foods has developed facilities management programs to administer the allocation of space in supermarket dairy cases. Kraft's power stems from the fact that the company accounts for 60 percent of dairy case volume, exclusive of milk, eggs, and butter.

For a small firm unable to take a leadership role in creating an administered channel, there are often strategic options available. First, the marketing manager can attempt to align the company with a dominant firm at a different level in the channel. A retailer, for example, could develop a relationship with a wholesaler or manufacturer. A second alternative is to form a contractual marketing channel that will offer the firm a legal power base to help secure channel member cooperation.[5]

Contractual systems. The third form of vertical marketing system is the **contractual system,** which may be defined as a system of independent firms at different levels (manufacturer, wholesaler, retailer) coordinating their distribution activities by contractual agreement. The objectives of a contractual system are essentially the same as those of an administrative system.

The franchise is a common form of the contractual system. A **franchise system** is the licensing of an entire business format where one firm (the franchisor) licenses a number of outlets (franchisees) to market a product or service and engage in a business developed by the franchisor using the latter's trade names, trademarks, service marks, knowhow, and methods of doing business.[6] (Franchising will be discussed in more detail in Chapter 15.)

HORIZONTAL SYSTEMS

A recent tendency for two or more companies to develop a joint marketing strategy to exploit new opportunities has been described as **symbiotic marketing.** One company, for example, may have developed a new product but lack the proper channel of distribution to reach the target market. Dr. Pepper found that the easiest way to break into many new market areas was to license existing Coca-Cola bottlers to bottle Dr. Pepper.

Magnavox found that Xerox had an excellent marketing organization to handle the telecopier Magnavox makes, and quickly entered into a marketing agreement with Xerox to handle its products. When A&P launched its massive modernization program, hundreds of stores were closed in marginal market areas. Southland recognized that A&P's 8 O'Clock brand of coffee had a strong consumer franchise. Southland entered into an agreement to sell the coffee at its 7-Eleven stores in trade areas vacated by A&P. Thus symbiotic marketing can result from changing distribution patterns, lack of capital, lack of marketing knowledge, or a desire on the part of two organizations to use their resources more efficiently.

Behavioral dimensions of distribution channels

A channel of distribution is more than a series of institutions linked by economic ties. Social relationships also play an important part in developing cohesiveness among channel members. The basic social dimensions of channels are member roles, power, and conflict. An understanding of how these concepts affect channel intermediaries will provide a better appreciation of channel systems.

MEMBER ROLES

Each channel member has a certain role to play if the distribution system is to function smoothly. Henry Tosi has said that

when channels of distribution are viewed as social systems, individual channel members are recognized as occupying distinct positions in the channel structure. A position pertains to the tendency for persons or organizations occupying a particular location in a system of social relationship to behave alike. One position becomes differentiated from other positions by virtue of the fact that the member exhibits predictable patterns of performance which elicit predictable responses from the other members.[7]

Every marketing channel must meet certain minimum role expectations in order to exist. For example, without some indication of what the wholesaler will do, the manufacturer would face a chaotic distribution system.

Each channel member tends to develop policies regarding services rendered, market served, and product offered. Each member must accept other members' functional domain, or conflict will result. As new marketing institutions evolve, they often force old intermediaries into new, different roles—or out of business. The supermarket, for instance, developed entirely outside the traditional channel for food. In fact, the old channel members actively fought the supermarket concept.

LEADERSHIP, POWER, AND CONTROL

As channel members jockey for power, control, and leadership roles within the system, conflict often results. **Channel power** may be defined as a firm's ability to achieve its goals in a state of conflict or potential conflict. Control occurs when one organization intentionally affects the behavior of another person, group, or organization. Leadership is the exercise of authority and power in order to achieve control. Power tends to be limited in scope, and issues to be specific. A manufacturer has control over new product designs and width of the product line. The retailer may possess power and control over the retail price, inventory levels, and quality of postsale service of the manufacturer's product. Power is rarely complete unless it is a corporate channel because of a lack of ownership of other channel members.

In any channel system there is a high degree of mutual dependence among channel members. Even the most powerful manufacturers depend on dealers to sell their product. It is also important to recognize that power depends on perception. A retailer, for example, may not recognize the power of a large, well-known manufacturer. Accordingly, the wholesaler may ignore the manufacturer's policies, suggestions, and directions. This could lead to serious conflict, with the manufacturer perhaps ultimately withdrawing the line from these distributors.

Power can be categorized into several forms:

1. *Reward.* A channel member believes that another channel intermediary can help the firm achieve its goals—for example, a manufacturer may give a wholesaler a full line to sell, therefore raising the wholesaler's profit potential.
2. *Coercion.* When a channel member feels threatened—for example, a threat by a wholesaler not to promote a manufacturer's product to a retailer. Slow vehicle delivery has been used as a means of coercion in the auto industry.
3. *Legitimate power.* The "right" of a channel leader to make decisions. Legitimate power usually results from the company's reputation. IBM, General Electric, and Xerox are perceived as natural leaders.
4. *Referent power.* A desire to join a channel—for example, independent motels like to be affiliated with a motel chain. Manufacturers often like to see their brands carried at prestige stores such as Neiman Marcus or Saks Fifth Avenue.
5. *Expert power.* Power based on the belief that a channel member's knowledge and expertise can result in a more efficient system. Small retailers often rely on larger, well-established wholesalers for advice.

CHANNEL CONFLICT

When channel members perceive that their goals are not being met or that they can achieve a stronger financial position, they may elect to exercise additional channel power. An attempt to exert power—for example, by changing required inventory levels or price policies or bypassing a middleman—can lead to conflict. In a broad context, conflict may not be bad. Often it arises because staid, traditional channel members refuse to keep pace with the times. The removal of an outmoded intermediary may result in a reduction of costs for the entire system.

The basic sources of conflict within channels can be grouped as follows:[8]

1. *Goal incompatibility.* The goal of a runner's shop is to sell as many shoes as possible to maximize profits. It carries Adidas, Puma, and Saucony. The manufacturer of Adidas wants a certain sales volume and market share in each market. The runner's shop and Adidas may have conflicting goals.
2. *Role incongruence.* A channel member has specific roles to fulfill. Burger King requires that its franchisees prepare hamburgers according to a certain procedure. If the franchisee decides to make the burgers in a different manner, role incongruence between the franchisor and franchisee has developed.
3. *Communication breakdowns.* When a manufacturer makes changes in the marketing mix and fails to notify other channel members, conflict can result. The failure to notify dealers of reduced warranty coverage from six months to three months could cause a major problem. Dealers could make repairs and expect reimbursement by the manufacturer, not knowing the warranties have expired.

4. *Different perceptions of reality.* A manufacturer may feel that the margins offered to the intermediaries are ample for the various demands it places on retailers and wholesalers. The intermediaries might view the situation as being just the reverse. Margins are low, so the space, service and sales effort they provide the manufacturer will be minimal.
5. *Ideological differences.* Channel members sometimes have different values or views of situations. The retailer may follow the policy of "the customer is always right" and have a very liberal return policy. The wholesaler or manufacturer may feel that many people "try to get something for nothing" or don't follow product instructions carefully. Its view of allowable returns would be at variance with that of the retailer.

RESOLUTION OF CHANNEL CONFLICT

When a conflict situation arises within a channel, someone must take a leadership role to resolve the problem. If this does not happen, the difficulties will fester and communication and channel efficiencies will decline. Conflict resolution usually takes one of the following forms:[9]

1. *Problem solving.* Mutual goals are assumed and the task is to find a solution which satisfies shared objectives.
2. *Persuasion.* Used by a powerful channel member to convince dissident channel members.
3. *Bargaining.* Using compromise to reach new agreements.
4. *Politics.* An attempt to create coalitions to alter the power structure — for example, auto dealers banded together to form the National Association of Automobile Dealers to fight perceived unfair practices of the manufacturers.

The Armstrong Cork Company is a good example of a manufacturer that stresses the partnership concept in building a highly motivated team of channel members. In its floor covering division, for example, all its products are sold through independent wholesale distributors whom Armstrong views as its "partners" in its quest to maintain its strong leadership position in many types of floor coverings.

This partnership concept has been a long-standing tradition of Armstrong's channel policy. A major feature of this relationship, which serves as a continuing reminder of the partnership, is the annual conference of Armstrong and its distributors. For the last fifty-five years Armstrong has sponsored this annual convention. In recent years these conventions have developed into meticulously planned programs designed to carefully reiterate the roles that each of the "partners" is expected to play in the marketing success of Armstrong floor products. This seminar is actually a very entertaining play performed by professional Broadway actors and actresses playing the roles of various Armstrong and distributor personnel. The times, places, and setting are, of course, changed to provide entertainment value. Though the play is very entertaining, Armstrong's intent is deadly serious—to show the roles that the channel members are expected to play in the channel partnership—in short, what Armstrong expects from its distributors and what the distributors can expect from Armstrong.[10]

Selecting a distribution channel

The task of channel selection is a critical decision for the marketer. If the wrong channel is chosen, the product will either die or, at the very least, not meet management's sales and profit expectations.

STEPS IN THE SELECTION PROCESS

Key steps in the channel selection process are shown in Figure 13.5. The need for changing or creating a channel can come from many factors: a new product, changing target audience buying habits, inefficiencies in existing channels, major changes in the marketing mix (a new price strategy may require the product to be sold in discount stores), new territories, or changing intermediary functions (supermarkets start carrying auto accessories, clothing, and small appliances).

Identify the target audience. Once the need for a change or new channel has been established, the first task is to identify the target customers. Who is most likely to purchase the product? Who are the heavy users? What are their demographic and life style characteristics?

Determine purchase habits. After the potential users have been identified, purchase habits need to be examined. Do they buy on credit? What type of financial arrangements are expected? Is delivery and maintenance required? Where do they expect to purchase the product? In order to counter competition in the small copier market, Xerox recently opened its first retail store. Small businesspeople were beginning to purchase copiers from office supply dealers and business machine dealers. Moreover, Xerox could not afford to send its highly trained and skilled sales staff out to call on small businesses; the margin did not cover such sales costs.

When a major candy company developed a new sugar-free line, the first question was, who is the target audience? As it developed, both individuals who were dieting and those medically restricted to sugar-free foods were potential customers. Management then had to determine if potential users expected to find the product in grocery stores or drugstores. It also had to determine if the new candies were viewed more like a medicine (stock it with drug

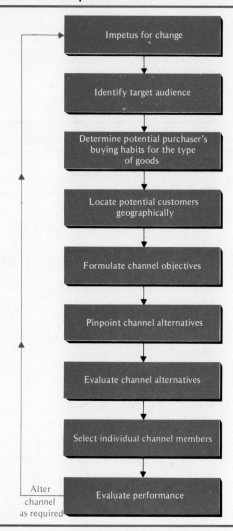

items) or more like a food (stock it next to other candies). A third choice was to stock the sugar-free candy in a separate area restricted to dietetic foods.

Locate customers geographically. The next step in creating a channel is to pinpoint potential users geographically. Perhaps heavy users are concentrated in specific regions. Sometimes buyers are found predominantly in small towns (major markets for home canning equipment are cities under 50,000 population); in other cases, markets are confined to large metropolitan areas. Home burglar alarms are sold almost exclusively in big cities. By locating customers geographically, managers can also determine modes of transportation, numbers and types of warehouses, and size and form of retail institutions available in the target regions.

Formulate channel objectives. After the marketing manager understands who the customers are and where they are, he or she should specify channel objectives. As with all marketing objectives, these should be specific, realistic, and measurable. A manufacturer of quality western belts might have the following objective: To ensure at least 75 percent of men and women between the ages of 14 and 65, living in its eighteen-state market area and spending at least $20 for a belt, have the opportunity to purchase its belts at least once out of every two occasions when they shop for a new belt. Marketing research can be used periodically to determine if the objective is being met or exceeded.

Channel objectives are sometimes expressed in levels of intensity of distribution. There are three basic degrees of intensity: intensive, selective, and exclusive.

Intensive distribution. **Intensive distribution** is maximum market coverage. The manufacturer tries to offer the product in every outlet where the potential customer might want to buy it. If a buyer is unwilling to search for a product (as is true of convenience goods and operating supplies), the product must be taken closer to the buyer. Assuming that the product is of low value and frequently purchased, a lengthy channel may be required. Candy, for example, is found in just about every type of retail store imaginable. It is typically sold in small quantities to retailers by a food or candy wholesaler. The cost to the Wrigley Company of selling its gum directly to every service station, drugstore, supermarket, and discount store that sells gum would be enormous.

Most manufacturers pursuing an intensive distribution strategy sell to a large percentage of the wholesalers that are willing to stock the product. Retailers' willingness—or lack of it—to handle the item tends to control the manufacturer's ability to reach intensive distribution at the retail level. For example, if a retailer is already carrying ten brands of gum, it may show little enthusiasm for another one.

Selective distribution. **Selective distribution** involves screening dealers to eliminate all but a few in any single geographic area. Since only a few retailers are selected, the consumer must be willing to seek out the product. Shopping goods and some specialty products are distributed selectively. Accessory-equipment manufacturers in the industrial goods market usually follow a selective distribution strategy.

Several screening criteria are used to find the "right" dealers. An accessory-equipment manufacturer may seek firms that are able to service its product properly. A television set manufacturer may look for service ability and a quality dealer image. On the negative side, poor credit risks and chronic complainers are quickly removed from consideration. If the manufacturer expects to move a large volume of merchandise through each dealer, it will select only those that seem capable of handling such volume. This may remove many smaller retailers from consideration.

RAYNAUD CERALENE
Limoges

Now, Raynaud Ceralene for
your very special gifts.
Because Raynaud Ceralene
exquisite design should not be
reserved for your dining table
alone.

At selected stores and **bACCARAT** 55 E. 57 St. N.Y.C.

Source: Courtesy of Baccarat Crystal.

Exclusive distribution. The most restrictive form of market coverage is **exclusive distribution** (see Figure 13.6). This normally entails establishing one or perhaps two dealers within a given geographic area. Since buyers may have to search or travel extensively to acquire the product, exclusive distribution is usually limited to consumer specialty goods, a few shopping goods, industrial installations, and accessory products at the retail level. Wholesale exclusive distributorships may cover a much wider array of products.

Sometimes exclusive territories are granted by new companies (such as franchisors) in order to obtain market coverage in a particular area. Retailers and wholesalers may be unwilling to commit the time and investment to promote and service a product unless the manufacturer guarantees them an exclusive territory. Limited distribution also may serve to create an image of exclusiveness for the product. If the product or service is successful in the long run, an area franchise can be very valuable.

If a wholesaler or retailer is expected to carry a large inventory or provide the extensive servicing, it may be granted an exclusive territory. This arrangement shields the dealer from direct competition and enables it to be the primary beneficiary of the manufacturer's promotional expenditures in that area. Channels of communication are usually well established, since the manufacturer deals with a limited number of dealers rather than many accounts.

Determine and evaluate channel alternatives. After channel objectives have been delineated, the marketing manager can pinpoint and evaluate channel alternatives. If the company considers a corporate chain, it will have to examine the required investment, sales potential, and availability of managerial resources to perform all the channel functions. On the other hand, a decision to go with existing channels requires that existing channels be evaluated to determine their compatibility with distribution objectives. If, for example, a company is selling a consumer convenience good, it will probably need a long channel. That is, producer ⟶ wholesaler ⟶ retailer ⟶ consumer. Such a channel is usually necessary to achieve intensive distribution for a convenience good like candy, pocket combs, milk, and so forth.

Select channel members. When a channel structure has been selected, the next step is to evaluate individual channel members. Key criteria for reviewing channel candidates are shown in Table 13.1. The various items may be weighted according to company needs and objectives: sales strength, product lines, and reputation, and the firms with the highest overall score are then approached for membership.

Performance evaluation. Channel determination is not a static procedure. Performance must be continually evaluated and channel policies changed as market conditions change. If customer purchasing habits or other key market considerations are altered, a new channel may be necessary. Good communications can help channel members adjust to change and minimize the need for drastic overhauls.

Factors that influence channel selection

Let us look at how two dramatically different firms—Westinghouse and Falcon Hang Gliders—are influenced by product and market factors in the channel selection process. Westinghouse can follow the procedure discussed above

1. Size of prospective channel member—sales, financial strength
2. Sales strength
   Number of sales personnel
   Sales and technical competence
3. Product lines
   Competitive products
   Compatible products
   Complementary products
   Quality of lines carried   .
4. Reputation
   Leadership
   Well-established
5. Market coverage
   Geographic coverage—outlets per market area
   Industry coverage
   Call frequency or intensity of coverage
6. Sales performance
   Performance with related lines
   General sales performance
   Growth prospects
7. Management
8. Advertising and sales promotion
9. Sales compensation
10. Acceptance of training assistance
11. Transportation savings
12. Inventory
    Kind and size
    Inventory minimums—safety stocks
    Reductions in manufacturer inventories
    Extent of postponement—speculation
13. Warehousing
    Supplied in field
    Ability to handle shipments efficiently
14. Lot quantity costs—willingness to accept our ordering policies

Source: Douglas M. Lambert, *The Distribution Channels Decision* (New York: National Association of Accountants; and Hamilton, Ontario: The Society of Management Accountants of Canada, 1978), p. 37.

and scientifically select a channel. Falcon is lucky if it can get any reasonable distribution at all.

THE ABILITY TO CHOOSE

A huge organization like Westinghouse, with an established reputation, tremendous financial resources, many existing distribution channels, and quality products has enormous channel power. Picking new members is rarely a problem. Falcon Hang Gliders (whose average output is two per month) is in an ill-defined market with virtually no financial resources. Assuming that a reasonable channel can be defined, it may be very difficult to enter the channel. The heart of the problem of small entrepreneurial manufacturers is often credibility—even for those that are well financed. How does a dealer know, for example, that the manufacturer will be able to supply quality merchandise whenever needed over the long run?

If the middleman is already handling a competing line, it usually makes it much harder for the entrepreneurial firm to gain acceptance. The problem of selecting the "best" channel may be a moot point. The question is, Will anyone handle the product? Many small manufacturers with good products have fallen into bankruptcy because they could not reach potential buyers.

PRODUCT-RELATED FACTORS

The nature of the product is a major determinant of its distribution channels. For example, except for supply items, industrial merchandise tends to be more expensive and technically complex than consumer goods. Usually, the higher the product's unit value, the shorter the channel, and vice versa. Also, the more technically complex the product, the greater the need for the producer to work directly with the end user, and thus the shorter the channel. Similarly, custom-made products usually flow through a very short channel. Westinghouse's nuclear power plants are sold by the firm's highly specialized field salespeople to a relatively small number of easily identifiable customers—electric utilities.

Bulky items, such as lumber, coal, and gravel, tend to move through shorter channels. Costs of storage and lack of storage facilities render lengthy channels unsuitable. With some products it is cheaper to move bulk quantities to central markets and package or reformulate the product there. For example, milk is gathered in bulk from the countryside and brought to large cities for final processing and packaging. Soft-drink manufacturers ship syrup in bulk to bottlers throughout the country rather than producing finished drinks at one plant. Similarly, some inexpensive wines are bottled by local distributors after being shipped in tank cars from the vineyards.

Another important product aspect of distribution channels is the extent of the product line. If a firm has an extensive product line, even if it consists of low-priced products, total sales to individual retailers may be high enough to justify direct distribution. Oscar Mayer sells a complete line of packaged meat products directly to supermarkets through company salespeople. This might not be economically feasible if the company sold only hot dogs. Generally speaking, the wider the product line, the shorter the channel—as long as the quantities justify such an approach.

MARKET-RELATED FACTORS

Returning to the hang glider manufacturer, its product is a consumer specialty good, or perhaps a shopping good, and by definition usually requires only a few dealers per area. Interested parties will search for the product until it is found and evaluated. But most hang glider enthusiasts live in California, and Falcon is located in Texas. Hang glider retailers have sprung up in larger West Coast cities to serve the growing market. Elsewhere in the country, hang glider retailers are virtually nonexistent. As you can see, geographic customer concentration is a key market consideration for Falcon. It has a limited number of potential buyers near its manufacturing facilities.

Buyers, particularly in industrial markets, often have widely varying needs even when they are purchasing the same product. Such a situation may call for multiple channels of distribution. The following statement by a Westinghouse executive illustrates the multiple-channel strategy:

Small motors are sold to original equipment manufacturers (OEM's), motor repair shops, industrial plants, and consumers. To reach all of these, we must use several different distribution channels.

For example, we sell and service very large OEM's directly. This is mainly because of the large number of motors involved, which leads to extreme competition—often to the point where we are negotiating for pennies. In addition, large OEM accounts need the technical expertise that specialized factory salesmen can best provide (the salesman in this case is, in effect, an application engineer). Various types of distributors, as well as chain stores, are used to sell small motors to other types of users.

The small motor division continuously analyzes the rationale used in selecting each distribution channel or combination of channels. They want the most effective way for getting the division's motors to the various market segments. Among the factors considered: required technical application assistance, inventory practices, advertising and sales promotion, and packaging.[11]

Consumer goods also flow through multiple channels because of differing needs of buyers. For example, Remington sells its shotguns through discount stores, sporting-goods stores, and gun shops, to name a few of its many outlets.

Customer order size is another important channel determinant. In industrial markets, operating supplies are commonly sold through industrial distributors because orders typically are not large enough to make direct sales economically feasible. Small hardware stores must rely on hardware wholesalers for similar reasons. Large orders make it possible to use shorter channels.

COMPANY-RELATED FACTORS

In addition to market and product factors, organizational considerations strongly influence channel strategies. Probably the most important of these considerations is financial strength or the lack of it. In the case of Falcon Hang Gliders, for example, the company was founded by two young men just out of college with a $5000 loan from one partner's father. Direct sales leads proved too costly, so in desperation Falcon turned to sporting-goods retailers and motorcycle shops. The company's poor financial condition meant that it could not supply inventory or even a single demonstration model to the eight retailers who agreed to sell the product. Instead, pictures and brochures were used as sales aids. After using the new channel for three months Falcon closed its doors. It had an unusual product, it's true; but it faced the distribution problems that have forced countless small entrepreneurial firms out of business.

Returning to our giant manufacturer, Westinghouse, the focus is on the other end of the financial spectrum. Well-financed companies may be able to set up corporate systems that remove the outside middleman from the picture. Or, as in the case of Westinghouse, it may establish its own wholesale operations and sell to independent retailers (such as electrical distributors) as well.

SUMMARY

A channel of distribution is a system of relationships among institutions involved in the process of facilitating exchange and consumption transactions. Since channel institutions such as manufacturers, wholesalers, and retailers tend to form buying and selling relationships among themselves, they may be viewed as a system. Middlemen are used to facilitate the flow of goods and services, reduce the number of transactions, and eliminate discrepancies of quantity and assortment. They also help locate buyers and engage in storage. Some institutions, such as truck lines and banks, facilitate channel flows, yet are not channel members because they do not perform negotiatory functions. These are referred to as facilitating agencies. There are a number of flows within a channel system. These include the physical flow of goods, plus promotion, title, communications, financing and payment, and negotiation flows.

There are many different kinds of channel systems. Services, unlike products, cannot be stockpiled, transported, or inventoried. They must be created and distributed simultaneously. Longer service channels can evolve when intermediaries other than the producer are utilized—for example, retailers who accept VISA are intermediaries for a bank's credit services.

Historically, channels of distribution have been unstable networks in which relationships were terminated with impunity and channel members behaved autonomously. In recent years, closer relationships have developed among channel participants, and vertically coordinated systems have evolved. There are three basic types of vertically coordinated systems: corporate, administrative, and contractual. As channel systems develop, social dimensions begin to evolve. Channel members develop roles, communication links, and power structures, and sometimes engage in conflict. Conflict is resolved through problem solving, persuasion, bargaining, or politics.

Selecting a channel is not always easy. Target consumers have to be identified and their buying habits examined; customers must be located geographically; and channel objectives must be formulated. Next, the firm must determine and evaluate channel alternatives. Channel members are then selected from available alternatives, or new channels are created.

Often, a small firm has little choice in the channels it uses. In fact, it may be lucky to obtain distribution at all. If channel alternatives do exist, the nature of the product, the type of market to be served, and company resources become important criteria for selection.

KEY TERMS

Channel of distribution	Administrative system
Discrepancy of quantity	Contractual system
Discrepancies of assortment	Franchise system
Sorting function	Symbiotic marketing

Channel flow
Vertical channel system
Horizontal channel system
Channel captain or system leader
Corporate distribution system

Channel power
Intensive distribution
Selective distribution
Exclusive distribution

REVIEW QUESTIONS

1. Explain the different functions performed by distribution channels.
2. What are the reasons underlying the use of a multichannel system? Identify its potential problem areas.
3. What is a channel of distribution? What is meant by a channel flow?
4. Describe the sorting process and state the benefits it provides.
5. State the forms of channel power and describe the basis of this influence.
6. What gives rise to channel conflict?
7. What steps are included in selecting a distribution channel?

DISCUSSION QUESTIONS

1. Discuss the factors that influence the number and type of channel intermediaries for a consumer goods company. How does your analysis change for industrial products?
2. Evaluate the following statement: "Regardless of the channel members used, the basic functions must be performed." Do you agree or disagree? Why?
3. What is channel power? How is it gained? Why is it such an important factor in channel systems and member relations?
4. How do product characteristics affect channel selection?
5. What criteria should a manufacturer establish for selecting channel members?
6. Why are decisions regarding channel management often more complicated than other marketing decisions?

NOTES

1. "G. Heileman Brewing, A Heady Growth in Stature," *Sales and Marketing Management,* January 14, 1980, pp. 14–15. Reprinted by permission from Sales & Management magazine. Copyright 1980.
2. Reavis Cox, Thomas F. Schutte, and Kendrick S. Few, "Towards the Measurement of Trade Channel Perception," in Fred C. Allvine (ed.), *Combined Proceedings 1971 Spring and Fall Conferences* (Chicago: American Marketing Association, 1972), pp. 190–191. By permission of the American Marketing Association.
3. John M. Ratmell, *Marketing in the Service Sector* (Cambridge, Mass.: Winthrop Publishers, 1974), pp. 109–110.
4. Bert C. McCammon, Jr., "Perspectives for Distribution Programming," in Louis P. Bucklin (ed.), *Vertical Marketing Systems* (Glenview, Ill.: Scott, Foresman, 1970), p. 43.
5. Bert Rosenbloom, *Marketing Channels: A Management Vow* (Hinsdale, Ill.: Dryden Press, 1978), p. 299.
6. Louis W. Stern and Adel El-Ansary, *Marketing Channels* (Englewood Cliffs, N.J.: Prentice-Hall, 1977), p. 408.
7. Henry L. Tosi, "The Effects of Expectation Levels and Role Consensus on the Buyer-Seller Dyad," *Journal of Business* 39 (October 1966): 516–529. Reprinted by permission of The University of Chicago Press.

8. The five conflict sources are from: Donald J. Bowersox, M. Bixby Cooper, Douglas M. Lambert, Donald A. Taylor, *Management In Marketing Channels* (New York: McGraw-Hill Book Company, 1980), p. 74.
9. The four basic techniques for conflict resolution are from Bowersox et al., pp. 108–109.
10. Bert Rosenbloom, "Motivating Independent Distribution Channel Members," *Industrial Marketing Management,* July 1978, pp. 278–279. Reprinted by permission.
11. S. C. Mulle, "Distribution Channel Strategies," in Earl L. Bailey (ed.), *Marketing Strategies: A Symposium* (New York: Conference Board, 1974), p. 78. Reprinted by permission.

◢ CASES

13.1 Welch Grape Soda

Welch has been producing grape products since 1869, when founder Thomas B. Welch first developed pasteurized "unfermented wine" for his church's communion service. This grape juice is still used in many Protestant churches today.

Welch's Foods has grown into an agricultural cooperative owned by 2000 grape growers. Between 1962 and 1976 the company introduced some 36 new products. One of them, carbonated grape soda, seemed to have great market potential as a soft drink.

The soft-drink industry's annual case volume totals about 4.6 billion cases. Grape soda's share of that market is about 3 percent. That's about $460 million for grape soda alone. However, there is no major national brand of grape soda. Perhaps this is because there is no nationally advertised brand.

Welch had several big advantages over other grape soda distributors. First, Welch was synonymous with grape products. Second, throughout its grape processing more than 25 separate inspections and analyses are made at plant laboratories for control over taste, purity, and uniform quality.

Welch tested the product and modified the formula continually over a five-year period before deciding that it was ready for introduction. At that point market tests showed that the product was strongly preferred over any of the existing competitive brands.

Welch had expected to tie into its own food store broker network, which used a warehouse delivery system. An alternative would have been to franchise an independent soft-drink bottler that could distribute the product via store delivery. Welch selected the first alternative because it believed that it would generate higher profits on a per-case basis. The wholesale cost was about $5 for 24 twelve-ounce bottles. At that price Welch was earning about a $2 margin. The product was put into a test market in Buffalo, New York. The results were very poor.

After examining the situation, Welch found that its problem was trying to crack a strong bottler delivery system. Bottlers control their shelf locations and shelf inventory. The bottler salespeople put the product on the shelf, thereby freeing store personnel for other tasks. The food broker salespeople were unable to get into retail outlets more than once a month. So they could not hold or check on the shelf space they needed. By means of frequent delivery, soft-drink bottlers

395

could obtain better shelf space. Primary shelf space was reserved for Coke, Pepsi, and 7-Up.

Franchising presented other problems. One was loss of control over product quality and distribution. A second problem was a much smaller return per case. However, bottlers dominate the shelf space and can produce a full line of package sizes. They also have huge inventories of merchandising hardware, including coolers, racks, vending machines, and the like, which could be used to support Welch's product outside the supermarket.

1. What should Welch do at this point to obtain distribution for its product?
2. How should it go about making the distribution channel decision?
3. Why wasn't the Buffalo failure foreseen?
4. How can these mistakes be avoided in the future?

13.2 Digital Equipment Corporation

Companies such as Digital Equipment Corporation (DEC), Wang, Apple Computer, Hewlett-Packard, TI, and others are all vying for a stronghold in the fast-growing market for small business computers. Their target is more than 4 million small businesses with fewer than 200 employees each, and the 6 million offices in the home that are beginning to display the same thirst for information processing equipment that the large industrial corporations and financial institutions have shown through the 1970s. But small computer prospects are more difficult to identify than their large corporate counterparts.

Compounding the difficulty of selling to smaller businesses are the lower profit margins on these systems compared with those on large, sophisticated computers. Although a small business computer costs a small fraction of the price of a larger machine, the first-time customer who buys one often needs more service and support than his or her large corporate counterpart. Classic distribution channels such as direct sales representatives or systems houses, which buy the bare bones computer, add software, and resell the package, are too costly to support a $10,000 to $20,000 system. Yet about 500,000 small business computers have been sold.

To compound the problem further, there are a number of submarkets or segments within the small business market. For example, a business with fewer than 25 employees now using paper and pencils for office chores approaches computerization with a vastly different attitude and requirements from a business with 150 to 200 employees. Some manufacturers are experimenting with retail stores, mail order, and local office supply dealers. IBM sells its small computers through its nationwide Business Computer Centers and its retail store in London. DEC is selling its inexpensive minicomputers through retail stores and authorized computer dealers, as well as through traditional systems houses. Xerox is experimenting with retail office products outlets that will sell everything from typewriter ribbons and copiers to computers. Apple Computer sells its machines in Computerland stores, Xerox retail outlets, and through office equipment dealers, and is now setting up its own distribution network with regional sales and service centers.

DEC is not fully satisfied with the existing channels of distribution. For example, it recently closed a retail store in Detroit and one in New York City, but at present has no intention of pulling out of the retail computer business. It is even trying sending out salespeople to call on prospective small business customers in a "Computer Van" loaded with equipment for hands-on demonstrations. Outsiders say DEC's problem is trying to move from a traditional manufacturing mentality to a retailing mind set.

Another option for DEC is to get into retail sales by signing on independent storeowners. In return for the storeowner's retailing knowhow, DEC could supply training supplies and service facilities.

1. What are the advantages and disadvantages of the various options open to DEC?
2. What would be some other distribution options?
3. Discuss some of the sources of power in the small computer distribution channels and potential sources of conflict.

14

Wholesaling

OBJECTIVES

To develop an understanding of the functions and roles of wholesalers.

To become aware of the various types of wholesalers.

To examine the task of managing the wholesale operation.

To gain insight into present and future trends in wholesaling.

Airwick Industries Professional Products Division manufactures and markets a variety of disinfectants, cleaning agents, odor counteractants, insecticides, and environmental sanitation products for hospitals, schools, nursing homes, restaurants, hotels/motels, government installations, retail sores, and industrial plants (see Figure 14-1). . . .

"The institutional supply side of Airwick has always done quite well," said John Updegraph, Professional Products Division president. "We have had a sales rate increase of 5% to 10% a year.

"But recently, with inflation running at 12% to 14% annually, we decided there was a need for a change in strategy. It became evident that if we were going to double sales or profits we'd have to do something unorthodox.

"In the beginning our products were marketed exclusively by independent distributors. Then, in the 1970s, we began to buy out the private distributors in the hope of someday dealing totally and directly with our customers through branch offices.

"Out of the hard rethinking about the best way to improve support for our distributors evolved the corporate strategy to divest ourselves of branch offices. We felt it was better to ride one horse successfully rather than risk falling on our faces riding two horses at the same time.

"So all 10 factory sales offices are being divided into 28 new distributorships. We'll now have a sales force of 93 independent entrepreneurs backed up with every sales aid we can supply.

"Sure, you relinquish some control when you have to rely on distributors," Updegraph explains. "It's nice if your company has the money to own every aspect of its business lock, stock, and barrel.

"In some ways, it is actually better to have the sales of your products handled by private entrepreneurs. These independent distributors run their own businesses and if anyone wants to turn a profit, they do. The more they push our products, the more money they make.

"Also, when you market your products through distributors, you eliminate numerous management headaches. In fact, we've found that Airwick is even stronger now because the distributors know we are behind them 100%."[1]

Source: Courtesy of Airwick Professional Products.

The Airwick story illustrates many of the important concepts discussed in Chapter 13. There was Airwick's desire to create a corporate vertical marketing system during the 1970s, and its finding in the 1980s that the costs of such a system were greater than the benefits. Channel conflict is also illustrated by the destruction of the old company sales branch system and the reinstalling of independent distributors. What role are industrial distributors supposed to play in a channel? What other wholesalers could Airwick have utilized? What elements are involved in managing a wholesale operation? Let us take a closer look.

The functions and roles of wholesalers

It is hard to develop an all-encompassing definition of wholesaling. We know that a wholesaler is an institution located somewhere within the channel system yet not at either end of the system (it is not a consumer or a manufacturer). Using this notion as a starting point, a **wholesaler** may be defined as an institution that

1. Sells finished goods to other institutions (primarily retailers) that will, in turn, resell it to the final user.
2. Sells to other institutions (hospitals, schools, manufacturers) that utilize the product in performing basic function. A hospital, for example, may purchase cleaning supplies from a wholesaler as part of its function of providing a relatively germ-free environment. A different example is the manufacturer that purchases grinding tools to be used in the product fabrication process.
3. Sells to institutions (mostly manufacturers) that will incorporate the item into a product. A small manufacturer of trailers may purchase tires from a tire wholesaler. The tires, of course, form an integral part of the trailer.

In a general sense, the distinction among wholesalers, manufacturers, and retailers may become blurred. A retailer may have its own warehouse facility and perhaps even sell some merchandise to other retailers. Its primary function, however, is to sell to final consumers. A manufacturer may sell merchandise to another manufacturer, thereby assuming the role of a wholesaler. In order to categorize an organization properly, we must determine its primary function. Is it basically a wholesaler that engages in limited manufacturing or a manufacturer that sometimes "wholesales" part of its output? Figure 14.2 illustrates the basic functions of wholesalers. As you might imagine, very few wholesalers perform all these functions. Most, in fact, perform only a limited number. Moreover, retailers and manufacturers perform some of the same activities.

◢ **FIGURE 14.2 Wholesaler functions.**

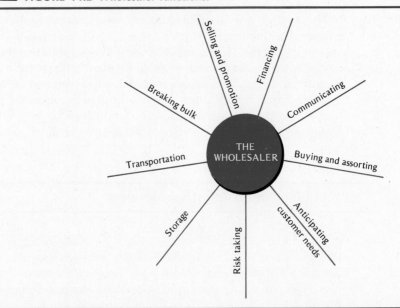

Anticipating customers' needs, buying, assorting, and communicating.
Wholesalers buy goods to resell to others. Firms that assume ownership
(acquire title) to the merchandise are called merchant wholesalers. Agents, by
contrast, may sell products for a manufacturer, but they never acquire title.

Buying the right mix of merchandise implies that the wholesaler has properly
anticipated the needs of its customers. A wholesaler must understand industry
trends, be informed about new product offerings, and even monitor changing
use patterns and attitudes of final consumers in order to purchase an appropriate assortment of goods at the wholesale level.

Selling and promotion. Perhaps the only function *all* wholesalers perform is
selling. In very small operations, the owner/agent may be the only salesperson.
Corporate wholesale operations sometimes employ several hundred salespeople.

Traditionally, most of the wholesaler's sales effort has focused on personal
selling. More progressive wholesalers such as wholesale druggists are utilizing
in-house telephone sales techniques to supplement the activities of the field
salesforce. Some drug wholesalers are taking 80 percent of their orders over the
telephone. Personal salespeople limit their calls to key accounts, special customers, and prospects that show high potential.

Wholesalers also supplement their sales efforts by mailing out flyers, catalogs, and brochures. The rapidly rising prices of the 1980s forced many firms to
print catalogs without printing a price next to the picture and description of the
merchandise. Monthly and sometimes weekly price list updates are mailed to
catalog recipients.

Financing. Although all wholesalers sell to customers, fewer than half offer financing to their clients. In some industries the practice of providing credit or
granting cash discounts is traditional. Other channels feature both cash-and-
carry wholesalers and wholesalers that are willing to provide financing. An unusual form of financing sometimes found in seasonal items such as toys and
beach play equipment consists of delivering the merchandise several months
before the season begins and not billing the retailer until the season is under
way. The wholesaler often must acquire and finance large inventories of its
own.

Storage. When a wholesaler develops an assortment of merchandise, it usually
must store the goods until they are ordered by the customer. Storage and inventory control are an integral part of financial management. Most wholesalers attempt to reduce lengthy storage times and increase product flow. Five basic
reasons why storage is necessary are (1) seasonal production, (2) erratic
demand requirements, (3) conditioning (such as the ripening of bananas), (4)
speculation (in the hope of an increase in product value), and (5) realization of
a special discount (for accepting delivery during an off season or reduced price
on closeouts).

Breaking bulk. Purchase of closeouts or large quantities often results in rail
carload or truckload shipments of merchandise. Not only does the wholesaler

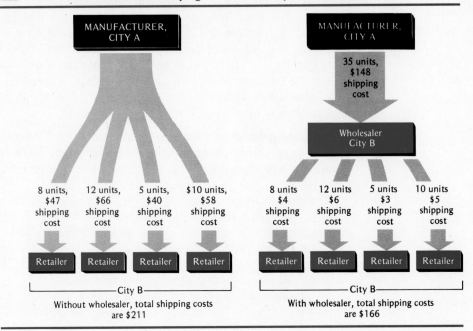

8 units, $47 shipping cost	12 units, $66 shipping cost	5 units, $40 shipping cost	$10 units, $58 shipping cost

Without wholesaler, total shipping costs are $211

8 units $4 shipping cost	12 units $6 shipping cost	5 units $3 shipping cost	10 units $5 shipping cost

With wholesaler, total shipping costs are $166

receive quantity and other special discounts for purchasing large amounts, but it also obtains a lower freight ratio for full-car or truckload shipments. Usually the wholesaler will store the goods and fill orders, one or several cases at a time, from inventory. This process is referred to as breaking bulk. Manufacturers and small retailers cannot afford the high cost of shipments of "less than carload" to individual retailers. It is more economical to sell in bulk to wholesalers, which, in turn, offer small quantities to local merchants (see Figure 14.3).

Transportation. Since the wholesaler tends to serve a limited geographic area, it is usually closer to the retailer than to the manufacturer. Consequently the retailer gets quicker delivery and perhaps a lower total cost of goods. The lower prices result from not having to buy goods in lots of less than a carload from the manufacturer. If the retailer can depend on the wholesaler for fast delivery, the retailer can reduce its inventory. Lower inventories mean lower working capital requirements and reduced risks of fire, theft, deterioration, and obsolescence to the retailer.

Risk taking. Carrying inventory involves some risk that the goods will not be sold. In addition, inventory requires the assumption of the other types of risk just mentioned. As the wholesaler increases inventory to avoid **stockouts** (when all inventory has been sold), it increases the risk of not selling all the goods that are stored. Ultimately a tradeoff must be reached between not having some items in stock (and perhaps losing a sale) and the risk of a large inventory.

Merchant wholesalers

Of the 382,837 wholesalers in existence in 1977, 307,264 were **merchant wholesalers.** These organizations accounted for $676 billion of the $1.258 trillion total of wholesale sales in 1977, the last year the Census of Wholesale Trade was taken.[2] A merchant wholesaler can be defined as an institution that

1. Purchases goods from manufacturers for their own account (as distinguished from the agent, who typically does not purchase for his own account) and resells them to other businesses, government agencies, and other wholesalers.
2. Operates one or more warehouses in which it receives and takes title to goods, stores them, and later reships them. In some cases, it may have goods shipped directly by the manufacturer to the customer, so the goods do not actually pass through the wholesaler's warehouse. Still, a good part, and usually all, of the goods the wholesaler handles do, in fact, pass through its warehouse.

Since merchant wholesalers acquire title to the goods, they have control over the items of sale—price, delivery date, and the like. Their customers are primarily small or moderate-sized retailers, but they may also promote their offerings to manufacturers and institutional clients.

Let us examine several types of merchant wholesalers. Some of the most common forms are these: single line, specialty, industrial distributor, rack merchandiser, drop shipper, and producers' cooperative.

SINGLE-LINE WHOLESALERS

Single-line wholesalers carry one or two, at most, lines of merchandise. Usually, they stock a full assortment of products within the line. For instance, a hardware wholesaler will handle a full array of tools, paints, fasteners, rope, chains, and the like. In addition to hardware markets, single-line wholesalers are common in the drug, grocery, and clothing markets.

The target market of this type of wholesaler is the single-line retailer, such as supermarkets, drugstores, clothing stores, and hardware stores. As retail chains continue to grow in size and market share, the single-line wholesaler tends gradually to lose market position. Retailers establish their own wholesale operations or purchase directly from the manufacturer.

SPECIALTY WHOLESALERS

Specialty wholesalers offer part of a line to target customers. An example would be a meat wholesaler or a fish and seafood wholesaler, as opposed to a single-line grocery wholesaler. The specialty wholesaler usually offers much greater depth within the scope of the product line than a single-line wholesaler. Customers, for example, are more likely to find unusual seafood at a seafood wholesaler rather than a grocery wholesaler.

Specialty wholesalers offer their customers several advantages in addition to greater variety. They usually have excellent product knowledge, which can be very important, for example, to a sausage packaging house when purchasing spices from a specialty spice wholesaler. There are literally hundreds of spices and combinations to choose from. A specialty industrial goods wholesaler may handle only ball bearings. Another may specialize in drilling bits. Each offers a complete product line and information to aid potential buyers. Another example of the specialty wholesaler is the supplier of fast-food restaurants.

The archetype of the fast-food service wholesaler who has elected to concentrate on the fast-food market segment is represented by Golden State Foods Corporation (GSF), located in southern California. GSF is unique in that it derives 92 percent of its volume, or some $250 million annually, by selling to 890 McDonald's restaurants in 17 states, Guam, and Hong Kong. The company distributes ground beef patties, soft drink syrups, milk shake mixes, condiments, mixes for sundaes, hamburger buns, and a variety of purchased-food paper products and other disposable items required for McDonald's operations. Approximately 17 percent of the food products are manufactured or processed by the company.

GSF has benefited from the growth in the number of McDonald's restaurants it serves and from the increase in the average sales per individual establishment. . . . GSF has been able to maintain its close association with its prime account without the benefit of any contracts or agreements that stipulate that the McDonald's or its licensees purchase their requirements from the company. Its success has been based on its ability to maintain low prices and to act as a complete supplier to the chain.[3]

INDUSTRIAL DISTRIBUTORS

Most, but not all, **industrial distributors** can be described as merchant wholesalers. Typically, they sell to manufacturers rather than to retailers. Full-service distributors usually have internal and external salesforces, offer credit, stock merchandise, provide delivery, and keep a full product assortment.

The products stocked by industrial distributors include maintenance, repair, and operating supplies (MRO items); original equipment (OEM) supplies, such as fasteners, power transmission components, hydraulic equipment, and small rubber parts, which become part of the manufacturer's finished product; equipment used in the operation of the business, such as hand tools, power tools, and conveyors; and machinery used in making raw materials and semi-finished goods into finished products. Distributors that carry a smorgasbord of industrial products (a general line) are called "mill supply houses" or "the supermarkets of industry." The growth of industrial distribution chains has created the classic channel power struggle described in the example below.

With nearly $25 billion in sales, Industrial Distribution (ID) is one of America's largest industries. It is in addition—because it supplies industry with such ubiquitous products as nuts and bolts, bearings, belts, power transmission equipment, and component parts for large pieces of equipment—one of the least known industries, anonymous to the average consumer and seldom mentioned in the general press.

However, the rise of distributor chains promises to bring it to national attention within the near future.

Chains are advancing, and with them is coming a shift of power paralleling that in food and drug retailing and also every bit as disruptive. Many thousands of suppliers, distributors, and end-users are all facing the same major—if not life-and-death—business decisions right now.

Like food and drug retailing, ID is tremendously fragmented: products, uses, and users are bewilderingly varied.

There are about 6,500 firms and 11,000 outlets. The small, privately-owned, single-warehouse firm did and still does form the core of the industry.

This enormous scattering and diversity makes the industry ripe for some clever entrepreneurs to come in and clean up. The method: buy or start up multiple outlets, and achieve significant economies of scale by establishing one highly sophisticated central inventory, purchasing, and distribution system. This is just what's happening. . . .

The merger trend is strengthening, particularly among bearing and power transmission distributors. Some chains have opened new outlets, but because personal service is a strong marketing factor, they prefer to buy out established distributors.

Private labeling is also gaining momentum, particularly in a few product lines such as bearings; electrical motors and equipment; and expendable maintenance, repair, and replacement supplies. For some distributors, private labels constitute far and away the bulk of total sales (for example, Associated Spring, almost 100 percent; W. W. Grainger, 75 percent; and Lawson Products, 90 percent).[4]

RACK MERCHANDISER

The **rack merchandiser,** or rack jobber, performs the functions of the merchant wholesaler and even some that are usually carried out by the retailer. Rack merchandisers serve drug and grocery retailers, in contrast to the industrial distributor, whose customers are manufacturers.

In addition to the normal full-service functions, rack merchandisers stock nonfood merchandise on racks or shelves for their retail clients. The toy racks and occasional clothing displays you see in a supermarket were probably placed there by a rack merchandiser.

The rack merchandiser sells on consignment in most cases, meaning that the jobber retains title to the goods and the retailer does not pay for the merchandise until it is sold. The delivery person employed by the jobber maintains inventory records, prices the goods, keeps the merchandise fresh, restocks the racks or shelves, and assembles any promotional display material that is used at the point of sale.

DROP SHIPPERS

Drop shippers do not inventory or physically handle the products they sell. Instead, orders are placed with the manufacturer and shipped directly to the customer. Drop shippers are usually found in the bulk industries, such as coal, lumber, bauxite, heavy equipment, and some agricultural products.

Like cash-and-carry wholesalers, drop shippers can offer lower prices because they perform relatively few wholesale functions. In this case, warehousing and storage are eliminated.

The drop shipper is still a merchant middleman even though it may never see the goods. It takes title to the merchandise and therefore sets the terms of the sale. Also, drop shippers arrange shipping terms and take the risks of ownership during the shipment; in addition, they locate suppliers and sometimes offer credit.

PRODUCERS' COOPERATIVES

Producers' cooperatives are nonprofit institutions established and operated for the benefit of their members. If any surplus revenues accrue, they are normally dispersed to the members at the end of the year. Farmland Industries, a huge supply cooperative, has annual sales which exceed $2 billion. If a member dies or retires, his or her share must be sold back to the cooperative.

Marketing coops are usually dedicated to improving product quality and promoting a coop brand name. Sun Maid raisins, Diamond walnuts, Ocean Spray cranberries, and Sunkist oranges and lemons are examples of brand names that coops have promoted to differentiate homogeneous products.

The tremendous growth of the coop movement during the 1970s created yet another major power conflict in the farm products distribution channels. Dairy coops, for example, have increased their share of the wholesale dairy market from 65 percent to 80 percent.[5] Coops today market 37 percent of the nation's cotton crop compared with 25 percent a decade ago. A new source of channel conflict is the construction of food processing plants, which could adversely affect companies like Kraft and Bordens. The coop retail stores have forced hundreds of independent suppliers out of business.

Other types of wholesalers

MANUFACTURERS' SALES BRANCHES

As manufacturers grow in size, they often establish wholesale operations similar to full-service merchant wholesalers. Yet these wholesale institutions, called **manufacturers' sales branches,** are managed, controlled, and owned by the manufacturer. Although manufacturers' sales branches and offices account for only about 13 percent of all wholesale institutions, they represent almost 37 percent of all wholesale sales.[6]

Since the late 1960s manufacturers' sales offices and branches have been the most rapidly growing type of wholesaling as manufacturers seek tighter control over their channels of distribution. The growth of manufacturers' sales branches is due partly to a general increase in the importance of inventory control at the wholesale level. This is particularly true in the automotive, transportation equipment, and lumber, millwork, and plywood industries. In cases in which inventory is not carried by the wholesaler, manufacturers' sales offices have grown at the expense of agents and brokers. This phenomenon is most noticeable in the drygoods and notions industries.

A third trend has been for manufacturers' sales branches to grow by forcing out merchant wholesalers. Lack of wholesaler promotion, high costs, the need for better control, and wholesalers' unwillingness to carry adequate inventories have prompted many manufacturers to create sales branches. This trend has been most noticeable in the drug, hardware, and commercial equipment industries.

Small producers that cannot afford to maintain a field salesforce often employ manufacturers' agents. Larger firms use agents to open new territories and then substitute company salespeople when volume justifies such action. If a territory does not have the long-term potential to support a salesperson, the manufacturer will develop a continuing relationship with the manufacturers' agent.

AGENTS AND BROKERS

Agents and brokers represent retailers, wholesalers, or manufacturers and do not take title to the merchandise. Title reflects ownership, and ownership usually implies control. A wholesaler that owns the merchandise can establish the terms of sale. It is then up to the buyer to decide whether the terms are acceptable. An agent or broker generally has little input into the terms of sale (except in the case of commission merchants). They facilitate sales but usually do not determine the conditions of the sale. Agents and brokers receive a fee or commission based on sales volume. Many perform fewer functions than limited-function merchant wholesalers. Agents and brokers account for less than 13 percent of all wholesale sales.

Broker. The **broker's** function is to bring buyers and sellers together. Brokers exist in markets where two parties would otherwise have difficulty locating one another. Brokers do not usually handle the goods involved in the sale or finance either the buyer or the seller. Their basic function is to represent the buyer or seller in finding another party to complete the sales transaction. Typically, a broker locates a potential buyer/seller and then lets the two parties work out matters such as price, quantity, delivery date, specifications.

The broker performs only the locating function and therefore operates on a very low margin. The fee is paid by the principal who engaged the broker, never by both parties.

Manufacturers' agent. Like brokers, **manufacturers' agents,** sometimes called manufacturers' representatives, rarely have much voice in the terms of a sales contract. They represent one manufacturer or several manufacturers of complementary lines and follow the terms established by the manufacturer. Agents work on a commission basis and therefore must be good salespeople if they want to earn an adequate living. They generally have excellent product knowledge and extensive knowledge of customer preferences within their territory. A manufacturers' agent primarily acts as a salesperson, whereas a broker simply brings the buyer and seller together. The example below shows how manufacturers' agents operate.

Corporations that recently have enlisted sales reps include, to name a few, General Electric, W. R. Grace, Raytheon, Honeywell, Carrier, and Cincinnati Milacron. Elliott Black, vice president, Dunmore Co., a manufacturer of machine tools and universal and permanent magnet motors, Racine, Wis., says, "To put a company salesman on the road, he must generate around $400,000 worth of business." Although in some cases the sales rep may be paid more than the company salesperson, perhaps 10% to 11% of sales compared with 8% for a full-time man, Black calls the rep "a true economic saving." The reasons he cites: (1) Manufacturers' reps get no fringe benefits. (2) They represent no expense when orders are down. (3) They work as hard as company salespeople and often harder because their commissions are at stake.

Instead of economics, Fred Holloway, manager of Yarway Corp.'s Metering Pump Div., Blue Bell, Pa., values the 20 sales rep companies that represent him for a simple marketing reason. Says Holloway, "Manufacturers' reps tend to be more knowledgeable about markets. They have a closer relationship with the key buying influences in the processing industry markets we want to penetrate. Sales costs are not the prime factor for us." Holloway admits that if he had a direct sales force, he would probably have stricter control over field selling; he also wishes that he did not have to compete for selling time with the other manufacturers whose products his reps also carry. "But our reps give us the market coverage we believe we could not win otherwise," he says.[7]

Commission merchant. **Commission merchants** (or houses) differ from manufacturers' agents and brokers in that they take possession of the merchandise. Usually they are not employed on a long-term basis but instead are used to sell specific lots of goods. They are given wide discretionary powers over price, delivery dates, and other terms of sale. In fact, merchants even collect the bills, deduct their fees, and remit the balance to the principal.

Commission merchants are most common in agriculture, where farmers cannot or don't want to sell their products locally. The merchant is located in central market cities and engages in many market transactions daily. The farmer rarely sets the specific price of the sale, but instead empowers the commission merchant to obtain the best price possible. Withholding produce or fruits from the market in order to obtain a higher price is often very risky because of the high perishability of such items. The merchant is expected to do the best it can under the circumstances. It may even grant credit to the potential buyer.

AGRICULTURAL ASSEMBLERS

The **agricultural assembler** is actually a merchant wholesaler that buys grain from farmers and assembles it into large quantities and sells it to governments, bakers, and other food processors.

The Census Bureau also lists petroleum bulk plants as a separate type of assembler–wholesaler because of their unique storage and distribution facilities. Actually they are either merchant wholesalers or manufacturers' sales branches, depending on their ownership. Petroleum bulk plants are engaged in the collection, storage, distribution, and sale of oil, gasoline, and similar petroleum derivatives.

AUCTION COMPANIES

A unique form of brokerage is performed by **auction companies.** Like agricultural assemblers and bulk plants, they account for a small portion of total wholesale volume but are very important in several industries. Whenever it is necessary for goods to be seen and inspected prior to purchase, auction houses provide a unique advantage. Buyers come together and bid against one another until only one bidder remains. Unless the bid is below a predetermined minimum, the products are sold to the highest bidder. Auctions are common in certain areas of agriculture, such as tobacco and livestock, and in industrial bankruptcies.

SELLING AGENTS

A final type of agent/broker is the **selling agent.** Actually the term *selling agent* is somewhat misleading, since the agent usually takes over the entire marketing operation of a company. In some industries, such as textiles, selling agents may even offer financial assistance to clients. They normally work on a commission basis and contract to sell the entire output of the manufacturer. Selling agents are used mostly by small firms. For example, some electronics firms, founded and managed by engineers who have little interest in marketing, depend on selling agents.

Institutions that facilitate wholesaling

Two institutions that facilitate the wholesale function are resident buyers and merchandise marts.

Resident buyers perform the purchasing function for small retailers. If a low-volume retailer is located hundreds of miles from a major market, it is difficult to keep abreast of rapidly changing styles and trends as new merchandise reaches the market. More important, it would be uneconomical to go to market and purchase in small quantities. This is where resident buyers come in. Since resident buyers are located in New York, Chicago, and other major market cities, they can easily monitor new trends and purchase for the retailer. Also, because resident buyers represent many retailers, they can purchase in large quantities and pass the savings on to the retailer.

When retailers "go to market" once or twice a year, their resident buyer generally acts as host, guiding them to the "right" manufacturers and arranging for the retailer to see sellers that might otherwise ignore a very small retailer. A resident buyer typically specializes in a single line such as a certain type of wearing apparel, toys, or furniture.

Often a retailer "goes to market" at a **merchandise mart.** Most merchandise marts are huge buildings containing hundreds of individual exhibition spaces leased by manufacturers. An entire mart may be devoted to one type of product, such as furniture or apparel. Merchandise marts are permanent showrooms that remain open throughout the year.

Fairs or shows are held several times a year in the market cities. Christmas gift and jewelry shows, for example, are usually held in July in such cities as New York, Los Angeles, Dallas, and Chicago. In addition to the permanent exhibitors at the merchandise marts, hundreds of temporary exhibitors set up booths at convention centers, auditoriums, or exhibition halls during the major shows.

The channel power of wholesalers

The examples we have given of industrial distributors, the Airwick story, and producers' cooperatives allude to the continuing struggle among channel members for power and control. Over the years the growth of nationally distributed manufacturers and retail brands, the huge size of manufacturer and retail operations, and the general lack of innovation at the wholesale level has resulted in erosion of the power of wholesale firms. Industrial distributor chains and producer cooperatives are gaining. There are several reasons why other wholesale organizations should be able to regain some channel power. These include:

1. Wholesalers have continuity in and intimacy with local markets. Being close to customers, they are in positions to take initial steps in the sale of any product—namely, identifying prospective users and determining the extent of their needs.
2. Wholesalers make possible local availability of stocks and thereby relieve suppliers of small-order business, which the latter can seldom conduct on a profitable basis. Also, they tend to have an acute understanding of the costs of holding and handling inventory in which they have made major commitments.
3. Within their territories, wholesalers can provide suppliers with a salesforce that is in close touch with the needs of customers and prospects. Also, by virtue of the fact that a wholesaler represents a number of suppliers, it can often cover a given territory at a lower cost than could the manufacturer's own salesperson.
4. Wholesalers can concentrate managerial talent on local marketing problems without having to worry about retailing and manufacturing difficulties. Production schedules, assembly line breakdown, sources of raw material, production line workers, and manufacturing technology are all problems of major concern to the producer. Expensive retail site locations, retail clerks, consumer credit, consumer advertising, local delivery to final purchasers, display racks and cases, foot-traffic flows, and mall tenant-lessor problems are indigenous to retailers.[8]

Managing the wholesale operation

Just because wholesalers have certain inherent advantages to achieve channel power does not mean they actually acquire that power. Like every other business, a wholesaling operation must be professionally managed and marketing-oriented to achieve success. For many years, this simply was not the case. Many wholesalers were small, undercapitalized, intermediate "storers" of merchandise. They were more concerned with physical movement of goods in and through their warehouses than with basic customer needs.

MEETING MANUFACTURER AND RETAILER NEEDS

Modern wholesale managers are in touch with the marketplace from both the manufacturers' and retailers' perspective. What do manufacturers want from their wholesalers? Research has shown that manufacturers' expectations vary depending upon the type of wholesale operation. Manufacturers evaluate agent wholesalers primarily on the basis of:[9]

◢ Their delivery service to retail customers.
◢ Product lines carried (if a manufacturer needs an intermediary who carries a broad line of products it will not usually favor an agent wholesaler).
◢ Adequate market coverage.

On the other hand, manufacturers select merchant wholesalers using these criteria:[10]

◢ Wholesaler operating procedures (minimum order policies, inventory management procedures, delivery speed).

◢ Adequate market coverage.

◢ Warehouse facilities.

An effective wholesale manager must understand the needs of the manufacturer and then develop a strategic plan to meet those needs. The same thing is true of retail customers. Retailers tend to pick wholesalers that:

1. Supply a majority of the lines needed by the retailer.
2. Carry the brand names desired by the retailers' market.
3. Carry assorted styles, sizes, price ranges, and varieties to meet retail customers' needs.
4. Provide rapid delivery.
5. Have few stock outages.
6. Offer reasonable extension of credit to the retailer.

STRATEGIC PROFIT PLANNING

In order to achieve profit goals, wholesale managers must adhere to the **strategic profit formula.**[11] The profit formula, management tasks, and strategic profit results are shown in Table 14.1.

Margin management. The first task for the wholesale manager is to achieve a reasonable margin of profit. Generally speaking, wholesalers tend to experience large changes in profits (up or down), with small changes in gross margins (sales less cost of goods sold) or expense ratios. To obtain a target profit margin, management must watch closely those factors that determine net profit (gross margin less operating expenses equals pretax profits less income taxes equals net profits). The wholesale manager must:

◢ Generate maximum sales at minimum costs.

◢ Manage the cost of goods sold and gross margin: supplier negotiations, pricing decisions, inventory mix decisions.

◢ Control major operating expenses: warehouse and delivery expenses, selling expenses, general and administrative expenses.

◢ **TABLE 14.1 The Strategic Profit Formula**

The management task	→	Margin management	×	Asset management	=	Return on assets	×	Financial management	=	Return on net worth
The strategic profit formula	→	$\dfrac{\text{Net profit}}{\text{Net sales}}$	×	$\dfrac{\text{Net sales}}{\text{Total assets}}$	=	ROA	×	$\dfrac{\text{Total assets}}{\text{Net worth}}$	=	RONW
Strategic profit results	→	Net profit margin	×	Asset turnover	=	ROA	×	Leverage ratio	=	RONW

Asset management. A wholesaler, unlike a manufacturer, usually does not have a huge investment in fixed plant and machinery. It can also minimize investments by leasing warehouse space, forklift trucks, computers, and similar capital items. The wholesale manager's asset management task focuses on accounts receivable and inventories. Managers should strive for a low number of average days accounts receivable are outstanding. The faster the wholesaler collects accounts receivable, the quicker the money can be "put back to work" —for example, in purchasing new inventories.

On the inventory side, management should strive to maximize inventory and total asset turnover. The more times a firm turns its inventory in a given period, the lower the average investment in inventory. A high inventory investment means greater warehousing costs, more interest on funds tied up in inventories, insurance, obsolescence, and so forth. The formulas for inventory turnover and total asset turnover are as follows:

$$\text{Inventory turnover} = \frac{\text{Cost of goods sold}}{\text{Average inventory}}$$

$$\text{Total asset turnover} = \frac{\text{Net sales}}{\text{Total assets}}$$

At this point, let us stop and examine a hypothetical wholesaler and its strategic profit situation. Presented below are the financial statements for Mid-American Wholesalers, Inc.

Mid-America profit-and-loss statement

Net Sales	$6,000,000 (100%)
Less: Cost of goods sold	5,000,000 (83%)
Equals: Gross margin	1,000,000 (17%)
Less: Operating expenses	800,000 (13%)
Equals: Pretax profit	200,000 (3.3%)
Less: Income taxes	80,000 (1.3%)
Equals: Net profit	120,000 (2.0%)

Mid-America balance sheet

Assets		Debt and net worth	
Current assets:		Current debt	$1,000,000
Cash	$ 40,000	Long-term debt	75,000
Accounts receivable	900,000	Total debt	1,075,000
Inventory	850,000	Net worth:	
Miscellaneous	60,000	Invested capital	300,000
Total current assets	1,850,000	Retained earnings	575,000
Fixed assets	100,000	Total net worth	875,000
Total assets	1,950,000	Total debt and net worth	1,950,000

The inventory turnover for Mid-America is:

$$\frac{\text{Cost of goods sold}}{\text{Average inventory}} = \frac{5,000,000}{850,000} = 5.9$$

Total asset turnover is:

$$\frac{\text{Net sales}}{\text{Total assets}} = \frac{6,000,000}{1,950,000} = 3.08$$

The asset turnover ratio of 3.08 means that for every dollar invested in Mid-America, sales of $3.08 are generated.

How does Mid-America compare with other wholesalers? Not bad, really. Its 2 percent profit margin is almost double the U.S. average for wholesale corporations of 1.1 percent. This is partly due to the 3.08 asset turnover ratio as compared with the average of 2.60.[12] In other words, Mid-America is achieving above-average sales on every dollar invested in the firm.

Financial management. The third aspect of strategic profit management for wholesalers is financial management—the company's debt-equity relationship. Debt financing means obtaining money from creditors, such as borrowing from banks and insurance companies, or issuing bonds. Equity financing is the owner's money. Net worth, of course, is ownership investment.

The leverage ratio is a very important measure of the wholesaler's financial health. The formula is:

$$\frac{\text{Total assets}}{\text{Net worth}} = \frac{1,950,000}{875,000} = 2.2$$

The leverage ratio for Mid-America is in the acceptable range. As the ratio exceeds 2.0 (equal amounts of debt and equity), debt financing becomes dominant. A highly leveraged wholesaler (above 2.5) is usually considered a possible lending risk.[13] Ronald Stevenson explains the importance of the leverage factor as follows:

Most wholesale firms are closely held and owner/managers do not wish to dilute their control via outside investment. Thus, new equity to fund growth is limited to the level of profit retained in the business. If all profits are reinvested, the firm's growth capacity is limited to its after-tax rate of return on net worth. The only means of growing faster than the return on net worth is to expand the leverage ratio. However, it is necessary to hold the leverage ratio within a healthy range.

Thus, control of growth and resulting leverage ratios are critical wholesale management functions. Low profits limit the earnings wholesalers have available for reinvestment. High leverage ratios mean that growth cannot be funded with new debt except at high interest rates, which further depress profits.[14]

Let us recap the strategic profit concept for wholesalers as applied to Mid-America. Recall that the basic formula is:

$$\frac{\text{Net profit}}{\text{Net sales}} \times \frac{\text{Net sales}}{\text{Total assets}} = \text{Return on assets} \times \frac{\text{Total assets}}{\text{Net worth}} =$$

$$\text{Return on net worth} = 2.0 \times 3.08 = 6.16 \times 2.2 = 13.6\%$$

The return on net worth figure is the profit on the owner's investment. Again, Mid-America fares well when compared to the average for U.S. wholesalers of

7.5 percent. Our hypothetical firm has done very well in margin and asset management. It has also used debt financing in a prudent manner to further enhance growth. In summary, the management of Mid-America has done an excellent job of strategic profit planning.

Trends in wholesaling

Progressive wholesalers view themselves as more than "bulk breakers" or "warehousers." Instead, they believe that wholesaling plays a vital role in effective distribution and requires full application of the marketing concept to their businesses. Many are adopting the strategic profit concept outlined above. Modern wholesalers examine the needs of their markets and determine how those needs can be fulfilled using contemporary marketing concepts. For example, grocery wholesalers have added a sales effort geared to growing institutional markets, including hotels, airport restaurants, hospitals, and schools. As they analyze their market segments, these wholesalers are sensitive to inventory requirements and new product lines.

Some wholesalers have found their markets so drastically changed that they have either set up their own chains (voluntary chains) or franchised retail operations. Super Value, Ace Hardware, Butler Brothers (Ben Franklin Stores), and Western Auto are all examples of this trend. Other wholesalers have moved back up the channel and entered manufacturing. Midas International, originally an automotive wholesaler, not only franchises retail outlets but manufactures mufflers as well.

Progressive wholesalers are using new techniques to build sales volume. One is promoting to the final consumer. Natually, this increases the retailers' sales, and they, in turn, order more merchandise from the wholesaler. Constantino Brokerage, a St. Louis grocery wholesaler, regularly uses multibrand coupons in newspaper inserts.[15] Sometimes, wholesalers will bear the entire cost of the promotion campaign, but usually part of the expense is carried by the manufacturer. A few wholesalers have carried promotion a step further by setting up their own in-house advertising agencies.

Wholesalers are also fostering sales growth through the establishment of outlets in new territories. Strong wholesaler networks have begun to develop where the distributor is selling relatively undifferentiated products coupled with excellent product line knowledge and familiarity with the local market. As noted in the discussion of industrial distributors, this has led to increased market power and channel control for the multibranch wholesalers. Naturally, many manufacturers are disturbed by the aggregation of wholesalers into fewer and larger companies. One manufacturer recently examined its distribution network and found that its wholesalers operate in 290 locations, that those locations belong to 60 wholesalers, and that 5 of those wholesalers operate half of the locations.

The computer has entered wholesaling in a big way. It has been a boon for inventory control, shipping schedules, managing accounts receivable, and the development of information systems. An example of computer applications in wholesaling is detailed in the Brian Supply Company story below.

"People we know have called us the quiet supply house and there's the reason," beams tall, white-haired Joe Brian, pointing to the blinking, quietly chirping CRT terminals.

"In fact," smiles the obviously proud Brian Supply Co. president, "it's all so quiet around here, they wonder if we've got much business until I show them our order volume." "Before we had [the computer], this place was the typical distribution madhouse. We were growing too fast and were slightly out of control."

The system was installed at Brian gradually. First, inventory was computerized, followed by receivables, payables and the general ledger. Now, all record processing, including that to and from the branches, is tied to the central computer. Twenty-three CRT terminals help facilitate routine inventory control, order filling, purchasing, expediting, billing, and receiving.

Joe Brian can be apprised of current sales volumes, expenses, status of receivables, even his bank balance via his portable CRT. If a customer wants to know if a particular item is in stock, the salesman need only ask the inventory computer module operator to check the computer. This check will reveal how much stock is on the shelves in the main location and in the branches.

Inventory levels are predetermined in the computer through programming. When supplies diminish to the preset reorder point, the computer will automatically reorder new stock. It keeps track of all sales, reflecting the most current inventory levels at all times.

As transactions are entered, the computer examines inventory and determines if Brian can fill the order or not from any location. If a customer wants 100 items but only 75 are in stock, the computer also provides the customer with the option of having goods shipped directly to him.[16]

Wholesalers have come a long way since their days as "merchandise storehouses." As success stories similar to Brian Supply Company continue to spread, more wholesalers will move into the computer age. Wholesalers are not a relic of the past, but a vital cog in tomorrow's distribution systems.

SUMMARY

Wholesalers sell finished goods to retailers and institutions. They do not sell directly to the final consumer. Wholesalers anticipate customers' needs and purchase accordingly for their target market. They are also expected to communicate with manufacturers and retailers regarding changing market trends. Many wholesalers provide financing for clients and store merchandise until the goods are ordered. They typically buy in large quantities and ship in smaller units to retailers and other buyers.

Merchant wholesalers are the largest category of wholesalers. They purchase goods for their own account, operate one or more warehouses, take title to the goods, store them, and later re-ship the merchandise. Merchant wholesalers can be subdivided according to their inventories (general line, single line or specialty wholesalers). Industrial distributors usually sell to manufacturers rather than to retailers. Full-service distributors often have internal and external salesforces, offer credit, stock merchandise, provide delivery, and maintain a full product assortment. Other merchant wholesalers include rack merchandisers, drop shippers, and producers' coops.

Large manufacturers often establish wholesale operations similar to that of merchant wholesalers. These are called manufacturers' sales branches. They account for almost 37 percent of all wholesale sales. Their growth has been due primarily to an increase in the need for better inventory control and sales efforts at the wholesale level.

Agents and brokers do not take title to the merchandise and generally perform fewer functions than merchant wholesalers. Other wholesaler institutions include agricultural assemblers, auction companies, and selling agents. Resident buyers and merchandise marts are not actually wholesalers, but they facilitate the wholesaling process.

Over the years, lack of innovation and other factors at the wholesale level have resulted in the erosion of wholesale firms' power. Because wholesalers have a continuous and intimate relationship with local markets, local availability of stocks, and often a salesforce that is in close touch with the needs of the customers, they should be able eventually to regain some channel power. Achieving channel power requires good management. That is, management needs to understand the needs of both the manufacturer and the retailer. Also, wholesale managers must adhere to the strategic profit formula.

Many wholesalers are awakening to the belief that their function plays a vital role in effective distribution and requires full application of the marketing concept. Some wholesalers are setting up their own chains and franchised retail operations. Others are using new strategies, such as promoting directly to the final consumer, to build sales volume. Many are now using computers for inventory control, shipping schedules, managing accounts receivable, and the development of information systems.

KEY TERMS

Wholesaler
Stockout
Merchant wholesalers
Single-line wholesaler
Specialty wholesaler
Industrial distributors
Rack merchandiser
Drop shipper
Producers' cooperative
Manufacturers' sales branches

Broker
Manufacturers' agent
Commission merchant
Agricultural assembler
Auction company
Selling agent
Resident buyer
Merchandise mart
Strategic profit formula

REVIEW QUESTIONS

1. What functions do wholesalers perform? Are these tasks common to all?
2. How are merchant wholesalers defined? Give their general characteristics and most common forms.
3. Differentiate among selling agents, brokers, and commission merchants by services provided.
4. Comment on the use of resident buyers and merchandise marts as a means of facilitating the wholesale function.
5. In what ways do modern wholesalers apply the marketing concept?

DISCUSSION QUESTIONS

1. Comment on the following statement: "Prices would be much lower if we could only eliminate the middleman." Do you agree or disagree? Support your answer logically.
2. How can small, independent distributors compete with industrial distribution chains? What economies of operation do these large chains realize?
3. Why have agricultural coop organizations formed, and what is their market power predicated on?
4. Explain the importance of asset and financial management to the efficient operation of the wholesaler.
5. With reference to manufacturer and retailer needs, what constitutes an effective wholesaler?

NOTES

1. Bernard F. Whalen, "Airwick Drops Sales Offices to Increase Sales," *Marketing News,* February 8, 1980, p. 6. Reprinted by permission of the American Marketing Association.
2. U.S. Bureau of the Census, *Census of Wholesale Trade, 1977* (Washington, D.C., 1980).
3. J. Robert Foster, "Supplying the Eating Out Revolution: Strategic Trends in Food Service Wholesaling," in Robert F. Lusch and Paul H. Zinszer (eds.), *Contemporary Issues in Marketing Channels* (Norman: The University of Oklahoma Press, 1979), p. 148.
4. "The Chain of Events in Industrial Distribution," *Marketing News,* January 30, 1967, p. 7. Reprinted by permission of the American Marketing Association.
5. "The Billion-Dollar Farm Co-ops Nobody Knows," *Business Week,* February 7, 1977, pp. 54–64.
6. U.S. Bureau of the Census, *Census of Wholesale Trade.*
7. Thomas C. Reinhart and Donald R. Coleman, "Heyday for the Independent Rep," *Sales and Marketing Management,* November 1978, pp. 51–54. Reprinted by permission from Sales & Marketing Management magazine. Copyright 1978.
8. The first three factors are from Louis W. Stern and Adel I. El-Ansary, *Marketing Channels* (Englewood Cliffs, N.J.: Prentice-Hall, 1977), p. 115.
9. James R. Moore, Donald W. Ekrich, and Richard M. Durand, "Correlates of Manufacturers' Attitudes toward Alternate Channel Intermediaries," in Robert S. Franz, Robert M. Hopkins, and Al Toma (eds.), *Proceedings of the Southern Marketing Association 1978 Conference,* University of Southwestern Louisiana, pp. 329–331.
10. Ibid.
11. This section on strategic profit management is adopted from P. Ronald Stephenson, "Wholesale Distribution: An Analysis of Structure Strategy and Profit Perform-

ance," in Arch G. Woodside, J. Taylor Sims, Dale M. Lewison, and Ian F. Wilkinson, *Foundations of Marketing Channels* (Austin: Lone Star Publishers, 1978), pp. 87–107.

12. Ibid.

13. Ibid.

14. Ibid., pp. 97–98. Also see: P. Ronald Stephenson, "High Profit Wholesaler Strategies: An Analysis of Marketing and Operational Strategies Producing Superior Profit Performance in Wholesaling," in Henry Nash and Donald P. Robin (eds.), University of Southern Mississippi, *Proceedings Southern Marketing Association 1977 Conference,* pp. 199–201.

15. David Berkus, "How Food Brokers Build Merchandising Muscle with Multi-Brand Coupon Ads," *Advertising Age,* September 17, 1976, p. 54.

16. "The House of Quiet Confidence," *Industrial Distribution,* December 1977, pp. 29–34.

◢ **CASES**

14.1 The Farmer Company

For many years the Farmer Company was a wholesaler of plumbing equipment and supplies throughout the state of Virginia. It handled all types of plumbing equipment and fixtures, heating and air-conditioning equipment, and hot water heaters. The Farmer Company had sales of approximately $21 million last year and was the largest plumbing wholesaler in the state.

Service to customers was a primary company objective and seemed to be one of the key factors in its long-run growth. In fact, service was offered without a great deal of attention to cost and growth.

Dan Smith, president of the Farmer Company, noticed several subtle changes during the past few years in manufacturer-wholesaler relationships. These began to worry him. In a few instances, for example, manufacturers had begun selling directly to large plumbing contractors. This was not considered a major problem, since the market was dominated by a large number of relatively small contractors.

There were other problems, however, that needed attention. First and foremost were sudden and substantial price increases. Many plumbing contractors use a bid basis for procuring new jobs. Bids, of course, are predicated on existing price levels. When unexpected large price increases come through, it may make existing construction and recently procured jobs unprofitable for the contractor. This creates ill will between the wholesaler and the contractor.

A second problem is unannounced and abrupt model changes. Often manufacturers discontinue models without warning, again creating ill will. Sometimes model changes are made without notice. Since most plumbing jobs are made to specifications, model changes may make it hard to find the right fixture. It also creates a problem with existing inventories, since once the new models come out, contractors no longer want to install the old models. It also means carrying additional parts for the discontinued items.

A third problem is defective or damaged merchandise received from manufacturers. At present over 15 percent of the porcelain-enameled fixtures received by

Farmer are damaged to some degree. Often it takes many months to obtain price rebates and adjustments from the manufacturer. However, the products are sold to the plumbing contractors within a short time at substantially reduced prices, a policy that creates cash flow problems for Farmer.

Still another problem is dissemination of new product information and training materials to the plumbing contractors. Many plumbers shun new items because they are unfamiliar with installation techniques or with the advantages of the new products over existing models. Thus the company's sales efforts often suffer.

1. It appears that the wholesaler is "caught in the middle." Do you believe this is a typical situation? What can be done to overcome this dilemma?
2. How would you suggest that the company solve its problems? Suggest a strategy the wholesaler can follow to avoid similar situations in the future.

14.2   Anixter Brothers

Anixter Brothers, of Skokie, Illinois, is one of the nation's largest distributors of electrical wiring and cable. The inventory is manufactured by 300-odd companies, and Anixter sells to just about every type of company, from utilities and oil firms to mining and manufacturing concerns. The company president noted: "We buy by the mile and sell by the foot." Anixter has 24-hour emergency service; handles a company's total inventory needs; provides technical advice; and stocks nearly every type of wire and cable — 6000 varieties in all. It has a nationwide distribution system and is expanding into Europe and Southeast Asia.

With its national accounts program, client companies arrange with Anixter to have it supply all their wire and cable needs. In some cases, this results in Anixter supplying all the maintenance, repair, and emergency wire and cable requirements of the company. When an agreement is reached, Anixter often takes over the company's existing wire and cable stock. From then on it supplies the companies from some 50 warehouses throughout the world.

Competition comes mainly from three types of companies: (1) general electric supplies distributors, which of necessity carry a more limited stock than Anixter; (2) manufacturers, which mainly handle bulk orders; and (3) a few small, regional imitators that have sprung up in recent years.

Anixter's subsidiary, Pruzan, is considered the Sears of the cable TV industry. Pruzan stocks over 9000 items, ranging from amplifiers to linemen's hardware to work gloves, and sells them mainly to cable TV companies across the country through a mail order catalog. Servicing the cable TV market has led Anixter into manufacturing specialized items such as antennas for microwave systems. In addition to the Pruzan antennas, Anixter manufactures cutting tools and such electrical transmission products as switchboards and power panels. Still, Anixter does not manufacture any electrical wire and cable.

1. Why do you feel that Anixter does not manufacture any electric wire and cable?
2. What are the advantages and disadvantages of Anixter moving into the manufacture of wire and cable?
3. What criteria should Pruzan use to determine whether or not it should manufacture any additional items it sells?

15 Retailing

OBJECTIVES

To understand the importance of retailing in the American economy.

To review the major methods of retail operations.

To understand the nature of franchising.

To study the tasks involved in retail management and planning; to learn the determinants of store patronage.

To gain insight into present and future trends in retailing.

Floyd Hall would like to see a TV award show for books along the line of the Academy Awards. "The exposure would be just the kind of promotion the industry needs," he says enthusiastically. Hall, 40, might add that it's precisely the sort of thing he's used for the past six years, as president of B. Dalton Bookseller, to put the Minneapolis company in the forefront of the fast-growing chain segment of the book-selling industry (Dalton and Walden Book Co., Stamford, Conn., are the big national chains; there are also some 25 regional chains). . . .

Typical of Hall's marketing style was the opening of Dalton's store on New York's Fifth Ave. At 25,000 sq. ft. and with 100,000 titles and 300,000 books, the store is the company's largest; indeed, it is one of the biggest in the world. The champagne reception opening had all the fanfare of a Hollywood opening. And as a goodwill gesture, the Dayton-Hudson Corp., Dalton's parent company, donated $100,000, plus $15,189.93, the proceeds from the store's opening day, to the New York Public Library. . . .

With an assist from a computerized inventory system, Dalton gets a wide assortment of books. The average outlet stocks 25,000 titles. "We want people to think of us as the place that'll have what they want," says Hall. A central computer, into which all sold books' code numbers are fed, allows the company to compile what it considers the country's "most accurate and current best-seller lists." Including the "Hot List"—books whose sales make them look promising—the lists are released weekly and are popular with other booksellers. The system enables Dalton's 20-odd buyers to spot trends quickly, stock best-sellers, and sweep slow-selling books from the shelves before other booksellers.

The company also likes to read about potential readers, using demographic studies of 36,000 cities with information broken down into census tracts. "The heaviest readers are between 21 and 49 years old," says Hall. "Most have a high school education and some college, a third have incomes over $20,000, and they're generally in managerial or professional positions. They're also predominantly female." The company has been tapping this market mainly through mall locations, but recently it's begun opening stores in free-standing buildings and central business districts as well.

Dalton's merchandising formula—"Nothing but books" (in "organized clutter," as Hall puts it)—is evident in each Dalton store. Books are everywhere: shelves go to the ceiling, walls are

421

covered with books, and books are stacked on the floors at the ends of display islands; even on glass walls, books are lined up on shelves across the top. Says Hall, "There's an awful lot of impulse buying in bookstores. Most people come in looking for a specific title or for any book in a specific area of interest. But the average purchase in a Dalton store is two books—half the time the second book is bought on impulse."[1]

As a college student not too many years ago, I never dreamed a bookstore could be an exciting place to work at or manage. In fact, the picture I usually conjured up was a dimly lit store on a not too-well-traveled side street that had an odor reminiscent of a musty basement. The B. Dalton story is indicative of retailing today—exciting, challenging, scientifically managed, creative, competitive, and growing. B. Dalton's is a marketing-oriented organization that knows its market target (21 to 49 years old, some college, with one-third having incomes over $20,000). Accordingly it puts stores where target customers are located, maintains a computerized inventory control system to deliver the right product in a timely fashion, and promotes with flair. This is the marketing-oriented retailing of the 1980s—it's the only way to survive.

How important is retailing to our economy? What distinguishes a discount store from a department store or a specialty store? Do they face similar problems? What has been the impact of franchising and shopping centers on retailing? What are the major tasks and decisions facing a retail manager? Let us take a closer look.

The importance of retailing

American retailing is ubiquitous: it affects all of us directly and indirectly every day. Over 28 million Americans are engaged in some form of retail activity, so it is a major source of income and employment. Almost 16 million individuals work in services such as barbershops, repair shops, and car washes. Medical services account for the largest percentage of service employment, followed by nonprofit organizations and educational institutions. **Retailing** may be defined as all activities directly related to the sale of goods and services to the ultimate consumer for personal, nonbusiness use.

Most retailers are quite small. However, less than 10 percent of all retail establishments account for over half of total retail sales and employ about 40 percent of all retail workers. Thus, the industry is actually dominated by giant organizations. Who are these giant retailers? Table 15.1 lists America's twenty-five largest retailers as of 1978. It probably comes as no surprise to find that Sears heads the list, with sales of over $17 billion. Sears is also the largest retail employer, with 430,000 employees. Safeway Stores had the second-largest volume—$12.5 billion. These sales required far fewer employees per dollar of

Company	Sales ($000)	Number of employees
Sears Roebuck (Chicago)	25,194,900	390,000
Safeway Stores (Oakland)	15,102,673	150,012
K-Mart (Troy, Mich.)	14,204,381	256,000
J. C. Penney (New York)	11,353,000	194,000
Kroger (Cincinnati)	10,316,741	124,642
F. W. Woolworth (New York)	7,218,176	196,527
Great Atlantic & Pacific Tea (Montvale, N.J.)	6,684,179	58,000
Lucky Stores (Dublin, Calif.)	6,468,682	65,000
American Stores Co. (Salt Lake City)	6,419,884	63,000
Federated Department Stores (Cincinnati)	6,300,686	116,600
Montgomery Ward (Chicago)	5,496,907	131,994
Winn-Dixie Stores (Jacksonville)	5,388,979	60,700
Southland (Dallas)	4,758,656	44,600
City Products (Des Plaines, Ill.)	4,462,378	58,000
Jewel Companies (Chicago)	4,267,922	55,000
Dayton-Hudson (Minneapolis)	4,033,536	70,000
May Department Stores (St. Louis)	3,172,976	66,000
Grand Union (Elmwood Park, N.J.)	3,137,612	33,000
Albertson's (Boise)	3,039,129	28,000
Wickes Companies (San Diego)	2,876,973	43,219
ARA Services (Philadelphia)	2,806,020	120,000
Carter Hawley Hale Stores (Los Angeles)	2,632,921	55,000
Supermarkets General (Woodbridge, N.J.)	2,628,851	30,000
R. H. Macy (New York)	2,373,531	45,000
Rapid-American (New York)	2,351,591	46,000

Source: Fortune, July 13, 1981, pp. 122–123.

sales than Sears' because supermarkets are less labor-intensive than department stores.

Major methods of retail operation

To appreciate more fully the environment facing retail managers, let us examine major retail operations from the standpoint of what they do. We will discuss department stores first, and then focus on discounters, mail order houses, and supermarkets.

DEPARTMENT STORES

A **department store** houses many departments under one roof to achieve economies in promotion, buying, service, and control. Each department is usually headed by a **buyer.** In effect, each buyer's department is treated as a separate profit center, and thus each department has a modicum of autonomy. A buyer not only selects the merchandise mix for his or her department, but may also be responsible for promotion within the department and for its personnel. Central management establishes broad policies regarding types of merchandise and price ranges in order to build and maintain a consistent, homogeneous store image. The central administration is also responsible for the overall advertising program, credit policies, store expansion, customer service, and so forth.

Because of their size and buying power, most department stores buy directly from manufacturers. In fact, it is not unusual for a manufacturer to produce merchandise under the store's brand name. Some department stores have so much buying strength that they literally dominate small manufacturers. The manufacturer's profit margins, delivery dates, merchandise specifications, and transportation methods are virtually dictated by the department store in some instances.

It is difficult to find a large independent department store today. Most are owned by large national chains. The five largest department store chains by 1979 sales were: Federated Department Stores—$5.4 billion, Dayton-Hudson—$3 billion, May Department Stores—$2.6 billion, Allied Stores—$2.2 billion, and Associated Dry Goods—$1.6 billion. Federated is huge: It operates 262 stores in 18 states.[2] Some of its better-known department stores are Bloomingdale's and Abraham & Straus on the East Coast, I. Magnin and Bullock's on the West Coast, Filene's in New England, Burdine's in Florida, Foley's and Sanger Harris in Texas, Shillito's in the Midwest, and Goldsmith's in Memphis. Many consumers are unaware of the dominance of department store chains because the parent company's name is not actively promoted.

Department stores have begun to experience some new problems since the mid-1970s, as well as having to contend with some nagging old ones. For years they attempted to be all things to all people. They carried wide ranges of both soft goods (clothing) and hard goods (appliances, sporting goods, hardware). Discounters have cut severely into the hard goods market, so that many department stores are cutting back on low-margin hard goods.

A second problem is personnel. Finding and retaining good salesclerks is an endless battle. But the problem does not stop there. Department store chains have a hard time attracting college graduates because of their low starting pay, poor training programs, and long, irregular working hours.

Even with these problems, expansion is continuing.

Despite more attention to bottom-line considerations and energy-related concerns, overall expansion plans for department stores in the early 1980s appear little changed from the overall patterns of the 1970s. These include:

- The rush to the Sunbelt, particularly the Southwest, but also other growth areas, especially the Northwest. Federated Department Stores have paced the major companies in expanding to the Sunbelt, others are catching up.

- Regional expansion of department store operating divisions into new markets, both with large full-line stores in major new marketing areas and smaller "specialty department stores" in smaller communities. Here too, Federated has set the pace.
- More long-distance jumps into new markets, half-way or even fully across the country, a strategy of those high-fashion retail companies whose names have national recognition. Marshall Field has joined this movement with its big plunge into Texas, following the lead of Associated Dry Goods, with Lord & Taylor, and high-end specialty operations such as Carter Hawley Hale's Neiman-Marcus and Brown & Williamson's Saks Fifth Ave.
- Expansion and remodeling of existing units, not only as a means of "internal expansion," but to bring them up to date with new merchandising directions and images, as well as to reflect the growth of their marketing areas.
- New attention to downtown units, not only in revitalizing existing units but, increasingly, replacing them with more modern facilities. Gimbels', Philadelphia, new downtown unit, the major overhauling of Jordan Marsh in Boston, and the planned replacement of Hudson's downtown Detroit flagship are recent examples. Additional downtown units undoubtedly will be replaced. Rich's in Atlanta is a prime prospect, among others.
- Diversification into specialty store retailing. Allied, with Bonwit Teller and Plymouth Shops, and Marshall Field, with Breuner's, joined the trend in recent months through these acquisitions.[3]

MASS MERCHANDISING SHOPPING CHAINS

Mass merchandising shopping chains such as Sears, Penney's, and Montgomery Ward are similar to department store chains in many respects. Yet their sheer size in terms of sales volume, promotional budgets, dealer brands, and number of stores sets them apart from regular department store chains. Sears is so large that it accounts for approximately 1 percent of America's GNP.[4] The company has 900 traditional stores, 1700 catalog stores, 13 huge distribution centers, and 124 warehouses. These organizations are vertically integrated, owning either all or part of many manufacturers that supply their merchandise. Sears also depends on 12,000 independent suppliers in addition to those it controls.

The mass merchandising shopping chains are high-volume operations that almost always purchase directly from manufacturers. They do not need to utilize wholesalers, since they are larger than any independent wholesaler and can purchase in larger volume. Most of their buying is centralized, but local managers are given limited purchasing authority.

Since Sears and Penney's cover most of the U.S. market, network television advertising is both feasible and economical for them. Heavy national television exposure also contributes to name identification and a strong company image. Network promotion usually centers on high-margin dealer-branded items such as the Diehard battery or Sears' steel-belted radial tires.

SPECIALTY STORES

The term **specialty stores** is used not only to refer to a type of store, but also to identify a method of retail operation. That is, such stores specialize in a given type of merchandise—children's clothing, men's clothing, candy, baked goods, sporting goods, pet supplies. A typical specialty store carries a deeper assortment of merchandise in its specialty than a department store would carry. In addition, it often offers more attentive customer service and more knowledgeable salesclerks.

Specialty stores face many of the opportunities and challenges that confront department stores. For example, specialty chains have become very powerful in apparel and other areas. A typical specialty chain is The Gap, a 192-unit chain that caters to the "jeans generation" in a 26-state market. Bonwit Teller, a 13-unit women's specialty retailer, caters to the affluent young professional woman with a blend of youth-oriented goods and designer merchandise.

Price is usually of secondary importance in fashion specialty outlets. Instead, the distinctiveness of the merchandise, the physical appearance of the store, and the caliber of the personnel determine shopping preferences.

DISCOUNT STORES

Today's **discount stores** still stress high volume and low prices. Chain discounters usually carry a complete line of well-known, nationally branded hard goods, such as RCA, GE, and Hamilton-Beach appliances, and an extensive selection of soft goods. They generally price well below the suggested retail price. The difference is easily recognized by most customers.

The major competitive advantages discounters have over department stores are these:

1. The lowest price lines and the lowest prices within the market area.
2. Wide breadth and depth of consumables, such as health and beauty aids and housewares.
3. Aggregate convenience, including location, parking, hours, and ease of purchase. They feature supermarketlike front ends, total merchandise display, wide aisles, easy-to-see-and-locate merchandise groupings, shopping carts, and usually a single display floor.
4. Advertising leverage in brand names.
5. Important leverage in a changing international environment because they buy in greater depth than the traditional department store.[5]

Like department stores, national chains dominate the discount industry. The largest, Kresge (K-Mart), had sales of $12 billion in 1980. Kresge operates over

1500 K-Marts. Other major discount chains include Treasury (J. C. Penney), Target (Dayton Hudson), Gold Circle (Federated), Venture (May), Almart–T. B. Hunter (Allied), and Woolco (Woolworth's). The early success of the discount chains led to rapid expansion and oversaturation in many markets. Management controls broke down as the chains attempted to cope with a large number of stores in a wide variety of markets: "High-priced artificial flowers don't move in a college town," grumbled one store manager. A lack of sound management control systems and poor planning led to the rapid decline of Korvettes in the Northeast.

The discounting giants and other mass retailers may well roll over their small-town rivals in many areas, but not in the South. In the past decade, a little-known discounter, Wal-Mart Stores, Inc., has so firmly entrenched itself in less-populated markets that it is emerging as the leader in small-town retailing.

At Wal-Mart Stores, Inc., headquartered in Bentonville, Arkansas, the regular 7:30 A.M. Saturday managerial meeting is going full blast. Amid tumultuous applause, the blushing "Buyer of the Month" has just received his plaque. Perhaps carried away by the moment, Sam Walton, chairman and chief executive, leaps up and bellows: "Who's No. 1?"

The deafening reply: "Wal-Mart!"

Wal-Mart is actually far from being No. 1. The meeting is typical, however, of the company's rah-rah style, a combination of pep rally and evangelical revival. Vice presidents recite homilies about last week's "honor roll" stores. The head of a "SWAT" team that swoops down to remodel stores testifies to a job well-done.

In many executive suites across the country, such team spirit would seem hokey. But here in the Ozarks, it has helped catapult Wal-Mart into the No. 4 slot among discount retailers. Wal-Mart posted unrivaled growth over the past decade to $1.6 billion in sales from less than $45 million and to profits of $55 million from $1.6 million. Wal-Mart wound up 1980 with 330 stores, an increase over a meager 18 in 1970.

Wal-Mart shunned the intensely competitive major metropolitan areas and concentrated on selling brand-name merchandise at low prices in small, rural Midwestern and Southern communities. By saturating its trade area with several stores, Wal-Mart prevented penetration by competitors. Other keys to success have been strategically placed distribution centers, state-of-the-art computer technology and highly productive employees.[6]

DIRECT RETAILING

If the 1960s and 1970s were the era of the discounter, the 1980s may be the era of the **direct marketer.** The direct marketer sells either by telephone, by mail, or through personal visits to customers. In 1980, direct marketing sales topped $100 billion.[7] Sears is the nation's largest direct marketer, with catalog and phone sales of about $2 billion. Each year Sears distributes about 16 million catalogs four times a year. The primary advantage offered by direct marketing is the convenience of ordering merchandise without leaving home. The lack of well-trained retail clerks, having to carry bulky heavy packages to the car, traffic jams and parking problems, crowded aisles, and expensive gasoline have all contributed to the growth of direct retailing.

In 1979, about 28 million direct mail pieces were sent to prospective buyers. Direct mail is not a cheap form of promotion. Postage, good paper, the cost of the mailing list, and return envelopes can average about $300 per 1000 prospective buyers. This compares with about $5 per 1000 for prime time network television. The reason direct marketers are willing to pay the cost is that they can hone in on a very specific market target. You can, for example, reach orthodontists living in Illinois who have purchased an oriental rug in the past 12 months. Such a specific mailing list would cost about $100 per 1000 names. An "average" mailing list generally sells for $60 per 1000 names. Some direct marketers are combining direct mail with local television advertising to increase their response rates. *Readers Digest,* for example, tells viewers to "look for the *Readers Digest* sweepstakes" coming in the mail.

Mail order retailers often develop warehouse-type operations for the sake of low overhead. Many specialty mail order retailers offer products that cannot be found in most communities. For some companies direct mail has been the most effective way to achieve adequate distribution.

Newspaper and magazine advertisements that ask the consumer to call in or send in a coupon are another popular form of direct marketing. Similarly, the use of preprinted newspaper inserts and magazine bind-in cards has become increasingly popular. Bound-in cards "flag the reader's attention" and are often printed on quality four-color presses and on better-quality paper stock than the magazine itself. Although inserts usually cost two to three times the rate of an ad placed directly in the publication, higher response rates can help justify the expense.

Door-to-door retailing is a third form of direct marketing. Usually the target consumers are in the middle and lower socioeconomic groups. Companies such as Avon, Fuller Brush, Amway, and World Book Encyclopedia depend on this technique. The trend seems to be away from cold door-to-door canvassing, however, with direct marketers relying instead on "party plans" in which one person acts as a "host" and gathers together as many prospective buyers as possible. Most parties are a combination social affair and sales demonstration. The underlying strategy is that the host will invite only people who are likely to buy something.

Telephone selling is becoming increasingly common in today's energy-short society. It is estimated that each of the 54 million "phone reachable" households in the United States receive an average of 19 calls a year from businesses selling various products and services.[8] Department stores have used the practice for years, but numerous other retailers have recently discovered the value of this form of retailing. Land developers, repair services, appliance marketers, and others rely heavily on telephone selling. However, many consumers resent telephone selling as an invasion of their privacy. "Canned" presentations and high-pressure appeals are also repugnant to many people. Nevertheless, the effectiveness of telephone solicitation cannot be denied, and it will probably continue to grow in popularity unless restrictive legislation is passed.

FRANCHISING

Franchise sales of goods and services totaled approximately $300 billion in 1980. The older types of franchises, such as automobile dealerships, service stations, and soft-drink bottlers, account for the bulk of the business, but newer types are gaining ground. Franchising is nothing new. Singer has used this approach since 1863, General Motors since 1898, and Rexall since 1901. A **franchise** is a continuing relationship in which the **franchisor** grants operating rights to a **franchisee.** The franchisor is the one with the trade name, product, methods of operation, and so forth. It receives revenues in one or more forms from the franchisee. There are three basic forms of franchises today: manufacturer-retailer, wholesaler-retailer, and service-sponsor-retailer. These are explained and illustrated in Table 15.2.

Usually there is an initial fee for obtaining the franchise. Mr. Steak, for example, charges $36,000, and 7-Eleven Stores charge $14,000. Generally speaking, the more successful the franchise, the higher the initial fee becomes. McDonald's has raised its fees and capital requirements continually over the years. A second source of revenue is royalties based upon sales volume. Howard Johnsons Motels receives $8.50 per room per month or 5 percent of gross sales, whichever is greater. McDonald's charges royalties of 8.5 percent. Another major source of revenue is the sale of supplies. Prior to 1970, most franchisors required franchisees to buy only from the franchisor. At one point, more than half of Kentucky Fried Chicken's profits came from such sales. After a federal court ruling, companies struck this clause from their franchise contracts. Today, franchisors usually offer to sell merchandise, but allow franchisees to buy elsewhere if strict quality standards are met. A fourth source of revenue for franchisors is charging a management fee. A franchisee is sometimes assessed for "brush-up" training courses or explaining new product offerings. On other occasions, the franchisee invites the franchisor to come in and act as a consultant, and a management fee is charged.

Why get a franchise? Franchising is supposed to offer the following advantages to the franchisee:

1. It gives the individual an opportunity to become an independent business-person with a "proven" business system.
2. The person obtains a product or service with a "positive" image.
3. Management skills are taught.
4. Often purchases are cheaper because of volume buying.
5. The arrangement includes the right to sell a product or service exclusively within a defined geographic territory.

▶ **TABLE 15.2   Franchising Structural Arrangements**

Types of retail structural arrangements	Examples	
A. Manufacturer-retailer Manufacturer gives right (through licensing arrangement) for independent businesses to sell product subject to conditions.	*Car/truck manufacturers* General Motors Ford Chrysler American Motors	*Petroleum refiners* Exxon Mobil *Farm equipment* John Deere
B. Wholesaler-retailer 1. Voluntary—wholesaler organizes a franchise system and grants franchises to individual stores.	VOLUNTARY *Auto* Western Auto	*Electronics* Radio Shack Lafayette
2. Cooperative—retailers set up franchise cooperative by owning and operating a wholesale organization	COOPERATIVE *Grocery* Associated Groceries Certified Grocery	

C. Service sponsor-retailer
Service firm licenses retailer to provide specific service package to ultimate consumer.
	Auto rental
	Avis
	Hertz
	National
	
	Fast foods
	McDonald's
	Burger King
	Orange Julius
	Chicken Delight
	International House
	  of Pancakes
	Dairy Queen
	Tastee Freeze
	Carvel
	Baskin-Robbins
	  31 Flavor Stores
		Motels
		Holiday Inn
		Howard Johnson
		
		Employment agencies
		Manpower
		Kelly Girl
		
		Lawn Care
		Lawn-a-Mat
		Lawn King

Source: Barry Berman and Joel R. Evans, *Retail Management: A Strategic Approach* (New York: Macmillan, 1979), p. 34. Used by permission. Copyright © 1979, Macmillan Publishing Co., Inc.

The franchisor obtains:

1. Company growth without providing capital.
2. Motivated store managers.

Franchise failure rates. Do franchises have lower failure rates than other kinds of businesses? Research data are inconclusive on this question. Individually, of course, the success of the franchise depends on the franchisee. Some, like Mc-Donald's, One-Hour Martinizing, and United Rent Alls, have an extremely low failure rate. On the other hand, Roy Rogers Roast Beef, Minnie Pearl's Fried

Chicken, and Joe Namath's Girls (an employment agency) have been less successful.

Some franchisors have used a short-run strategy by planning to make their money "off of the front end." That is, they viewed the initial franchise fee as their major source of revenue, rather than long-run royalties. This type of franchisor usually relies on a gimmick, such as a well-known personality's name, to sell the franchise. The product or service is often of poor quality and the franchisor offers little, if any, training, site location help, and so on. This naturally leads to failures. One study found that 68 percent of the franchisees in the fast-food industry had never owned a business prior to their franchised business, half had incomes below $10,000, and 39 percent had failed to consult a lawyer prior to signing a franchise agreement.[9] Low incomes mean that the franchisee must usually live off the franchise initially, thus further lowering the chance of success.

Franchising has reached a level of maturity. Most of the "get rich quick" artists have long since left the industry. As the risk of acquiring a major franchise declines (how many McDonald's have failed recently?), the demands of the franchisor for acquiring a quality franchise will increase. Although there will be numerous opportunities for the small businessperson in franchising during the 1980s and 1990s, the price of entry will be very high.

Shopping centers

Some franchisors such as Hickory Farms, Swiss Colony Cheese, and Orange Julius tend to prefer shopping center locations. The tremendous growth of shopping centers began after World War II as the U.S. population started its migration to the suburbs. The first shopping centers were **strip centers,** typically located along a busy street and including a supermarket, a variety store, and perhaps a few specialty stores.

Next came the larger **community shopping centers** with one or two small department store branches, more specialty shops, a restaurant or two, and several apparel stores. These centers offer a wider variety of shopping, specialty, and convenience goods, have large off-street parking lots, and usually range in size from 75,000 to 300,000 square feet.

Finally, along came the huge **regional malls.** Randall Park Mall in suburban Cleveland, Ohio, is the largest shopping mall in America. It sprawls over 143 acres and has room for five major chain or department stores and about 250 smaller shops. Regional malls are either entirely enclosed or roofed to allow easy shopping in any weather. Many offer benches, trees, fountains, sculptures, and similar items to enhance the shopping environment. Acres of free parking are characteristic of malls. The "anchor stores" or "generator stores" (Penney's, Sears, or a major department store) are usually located at opposite ends of the mall to create a heavy pedestrian traffic flow.

In 1980 retail sales in shopping centers amounted to approximately $200 billion and accounted for one-third of all retail sales. Mall and shopping center development seems to be reaching a saturation point, however. Sales per square foot are dropping, vacancy rates are climbing, and some centers and malls have declared bankruptcy. As major markets become saturated, new construction will be highly selective and concentrated in fast-growing areas like the Southwest. Future malls will be smaller, probably in the 400,000-square-foot range, as developers concentrate on medium-sized and smaller cities. A spokesman for Arlen Realty and Development, a major shopping center developer, says, "We don't build in Cleveland, Ohio, but we will in Cleveland, Tennessee."[10]

In addition to the trend toward "midmarket" towns, some developers are creating mixed-use centers. The idea is to blend recreational and community facilities with retail stores to create a focal point of community life and activities. For example, University Towne Centre in San Diego has an ice skating rink, a preschool day care center, folk art museum, discotheque, community meeting room, classrooms for university extension courses, and YMCA/YWCA exercise classes. Such developments tend to create a modern day village square.

Retail management and planning

The key tasks in retailing management and planning are these: (1) defining a market target, (2) developing a product/service offering, (3) creating an image and promotional strategy, (4) selecting a proper location, (5) determining price levels, and (6) controlling the retailing mix (see Figure 15.1). Each managerial task is discussed below.

◢ **FIGURE 15.1 The tasks of retail management.**

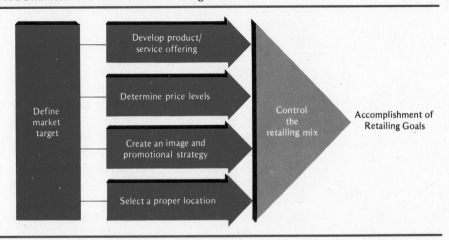

DEFINING A MARKET TARGET

In order to reach company profit, market share, and growth objectives, retailers must begin their strategy by deciding who they want to serve. Essentially this is nothing more than the process of market segmentation discussed in Chapter 4. It is important to enter markets where there is a reasonable opportunity to achieve a significant market share. Retailers with an 8 to 14 percent market share have an average return on investment of 20 percent, and businesses with market shares of less than 8 percent have an average return on investment of slightly over 8 percent.[11] The fragmented and diversified nature of retailing rarely results in a market share larger than 15 percent.

Target audiences are often defined on both demographic and life style dimensions. J. C. Penney has determined its target: (1) young juniors who are fashion conscious; (2) contemporaries who spend more money than any other segment on quality clothing; and (3) conservatives who want comfort and value. J. L. Hudson's typically appeals to an older consumer. Yet after conducting research the store found that it needed to generate more business from the 25 to 40 market. 7-Eleven defines its primary target customer as married men under 35 years of age. These men also earn over $10,000 per year and have two young children.[12]

DEVELOPING PRODUCT/SERVICE OFFERINGS

A second basic task of retail management is to develop its product/service offering, which is called the merchandise mix. The first task is to create a buying organization. In large retail firms, a formal buying department is often established with well-defined purchasing authority and responsibility. In smaller firms, there is an informal buying organization which is not separate from the rest of the firm and does not require additional personnel. In very small companies, buying may be delegated to an outside firm. Outside purchasers operate in major market cities and have excellent sources of supply and knowledge of market trends.

After the buying organization is established, the retailer must determine what to buy. This decision is based upon traditional market research, what has sold in the past, fashion media, customer requests, and other sources. As the vice-president of marketing for May Department Stores notes: "It's not enough to know what customers buy—we have to learn what they would rather buy."[13] After target customer desires are determined, sources of supply must be procured and their wares evaluated. When desirable products are found, a purchase contract is negotiated. The goods must then be physically moved from the seller to the retailer. This involves shipping, storing, and stocking the inventory. The inventory must be managed to take timely price reductions to move slow goods and to avoid stockouts of hot items. As in all good systems, the final step in merchandising is to reevaluate the entire process on a periodic basis to seek greater efficiencies and eliminate problems and bottlenecks.

HERE'S ANOTHER ANCIENT ORIENTAL ART FORM: HAND WEAVING.

THIS PEKING PICTURE RUG IS ONE OF A PRIZE COLLECTION WE FOUND INSIDE CHINA.

Because our buyer is one of the few Westerners ever permitted into the antiques warehouses of the **People's Republic**, we believe our just-arrived shipment of old Chinese carpets is worth a connoisseur's serious consideration.

The rug shown is an exceptionally **rich indigo** blue, high lit with pale blues, beiges and a stroke of red. It's pure wool of course and measures 2'8" by 5'3", the price is 1995.00 and you'll find it in Oriental Carpets on our fifth floor, where our entire **art collection** of Chinese hand-wovens is on display. You can choose from small scatter sizes, gallery sizes and large area rugs. Most are scenics like this one, some are geometrics and colors range from subtle naturals to violets, mauves, pinks and corals. Every one is a unique opportunity **to invest** in rare beauty.

More beauty at Altman's? Almost everywhere you look, from the latest **designer fashions** to old and antique books. Even Waterford crystal so you can toast St. Patrick's Day in style. And that's just a hint of the pleasures at Fifth Avenue's **only department store**.

Out of town, call toll-free (800) 228-5444, in Nebraska (800) 642-8777. The American Express Card is welcome at Altman's.

B.Altman&Co

It's always a pleasure.

361 Fifth Avenue, New York, N.Y. 10016, White Plains, Manhasset, N.Y., Short Hills, Ridgewood/Paramus, N.J., St. Davids, Pa.

Source: Courtesy of B. Altman & Co.

CREATING AN IMAGE AND PROMOTIONAL STRATEGY

The third task in retail management is to create an image and promotional strategy. Promotion, combined with the store's merchandise mix, service level, and atmosphere, make up a retail image. Atmosphere refers to physical layout and decor, which create a relaxed or busy feeling, a sense of luxury, a friendly or cold attitude, or a sense of organization or clutter.

The consumer then develops an impression and positions one store against another in his or her frame of reference. Progressive retailers are mindful of this and therefore establish positioning objectives. Price levels, merchandise mix, promotional strategies, location, and other image components are manipulated to create the desired positioning. An example of strategic positioning is the Limited retail chain, which aims directly at the 18- to 35-year-old woman who is style and fashion conscious and willing to pay moderately high prices to satisfy her desire for tasteful apparel. Its entire marketing effort is geared toward this market segment. It carries primarily junior sizes and emphasizes coordinated outfits; its displays are casual and youth-oriented; and its employees are in the same age category and project the same life style as the target customers. Effective positioning will enhance store loyalty and perhaps shield a retailer from direct competition.

Promotion enhances positioning by telling target customers "this is who we are, what we are, and how we can serve you" (see Figure 15.2). New York's Bloomingdale's is a prime example of effective use of promotion for positioning.

"Positioning the store as a unique entity is the only solution" to the "awesome dilemma" retails face, said George P. Kelly, president of Marshall Field's. "[Bloomingdale's] is located in the midst of a booming, affluent, young and 'swinging' customer audience. But as public and well publicized as this group was and is, they alone could not have made the store as successful as it has become.

"I would guess that 70% to 75% of all the merchandise in the store at 59th and Lexington in New York City is available in any other major department store in New York or the country. It is the other 25% to 30%, along with sometimes outrageous windows, continually changing decor, exciting advertising and great publicity that makes the store 'go.' And many of those who shop there do so because they consider themselves 'swingers,' even though in real life they are accountants and dentists five days out of seven.

"Positioning," said Mr. Kelly, "really treats the store as the product itself and its position is determined by how management decides to 'package' the product." He added it involves careful planning of merchandise assortments, media choices, sophistication of display and "even to the posture that the CEO takes with regard to involvement in the community."

Before undertaking a positioning effort, a retailer must conduct extensive research on its trading area, and after the position is

435

taken, Mr. Kelly said, the retailer must periodically measure customer attitudes to make sure "management is on the right track."

But the Marshall Field executive made it clear that the large retailer has no choice. Positioning, he said, "is an absolute requirement for the future viability of today's department store in tomorrow's world."[14]

SELECTING A PROPER LOCATION

Another major task of retail management is site location, which can be a major component of a retailer's image. Is the store convenient or inconvenient, in a high-rent area or warehouse district? Many factors enter into the location decision. First, a community must be chosen. This decision depends upon economic growth potential and stability, the nature of the competition, political climate, and so forth. After a geographic region is determined, a specific site must be selected. Growth potential, socioeconomic characteristics of the inhabitants, traffic flows, land costs, zoning regulations, existing competition, and public transportaiton are among the most important site location factors.

Several sophisticated mathematical models have been developed to aid in site selection. 7-Eleven store locations are determined using an elaborate quantitative model. And since the organization began using the model, the number of new store failures has dropped dramatically.

DETERMINING PRICE LEVELS

The strategy of pricing has already been discussed in Chapters 11 and 12. Retailers, like other marketing managers, must establish pricing goals and understand both cost and demand. Price is a critical element in the store's image and positioning strategy. Higher prices often denote an air of quality and also dictate the type of clientele the store will attract. Lord and Taylor, Saks Fifth Avenue, Gucci, Cartier, and Neiman Marcus all use price effectively to position themselves as quality, high-class retailers. On the other hand, K-Mart, WalMart, and Target use price to convey "good value for the money."

CONTROLLING THE RETAIL MIX

Every activity that can affect the accomplishment of the retailer's objectives must be controlled. Two very important activities that have a major impact on success are cost of goods and operating expenses. In order to control the latter, expenses must be classified (payroll, depreciation, bad debts) and then distributed to departments or profit centers. Next, an expense budget must be drawn up for each department or profit center. If a department goes over its expense budget, the additional costs must be justified to higher management. The cost of goods is managed by astute bargaining with suppliers and goods inventory control techniques. (We will discuss inventory control in the next chapter.)

In addition to daily expense and control, retail managers should also periodically undertake a marketing audit. Topics covered in the audit include company growth potential, customer relations, personnel management, inventory control procedures, budgetary controls, buying, price strategies, advertising and sales promotion, display, equipment and layout, cash flow, credit policies, insurance, and legal obligations. (We will discuss the marketing audit in detail in Chapter 22.)

Trends in retailing

Good management techniques such as those just described are a requisite for successful retailing because of the dynamic nature of the industry. Retail institutions, especially today, are in a continual state of change.

THE WHEEL OF RETAILING

The perennial state of flux in retailing has been conceptualized as the **wheel of retailing.** The traditional theory states that new retail institutions enter the market as low-cost, low-price operators. Over a period of time, the institution "trades up" by moving to better locations, offering higher-quality merchandise, installing better fixtures, supplying more services, and, of course, raising prices. Trading up leaves a gap in the lower end of the market, creating a vacuum that is ultimately filled by new low-priced institutions. Some of the reasons for retailers' trading up include these:

1. *Demographic trends.*   As the standard of living increases, retailers are naturally attracted by market segments with higher levels of income.
2. *Imperfect competition.*   To avoid direct price competition, emphasis is placed upon additional services, which mean higher margins.
3. *Scrambled merchandising.*   As merchandise assortments are diversified, they tend to add higher-priced items.
4. *Managerial evaluation.*   As second-generation management replaces early founders, cost consciousness gives way to concern over store appearance and image, thus creating an upward pressure on price.[15]

The wheel of retailing concept can be seen in Figure 15.3. A low-cost operator begins at *A* on the *O–W* curve. The curve denotes that as service levels (our generalized example for trading up) rise, prices must follow. *F,* for example, is unattainable at the present level of technology. Only a cost-reducing innovation will make *F* possible. As *A* trades up to *A'*, it will begin cutting into *B*'s market. *B,* however, may also trade up and capture part of *C*'s customers. If *C* continues to trade up as the standard of living rises, it may continue to capture the cream of the upper-class market. The continual trading up leaves a gap at the lower end of the the market around point *A.*

Do stores really follow the wheel of retailing? The answer seems to be yes. Department stores, supermarkets, and discounters have been shown to generally trade up over a period of time.[16] New stores, however, do not always enter with a no-service and low-status profile. And it is forecasted that electronic shopping via home television screens and computer terminals will create the biggest shift in the wheel of retailing ever.[17]

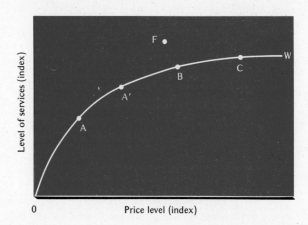

ELECTRONIC SHOPPING

Electronic shopping is already beginning to enter the retailing system. The biggest hurdle these new retailers face is not the hardware for such a system, but changing peoples' buying habits and attitudes. Some examples of electronic buying systems are discussed below (see also Figure 15.4).

The Source Telecomputing Corp., based in McLean, Virginia, is offering subscribers nationwide a computer time-sharing service that makes shopping a living-room activity. Using a home computer linked over phone lines to the system's 2000 information banks, a customer can purchase cameras, furniture, appliances, and other products. The customer pays for the equipment and the time spent using the system, plus a one-time fee.

In Coral Gables, Florida, Knight-Ridder Newspapers is spending $1.7 million to test a service called Viewtron. Some 200 homes will each get a TV screen, a typewriter keyboard, and a Touch-Tone keypad. By following simple instructions on the screen, the chosen few will be able to check flight schedules of Eastern Air Lines, pay bills through a local bank, and draw on a mass of stored information, from wire-service news to Spanish lessons.

Theoretically, a full-scale "viewdata" system can hold an infinite number of video frames, swallowing catalogues bigger than Sears' without so much as a burp. But for the first experiment, Sears and other suppliers such as Grand Union and B. Dalton Bookseller will offer participants a relatively limited selection of products. Once a customer decides to place an order, the computer, always eager to close a sale, will display a form on which only two variables remain: How many do you want? How do you prefer to pay?[18]

THE COMPUTER

The biggest increase in computer usage in retailing is occurring at the point of sale. Computers are often used in conjunction with optical scanning equipment. This equipment is used to read a **universal product code,** a standardized bar code stamped on packages which can be read by scanners at checkout counters. The code identifies the size and brand of the product.

Small retailers are acquiring stand-alone register/terminals equipped with a magnetic tape cassette or a continuous tape. As data are accepted by the register, they are recorded on the tape and later transferred either directly or by phone lines to a central computer. These registers calculate taxes, discounts,

◢ **FIGURE 15.4 Full-scale "Viewdata" system.**

Source: Courtesy of Sears, Roebuck and Co.

and multiply price/quantity information. The system makes merchandise classification more comprehensive:

- ◂ Scanners allow the store to capture real item sales as they happen, as opposed to making the assumption that merchandise shipped from the distribution center "is sold."
- ◂ Management can have easy access to item movement to answer a variety of "what if" questions: What happens to item unit sales when the price of an item is changed? What happens if an item is relocated with a category display? What types of promotions are most effective? At what types of stores?

Larger retail stores are moving to on-line real-time computer systems. These computer systems have register/terminals that are actually input/output terminals that are on-line (communicating directly) with a central computer. This system can respond almost instantly with information requested by the user of any terminal in the system. It provides a picture of what is happening immediately, rather than capturing data on tape and sending it to the computer at the end of the day.

Computers are also being used in increasingly sophisticated management decision making. Planning models, store location models and "what if" store environment simulations will be increasingly used during the 1980s.

THE GROWTH OF SPECIALTY RETAILING

Another important retailing trend is the growth of specialty retailing. Specialty stores will segment and resegment their markets, often catering to a very narrow market target. Examples include The Limited (junior apparel), Mervyn's (family apparel), Aaron Brothers (artists' supplies), and Hickory Farms (specialty foods). Many specialty stores will concentrate not only on fashion merchandise, but on "life style goods" as well. Items such as recreational equipment, cameras, gourmet cooking equipment, and arts and crafts materials will provide the bases for numerous specialty outlets.

WAREHOUSE RETAILING

Perhaps less glamorous, but no less important, is the growth of **warehouse retailing.** The key to the success of this form of retailing is its ability to undercut prices of conventional retailers by from 10 to 30 percent.[19] Firms like Levitz and Best Products will continue to be a major force in this form of retailing. The warehouse grocery will prosper as more consumers seek bargain food prices. In 1980, there were about 500 of these limited assortment, no-frills grocery stores. Typically the food is left in its original packing cases, and the shoppers bag their purchases themselves. Cashiers periodically check to make sure that the price on the outside matches the goods inside. This is essentially an honor system designed to cut costs.

Along similar lines, there are more "factory outlets" springing up around the country. There were over 8000 outlets in the United States in the early 1980s, with sales approaching $1 billion.[20] In order to avoid channel conflict, many manufacturers deliberately set up their factory outlets in rural areas some distance from their major department and specialty store customers.

SUMMARY

Retailing permeates our lives. It is one of America's largest industries, employing over 28 million people, but a very small percentage of retail establishments account for a majority of retail sales.

Department stores constitute one of the most important forms of retail operation. They are dominated by large national chains. Department stores historically have experienced problems in choosing an appropriate merchandise mix and hiring capable personnel.

The mass merchandising shopping chains include Sears, Penney's, and Montgomery Ward. Their huge size, promotional budgets, dealer brands, and numerous stores set them apart from regular department store chains. Mass merchandising shopping chains have extensive market coverage. This makes network television advertising an economical way of promoting their own brands.

Specialty stores, like department stores, are also becoming dominated by chains. They usually specialize in a specific type of merchandise, such as men's clothing, candy, or sporting goods. Specialty stores face many of the same opportunities and challenges that confront department stores.

Discounters first entered the market after World War II. Chain discounters usually carry a complete line of well-known nationally branded hard goods. Major chains include K-Mart, Target, and The Treasury.

Direct marketing has also grown during the 1980s. Sears is the nation's largest direct marketer, with catalog and phone sales of about $2 billion. The primary advantage of direct marketing is the convenience of ordering merchandise without leaving the home.

Franchising's major period of growth was during the 1970s. The franchiser grants operating rights to the franchisee for an initial fee plus a monthly royalty. Franchising increases opportunities for independent businesspeople, and franchises typically have lower failure rates than other businesses. Some franchisors, such as Hickory Farms, tend to prefer shopping center locations.

The 1970s was the era of the huge regional malls. Many malls contain over 200 retail specialty shops and several major department store chains. Their rapid growth seems to have brought them close to the saturation point. Today, they account for approximately one-third of all retail sales.

The key tasks in retailing management are defining the market target, developing the product or service offering, creating an image and promotional strategy, selecting a proper location, determining price levels, and controlling the retailing mix. Good management is necessary due to the dynamic nature of retailing. Retail institutions are in a continual state of evolution—a situation known as the wheel of retailing. Electronic shopping has already entered the retailing system and will continue to show tremendous growth during the 1980s. And point-of-sale computer terminals, in conjunction with optical scanning equipment, have revolutionized retail recordkeeping and inventory management.

KEY TERMS

Retailing
Department store
Buyer
Specialty store
Discount store
Direct marketer
Franchise
Franchisor

Franchisee
Strip center
Community shopping center
Regional mall
Wheel of retailing
Universal product code
Warehouse retailing

REVIEW QUESTIONS

1. Describe the major methods of retail operation. What differentiates them? Are their distinctions rigid?
2. Evaluate the advantages and disadvantages of becoming a franchisee instead of being an independent, unaffiliated retailer. How have the recent court rulings increased the freedom of operation of franchisees?
3. Comment on the merits and shortcomings of free-standing versus shopping center locations.
4. Review the key managerial tasks of retail management and planning.
5. How is price used in positioning? Why is it of such importance to retailers?
6. What is meant by controlling the retail mix? What activities are involved?

DISCUSSION QUESTIONS

1. How does the retailer apply market segmentation to retail management?
2. What are the competitive advantages enjoyed by the major discount chain stores? Give detailed attention to centralized buying, economies of operation, and bargaining power with suppliers.
3. Discuss the factors likely to lead to increased use of telephone, mail order, and electronic shopping. How will these developments alter retailers' present operations?
4. What factors would you consider important in selecting a retail location? How would you go about collecting the necessary information?
5. What factors move the wheel of retailing?
6. Discuss the impact computers have made on retail management.

NOTES

1. John Mutter, "B. Dalton Bookseller—A Novel Approach to Retailing," *Sales and Marketing Management,* May 14, 1979, pp. 49–51. Reprinted by permission from Sales & Marketing Management magazine. Copyright 1979.
2. "Federated: The Most Happy Retailer Grows Faster and Better," *Business Week,* October 28, 1976, pp. 74–80.
3. Edward S. Dubbs, "Planning into the 1980's: Retail Expansion," *Stores,* August 1979, p. 24. Reprinted from Stores magazine. National Retail Merchants Association, copyright 1979.
4. "Sears' Identity Crisis," *Business Week,* December 8, 1975, p. 52.
5. Morris L. Mayer and J. Barry Mason, "Discount Department Stores Will Prosper in

80's Despite Intense Competition," *Marketing News,* March 7, 1980, p. 6. Reprinted by permission of the American Marketing Association.

6. Partially adapted from Lynda Schuster, "Wal-Mart Chief's Enthusiastic Approach Infects Employees, Keeps Retailer Growing," *Wall Street Journal,* April 20, 1981, p. 27.

7. Walter McQuade, "There's a Lot of Satisfaction (Guaranteed) in Direct Marketing," *Fortune,* April 21, 1980, p. 110.

8. Ibid., p. 112.

9. Gilbert Churchill, Jr., and Shelby Hunt, "Sources of Funds and Franchise Success," *Journal of Business Research* 1 (fall 1973): 157–164.

10. David Elsner, "Shopping Center Boom Appears to be Fading due to Overbuilding," *The Wall Street Journal,* September 7, 1976.

11. Robert D. Buzzell and Marci K. Dew, "Strategic Management Helps Retailers Plan for the Future," *Marketing News,* March 7, 1980, p. 1.

12. The target market examples are taken from Ronald D. Michman, "Changing Patterns in Retailing," *Business Horizons,* October 1979, pp. 35–36.

13. "Department Stores Redefine Their Role," *Business Week,* December 13, 1976, p. 47.

14. "Positioning Termed Salvation of Department Store," *Advertising Age,* February 12, 1979, p. 18. Reprinted with permission. Copyright 1979 by Crain Communications, Inc.

15. These four factors are taken from William Davidson, Albert Bates, and Stephen Bass, "The Retail Life Cycle," *Harvard Business Review* 54 (November–December 1976): 89–96. Copyright © 1976 by the President and Fellows of Harvard College; all rights reserved.

16. Ariel Goldman, "The Role of Trading-Up in the Development of the Retailing System," *Journal of Marketing* 39 (January 1975): 54–62.

17. Malcomn P. McNair and Eleanor G. May, "The Next Revolution of the Retailing Wheel," *Harvard Business Review* 56 (September–October 1978): 81–91.

18. Stratford P. Sherman, "A Supermarket at Your Sofa," *Fortune,* April 12, 1980, p. 121.

19. See James Kenderine and Bert McCammon, "Structure and Strategy in Retailing," in Henry Nash and Donald Robin (eds.), Southern Mississippi University, *1975 Proceedings: Southern Marketing Association,* pp. 117–119.

20. John L. Moore, "More Companies Open Factory Outlet Stores for Discount Shoppers," *The Wall Street Journal,* December 24, 1978, p. 1.

◢ **CASES**

15.1 Everfast Printing

Marjorie Ellis is a successful insurance salesperson currently living in Milwaukee, Wisconsin. At 42 years of age, Marjorie has amassed approximately $100,000 in savings and is considering embarking on a new career. She hopes to find something that will give her personal freedom and a sense of accomplishment. Marjorie noticed an ad in *The Wall Street Journal* for an Everfast Printing franchise.

The advertisement noted that Everfast would enable the owner to run a business, not a printing press. The company has over 500 franchisees throughout the world. The franchisor will provide market research, site selection, and lease negotiation. It also offers three weeks of comprehensive training, including transportation and lodging. Other benefits are a fully equipped color-coordinated facility and use of a copyrighted logo. Naturally, the franchisee has to pay for the facility. Everfast also provides accounting systems and inventory control programs, plus money-saving national account purchasing. A down payment of $25,000 is required on a franchise fee of $45,000. Total investment ranges from $80,000 to $100,000, which includes working capital.

1. Marjorie is preparing to write the Everfast Corporation. What questions should she ask the company?
2. Would you recommend instead that Marjorie simply buy her own printing equipment and set up an independent operation? What are the advantages and disadvantages of doing so?

15.2 University Food Service

The North Central A&M University Center Food Service broke even in 1979, lost $5,000 in 1980, and lost $35,000 in 1981. In order to examine user attitudes toward UC food services, a quota sample was undertaken. Quotas were established in proportion to the student population (male-female, day-night, student classification, and major). Four hundred interviews were completed. The results are shown below:

1. Are you aware of the upstairs dining facility, the Caprock, in the University Center? *Yes 50%   No 50%*
2. Are you aware of the Sweet Shoppe in the University Center? *Yes 62%   No 38%*
3. Are you aware of the cafeteria facility, the Table Top, in the University Center? *Yes 67%   No 33%*
4. Are you aware of the grill and sandwich hot meal facility in the University Center? *Yes 73%   No 23%*
5. Do you use the food service facilities in the University Center? *Yes 64%   No 36%*
6. When you use the food service facilities, do you usually buy a meal? *Yes 28%* A snack? *Yes 36%* A beverage only? *Yes 36%*
7. How many times do you use the food service facilities in the University Center per week? *1–2? 43%   3–4? 14%   5–6? 4%   More than 6? 3%   Never 36%*
8. What days do you use the food service facilities in the University Center? (check all applicable) *Monday 33%   Tuesday 68%   Wednesday 32%   Thursday 55%   Friday 25%   Weekends 2%*
9. What time of day do you use the food service facilities in the University Center? *7 a.m. to 11 a.m. 23%   11 a.m. to 2 p.m. 54%   2 p.m. to 4 p.m. 6%   4 p.m. to 7 p.m. 17%*
10. What single area needs the most improvement? *Decor 12%   Price 21%   Food preparation 29%   Food variety 18%   Service 3%   Hours of operation 4%   Don't know 13%*

11. What do you like most about the food service? *Convenience 45%* *Service 9%* *Quality of food 5%* *Decor 6%* *Price 7%* *Variety 9%* *Nothing 19%*
12. What do you dislike most about the food service? *Convenience 2%* *Service 8%* *Quality of food 27%* *Decor 3%* *Price 21%* *Variety 15%* *Other 24%*

1. As the University Center Food Service manager, you must take this survey and make recommendations to the vice-president in charge of student affairs. What recommendations would you make? Defend those recommendations.
2. Which questions are most helpful to you in developing a strategy? Why?
3. What additional information should have been gathered on the questionnaire?

16

Logistics and distribution management

OBJECTIVES

To understand the logistics concept and associated elements.

To become aware of the costs of distribution.

To examine several key functions of logistics.

To learn about the institutions that facilitate physical distribution.

To present an introduction to logistics management.

To gain insight into present and future distribution trends.

Robert Johnson walked into Walter S. Mack's Park Ave. office with a business proposition: he wanted to distribute Mack's King-Cola, a would-be competitor to Coca-Cola and Pepsi, in his native Sierra Leone and six other West African countries. Mack's response: the distribution rights would cost $1 million—half of it in cash and half payable over the next 10 years. Johnson asked for 90 days to raise the cash.

Meetings like that occurred daily as King-Cola worked to establish international distribution and, more importantly, planned for its national rollout in 1979.

Under the chairmanship of Mack, who was Pepsi's first president (from 1938 to 1951), Coke and Pepsi alumni formed King-Cola to give consumers a cola they insist is as tasty as its two competitors, but thanks to a streamlined distribution system and sales force, costs significantly less.

Mack notes that Coke established its 1,100 franchises in the "horse-and-buggy days," when territories had to be small enough to be covered by that delivery method. Pepsi, established in the era of auto transportation, split the U.S. into 550 areas. "Someone has to bring the industry up-to-date," says Mack, 83. Thus King-Cola has divided the U.S. into a mere 29 franchise areas, called kingdoms by Mack, which sell for $1–$2 million.

Along with the simplified franchises goes simplified distribution. Rejecting the "store-door" system of Coke and Pepsi, among others, King-Cola delivers to chain store warehouses, as do most marketers of nonperishables. There are advantages to that: eliminating driver-salesmen means also eliminating their supervisors and the fleet-maintenance team, thus cutting costs substantially. Instead of the traditional sales force, each "kingdom" is expected to have a "marketing manager" who will make sales calls to chain headquarters, and four to eight merchandisers who will make stock-checking calls on individual stores.[1]

Why would Robert Johnson pay $1 million for King-Cola distribution rights? What makes distribution so important? How can distribution save a company money or, on the other hand, cause it to lose profits and market share? What tasks are involved in distribution?

The King-Cola story speaks of the never-ending quest for a better way to get products to consumers and users. "Better" in physical distribution and logistics can be summarized as faster and cheaper. Another example of the importance of good logistics occurred when Kodak announced a new line of instant cameras and film to compete against Polaroid. Introductory promotion was splashy, dramatic, and heavy. A five-page spread in *TV Guide* dramatically announced, "It's here! The Kodak Instant." Yet a key marketing element had hit a snag — physical distribution. Most dealers had only a few cameras, and many had none. One buyer for a major department store chain noted that "people aren't inclined to wait — they will switch to Polaroid instead. So, the situation seems to be that Kodak is advertising for Polaroid." In fact, the buyer added, "We've been urged by Polaroid to stock up on their material in anticipation of nondelivery of the Kodak item."

This chapter begins with some definitions of basic distribution concepts. Next we will look at the costs and objectives of physical distribution, and then explore the managerial tasks required to meet distribution objectives, including the planning and organization of physical distribution departments. We conclude with a look at trends in distribution.

The logistics concept

Logistics consists of two key areas: operations and coordination.[2] **Logistics** is the process of managing the movement and storage of materials, parts, and finished inventory from suppliers, between enterprise facilities, and to customers. **Logistical operations** is the management of the movement and storage of enterprise materials and finished products. **Logistical coordination** is the management of finished product and raw material movement. Movement problems vary with order size, inventory availability, and urgency of movement.

The logistics concept is illustrated in Figure 16.1. The left side of the figure is logistical operations. It starts with procurement of raw materials needed for manufacturing and continues through shipment of the final product to the consumer. The broken lines on the right side of the diagram represent information flows, in contrast to the physical flows denoted by solid lines. Information flows both ways in the system to facilitate coordination. For example, a supplier may call the manufacturer and say that the raw materials ordered will be a day late in arriving. This necessitates adjustments in the manufacturer's production schedule.

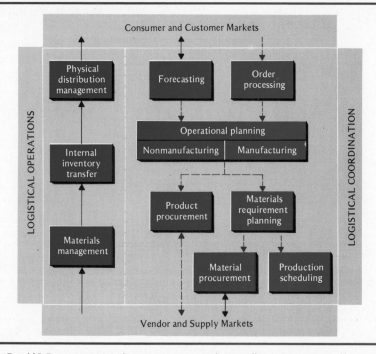

Source: Donald F. Bowersox, *Logistical Management* (New York: Macmillan, 1978), p. 18. Used by permission.

OPERATIONS

Logistical operations can be divided into three subareas: physical distribution management, materials management, and internal inventory transfer.

Physical distribution consists of all business activities that are concerned with transporting finished inventory and/or raw material assortments so that they arrive at the designated place when needed and in usable condition. Physical distribution managers are responsible for getting the finished product to the consumer or user. This is an integral part of the total marketing mix. You don't sell products that you can't deliver, and salespeople don't (or shouldn't) promise deliveries that they can't make. Of course there are exceptions, but such promises usually mean the loss of a customer. The physical product is inseparable from accurate order filling, billing, timely delivery, and arrival in good condition. It is also part of the price of the product.

Materials management, the second area of logistical operations responsibility, is concerned with finding sources of supply, acquiring raw materials to keep the production line running smoothly, and getting them at a reasonable cost. Whereas physical distribution managers are concerned with outbound goods, materials managers are responsible for the proper raw materials assortment being where and when it is needed. Materials management is a critical function of any manufacturer. Consider the case of Dayton Industries, a small electric motor manufacturer, whose average product contains over 100 individual parts. If any single item is not available, the entire production line grinds to a halt. The importance of distribution in a service organization is discussed in the example below.

The Rhode Island Hospital is a large New England hospital with 700 beds, a budget of over $38 million, and a staff of 3800 persons. It provides the typical medical and surgical services of a hospital plus medical research projects and medical education programs. To support this level of activity, the hospital has an investment in inventories of $745,000 and purchases over $8 million in materials per year (about 22% of total operating costs) with 25,000 to 30,000 purchase orders.

The material management organization consists of four departments: Purchasing, General Stores and Inventory, Central Services, and Laundry. They are integrated into the Materials Management Department, whose mission it is to balance and coordinate the independent materials functions into a single work force in order to achieve high-quality service at lowest cost. The focus of the department is on transportation and processing efficiency through the integration of functions and on the awareness of the total cost of supplying items to patients, including purchase, receiving, storage, and final disposal.

Purchasing is a key materials-management activity in the hospital, because purchasing expenditures account for roughly one-quarter of operating costs. Purchases are made directly from suppliers, but this hospital and others are able to secure better prices on some items by collectively buying in volume through two cooperatives: the Hospital Association of Rhode Island and the Hospital Bureau. Advance buying is a common hospital purchasing practice. Although inventory storage costs increase, the benefits of buying before price increases can more than offset these added inventory costs. With the large number of purchase orders that are processed annually, the hospital computer controls its inventory levels system and types purchase orders automatically from the machine.

The General Stores and Inventory group is responsible for the receiving and storekeeping activities as well as delivery of the material to nursing stations. This group, under the Director of the Materials Management Department, is responsible for 65% of the total inventory investments. Unique to the hospital setting is that departments outside the control of materials management maintain their own inventories. In this case, the Dietary Food and Pharmacy Departments carry and keep close control over stocks for their own purposes. Inventory levels are controlled by scientific procedures and computerized record keeping.

Central Services is a function that is unique to hospital materials management. In effect, it is the management of sterile goods inventories. Inventories in a hospital are of two types: sterile and nonsterile. The nonsterile stocks are managed by the General Stores and Inventory groups in much the same way as they are in an industrial firm. However, sterile goods must be handled more carefully to prevent contamination. The Central Services group, in addition to stock keeping, prepares "kits" of dressing and sterile materials for burn patients, operating rooms, nursing units, and other special purposes.

The Laundry group would be classified in an industrial setting as a manufacturing operation rather than a supply activity. The major reason for including it in the Materials Management Department is that the hospital is moving more toward the use of disposable materials that previously were laundered.[3]

Internal inventory transfer is the third component of operations. It is the control of semi-finished goods as they move through various stages of manufacturing. Since it is strictly an internal function, it is not subject to random external factors, such as customer order variations and vendor's shipping dependability. Thus internal inventory transfer should be well planned and organized.

COORDINATION

Coordination is a critical element of effective management. The coordination effort depends heavily on forecasting to develop plans for incoming items, production scheduling (in-plant holding and moving), and the monitoring of materials and finished goods inventories. The specific functions involved in coordination are product-market forecasting, order processing, operational planning, and procurement. We will discuss forecasting in detail in Chapter 21; here we will look at the other functions.

Order processing is the mechanical function of correcting, transmitting, and filling items that have been sold to a customer. For complex industrial goods, an order may literally be hundreds of pages long. (We will have more to say later in the chapter about order processing.) Operational planning is based on sales forecasts. In a manufacturing operation it is the coordination of production scheduling and overall materials and supplies procurement into a smooth, integrated system. In retailing operations, planning involves obtaining the "right" merchandise mix in a timely manner. The last function of logistical coordination is procurement or materials requirement planning. If it is a wholesaler or retailer buying a finished good for resale, the process is called product procurement. If raw materials are being bought for production, the process is called materials requirement planning. In either case, buying finished goods or raw materials depends upon forecasted sales of final products. In the building of new homes, for example, the number of fixtures to buy depends upon the quantity of homes the builder can expect to sell.

Critical path method (CPM) is a time and activity sequence technique often used in manufacturing to determine when certain raw materials are needed. The technique recognizes that some activities can take place only after others are completed. Materials orders can then be placed ahead of time so that supplies are always available.

Distribution: costs, objectives, importance

Logistics encompasses a large number of activities within the firm, but it is only in recent years that these activities have been brought together as a single organizational unit. As distribution departments have evolved, their emphasis has changed from obtaining the lowest transportation rates to minimizing total distribution costs, both explicit and implicit, relative to a pre-determined level of service. In fact, the ability to achieve significant cost savings has been one of the primary reasons for the establishment of physical distribution departments. Distribution costs can act as a constraint on territory covered and therefore on the firm's market potential.

A National Council of Physical Distribution Management study completed in 1979 concluded that virtually every distribution activity in the country has an improvement opportunity of at least 10 percent, or $40 billion a year nationwide. The percentage breakdown of total distribution costs is this: transportation (45 percent), customer service and administration (10 percent), production and inventory planning (25 percent), and warehousing (20 percent).[4] But a firm must be careful not to embark on random cost cutting. One health care products firm cut its distribution costs to 5 percent below the industry average. During the same period, the firm's primary competitor had increased its distribution costs. The cost-cutting health care products firm was still using wholesalers, whereas the competition was going direct to major drug chains. While the competition was reducing turnaround time on orders and increasing inventory, the firm continued its cutbacks. When it finally realized what was happening, significant market share had been lost. In contrast, a household product manufacturer overspent by catering too much to customers. It set a three-day delivery schedule and increased inventory 15 percent to meet it. This meant increased prices. When the company found that its customers were happy with a ten-day delivery, it realized it could cut inventory and transportation costs.

At this point the following caveat is apparent: Cost minimization per se can have disastrous results. Marketing managers must consider the impact of any cost saving on the quality of the distribution system. The objective of physical distribution is to provide good service at low cost. Good service increases the probability of repeat sales, a high customer retention rate, and the addition of new customers.

Perhaps the best measure of distribution service is **order cycle time.** This is the elapsed time between the initial effort to place an order and the customer's receipt of the order in good condition. A buyer may feel that the availability of

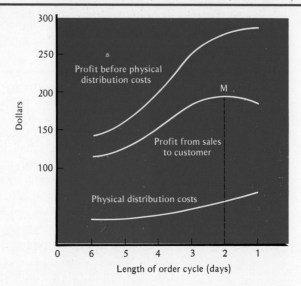

Schedule of Profit Differentials as a Function of Varying Order Lengths (One Customer)[a]

Length of order cycle in days	Probability supplier will receive customer's orders [b]	Annual revenue from customer	Profits before physical distribution costs	Total physical distribution costs [c]	Profits from sales to customer
1	.158	$774	$271	$85	$186
2	.155	736	258	66	192
3	.150	675	236	51	185
4	.140	560	196	36	160
5	.130	455	159	26	133
6	.125	406	142	20	122

[a] Based on hypothetical data.
[b] Assumes a single acceptable level of consistency in order cycle lengths.
[c] Includes placement costs (where covered), processing costs, transportation costs, and control costs.
Source: Ronald Stephenson and Ronald Willet, "Selling with Physical Distribution Service," *Business Horizons,* December 1968, pp. 78–79. Copyright 1968 by the Foundation for the School of Business at Indiana University.

timely and reliable order status information is an important part of the "total product." Generally speaking, distribution managers set service policies and objectives in the following areas:[5]

Minimum order size   Counter pickups   Delivery schedules
Ordering methods   Credit   Returned goods
Lead time requirements   Releases   Claims
Service charges   Expediting   Complaints

How important is physical distribution service? Although measures are lacking in the consumer market, a survey of 400 purchasing agents for large manufacturers revealed that distribution service is second only to product quality.[6] In fact, it is more important than price! The same study indicated that 25 percent of the purchasing agents surveyed canceled back orders more than 35 percent of the time. Inability to make on-time deliveries often translates into lost revenue for the seller.

One may quickly jump to the conclusion that a company should never be out of stock. But this is not the case. Each unit of increased customer service requires greater incremental expenditure. For example, a firm that strives to support a service standard of overnight delivery at 95 percent consistency may confront costs that are nearly double the total cost of implementing a program of second-morning delivery with 90 percent consistency.[7] Thus the shortest order cycle time (one day in Figure 16.2) is not always the most profitable policy.

Let's look again at the concept of total distribution costs. Physical distribution managers should examine the interrelationship of such factors as number of warehouses, finished-goods inventory, and transportation expenses. Each component of distribution expense should be examined in light of the other cost centers in the system. Finally, the cost of any single distribution system should be analyzed relative to its order cycle time. One classic study justified the high cost of air transportation when viewed in a systems context.[8] The rapid delivery capabilities of air freight drastically reduced the number of warehouses required at distant locations as well as outlying inventory requirements. Thus the cost increase of using air freight was more than justified by the savings in inventory and warehouse expenses.

Figure 16.3 illustrates the interrelationship among transportation, inventory

---

◢ **FIGURE 16.3 Distribution costs versus number of warehouses.**

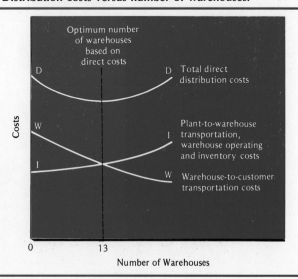

carrying cost, and number of warehouses. The WW curve declines as the number of warehouses increases. The more warehouses a firm has, the lower the transportation cost from warehouse to customer. If Jones Manufacturing, our theoretical company, serves fifty markets and has a warehouse in each one, the warehouse-to-customer transportation costs are going to be low. If the company has only one warehouse, the transportation expenses will be much higher. The II curve represents plant-to-warehouse transportation and warehouse operating and inventory costs. Plant-to-warehouse costs will rise as the number of warehouses increases because the plant will be forced to make small shipments to numerous points (small shipments generally cost more than carload or truckload shipments via a common carrier). Warehousing and inventory costs rise because of the duplications in overhead at each location. As you can see, the decline in WW is ultimately offset by the increase in II such that total distribution costs (DD) begin to rise. The lowest point of DD corresponds to 13 warehouses, yielding the lowest total distribution cost.

Major logistical functions

Key functions of logistics include determining warehouse location and type of warehouse, establishing a materials-handling system, maintaining an inventory control system, establishing procedures for processing orders, and selecting modes of transportation (see Figure 16.4). Channels of distribution create trans-

◢ **FIGURE 16.4 Logistics as part of the marketing mix.**

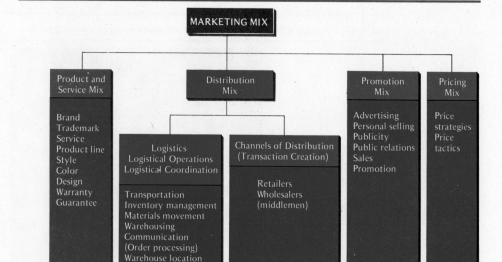

actions (buying and selling), and logistics aids in creating the product and in physical fulfillment of the customer's need.

DETERMINING WAREHOUSE LOCATION AND FORM

Warehousing is sometimes called "the second oldest profession," because the biblical Joseph developed a storage program based upon seven good years and seven poor years of harvest. Joseph probably didn't have to worry, however, about warehouse location and the type of warehouse to use or construct. Warehouse location, like distribution center site selection, is primarily a function of markets to be served and the location of production facilities. But there are other important considerations:

- Quality and versatility of transportation
- Quantity and quality of labor
- Cost and quality of industrial land
- Taxes
- Community government
- Utilities

There are also several types of warehouses.

Public warehouses. Sometimes a manufacturer must choose between building its own warehouse or using a public warehouse. **Public warehouses** are independently owned and often specialize in handling certain products, such as furniture or refrigerated products, and household goods. The use of public warehouses enables a producer to place inventories close to key customers. This means quick delivery without the cost of building a private facility. Other reasons for using public warehouses include (1) avoiding investment in new capital structures, (2) reducing distribution risks and increasing flexibility when entering new markets, and (3) meeting seasonal demand.

Distribution centers. **Distribution centers** are a special form of warehouse. The emphasis is on making bulk (consolidating shipments) or breaking bulk, and not on storage. Conceptually, a distribution center strives for rapid inventory turnover, as opposed to serving as a long-term merchandise depository.

A distribution center can be distinguished from a warehouse in a number of ways. It is a centralized warehousing operation that

Serves a regional market.
Consolidates large shipments from different production points.
Processes and regroups products into customized orders.
Maintains a full line of products for customer distribution.
Is primarily established for movement of goods, rather than for storage.
Provides services for shippers and consignees of goods.
Usually employs a computer and various materials-handling equipment, and may be automated rather than labor intensive.
Is large and single- rather than multistoried.[9]

The role of the computer in maintaining an efficient flow of merchandise into and out of the distribution center cannot be overemphasized. In fact, the computer is often cited as the key to the success of the distribution center concept. Let us see how one large company incorporates the computer into its distribution center network.

Norwich Pharmaceutical Company is the pharmaceutical division of Morton-Norwich Products, Inc., a diversified, consumer-product oriented corporation marketing pharmaceuticals, cosmetics, food service and household products, specialty chemicals, and industrial and ice-control salt through a number of marketing divisions.

The new teleprocessing system puts the company's five distribution centers across the country as close as a keyboard to central headquarters. Sales, distribution and invoicing are handled "on location," communicating constantly with centralized inventory, accounts receivable and credit files. Major files are linked; on-line processing keeps them always up to date. The result is a dynamic new operating environment.

As orders are received, operators at the distribution center enter them through the keyboard terminals and inquire into headquarters files on inventory status, customer credit ratings and other customer data.

Responses appear on the local terminal screen. Problems, if any, are flagged in headquarters. Finally, assuming the order can go through, the complete order document is flashed on the screen at the distribution center for the operator's inspection. Once OK'd, it is printed out, along with shipping papers, on the printer next to the terminal. From there, it goes directly to the warehouse for picking.

Norwich can now pull, pack and ship each order much faster than before. All bill-of-lading and delivery information is in the shipping papers, so the man at the warehouse need only enter data in the correct boxes on the bill-of-lading. And the invoices, which used to be prepared and mailed in Norwich, are now ready and can either go directly with the shipment or directly into the mail.

If an order should be flagged for credit reasons, a printout in the credit department gives the name of the customer, distribution point where the order was entered, and a code indicating a past due bill, a credit limit overage or an account that requires special handling—a rush order, for example.

This printed information goes to the credit director or one of his six credit managers. Based on a detailed display of the customer's account, which they call out on a nearby 3270 visual display terminal, they can decide whether the order should be shipped or held.[10]

Just as important as the computer is the **flow-through concept** in distribution center design. The idea is to move goods in and out of the system as rapidly as possible while meeting customer service needs. Consider, for example, the Coast-to-Coast Corporation, a wholesale hardware chain that supplies over 1100 independent hardware stores. It is the policy of Coast-to-Coast to maintain a very high service level for each individual store.

Coast has built distribution centers in Oregon, Indiana, and Brookings, South Dakota. The Brookings distribution center is the newest and biggest, with 375,000 square feet of high-cube warehouse space and 15,000 square feet of office space.

The most important feature of the distribution center, however, is the method of arranging items in storage. So says Robert Gambill, divisional vice president, who heads up the operation.

"Most warehouses arrange merchandise by stock number, but here we arrange everything by popularity," says Mr. Gambill. "Items in greatest demand sit right on the aisle. Order fillers have 80 percent of items within arm's reach."

The center is divided into ten sections and, because arrangement corresponds with demand, many items are shifted within a section season by season. For example, electric trains sell big at Christmas time but fall off sharply after that. The storage bin in the "Toys" section that held trains during Christmas season will hold baseball equipment in early spring, and fishing tackle later in the year.[11]

ESTABLISHING A MATERIALS-HANDLING SYSTEM

The Coast-to-Coast example points out the importance of proper design. It also implies that a good materials-handling system is essential to move the inventory rapidly. American businesses spend over $300 million a year for materials-handling equipment such as power-lift trucks, automated high-rise storage, racks and shelving, conveyor equipment, and packaging, weighing, and marking equipment.[12] One of the major goals of materials managers is to reduce item handling. It is estimated that in a factory warehouse, a product is typically handled 16 times.[13] And each movement of a product is an opportunity to damage it, and each lifting of the item fatigues the package. So the goal of a good materials-handling system is to move items as quickly as possible while handling them as little as possible.

A discussion of materials handling would not be complete without a mention of **containerization,** putting the goods in a box for protection and ease of handling. This form of distribution has become extremely popular in international shipping, and approximately 60 percent of all international shipments now move this way.[14] A container, often a special form of truck trailer body, can be loaded and locked in Yuma, Arizona. A truck tractor then hauls the load to

Phoenix, where the container is placed on a special railroad flatcar. The train arrives at the port of embarkation, say, San Diego, where giant cranes lift the container onto special container ships. The reverse process occurs at the port of destination. The process can be repeated many times, since the average container has a life expectancy of ten years and can be repaired if damaged. Today over 2 million containers are utilized in world shipping.

MAINTAINING AN INVENTORY CONTROL SYSTEM

The third important function of logistics is the establishment of an inventory control system. Inventory levels are subject to many internal pressures, depending on the goals of the operating department. The following passage illustrates those pressures:

The field salesman will try to convince you to maintain large stocks so that none of his customers will have to wait. Purchasing agents will tend to buy in large quantities in order to take advantage of quantity discounts and price speculations, and to hedge against a cut-off in supply, perhaps caused by labor problems. The traffic specialist will also opt for large shipment quantities to take advantage of lower freight rates. All these are forces at work in a firm which tend to increase the amount of inventory on hand, as well as the quantity ordered.

Then there are opposing forces pushing for low inventory levels. The firm's financial officers, for example, will pressure for reduced inventory levels. Less inventory not only means less capital tied up, but also lower warehousing costs.[15]

Who is right? In a general sense, everyone is. All these objectives should be considered in designing an inventory control policy.

Three basic elements are at the heart of an inventory control system: ordering costs, inventory carrying costs, and the costs of lost sales or stockouts. The last element may necessitate safety stocks. Unpredictability of usage or unreliability of supplier delivery times may cause lost sales if safety stocks are inadequate. The level of inventory that should be ordered at any one time is guided by the **economic order quantity (EOQ).** EOQ minimizes the sum of the ordering cost and the inventory carrying costs (see Figure 16.5).

Ordering cost. **Ordering cost** is the total of operating expenses for the ordering or purchasing department, the follow-up required, the operating expenses for the receiving department, the expenses incurred in paying invoices, and an allocation of the data-processing costs related to purchasing and acquisition of inventory. The cost is then divided by the number of orders placed per year to arrive at an ordering cost per order.

Carrying cost. **Carrying cost** is the total of all expenses involved in maintaining inventory. Such expenses include the cost of capital tied up in idle merchandise, the cost of obsolescence, space charges, handling charges, insurance costs, property taxes, losses due to depreciation, losses stemming from

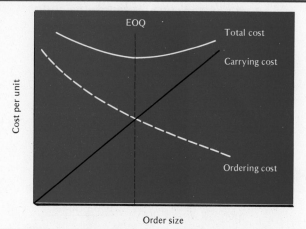

deterioration, and losses resulting from inability to use the capital involved in other ways. In the examples that follow, we will use 24 percent per year (2 percent per month) of the unit cost per year—a fairly typical figure for most businesses.

You can compute the EOQ using this formula:

$$EOQ = \sqrt{\frac{2 \times \text{average usage} \times \text{ordering cost}}{\text{unit cost} \times \text{carrying cost (\%)}}}$$

Average usage (units sold)—600 per year*
Ordering cost—$48 per order
Unit cost (not selling price)—$24
Carrying cost—24% per year*

$$EOQ = \sqrt{\frac{2 \times 600 \times 48}{24 \times 0.24}} = 100 \text{ (or two months' usage)}$$

* Must be in same time units.

EOQ should be used carefully. The basic assumptions of the economic lot size or economic order quantity model are as follows: (1) Usage is at a constant rate throughout the year; (2) the price of inventory items is constant—that is, no quantity discounts are available; and (3) carrying costs are linear, based on the average inventory.

The basic effects of using EOQ are these:

1. An increase in units sold or order cost will increase EOQ, but at a slower rate— namely, the square root of the increase.
2. An increase in unit cost or carrying cost will reduce the EOQ, but may increase investment in inventory, with the same effect as an increase in usage volume.[16]

Reorder point. Assuming that a firm has satisfactorily established an EOQ system, the next question is when to order. Put another way, how low should stocks fall before the **reorder point (ROP).** The formula for determining ROP is as follows:

$$ROP = SS + \frac{(A)L}{365}$$

where: ROP = Reorder point
  SS = Safety stock
  A = Annual usage of inventory item
  L = Lead time in days
If: SS = 4,000
  A = 120,000
  L = 20 days

then: $ROP = 4,000 + \dfrac{(120,000)(20)}{365}$

  $ROP = 4,000 + 6,575$
  $ROP = 10,575$ units

The usefulness of ROP depends upon determining an optimum safety stock. If the safety stock is too large, excessive inventories will be maintained and merchandise will be reordered before it is needed. On the other hand, safety stocks that are too low will cause a stockout, with all its problems.

Because inventory management is so quantitatively oriented, the question arises as to whether the system should be computerized. Fingerhut Corporation, a large direct mail merchandiser of consumer goods, installed an IBM data-base inventory management system and within two years cut inventory about 60 percent and eliminated $57 million in debt. The system keeps up-to-the-minute records on order volume, and adjusts inventories and production schedules accordingly. Fingerhut has cut order cycle time in half.

ESTABLISHING PROCEDURES FOR PROCESSING ORDERS

An efficient inventory control system goes a long way toward reducing order cycle time. Another important activity is the establishment of an effective order-processing system. The starting point of an order-processing system is the placement of an order by a customer. A salesperson transmits the order to the office (this is the order transmittal time), usually on a standardized order form. As the order enters the system, management must monitor two flows: the flow of goods and the flow of information.

The importance of proper order processing cannot be overemphasized. Slow shipment, incorrect merchandise, or partially filled orders can create just as much dissatisfaction as stockouts or slow delivery. The flows of goods and information must be continually monitored so that mistakes can be corrected before the bill is submitted to the customer and the merchandise shipped.

Mode	Billions of ton-miles[a]	Percentage
Rail	868	36%
Air	5	—
Water (domestic)	375	15
Pipeline	586	24
Truck	602	25
Total	2,436	100

[a] A ton-mile is the movement of 1 ton (2000 pounds) of freight for the distance of 1 mile.
Source: Statistical Abstract of the United States, 1980, p. 639.

SELECTING MODES OF TRANSPORTATION

Shipping brings up the question of which mode of transportation should be used. The usage rates of the five major modes of transportation are shown in Table 16.1. Let us examine some of the unique advantages and problems each mode of transportation offers a logistics manager.

Railroads. Railroads have long been the backbone of United States freight transportation, but competition from trucks has virtually eliminated rail service to minor markets. Most service is relatively slow and limited from terminal to terminal. As compared with other carriers, rail rates are low on carload lots. But rough handling and lack of speed make raw materials more suitable for rail transportation rather than finished goods.

A main advantage rail offers over other modes is reliability: weather rarely interrupts rail freight schedules. With proper scheduling, railroads can be turned into "rolling warehouses," providing additional savings.

The future of the railroad system in America is secure. Transportation officials are preparing to spend about $20 billion during the 1980s to reengineer the national rail network. This will include mergers, abandonment of unneeded lines, upgrading the many miles of deteriorated track, and rebuilding dilapidated yards and terminals. At present, it is estimated that America uses only 25 percent of its total rail capacity because of duplication. Eventually, we may see four transcontinental railroads and perhaps a half-dozen north-south lines carved from today's 67 major railroads (see Figure 16.6).

Inland waterways. Inland waterways have made a dramatic comeback since the mid-1950s, when they hauled roughly 3 percent of the nation's freight. New towboats have greatly increased the capacity of many carriers. Special barges now handle refrigerated commodities; others contain steam coils for asphalt; and traditional tank barges now have special linings for hauling chemicals.

Routes, of course, are limited. High fixed costs necessitate heavy traffic from point to point in order to achieve economies of scale. Often, locks and channels in major industrial areas are overtaxed, creating costly delays. Even without the bottlenecks, service is usually slow, and in some northern areas,

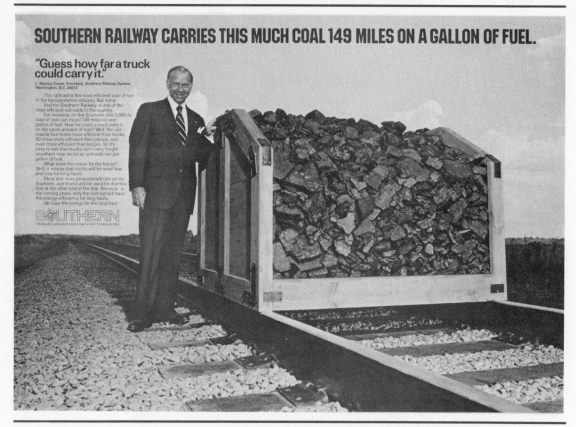

SOUTHERN RAILWAY CARRIES THIS MUCH COAL 149 MILES ON A GALLON OF FUEL.

"Guess how far a truck could carry it."

L. Stanley Crane, President, Southern Railway System, Washington, D.C. 20013

The railroad is the most efficient user of fuel in the transportation industry. Bar none.

And the Southern Railway is one of the most efficient railroads in the country.

For instance, on the Southern, this 3,000-lb load of coal can travel 149 miles on one gallon of fuel. How far could a truck carry it on the same amount of fuel? Well, the railroad is four times more efficient than trucks, 60 times more efficient than planes, and even more efficient than barges. So it's easy to see that trucks can't carry freight anywhere near as far as railroads can per gallon of fuel.

What does this mean for the future? Well, it means that trucks will be used less and less for long hauls.

More and more products will ride on the Southern, and trucks will be used for distribution at the other end of the line. Because, in the coming years, only the railroad will have the energy-efficiency for long hauls. *We have the energy for the long haul.*

SOUTHERN
THE RAILWAY SYSTEM THAT GIVES A GREEN LIGHT TO INNOVATIONS

Source: Courtesy of Southern Railway System.

heavy icing problems cause further delays. But even though service is slow, water is still one of the cheapest means of moving raw materials and some semi-finished goods on a regular basis over long distances. The growth of containerization and improved port facilities will mean continued growth for inland waterways transportation.

Pipeline. Pipelines also are quite slow but offer continuous product flow. There is no route flexibility, and route capacity is limited by the diameter of the pipe. Gases, liquids, and some solids (movable in slurries) constitute the market for pipelines. Routes are one-directional, with storage terminals required at the receiving end. Perhaps the greatest advantage of pipelines, other than cost, is dependability: they are almost never affected by the weather. Pipelines are also the lowest consumers of energy.

Trucks. The nation's motor carriers constitute our most flexible freight hauling mode. Many provide door-to-door service, thus reducing packing costs. Rates

◢ **TABLE 16.2 Service Rankings of the Basic Modes of Transportation**

Speed	Frequency	Dependability	Payload flexibility	Points served
Air	Pipeline	Pipeline	Water	Highway
Highway	Highway	Highway	Rail	Rail
Rail	Air	Rail	Highway	Air
Water	Rail	Water	Air	Water
Pipeline	Water	Air	Pipeline	Pipeline

Source: Adapted from J. L. Heskett, Robert M. Ivie, and Nicholas A. Glaskowsky, Jr., *Business Logistics* (New York: Ronald Press, 1974), p. 71. Used by permission.

are usually economical over the short haul, and speed is better than most other modes.

Service can be affected by the weather, and there are size and weight limitations. However, minimal handling and generally smooth rides make trucking desirable for finished goods and fragile items. Carriers are improving terminal facilities for handling less-than-truck load shipments and buying computers to cut paperwork. As a result, trucks will continue to be the mainstay of the short-haul public shipper.

Air. Air freight offers the fastest, but the most expensive, means of moving freight. Expense, of course, refers to transportation costs, not the total costs of distribution. Speed and limited handling enable shippers to utilize limited packaging in air freight. Generally, the market is limited to merchandise of high value and certain perishable items.

Specialized cargo planes with swing tails, roll-on containerization, and efficient ground-time cargo operations have helped reduce the cost of air freight. However, the overall low weight capacity of the aircraft compared to other modes such as barge or rail will always be a major factor in limiting air freight growth. Weather and a lack of adequate runways in smaller communities may also affect service quality.

The modes of transportation actually selected by the firm will depend upon the needs of the shipper. All shippers are concerned with costs of service, delivery time and variability, freight loss and damage, speed, and points served. Table 16.2 summarizes the advantages of each mode of transportation.

Carriers

Many shippers find that carriers specializing in small packages are uniquely suited to their needs. Other shippers rely on freight forwarders to lower their transportation costs.

SMALL-SHIPMENT CARRIERS

During the OPEC oil embargo, jet fuel increased dramatically in price, causing a corresponding increase in air freight rates. Airlines cut schedules, making deliveries of lightweight high-value items less timely. This was particularly true of night schedules, when most freight moves. The company that first sensed the problem and developed a potential solution was Federal Express.

The key to Federal's success was the acquisition of its own private fleet of jets that fan out from Memphis, Tennessee, every evening. All freight is returned to Memphis late at night, resorted, and flown to its new destination before the beginning of working hours on the next day. Thus a Federal truck will pick up merchandise in, say, El Paso at 5:00 P.M., and it will be sitting on the client's desk in New York early the next morning. Federal is not without competition. Emery, Federal's closest rival, concentrated on slower-moving, larger freight shipments over regular scheduled airlines until 1978. Now Emery also has its own fleet of jet freighters.

FREIGHT FORWARDERS

Freight forwarders collect less-than-carload shipments from a number of shippers and consolidate them into carload lots. Their rates are equivalent to less-than-carload rates, but the forwarder pays carload rates; thus their profit comes from the difference between the two rates. Unlike Federal Express, forwarders do not own their long-haul equipment. Instead, they use available modes of transportation. Most offer pickup and delivery service, along with the speed and efficiency of handling carload merchandise. Historically, ground freight forwarders have handled consumer durable goods such as clothing, sporting equipment, and appliances.

LEGAL DEFINITIONS OF CARRIERS

Private carriers. Some shippers may decide to provide their own transportation—**private carriers**—rather than using other carriers. Private carriers (company-owned transportation equipment) normally cannot haul goods for other firms, since they are not in the transportation business. When customized operations are necessary or special equipment is required, private ownership may be the only solution to a company's problem. Generally, however, an economical operation requires that shipment be limited to a relatively few destinations and that volume be sufficient to justify the costs of private carriage. Better control, reliability of delivery, and rate increases by public carriers have stimulated greater utilization of private ownership.

Common carriers. At the other extreme is the **common carrier.** Common carriers offer to transport goods for hire without discrimination among shippers. Rates are published and are identical for the same quantities and types of freight among all shippers. Common carriers are highly regulated, resulting in a complex array of regulations, operating routes, and time schedules.

The number of common carriers—there are over 17,500 regulated motor carriers, for example—means that flexibility and availability of service are very high. This is often a powerful incentive for shippers to use common carriers rather than establishing their own fleets. Partially loaded trucks, empty back-hauls, and uneconomical routing have long been the nemesis of private carriers.

Contract carriers. **Contract carriers,** a third type of legal carrier, limit their service to one or a few shippers. Contract times may range from a few months to several years. If goods are moved across state lines, the contract carrier is subject to many of the same regulations that govern common carriers. Some shippers prefer contract carriers because they gain most of the advantages of private carriage without the costs of equipment ownership.

Exempt carriers. **Exempt carriers** need only conform to the licensing and safety laws of the states in which they operate. Exempt carriage had its origin in agriculture, in which unprocessed farm products could be hauled to major processing centers under certain exemptions. Today such exemptions cover many product categories, as well as certain geographic regions (usually around metropolitan areas). For example, it would be almost impossible to "keep up" administratively with all local delivery trucks in a big city.

Logistics management

We have seen how logistics can help increase profits through better cost control and how good distribution can provide a high level of customer service that will lead to repeat business. We have also examined some key logistics functions. Now we face the question of how to put it all together to make distribution work. It isn't easy.

EVOLUTION OF DISTRIBUTION SYSTEMS

Bernard LaLonde, a logistics expert, has identified three stages in the evolution of distribution systems: primary integration, functional integration, and total integration. They are described as follows:

1. *Primary integration.* The integration of traffic and warehousing, usually the first step in moving toward the logistics concept. These functions deal directly with the physical storage and movement of goods. In most companies, any reorganization at this level usually brings only small corporate "shock waves."
2. *Functional integration.* The second stage of integration: order processing and finished goods inventory management responsibility are integrated with traffic and warehousing. Also at this stage, the distribution interface with marketing, production, and data processing becomes much more prominent; the chief distribution executive will find his or her focus being shifted to external corporate rather than internal departmental affairs. The "systems approach" and the use of data processing in a systems context are typically characteristic of the departmental thrust.

3. *Total integration.* The third stage, total integration of the materials-flow system. Procurement, production planning, packaging, as well as other functions are added to plan and administer materials flow from raw materials acquisition to end user. This level of integration is obviously the most difficult to implement, since it extends the boundaries of the distribution function into areas traditionally restricted to the production and procurement function.

This level of integration is probably the most efficient method of achieving an optimum cost-service mix, but not all firms can or should regard this level of integration as a goal.[17] Most firms are still at the primary level, and many top executives are not satisfied with their logistics departments. But without a total commitment to a strong distribution organization, the logistical function is usually doomed to mediocrity.

THE LOGISTICS DEPARTMENT

If a commitment to the distribution concept is made, the resulting department will resemble the one shown in Figure 16.7. It should be noted that the role of logistics planning is given special attention in a fully integrated operation. The distribution-logistics department can pinpoint basic service-cost relationships for top management so that efficient service strategies can be developed. Top

◢ **FIGURE 16.7 A totally integrated logistics organization.**

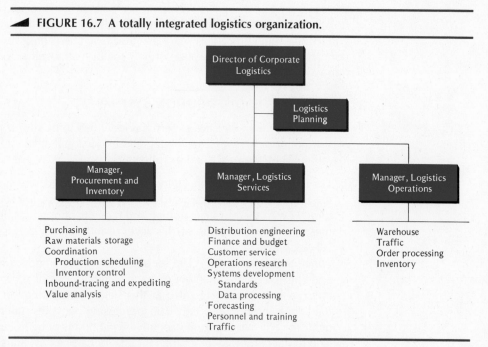

Source: Bernard LaLonde, "Strategies for Organizing Physical Distribution," *Transportation and Distribution Management,* January–February 1974, p. 24. Used by permission.

Chapter 16 LOGISTICS AND DISTRIBUTION MANAGEMENT

management needs guidelines that will tell it the cost of each element of customer service, and the cost impact of any increase or decrease in that service.

Trends in physical distribution

One important trend in distribution is the broadening of the scope, functions, and power of distribution/logistics managers. The need for better service and cost control in most companies will continue to amplify the importance of distribution. Distribution managers will begin to undertake periodic strategy audits to strengthen their departments. Questions such as the following will be asked: What levels of service do our customers expect? How do competitors achieve the service levels we think they achieve? Are our plants located and focused properly to support corporate strategy? What implications do technological and regulatory trends have for our company?

Changing transportation modes. The continued reliance on petroleum will cause a dramatic shift back to rail as the most common transporter of goods. Trucks will be used mostly for short hauls under 300 miles. Late in the 1980s batteries with better storage and charge characteristics will make electric intercity freight vehicles a reality. Piggyback freight (truck trailers carried on railroad flatcars) will increase dramatically, as well as the average railcar capacity tonnage.

Dominant role of the computer. Over 80 percent of America's manufacturers will use a computer in their distribution operations in the 1980s. Current applications are concentrated in accounting, inventory control, shipment routing, tracing, and carrier payments. More companies will begin using their computers for vehicle routing, shipment forecasting, warehouse modeling, and "what-if" type total distribution system simulations.

Shared services. Another trend is toward greater use of shared services. Increased use of freight forwarders, shippers' associations, and other freight consolidators exemplifies this trend. The growth of public warehousing and the establishment of national chains of public warehouses testify to the economies that may stem from sharing facilities and carriers. Tight money in this capital-intensive function is a further inducement for logistics managers to share services. Such sharing will occur in the areas of data processing, pallet exchanges, and freight bill payment systems.

New technology. New materials-handling technology will be developed as labor costs continue their upward climb. Energy-efficient conveyor systems, lifts, and protective packaging will further reduce the need for human cargo handling. These will be more automatic storage and retrieval systems, high-speed sorting systems, and item-picking machines.

The role of consumerism. Consumerism will create a demand for better handling to reduce the quantity of damaged merchandise. The importance of sanitation in distribution will also expand. Already several major food chains have been placed under criminal indictment as a result of insanitary conditions in their warehouses.

Some manufacturers are constructing systems for tracing and recalling everything they produce. This will present even greater challenges to logistics managers. Model numbers will no longer suffice — now it is often necessary to know the package number, the city where the item was sold, and to whom it was sold. All this recordkeeping will, of course, mean greater reliance on computers to keep the company from drowning in paper. It should also, however, lead to faster, safer, and better service.

SUMMARY

Logistics consists of two key areas: operations and coordination. Logistics is the process of strategically managing the movement and storage of material, parts, and finished inventory from suppliers, between enterprise facilities, and to customers. Logistical operation is the management of the movement and storage of enterprise material and finished products. Logistical coordination is the management of finished products and raw materials movement.

Operations can be segmented into three subareas: physical distribution management, materials management, and internal inventory transfer. Physical distribution consists of all business activities concerned with transporting finished inventory and/or raw material assortments so that they arrive at the designated place when needed and in usable condition. Materials management is concerned with finding sources of supply, acquiring raw materials to keep the product line rolling smoothly, and getting them at a reasonable cost. Internal inventory transfer is the control of semi-finished goods as they move through the various stages of manufacturing. The specific functions involved in coordination are product market forecasting, order processing, operational planning, and procurement.

The goal of physical distribution is to minimize total distribution costs relative to a predetermined level of service. Cost minimization alone can lead to disastrous results unless the impact on the quality of service is considered. The best measure of good distribution service is order cycle time — the elapsed time between the initial effort to place an order and the customer's receipt of that order in good condition.

In order to lower distribution costs, one must consider the interrelationships among many factors, such as finished goods inventory, number of warehouses, fixed warehouse expenses, and transportation costs. Sometimes, for example, the high cost of air transportation is offset by the reduction in the number of warehouses needed and in inventory requirements.

Some key functions of logistics include determining warehouse location and type of warehouse, establishing a materials-handling system, maintaining an inventory control system, establishing procedures for processing orders, and selecting modes of transportation.

Small shipment carriers concentrate on deliveries of lightweight, high-value items overnight. Freight forwarders collect less-than-carload shipments from a number of shippers and consolidate them into carload lots.

Several types of legal carriers exist to serve shippers. There are private carriers that do not haul goods for other firms; common carriers that offer to transport goods for hire without discriminating among shippers; contract carriers that limit their services to one or a few shippers; and exempt carriers that conform only to the laws of the states in which they operate. The many types of carriers and vast array of products carried have led to an extremely complex set of freight rates and regulations.

Logistics departments and distribution systems tend to evolve over time from primary to functional integration, and ultimately to total integration. Most firms are still at the primary level.

In the future, we will see better logistics organization, and many logistics managers will begin to undertake periodic strategy audits to strengthen their departments. There will be a changing emphasis on modes of transportation, as shippers revert to those that are more energy efficient. The computer will play a dominant role throughout the 1980s in virtually all aspects of logistics, including modeling and "what if" type distribution system stimulation. Shared services, new technology, and the consumer's demand for better handling to reduce damage will also be evident during the 1980s.

KEY TERMS

Logistics
Logistical operations
Logistical coordination
Physical distribution
Materials management
Internal inventory transfer
Critical path method (CPM)
Order cycle time
Public warehouse
Distribution center
Flow-through concept

Containerization
Economic order quantity (EOQ)
Ordering cost
Carrying cost
Reorder point (ROP)
Freight forwarder
Private carrier
Common carrier
Contract carrier
Exempt carrier

REVIEW QUESTIONS

1. What factors are included in the logistics concept?
2. What are the distinctions between operations and coordination?
3. State the sequence of tasks included in coordination.
4. What is meant by economic order quantity? State the formula and identify the costs comprising the firm's ordering costs and carrying costs.
5. What are the underlying assumptions of the EOQ model?
6. Name several of the institutions that facilitate physical distribution. Why have they achieved market acceptance and what functions do they perform?
7. What factors should a distribution/logistics manager take into consideration when evaluating transportation alternatives?

DISCUSSION QUESTIONS

1. What is the overall objective of distribution management? What service policies must be established?
2. Discuss the relationship between total distribution costs and customer service. How does a firm select an optimal level of service? What factors are considered?

3. Why would a company elect to use a public warehouse over its own distribution facilities?
4. How do companies determine the correct amount of safety stock? In your opinion, should this level remain constant throughout the year? Explain fully.
5. What is the purpose of the EOQ model? How can this general concept be applied to other areas of distribution policy?
6. Why do costs tend to rise as the length of the order cycle is shortened?

NOTES

1. "Now the King-Cola Challenge," *Sales and Marketing Management,* November 1978, pp. 22–24. Reprinted by permission from Sales & Marketing Management magazine. Copyright 1978.
2. This section is taken from Donald F. Bowersox, *Logistical Management,* 2nd ed. (New York: Macmillan, 1978), pp. 12–16.
3. Ronald H. Ballon, *Basic Business Logistics* (Englewood Cliffs, N.J.: Prentice-Hall, 1978), pp. 58–59.
4. "Distribution Can Greatly Boost Productivity," *Distribution Worldwide,* January 1979, pp. 39–40.
5. "Customer Service . . . Its People, Product and Policies," *Industrial Distribution,* May 1978, p. 59.
6. The terms in this paragraph are taken from William Perreault and Frederick Russ, "Physical Distribution Service in Industrial Purchase Decisions," *Journal of Marketing* 38 (April 1976): 3–10; see also their "Physical Distribution Service: A Neglected Aspect of Marketing Management," *MSU Business Topics,* summer 1974, pp. 37–45.
7. Ibid.
8. Donald Bowersox, "Physical Distribution Development, Current Status, and Potential," *Journal of Marketing* 33 (January 1969): 63–70.
9. Marjorie Person and Diane Mitchell, "Distribution Centers: The Fort Wayne Experience," *Business Horizons* 18 (August 1975): 89–95. Copyright 1975 by the Foundation for the School of Business at Indiana University. Reprinted by permission.
10. From Vincent Gallagher, "Distributing Line," *Transportation and Distribution Management,* May–June 1974, pp. 50–51; used by permission. See also Arthur M. Geoffrion, "Better Distribution Planning with Computer Models," *Harvard Business Review* 54 (July–August, 1976): 92–99.
11. "Efficiency Key to Distribution Center Success," *Handling and Shipping,* March 1978, pp. 70–71. Used by permission.
12. "Material Handling for Distribution," *Handling and Shipping,* January 1976, p. 39.
13. Kenneth B. Ackerman and Bernard T. LaLonde, "Making Warehousing More Efficient," *Harvard Business Review* 58 (March–April 1980): p. 95.
14. Jacob Merriwether, Gunnary Sletmo, and Orville Goodin, "Distribution Efficiency and Worldwide Productivity," *Columbia Journal of World Business,* winter 1974, p. 90.
15. C. G. Chentnik, "Inventory: Controlling Its Costs," *Transportation and Distribution Management,* May–June 1976, p. 23. Reprinted by permission.
16. D. B. Moritz, "Cut Costs by Controlling Inventory Level," *Supervisory Management,* September 1975 (New York: AMACOM, a division of American Management Associations, 1975), p. 19.
17. Bernard LaLonde, "Strategies for Organizing Physical Distribution," *Transportation and Distribution Management,* January–February 1974, pp. 21–25.

16.1 Indiana Quality Manufacturing

Indiana Quality Manufacturing is broken down into two divisions. The high-voltage group produces sophisticated high-voltage switch gear and other protective devices essential for dependable power transmission and distribution. The electronic hardware group produces small electrical items, such as switches and outlets used by home builders and do-it-yourselfers.

At this time, inventories in the high-voltage group are controlled by managers of the sales regions, who report to the vice-president of marketing. The electronic hardware group is headquartered in Bloomington. Production management handles procurement and customer service. The plant is naturally devoted to mass production and bulk shipments. The smaller, less than truckload, orders have second priority. At present, the electronic hardware group's salesforce is requesting its own warehouse. To complicate matters further, inventory costs have increased dramatically in the past five years.

There are 220 items produced or assembled at the Bloomington plant. Inventory stock of some merchandise amounts to well over a year's supply. For fast-moving items, it is not uncommon to run completely out of inventory once every six or eight weeks. It then usually takes a week to two weeks to replenish this supply, depending upon the production cycle. The inventory is currently controlled by a manual card system.

1. Recommend a logistics organization structure for the corporation.
2. How might the firm gain better control over its inventories?
3. What would be the advantages of moving to a computerized system?

16.2 Klip Klean, Inc.

Klip Klean was started in 1962 as a lawnmower repair service by two brothers. Over the years, the business grew and the brothers began repairing chainsaws and snowmobiles as well as lawnmowers. Their next move was to acquire a Lawn-boy and Toro franchise. This proved to be a wise decision. In 1980, Klip Klean sold over 3000 lawn mowers from three locations.

Bob Moore, one of the founding brothers, acts as the company bookkeeper and purchasing agent. He is in the process of reordering his single most popular mower, the RX-421. His records reveal the following:

Units of RX-421 sold in last 12 months	450
Ordering cost per order	$32
Unit cost	$81
Carrying cost	24% per year
Safety stock	10 units
Order lead time	40 days

1. How many units should Bob order? Why?
2. What is the reorder point? Why?
3. What additional factors should Bob consider before reordering?

Kingsley Humidifier*

Humidifiers are usually purchased by consumers for health reasons, for comfort, or to reduce home maintenance costs. Consumers have become exceedingly health conscious in recent years. The sale of vitamins and health foods has been soaring. Consequently, Edward Kingsley, an engineer by profession and an inventor by avocation, decided that a new type of humidifier was needed that would not be a large or noticeable piece of furniture, or require constant attention.

The Kingsley humidifier operates from any hot water source and can be located anywhere in the room. The humidifier is 3 feet in length and designed to fit behind a baseboard heating covering, thereby occupying an inconspicuous space. The hot water supply line provides heated water for the trough, eliminating the necessity of constant hauling of water for refilling. A drain and overflow pipe is provided for cleaning and emergency situations.

The selling price of the Kingsley humidifier ranges from $70 to $200 per unit for semi-automatic and fully automatic systems. The customer can install the system, and maintenance is negligible. The market potential would include not only homeowners, but builders and contractors, government agencies, designers, architects, and engineers. The product, with some modification and enlargement, could also be sold to the commercial and industrial field.

Edward Kingsley made an appointment with a national chain store organization so that their executives could see the product. The executives were pleased with the product, but negotiations broke down when they wanted to see a sales record for the humidifier. Kingsley was advised that the product needed to be test-marketed in a pilot city before it could be considered further. Kingsley had only limited financial resources, and high expenses were anticipated. The national chain did make Kingsley an offer to purchase all rights to the humidifier, but Kingsley declined because the offer was too low.

It was at this point that Kingsley contacted the college where he received his engineering degree and was referred to the senior marketing professor. They both agreed that a preliminary study of the market was necessary, and the professor was engaged to conduct a market research survey. The professor pointed out that it would not be possible to survey multiple markets simultaneously. Kingsley believed that the consumer market might be the most lucrative and therefore preferred to have this market studied first. The survey was designed to answer the following quesions: (1) Is there a need for the product? (2) Is the product the best of its type? (3) What is the attitude of consumers toward the product? (4) Are there any buying habits that would have an impact on the distribution of the product? (5) What would be the best channels for distribution? The survey was to be taken among consumers who already owned a humidifier or planned to buy one. The questionnaire that was used is shown in Figure 1.

A total of 120 households was included in the survey. Six interviewers were employed, and each interviewed 20 households. Households that neither owned

---

* Case prepared by Professor Ronald D. Michman, Shippensburg State College, Shippensburg, Pennsylvania.

PLEASE MARK AN X OR COMPLETE THE APPROPRIATE BLANKS AS INDICATED:

1. Do you have a humidifier in your home?

    1. Yes   2. No

2. Are you interested in buying a humidifier in the near future?

    1. Yes   2. No

3. Would you have any objections to having a permanent humidifier hooked to your hot water supply or heating system, if the humidifier and its hookup were inconspicuous? This is in lieu of a portable or furnace type installation.

    1. Yes   2. No

If not, why not? _____

_____

4. Do you use a consumer check for performance certification, seals of approval, recommendations, ratings, guarantees, etc., when purchasing items?

    1. Yes   2. No

5. How much effect on your decision to purchase do the above items have?

    1. None   3. Considerable
    2. Some   4. Will only purchase this way

FOR THOSE WHO HAVE HUMIDIFIERS IN THEIR HOME:

6. The type of humidifier you presently own is:
    1. A portable   3. Other (please specify) _____
    2. Furnace-attached
                             _____

7. The type of humidifier you presently own is:
    1. Automatic   3. Manual
    2. Semi-automatic

8. In what type of store did you purchase your humidifier?
    1. Department store   4. Hardware store
    2. Discount house   5. Plumbing and heating supply
    3. Mail order   6. Other (please specify) _____
                             _____

9. Where did you first come in contact with the humidifier you purchased?
    1. Home show   4. Mail order catalog
    2. Neighbor   5. Local supplier
    3. Magazine ad   6. Other (please specify) _____
                             _____

                             _____

10. What is the brand or make of your humidifier?
    1. Arvin   5. Sunbeam
    2. General Electric   6. Wards
    3. Presto   7. Westinghouse
    4. Sears   8. Other (please specify)

11. Approximately how old is your present humidifier?
    1. Under 3 years   3. 6–10 years
    2. 3–5 years   4. Over 10 years

12. The capacity of your humidifier is:
     1. Under 6 gallons   3. 10 or more gallons
     2. 6–9 gallons   4. Don't know

13. In which room is your humidifier placed most of the time?
     1. Living room   4. Dining room
     2. Bedroom area   5. Recreation room
     3. Kitchen   6. Other (please specify) ————————
     ————————————————————————————————————

14. Why did you purchase your humidifier?
     1. Health reasons
     2. Comfort
     3. To reduce home maintenance costs
     4. All of the above
     5. Other (please specify) ————————————————

15. What was the price range of your present humidifier?
     1. Under $30   4. $90–119
     2. $30–59   5. Over $120
     3. $60–89

16. The problem with your present humidifier (if any) is:
     1. Noisy   4. Awkward piece of furniture
     2. Must be filled   5. No problem
        manually   6. Other (please specify) ———————————
     3. Not efficient

17. What reason or reasons caused you to go to the dealer you purchased your humidifier
    from? (If more than one, please rank in order of importance.)
     1. Previous dealings with dealer
     2. Contacted by salesman
     3. Just shopping around
     4. Reputation of dealer
     5. Dealer location
     6. Dealer advertising
     7. Dealer service
     8. Replacement
     9. Other (please specify) ————————————————

18. Did you visit other dealers before buying your humidifier?
     1. Yes   3. Don't remember
     2. No
    If yes, what caused you not to buy from them?
     1. Price terms
     2. Poor job of selling by salesmen
     3. Product itself, certain features
     4. Manufacturer of product
     5. Service department
     6. Other (please specify) ————————————————

FOR THOSE INTERESTED IN BUYING A HUMIDIFIER:

19. Why are you interested in purchasing a humidifier?
     1. Health reasons
     2. Comfort
     3. Reduce home maintenance costs
     4. All of the above
     5. Other (please specify) ————————————————

20. Where do you think that you would be most likely to purchase a humidifier?
    1. Department store   4. Hardware store
    2. Discount house   5. Plumbing and heating supply
    3. Mail order   6. Other (please specify) _____
                                 _____

21. What type of humidifier are you interested in buying?
    1. Portable   3. Other (please specify) _____
    2. Furnace attached   _____

22. What price would you consider paying for a humidifier?
    1. $60–$89   3. $120 or over
    2. $90–$119   4. Don't know

23. Do you prefer any special brand?
    1. Yes   3. Undecided
    2. No
    If yes, which brand? _____

24. What feature do you want on the humidifier?
    1. Automatic   3. Manual
    2. Semi-automatic   4. Don't know

25. Who would you consult before buying a humidifier?
    1. Family and friends   4. Plumbing and heating supply
    2. Newspaper or other   5. Other (please specify) _____
       advertising   _____
    3. Retail salesman

TO BE ANSWERED BY ALL:

26. Please look at the picture of the Kingsley humidifier. If the price and terms are compara-
    ble to name brand humidifiers, would you be interested in buying the Kingsley?
    1. Yes   2. No
    Why or why not? _____
    _____
    _____

                                                            THANK YOU

or were not interested in buying a humidifier in the future were eliminated. It was
believed that in this phase of exploratory research it was necessary to question
consumers who had some knowledge of the product type. The interviewers' work
was validated through a random sample of telephone calls to respondents.

A few limitations to this survey were reported. (1) Respondents were shown pictures of the Kingsley humidifier and its principles of operation were then explained to them. However, respondents were unable to see the product itself. (2)
Only final consumers were included in this survey. No attempt was made to contact contractors, hospitals, industrial distributors, or other commercial establishments that could use the product. (3) The survey was conducted in an upstate
New York community of approximately 100,000 population, with a trading area of
250,000, and may not necessarily be representative of areas in which humidifiers
are purchased in great quantities.

In the upstate New York community, such brands as Sears and General Electric appeared popular, but a particular brand did not have a commanding share of the market. Other brands that were reported purchased in this survey were Hankscraft, Lennox, Presto, Arvin, Sterling, Sunbeam, and Westinghouse. The prestige of the seller or the confidence the consumer had in the seller at point of purchase was the most important buying motive. Consequently, while such reasons as health, comfort, and reduction of home maintenance costs were important motivations, patronage was also important in the decision-making process.

Aside from manufacturing a new product, distribution is probably one of the most difficult aspects of launching a new product. About half of the respondents included in the survey purchased their humidifiers from a department store (see Figure 2). Among those consumers who already owned a humidifier, about 20 percent had purchased it at a discount store, and another 20 percent at a plumbing and heating supply store. The others had purchased their humidifiers by mail order, at hardware stores, or at trade shows. Approximately 80 of the respondents desired a portable, automatic humidifier. The balance of the respondents owned or desired a furnace-attached humidifier.

The high percentage of consumers purchasing or wanting to purchase a humidifier through a department store might indicate that department stores have a reputation for service and making adjustments should the merchandise warrant it. The upstate New York area did have a Sears and other department stores with good reputations for product quality.

Consumer interest in purchasing the humidifier at a discount store probably reflects the desire to purchase this product on the basis of price. Since brand does not appear to be a strong factor in the purchase decision, a relatively unknown brand might be purchased provided the price was reasonable.

The interest in the plumbing and heating supply stores in Figure 2 might reflect

◢ FIGURE 2 Channels of distribution, Kingsley humidifier.

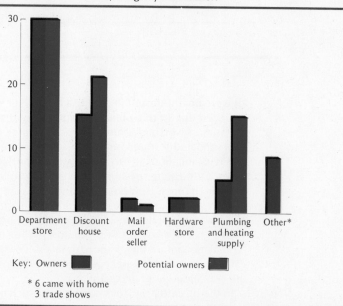

Chapter 16 LOGISTICS AND DISTRIBUTION MANAGEMENT

the sentiment on the part of consumers that expertise might be needed and that sales personnel in discount and department stores might not have this expertise. Some consumers might also believe that the humidifiers sold in plumbing and heating supply stores are of quality that is unknown to them but definitely known to the retailer.

A great variety of communication vehicles were specified by the respondents as influential in the buying process, but no one source predominated. Word-of-mouth from family and friends and newspaper advertising were among the leading sources of information. The need for credibility is necessary in selling this type of product. At least half the respondents desired some measure of performance certification. Therefore, certification from a bureau of standards or a good writeup in *Consumer Reports* would be helpful in marketing the product. Many consumers found the constant manual filling of their humidifiers to be a burdensome chore. Others complained that their humidifiers were noisy. Since the Kingsley humidifier can operate automatically and is not noisy, these were viewed as positive competitive features.

The price that respondents have already paid for their humidifier or are willing to pay is in accord with the price of the Kingsley humidifier. Since Kingsley is not a well-known brand, the price should be below national brands or much higher. A lower or higher price for the Kingsley would establish the brand in specific markets.

1. Analyze the questionnaire in Figure 1. Would you have included any other questions?
2. Which channels of distribution should be selected to market the Kingsley humidifier?
3. What other considerations should Kingsley be advised about in formulating a marketing strategy?

PART Six

Promotion concepts

17

Marketing communication: promotion strategies

OBJECTIVES

To develop a basic understanding of the communication process.

To identify the various goals of promotion.

To understand the approaches and basic forms of promotion.

To analyze the role of the hierarchy of effects concept in the promotional blend.

To develop an awareness of the factors that affect the promotional mix.

To understand the steps involved in the development and implementation of the promotional plan.

As business meetings replace lunch-hour browsing on the working woman's calendar, retailers find themselves facing a new, more sophisticated and a more demanding consumer.

With the change in American lifestyle, Spiegel faced the question: "How do you get the contemporary woman to buy from the same 'mail-order house' that mom and pop used?"

Spiegel answered by changing its merchandise, seeking new sources and emphasizing well-known and prestigious brand names.

To support the new marketing mix, Spiegel had to communicate their changes to the target market.

The initial advertising had two objectives: To get a copy of the new catalog in the hands of the right women; and to develop Spiegel's new image in the marketplace as an upscale, fashion-oriented, nonstore retailer. Further, Spiegel decided that these objectives could best be accomplished in two phases.

Since most of its customers are women, the target audience was easy to define. In the first phase of the campaign, Spiegel aimed at a broad group of women, using such general circulation magazines as *Woman's Day* and *Family Circle*.

During the second phase of the campaign, which ran from 1977 through 1980, Spiegel used full-page magazine inserts that emphasized the convenience of catalog shopping. For $3, Spiegel offered its catalog and a $3 merchandise certificate good toward the first purchase. Each insert carried a coupon and reply device to aid response.

Results were fine, but additional market research resulted in Spiegel's recasting its copy platform for phase two of the campaign.

Spiegel narrowed its target audience to include only the more affluent working woman.

This meant moving the advertising out of the more general women's magazines and into more targeted women's magazines. By using *The New Yorker, Vogue, Harper's Bazaar, Cosmopolitan* and *House Beautiful*, Spiegel felt it would not only deliver its message to the "right" women, but reinforce its position as a prestige retailer as well.

This, in turn, meant changing its copy platform dramatically. Instead of emphasizing convenient, stay-at-home, leisurely shopping, Spiegel's new ads emphasized fashion, style and quality.

The graphics and photography in the new ads are also designed primarily to promote Spiegel's "department store-in-print" image.

No longer will the ads depict a woman on the telephone with a catalog in her lap or silhouetted photographs floating in space — instead, the ads' high quality, mood-setting photography says "fashion."[1]

The Spiegel story illustrates the importance of promotion to a firm. Without a good promotion strategy, the target audience might have slowly (or rapidly) drifted away. The new Spiegel promotion campaign promises that the firm is just as contemporary as today's working women.

What is promotion and how does it fit into the overall communications process? What are the goals of a promotional program? What factors influence how much is spent on advertising in comparison to other means of promotion? How does one develop a promotional plan? All these questions are considered in this chapter.

What is the communication process?

When a company develops a new product, changes an old one, or simply wants to increase sales of an existing product or service, it must transmit its selling messages to potential customers. Let us begin by examining the basic process of communication and its relationship to promotion.

Communication is a process by which meanings such as feelings, attitudes, and emotions, are exchanged between individuals through a common system of symbols. It may be divided into two major categories. **Explicit communication** involves the use of language to establish common understandings among people. The second category, **implicit communication,** involves "intuitive interpretation" of the "relatively unconscious symbolisms of gesture and the unconscious assimilation of the ideas and behavior of one's own culture." Implicit communication can add meaning to explicit communication in three ways.[2] First is the amplifier phenomenon, in which nonverbal communication supports, modifies, or emphasizes the meanings of explicit communication. Some examples of high- and low-status and positive and negative forms of nonverbal communication are shown in Table 17.1. If I ask you how you are going to do on the next marketing exam you might say, "I'm going to make an A." If you look at the floor, shuffle your feet, and bite your lower lip, you have modified (negated?) your explicit communication. On the other hand, if you look me in the eye, bang my desk, and tell me you're going to make an A, you have reinforced your explicit communication. A second phenomenon of implicit communication is the unintentional display effect. Sometimes nonverbal actions will tell more about your attitudes, emotions, and feelings than what you say. The third phenomenon is the consistency factor. It involves the matching of a person's explicit and implicit communications to discover the sincerity or depth of a message. We have probably all used the consistency factor when we

TABLE 17.1   Selected Forms of Nonverbal Communication

Mouth region	Droop	Caress
Broad smile	Wink	Rub
Wry smile	Stare	Pick
Grin	Widen	Fumble
Mouth corners tremble	Tears	Tap
Mouth corners back		Digit suck
Intentional bite	**Gaze direction**	Cover eyes
Lip up	Look at	Beat
Sneer	Look away	Hand on neck
Biting lips	Look down	Arm over face
Lower lip out	Look up	Clap
Open mouth	Look around	Pound
Spit		Palms up
Kiss	**Other facial**	Fist
Chew	Grimace	Grasp
Tongue between lips	Twitch	Hands behind back
Tongue out	Sweat	Punch
Lick	Facial reddening	
Lower lip trembles		**Lower limbs**
Yawn	**Head movement**	Cross legs
	Chin out	Shuffle
Eyebrows	Head to side	Tap floor
Raise	Nod	Leg tremor
Angry frown	Shake	Swing
Sad frown	Chin in	
	Hang	**Trunk**
Eyelids and eyes		Slope
Shut	**Hands and arms**	Crouch
Blink	Shrug	Punch
Narrow eyes	Sit on hands	
	Scratch	

are told "I love you" by someone we care about. In marketing, this factor is applied when evaluating a salesperson's message.

Communication requires a common understanding, which in turn requires overlapping frames of reference. If you said "Let's go eat at the golden arches" to a person from the Soviet Union, it is doubtful that meaning would be shared. Since McDonald's is unknown in the Soviet Union, the visitor would not understand your frame of reference. The act of communication would be even more difficult if our foreign friend could not speak English. We sometimes miscommunicate because of subtleties of meaning. Differences in age, social class, or ethnicity also often lead to lack of understanding.

If a communication is going to affect a person, he or she must care about what is being said. In advertising, for example, the marketing manager needs to understand the audience and its motivations and attitudes in order to communicate effectively. If it is determined that the audience has little interest or involvement in the factor being communicated, the advertiser probably will not accomplish its objectives. For example, many people feel the United States does not really face an energy crisis. There has been low personal involvement with the concept. Others failed to accept or believe that there was a significant relationship between fuel consumption and speed of driving. Another large segment simply felt that slowing down was not worth the cost of lost time. As a result, the 55 mph speed limit promotion campaign met with almost complete failure.

THE COMMUNICATIONS FLOW

Communication consists of five components. These are (1) the source, (2) encoding, (3) the transmission channel, (4) reception, and (5) decoding (see Figure 17.1). Note that the overlapping circles imply a common frame of reference — the necessary ingredient for understanding.

The **source** is the originator of the message. It may be a person or an organization. In the 55 mph campaign, government was the source. **Encoding** requires the conversion of the source's ideas and thoughts into message form. As I write this material I am encoding my thoughts, just as I would if we were engaged in a two-way conversation. If the source happened to be a business trying to sell a good or service, the firm might rely on an advertising agency to act as an encoder. The 55 mph advertising campaign, for example, was developed by an advertising agency acting as an encoder.

Transmission of a message requires a channel such as a voice, radio, newspaper, or any other communication medium. A changed facial expression can also serve as a channel. **Reception** occurs when the message is detected by the receiver and enters his or her frame of reference. Reception is normally high in a two-way conversation. But the message of mass communication may or may not be detected by the desired receivers; it is a shotgun approach. For example, some members of the desired audience (those driving over 55 mph) may be watching a certain TV program, and others almost certainly will not be. Reception may be hindered by noise. **Noise** is anything that interferes with, distorts, or slows down the transmission of information. Competing ads can be a source of noise. News stories in a newspaper may be noise preventing reception of a newspaper advertisement. A child playing in a room where adults are watching television can be an obvious form of noise.

Decoding involves interpretation of the language and symbols sent by the source through a channel. Again, without common understanding and overlapping frames of reference, the message will not be understood. Just because a message is received does not mean that it will be properly decoded. If you see

◢ **FIGURE 17.1 The basic communication process.**

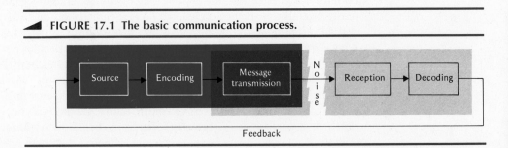

an advertisement written in Chinese, you cannot decode it unless you read Chinese. Face-to-face communication also involves **feedback.** Feedback to the source may be verbal, as in "I agree," or nonverbal, as in a nod, smile, frown, or gesture. A mass communicator is cut off from direct feedback and must rely on market research or sales trends for indirect feedback.

THE INFORMATION TRANSFER PROCESS

The application of behavioral science techniques to the study of communication has enabled scholars (and marketers) to understand the total information transfer process much more clearly. Involved in the process are perception, learning, and persuasion.

Communication and perception. Perception theory provides important insights into the nature of communication. People tend to organize their conscious perception of the environment in terms of the highest available level of organization. For example, when a person looks at a refrigerator, he or she does not view it as a combination of sheet metal, insulation, tubing, and a motor, but as a refrigerator. Organized perception has led to advertising campaigns such as this one for Salem cigarettes: "You can take Salem out of the country, but you can't take the country out of Salem." This jingle was played one and a half times; on the second round, the silence after "You can take Salem out of the country, but . . ." invited the listener to complete the message mentally.

Perception is also selective. People cannot possibly perceive every stimulus in their environment. One study showed that of all the promotions to which consumers are subjected every day, only between 70 and 80 are perceived out of 1,500 to 2,000 messages per day.[3]

The color of an advertisment, the familiarity of a brand, the contrast in a picture, movement, intensity (such as increased volume), and of course the message itself influence perception. A recent study in which individuals were told that a drink would taste sweet found that these people were more likely to perceive the drink to be sweet than people who were not exposed to the test. The next step for a beverage bottler would be to determine the importance of sweetness to the target market.

Communication and learning. Learning, like perception, is an integral part of communication theory. We may subdivide learning into two types: intentional learning and incidental learning. A person who intends to learn is more perceptive of message content than a person who happens to learn while engaged in another activity. Promotional learning is almost always incidental to entertainment, but a person searching for a good or service may actively utilize various media for intentional learning. For example, one of my students recently purchased a new Panasonic stereo system. He told me he read every newspaper ad, brochure, and hi-fi magazine advertisement for stereo systems that he could get his hands on for approximately a two-month period prior to purchase.

After learning takes place, we begin to forget almost immediately. Losses from memory are very great at first, and then slowly level out. The greater the complexity and length of the message communicated, the greater the amount of repetition necessary to produce retention. Noise or interference may increase forgetting—for example, competing messages may increase the time necessary to produce retention.

As we all know, promotional repetition can sometimes be carried to an extreme. The message may become boring, and thus reduce perception and learning. Unfortunately, research has not produced a magic number that, if exceeded, will hinder the learning process. But we can draw some conclusions about retention:

1. Retention increases with repetition. However: (a) repetition distributed over several periods leads to greater retention than repetition concentrated in a single period; (b) variation in form, style and expression during repetition, together with repetition of main points, may result in greater retention than repetition of the identical message; (c) the greater the complexity and length of the message, the greater the amount of repetition necessary to produce retention; and (d) the greater the interference from competing messages, the greater the amount of repetition necessary to produce retention.
2. More meaningful or more vivid material is better retained than less meaningful or less vivid material.
3. The more completely material is initially learned, the greater is retention.
4. Material presented first (primacy) or last (recency) is better retained than material presented in the middle.[4]

Communication and persuasion. In order to be persuaded by a given message, consumers must first receive the message and then comprehend it. After that they must yield to it; that is, change their attitudes accordingly. If marketers are interested in changing long-run behavior patterns, the receiver must also retain the information. Finally and (usually) most important, the receiver must act or take a position based on the new attitude. This is **persuasion.** For example, the March of Dimes may have convinced us that birth defects are bad, yet the organization has not achieved its goals until young people take positive action to prevent birth defects.

Research on persuasive communication has taught us several things. For example, overemphasis on yielding (getting someone to give in to your position) can be a serious error.[5] Persuadability tends to increase with intelligence and education. Although more intelligent people are more resistant to persuasion, their increased attention to and comprehension of the message make them more vulnerable. It has also been determined that males low in self-esteem or self-confidence are more readily persuaded than males high in self-esteem. This finding has not typically held for females. Individuals of low self-confidence—with regard, for example, to buying clothes—are more readily persuaded by friends or a salesclerk than individuals with high self-confidence. This finding typically holds for both males and females.[6]

Many research dollars are expended trying to determine if a person has credibility with an audience. For example, STP Corporation undertook an exhaustive search to find "the right" spokesperson for their gasoline additive. The person who purchases STP seemed to have difficulty identifying with and believing the run-of-the-mill superstar. Robert Blake was finally determined to be the person to whom the target audience could best relate. He made more money from some of the commercials than from several episodes of *Baretta*.

The goals of promotion

The STP Corporation obviously established some specific goals and then set out to accomplish them in a logical fashion. Let us examine the goals of promotion in more detail. People communicate for many reasons. They seek amusement, ask help, give help or instructions, provide information, and express ideas and thoughts. Promotion, on the other hand (see Figure 17.2), seeks to (1) modify behavior and thoughts (get you to drink Pepsi rather than Coke) or (2) reinforce existing behavior (get you to continue to drink Pepsi once you have converted). The source (the seller) hopes to create a favorable image for itself (institutional promotion) or to motivate purchases of the company's goods and services.

PROMOTIONAL TASKS

All promotions have the tasks of informing, persuading, or reminding the target market about the firm's offerings. Often a company will attempt to accomplish several of these tasks simultaneously.

Informing. Informative promotion is generally more prevalent during the early stages of the product life cycle. It is a necessary ingredient for increasing

◢ **FIGURE 17.2 Promotional goals and tasks.**

primary demand. People typically will not purchase a good or service until they know what it will do and how it may benefit them. Consumerists and social critics generally applaud the informative function of promotion, since it aids the consumer in making more intelligent purchase decisions. An example of informative promotion is presented below.

Milton Bradley, which claims to have the largest R&D department in the toy industry, had two successful electronic entries on the market as early as 1977: Electronic Battleship and Comp IV. But it burst into prominence in the 1978 Christmas season, when it introduced Simon, a flying-saucer-shaped game that challenges players to duplicate its increasingly complex sequences of lights and sounds. Response was so overwhelming that the company could not meet demand because of the shortage of microprocessor chips, which are the heart of the electronic products. Even so, Bradley probably sold close to two million Simons during 1979.

George Ditomassi, Senior VP Marketing, says that when Bradley moved into electronics, ''we made sure our advertising and marketing were better than anything we'd ever done. Because of the prices of the games [retail range: $35–$60], we had to tell consumers what they did. Otherwise, consumers wouldn't think they were worth the price.'' The advertising budget, which was $22.5 million in 1978, was about $27 million in 1979. Also, when Simon was introduced, management recognized its potential appeal to adults as well as children, and organized an introductory party for dealers, distributors, and salespeople at New York City's Studio 54 (in the days before its notoriety). In the months that followed, sales of Simon took off beyond the company's wildest—and fondest—expectations.[7]

Persuading. Persuasive promotion is not viewed in a favorable light by many consumerists. Yet most promotions attempt to persuade because persuasion is a legitimate and logical tool to accomplish promotional goals. Persuasive promotion is designed to stimulate purchase. Often the firm is not attempting to obtain an immediate response, but rather to create a positive image in order to influence long-term buyer behavior. Persuasion normally becomes the primary promotion goal when the product enters the growth stage of the product life cycle (see Figure 17.3).

Reminding. Reminder promotion is used to keep the product brand name in the public's mind and is prevalent during the maturity stage of the life cycle. Coca-Cola, Pepsi-Cola, Bell Telephone, and the FTD florist association use large amounts of reminder promotion. This form of promotion tacitly assumes that the target audience has already been persuaded of the merits of the good or service. It simply serves as a memory jogger (see Figure 17.4).

Source: Courtesy of Foodway National Inc.

SPECIFIC OBJECTIVES

The tasks of informing, persuading, or reminding serve as general guidelines for promotional campaigns and strategies. However, they are not sufficient for measuring the results of promotion. Russel Colley has developed a technique known as DAGMAR—Defining Advertising Goals, Measuring Advertising Results—that is predicated upon lucid advertising (or promotion) objectives. Colley writes:

Advertising's job purely and simply is to communicate, to a defined audience, information and a frame-of-mind that stimulates action. Advertising succeeds or fails, depending on how well it communicates the desired information and attitudes to the right people at the right time and at the right cost.[8]

You loved it as a kid.
You trust it as a mother. Kool-Aid.

Source: Reproduced with permission of General Foods Corporation, © 1981.

In order to be measurable, goals should be defined in the following manner:

1. To increase brand awareness among 21- to 30-year-old males with two or more years of college by 10 percent between November 15 and April 1.
2. To obtain a 5 percent increase in retail distribution in all southwestern communities with populations over 5000 by June 15.

These objectives are precise, quantified, and measurable, and have a specific time frame. Marketing research can be used to determine whether or not the first goal was achieved. A syndicated audit service such as the National Retail Tracking Index or Neilsen reports may be purchased to evaluate the second objective. Firms like General Motors, Shell Oil, Exxon, and Rockwell-Standard all use the DAGMAR approach in setting and measuring promotional goals.

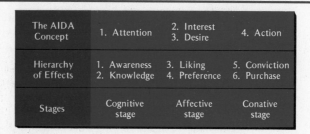

The AIDA Concept	1. Attention	2. Interest 3. Desire	4. Action
Hierarchy of Effects	1. Awareness 2. Knowledge	3. Liking 4. Preference	5. Conviction 6. Purchase
Stages	Cognitive stage	Affective stage	Conative stage

AIDA AND THE HIERARCHY OF EFFECTS

The objectives of promotion require the target comsumer to pass through a series of stages that lead to purchase behavior (see Figure 17.5). The first stage is **cognitive** — this is when a message is received and interpreted. The second stage is **affective** and requires the formulation of a positive product image. The final, **conative** stage consists of motivation and purchase.

E. K. Strong developed the AIDA (Attention–Interest–Desire–Action) concept in 1925. First, the marketing manager obtains a person's attention by means of a greeting and approach (personal selling) or loud volume, unusual contrasts, bold headlines, movement, bright colors, and so forth (mass media). Next, a good sales presentation or promotional copy creates interest in the product. Illustrating how the product's features will satisfy the consumer's needs creates desire. Finally, a special offer or simply a strong closing sales pitch may be used to obtain purchase action. The hierarchy of effects theory is basically an updated version of the AIDA concept.

The three-stage approach to purchase behavior suggests that promotional effectiveness can be measured in terms of people moving from one stage to the next. Certainly there cannot be conviction without knowledge or knowledge without awareness. Also, measuring the effectiveness of promotion at various stages avoids the problem of directly relating promotion and sales. One early study failed to confirm that movement from one stage to another increases the probability of purchase.[9] However, more recent studies have proved more promising. A Sears, Roebuck project found positive relationships between advertising recall and purchase intention. Sears also found a positive relationship between purchase intention and actual purchase.[10] Another study found that awareness exists before attitude change and that intention to purchase exists before purchase.[11]

The promotional mix

Rarely will a single communication resource be the most effective means of accomplishing the firm's promotional objectives. Instead, a blend of various factors must be used to reach the target market. That blend is called the **promotional mix.** The four major tools that make up a promotional mix are these:

1. *Advertising.* Any paid form of nonpersonal presentation and promotion of ideas, goods, or services by an identified sponsor.
2. *Personal selling.* Oral, face-to-face presentation in a conversation with one or more prospective purchasers for the purpose of making sales.
3. *Sales promotion.* Marketing activities, other than personal selling, advertising, and publicity, that stimulate consumer purchasing and dealer effectiveness, such as displays, shows and exhibitions, demonstrations, and various nonrecurrent selling efforts not in the ordinary routine.
4. *Public relations.* The marketing function that evaluates public attitudes, identifies the policies and procedures of an individual or an organization with the public interest, and executes a program of action to earn public understanding and acceptance.

The role of promotion in the total marketing mix is shown in Figure 17.6 (some experts include packaging, since it can serve as a means of communication).

ADVERTISING

Advertising is a form of impersonal one-way mass communication. It may be transmitted by many different media, including television, radio, newspapers, magazines, books, direct mail, billboards, and transit cards. Since advertising lacks a direct feedback mechanism, it cannot adapt as easily as personal selling to the changing preferences, individual differences, and personal goals of the consumers.

Advertising has two main decision areas: (1) determining the message to be

---

◢ **FIGURE 17.6 Promotion as a component of a master marketing strategy.**

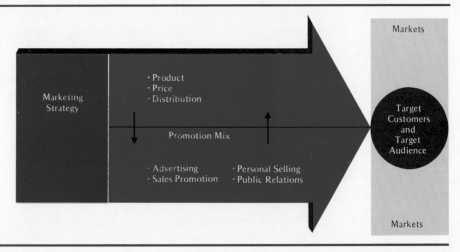

transmitted to the target market, and (2) selecting the media. Neither choice is easy, and both involve a number of different dimensions. We will examine these in detail in Chapter 18.

PERSONAL SELLING

Advertising dollars are spent primarily on the promotion of consumer goods, whereas **personal selling** is more prevalent in the industrial goods field. Industrial products are less homogeneous and often do not lend themselves to mass promotions. Instead, many products must be tailored to the needs and financial status of the buyer. In order to design and sell a custom-made product, rapid buyer feedback is necessary. Thus personal selling must be used rather than advertising. The role of advertising may be to create general buyer awareness and interest through advertisements in trade media. Print media advertising often includes coupons soliciting the potential customer to "fill this out for more detailed information." In this manner advertising can be used to locate potential customers for the salesforce.

Effective sales presentations are not cheap. The cost of face-to-face selling of industrial goods climbed to over $80 per sales call in 1980. Weekly lodging, auto rental, and meal expenses were $552 in 1980. And this figure does not include the salesperson's compensation.[12]

SALES PROMOTION

Sales promotion is a catchall category that consists of all promotions other than personal selling and advertising (see Figure 17.7). The following list includes many of the tools used in sales promotion:

Trial-size bottles and cans	Tours
Free samples	Point-of-purchase displays
Coupons	Contests
Trading stamps	Free use of products in movies
Catalogs	Cents-off packages
Directories	Cash refund offers
Badges	Gifts for secretaries and
Decals	executives
Premiums and giveaways	Calendars
Demonstrations	Packages with secondary uses
Trade shows	Toll-free numbers
Free films	

A major promotion campaign may involve the use of several sales promotion tools as well as advertising and personal selling. Sales promotion is generally a short-run tool used to stimulate immediate increases in demand. Research shows that sales promotion complements advertising by yielding faster responses in terms of sales. Promotions appeal to the consumer looking for a

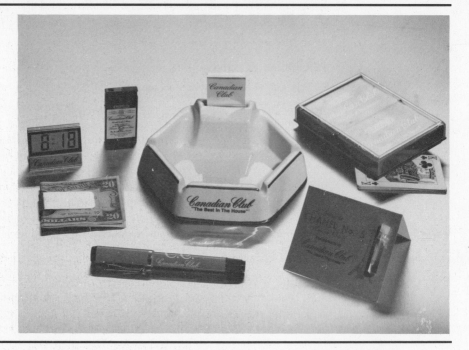

Source: Courtesy of Hiram Walker Incorporated.

deal, who often sees all products as equal or is willing to sacrifice quality for price.

PUBLIC RELATIONS

Corporations are concerned about their public images and often spend large sums of money to build a positive consumer image. Too many firms have found that a negative industry and/or company image often leads to new and restrictive governmental legislation. Automobiles, toys, and cereals are three prime examples.

Publicity is public information about a company, product, or service that is not directly paid for or placed in commercial media. While good publicity is expensive, bad publicity is often free. When a firm pollutes a stream, produces a defective product, has executives who are engaged in payoffs or bribes, or becomes involved in other undesirable acts, the world hears about it through the mass media. Bad publicity can often be avoided by conducting a social responsibility audit. The audit examines company activities that are socially desirable and those that have potential for negative publicity. With good **public relations,** management can take the offensive and eliminate sources of potential trouble before they occur.

THE HIERARCHY OF EFFECTS AND THE PROMOTIONAL MIX

Figure 17.8 depicts a general relationship between the promotional mix and the hierarchy of effects model. Advertising seems to be most effective in the awareness/knowledge stage of the hierarchy model. This is not to say that advertising does not have an impact in the latter stages, but in general its greatest thrust is in creating awareness and knowledge about goods or services. Personal selling reaches fewer people initially, but once the salesperson enters the picture, he or she is more effective at developing preferences for merchandise and gaining conviction.

A good sales promotion campaign can create awareness of a new product. The classic example is the creation of the Bloody Mary for the then new Smirnoff Vodka. It also can create strong purchase intent. For example, Stanley Tools stocked 1800 of its best retail accounts with supplies of its ten best-selling tools. Each had a special Lake Placid Olympics tag. Purchasers could return the tag and $2 and receive a cap bearing the Winter Olympics and Stanley logos. The sales promotion created $17 million in additional sales during winter months, when most "do-it-yourselfers" are in hibernation.

Public relations has its greatest impact in creating awareness about a company, good, or service. As I mentioned before, this knowledge can be good or bad. Many air travelers tended to avoid the DC 10 after the plane crash in Chicago in the late 1970s. Good publicity, on the other hand, can aid in developing a preference for a product or service. Coca-Cola, for example, sponsors the Special Olympics, its first major private philanthropic activity. Coke's sponsorship is designed to create a good image of the firm and its products in the minds of the consumer and potential consumer.

◀ FIGURE 17.8 The hierarchy of effects model and the promotional blend.

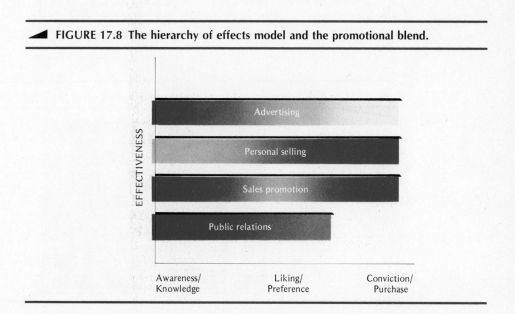

Factors that affect the promotional mix

Promotional blends vary significantly from one product and industry to the next. Figure 17.9 illustrates this differential emphasis for advertising and personal selling. Normally, these two resources are the primary product and service promotional tools and are, in turn, supported and supplemented by sales promotion. Public relations aids in developing a positive image for the organization and the product line.

The promotional blend depends upon the following factors: the nature of the product, market characteristics, available funds, push and pull strategies, and the stage of the product life cycle. Each of these factors will be discussed below (see Figure 17.10).

THE NATURE OF THE PRODUCT

Research has identified the relative importance of several facets of the promotional mix.[13] Personal selling is most important in industrial goods and least important in consumer nondurables (mostly convenience goods). Broadcast advertising is used heavily in consumer goods promotion, particularly for nondurables. Print media, on the other hand, are employed for all three product categories. Industrial goods are advertised primarily through special trade magazines. Consumer goods, in contrast, are advertised through newspapers and various consumer-oriented magazines. Sales promotion, branding, and packaging are approximately twice as important for consumer goods as for industrial goods.

Industrial goods. Producers of industrial goods, with the exception of supply items, tend to rely more heavily on personal selling than on advertising. Consumer goods, on the other hand, are promoted primarily through advertis-

◀ **FIGURE 17.9 Promotional blends that are dependent upon the nature of the product.**

High Advertising Low Personal Selling	Many specialty and convenience goods Cereals Liquor and beer Cheaper lawn mowers	Computers Control devices Automobiles Many shopping goods Better wines	High Advertising High Personal Selling
Low Advertising Low Personal Selling	Many farm products and convenience goods Pocket combs Bobby pins Nails	Many industrial goods Industrial equipment Paper specialty items	Low Advertising High Personal Selling

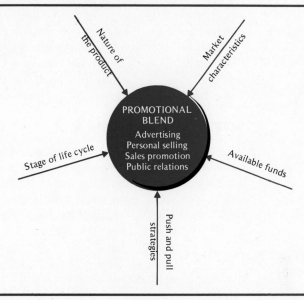

Nature of the product

Market characteristics

PROMOTIONAL BLEND
Advertising
Personal selling
Sales promotion
Public relations

Stage of life cycle

Available funds

Push and pull strategies

ing. Persuasive personal selling is also important at the retail level for shopping goods such as automobiles and appliances. Informative personal selling is common in better furniture stores and with specialty goods, as well as for industrial installations, accessories, and component parts and materials.

Convenience goods. Convenience goods and supply items, such as pencils and soft drinks, are usually simple to understand and use. Moreover, these products are not custom-made and do not require a company representative to tailor them to the user's needs. Attractive displays and brand familiarity advertising are often all that is required for effective promotion.

Level of social risk. Convenience goods and industrial supplies are not products of great social importance—they are not indicative of social position. We do not experience much social risk in the purchase of a loaf of bread or a bar of candy. Quite the opposite is true in the purchase of some shopping goods and many specialty goods such as jewelry and clothing. Many consumers depend upon sales personnel for guidance and advice in making the "proper" choice.

Cost. Items that are a relatively small part of a firm's budget (supply items) or a consumer's budget (convenience goods) do not require a salesperson to "close the sale." In fact, inexpensive items cannot support the cost of a salesperson's time and effort unless the potential volume is high. Expensive, complex machinery, new buildings, cars, and new homes represent a considerable investment to both businesses and consumers. Assurances must be forthcoming from a salesperson that the funds are being spent wisely and that the buyer is getting the best value for the money.

Distinguishable features. Products with easily distinguishable features, including automobiles, business aircraft, and forklift trucks, use advertising to reinforce their differences. Personal selling meshes with advertising to further differentiate a specific brand and actually close the sale.

Other products with few distinguishing characteristics like many pain remedies, soft drinks, milk, and other convenience goods use advertising to build a product image and create psychological distinctions among brands. These items, however, do not depend upon personal selling at the retail level.

MARKET CHARACTERISTICS

Widely scattered potential customers, highly informed buyers, and a large number of brand-loyal repeat purchasers generally require a blend of more advertising and sales promotion and less personal selling. Sometimes personal selling is required even when buyers are well informed and geographically dispersed. Industrial installations and component parts may be sold to extremely competent individuals with extensive education and work experience. Yet the salesperson must still be present to explain the product and work out the details of the purchase agreement. Often firms sell goods and services in markets where potential customers are difficult to locate. Advertising is used to locate potential customers by inviting the reader to "call collect" for more information or "fill out the coupon" for a detailed brochure. Salespeople are sent to the potential customers as the calls or coupons are received.

Another market characteristic that may dictate the use of salespeople depends on whether physical stocking of merchandise (detailing) is traditional for a product class. Milk, bread, and other convenience goods, for example, are generally stocked by the person who makes the delivery. This practice is becoming increasingly common in the convenience good field as sellers strive to ensure attractive display and adequate shelf space for their wares.

AVAILABLE FUNDS

Money, or the lack of it, may easily be the most important factor in determining the promotional blend. A small, undercapitalized manufacturer may rely heavily on free publicity if its product is unique. If the situation warrants a salesforce, the financially strained firm may turn to manufacturers' agents who work on a commission basis, with no advances or expense accounts. Even smaller, well-capitalized organizations may not be able to afford the advertising rates of publications such as *Better Homes and Gardens, Reader's Digest,* or *The Wall Street Journal.* The price of a single advertisement in these media could often support a salesperson for a year.

If potential buyers are easily identified, direct mail with color brochures may be an efficient alternative to print media advertising. Although a smaller audience will be reached with direct mail, a good mailing list will enable the firm to reach a higher ratio of potential buyers. For example, if a firm that manufactures luggage advertises a travel case in *Business Week,* it may reach 25 individuals per 1000 who are in the market for such a product. A mailing list comprised of people who have bought luggage through the mail in the past six months might contain 75 potential customers per 1000.

When promotional funds are adequate to optimize a promotional blend, the firm should continue to promote until the marginal promotional dollar cost is equal to the marginal revenue received from promotion. Also, it has been held that the firm should set up its promotional blend so the cost per message received by the audience divided by the cost of the promotional tool is the same for all tools in the blend. In other words, where

MR_a = the number of people who received the message via tool A
MC_a = cost of tool A

and

$$\frac{MR_A}{MC_A} = \frac{MR_B}{MC_B} \cdots \frac{MR_0}{MC_0}$$

If, for example, promotion tool A, a large sales promotion display, reaches 10,000 individuals who read and understand a firm's message at a cost of $5,000, then the cost per receiver is $0.50. If tool B, an ad in a regional magazine, reached 15,000 people at a cost of $9,000, the cost per receiver would be $0.60. Therefore funds should be shifted from B to A.

Before you read on, let me point out several key flaws in this concept. First, if tools A and B are reaching different audiences, you would lose 15,000 potential receivers by shifting out of B. Furthermore, additional expenditure on A may reach very few new receivers. Second, sometimes a blend of all four tools is necessary to create a proper image and sell a product. Each has its own unique function in the blend, even though one may cost more than the other. Often one medium reinforces another. Advertising, for example, can create company and product awareness prior to a salesperson's call. Research has shown that industrial advertising which builds a firm's reputation enhances the probability of a salesperson making a sale.[14]

PUSH-AND-PULL STRATEGIES

The use of aggressive personal selling and trade advertising by the manufacturer to convince a wholesaler and/or retailer to carry its merchandise is known as a **pushing strategy.** The wholesaler, in turn, must often "push" the merchandise forward by persuading the retailer to handle the goods. The retailer then uses advertising, displays, and other forms of promotion to convince the consumer to buy the "pushed" products.

At the other extreme is a **pulling strategy** to obtain product distribution. Rather than attempting to sell to the wholesaler, the manufacturer focuses its promotional efforts on the final consumer. As consumers begin demanding the product, the retailer orders the merchandise from the wholesaler. As the wholesaler is confronted with rising demand, it places an order for the "pulled" merchandise with the manufacturer. Thus, stimulating final consumer demand pulls the product down through the channel of distribution. Heavy sampling, introductory consumer advertising, cents-off campaigns, and couponing are indications of a pulling strategy. In contrast, a pushing strategy relies more on extensive personal selling to channel members and trade advertising. Rarely does a company use a pulling or pushing strategy exclusively. Instead, the mix of the two will lean in one direction or the other. Tradition, salesforce availability, and type of product all play an influential role in determining whether a product is pushed or pulled.

Push-and-pull strategies are not limited to new products. If a mature product is not reaching its full potential, an aggressive pushing or pulling strategy may be undertaken. An example of aggressive pulling strategy is presented below.

Folger's had a goal of obtaining 15 percent of the East Coast market for ground roast coffee.

Folger's weakest performance is in the coffee-loving New York area—the nation's biggest single market—where it had held a mere 6.9 percent share.

Procter and Gamble, Folger's parent company, decided to offer consumers a "rich" coupon—that is, one really offering a hefty discount.

Folger's coupon would certainly seem to qualify for that adjective. It was worth 45 cents a can, and it wasn't buried on the back pages of the newspapers or in one of those messy direct-mail envelopes that are stuffed with script for dozens of different products. This coupon went out in its own mass mailing to millions of consumers—to 70 percent of the six million households in the New York area, for example. P&G figured that about 40 percent of the New York coupons would be redeemed at the stores.[15]

As an epilog to the Folger's pulling-strategy story, it should be noted that the massive campaign failed. The 45 cents offer was not big enough to induce a significant rate of trial.

STAGE OF THE LIFE CYCLE

The stage of the product life cycle can also be an important determinant of a product's promotional blend. Any new product promotion will be strongly influenced by the decision to push or pull to obtain distribution. If the product reaches the growth stage of the life cycle and obtains adequate distribution, the promotional blend may shift. Often a change is necessary because different types of individuals become a relevant part of the target market.

As noted in the discussion of diffusion of new products, innovators and early adopters differ significantly from the majority of adopters and late adopters. Late adopters are virtually immune to promotion and depend almost solely on word-of-mouth advertising. Thus, the promotion blend in the later stages of the life cycle might switch more to personal selling in the channel to maintain adequate distribution and various sales promotion techniques to stimulate repeat purchases and top-of-the-mind awareness among potential late buyers.

Further complicating the situation is the fact that different media exhibit varying degrees of effectiveness in reaching innovators and early adopters.[16] Radio and television often do not provide concentrations of innovators. Magazines, as a group, are much more selective in their appeal to the consumer product innovator. For example, there seems to be a strong relationship between package food innovators and high women's magazine readership. The same is true for women's clothing and women's fashion magazines. Newspapers, although positively related to small and large appliance innovators, are so widely distributed that they preclude a substantial concentration of innovators.

Innovators often like to learn more about a product's features and its functions than later buyers, so they may require more personal attention (personal selling) than the early and late majority. The latter two groups tend to enter the market after the product leaves the growth stage of the life cycle. Late adopters often do not enter until maturity or even the decline stage of the life cycle.

Implementing the promotional plan

A promotional plan involves several distinct steps: (1) setting objectives, (2) identifying the target audience, (3) developing a budget, (4) choosing a message, (5) determining the promotional mix, (6) selecting the media mix, (7) managing the promotion, (8) measuring effectiveness, and (9) following up and modifying the promotion campaign (see Figure 17.11). Each step follows in a logical sequence, resulting in a promotion campaign that is geared to specific objectives.

◢ **FIGURE 17.11 The promotion plan.**

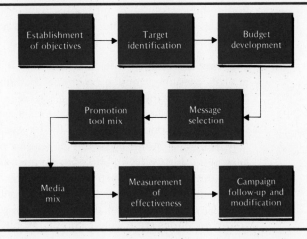

Several steps require the completion of an earlier task before they can be undertaken — for example, the setting of objectives should come before budget development. Others can occur simultaneously and, in fact, may occur in reverse order. This is particularly true of message selection, choice of promotional mix, and media selection.

Setting objectives. The need for specific, realistic objectives has already been discussed and needs little elaboration. It is the starting point for any promotional campaign. Indeed, it is impossible to plan a promotional program unless the marketing manager knows what goals he or she is trying to achieve.

A corollary to the establishment of specific objectives such as level of message awareness or number of sales completed as a percentage of sales calls made is the development of positioning goals. All four promotional tools must be developed and utilized in terms of a specific "positioning" goal for the good or service in question. Each tool, whether it is publicity, personal selling, advertising, or sales promotion, should aid in placing the good or service at a specific point on the positioning continuum for a specific target market. A woman's handbag premium offer would hardly aid in positioning Marlboro cigarettes.

Identifying the target audience. The market segment the firm wants to reach in a given promotional campaign should be explicitly defined both demographically and perhaps psychographically through market research. Naturally, the target audience should consist primarily of the individuals who are most likely to purchase the product within a relevant period. For a new product, in-home use tests, test marketing, and focus groups provide valuable insights into characteristics of potential buyers.

Developing a budget. After a marketing manager has specified the promotional goals and identified the relevant market segments, a concrete promotional budget can be developed. This is no simple task, nor is there a "cookbook approach" that will lead to an optimal promotional budget. Top-management decision making is usually required to define the role of promotion in the marketing mix. The importance of promotion is determined largely by things such as competitors' actions and type of product. Several budgeting methods will be discussed in Chapter 19 on advertising management.

Choosing a message. After promotional objectives have been created, target markets identified, and promotional budgets established, management can begin preparing the "right message" to reach the target. The nature of the message will vary, of course, depending on the goals of the promotion. If the product is in the introductory phase of the life cycle, product information will probably be the major message. More persuasive promotional themes are addressed later in the life cycle; in addition, an attempt may be made to communicate with "new" target audiences (the late majority).

Messages are channeled to consumers from a number of sources. Many messages leave a negative impression or no impression at all. Some promotional communications are boring or uninteresting, and the reception process is further complicated by the noise problem. Consumers are also selective in the message-receiving process and comprehend information selectively. Selective comprehension of messages has been found to cause:

1. Distortion and misinterpretation of appeals to make them consistent with attitudes.
2. Rejection of the source and message as being biased.
3. Communication of factual information but short-circuiting of the persuasive appeal.[17]

An example of the latter phenomenon occurs when a consumer might remember an appeal from the American Cancer Association to have a yearly checkup but forgets the persuasive communication to make a donation. In other words, the person remembers only the latter half of the slogan, "Fight cancer with a check and a checkup!"

Determining the promotional mix. Often different message themes are developed for each promotional tool. For example, public relations may be charged with creating a positive corporate image among target customers. Advertising will focus on developing corporate and product awareness to complement personal selling. The function of personal selling will be to interact with the customer by amplifying and explaining the advertising messages and designing the right product or service to meet the specific needs of the customer. Sales promotion may come into the picture by communicating a "special discount" to prospective buyers if they purchase now. Thus public relations, advertising, and sales promotion are all aimed toward increasing sales effectiveness.

A study of the promotion of 129 brands of 23 products in the utility, commodity, electronic, metalworking, and chemical industries revealed that advertising exposure increased positive buyer attitudes and sales response.[18] Dollar sales per sales call were much higher for customers who had been exposed to advertising before the sales call than for those who had not. Other research has shown that a positive company image increases the effectiveness of industrial salespeople.[19]

Selecting the media mix. The advertising media mix to be used in conjunction with the other three promotional tools will be discussed fully in Chapter 18. At this point you should know that different types of media tend to appeal to different audiences. Also, different specific media, such as country and western radio stations, will have different audiences than other specific media, such as stations playing only classical music.

Measuring effectiveness. It is incumbent on promotion managers to measure the effectiveness of their promotional campaigns. Since the effectiveness of various tools is measured quite differently, this concept will be discussed in detail in Chapter 18. Without some measurement of the outcome of promotional campaigns, there would be no way of determining whether objectives are being met.

Following up and modifying the promotion campaign. After measuring the outcome of a promotional endeavor, it may be necessary to change the promotion plan. Change often occurs in the promotional blend, the media mix, the message, the total promotional budget, or the way the budget is allocated.

Follow-up must also ask the question, What do we know now that we did not know before we began the promotional campaign? The firm should learn from its mistakes and ensure that policies are established so that the same mistake can be avoided in the future.[20]

SUMMARY

Communication can be explicit, or implicit. The communication process requires a common understanding, which necessitates overlapping frames of reference. It consists of five components: a source, encoding, a transmission channel, reception, and decoding. Reception may be hindered by noise—anything that interferes, distorts, or slows down the transmission of information.

Perception theory provides important insights into the nature of communication. People tend to organize their conscious perception of the environment in terms of the highest available level of organization. Perception is also selective.

Learning is an integral part of communication theory. Promotional learning is almost always incidental to entertainment. After learning something, we begin to forget almost immediately. Retention increases with repetition, meaningful material, and the order in which the message is presented.

In order to be persuaded by a message, consumers must first receive and then comprehend the message. Next, they must yield to it; that is, change their attitudes accordingly. Most important, the receiver must then act or take a position based on the new attitude.

The goal of promotion is to modify behavior or to reinforce existing behavior. This is accomplished through several promotional tasks: informing, persuading, and reminding. To accomplish promotional objectives, an advertisement must first procure the attention of the consumer. Second, it must increase or generate interest. Next, it should create a desire for the good or service. Finally, a purchase should result.

A blend of several forms of promotion is usually necessary. This is called the promotional mix. The four basic forms are advertising, personal selling, sales promotion, and public relations. The nature of the product, market characteristics, the funds available for promotion, the use of push or pull strategies, and the stage of the life cycle all affect the promotional blend.

A promotional blend begins with the establishment of objectives and the identification of target customers. Next, a budget is developed, a message chosen, and a promotional mix established. The media mix is then determined; promotional management is established; and effective measures are established and monitored. The process concludes with campaign follow-up and modifications where necessary.

KEY TERMS

Communication   Cognitive stage
Explicit communication   Affective stage

Implicit communication   Conative stage
Source   Promotional mix
Encoding   Advertising
Transmission   Personal selling
Reception   Sales promotion
Noise   Publicity
Decoding   Public relations
Feedback   Pushing strategy
Persuasion   Pulling strategy

REVIEW QUESTIONS

1. Explain the communication process. What is necessary for understanding between participants to occur?
2. For communication goals to be measurable, how should they be defined?
3. What is the ultimate goal of promotion? How is this related to the hierarchy of effects model?
4. Why does the promotional blend for a product change over time?
5. In what ways does the nature of the product influence the promotional blend?

DISCUSSION QUESTIONS

1. Why is an understanding of the learning process of vital importance to communication theory?
2. Explain the role of promotion in the marketing mix. Describe environments in which its role is lessened or heightened.
3. In your opinion, what promotional mix would be required to gain consumer acceptance of a new convenience item? How important is personal selling in this instance?
4. Why might a new consumer products company rely heavily on a pull strategy to gain retail distribution?
5. With regard to promotion, why is it important for marketers to understand their target market's awareness and predispositions toward the product?
6. Evaluate the role of personal selling for each of the following product classifications. What reasons support its use as a major or minor component of the communication process?
   a. Home video recorders.
   b. Laundry detergents.
   c. Aircraft guidance systems.
   d. Packaged food products.
   e. Photocopy machines.

NOTES

1. Edward J. Spiegel, "Spiegel," *Advertising Age,* December 22, 1980, pp. 28–29.
2. Thomas Bonoma and Leonard Felder, "Nonverbal Communication in Marketing: Toward a Communicational Analysis," *Journal of Marketing Research* 14 (May 1977): 170.
3. Beverlee B. Anderson and J. P. Culea, "The Influence of Information Cues on Expectations and Taste Perceptions," in Robert L. King (ed.), *Proceedings: Southern Marketing Association, 1973 Conference,* Virginia Polytechnic Institute and State University, pp. 98–101.

4. Thomas S. Robertson, *Consumer Behavior* (Glenview, Ill.: Scott, Foresman, 1970), pp. 28–29.

5. William J. McGuire, "Persuasion," in George A. Miller (ed.), *Communication, Language and Meaning* (New York: Basic Books, 1973), pp. 243–255.

6. Ivan Preston, "Inconsistency: A Persuasive Device," in *Dimensions in Communication,* eds. James H. Campbell and Hal W. Hepler (Belmont, Calif.: Wadsworth, 1965), p. 115.

7. "Milton Bradley—Simon Says It's a Winner," *Sales and Marketing Management,* January 14, 1980, pp. 18–19. Reprinted by permission from Sales & Marketing magazine. Copyright 1980.

8. Russell H. Colley, *Defining Advertising Goals* (New York: Association of National Advertisers, 1961), p. 21.

9. Kristian S. Palda, "The Hypothesis of a Hierarchy of Effects, A Partial Evaluation," *Journal of Marketing Research* 3 (February 1966): 13–24.

10. "G & R Research Links Recall, Buying Intent," *Advertising Age,* August 16, 1971, p. 3.

11. Terence O'Brien, "Stages of Consumer Decision Making," *Journal of Marketing Research* 8 (August 1971): 283–289.

12. Thayer C. Taylor, "Selling Costs Climb A Record 15.5%," *Sales and Marketing Management,* February 25, 1980, p. 10.

13. Jon G. Udell, "The Perceived Importance of the Elements of Strategy," *Journal of Marketing* 32 (January 1968): 34–40.

14. John E. Morrill, "Industrial Advertising Pays Off," *Harvard Business Review* 48 (March–April 1970): 4–14.

15. Hugh D. Menzies, "Why Folger's Is Getting Creamed Back East," *Fortune,* July 17, 1978, pp. 68–76. By permission.

16. John O. Summers, "Media Exposure Patterns of Consumer Innovators," *Journal of Marketing* 36 (January 1972): 46–47.

17. James F. Engle, Hugh G. Wells, and Martin R. Warshaw, *Promotional Strategy,* 3rd ed. (Homewood, Ill.: Irwin, 1975), pp. 69–70.

18. John E. Morrill, "Industrial Advertising Pays Off," *Harvard Business Review* 48 (March–April 1970): 4–14.

19. Theodore Levitt, *Industrial Purchasing Behavior: A Study of Communications Effects* (Boston: Harvard University, Graduate School of Business Administration, Division of Research, 1965).

20. Engle, Wells, and Warshaw, *Promotional Strategy,* p. 545.

◢ **CASES**

17.1 Cumberland Packing

Cumberland Packing, the producer of Sweet 'n' Low sugar substitute, has been searching for a way to diversify ever since it lost $1 million as a result of the cyclamate ban in 1969. In 1980, it felt it had come up with an answer to its new product needs. The company had tried gum, chocolates, soda, and desserts, among others, but had not been able to ease its dependence on Sweet 'n' Low. The new product is entitled Butter Buds, which are butter-flavored granules. The product is low-calorie, has low-cholesterol benefits, and its price (about $1 for a 4 ounce box that provides the flavor of 2 pounds of butter) is economical. A 4 ounce box has 384 calories, compared with 6,400 for an equivalent 2 pounds of butter or margarine. The cholesterol content is 25 mg compared with 2,240 in butter and zero in margarine.

The flavor granules are packaged in single-serving packets and are designed to be mixed with hot water as a flavoring for vegetables, pasta, fish, and so forth. Butter Buds cannot be used as a spread, or as a frying agent or for baking when the fat, as well as the flavor, is needed. The question at this point is how to devise a promotional strategy for the new product. It has many new attributes that will require extensive consumer education, and will also require explanation on how the product should be used.

The firm planned to spend about $4 million on promotion during the first year and expected sales of about $1 million. The president thinks it will take at least three years for Butter Buds to become a well-known product. The only other way to speed up the education process would be to license other large companies to use the Butter Buds patents. The patents are so strong that the firm does not expect competition any time soon and is not interested in licensing the product.

The plan has been to introduce the product in markets one at a time, since production can only be expanded relatively slowly. The president noted that as the firm goes into each new market, it has experienced difficulty in gaining shelf space in the supermarkets.

1. What promotional mix would you recommend for the company?
2. What are some of the product attributes the firm should stress?
3. How can the company overcome its distribution problems?

17.2 Dr. Pepper

Dr. Pepper was created by chemists who perfected a drink of 23 fruit flavors (no prunes) and began bottling it. By 1954, the beverage had attained a number eight position in the soft drink industry and enjoyed a significant degree of regional popularity. By 1970, Dr. Pepper was number seven in the soft drink business but was still marketed only in the South and Southwest. At this point, the firm set a goal of becoming number four nationwide. Dr. Pepper's first task was to become franchised nationwide. To do this, the firm utilized an aggressive "push" strategy. The parent sought to give (not sell) the franchises to the strongest bottler in each market area. By targeting franchises to the strongest bottlers in new markets, Dr. Pepper has tended to gain greater consumer acceptance and more sales, since strong bottlers can obtain more trucks and vending machine outlets.

The company operates incentive programs for bottlers to focus their energies on Dr. Pepper. Route salesmen who reach or exceed their sales quotas may get points. Accumulated points can be redeemed for prizes displayed in company catalogs. Bottlers who attain their marketing goals can send their personnel on various trips at Dr. Pepper's expense.

In keeping with the firm's desire to become the number four soft drink, it was decided that a unique product image had to be established. Coke spends five times as much on promotion as Dr. Pepper; thus the promotional campaign had to be very different in order to succeed. It also had to be well-coordinated with

Dr. Pepper's bottlers. Dr. Pepper's first major advertising theme from 1970 to 1973 was directed to bottlers as much as consumers. It said Dr. Pepper was "the most mis-understood soft drink" and went on to say "it's not a cola, not a root beer, it's something much much more." In 1974, the company's ad campaign underwent major changes. The new theme was "the most original soft drink ever in the whole wide world." Around the country, Dr. Pepper's franchise bottlers responded to the revamped advertising with great enthusiasm. By 1975, the company achieved its goal—Dr. Pepper replaced Royal Crown Cola as the number four soft drink. The company also began using many musicals in its advertising campaigns. Dr. Pepper soon set its sights on the number three soft drink position occupied by Seven-Up. Advertising and other promotions sought to generate trial of the drink by those who had never used it and retrial by those who had used it infrequently, and also tried to convert brand triers to brand users.

In 1977, ads began to emphasize people who drink Dr. Pepper regularly. This marked the beginning of the "be a Pepper" theme. Research indicates that consumer recall of "be a Pepper" ads is more than twice that of the average soft drink commercial. In addition, the theme has been expanded to a wide variety of items such as T-shirts, buttons and caps. In 1980, more than a million "Pepper" items were distributed. Other types of promotion include permanent display pieces, scoreboards, clocks, calendars, illuminated and nonilluminated signs, menus, and recipes using Dr. Pepper. It also supports activities of the North American Soccer League with the Soccer Pepper Youth Competition program and has developed a highly regarded soccer skills training film for coaches and players.

David Naughton, the Pied Piper of Dr. Pepper's "be a Pepper" campaign, has developed a national image. Dr. Pepper management refers to him as the "perfect composite Pepper." By early 1981, Dr. Pepper and Seven-Up were running neck and neck.

1. Comment on Dr. Pepper's promotional program through the years. Do you feel it could have become larger earlier in the company's history if it had undertaken a more aggressive campaign?
2. What additional promotional steps would you recommend to Dr. Pepper to help it overcome Seven-Up?
3. You are the promotional manager for Seven-Up. What promotional strategies would you recommend to slow down Dr. Pepper's momentum?

18

Advertising, sales promotion, and public relations

OBJECTIVES

To develop an appreciation of the importance of advertising.

To review the major types of advertising.

To develop an awareness of the factors considered in media selection.

To identify media characteristics and trends.

To examine the objectives, trends, forms, and problems of sales promotion.

To understand the role of public relations.

In the high-stake game of cigaret marketing, money can't buy everything. The country's largest tobacco company has learned that lesson the hard way.

R. J. Reynolds Tobacco Co. spent $40 million to introduce an "all natural" cigaret called Real. That was the most ever spent on a new brand of consumer packaged goods. The money went for some 130 boxcars of display materials, thousands of newspaper and magazine ads and 25 million sample packs of Reals that pretty girls handed out on street corners around the land.

Real still struck out; it managed to corral less than one-half of 1% of the U.S. cigaret market. After one final effort in early 1980 to revive Real, R. J. Reynolds seems to have decided to pull the plug. Although the company won't say that officially, rumors are widespread—and advertising spending has been slashed. "Real is to cigarets what the Titanic was to sailing," says a New York tobacco advertising executive.

Marketing has been deemed one of R. J. Reynolds' strong points. Why, then, a fiasco that tars the company's reputation and threatens to sour its customers on any new brands? Marketing men and securities analysts offer several explanations. One is that Real advertising failed to exploit the market turn to low-tar brands. The first Real ads didn't note that, at nine milligrams, Real was low in tar content. Another explanation lies in timing: Real went on the market toward the end of a flood of new-product entries—26 low-tar brands in 1977—by other cigaret companies. "Real just got lost in the shuffle," says Jane Gilday, a tobacco analyst at Faherty & Faherty Inc., New York.

R. J. Reynolds may have erred the most in calling Real "all natural." That, a marketing man for a competitor says, "might have appealed to health nuts and yogurt eaters, but they aren't the kind of people who smoke cigarets." After a year, R. J. Reynolds dropped the all-natural theme. Ads began to tout Real as "strong tasting." By then, however, retailers had had enough of Real.

All this occurred despite elaborate research. It took four years and more than $1 million to develop Real. R. J. Reynolds took dozens of consumer polls. More than 10,000 smokers were asked to try Reals, and one test showed smokers liked them better than Phillip Morris' enormously popular Merits. Indeed, when R. J. Reynolds introduced Real, executives predicted that it would become the next Winston or Marlboro. At a rock-bottom minimum, they said, it would get 1% of the cigaret market—and 1% of that market is worth some $100 million a year in revenues.[1]

507

Doesn't a huge advertising and promotion budget normally guarantee success? How much money does American industry spend on advertising? Who spends it and where? What advantages does one form of media have over another? Where do sales promotion and public relations fit into the picture?

Advertising, which many people consider the most glamorous function of marketing, grows in dollar volume each year. U.S. advertising expenditures were estimated at $49.8 billion in 1979.[2] But while advertising expenditures may seem large, the industry itself employs only approximately 500,000 people. This figure includes not only people who work in the advertising departments of manufacturers, wholesalers, and retailers, but also the employees of America's 5000 advertising agencies as well as the media (radio and television, magazines and newspapers, and direct mail firms).

People are often amazed at the magnitude of the advertising budgets of American firms. Procter & Gamble, for example, spends over $400 million on advertising a year. Approximately 30 additional companies spend over $100 million each per year. It is even more astounding when one realizes that these figures do not include the costs of sales promotion, personal selling, or public relations. They are larger than the budgets of all but a handful of American cities. Newspaper advertising attracts the largest single share of the advertising dollar, followed by television and direct mail (see Table 18.1). Let us see what all this money does.

What can advertising do?

Even though advertising has shown a tendency to grow steadily, in the long run it is not a panacea. Its impact on America's socioeconomic system has been subject to extensive debate by economists, marketers, sociologists, psychologists, politicians, professors, homemakers, consumerists, bureaucrats, and other assorted groups. With something like 1700 newspapers, 3000 magazines, 6000 AM–FM radio stations, 600 television stations, billions of pieces of direct mail, and thousands of billboards, advertising and promotion must have an impact on us. The question is, What is that impact? Perhaps the best approach to answering this question is to divide the answer into macro and micro components.

THE MACRO IMPACT

Effect on attitudes and values. Vance Packard, a popular writer on socioeconomic phenomena, claims that "there are large-scale efforts being made through advertising, often with impressive success, to channel our unthinking habits, our purchasing decisions, and our thought processes by the use of insights

TABLE 18.1 Advertising Volume in the United States, 1979 and 1980

Medium	1979 ($ millions)	Percentage of total	1980 ($ millions)	Percentage of total	Percentage change
Newspapers					
Total	14,493	29.3%	15,615	28.5%	+ 7.7
National	2,085	4.2	2,335	4.3	+12.0
Local	12,408	25.1	13,280	24.2	+ 7.0
Magazines					
Total	2,932	5.9	3,225	5.9	+10.0
Weeklies	1,327	2.7	1,440	2.6	+ 8.5
Women's	730	1.5	795	1.5	+ 9.0
Monthlies	875	1.7	990	1.8	+13.0
Farm publications	120	0.3	135	0.3	+12.0
Television					
Total	10,154	20.5	11,330	20.7	+11.6
Network	4,599	9.3	5,105	9.3	+11.0
Spot	2,873	5.8	3,260	6.0	+13.5
Local	2,682	5.4	2,965	5.4	+10.5
Radio					
Total	3,277	6.6	3,690	6.7	+12.6
Network	161	0.3	185	0.3	+15.0
Spot	659	1.3	750	1.4	+14.0
Local	2,457	5.0	2,755	5.0	+12.0
Direct mail	6,653	13.4	7,655	14.0	+15.0
Business publications	1,575	3.2	1,695	3.1	+ 7.5
Outdoor					
Total	540	1.1	610	1.1	+12.8
National	355	0.7	400	0.7	+13.0
Local	185	0.4	210	0.4	+12.5
Miscellaneous					
Total	9,776	19.7	10,795	19.7	+10.5
National	5,063	10.2	5,690	10.4	+12.4
Local	4,713	9.5	5,105	9.3	+ 8.3
Total					
National	27,075	54.7	30,435	55.6	+12.4
Local	22,445	45.3	24,315	44.4	+ 8.3
Grand total	49,520	100.0	54,750	100.0	+10.6

Source: "Fast Facts," *Advertising Age,* February 16, 1981, p. S-4. Copyright 1980 by Crain Communications, Inc. Reprinted with permission.

gleaned from psychiatry and the social sciences."[3] Although this claim sounds impressive, it is more fiction than fact.

An attitude that stems from an individual's basic value pattern (good or bad, right or wrong) and is strongly supported by his or her culture will be almost impossible to change through advertising. Advertising cannot change strongly held values and therefore cannot manipulate society against its will. All the advertising in the world is not going to convince Moslems to eat pork or Americans to eat horsemeat or to let elderly citizens starve to death.

Advertising can influence product and brand selection when a neutral or favorable frame of reference already exists. For example, Revlon can influence women to buy Charlie perfume through advertising because society perceives a pleasant body odor as a desirable trait. On the other hand, Revlon would find it difficult indeed to convince American women to purchase "the new Revlon nose ring" because our society does not view nose rings as acceptable jewelry.

But even though advertising cannot change strongly held values, critics point out that it does create a preoccupation with material goods and services. It is argued that advertising changes social priorities by encouraging expenditures in the private sector of the economy at the expense of public goods (better parks, highways, police departments, and so forth). In a similar fashion, antiadvertising forces claim that promotion persuades consumers to buy things they do not need instead of devoting a larger share of their productive labor and income to the accomplishment of social goals such as crime prevention, antilitter campaigns, clean air, and efficient public transportation.

On the other hand, advertising does reflect our own values, or it would not be effective. Although the critics may hold that advertising creates materialism, it is perhaps more accurate to say that advertising appeals to values which already exist. Even in the most primitive societies, people tend to adorn themselves with "objects of beauty" and accumulate possessions.

Economic consequences. Although advertising cannot reverse strongly held attitudes, economist John Kenneth Galbraith and others believe that advertisers "manage demand" and that this has negative economic consequences. To "manage demand" means that a firm can increase demand and/or its elasticity by spending large sums of money for advertising. The chain of logic leading to this conclusion is shown on the left side of Table 18.2. That is, advertising ultimately blocks other firms from entering an industry (barriers to entry), leading to market power for the firm and ultimately to higher prices. Jean-Jacques Lambin's research, also outlined in Table 18.2, generally refutes this contention.[4]

Higher prices as a consequence of advertising are typically illustrated through parity products. These are goods or services with the same basic characteristics, such as travel, aspirin, milk, and bleach:

The prototype illustration might come from a campaign for blended whiskey that ran some years ago. The advertising-agency copywriter on the account was simply unable to find a single good copy point to distinguish his client's product from any of its competitors. Having sought in vain for evidence of superiority, he came up with a slogan that the client loved that ran for years. It was persuasive without being in the least deceptive. The slogan was "If you can find a better whiskey, buy it."[5]

Do huge advertising expenditures lead to market power? Does the sheer weight of the advertising rather than the content become the prime determinant of market position? The answer to these questions has been the subject of extensive debate. Studies have, in fact, produced contradictory results.[6] If sheer

Steps in the advertising controversy	Assumed roles or effects of advertising	Observed roles or effects of advertising
1 Advertising	Large companies advertise in order to create a preference for their brands Consumers perceive real or apparent differences among brands and develop preferences	**Yes, but . . .** they also use advertising to perform communications tasks required by the market situation; large-scale advertising has no built-in advantage for the large companies, although a threshold level exists that may privilege the deep purse.
2 Consumer buying behavior	Preferences lead to brand loyalty, or consumer inertia, that constitutes a barrier to entry of new brands into the market	**Yes, but . . .** the advertising effect is modest in both absolute and relative value; consumers are less responsive to noninformational advertising
3 Barriers to entry	Protected brand positions reduce active rivalry and give the company more discretionary power	**Yes, but . . .** many other factors explain consumer inertia or loyalty; where consumer inertia is high, advertising intensity is not necessarily also high
4 Market power	Discretionary power allows the company to ignore more tangible forms of competition (price and product quality) and lets it charge higher prices Higher prices result in high profits that furnish incentive to continue advertising	**No . . .** we observed no basic incompability between the presence of intensive advertising in a market and the degree to which that market exhibits active rivalry **but . . .** advertising escalation does not benefit the consumer as does a price war or a technological race
5 Market conduct		**No . . .** consumer responsiveness to price and product quality remains high in advertising-intensive markets; a company may react to rival advertising by advertising, price, or even quality adjustments
6 Market performance		**Yes . . .** advertising increases the capacity of the company to charge higher prices to the consumer **but . . .** no continuous association is observed between market concentration and advertising intensity; sales maximization under profit constraints seems to be the company's objective, although long-term profitability is likely for several brands

Source: Jean-Jacques Lambin, "What Is the Real Impact of Advertising?" *Harvard Business Review,* May–June 1975, p. 145. Copyright © 1975 by the President and Fellows of Harvard College; all rights reserved.

▲ TABLE 18.3   Slogan Identification and Advertising Expenditures

Brand	Percentage correctly identifying slogan	Start of current slogan promotion	Total advertising since start of current slogan promotion
Charmin	82%	Jan. 1968	$ 36,802,000
Alka-Seltzer	79	Jan. 1976	11,730,000
Chiffon	58	Jan. 1970	12,916,000
Morton's (salt)	57	Sep. 1914	42,873,000
Contac	55	Oct. 1972	44,498,000
Hertz	47	Sep. 1975	5,511,000
Ragu	45	Jan. 1973	16,490,000
Meow Mix	41	Dec. 1973	11,512,000
McDonald's	38	Apr. 1975	129,408,000
Dynamo	37	Feb. 1972	18,824,000
Aim	33	Nov. 1974	24,590,000
Schlitz	23	June 1976	9,470,000
Coca-Cola	16[a]	May 1976	31,148,000

[a] In addition, Coca-Cola's old slogan was correctly identified by 59 percent.

Source: Leo Bogart, "Is All This Advertising Necessary?" *Journal of Advertising Research* 18 (October 1978): 21. Reprinted by permission. © Copyright 1978, by the Advertising Research Foundation.

advertising volume is directly related to increased sales, it seems that advertising would first have to create product visibility through brand and slogan recall. If you are unaware of a product or its characteristics, you are unlikely to purchase it except on an impulse basis. Table 18.3 shows a range of slogan identification for major brands ranging from 16 percent to 82 percent.[7]

Quality. Firms advertise to accomplish a variety of goals in addition to brand identification. Generally, large-scale advertising makes sense only if the advertiser can expect repeat purchases. Heavy advertising normally implies that the seller is counting on acceptance and repeat business. Naturally, consumers will buy a product again only if it meets their expectations. Thus it is apparent that the advertiser has built some quality into the product. If it were of poor quality, the advertiser would not expect repeat purchases. This is one reason why the words "nationally advertised" are prominently shown on many displays and packages. In a sense, the seller is assuring the purchaser of product quality.

Economic growth. Not only does advertising induce the production of quality merchandise; it also stimulates economic growth. Sales that take place due to persuasion, informative, and reminder advertising give management a more rapid return on its investment. A faster return stimulates more investment, which in turn creates economic growth. Economic growth means more jobs creating more demand and a higher standard of living for everyone. Indeed, advertising has been called "the engine of growth."

MICRO EFFECTS

So far we have examined how advertising affects society as a whole and economic activity in general. Now our attention will turn to the firm.

What can advertising do? In one case a German electric-shaver manufacturer tripled its advertising budget and doubled its market share while maintaining good product quality and keeping prices stable. In Belgium, Italy, and Denmark major gasoline marketers overspent on advertising with little improvement of market share. These and other examples often lead to quick conclusions regarding a firm's advertising. In the first example it seems that advertising had a strong positive effect on sales; the second example appears to have had the opposite effect.

Effect on sales. Studies have found that additional increments of advertising yield increasing sales returns, up to a point, in most situations.[8] It may, for example, force competing firms to raise their promotion budgets in order to maintain market share. Wendy's and Jack-in-the-Box have recently raised their advertising budgets in an attempt to regain profits and market share.

But although advertising is a powerful determinant of demand, it usually has less impact than environmental factors such as population and income.[9] On repeat purchases advertising is usually less important than product quality, distribution, and price.[10] In other words, long-run sales are predicated on a sound total marketing mix, not just advertising.

Impact on market share. Brands with a small market share tend to spend proportionately more for advertising than those with a larger market share.[11] This is probably due to two factors: (1) Beyond a certain volume of advertising expenditure, diminishing returns set in, causing firms with large market shares to hold back on advertising. (2) There is a minimum level of exposure needed for advertising to have a measurable effect on purchase habits. But that threshold varies from one product to another.

Other micro effects. Advertising helps increase the effectiveness of the salesforce. Advertising builds brand, product line, and company familiarity and thus makes the sales job easier. It also may lower a buyer's price resistance, thereby enabling the salesperson to close a sale that might otherwise not have been made. An advertisement cannot usually close a sale, whereas a personal call can.

With industrial products, many people are often involved in the purchase decision. But research has shown that an industrial salesperson typically only reaches three to four out of ten "influentials" (persons with purchasing influence). For example, of 40 firms that ship freight by air, American Airlines salespeople had *not* "called on" 28 out of the 40 in the previous three months; Emery did *not* call on 29 of them; TWA did *not* call on 37 out of the 40; and United did *not* call on 32 of these air freight customers in the preceding 90 days.[12] Advertising can communicate the existence of a product to the members of ad hoc buying committees, even when the salesperson does not know who or where they are.

The major types of advertising

Advertising goals are the major determinant of the type of advertising used by the firm (see Figure 18.1). If the goal is to build up the image of a product, service, company, or industry, the advertiser will use institutional advertising. When the objective is to sell a specific product, service, or cooperative mark, an advertiser will utilize product or institutional advertising.

INSTITUTIONAL ADVERTISING

Institutional advertising, in contrast to product advertising, is not always directed only to consumers of the company's products and services. Instead, it may be aimed at any of the various publics (stockholders, consumerists, legislators) that may have an impact on the firm. It is not product-oriented; rather, it is designed to enhance the image of the company. Institutional advertising usually asks for no action on the part of the audience beyond a favorable attitude toward the advertiser and its goods and services.

Advocacy advertising. One aspect of institutional advertising that is becoming more popular is **advocacy advertising.** The objective is to propagate ideas and advocate certain positions on controversial social and economic issues. Advocacy advertising has sometimes been referred to as grassroots lobbying. Many companies (particularly energy and resource firms) have felt that the press has not always accurately presented their views and actions on a number of issues. They also believe that many of the values upon which American business was founded—incentives, reward, profit—were being legislated out of existence. Thus they turned to advocacy advertising.

◀ **FIGURE 18.1 Types of advertising.**

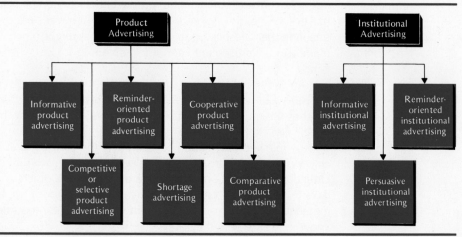

No. 5 in a series.

Who profits from Exxon's profits?

Millions of Americans. Perhaps you.

Exxon's profits are split two ways. So far this year, 42% of our profits have been paid out in the form of dividends on Exxon common stock. The remainder was retained by Exxon, primarily to help pay for new energy projects. You may benefit from both uses of our profits:

Dividends	Reinvested Profits
Millions of Americans have either a direct or indirect share in Exxon profits in the form of dividends. Beyond the 625,000 individuals who have a direct ownership in Exxon, there are 60,000 institutions such as pension funds, trust funds, colleges, foundations and insurance companies in which millions of people have a stake. In 1979, Exxon's total dividends will give our shareholders a return of about 7% on the current price of Exxon stock.	Over the past ten years, more than half of Exxon's profits have been reinvested in the business, primarily to develop new supplies of oil and natural gas, coal, uranium, solar power and synthetic fuels. But the amount we must spend on these projects far exceeds our profits. We make up the difference mainly by borrowing money and from money set-aside to replace worn-out facilities. So far in 1979, Exxon's investments in the energy business have been nearly 1½ times as large as our profits—investments that will help to supply energy to millions of consumers.

Toward a National Energy Policy

An Energy Manifesto

America needs a national energy policy. As last winter's crisis showed, our country is too dependent on foreign oil—expensive foreign oil. Too much of our money is draining abroad for the health of the U.S. dollar and the international monetary system. Money that would be better invested in the U.S.

Government agencies, Congressional committees, foundations, and other public and private groups are working on energy policy. We at Mobil feel we have an obligation to speak out on this subject.

We want to spell out today what we think the major emphases of a national energy policy should be. Later in this series, we shall discuss specific issues in more depth.

Here are the main points of our "energy manifesto":

• The nation's objective for the coming decade should be substantially greater energy self-sufficiency. This means increasing domestic production of conventional crude oil, natural gas, and coal. The resources are there. They must be developed.

• A return to a free market for oil and natural gas should be a near-term goal. This is the most immediate step our country can take to bring about greater energy self-sufficiency; there is no effective substitute for having incentives at the right level. We know of no better mechanism for fine-tuning incentives than the marketplace. If higher energy costs bear too hard on the poor, this can be ameliorated through tax relief or other means. But arbitrary and misguided controls that delay the development of additional supplies will only exacerbate the under-employment and other problems of the poor.

• Timetables on environmental objectives must be related to energy needs and other national priorities. There is no irreconcilable conflict between additional energy supplies and a cleaner environment.

• For the long term—by 1990 or thereabouts—we should aim for some surplus in domestic energy supplies, as the best guarantee of reasonable prices.

• To help minimize dependence on foreign oil, we must conserve energy by eliminating wasteful use of it. But we should distinguish between cutting out fat and cutting into muscle. To retain the muscle—i.e., to maintain a dynamic economy and to create more jobs—we will need *more* energy.

• The price of "new" natural gas should be decontrolled, to provide an economic incentive for accelerated exploration for this fuel and to discourage wasteful use of it. This can and should be done now.

• The Atlantic and Pacific sectors of our outer continental shelf should be opened up for exploration on an orderly, continuing basis. Obviously, we won't know how much oil and gas is there until we drill. But we clearly should avail ourselves of the opportunity to find whatever additions to our national reserves may be located in those areas. Environmental controls on drilling should continue to be strict, but excessive restrictions and litigation should not be allowed to hold up projects to provide additional energy.

• U.S. companies should be encouraged to search for oil and natural gas throughout the world, for the maximum diversification of foreign sources of supply. Those supplies are going to be required in the period before we can achieve a surplus. Our government should continue to give U.S. companies the same tax treatment that other major countries accord their companies operating abroad.

• Deepwater terminals enabling the largest tankers to deliver foreign oil to the U.S. should be built without delay, for environmental reasons as well as to provide the lowest transportation costs for the large volumes of oil we will have to import for at least the next decade.

• Provision should be made for security stockpiling of oil to help tide us over if another supply disruption occurs.

• Public transportation should be improved through the development of a comprehensive National Master Transportation Program that would take into account all of the nation's transportation needs and would provide enough money to do an adequate job nationwide.

• Goals and scheduled programs should be set for commercial development of alternate energy sources—primarily coal in liquid or gaseous form, nuclear and solar energy, and possibly oil from shale—so they can carry an important share of the energy load as soon as possible.

These strike us as the major items the nation needs to be thinking about now. Look in this newspaper on succeeding Sundays for a fuller discussion of various of these issues.

Next: "Setting the objectives"

Mobil

© 1974 Mobil Oil Corporation

Source: Exxon ad courtesy of Exxon Corporation. Mobil ad © 1974 Mobil Corporation.

Two examples are presented in Figure 18.2; both are petroleum corporation advertisements. Mobil's advertisement is a strong advocacy ad, whereas the Exxon ad is simply institutional in nature. In 1978 Mobil spent $4 million on advocacy advertising. During that year, 90 percent of administration, congressional, and other government leaders had read a Mobil advocacy ad. Whether this is good for society is the subject of heated debate; but only one-third of the leaders said they found the ads useful.[13]

PRODUCT ADVERTISING

A good image often enhances the effectiveness of **product advertising.** Perhaps you have observed that some product advertisements are much more informative than others. This is a normal characteristic of advertising used to create primary demand—that is, demand for a product category rather than for a specific brand. **Pioneering advertising** is intended to stimulate primary demand for a new product or product category. It is heavily utilized during the introduction stage of the product life cycle. Recently, for example, manufacturers of home video recorder/player equipment have been attempting to educate Americans on the advantages of owning such equipment.

SELECTIVE/COMPETITIVE ADVERTISING

When a product enters the growth phrase of the life cycle and competitors begin to enter the marketplace, advertising becomes **competitive** or **selective.** No longer is the main emphasis on building general primary demand. Now the goal is to influence demand for a specific product or service. Often promotion becomes less informative and more emotional during this phase. Advertisements may begin to stress subtle differences in brands, with heavy emphasis on building brand name recall. Price often becomes a key promotional weapon as products become very similar. As the home video recorder/player market matures, we hear less about why we should own the equipment and more about why RCA is better than Magnavox, which is better than Sony, and so forth.

When products are in the maturity or decline phase of the life cycle, advertising is mostly reminder promotion. The primary purpose of the campaign is to maintain awareness (see Figure 18.3).

COMPARATIVE ADVERTISING

A highly controversial trend in competitive advertising is the growth of comparative advertising. When an advertisement compares two or more specific brands in terms of product/service attributes, it may be defined as **comparative advertising.** This isn't really new; 1931 Plymouth ads suggested that the consumer "Look at All Three" before buying. The Avis–Hertz battle of the 1960s also involved comparative advertising. As recently as 1973–1974, only 1 out of 30 commercials on prime-time television was of this type. By the end of 1975, however, the number was 1 out of 12 and growing. A major reason for this growth is the Federal Trade Commission's fostering of comparative advertising. Joan Bernstein, assistant director of the FTC, has stated that comparative advertising "delivers information not previously available to consumers" and also that "advertisers and agencies are more skillful than the government in communicating information."[14]

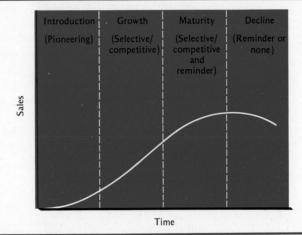

Even though comparative advertising has received the FTC's blessing, not everyone is for it. Andrew G. Kershaw, chairman of Ogilvy and Mather, one of the world's largest advertising agencies, says, "If the FTC told us it was permissible to jump out of the window, I for one would not jump."[15] Why the controversy? There is general disagreement on the effects of comparative advertising. Perhaps the recent flurry of comparative advertising can be traced to Schick's naming of its competitors in ads for the Fleximatic electric shaver. Its market share rose from 8 percent to 24 percent, with a net sales gain of $28 million.

Is comparative advertising effective? Academic research on the subject has shown:

1. The message recall effectiveness of the comparison advertisement was higher than that of its "brand X" counterpart.
2. Brand recall effectiveness was equal.
3. Claim recall effectiveness was considerably higher for the comparative advertiser.[16]

SHORTAGE ADVERTISING

Comparative advertising reveals the intensity of competitive advertising. When shortages occur, advertising often disappears into the background. When the oil crisis hit in 1974, petroleum advertising virtually disappeared. Yet enlightened marketers have found that **shortage advertising** is a viable marketing tool. Instead of decreasing the advertising budget, marketers change promotional objectives. Their new goals might include (1) educating the user on more efficient means of utilizing the product, thus reducing demand; (2) explaining the firm's situation, thereby helping reduce customer pressure on the salesforce; (3) improving good will; and (4) informing the market about how the firm's products will save resources.

Many companies were quick to position themselves around the energy crisis. General Electric introduced a new product as "the first fluorescent lamp specially designed for the energy crisis." The Bell System has taken advantage of the fuel shortage by promoting long-distance phone calls as an alternative to travel. Textron pushes solar power for such things as offshore drilling platforms. Bechtel promotes the environmental advantages of nuclear power, and investor-owned electric light and power companies advertise the impressive safety records of nuclear power plants.

Institutional rather than product advertising is still another approach to shortage situations. For example, Allegheny Ludlum's ad goes, "Allegheny Ludlum Industries: A group of our companies makes light work of supplying energy." St. Joe Minerals says, "We're growing with three kinds of energy. Energy is a growing business. We're in on the ground floor."[17]

COOPERATIVE ADVERTISING

Cooperative advertising involves payments by manufacturers to retailers (and sometimes to wholesalers) for advertising products through local advertising media (see Figure 18.4). For example, the local television retailer receives a check for $200 as partial compensation for an ad placed in a local newspaper advertising the availability of the manufacturer's sets at the local store.

Use of coop advertising by manufacturers is almost universal. One recent study revealed that over 90 percent of all manufacturers engage in cooperative advertising.[18] Often cooperative advertising budgets are quite large. Expenditures on cooperative advertising in 1980 were estimated at over $4 billion. Normally the manufacturer gives the dealer a rebate based on the number of units or dollar amount purchased. In either case, it is traditional for the dealer to pay half the actual cost of the ad. Most coop advertising is confined to the print media. However, more firms like True Value Hardware, International Harvester and many department stores are now using coop dollars in television advertising.

One reason manufacturers use cooperative advertising is the impracticality of listing all their dealers in national advertising. Also, coop advertising encourages the dealer to devote more effort to the manufacturer's lines. If a new product is involved, it helps the dealer develop demand and thus encourages adequate stocking of the new item. Sometimes coop advertising ties the dealer closer to the manufacturer and aids in developing good will. Most important, the manufacturer obtains more total promotion, since the dealer is sharing part of the expense.

The inability to verify the actual running of an advertisement on radio or television has been a big reason for a lack of coop dollars going to the broadcast media. One study of firms with large cooperative advertising budgets revealed that 50 percent of the advertisers felt that radio did not furnish sufficient documentation to justify their reimbursement of dealers for radio coop.[19] The following example shows how one manufacturer handled its cooperative advertising.

Tired of cleaning your swimming pool?

Let the Arneson Pool-Sweep® do it automatically.

You'll never have to clean your swimming pool again. Because the Arneson Pool-Sweep® does it automatically, 365 days a year. For just pennies a day.

Your pool will be cleaner than it's ever been. And it will stay that way. Because the Arneson Pool-Sweep is the most thorough, automatic pool cleaner available. Come in today and we'll show you the amazing Arneson Pool-Sweep. It's like having a self-cleaning pool.

ARNESON
Pool **Sweep**®

DEALER NAME
Address
Phone Number

Source: Courtesy of Arneson Products.

Arneson Products, which sells its Pool-Sweep automatic swimming pool cleaner through some 2,500 dealers and builders, recently remodeled its co-op plan when it found that many of the dealers and builders weren't taking part in the program at all. A major complaint, especially from small dealers: Instead of making its reimbursements in cash, Arneson credited the dealer in spare parts. Inasmuch as most of its accounts have a limited demand for Pool-Sweep parts, they didn't do much cooperative advertising under this system.

To get things moving, Arneson threw out the parts-payment idea and set up a program that pays 75% of the co-op cost and, in an unusual provision, puts no limit on the total amount of funds available to a store during the year. The principal media being used are newspapers and direct mail, and Arneson makes most of the buys. This is somewhat of a departure in that retailers often can get a lower rate from the local paper than a manufacturer, but Bruce Martin, marketing product manager, explains that many of his dealers have done little or no advertising before and thus look to Arneson for guidance.

Arneson further simplified the procedure by having its 20 sales representatives work out co-op campaigns with their accounts on the spot. Once the details are arranged, the salesman picks up the phone and calls a special co-op WATS number at the company's Corte Madera, Cal., headquarters to tell the advertising department where the ad should run and how often. The dealer then gives him a check for 25% of the cost, and the transaction is complete. If the retailer wants to place the ad himself, he merely submits a tear sheet and a copy of the newspaper invoice to Arneson for reimbursement after the ad has run.[20]

Media selection

Promotional objectives and the type of advertising a company plans to use will have a strong impact on the selection of media channels. A number of factors enter into media selection. Basically, management must determine what it wants to say and how (by what media) it wants the message delivered.

Costs and audience. Two of the most important criteria of media selection are costs and audience. If marketing managers are trying to reach female teenagers, they would not select *Barron's* financial paper but might select *Teen* magazine. Even when audience profiles match media profiles, other factors, such as circulation and image, must be considered. For example, *Teen* magazine might reach part of the "right" market, but this might be only a small fraction of the firm's market. Also, how do teenagers perceive *Teen* magazine? Perhaps it is a "how to" magazine and is used as a reference guide by many teenagers. If this is true, it should strengthen advertiser credibility.

Other criteria. No two media are the same, yet all can be evaluated by certain selection criteria. Table 18.4 combines a number of important factors used in media selection. **Cost per contact** is the cost of reaching one member of the audience. Naturally, as the size of the audience increases, so does the total cost. We will discuss cost evaluation in more detail in Chapter 19.

Market selectivity is another important media characteristic. Some media, such as general newspapers, appeal to a wide cross-section of the population. Others, such as *Flying,* the *Journal of Marketing,* and *Architectural Record,* appeal to very specific groups. Geographic selectivity refers to coverage of a specific area. Local radio, newspapers, and television all cover limited geographic areas. Network television and many magazines offer nationwide coverage. Other magazines, such as *New West, Sunset, Southern Living, Texas Monthly,* and *Chicago,* offer good coverage in limited areas.

Although a lot of work still needs to be done, some generalizations can be made regarding source credibility (trust). Radio, for example, tends to have lower credibility than major retail catalogs. Trade and professional magazines generally offer the highest level of reader trust and believability.

Because of printing timetables, paste-up requirements, engraving, and so forth, some magazines require final ad copy several months before publication. The advertiser thus loses flexibility and is unable to adapt to changing market conditions. Radio, on the other hand, provides maximum flexibility, usually enabling the advertiser to change the ad on the same day.

Another important media characteristic is "noise level." Television, for example, often requires both audio and visual attention for the promotional message to be understood. It is often viewed in the presence of other individuals, who may contribute to the noise factor. In contrast, direct mail is a private medium. There are no other advertising or news stories to compete for the reader's attention. Generally, direct mail offers a very low noise level.

Some media have relatively long life spans, whereas those of other media are quite short. When a radio commercial is over, it's over. You can't repeat it unless you've taperecorded the program. Advertisers overcome this problem by repeating their ads often. A trade magazine, in contrast, has a relatively long life span. A person may read several articles, put it down, and pick it up a week later to continue reading. Some families naturally save back issues of *Playboy, Gourmet, National Geographic,* and similar magazines. Magazines and catalogs often have a high "pass-along rate." One person will read the publication and then give it to someone else.

Media characteristics and trends

Table 18.4 presents a good overall view of the major media. Now we will take a brief look at some current media trends and characteristics.

◢ **TABLE 18.4   Key Media Characteristics (0 = nonapplicable; L = low; M = moderate; H = high)**

	Cost per contact	Total cost	Market selectivity	Geographic selectivity	Source credibility	Visual quality	Noise level	Life span	Pass- along rate	Timing flexibility
Television	L	H	M[a]	M–H	L–M	H	M–H	0	0	L–M
Radio	L	L	M[b]	H	L–M	0	M–H	0	0	H
Newspaper	L	L	L	M[c]	L	L–M	H	L	L	H
Magazines	M–H[d]	M–H	M–H	M–H[e]	M–H	M–H	M	M–H	M–H	L
Direct mail	L–H[f]	M–H	H	H	L–M	M–H	L	L–M	L	M–H
Billboard	L	L	L	M	L	M	H	L	0	M
Catalog	M–H	M–H	H	H	M	M–H	L–H	M–H	M–H	L

[a] Market selectivity by correlating program audience profiles with target markets.
[b] Selective for broad groups: black, teen, adult.
[c] Some geographic selectivity, but not for a small area such as a particular suburb.
[d] Higher cost per contact than newspaper, but lower cost per potential customer.
[e] Some magazines, such as *Time,* have over 50 regional breakdowns.
[f] Cost depends on quality of mailing list.

NEWSPAPERS

After 275 years, newspapers are still America's basic communication medium. Newspapers are read by nearly nine out of ten Americans, and roughly half of all American adults read a paper every day. One of the problems radio and TV have in competing with newspapers is that people like to turn the pages and determine their own "program content" when they monitor the world for news, information, and entertainment.

Newspaper readers contributed nearly $5 billion in 1980 to purchase 62 million copies daily and over 54 million Sunday editions.[21] Many of the same reader-customers will account for part of the $4.4 billion invested in newspaper classified advertising. Retail advertising customers spent $7.6 billion, and national rate advertisers invested over $2 billion in newspapers in 1980.

Automobiles, transportation, tobacco, and food are the largest newspaper advertising categories. These large-volume advertisers continue to consider newspapers, the largest medium in terms of circulation, most attractive. Cards and color inserts are also becoming a significant form of newspaper promotion. It is estimated that over 15 billion advertising pieces are inserted into newspapers each year.

Newspaper ads can usually be prepared quickly and at a reasonable cost, so local merchants can reach their target audiences on almost a daily basis. On the other hand, newspapers may be quite costly if a marketer is trying to reach a very narrow market. For example, local newspapers are perhaps not the best media for reaching purchasers of specialty steels or even janitorial supplies. Newspaper advertising also has a lot of "noise" from competing ads and news stories. Thus visibility for one company's ad may be difficult to obtain.

MAGAZINES

Although magazines' cost per contact is usually higher than that of other media, their cost per potential customer may be much lower. This difference is due to the specialized nature of magazine audiences. Magazines fall into two general categories: (1) consumer and (2) trade and professional. Among the fastest-growing publication areas are in-flight, mechanical and science, and home and apartment magazines.

There are magazines for virtually every interest group (market segment). For example, there are magazines on sewing, waterskiing, golfing, dogs, aquarium ownership, art, and hundreds of other subjects. If a seller has a unique new breeding grass for tropical fish, chances are the potential purchaser will more likely be found reading *Tropical Fish* than *Dun's Review*. Magazines are an ideal media for reaching narrow target audiences. At present there are approximately 1150 consumer magazines, 210 farm publications, and 3450 business magazines. There are magazines for virtually every business. For example, department stores, chain stores, car washes, taverns, funeral homes, grocery stores, and many others have magazines that appeal specifically to their industries. These target audiences often cannot be reached through any other media.

Magazines can also create an air of sophistication for a good or service or lend credibility to the product. Advertising in *Town and Country* or *Bon Appetit* gives the product "respectability" not attainable through other media. *Parents* and *Good Housekeeping* help their advertisers project a quality image by allowing them to use the magazine's "seal of approval." It is not uncommon to see "as advertised in *Good Housekeeping*" on a package label.

The long-run prognosis for magazines is good. Advertising in this medium should easily reach $4 billion before 1985. A rising level of education, coupled with an ever-increasing number of special interest areas, provides ample opportunities for magazine growth. But some disadvantages of magazines may temper the estimated 1985 sales figure. For example, magazines lack the flexibility of newspapers, radio, and TV. Often ads must be in final form two to three months prior to publication. This can sometimes cause a loss of "freshness" as world events change. Some magazines have limited geographic audiences, thus leaving gaps in coverage for national advertisers. General interest magazines may be too broad and include many readers with little or no interest in an advertiser's product. Finally, other advertisements and articles offer significant competition for the reader's attention.

RADIO

In major metroplitan markets, radio provides a station for just about every taste. Denver, for example, has 12 stations, and Phoenix is licensed for 49. There is no area of the country that cannot be reached by one of America's 7000 radio stations. Like television, radio offers network (though limited), spot, or local advertising. The major networks are CBS, NBC, Mutual, and the four ABC networks devoted to contemporary living, information, entertainment, and FM. In **network advertising,** one central organization produces and supplies programming to its affiliates. Affiliates are local stations that haven't the money, access to production facilities, or inclination to produce those programs themselves. **Spot advertising** means that the advertisers "spot" or select certain stations for their campaigns. **Local advertising** refers to local radio advertisements by retailers and other groups. Radio stations often develop loyal followings and "radio personalities." Some advertisers can increase their effectiveness by using radio personalities in spot and local radio advertisements.

Louis T. Hagopian, chairman of the giant N. W. Ayer Advertising Agency, calls radio "a medium for advertisers that reaches key life styles with emotional selling power."[22] It has the one-on-one intimacy lacking in many other media. Television, for example, is often watched by several members of the family. There are an average of almost six radios in every home, plus a receiver in virtually every car. Thus, each family member can listen to the station that best suits his or her taste.

Radio programs are now segmented on an ever increasing variety of factors: age, race, income, life style, and others. It is primarily a local medium catering to local tastes.

Radio commercials are relatively inexpensive and easy to prepare. There is not a long lead time, as with magazines and television. The biggest disadvantage of radio is the lack of visual appeal. Also, unless a national advertiser chooses a network, selecting stations for a nationwide campaign can be complex and time-consuming.

TELEVISION

From its takeoff period in the late 1940s through the mid-1970s, television advertising has grown continuously. In 1979, almost $10.2 billion was spent on television advertising.[23] Pepsi-Cola spent an average of over $125,000 every day of the year on television advertising during 1980. Certainly it is a lot of money, but remember the company is vying for a significant share of the $15 billion a year soft drink industry.

Why this popularity? Mass audiences, low costs per contact, ease of getting viewers' attention due to lack of competition from other stories and advertisements, and most of the advantages of personal selling (sight, sound, and demonstration). Also, television reaches just about all of us. One study showed that television is viewed by 95 percent of all adults and children.[24] Television also delivers huge audiences. For example, when *Roots* was presented for the first time on eight consecutive days, it reached an average of 32 million homes a night, or almost 45 percent of all homes in America. An average prime time program delivers about 12.5 million homes.[25]

Spot and local television expenditures together total slightly more than network advertising. Spot advertising is highly popular with regional advertisers and with national advertisers attempting to reach selected markets. Local television is dominated by companies that serve a single city or county.

Television's latest growth market is pay TV, both cable and over-the-air (satellite). By the end of 1980, there were approximately 4 million subscribers. New customers were added during 1980 at a rate of over 100,000 households per month.[26] Many cable operators currently are originating their own programming in one form or another. Programs such as local sports, city council meetings, and local news are being produced and distributed by cable operators. Some operators set aside one or more channels to offer mechanical information sources as stock market ticker tapes, news wire services, and/or time and temperature. Cable operators have also turned to another source of programming called "pay cable." This involves the purchasing of programming from outside independent sources that sell special programs to subscribers. Such programs commonly consist of movies, sports, and special features.

Television is not without problems. The cost of advertising time has been rising by 15 to 30 percent per year, forcing many advertisers to turn to other media. In 1980 Warner-Lambert boosted its TV advertising budget 10 percent and found that it would buy less time than in 1979. Heublein's Kentucky Fried Chicken restaurants continue to increase their use of other media. TV advertising can involve huge production costs as well. For example, one commercial for Great American Soups cost over $200,000 to make. And the cost of running such a commercial during a popular prime-time program may be $100,000 or more.

The increasing pace of new-show introductions and cancellations makes it difficult to evaluate audiences and build brand loyalty among viewers. As an executive with Norton Simon Communications has put it, "Magazine rates have been holding relatively well over the years, and this continues to make print more and more desirable." Other advertisers are concerned about the quality of network programs. Borden, for example, has shifted its emphasis to fully sponsored network specials. One of its marketing managers says, "We want our brands to be associated with wholesome, family entertainment."

DIRECT MAIL

Direct mail can be the most efficient medium an advertiser uses or the least efficient, depending on the quality of the mailing list and the effectiveness of the mailing piece. Good mailing lists are available from list brokers for about $50 per 1000 names. Prestigious lists or lists of people who have bought merchandise through the mail in the past few months normally cost $100 per 1000 names.

Many of America's largest firms are just beginning to experiment with mail order promotions. General Foods, General Mills, and Avon have recently begun to utilize direct mail. Other companies have long been committed to direct mail and spend huge sums of money on this medium each year. Direct mail is not limited to consumer goods and inexpensive industrial goods marketing. General Automation, a minicomputer manufacturer, traced the sale of a $100,000 computer system to a direct mail piece.

Direct mail is a very flexible medium. Brokers can provide firms with lists broken down by very specific socioeconomic characteristics. If a marketing manager wanted to purchase a list of persons living in the Midwest with an interest in gourmet cooking who earn over $40,000 a year, it could easily be obtained. Often a seller will buy lists with the characteristics just described on a test basis from several different brokers. The seller will then code the order blanks to determine which list gave the best response rate. A major "buy" will then be made from the most profitable lists.

Even with a good mailing list, costs per thousand (CPM) persons contacted is higher than for other media. In 1979, typical costs per thousand were direct mail—$25, newspapers—$12, magazines—$7, television—$5.50, radio—$2.50, and outdoors—$1.[27] Direct mail has three primary costs: the mailing list, the brochure and other printed matter, and postage. Remember that TV has high initial costs, but these are spread over millions of people. Direct mail is usually sent to much smaller audiences.

OUTDOOR ADVERTISING

Outdoor advertising is a flexible, low-cost medium. Often advertisers make large purchases on an area basis (city, county, or SMSA). Large outdoor buys are referred to as "showings." A showing of 100, the maximum, is defined as reaching 90 percent of all adults in a given market in 30 days.

Outdoor advertising reaches a broad and diverse market, and therefore it is normally limited to convenience goods and select shopping goods. Advertisers usually base their billboard use on census tract data. They assume that the people who are most likely to see a certain billboard will have demographic characteristics similar to those of the tract in which the billboard is located. Outdoor advertising is proving to be a flexible medium for targeting a message to a specific metro market or ethnic group; for near point of purchase coverage of supermarkets and shopping centers; and in reaching the high-income or the younger, affluent consumer.

Traffic count data are supplied by the Traffic Audit Bureau (TAB)—they enable the advertiser to determine the total number of potential exposures per site. Recently TAB has come under increasing criticism for providing questionable data.[28] For example, TAB audits traffic flows once every three years. Major changes in traffic patterns can occur during such a long period.

CATALOGS

Catalogs offer the opportunity to pinpoint specific audiences (existing store customers or extensive users of certain types of products such as electronics, fishing equipment, or office supplies). The readership rate is usually high, and so is the pass-along rate. Spiraling costs (usually over $8 each for major seasonal catalogs) have forced retailers to maintain careful control over distribution. Cards are sent to customers informing them they can now pick up their copy of the catalog in the store. Mailing lists are carefully pruned in order to remove the names of people who do not order a specified volume of merchandise. Montgomery Ward has even opened its catalog to noncompetitive outside advertisers. Time-Life Books, Encyclopedia Britannica, and Columbia Records have experimented with this medium.

Let us turn our attention now to some other important forms of promotion—sales promotion and public relations.

Sales promotion

American businesses will probably spend about $40 billion per year on sales promotion by 1985. Consumer products manufacturers spend about 40 percent of their promotion budgets on advertising and 60 percent on sales promotion. Yet these firms spend 25 times as much creating and evaluating ads as they do managing promotions.[29] As you will see, sales promotion is marketing's stepchild. But premiums and point-of-purchase displays are furnishing the major impetus for growth. Some examples of sales promotions are shown in Figure 18.5.

Sources: Post Cereals ad courtesy of General Foods Corporation. Coke photo courtesy of The Coca-Cola Company. White Cloud ad courtesy of The Procter & Gamble Company.

TABLE 18.5 Tools for Reaching Sales Promotion Objectives

Objective	Tool
Increase trial	Sampling
	Couponing
	Price packs
	Bonus packs
	On-pack, in-pack, or near-pack premiums
	Refund packs
	Free mail-in premium
Increase consumer inventory	Bonus packs
	"Two-for" packs
	Price packs
	Prepriced packs
	Multiple-proof premiums or refunds
Encourage repurchase	Price packs
	Bonus packs
	Contests, sweepstakes
	On-pack, in-pack, or near-pack premiums
	Refund packs
	Self-liquidating items
	On-pack couponing good on next purchase
	Multiple-proof free premiums or refunds

Source: *Marketing and Sales Promotion* (New York: Sales and Marketing Management, 1979), p. 13. Reprinted by permission from Sales & Marketing Management magazine. Copyright 1979.

OBJECTIVES

Immediate purchase action or attitude modification is usually the goal of sales promotion, regardless of the form it takes. Specifically, the promoter is attempting to increase trial, increase consumer inventory, or encourage repurchase (see Table 18.5). A corollary objective may be to further increase the effectiveness of advertising. Often the two interact to produce higher sales than an equivalent investment in either alone.

In contrast to **consumer promotions,** which *pull* a product through the channel (by creating demand), **trade promotions** *push* a product through the channel. Trade discounts may be offered in order to obtain shelf space for a new product or to induce wholesalers and retailers to purchase during off seasons. Sometimes trade deals are offered "because everyone else does." This is difficult to justify, since research has shown that consumer promotions are normally more effective than trade promotions.[30]

COUPONS, PREMIUMS, SAMPLES

Premiums, coupons, and samples are at the heart of sales promotion.

Coupons. A. C. Nielsen Co. estimates that 81.2 billion coupons, or about 1200 per household, were distributed in 1980. Consumers redeemed 4 percent of them.[31] How can companies increase coupon use? Ralston Purina tried a lottery promotion. In each box of its Meow Mix, customers find a coupon with a ruboff spot. When removed, it shows the coupon is worth 40 cents, a 7-pound bag, or a year's supply of the cat food. Miles Laboratories, Inc., uses "instant coupons" for Alka-Seltzer. They are easily detachable and can be used to buy that package immediately. In effect, **couponing** is controlled price reduction. Women do most of the redeeming—63 percent of all adult females redeem coupons, while only 35 percent of the males do.[32]

A new program that will eventually replace some coupon offers has been developed by Universal Product Dollars. Shoppers collect coded symbols of various values from grocery products (universal product codes) and send them in for redemption. This saves the retailer time and money, since it does not have to handle the coupons, and redemption is facilitated because consumers are returning coded symbols that are quickly read by optical scanners. Perhaps another trend will be direct store distribution of coupons. Carol Wright is the registered trade name of a coupon distribution service. Six times a year, it sends packets of coupons to 21 million frequent users of several grocery store product categories. In 1980, it began stationing people in store entrances on "Carol Wright Value Days" distributing books of cents-off coupons. The company feels that in the long run, the redemption ratio will be three times higher than average.

Premiums. Sometimes a premium is tied to a product or service—notice the plethora of Budweiser items, from hot-air balloons to T-shirts. People in places as far away as Tanzania have sent $7.95 to Olympia Brewery for its logo-bearing backpacks. And 100,000 buyers paid $2.95 for a 4½-foot inflatable Dole banana. Some companies are now publishing catalogs of their premiums. Burger Chef's outlets increased their average sales volume 22 percent during a promotion offering a free *Star Wars* poster with every order of a large Coke, jumbo fries, and hamburger.

Manufacturers are also offering more "immediate-reward" **pack premiums** on packs, in packs, or as bonus packs. "Free" immediate-reward premiums are also increasing in use as a substitute for straight cents-off deals. Pack premiums give consumers greater perceived value than the same amount spent by consumers for cents-off promotions.[33] The FTC found that many retailers were not passing the full "10¢ off regular price" rebate on to the consumer. As a result new, strict guidelines have been established for cents-off trade deals, and the use of such deals has dropped sharply. One classic pack premium is that in every box of Cracker Jacks.

Although many companies continually search for sales promotions that are new and different, Cracker Jack has stuck to the same promotion for 66 years. In fact, the toy packed inside each box of the candied popcorn and peanuts has become so much a part of the product that Ken Strottman, product manager for the Borden subsidiary, says, "We don't view it as a promotion any more; we consider it part of the cost of goods."

Unlike the edible part of the product, the 107-year-old brand's in-pack premium has changed "radically" over the years, Strottman says. During World War II, for example, the use of metal toys had to be discontinued, and today, with the growing concern for consumer safety, more of the toys are made of paper. Nonetheless, Strottman claims that the quality of the premium has improved over the years, even though its value relative to the cost of the product (about 25¢ at retail) has stayed the same all this time.

To maintain the toy quality they're after, Cracker Jack marketers test prototypes of new items among children, who rate their acceptability—and they're tough critics. Of 40 items recently tested, Strottman says, only 2 were acceptable. The company pretests the toys to be sure they meet stringent legal requirements. Such restrictions don't seem to inhibit creativity, however; 600 *different* toy surprises are packed into Cracker Jack boxes each day, and a total of 450 million are packed each year.

"Consumers expect to find the toy in Cracker Jack just as much as they expect to find the peanuts," Strottman says. And we all know what happens when you start eating peanuts.[34]

Sampling. Free door-to-door sampling has dropped considerably owing to the high cost of this technique. Some manufacturers are turning to **coop sampling,** in which several different products are delivered in the same container or at the same time. The distribution costs are shared by the various manufacturers.

Another sampling trend is toward "trial-size" containers of **salable samples.** Minibottles or cartons of a product, such as shampoo or salad dressing, are offered in stores at nominal prices. Retailers like this form of promotion, since it keeps the profit in the store. Consumers also appreciate being able to buy trial-size containers. It reduces the risk (cost) of trying new products.

POINT-OF-PURCHASE DISPLAYS

Point-of-purchase (POP) displays consist of display materials and signs placed inside retail stores, usually next to the advertiser's merchandise. The primary value of POP materials is that it places the promotion close to the point of sale. POP materials act as a last-minute inducement to buy the product. POP can be very effective if it is done properly. In one test conducted by a major drug chain, manufacturer-supplied POP material increased dollar sales of the items an average of 103 percent over the test period.[35]

The biggest problem with POP materials is getting retailers to use them. Each year millions of displays, signs, posters, and so forth are discarded without being put up. Limited space and the quantity of materials to choose from have often produced a callous attitude toward POP materials. Manufacturers are attempting to offset this problem by building better-quality POP materials. Cheap paper signs and crude, ill-conceived displays are vanishing. POP material is often tied in with television or print messages to increase effectiveness. Recent studies indicate that reinforced POP materials generate more sales dollars than nonreinforced materials.[36]

BUSINESS MEETINGS, CONVENTIONS, AND TRADE SHOWS

Trade association meetings, conferences, and conventions are an important aspect of sales promotion. It is estimated that 5600 trade shows, conventions, and industrial expositions are held each year.[37] These meetings give manufacturers and wholesalers an opportunity to display their wares to a large audience of potential buyers at relatively low cost. Approximately 80 million people attend trade association conventions each year.

In probing 1000 visitors at 49 different trade shows, the Bureau of Exhibit Surveys found that, on average, 83 percent had not received calls from salespeople about the products and services they discovered at exhibit booths. Exhibitors of components and materials benefited most from trade shows: 89 percent of their exhibit visitors represented new prospects. Medical products exhibitors gained least: only 49 percent of their book visitors had received calls from salespeople. In other areas, trade shows brought:

79 percent new prospects to office/computing/accounting machines marketers.
82 percent new prospects to exhibitors of capital equipment priced under $5000.
79 percent new prospects to exhibitors of capital equipment priced over $5000.
54 percent new prospects to markets of consumable products.[38]

SPECIAL FORMS OF SALES PROMOTION

Many unique and special forms of promotion tend to be highly effective. One example is sponsorship of sporting events. Philip Morris, for instance, sponsors the Marlboro Cup horse race and the Virginia Slims women's tennis tournaments. Both events have provided a high degree of visibility for Philip Morris products. Many of America's large rodeos are sponsored by a competitor of Philip Morris—Winston cigarettes.

Harrah's of Reno engages in a unique form of promotion without ever naming its product. With 3655 slot machines, 544 bingo seats, two sports-betting facilities, four parimutuel wheels, and 159 games of "21," 23 of craps, 11 of roulette, 12 of baccarat, 9 of keno, and 4 of poker, the product becomes rather obvious. But mentioning gambling would violate postal and broadcast regulations. Thus Harrah's relies on quantity entertainment as its major form of promotion. In one instance, the casino offered Frank Sinatra and John Denver in one big show each evening for a week. In addition to the entertainers' fees, Harrah's spent $105,000 advertising the "happening" in various media. The response was overwhelming; 586,000 "parties" were turned away during the week because of overflowing crowds.

Another special, albeit less exotic, form of promotion is a newly established network of regional shopping malls that will enable marketers to move their promotions from one center to another. Each mall in the network offers guaranteed weekend traffic of at least 30,000 shoppers. The mall will offer a new display medium that is relatively inexpensive and will reach a fairly homogeneous group of shoppers.

SALES PROMOTION MANAGEMENT

Sales promotion is often considered a stepchild of the total promotional effort. Often responsibility for the function is given to the newest and most inexperienced member of the marketing management team. As a result, effective long-range planning for the optimum mix of advertising and promotion seldom occurs. Also, promotion spending is not evaluated in a consistent and objective way. Jack Worth, vice-president–creative director of V&R Enterprises of New York, says: "Promotion is suffering from a 'how-much syndrome.' Too often sales promotion programs emphasize cost rather than marketing objectives."[39] In more enlightened companies, the situation is changing. Better-qualified executives are being hired to supervise the promotion function. New staff positions are being created at the corporate level and established positions, such as supervisor of point-of-purchase materials, are being upgraded to entail broader responsibility.

Some of the problems of sales promotion have stemmed from the use of product managers. Product managers who were interested in rapid promotion found that sales results could be achieved more rapidly through heavy emphasis on sales promotion rather than advertising. While it may be effective in building short-term sales, overemphasis on sales promotion at the expense of advertising can mean the lack of a strong nucleus of brand loyal customers.

Without objectives, effective promotion management becomes virtually impossible. Budgeting becomes a question of "How much did we spend last year?" Another common approach is the "leftover approach." Anything that is left over after the advertising budget has been set goes to promotion. It is known that advertising and sales promotion have a positive interactive effect. Yet in many firms the advertising and promotion budgets are prepared independently.

Market research pretesting and posttesting is quite common in advertising but rare in sales promotion. This is rather strange, since premiums can be tested reliably very quickly and at a low cost. Trade allowances are also a problem; many companies fail to check on whether performance requirements are met. In effect, they consider the allowance just a way of buying shelf space.

In addition to improving the caliber of sales promotion personnel, elevating the function to a higher organizational level, and setting specific realistic objectives, several other things can be done to improve promotion management. Robert A. Strang suggests the following steps: analyze spending, select appropriate techniques, pretest, and evaluate in depth.[40]

Strang notes that after specific objectives have been determined, appropriate techniques for achieving them can be selected. Many techniques satisfy more than one objective (refer back to Table 18.5). All techniques should be evaluated in terms of total costs and sales impact. The possibility of using special packages, the possible loss of sales from complementary items, and the like must not be overlooked.

Pretesting the new promotion is just as important as pretesting a new advertising campaign. Unfortunately, promotion sales effectiveness is just as difficult to measure and predict as advertising effectiveness. For example, redemption rates for a coupon promotion may range from 2 to 25 percent, depending on the value of the coupon and the way it is distributed.[41] The effectiveness of any sales promotion program should be evaluated thoroughly. Sales increases can be due to many factors. Research at the pretest phase alone will not be adequate. Posttesting to gauge whether or not the promotion objectives have been reached should also be undertaken.

Public relations

Public relations, like advertising and sales promotion, is a vital link in a progressive company's marketing communications mix.

GOALS AND FUNCTIONS

The following lists enumerate the goals and functions of public relations.

◄ *Ultimate Consumers*
Dissemination of information on the production and distribution of new or existing products.
Dissemination of information on ways to use new or existing products.
Establishing a consumer correspondence function to answer consumer inquiries about any matters regarding the organization.
Satisfying consumer or client dissatisfaction through promptly handling complaints, correcting whatever it was that caused the complaint, and making any needed adjustments in the policies, practices, or products of the firm or organization.

◄ *Company employees*
Training programs to stimulate more effective contact with the public.
Encouragement of pride in the company and its products.
Working with the personnel in advertising, sales promotion, and personal sales to create consistent, effective, honest, and persuasive messages for all the firm's publics. Providing any assistance needed to adjust the goals, policies, practices, and products of the firm to meet the needs of changing social markets.

◄ *Suppliers*
Providing research information for use in new products.

Dissemination of company trends and practices for the purpose of building a continuing team relationship.

◢ *Stockholders*

Dissemination of information on: (1) company prospect, (2) past and present profitability, (3) future plans, (4) management changes and capabilities, and (5) company financial needs.

◢ *The community at large*

Promotion of public causes such as community fund-raising drives.

Dissemination of information on all aspects of company operations with the purpose of building a sense of unity between company and community.

Providing speakers for educational, social, civic, and other community groups to teach the public about the organization and to answer or to seek answers to their questions.

Demonstrating to society that the organization is listening, reacting, adjusting, and progressing in its attempts to promote optimum satisfaction to its diverse publics.

Maintaining liaison with consumer groups, civic groups, and other concerned citizen groups to answer any questions and to provide information about the firm or organization.

Listening to various organizational publics to determine their attitudes about the organization and its policies, programs, products, personnel, and practices.[42]

Public relations media for internal use

◢ *Print*

Management letters to employees, employee newspapers and magazines, bulletin board announcements, annual and interim financial reports, employee handbooks or manuals, management bulletins for executives and supervisors, pay-envelope inserts, booklets explaining policies and procedures, daily news digests, reading racks, indoctrination kits, posters, and policy statements.

◢ *Oral*

Employee and executive meetings, public address systems, open houses, plant tours, family nights, informal talks by key executives on visits to departments, new-employee orientation meetings, employee counseling, panel discussions, grievance and employee-management committees, recordings, and employee social affairs.

◢ *Audiovisual*

Motion pictures, color slides, and filmstrips, closed-circuit television, sound slide film, flip charts, easel charts, posters, maps, flannelboards, and product exhibits.

Public relations media for external use

◄ *Mass media*

Newspapers, magazines, radio, television, annual and interim reports, correspondence, booklets, reprints of executive speeches, program kits and study materials for clubs, educational materials, library reference materials, manuals, and handbooks.

◄ *Oral*

Meetings with shareholders, consumers, dealers, suppliers; opinion leaders in plant communities, educators, and legislators; open houses; plant tours; business education days; speeches by employees and executives; visits to community institutions and suppliers; radio and television broadcasts; and community social affairs.

◄ *Audiovisual*

Displays and exhibits, motion pictures, sound slide films, charts, maps, posters, slides, television broadcasts, models and construction, and demonstration devices.[43]

Traditionally, public relations has been viewed as little more than image building. As such, it has often been divorced from marketing and other operating units. Although image building is still a basic function of publicity, its role has been expanded and integrated into the total marketing effort. Publicity, for example, is used to establish the credibility of a firm and its products before a sales representative calls on a customer. Public relations managers help key salespeople and sales managers obtain speaking invitations and then follow through with interesting talks. Public contact by sales managers and representatives helps build company and product familiarity and increases customer receptiveness to an initial sales call.

BUILDING ADVERTISING CREDIBILITY

Public relations complements the role of advertising by building product/service credibility. *Public Relations News* states:

The consumer will increasingly choose products on the basis of corporate preference—especially when choosing new products. This is only human nature; people naturally prefer to deal with companies they know, understand and trust.

Consumers want knowledgeable, straightforward and credible advertising, but they also want credibility reinforcement.[44]

Editorial exposure, such as an endorsement for a specific product or service, is highly valuable, as a promotion manager has noted:

A message sanctified through acceptance by 'third party' editors, when perceived by the viewer or reader in the editorial or nonpaid segments of a medium, has more persuasiveness and believability than the advertising, where the sponsor of the message is identified.[45]

An example is the classic introduction of the original Ford Mustang. Everyone first learned about it via editorial exposure. The same is true of the Wankel engine and, by extension, the Mazda. Many years ago an editorial mention of Vicks, and more recently one for Kent cigarettes, created an avalanche of sales.

AIDING IN PRODUCT DIFFERENTIATION

Public relations can help an advertiser differentiate its product in a relatively homogeneous market. In the liquor industry, for example, it was a National Mixed Drink Contest for professional bartenders that produced a cocktail that was later named the Pussycat and gave a creative headline writer the opportunity to entitle a story, "How the Pussycat Became a Tiger."

Public relations can play a vital role in any firm's marketing mix. Failure to recognize its potential and integrate it into the communication mix can only reduce the effectiveness of the total marketing effort. Some companies have failed properly to utilize public relations because they claim that the consequences of publicity are difficult to measure. Yet new techniques similar to those used in measuring advertising effectiveness are beginning to overcome the measurement problem.

MEASURING RESULTS

The traditional and still most common way to measure the results of public relations is the number of exposures created by the various media. Thus a newspaper clipping service would provide the number of column inches of news and photograph spaces. In addition, the minutes of radio and TV times would be counted. The assumption, of course, is that the greater the exposure, the more effective the public relations campaign. However, attempting to translate exposures into direct dollar sales is a difficult if not impossible task. As an alternative, public relations executives will convert the number of exposures to an equivalent cost if the firm had purchased the time through advertising. Thus, the executive might say the total exposures for the City of New York's "I love New York" image campaign was worth $82 million.

Because public relations objectives are difficult to quantify, many firms find establishing a public relations budget quite perplexing. Many simply use last year's budget plus an increase to cover any new tasks and inflation. Other companies use a residual approach. After advertising and sales budgets are deducted from the total promotional budget the remainder (whatever it is) is divided between public relations and sales promotion. The budgeting process will be discussed in more detail in the next chapter.

SUMMARY

Advertising can reinforce positive attitudes and influence neutral attitudes. It cannot, however, change basic value patterns. Advertising does not manage demand or block entry. Extensive advertising often implies that a seller is counting on product acceptance and repeat business; it is the implicit guarantee of quality.

From a macro perspective, advertising fosters sales through persuading, and through informative and reminder advertising. This gives firms a more rapid return on their investment. Faster and greater financial returns stimulate additional investment, which in turn creates economic growth. Advertising may or may not increase sales and market share for a specific company; it depends upon the quality of the advertising.

Institutional advertising is not oriented toward a product or service, but instead is designed to create good will for a company. Many firms are now engaging in advocacy advertising. The objective is to propagate ideas and to advocate certain positions on controversial social and economic issues.

Product advertising often begins with pioneering promotions. Emphasis is on building primary demand for a product type rather than for a specific brand name. As the item enters the growth stage of the life cycle, advertising becomes more competitive. Competitive advertising is designed to increase sales of a specific brand rather than general category of products.

When shortages occur, some firms cut back or eliminate advertising. Shortage advertising informs the consumer on how to use the product more efficiently, explains the firm's shortage situation, and tries to improve good will. Some companies use shortage advertising to describe how their products will save natural resources.

When manufacturers pay retailers and wholesalers for advertising the manufacturers' product through local advertising media, it is called cooperative advertising. Cooperative advertising expenditures are over $4 billion annually.

The following factors should be considered when selecting advertising media: objectives, costs, market selectivity, source credibility, reproduction capabilities, time factors, noise level, life span, pass-along rate, and timing flexibility.

Sales promotion has generally been considered a stepchild of advertising and personal selling. Yet sales promotion is growing at a faster rate than advertising, with estimated expenditures of approximately $40 billion per year by 1985. Both premiums and point-of-purchase displays are furnishing the major impetus for growth. The objective of sales promotion is usually immediate purchase action or attitude modification, rather than long-run behavior modification. Important forms of sales promotion include coupons, trade association meetings, conferences, and conventions, as well as free samples and premiums.

Sales promotion management has generally been considered an undesirable position as opposed to advertising management. As a result, effective planning and organization are often lacking. The situation is improving, however, as more companies recognize the importance of sales management.

Public relations also plays a unique role in the overall promotional mix. Traditionally, public relations has been viewed as little more than image building. Today, however, the goals of public relations are expanding. Public relations complements advertising by building product and service credibility. Editorial exposure, for example, provides credibility that is not available through advertising. Good public relations can also aid in new product introduction.

KEY TERMS

Institutional advertising	Network advertising
Advocacy advertising	Spot advertising
Product advertising	Local advertising
Pioneering advertising	Consumer promotions
Competitive advertising	Trade promotions
Comparative advertising	Couponing
Selective advertising	Pack premiums
Shortage advertising	Coop sampling
Cooperative advertising	Salable samples
Cost per contact	Point of purchase (POP) displays
Market selectivity	

REVIEW QUESTIONS

1. To what extend can advertising influence one's behavior? In what instances is advertising most effective?
2. In what ways does the communication message change over the product's life cycle?
3. Why is coop advertising beneficial to both manufacturer and retailer?
4. What are the advantages and disadvantages of the use of newspapers? Network TV?
5. Why are regional editions of national magazines offered?
6. What benefits can be derived through effective public relations?

DISCUSSION QUESTIONS

1. What factors are responsible for the increased use of comparative advertising? Describe the various requirements and precautions regulating its use.
2. Why are the more selective magazines able to charge higher advertising placement rates despite lower circulation?
3. How does editorial content influence advertising effectiveness?
4. Regional editions of national magazines usually charge advertising rates that are proportionately above the cost of national exposure based upon cost per contact. What factors allow for these increased rates?
5. Why would a major manufacturer with nationwide product distribution select regional advertising coverage?
6. Discuss the importance of publicity and public relations in relation to the firm's overall marketing efforts.

NOTES

1. John Koten, "Real Cigarets Prove True Disappointment despite Their Merits," *The Wall Street Journal,* February 26, 1980, p. 26.
2. Robert T. Coen, "A Down Year? Not in Advertising Growth," *Advertising Age,* December 31, 1979, pp. 51–52.
3. Vance Packard, *The Hidden Persuaders* (New York: McKay, 1957).
4. Jean-Jacques Lambin, "What Is the Real Impact of Advertising?" *Harvard Business Review* 53 (May–June 1975): 139–147.
5. Leo Bogart, "Is All This Advertising Necessary?" *Journal of Advertising Research* 18 (October 1978): 19. Reprinted by permission, © copyright 1978 by the Advertising Research Foundation.
6. William S. Cornamor and Thomas A. Wilson, *Advertising and Market Power*

(Cambridge, Mass.: Harvard University Press, 1974); for the rebuttal, see Harry Block, "Advertising and Profitability: A Reappraisal," *Journal of Political Economy* 82 (March–April 1974): 267–286.

7. Bogart, "Is All This Advertising Necessary?" p. 20.

8. Robert S. Weinberg, *An Analytical Approach to Advertising Expenditure Strategy* (New York: National Association of Advertisers, 1960); see also Gary L. Lilien, Alvin J. Silk, Jean-Marie Choffray, and Murlidhar Rao, "Industrial Advertising Effects and Budgeting Practices," *Journal of Marketing* 40 (January 1976): 16–24; and Peter Doyle and Ian Fenwich, "Planning and Estimation in Advertising," *Journal of Marketing Research* 12 (February 1975): 1–6.

9. Lambin, "What Is the Real Impact," p. 142.

10. Ibid.

11. Ibid., p. 144.

12. Richard Manville, "Why Industrial Companies Must Advertise Their Products — And Consumer Companies Should Advertise Theirs," *Industrial Marketing,* October 1978, pp. 46–50.

13. "How Good Are Advocacy Ads?" *Dun's Review,* June 1975, pp. 76–77.

14. William L. Wilkie and Paul W. Farris, "Comparison Advertising: Problems and Potential," *Journal of Marketing* 39 (October 1975): 7–15.

15. Andrew G. Kershaw, "Against Comparison Advertising," *Advertising Age,* July 5, 1976, pp. 25–26.

16. V. Kanti Prasad, "Communications-Effectiveness of Comparative Advertising: A Laboratory Analysis," *Journal of Marketing Research* 13 (May 1976): 128–137.

17. Examples are taken from Al Ries, "Today's Crises — New Opportunity for Advertisers?" *Management Review* 63 (September 1974): 29–33.

18. "Marketing Briefs," *Marketing News,* June 18, 1976, p. 2.

19. "New Hope for Co-op Funds," *Broadcasting* 88 (June 23, 1975): 40.

20. "The Cry in Co-op: Ready, Set, Charge," *Sales and Marketing Management,* July 11, 1977, p. 30. Reprinted by permission from Sales & Marketing Management magazine. Copyright 1977.

21. C. D. J. Lafferty, "1980's Newspaper Evolution Will Focus on Marketing," *Advertising Age,* October 8, 1979, p. 54.

22. Elino Ellis, "Radio Is Hot Marketing Tool," *Advertising Age,* October 8, 1979, pp. 523–533.

23. Coen, "A Down Year," p. 52.

24. *BBDO Audience Coverage and Cost Guide,* 14th ed. (New York, 1975), p. 8.

25. William Weilbacher, *Advertising* (New York: MacMillan, 1979), p. 361.

26. Louis Wolson, "Pay TV Experiences Geometric Growth," *Advertising Age,* October 8, 1979, p. 533.

27. Al Ries, "What Ad Planners Learn from War," *Marketing Times,* July–August 1979, p. 29.

28. "Need Outdoor Numbers, TAB Told," *Advertising Age,* February 3, 1975, p. 4.

29. "Business Bulletin," *The Wall Street Journal,* February 21, 1980, p. 1.

30. Roger A. Strang, "Sales Promotion, Fast Growth, Faulty Management," *Harvard Business Review* 54 (July–August 1976): 115–124.

31. "Business Bulletin," *The Wall Street Journal,* February 21, 1980, p. 1.

32. "Clip, Clip," *Fortune,* January 1977, p. 26.

33. William Robinson, "Twelve Basic Promotion Techniques," *Advertising Age,* January 10, 1977, pp. 50–55.

34. *Marketing and Sales Promotion* (New York: Sales and Marketing Management, 1978), pp. 66–67. Reprinted by permission from Sales & Marketing Management magazine. Copyright 1978.

35. "How To Use Point-Of-Purchase Materials More Effectively," *Drug Topics,* November 15, 1977, p. 50.

36. Eugene Mahany, "Package Goods Clients Agree: Promotion Importance Will Grow," *Advertising Age,* April 14, 1975, p. 46.

37. Rollie Tillman and C. A. Kirkpatrick, *Promotion: Persuasive Communication in Marketing,* rev. ed. (Homewood, Ill.: Irwin, 1972), p. 312.

38. "Exhibits Tap 80% New Buyers," *Marketing Times,* May–June 1979, p. 3. Reprinted from Marketing Times, business update for the management professional, published by Sales and Marketing Executives International.

39. "Promotions Lack Proper Planning," *Advertising Age,* April 21, 1975, pp. 2ff.

40. Strang, "Sales Promotion," pp. 121–122.

41. Ibid., p. 122.

42. Some of the goals are taken from William G. Nickles, *Marketing Communication and Promotion,* 2nd Edition (Columbus, Ohio: Grid Publishing Company, 1980), pp. 221–222.

43. James Engel, Hugh Wales, and Martin Warshow, *Promotional Strategy,* 3d ed. (Homewood, Ill.: Irwin, 1975), pp. 489–491.

44. Donald G. Softness, "What Product PR Can Do for You in Today's Advertising World," *Advertising Age,* August 2, 1976, p. 19. Copyright 1976 by Crain Communications, Inc.

45. Ibid., p. 20.

◢ **CASES**

18.1 RSVP Restaurants

RSVP Restaurants is opening two new restaurants, one in Kansas City and the other in St. Louis. The theme of the restaurants is "the total concept of dining." This encompasses the entire dining experience—atmosphere, food, and service. The European atmosphere emphasizes intimacy. The menu is oriented toward the expanding interest in gourmet foods. A typical dinner begins with a tureen of hot or cold soup (depending on the season) complemented by hot bread. A green salad follows, topped by one of the restaurant's three specially prepared dressings. An assortment of entrees is offered, such as veal cordon blue, beef stroganoff, breast of chicken bordeaux, and shrimp barsac, accompanied by freshly cooked vegetables served in typical European style. A dessert cart comes to the table after the meal, offering such choices as strawberries quorum, rum cream pie, and zqetchgenknodel (Bavarian plum dumplings) for an additional charge.

RSVP Restaurants' target market is the middle- to upper-income individual. Research reveals that the average customer spends between $25 and $40 on a meal, including cocktails, dinner, and wine. After an introductory period of six months, RSVP Restaurants in Denver, Colorado Springs, and Phoenix had built up enough business to seat customers by reservations only.

Irene Colby, director of marketing, is reponsible for deciding which media to use in the advertising campaign.

1. What media would she choose for the introductory period?
2. What media would she choose for a continuing advertising campaign? Explain your selections.

18.2 Dow Pharmaceuticals

Dow Pharmaceuticals planned to introduce a new oral/nasal decongestant to pediatricians. In order to distinguish between the advertiser's new Novafed brands and others in the crowded decongestant market, the sales promotion manager had created a digital "clown" thermometer that could be hung in examination rooms where it would be visible to both mother and physician. Mounted on a plastic placard imprinted with the brand name and company name, the thermometer was illustrated with a clown holding six balloons. Numerals in the balloons ranged from 68 to 78, each activated by temperature-sensitive crystals to indicate the room temperature. On the reverse of the thermometer was complete product information. The sales promotional item was distributed to 15,000 pediatricians.

The company has now produced a microcrystalline polymer to be used in controlling hemorrhaging and to aid in clotting blood. The product was somewhat revolutionary—it appeared to be more effective than any other similar item on the market. It was virtually nontoxic and appeared to have no adverse side effects. Not only was it clinically superior to competitive products for routine uses—such as wounds of the liver, controlling bleeding ulcers, and cardiovascular bleeding—but also it made possible surgery that was previously impossible. Spleen surgery repairs, certain types of brain surgery, liver surgery, and bone bleeding were now possible.

1. Suggest some additional sales promotional items for the decongestant.
2. What other factors should be used in the promotional mix to sell the decongestants?
3. As the sales promotion manager, what devices could you use to promote the new blood clotting drug?
4. Should the company rely strictly on advertising for the new blood clotting drug? Why or why not?

19 Advertising management

OBJECTIVES

To understand the various facets of advertising management.

To analyze the qualitative and quantitative aspects of media selection.

To learn some of the techniques of measuring advertising effectiveness and media audiences.

To understand the role of advertising agencies.

The battle began 47 years ago.

Pepsi-Cola Co., a David in the soft-drink business, challenged Goliath Coca-Cola by slashing the price of a 12-ounce drink to five cents from 10 cents and advertising it with a catchy jingle:

Pepsi-Cola hits the spot.
Twelve full ounces, that's a lot.
Twice as much for a nickel, too.
Pepsi-Cola is the drink for you.

Pepsi has narrowed the gap, and the battle is fiercer than ever. Aided by a "Pepsi challenge" advertising campaign wherein consumers in blind taste test choose Pepsi over Coke, Pepsi-Cola captured first place in the increasingly important segment of the market measured by A. C. Nielsen Co.—sales in major food stores.

A series of ads that ran in the late 1970s—"Give me a smile with everything on it, and I'll pass it on" was widely regarded as ineffective. A new campaign was ordered.

This directive led to a panic-inspired brainstorming session at McCann-Erickson, Coke's advertising agency. Under pressure to come up with a much better campaign or lose the prized account, the agency flew teams of its ad people to New York from around the world to seek ideas. From suggested themes such as "Grab the world with a Coke" and "The family of man is the family of Coke," McCann picked the new theme: "Have a Coke and a smile." A backup campaign was also prepared.

Several ads based on the theme were shown to the bottlers. They liked what they saw. The biggest hit was a commercial that featured "Mean Joe" Greene of the Pittsburgh Steelers football team. (This commercial alone, in which Mr. Greene is decidedly not mean to a young fan who offers him a Coke, took 12 hours and 125 takes to film and cost more than $100,000 to produce.)

One attempted solution: "Project Mordecai." Named after the Biblical figure who saved the Jews from a plot to destroy them, the project amounted to an attempt to intimidate Pepsi with a network roadblock. Advertising slots at the same time on all three television networks were purchased for a 60-second commercial with the slogan: "One third of all consumers prefer Fresca to Pepsi." Anxious Coke bottlers were told a solution had been found to the Pepsi challenge.

It hadn't. "We just laughed at the Fresca ad," a Pepsi executive says. "If anything, it encouraged us to press on. We knew Coke didn't have an effective response to our ads." Pepsi hasn't taken its "challenge" campaign nationwide, however, preferring instead to concentrate on areas where it is running well behind Coke.

Another Coke ad campaign used a chimpanzee to poke fun at Pepsi's commercials, and still another had a drugstore character named Mr. McAllister tell viewers they should drink Coke because it has 5% fewer calories than Pepsi. But all of the campaigns bombed.

"Coke has never come up with a successful response to the Pepsi challenge," says Mr. Lupton, the Coke director and bottler. "But we're still working on it."

Pepsi recently introduced its own new ad campaign featuring a series of well-crafted mini-dramas. Even Coke seems pleased with the Pepsi campaign — if only because it feared Pepsi was instead about to go nationwide with the "Pepsi challenge" campaign. Coke's salvation may be that Pepsi may become as smug as Coca-Cola once was.[1]

Advertising management, particularly evaluating the effectiveness of an existing or proposed campaign, is still to some degree an art, as the case of Pepsi and Coke shows. There is no cookbook approach that will guarantee a successful campaign. Why? Because advertising involves a lot of creativity, and creativity is hard to quantify. This is not to say that measuring advertising effectiveness is sheer guesswork. As you will see, we have many tools to measure advertising effectiveness. The "right" campaign can dramatically increase market share and profits. Inability to counteract a successful campaign can result in millions of dollars of lost revenue for an advertising agency and the advertiser. Note that Coke's ad agency flew in executives from all over the world to salvage the Coke account.

What is involved in developing the "right" advertising campaign? How does management establish advertising budgets? How can advertising media and campaigns be evaluated? What are the functions of an advertising agency? These are the kinds of questions we address in this chapter.

The advertising management process

Advertising management is a subset of promotion management and generally follows the same procedures (see Figure 19.1). First, advertising goals are established. These should be a logical derivative of overall promotional objectives. When advertising goals are accomplished, it should also mean that promotion goals are being met. After objectives are set, target audiences should be identified. Again, these audiences should be all or part of the audience identified in the promotion plan. Budgets are then developed. Often the overall

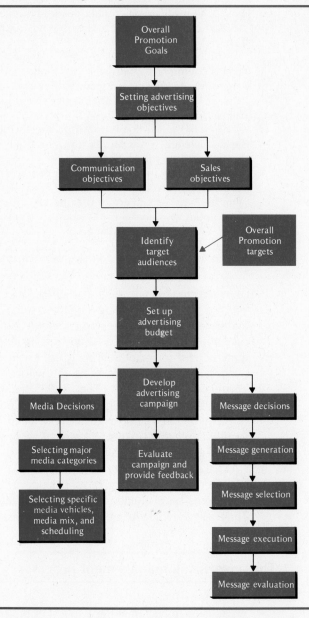

promotion budget is set using one of the techniques described below. In some companies, a build-up promotion budget plan is used. A budget is set for each form of promotion and then all are added together to get the total promotion budget.

The next step is creating an advertising campaign. The message or theme is developed, media are chosen, and schedules established. Finally, the effectiveness of the campaign must be measured. The advertising agency enters the picture at various stages of the managerial process. For example, the agency may have input in establishing promotional objectives or establishing target markets. In other firms, the agency may not have input until planning for a campaign begins.

SETTING GOALS

Effective advertising management requires the establishment of goals as a first step. These goals will provide a basis for planning and evaluating advertising efforts. Like promotional goals, advertising objectives usually involve behavior modification or reinforcement of existing behavior.

Communications and sales objectives. Effective planning cannot take place without specific objectives. These objectives can be either (1) communications goals or (2) sales goals. A **communication goal** is one of information, or maintenance of awareness. For example, research by the Potato Board found that people viewed potatoes as being not very nutritious and fattening. The board's research indicated that one-third of potato consumers felt potatoes had too many calories. Specific communication objectives were established to reeducate the potato eater. Two years later, only one-fourth of the consumers viewed potatoes as having too many calories. Also, the number of people who believed potatoes were nutritious grew from 55 percent of the eaters to 81 percent. Most important, potato consumption rose 18 percent during the two-year period—the first rise in 25 years. The objectives of the Potato Board were first attitude modification and then behavior modification.

The assumption of communication's goals is that if they are reached, the result will be higher sales, a better image, or both. Rather than attempting to reach specific communications goals (which at best are difficult to measure), such as increasing brand awareness 5 percent in Evansville, Indiana, during the next 60 days, some marketing executives attempt to measure the end result—changes in sales. They set a **sales goal.** Total sales volume and market share are widely used sales indices offered by firms such as A. C. Nielsen Company and Audits and Surveys, Inc. Market Research Corporation of America measures the flow of products into homes by the means of purchase diaries, and Selling Areas-Marketing, Inc., records the withdrawal of goods from warehouses.

Setting proper goals. Directly measuring sales results from advertising is not easy. In fact, it is costly and must usually be done under experimental conditions. Once the effect is experimentally measured, then marketing executives can decide if it is feasible to run the campaign for the entire market. Let us look at a real but disguised example. The National Fertilizer Company, a large manufacturer of mixed fertilizers for agricultural and professional gardeners, introduced Gardeneye. The new plant food product contained extra ingredients that reduced weeds and killed insects and fungus diseases. The firm decided to measure the relative efficiency of local television and newspaper advertising using increased market share (sales) as a measure of success.

The experiment involved nine combinations of newspaper and television exposure in 27 markets. Results of the research were these:

1. The overall campaign theme was judged successful. The company market share to the home plant food market increased from 6 to 11 percent.
2. Newspaper advertising increased market share 4.4 percent for every 10,000 lines of advertising.
3. TV advertising increased market share 1.7 percent for every 1,000 accumulated rating points.

On a cost-corrected basis, newspaper advertising sold about three times more efficiently than television. This $32,000 study, plus $250,000 for media time, enabled National Fertilizer to establish realistic and specific nationwide market share objectives for the coming year. Through more efficient media use, the advertising budget was cut by $700,000 and the firm was able to reach its market share objectives. The advertising experiment resulted in significant savings for National Fertilizer.

Specific goals. The variety of advertising objectives can be bewildering. Some of the general areas in which specific objectives might be set are shown in Table 19.1. Again, these objectives must ultimately be geared to increased sales and profits. A few years ago, 97 top advertising executives were asked to

---

▲ **TABLE 19.1 Areas for Specific Advertising Objectives**

Inform	Persuade	Remind
1. New product introduction	1. Persuade to purchase now	1. Maintain awareness
2. Build company image	2. Aid the salesforce	2. Maintain product and company image when salesperson is not available
3. Reduce consumer's fears of risk involved in purchase	3. Change relative importance of product attributes	3. Maintain image during off seasons
4. Suggest new uses of the product	4. Persuade to let salesperson make presentation or demonstration	4. Remind users where to buy product
5. Inform of change in marketing mix, e.g., price	5. Build brand preference	5. Remind consumers that the product will be needed in the near future
6. Tell consumers who is using the product now	6. Increase switching to advertiser's brand	
7. Explain how the product works	7. Attempt to offset competitors' advertising	
8. Explain various uses of the product or service	8. Build employee morale	
9. Correct false impressions		

Think small.

Our little car isn't so much of a novelty any more.

A couple of dozen college kids don't try to squeeze inside it.

The guy at the gas station doesn't ask where the gas goes.

Nobody even stares at our shape.

In fact, some people who drive our little flivver don't even think that about 27 miles to the gallon is going any great guns.

Or using five pints of oil instead of five quarts.

Or never needing anti-freeze.

Or racking up about 40,000 miles on a set of tires.

That's because once you get used to some of our economies, you don't even think about them any more.

Except when you squeeze into a small parking spot. Or renew your small insurance. Or pay a small repair bill. Or trade in your old VW for a new one.

Think it over.

Dealer Name

5-057-2

Source: Courtesy of Volkswagen of America.

pick the "best ads ever." Although their decisions are naturally somewhat subjective, and other good ads have been produced in five years since the contest, it is interesting to see what they chose as "some of the best." Their selections of best persuasive, informative, and reminder advertisements are shown in Figures 19.2, 19.3, and 19.4.

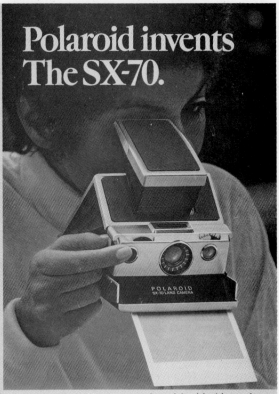

Polaroid's SX-70 explained.

just an interesting hobby, can now become a spontaneous and recurring pleasure in your daily life.

What it does for you.
The new SX-70 probably includes more technological advancements than any other consumer product in the world today.

It is a single lens reflex camera. Your eye sees what the camera lens sees, because you're actually looking through the camera lens.

And, the SX-70's unique 4-element lens allows you to focus on objects from 10.2 inches to infinity.

The 10-exposure film pack contains a revolutionary wafer-thin battery to provide fresh power to operate the camera every time you load fresh film.

A 10-shot GE FlashBar array lets you take flash pictures from 10.2 inches to 20 feet or more away. And you can shoot a sequence of pictures almost as quickly as you can touch the red electric button.

Nothing being left to chance, the SX-70 scans the FlashBar electronically, picking the next flash to be fired. A unique, tiny

The SX-70, quite simply, can reveal the world to you as you have never seen it before.

Slim, graceful, balancing lightly in your hand at only 24 ounces, this remarkable package of more than 200 transistors, elegantly wrapped in top-grain leather, scarcely hints at the wonders it can perform.

What you do.
One motion and the camera's open, ready at a finger's touch to propel picture after picture into your hands.

Just frame, focus and touch the red electric shutter button. Your picture is automatically ejected in less than 2 seconds, to come itself and develop into a color photograph of a depth and brilliance unparalleled in amateur photography.

What once might have seemed a family duty, or even

picture counter located on the back of the camera prevents the FlashBar from firing after your last exposure.

The pictures themselves are exceptionally durable. As soon as they are ejected from the camera, you can handle them, stack them, put them in your pocket.

Where and when.
The SX-70, with a suggested list price of $180, is available now in limited quantity at Polaroid Land camera dealers. We are increasing the supply as quickly as possible. Meanwhile, visit your dealer to see a demonstration, and to place an order for your own SX-70.

Polaroid invents The SX-70.

Just touch the red electric button and...

Source: Courtesy of Polaroid Corporation.

IDENTIFYING TARGET AUDIENCES

After objectives have been established, specific target audiences must be identified. In many cases, the target audience for an advertising campaign can be derived from overall promotional target groups that have been previously established. A number of firms identify their target audiences during the objectives-setting process. That is, their specific objectives will contain a statement which identifies the target audience.

THE ADVERTISING BUDGET

After objectives have been established and a target audience identified, an advertising budget must be developed. Theoretically, the budget needs to be set at a point where the last dollar spent on advertising equals profits from the sales

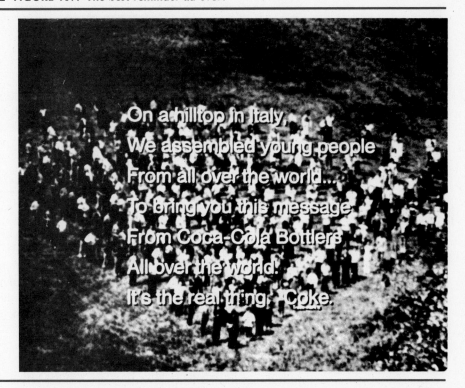

On a hilltop in Italy,
We assembled young people
From all over the world...
To bring you this message
From Coca-Cola Bottlers
All over the world:
It's the real thing. Coke.

Source: Courtesy of The Coca-Cola Company.

produced by that dollar. In practice, because of the immensity of the problems involved, it is not easy to apply this marginal concept. Common techniques for setting budgets are arbitrary allocation, percent of sales, market share, competitive parity, and objective task (see Figure 19.5). These traditional techniques of budget setting, while they are practical, rarely lead to an optimal dollar quantity or an optimal blend. In fact, an optimal technique has yet to be developed.

Arbitrary allocation. The easiest way to set an advertising budget is simply to pick a number. This is called **arbitrary allocation.** An offshoot of a recent study by the author among seven moderate-sized commercial banks found that in all cases but one, the advertising budget was set arbitrarily. One bank had allocated a constant dollar amount to advertising for eight years. Discussions with a number of bank officers did not reveal why that specific amount had been chosen. No one knew! Another bank simply followed the recommendation of its advertising agency. If the amount seemed too high, the board of directors would "lop off" a certain amount. Perhaps the reason for this illogical approach to budget setting is the difficulty of measuring the effectiveness of advertising.

FIGURE 19.5 Techniques for setting advertising budgets.

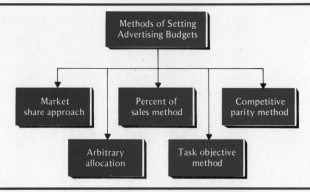

Competitive parity. A second approach for establishing an advertising budget is called **competitive parity.** That is, the firm allocates enough money to meet the promotional challenge of the competition. If competitor A spends $1 million, then your organization allocates $1 million for advertising. Perhaps the biggest problem with this technique is that it ignores creativity and media effectiveness. If the money is spent in the wrong media or if the campaign is ineffective, spending $10 to $50 million might not give the firm competitive parity. General Foods, for example, spends about three times as much on advertising as Kraft Foods but has sales less than 1.5 times as large as Kraft. Perhaps the only advantage of the competitive parity technique is that it does force the firm to examine competitors' actions.

Percent of sales. Another method of establishing a promotional budget is to use a certain percentage of total sales. In other words, promotion dollars $= n\%$ $\times$ total sales. The **percent of sales approach** is not limited to total sales; it can also be based on sales by product, territory, customer group, and so forth. The inherent weakness of this approach is that the budget becomes a consequence of sales rather than a determinant of sales. As sales go down, the promotion budget falls proportionately. Yet research has shown that industrial advertisers that maintain their promotional budgets during recessionary periods have better sales than those that do not.[2]

The appeal of the percent of sales technique is its simplicity. Even large firms like Beatrice Foods base their promotional budgets on sales. It is obvious that many others follow this practice, since advertising expenditures tend to rise and fall with the business cycle.[3] The technique is easy to use and easy for managers to understand, since they often view costs in percentage terms. It also gives the illusion of definiteness. Selected advertising-to-sales ratios by product category are shown in Table 19.2. One study showed that many firms that use this approach use the same percentage year after year.[4]

Some firms use average sales for their industry as a basis for budgeting. There are certain fallacies in following industry averages, however. The fact that one

Ad rank	Company	Advertising	Sales	Percentage of sales
	Airlines			
68	Trans World Corp.	$ 61,994,900	$ 4,334,000,000	1.4
77	UAL Inc.	52,461,900	3,831,523,000	1.4
88	Eastern Air Lines	40,400,000	1,881,526,000	1.4
96	American Airlines	35,039,800	3,252,532,000	1.1
97	Delta Air Lines	33,500,000	2,654,026,000	1.3
	Appliances, TV, radio			
24	RCA Corp.	158,600,000	7,454,600,000	2.1
31	General Electric Co.	139,407,500	22,460,600,000	0.6
84	North American Philips Corp.	44,179,375	2,409,003,000	1.8
	Automobiles			
4	General Motors Corp.	323,395,900	66,311,200,000	0.5
10	Ford Motor Co.	215,000,000	1,409,003,000	0.5
40	Chrysler Corp.	118,000,000	12,000,000,000	1.0
57	Toyota Motor Sales U.S.A.	80,256,200	13,460,000,000	0.6
65	Nissan Motor Corp.	66,082,900	13,079,598,000	0.5
75	Volkswagen of America	44,611,600	3,117,049,000	1.4
83	American Motors Corp.	44,611,600	3,117,049,000	1.4
85	American Honda Motor Co.	44,000,000	3,619,000,000	1.2
100	Mazda Motors of America	28,365,600	900,000,000	3.2
	Toiletries, cosmetics			
8	Warner-Lambert Co.	220,242,500	3,217,208,000	6.8
12	Bristol-Myers Co.	210,600,000	2,752,777,000	7.7
13	American Home Products Corp.	206,000,000	3,649,476,000	5.6
35	Gillette Co.	126,960,200	1,984,722,000	6.4
44	Chesebrough-Pond's	107,342,000	1,174,274,000	9.1
82	Beecham Group Ltd.	46,704,500	2,300,000,000	2.0
89	Noxell Corp.	40,216,285	179,700,000	22.2
	Wine, beer and liquor			
19	Seagram Co. Ltd.	168,000,000	2,554,096,000	6.6
22	Anheuser-Busch	160,524,000	3,263,744,000	4.9
26	Heublein Inc.	155,000,000	1,769,074,000	8.8
62	Jos. Schlitz Brewing Co.	71,551,000	894,156,000	8.0
79	Brown-Forman Distillers	50,000,000	675,823,000	7.4
	Soaps, cleansers (and allied)			
1	Procter & Gamble	614,900,000	10,772,186,000	5.7
23	Unilever U.S. Inc.	160,000,000	2,124,000,000	7.5
37	Colgate-Palmolive Co.	122,500,000	4,494,000,000	2.7
60	Clorox Co.	72,590,000	565,400,000	12.8
90	S. C. Johnson & Son	40,204,000	650,000,000	6.2

Source: "100 Leaders' Advertising as Percentage of Sales," *Advertising Age,* September 11, 1980, p. 8.
Copyright 1980 by Crain Communications, Inc. Reprinted by permission.

firm's promotion budget is 5 percent of sales and another's is 10 percent does not necessarily indicate that the latter's promotion is twice as effective. Percentages do not account for quality. They also ignore the base on which they are calculated. Procter & Gamble has one of the lowest percent of sales ratio among major producers of soaps and cleaners, yet it spends over $500 million on advertising—the largest advertising budget in the world.

Finally, an average is just that—an average. When a nonswimmer wades across a river that averages one foot in depth, there is still a good chance that he or she will drown! One student of advertising determined that 20 percent of the marketing budget should be spent on promotion and that until 20 percent is reached, the firm has not reaped the full benefits of its promotion.[5] This is a simplistic approach and at best should serve only as a rough guideline.

The market share approach. Another frequent approach to budgeting is based on trying to maintain a given market share or obtain a certain target share. This is the **market share approach.** If a firm is satisfied with its market share, it may decide to spend the dollar amount or percentage it spent previously. If the organization plans to increase its market share, it can increase its expenditures accordingly.

Like the percent of sales technique, this method ignores quality and creativity. Who is to say that spending $5 million this year will be more or less effective than last year's expenditures? Also, the firm is letting its competition set the parameters of its promotion budget. The market share approach also ignores potential new product offerings. Generally, a new product requires a heavier promotional budget to educate the target market and build product awareness. Aside from recognizing the importance of competition for market share, this approach does not improve much on the methods already discussed.

Borden uses a market share approach coupled with a formal working relationship between its top management and its advertising agency. The agency is answerable for every dollar of ad spending and the achievement of specific market share objectives. Recently, Borden spent $1.7 million on Cracker Jack advertising compared to $1.5 million the previous year. Its goal was to increase market share from 59 to 63 percent. It calculated the cost of four additional percentage points of market share at $200,000 worth of advertising.

Objective and task. The most popular and scientific approach to setting an advertising budget is the **objective and task approach** (see Table 19.3).

The approach offers management a sound technique for setting a promotion budget. First, objectives are established. Second, the communication tools required to achieve those objectives are delineated. Then a budget is built by adding the costs of the promotional activities and programs required.

This approach implies managerial understanding of the effectiveness of various promotional tools in eliciting the desired audience response. It also assumes that achieving the objectives will be worth the costs. Missouri Valley Petroleum used the objective and task approach to test promotion effectiveness. It found that approximately doubling its promotion budget had a profound effect

Percentage of sales	24.8%
Arbitrary	27.7
Other	11.9
Task	35.6
Total	100.0%

Source: Murray Harding, "Project Future: More Advertisers Mad Than Glad about Budget Policy," *Industrial Marketing* 53 (August 1978): 58.

on demand. Tripling the budget led to only minimal further increases. An-heuser-Busch also used the objective-and-task approach. It showed that it could often reduce promotion expenditures and still increase sales. Promotion dollars were utilized more effectively, and this accounted for the sales increases.

Developing an advertising campaign

After promotional objectives have been established, target audiences identified, and an advertising budget determined, the advertising campaign can be planned. An **advertising campaign** is a carefully planned sequence of advertisements designed around a common theme. The goals of a specific program will vary, depending on whether it is a product/service campaign or an institutional campaign. Every campaign requires a theme or message, the selection of a media mix, media scheduling, and measurement of the campaign's effectiveness. Research has shown that an effectively designed campaign will have a significant impact on sales.[6]

THE MESSAGE

Messages are developed in three stages: (1) generation, (2) evaluation, and (3) execution. **Message generation** is the creative development of things to say about the good or service. Message generation is undertaken in light of promotional objectives, the product's current image, and the desired positioning of the product. As the marketing environment changes, so must the basic campaign theme. In 1980, Braniff Airlines switched to a new theme in response to increased competition and rapid expansion into new markets. Braniff's new slogan was: "We had better be better—we're Braniff." In order to sell employees on the new concept of excellence, each advertisement features one or more Braniff employees.

Developing advertising messages as themes is not an easy task. Typically it is up to the "creative people" in the advertising agency to develop a theme. Often themes are quite general, thus allowing the advertiser to develop a number of subthemes or minicampaigns. Examples include: Datsun—"We are

TABLE 19.4 Seven Key Factors in Successful TV Commercials

Product	Campaign results	Star	Central character	"Look"	"Word"	Jingle	Story	Demo
Budweiser beer	No. 1 in U.S.; in world	Lou Rawls; Ed McMahon	Clydes-dales			This Bud's for You	Sport	
Contac	No. 1 in world			Tiny Time Pills				Pills in slow motion
Dr Pepper	Up 15% a year for last six years			Youthful	Pepper	I'm a Pepper		
Esso "Tiger"	Gained 12%; 28% in first year		Tiger			Hold that Tiger	Lady & tiger	
Great Western Savings	$15,000,000 deposits in first 2 weeks	John Wayne		Outdoor			Of the West	
Kellogg's sugar flakes	Part of Big No. 1; "Tony" 23 Yrs. Old		Tony the Tiger		Great		Tony's strife	
Kool-Aid powdered drink	Passed 10,000,000 packs a day		Face on pitcher			Kool-Aid Kool-Aid	Pitcher's arrival	
L'eggs hosiery	Won 30% share against 600 under-4% rivals	Juliet Prowse				L'eggs! L'eggs!		Gals show advantages
Levi's	Way out No. 1 again after 150 years			Sharp cartoon			Heritage/-youth	—as on label
Marlboro cigarets	Moved to No. 1 U.S.		Cowboy	Western	Filter, Flavor, Flip Top	Lot to like	Lone hero	
Maxwell House coffee	No. 1 against rivals		Cora		Good to last drop		Cora convinces	
Minute Maid	"He made it No. 1" —Client	Bing Crosby		Famous family			Family fun	
9 Lives cat food	Owns 25% of canned cat food market		Morris the cat		Unique cat voice		Finicky fun	
Parkay Margarine	No. 1 in margarine				Butter? Parkay!			
Pillsbury "Doughboy"	Valued at $20,000,000		Doughboy			Nuthin' says lovin'		Baking time lapse
Pine-Sol cleanser	Has gone up to No. 1			Graffiti		Pine-Sol theme		Wipe-offs
Polaroid cameras	Sold 2,000,000 "One Steps"	J. Garner & "wife"					Hubby-wife	Camera at work
RCA TV	Has passed Zenith, No. 1	Leslie Caron + more						Color emphasis
Shake n' Bake	Quick national intro success		Pete the butcher				Pete's point	Moist results
Vaseline Intensive Care	Passed Jergens, 25-yr. leader			Dry leaf			Leaf's dryness	Supple leaf
Visine Eye Wash	Passed Murine, 25-yr. leader			Frenetic edit	Gets the red out		Day's irritation	Red clears up
Winchester small cigars	Tripled market; then took 70% of it!		Winchester man			Hero wins gal	Farce situation	
Wisk detergent	Now No. 3 detergent; & No. 1 liquid!				Ring around collar		Problem/solution	Results

Source: Harry Wayne McMahon, "The 7 Factors to Creative Successes," *Advertising Age,* December 17, 1979, p. 42. Copyright 1979 by Crain Communications, Inc.

driven"; "Ford has a better idea"; and Goodyear—"Out front and pulling away." Marketing research is used to develop the perceived benefits of a product and a relative ranking of these benefits. Often creative people will take this information, along with the advertising objectives, and create the theme.

Message evaluation normally also involves market research to determine the best theme among those that have been developed. Evaluation criteria include desirability, exclusiveness, and believability. The message must first make a positive impression on the target audience. It must also be unique; consumers must be able to differentiate the advertiser's message from those of competitors. Most important, it should be believable. A theme that makes extravagant claims not only wastes promotional dollars, but also creates ill will for the advertiser.

Message execution means developing the copy and illustrations for the campaign. **Copy** is the written or spoken material. Illustrations (drawings, photographs) are used to complement and reinforce the advertising copy. Finally, the advertising format must be developed for print media and television. Copy and illustrations must be balanced on the page or screen, headline sizes determined, and colors chosen.

David Ogilvy, a leading advertising practitioner, has developed eleven rules for message creation:

Here, then, are my recipes for cooking up the kind of advertising campaigns which make the cash register ring—eleven commandments which you must obey if you work at my agency:
1. What you say is more important than how you say it. . . .
2. Unless your campaign is built around a great idea it will flop. . . .
3. Give the facts. . . .
4. You cannot bore people into buying. . . .
5. Be well-mannered, but don't clown. . . .
6. Make your advertising contemporary. . . .
7. Committees can criticize advertisements, but they cannot write them. . . .
8. If you are lucky enough to write a good advertisement, repeat it until it stops pulling. . . .
9. Never write an advertisement which you wouldn't want your own family to read. . . .
10. The image and the brand. Every advertisement should be thought of as a contribution to the complex symbol which is the *brand image*. . . .
11. Don't be a copy-cat. . . .[7]

Some examples of successful TV campaigns and the factors that made them successful are shown in Table 19.4. Note that the theme can be transmitted any number of ways—through a central character, word, jingle, story, demonstration, or a combination of factors.

Changing the message. When should a message be dropped or changed? The following example contains suggestions made by Richard Pinkham, vice-chairman of Ted Bates and Company, Inc., the ninth largest advertising agency in the world.

First, *when there's a significant change in your product*. Tire manufacturers would have been out of their minds had they not changed their advertising when radial tires came in.

A second reason is *when, through market research, you find you can expand your target audience*. This has happened in many subsegments of the cosmetic and hair care fields where older women used to be the prime prospects. Now, for example, *everybody* seems to be dyeing their hair. And have you seen the Geritol advertising lately? It used to be sold to grandparents. Then the grandmothers became young enough to be movie stars and now we have young marrieds taking the stuff. I wouldn't be a bit surprised to see my teen-age daughter hooked on the tonic when she comes home for Thanksgiving.

A third reason is *when the market changes*. This happens most often *when a new product is successfully introduced and establishes a strong identity which provides consumers with a new alternative*. Sometimes it's a new competitor. Sometimes it's a new appliance. Mr. Coffee and other automatic dripolators have forced a change in the marketing position of many brands of the coffee itself. Where they used to advertise they were best for the electric percolators, now they are saying they're best for the automatic dripolators.

A fourth good reason to change is *when the value systems of the market change*. Anybody selling to youth today knows you can't sell them in the same way you did ten years ago. They've changed, so the marketing must change. Toy marketing was dramatically changed as a result of consumer and FTC pressure.

Fifth and finally, a marketing point must be changed *when it's a bummer; when it's not working; when sales lag and you have made a mistake*. When this happens, you must start all over again, rewrite the whole 100-page marketing plan from scratch and change not only the message but the marketing plan, the marketing goal, the marketing strategy and the resulting advertising campaign. You have to completely reposition your brand.

A classic example of this is Kool cigarettes. Kools was already a 30-year old brand back in 1962 which for many years was sold as a specialty cigarette. It had only a tiny share of the market. Remember Willie the Penguin saying smoke Kools, smoke Kools, smoke Kools? Most of its customers had colds, smoked the cigarette as an occasional change from their regular brand.

To take Kools out of the specialty class and get it into the mainstream of the market to ride the tide of filters and new mentholated competition, everything was changed—product, market strategy, marketing point and, of course, the advertising. Willie the Penguin hit the dust—or perhaps—the glacier.

The new market strategy was based on Kools' higher mentholated content. The new message was "Come up to Kools for the taste of extra coolness."[8]

MEDIA SCHEDULING

Media scheduling usually has the objective of maximizing reach or frequency. **Reach** is the percentage of different target consumers exposed at least once to a commercial. **Frequency** is the number of times an individual reached is exposed to a brand message. For new product introductions or objectives to increase brand awareness, emphasis is usually placed on reach. Yet high reach levels do not necessarily mean high degrees of brand awareness or advertising recall. It is not unusual for a campaign to achieve a 90 percent reach but find only 25 percent of the target audience could provide top-of-the-mind brand awareness.[9] What is the problem? Reach is a potential measurement; that is, a 90 percent reach means that 90 percent of an audience had an opportunity to see or hear a message. In watching TV, for example, only about 70 percent of the program audience is available to view a commercial, and only about 20 to 25 percent of those viewers can recall anything about the commercial.[10]

Only a small portion of any commercial is perceived at one time. Research sponsored by the Du Pont Company showed that message learning tends to peak somewhere between three and five perceived messages. Once the amount of information is maximized, additional exposures tend to be rejected by consumers, and commercialization beyond this threshhold level may increase negative reaction.[11] Herbert Krugman has developed a "three hit" theory: if a person has perceived a commercial three times, he or she has learned what the product is, the benefits to be gained, and whether the product meets their needs and budget. A "hit" is when a consumer receives the message and one or more of the points in the advertisement is communicated and absorbed.[12] Thus three hits are all that are needed to make a campaign a success.

Scheduling strategies. Actual scheduling of media depends upon campaign objectives, opportunities to purchase time or space, competitors' actions, and the advertiser's past success with various scheduling techniques. Key scheduling strategies are shown in Figure 19.6. Some products are in the latter stages of the product life cycle and are advertised on a "reminder basis" at a constant level. Margarines, soft drinks, and cigarettes are examples. Others, such as cold tablets and suntan lotions, tend to follow a concentrated strategy. The continuous increasing strategy is sometimes used for a new product as long as it is in the introduction and growth stages of the life cycle.

Evaluating media alternatives. Media selection may require a kind of managerial judgment that defies quantification. Perhaps management feels that an endorsement is important; this requires the use of *Parents' Magazine* or *Good Housekeeping* seals. If quality is important, management should shy away from cheap magazines and some independent low-budget television stations. Some media tend to have a lower quality image than others — telephone sales pitches, match book covers, and posters on abandoned buildings. Others, like *Town and Country* magazine, denote quality and snob appeal. If an advertiser has a detailed or complex story to tell, it will limit the media choice. For example,

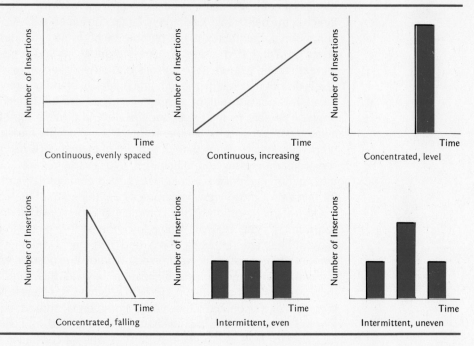

the advertisement in Figure 19.7 does not lend itself to television (due to cost), radio (because of the complexity of the message), or billboards.

Cost per thousand (CPM) is the standard criterion for comparing media. The formula is

$$CPM = \frac{\text{Price of a single ad}}{\text{Audience size (in thousands)}}$$

If the cost of an ad is $50,000 and the audience is 24 million people, CPM is $2.08. The costs of all media have been rising rapidly since 1970. Sunday magazines, newspaper advertising, and spot radio have shown the greatest CPM increases. Naturally, this improves the cost attractiveness of competing media.

There are several problems with CPM comparisons. First is the question of audience measurement. Does the figure include the pass-along rate or is it base circulation? Pass-along rate refers to the number of actual readers per issue. A large pass-along rate can drop CPM substantially. CPM data also make the tacit assumption that everyone in the audience is part of the target market. Rarely is this the case. Finally, media are so different in form, content, reputation, editorial content, display quality, audio capabilities, and so forth that cross-media comparisons based only on CPM become meaningless.

Another factor that complicates the media selection process is **audience duplication.** Assume that *Newsweek* has a circulation of 3.4 million and *Time* has a circulation of 4.5 million. If 800,000 people subscribe to both publica-

Source: Courtesy of Arnold Bernhard & Co., Inc.

tions, the nonduplicated circulations are 2.6 million and 3.8 million for *Newsweek* and *Time,* respectively (see Figure 19.8).

Usually the greater the number of media selected, the greater the problem of duplication. If an advertising campaign does not have dual exposure among its goals, duplicated circulation results in wasted advertising dollars.

Media selection models. Early approaches to modeling the media selection process centered upon linear programming. The objective of such models is usually to maximize total exposure. Again, these models ignore the problem of audience duplication, media discounts, and the marginal value of multiple insertions.

A refinement of basic linear programming models involves the weighing of the various media by executive perceptions of media properties, CPM, reach and frequency to reach certain audiences. Recently, more sophisticated heuristic models such as MEDIAC have been developed. They incorporate information on market segments, sales potential, exposure probabilities, media costs,

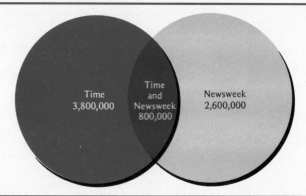

forgetting, seasonality, individual response to exposures, and vehicle exposure values into the selection process.[13]

Field survey media selection techniques. An alternative to modeling a media selection technique is field research. The area field method is the process of using one medium in one area and a second in a different area. A second technique, the response function method, requires only one area and measures different exposure levels by media. For example, medium A may average three exposures to the target audience and medium B five exposures during the test period. These data are then compared with cost data to select a given media. If unduplicated audiences, both part of the target market, are being reached, then perhaps both media will be utilized. Renault, the French automobile manufacturer, successfully used the response function technique to select its media.

EVALUATING THE ADVERTISING CAMPAIGN AND PROVIDING FEEDBACK

The last step in the advertising management process is the evaluation of the campaign. This can be done before it is actually "rolled out," during the campaign, and after the campaign. After a campaign has been created, tests may be run to fine-tune it prior to "roll out." When a campaign is underway, several monitoring techniques may be utilized to determine whether or not it is meeting goals. Even if a campaign is highly successful, a postcampaign analysis is typically undertaken to ascertain how it might have been done more efficiently and what factors contributed to its success.

Arthur W. Schultz, chairman of the board of Foote, Cone and Belding, says, "The biggest waste in advertising is in the advertising itself—because advertising doesn't do what it is supposed to do."[14] Obtaining the proper media mix is only half the battle; the "right" message must reach the target market. Any message that aids in accomplishing the advertising goal is the "right" message. An advertisement can be evaluated before it is placed in the media (pretest) or afterward (posttest). Of course, actual sales effectiveness must be measured after the campaign has been run.

Sales effects may be forecast, however, by using simulation models. To date most advertising simulation models have been of minimal use in measuring effectiveness. Simulation models are not of much value to creative personnel because they do not explain why an ad or a campaign was successful or unsuccessful. As one advertising executive has said, "I know that fifty percent of my advertising is ineffective; the problem is that I don't know which fifty percent."

Tests of communication effectiveness. How effective a campaign is can be tested with a number of techniques: recall tests, recognition tests, attitude measures, physiological tests, and experimental design sales tests.

Recall tests can be pretests that compare several ads or posttests that determine the amount of information learned by the target consumer. A pretest can take place in the home, in a shopping center, or in a laboratory situation. One form of recall testing in which the author was involved centered on measuring recall for two convenience grocery commercials. Participants were shown a 30-minute television program interspersed with the normal array of commercials, including the test commercials.

First, unaided recall was measured by asking the respondents to write down all the commercials they remembered. Next, they were asked to write down whatever details of the commercials they recalled. Answer papers were collected, and a series of aided-recall papers were distributed sequentially. Aided recall provides certain cues to jog the interviewee's memory—for example: "What do you remember about the grocery shopping commercials?" "What did the man say to the clerk?" "What was the theme of the customer-clerk grocery commercial?" An implicit assumption of recall tests is that higher recall ultimately leads to behavior or attitude modification.

Gallup-Robinson, a major marketing research firm, uses aided recall in both print media and television tests. Print tests (magazine readership) require first that the person interviewed recall at least one feature article in the magazine. The respondent is then handed a series of cards with advertisers' names on them. The interviewee is then asked to pick which ones were advertised in the magazine. When advertised products are correctly identified, the respondent is questioned in depth. Next, the issue is opened to the ad in question and aided-recall questions are asked.

Hooper-Starch, a market research company, conducts posttest magazine research that also requires recall but is referred to by Starch as a **recognition test.** Each interviewer carries a portfolio of sample pages and advertisements of up to 16 magazines. The researcher goes to the respondent's home and asks whether he or she has read a particular periodical. If the answer is yes, the interviewer will show the respondent an ad and ask: "Did you see or read any part of this advertisement?" Starch reports three basic findings:

1. *Noted.* The percentage of respondents who remember seeing the ad.
2. *Seen associated.* The percentage of respondents who recall seeing or reading part of the ad.
3. *Read most.* The percentage of respondents who reported reading at least half the ad.

One problem with Hooper-Starch data is that the respondent may not tell the truth about remembering the advertisement. More important, heavy readers are taken through a large number of portfolios. As a result, the interview may last 2½ to 3 hours, resulting in interviewee fatigue and poor responses.

Often **attitude measures** are incorporated into recall and recognition tests. Interviewers may ask interviewees to tell them whether an ad is believable, convincing, dull, imaginative, informative, phony, realistic, silly, and so forth. They may also ask: "How did the ad affect your desire for the product: (1) increased very much, (2) increased somewhat, (3) unaffected, (4) decreased somewhat, (5) decreased very much."

The "Come to Shell for Answers" advertising campaign has been a major success because of advertising research, according to Rene Zentner, manager of opinion research, Shell Oil Company.

There are three ways in which we employed survey research in connection with the program. First, we found such research central to selecting a corporate advertising theme. Second, once we had chosen a theme, survey research helped us define a program embodying the theme. Finally, survey research has helped us maintain the vigor and interest of the program since its inception. While the application of survey research in corporate communications is not new or unique to Shell, we believe our extensive use and selection of particular survey methods to address the multi-faceted elements of corporate advertising campaigns has made significant contributions to the overall effectiveness of our program. . . .

One thing that many studies had shown us with remarkable unanimity was the low credibility of the oil industry on energy topics. Since 1974 the oil companies have been held principally responsible for the oil embargo, its attendant gasoline shortages, and its consequent high refined-product prices. Moreover, oil industry spokesmen rated comparatively low on all scales we reviewed, and oil company issue advertising was among the least believed forms of public communication. . . .

. . . Because Shell for many years has had sensitivity to customer needs, we decided that there might be a good match between our consumer-oriented corporate policies and an advertising program responding to the needs of American drivers for better information on the care, maintenance and use of their automobiles — an area in which we have expertise.

Thus, the theme of the consumer-oriented "Come to Shell for Answers" arose from matching information on public needs to our own strengths and advertising history.

For some time, Shell and Ogilvy & Mather had been developing a strategy for such a program. When the idea of using booklets as the basis of the program emerged, we used research to test the booklet concept, the booklet content and the booklet topics. By carefully pretesting the elements of the campaign, we were able in May of 1976 to initiate the "Come to Shell for Answers" campaign with some assurance that it would reply to the needs of the American motorist. From the program's beginning, our tracking research indicated the advertising was performing as we had hoped. In that research, we periodically conduct interviews across the nation with samples of over a thousand motorists. The surveys showed that awareness of the campaign more than doubled in the first year, from 20 percent of the public in second quarter 1976 to 41 percent in second quarter 1977. And recall continues to rise. Moreover, perceptions of Shell as a consumer-oriented company increased in a similar fashion.[15]

In order to avoid the bias that is sometimes encountered in recall, recognition, and attitude tests, some advertisers have turned to **physiological testing.** Galvanic skin tests, eye movement experiments, pupil dilation measurement, and so forth are used as measures of advertising awareness and interest. Most advertisers have failed to prove satisfactorily that there is a strong relationship between the findings of physiological tests and actual purchase behavior.

Perhaps the only way to truly measure the effect of advertising on sales is through a good experimental design. These are often very costly, however, as well as time-consuming. A simpler experimental design such as the before and after design with a control group is often used. Such an experiment is described in Table 19.5. Companies such as Monsanto and Du Pont often use experimental designs to measure advertising sales effectiveness.

◀ **TABLE 19.5   A Two-City Test to Measure the Effects of TV Advertising**

Background

Consumption of prepared barbecue sauces in the southern market has typically been very low, even though there is a high incidence of backyard cookouts. An earlier small-scale test indicated the effectiveness of spot TV as a sales stimulant for Cowboy Barbecue Sauce in markets with similar consumption characteristics where competitive sauces were virtually nonexistent. To verify this proposition, a broad-scale test was designed utilizing Houston as a test city, with Atlanta selected as the control city. In addition to the regular media pressures levied in both markets, Houston received added media weight through six TV spots a week over a ten-week period. The results were measured by store audits over five months, plus before-and-after telephone surveys.

Telephone surveys

Residential telephone surveys aimed at measuring awareness and usage of Cowboy Barbecue Sauce were conducted in each market. Pre- and post-advertising measures were taken, six months apart. Almost 2100 telephone contacts with housewives were made during both stages of the test.

	Total telephone contact	
	Pre-advertising	Post-advertising
Control market (Atlanta)	492	538
Test market (Houston)	525	532
Total respondents	1,017	1,070

Awareness

In the test city, Houston, awareness of Cowboy Barbecue Sauce increased 30 percentage points between the pre- and post-advertising checks. In the control city, Atlanta, awareness decreased 2 percentage points.

Usage

In Houston, the percentage of respondents who had ever used Cowboy Barbecue Sauce increased from 10 to 27 percent. In Atlanta, the percentage of respondents who had ever used the sauce was 22 percent in both surveys.

Store audit results

Here are the results from our 20-store panel in each area, based on unit sales per store per week:

Average sales per store per week

	9/3 to 10/1	10/1 to 10/29	10/29 to 11/26	11/26 to 12/17	12/17 to 1/14
Houston (ad area)	15.0	17.4	17.9	21.6	23.2
Atlanta	12.9	13.5	14.5	13.5	12.9

Indexing the base period (prior to advertising) at 100 in each market, here is the comparative trend:

	Houston vs. Atlanta				
	9/3 to 10/1	10/1 to 10/29	10/29 to 11/26	11/26 to 12/17	12/17 to 1/14
Houston (ad area)	100	116	119	144	155
Atlanta	100	105	118	105	100

Summary

Our spot TV certainly seems to have stimulated increased awareness and usage of Cowboy Barbecue Sauce in the Houston market. As far as we can determine, television was the only variable evident in the profile of the two areas. The continued sales growth suggests the conversion of triers to repeat users. We may well expand this type of activity into other relatively undeveloped Cowboy Barbecue Sauce markets, for the dollars involved in this schedule could well play out in a reasonable time.

Although our example in Table 19.5 uses different cities, some print media offer split runs that enable advertisers to use an experimental design in a single city. A **split run** involves stopping the presses for a magazine or newspaper and inserting a different ad in place of the original one. Thus, one area of town will receive ad A and the other ad B. Several large metropolitan newspapers now offer split runs.

A major advance in coupling experimental design methodology and cable television has been accomplished by AdTel. The techniques use a dual-cable CATV system and two consumer purchase diary panels. The system results in a highly controlled but realistic testing environment. By using different ads on the dual-cable system, AdTel can measure sales response. The more detailed information recorded in the diary provides additional insight into why a test succeeded or failed.

Audience size measurement. Audience measures are generally made by the same research organizations that gauge advertising effectiveness. In addition to Starch, TGI specializes in periodic magazine audience studies. Another organization, the Audit Bureau of Circulation (ABC), audits the paid-circulation figures of both magazines and newspapers. Arbitron is the largest research firm specializing in radio audience measurement. Information is gathered by consumer diaries sent to randomly selected households. In 1980, no other researcher provided a nationwide radio audience survey.

Newspaper audience measurement is not dominated by any single firm. Beldon Associates and Markets In Focus probably conduct more newspaper research than any other company. Newspaper audience data are usually gathered through telephone or in-home interviews. Consumption patterns and demographic profiles are also obtained for promotional purposes. A trade ad may then read, "Ninety-three percent of all Detroit scotch drinkers read the Detroit Daily News."

Television audience data are usually gathered by means of consumer diaries. A. C. Nielsen and the American Research Bureau (Arbitron) dominate the syndicated measurement studies. When quick audience results are needed, telephone interviews are taken by A. C. Nielsen and several other research companies. In addition to diaries and telephone surveys, Nielsen also uses an audiometer that measures the number of sets tuned in to a particular station.

Nielsen's national television sample consists of only 1170 out of a total of 68.5 million TV-owning households in the country.[16] Each set in the sample has an audiometer that feeds channel selection information into Nielsen's computers over special telephone lines. Audiometer data are "reinforced" by the 100,000 families a year who fill out television diaries on a weekly basis. According to Nielsen's management, "the diary and meter results are consistently almost identical."[17] Accuracy is of extreme importance to television networks, since a percent rating change (a Nielsen point) was worth an average of $19 million or more during the winter of 1980.[18]

Advertising agencies

Advertising agencies occupy a unique position in the business environment. No other function of business is delegated to outside organizations to the extent that advertising is. Let us look at how advertising agencies function, and at how they interact with the business firm.

AGENCY FUNCTIONS

Full-service advertising agencies generally perform five functions: creative services, media services, research, merchandising counsel, and advertising planning. The largest full-service agencies are listed in Table 19.6.

565

TABLE 19.6   The Ten Largest U.S. Full-Service Advertising Agencies

Rank	Agency	1980 (millions)	1979 (millions)
1	Young & Rubicam	$2,273.2	$1,921.1
2	J. Walter Thompson Co.	2,137.7	1,693.0
3	McCann-Erickson	1,792.1	1,670.3
4	Ogilvy & Mather	1,661.9	1,392.6
5	Ted Bates & Co.	1,404.1	1,203.0
6	BBDO Int'l	1,305.0	985.5
7	Leo Burnett Co.	1,144.8	959.7
8	Foote, Cone & Belding	1,117.6	919.6
9	SSC&B	1,111.8	1,021.6
10	D'Arcy-MacManus & Masius	1,058.9	853.6

Source: John O'Connor, "Income Reaches $4.7 Billion," *Advertising Age* (March 18, 1981) p. 1.

Creative personnel conceive promotional themes and messages, write copy, design layouts, and draw illustrations. Media service departments aid in selecting the media mix, scheduling, and controlling the media program. Several major agencies are now subcontracting television buying to media purchasing boutiques because of the complexity of television advertising.

Larger advertising agencies also aid in the formulation and analysis of market research studies. Often the agency goes far beyond media research by aiding in new product development research, positioning research, and the like. In virtually every case, the actual research and most of the design work are done by a marketing research subcontractor. Some agencies also develop contests, premium offers, point-of-purchase displays, and other forms of sales promotion for clients. They also prepare brochures for the salesforce and aid in package design.

Almost all full-service agencies work with clients in campaign design and planning. Promotional goals are established, positioning strategies defined, promotional alternatives examined, and campaigns created. The agency also aids in developing control procedures to measure campaign effectiveness.

The responsibility for maintaining a channel of communication between the agency and the advertiser rests with the account executive. Account executives transmit plans, objectives, and concepts to the agency's creative personnel and present proposed campaigns to the advertiser. Usually, account executives are also the agency's salesforce and are expected to make presentations to potential new accounts.

AGENCY COMPENSATION

Historically, advertising agencies have been paid a standard 15 percent commission on the cost of media time and space. In the late 1960s the industry began to realize that some advertisers were not getting their money's worth, whereas others received far more than a 15 percent commission would justify.

Today the fee system is rapidly replacing the standard commission. Advertisers are charged a fee for services actually rendered rather than a fixed percentage. The president of one moderate-sized advertising agency noted, "I've got several clients billing under a half million dollars each, and at 15 percent commission, I'm losing money on every one of them."[19] Some large advertisers have switched to a cost-plus system that will provide the agency with a 1 percent net profit. At present, this is approximately the industry average net profit on billings.

CAMPAIGN FRANCHISING

A growing trend of the 1980s is **campaign franchising.** Since certain types of firms tend to have common goals and problems, agencies are designing a single campaign that can be used by any company. The Golnick agency franchises one campaign to 800 banks and savings and loans and another to 1000 local car dealers throughout the country. Golnick charges an annual fee that averages $4500. The client receives exclusive use in its market of a set of newspapers and radio ads, plus pennants, decals, window streamers, and billboard ideas. Typically, Golnick prepares six new campaigns a year and reuses popular older ones.

AGENCY SWITCHING

Perhaps because of the difficulty of measuring advertising effectiveness and/or advertiser demand for creative freshness, advertisers often switch agencies. Sometimes a change of agencies is justified because promotional goals have not been achieved. In other cases, advertisers with internal capabilities are dropping full-service firms in favor of boutiques. **Advertising boutiques** are typically small firms that specialize in some aspect of the creative function, such as the creation of copy for print media. All too often, however, advertisers change for emotional rather than rational reasons. And such shifts are not limited to small advertisers: It is not uncommon in a single year to find over 200 half-million-dollar or larger accounts switching agencies. Recently, for example, Toyota switched a $30 million account and Datsun, a $45 million account.

SELF-CONTROL IN THE ADVERTISING INDUSTRY

In addition to rapid account changes, advertising agencies have to cope with the growing role and scope of advertising regulation (see Chapter 3). To avoid increasing governmental regulation, the advertising industry set up procedures for regulating itself in 1971. The National Advertising Division of the Council of Better Business Bureaus (NAD) is intended to serve as a consumer complaint bureau, while the National Advertising Review Board (NARB) serves as an appeals board should NAD rule in favor of the complainant. Figure 19.9 traces the regulatory procedure and the results of self-regulation.

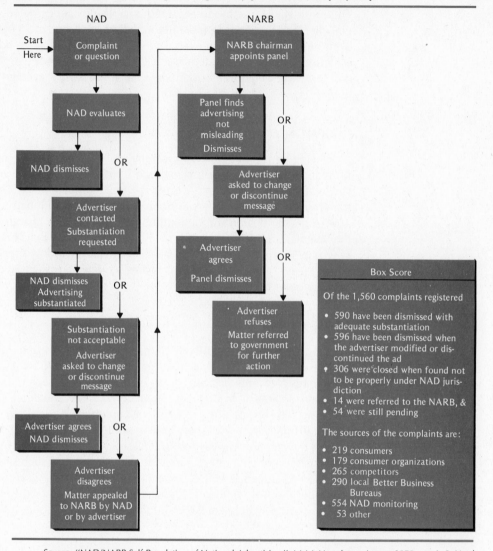

Source: "NAD/NARB Self-Regulation of National Advertising," *AAAA Newsletter,* August 1979, pp. 1–2. Used by permission.

SUMMARY

Advertising management begins with the establishment of realistic goals. These goals can take the form of communication or sales objectives. Regardless of the type selected, they should be specific and measurable.

After objectives have been established, an advertising budget should be developed. There are several techniques for setting budgets. Arbitrary allocation, the easiest to use, is also the least scientific. The percentage of sales approach makes advertising a consequence rather than a determinant of sales. The market share technique is predicated upon the desired level of market penetration. This approach may ignore quality and creativity. It also does not account for potential new product offerings. The objective and task approach is the most scientific and popular. Objectives are stated and tasks delineated; promotional dollars are then allocated to accomplish the necessary tasks.

After objectives have been established and an advertising budget determined, the campaign can be planned. Every campaign requires a theme and a message, selection of the media mix, media scheduling, and measurement of campaign effectiveness.

Media selection is often a difficult task. Audience duplication may complicate the process. Advertising recall tests, recognition tests, psychological tests, and attitude measures are common ways of examining the effectiveness of advertising. Experimental design sales tests are the most effective means of measuring the impact of advertising on sales. These experiments, however, are often time-consuming and costly.

No function of business is delegated to outside organizations more than advertising. This is due to the creative aspects of the process and the large number of specialized personnel required. A full-service advertising agency provides creative services, media services, research, merchandising counsel, and advertising planning.

In the future we will see a continuation of agency switching and a growth of advertising boutiques. In addition, the trend toward self-regulation of the industry will continue.

KEY TERMS

Communication goal	Reach
Sales goal	Frequency
Arbitrary allocation	Cost per thousand (CPM)
Competitive parity	Audience duplication
Percent of sales approach	Recall test
Market share approach	Recognition test
Objective and task approach	Attitude measure
Advertising campaign	Physiological testing
Message generation	Split run
Message evaluation	Campaign franchising
Message execution	Advertising boutique
Copy	

REVIEW QUESTIONS

1. List the various approaches to set advertising budgets and discuss the advantages and disadvantages of each.
2. Why is the use of a percent of sales method for budget determination said to involve circular reasoning?
3. What types of products require high reach levels?
4. Delineate the various methods of measuring advertising effectiveness. How is audience measurement done for the major media?

5. When should the firm's advertising message be changed? Why?

6. Why do most firms use advertising agencies? What services do these agencies render? How are they compensated?

DISCUSSION QUESTIONS

1. Explain the objective and task approach to setting advertising budgets. What kinds of objectives should be used? Is there any way to determine the objective's worth and the task(s) required?

2. Why is the CPM measure of such importance in media selection? How can this measure be improved upon to yield a more valid index of media efficiency?

3. How does audience duplication affect the reach and frequency of an advertising campaign?

4. During the introductory period of market entry, a new product is allocated a disproportionate share of the product's yearly advertising budget. Why?

5. What knowledge and insight does the advertiser hope to gain from the measurement of advertising effectiveness? How can this information benefit the campaign?

6. Why is it so difficult to measure advertising effectiveness?

NOTES

1. John Koten, "Coke's Challenge," *The Wall Street Journal,* March 6, 1980, pp. 1, 19.

2. *Advertising in Recession Periods 1949, 1954, 1958, 1961 — A New Yardstick Revisited* (Chicago: Buchen Advertising, 1970).

3. "Advertisers' Spending Is Stepped Up as the Economy Gains," *Advertising Age,* April 19, 1976, p. 1.

4. David L. Harwood, "How Companies Set Advertising Budgets," *The Conference Board Record* 5 (March 1968): 34–41.

5. John W. DeWolf, "A New Tool for Setting and Selling Advertising Budgets," paper presented at the Eastern Regional Meeting of the American Association of Advertising Agencies, New York, November 7, 1973, p. 21.

6. Peter Doyle and Jan Fenwick, "Planning and Estimation in Advertising," *Journal of Marketing Research* 12 (February 1975): 1–6.

7. David Ogilvy, *Confessions of an Advertising Man* (New York: Atheneum, 1963), pp. 93–103.

8. Speech by Richard Pinkham entitled "Sticking to the Marketing Point," presented before the National Industrial Conference Board, October 20, 1976.

9. Howard Kamin, "Frequency, Not Reach, Is Key to Lifting Brand Awareness," *Advertising Age,* October 9, 1979, pp. 535–536.

10. Ibid.

11. Howard Kamin, "Advertising Reach and Frequency," *Journal of Advertising Research* 18 (February 1978): 22.

12. Herbert Krugman, "What Makes Advertising Effective?" *Harvard Business Review* 23 (March–April 1975): 96–103.

13. See Arch Woodside and David Reid, "Is CPM Related to the Advertising Effectiveness of Magazines?" *Journal of Business Research* 3 (October 1975): 323–334.

14. Arthur W. Schultz, "Stretching the Advertising Dollar," in *Marketing Strategies, A Symposium* (New York: Conference Board Record, 1975), p. 38.

15. Rene Zentner, "Measuring the Effectiveness of Corporate Advertising," *Public Relations Journal,* November 1978, pp. 24–25.

16. David M. Elsner, "A. C. Nielsen Co. Does a Lot More Than Just Rate Television Shows," *The Wall Street Journal,* August 2, 1976.
17. Ibid.
18. Letter to author from A. C. Nielsen Corporation dated March 18, 1980.
19. Richard C. Douglas, "Client: Are You Paying Your Agency Too Much or Too Little?" *Advertising Age,* March 27, 1978, pp. 56, 57.

◢ **CASES**

19.1 Northeast National Bank

Northeast National Bank is a progressive Buffalo, New York, bank with $180 million in deposits. John Nash, vice-president for marketing, came up through the commercial loan department and, at 41 years of age, had hopes of becoming president of the firm by the age of 45. One area that he had trouble "tying down" was advertising effectiveness. With a budget of slightly over $100,000 per year, he wondered just what the bank was getting for its money. He decided that the only way to really understand the situation was to delve into it himself.

As a first step, Nash reviewed the minutes of the advertising committee for the past six months. Although he was a member of the group, he normally took a passive role and let Erma Fine, the promotion manager, set the tone of the discussion. The minutes were skimpy at best and dwelled basically on future advertising themes brought up by committee members. Most of the meetings were dominated by George Yob, the account executive for Cranston-Yost, the bank's advertising agency. Fine opened the meetings; Yob told the committee what the agency was doing and what it planned to do for the next two months; Fine then asked several questions, and then the campaign was routinely approved. Table 1 shows the media mix and themes approved for the months of June and July.

◢ **TABLE 1 Schedule of Media Mix and Message**

Media	Percentage	Description
Billboards	33⅓%	24 locations in southwest quarter of metropolitan Buffalo in points of high traffic flow.
Radio	33⅓	30-second commercial on two different stations—station choice based on listener characteristics.
Newspapers	33⅓	Ads in three newspapers in area of from 300 to 600 agate lines; two separate ads on same theme.

Advertising message during test
1. Loans for home improvements
2. Loans for new automobiles
3. High interest on savings deposits
4. General bank image—"Home of the Free"

Nash decided that some information would be better than none, so he designed a short questionnaire for new accounts covering media, theme recall, and bank services used. The services the respondents mentioned are listed in Table 2; the media selected are shown in Table 3. A final question proved to be the real shocker. Each person was asked why he or she had chosen Northeast National. These results are presented in Table 4.

◀ **TABLE 2   Services Used**

Type	Percentage
Checking accounts	48%
Savings accounts	23
Safe deposit box	5
Installment loan	24

◀ **TABLE 3   Media Chosen**

Medium	Percentage
Radio	55%
Billboards	10
Newspapers	35

◀ **TABLE 4   Why Northeast Was Chosen**

Reason	Percentage
Personal recommendation	26%
Special services	14
Location of the bank	48
Bank employee was known or a friend	6
Advertising	3
Other reasons	3

Nash, who tends to be impulsive, fired off a copy of his results to Fine along with a curt note stating that Northeast should immediately begin a search for a new advertising agency. Fine, who is rather bullheaded, decided that changing agencies would not solve the problem.

1. Prepare Erma Fine's reply to John Nash.
2. How could the advertising study be improved?
3. Was George Yob performing his job properly?
4. Should the media mix be changed? How?
5. Has Nash analyzed his study thoroughly?

Chapter 19   ADVERTISING MANAGEMENT

19.2 The U.S. Bacon Institute

Americans purchase about $5.5 billion worth of bacon every year. Bacon is used in about 83 percent of all U.S. households. Yet all is not well in the bacon industry. Per capital consumption of bacon dropped from 41 pounds per year in 1945 to under 30 pounds per year in the mid-1970s. In 1978, the U.S. Bacon Institute decided to take on the task of steadying or reversing the downward trend in per capita consumption.

The decrease in consumption was seen as a result of a number of factors:

1. Changing life styles—breakfast habits were changing: They were eating smaller breakfasts or no breakfast at all.
2. Increased competition—there is an ever-widening selection of breakfast alternatives available, from cold cereals to instant breakfasts.

The positive attributes of bacon are as follows:

1. High-quality protein.
2. A nutritious food.
3. Moderate in calories.
4. Bacon and bacon dishes are very good for snacks and sandwiches.
5. Bacon is a good value for the money.

Research found that bacon enthusiasts consume 23 percent more bacon per capita. Some breakfast skippers like bacon but lack time. Some people simply do not like the taste of bacon.

1. Suggest a promotional theme or themes for a bacon campaign.
2. Who would be your target audience? Why?
3. What media would you select?
4. How would you pretest your campaign?
5. How would you measure the results?

20

Personal selling and sales management

OBJECTIVES

To understand the nature and importance of selling to the company and to society.

To become aware of the contributions of the behavioral sciences to understanding the selling process.

To review the steps in the selling process.

To describe the function of sales management.

To study the effects of a changing economy on selling.

Selling Pall Industrial Hydraulic's filter systems to U.S. manufacturers and users of industrial equipment is a bit like selling dentistry to hill folk; the prospects have to be convinced that there is a problem before they'll consider investing in a solution. The problems Pall IH proposes to prevent are premature equipment wearout, high warranty costs and excessive downtime.

The marketing challenge for the twelve-year-old Pall IH is to convince key buying influences, such as project engineers who may routinely replace $5,000 pumps once a month, that its filter systems can extend the "normal" life of their equipment by 10–100 times. The systems, which cost anywhere from $100–$20,000, remove microscopic silt particles from the hydraulic systems of such things as cranes, drilling rigs and production-line machinery.

Pall IH claims to have become the No. 1 supplier of industrial, high-pressure filtration in the U.S. and the world.

Company officers decide whether a market segment will be covered by the regional sales managers or by a specialist. The regional managers' duties include calling on key accounts, training distributor salespeople, helping distributors develop new accounts, and seeing to it that distributors get both the scientific and servicing backup they need. They also clear and coordinate all visits by marketing specialists within their territories.

The specialists typically work with distributors to develop prototype sales in the automotive, mining, oil field equipment, or steel mill and foundry equipment markets. The distributors may ask for a specialist's assistance, or the specialist may go in on his own. Pall IH adopted a key accounts program for the regional sales managers. It directs them to spend 80–85% of their time calling on customers with a potential of $50,000–$8 million.

Sales vice president Ohm, who spends 60% of his time on the road calling on large accounts, leading seminars on technical applications and meeting with his field team, evaluates the regional managers' performance on the basis of the following factors:

- Sales
- Incoming bookings
- Distributor performance
- Feedback on needed changes and developments in the product line.

"The line we have today," he explains, "came from the input of our distributors and managers. We depend on them to be our eyes and ears."

Marketing vice president Ogg, who spends about one-third of his time on the road, evaluates his specialists in terms of these criteria: new applications; prototype sales; and getting Pall IH filters written into OEM (original equipment manufacture) equipment specifications. Specialists and sales managers, he says, are both compensated with salary and incentive.[1]

The Pall Industrial Hydraulic's story exemplifies what a well-organized, efficient marketing and sales program can accomplish. In a period of 12 years, the firm went from zero sales to the world's largest distributor of industrial high-pressure filtration systems. Something like this does not just happen. Pall IH's success results from good sales management. What functions are involved in sales management? What steps are involved in making a good sales presentation? The first segment of this chapter introduces the field of personal selling. The remainder of the chapter explains the nature of sales management.

The nature of selling

In a sense, all of us are salespeople. One may become a plant manager, a chemist, an engineer, or a member of any of a multitude of professions, and yet still have to sell. To reach the top in most organizations, individuals will have to sell ideas and concepts to peers, superiors, and subordinates. They will be expected to sell the company to stockholders, customers, and other public groups. Most important, a person must sell himself or herself and his or her ideas to just about everyone with whom he or she develops a continuing relationship and to many other people whom he or she will see only once or twice. The question is not whether a person sells—it is how well he or she sells.

SELLING AS A COMMUNICATION PROCESS

It is easy to understand that selling is a form of communication (see Figure 20.1). The source is the salesperson, who encodes the presentation on the basis of the perceived needs of the consumer. The message is usually transmitted to the potential buyer through the spoken word. Sales representatives will often reinforce the message through visual aids, such as a brochure or product demonstration. The salesperson's facial expressions, gestures, voice inflection, dress, and mannerisms serve as nonverbal forms of communication.

If the salesperson has properly ascertained the needs of the prospective buyer and has effectively communicated those needs in the sales message, the response may be a sale. Perhaps the response will be a request for more information or an objection to some aspects of the sales message. Unlike advertis-

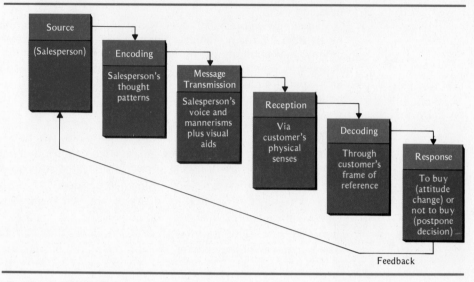

ing, personal selling often involves a reversal of communication roles. The salesperson becomes a receiver and the prospect becomes the source. The representative usually receives rapid feedback because of the face-to-face nature of the situation. The message can then be altered in a further attempt to make the sale. The better the sales representative understands the product or service and the needs and personality of the potential customer, the more effective the sales message will be. Naturally, this does not guarantee a sale. Other salespeople may make a better presentation, offer a superior product, or offer a comparable product at a lower price.

THE ROLE OF SELLING

Generally speaking, as the number of potential customers decreases, the complexity of the product increases. And as the value of the product grows, the role of personal selling becomes more important (see Figure 20.2). About 6 million people are engaged in personal selling in the United States; over 3.3 million of them are male.[2]

This figure reflects all sorts of sales occupations, from the salesclerks who take your orders at fast-food restaurants to engineers with M.B.A.'s who design large and complex production line systems for major manufacturers. Nevertheless, the sheer size of the group of people who earn a living from sales is tremendous compared, for example, with the advertising industry, which employs only a half-million workers. Chances are that if you are a marketing major, you may start your professional career in sales.

FIGURE 20.2 Determinants of the importance of advertising and personal selling.

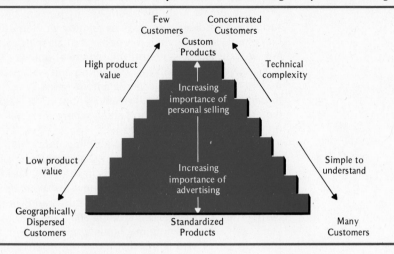

WOMEN IN SALES

Because of the relatively high salaries, government pressures, and lack of opportunity in some other fields, more women are moving into sales. In 1978, there were over 100,000 women in manufacturing and wholesale sales.[3] Since that time, the figure has increased dramatically. The barriers are slowly crumbling. Such industrial companies as Republic Steel, Exxon, and Diamond Shamrock now employ women in the field to sell their products.

How do women do in industrial sales? On the whole, very well. One expert says that if all else is equal, a woman is usually more effective than a man.[4] Women, he contends, not only tend to be more adept at nurturing personal relationships, but also are usually better listeners and have better verbal skills. On the other hand, an academic study found that the average performance of females was lower than males in industrial selling.[5] The authors note that the difference may be due to male-oriented supervision and evaluation systems. Another study found that women tend to receive the same level of job satisfaction as men in industrial selling.[6] Let us look at an example.

For five years, Christine Strittmatter labored in a dead-end job typing letters for a Washington, D.C., trade association. Then, a visiting salesman told her about an opening on the sales force of Wang Laboratories, a maker of computerized word-processing equipment. Mustering her courage, Strittmatter applied for the job and landed it. She soon caught management's attention by out-selling her colleagues, and within eighteen months, was Wang's top sales representative. Today, Strittmatter manages the Washington-Baltimore-Philadelphia territory—Wang's biggest— and has her eye on a vice-presidency.

To be sure, women still have a tougher time than men landing sales jobs, as they do in many other areas of business. Personnel experts estimate that only about twenty percent of all manufacturing and wholesale companies employ women sales representatives and that less than ten percent of all sales representatives are women. At latest count, there were about 100,000 women sales representatives in manufacturing and wholesaling, but the majority are in such so-called glamour fields as fashion and communications; there are still relatively few in such industries as paper, heavy equipment and steel, where informal restrictions on women are still widespread.

But, the barriers are slowly crumbling. Such industrial companies as Republic Steel, Exxon and Diamond Shamrock now employ women to sell their products in the field, and two years ago, 22-year-old Ann Manix made news in the machine-tool industry by becoming the first woman sales representative at staid old Warner & Swasey Co. Traveling 500 miles and more a week, Manix sells giant turning machines to manufacturing companies, and now ranks among her division's top producers.[7]

Sales positions

SELLING TO WHOLESALERS AND RETAILERS

Serving as a manufacturer's salesperson (selling to wholesalers and retailers) or as a wholesaler's salesperson (selling to retailers) may not be very challenging for a college graduate. Although the purchasing motives of wholesale and retail buyers are rational rather than emotional, and some creative selling may be involved, the job often involves little more than taking orders. When a firm buys products for resale, its main concern is usually purchasing the "right" product mix, making sure it has an adequate supply, and reordering merchandise promptly when necessary. Often the retailer expects the manufacturer's salesperson to stock the merchandise on the store's shelves and set up promotional materials approved by the store. Sometimes these sales jobs are entry-level training positions that can lead to more challenging and demanding opportunities.

SELLING TO PURCHASING AGENTS

A **purchasing agent** is in charge of procurement for all or part of an organization. Purchasing agents are found in government, manufacturing, and the institutional market (hospitals and schools). They are sophisticated buyers who know their needs and the capabilities and limitations of many products that can fill those needs. Thus selling to a purchasing agent often amounts to disseminating information. That is, it involves telling the agent how the product or service can benefit the agent's firm. The purchasing agent looks for credibility (can the salesperson deliver merchandise of the proper quality when needed?), service after the sale, and a reasonable price. The message the salesperson must get across is one of dependability and reliability.

Often purchasing agents rely on **hidden buyers** such as engineers, general managers, secretaries, or other "experts" who may actually specify characteristics of the product or service that the purchasing agent buys. Sales representatives must be aware of hidden buyers and attempt to "read" them as well as the purchasing agent.

SELLING TO COMMITTEES

Perhaps the most demanding form of selling in terms of professionalism and creativity is selling to a committee. When a purchase decision is so important that it will have a substantial impact on the buyer's long-run profitability and success, it is usually made by a committee. The committee may be the board of directors, a group of top executives, or the top executives and subordinates who will be most closely involved in the use of the proposed product or service. Purchases of new plant locations, buildings, major capital equipment, long-term supply contracts, and so forth often require a committee decision.

Usually a committee sales presentation is based on extensive analysis of the potential buyer's needs. An elaborate audiovisual presentation is common. Sometimes prospects are taken to existing installations of the product so that its major characteristics and advantages can be demonstrated. Question and answer sessions follow the formal presentation. After the buyer has heard several presentations from competing potential suppliers, each alternative is weighed before the purchase decision is made.

Committee selling is often time-consuming and demanding. The stakes are high, and sales may be spaced far apart owing to the limited size of the market. When a sale is made, however, the salesperson often receives a generous award. Kim Kelly, a Honeywell computer salesman, spent three years closing an $8 million sale. His commission was $80,000.

SELLING TO PROFESSIONALS

Another form of informational selling is selling to professionals. Individuals who sell to the medical profession are called **detail men.** Their job is to build good will among physicians and to explain the new products offered by pharmaceutical houses. College graduates in fields related to medicine are typically preferred by manufacturers for this type of selling because they can discuss the medicines intelligently and establish rapport with the physician. Detail men also call on select drugstores for promotional support and to sell nonprescription items.

SELLING DIRECTLY TO FINAL CONSUMERS

Direct selling to consumers may be done in retail stores, over the phone, or door to door. Retail selling is rarely attractive to college graduates and typically offers low pay, few advancement opportunities, and little job satisfaction. There are exceptions, such as the management training positions offered by J. C. Penney's and Sears, as well as some real estate sales positions.

Door-to-door selling is probably the most grueling form of selling. Yet it is a very big business. For example, Avon has 800,000 salespeople worldwide and over 50 million customers. Fuller Brush, another large door-to-door retailer, has recently increased the size of its salesforce. According to a spokesman for the brush manufacturers, "We are selling high-quality merchandise at moderate prices without fancy gimmicks."

Door-to-door selling is often characterized by high-pressure tactics, deceptive entrance ploys, and shoddy merchandise. Despite these problems, door-to-door selling offers several advantages to the consumer: the entire family can be consulted; some firms allow trial before purchase; and there is the convenience and comfort of in-home buying.

Another and inexpensive form of direct selling is by telephone. Sears has used phone sales for two decades to remind people to use its catalogs. As the costs of personal selling and direct mail continue to rise, more firms are turning to direct phone selling. Such different organizations as *Women's Wear Daily,* the U.S. Postal Service, and the Center for the Study of Democratic Institutions utilize phone selling. A major tire company has 40 people continually phoning customers who are too small or isolated to be visited by a sales representative more than once or twice a year. It has reportedly added millions of dollars to its annual sales total. In any 30-day period, 53 percent of adult Americans are solicited at home by a telephone salesperson, and 15 percent of those contacted buy something.[8] In contrast, party plan direct selling, such as Tupperware, results in approximately 45 percent of the participants buying something.

Who are professional salespeople?

Not everyone who sells is a professional salesperson. A professional sales representative should have two dominant characteristics: complete product knowledge and creativity.

The professional salesperson knows the product line from A to Z and understands each item's capabilities and limitations. He or she also understands how to apply the product or service mix to customers' needs. For example, a sales representative may devise a new way of installing the firm's conveyor equipment that will lower the cost of a prospect's intracompany product movement. As a sales representative for IBM puts it:

I get inside the business of my key accounts. I uncover their key problems. I prescribe solutions for them, using my company's systems and even, at times, components from other suppliers. I prove beforehand that my systems will save money or make money for my accounts. Then I work with the account to install the system and make it prove out. Every success I have sells my next system for me. I may never have to "sell" again.[9]

Other factors naturally come into the definition of a professional salesperson —being well organized, having a pleasant personality, being able to converse intelligently about many topics, having an optimistic attitude and a strong desire to sell. The professional sells ideas and concepts and the buyer purchases satisfaction. It is an old adage that a good sales representative "sells the sizzle, not the steak."

Professional sales representatives and even some order takers receive support from missionary salespeople and technical representatives. Both types can be vital to the sales effort, yet neither takes the sales order itself. Almost all supporting sales representatives are employed by manufacturers.

Missionary salespeople are common in consumer packaged-goods industries such as food and drug products. Their job is to stimulate good will within the channel of distribution and to support their company's sales efforts. A missionary sales representative may travel with a wholesaler's representative for a while to reinforce the promotional effort for the product. Sometimes a missionary salesperson will work with the manufacturer's new sales personnel to help them learn the territory and the accounts.

At the retail level, missionary sales representatives may set up displays, check the stock and shelf space, and explain new product offerings to retailers. Usually they are "old hands" who know the territory and product well. In the area of industrial goods, they usually perform a communication function between the manufacturer and key accounts. Any problems that arise are relayed back to the manufacturer via the missionary representative, and new products or product applications are passed forward to the customer.

Technical specialists have backgrounds in chemistry, engineering, physics, or the like. They work out the details of custom-made products and communicate directly with the technical staff of the potential buyer. The sales representative may make an initial presentation to a purchasing committee, with the technical specialist's presence required only for the question and answer phase.

If interest in the seller's product develops, the specialist plays a larger role in planning the product specifications and installation procedures and overseeing the installation. After the sale has been made, the sales representative usually relies on feedback from the technical specialist about installation dates, debugging time, and similar information.

Smaller firms may not be able to afford both sales representatives and technical specialists. In fact, some large firms may feel that the job is best handled by one person. In this case, the company may look for a person with the appropriate undergraduate degree plus an MBA.

Steps in the selling process

If a person enters the field of industrial selling, he or she will generally follow the same basic selling process. The steps in selling are (1) prospecting and qualifying, (2) the sales approach, (3) the sales presentation, (4) demonstration, (5) handling objections, (6) the closing, and (7) follow-up (see Figure 20.3). Like other forms of promotion, selling follows the AIDA concept. Once a salesperson has located a prospect with the authority to buy, an attempt is made to secure attention. Interest is generated by means of effective presentation and demonstration.

When initial desire is generated (preferably during the presentation and demonstration), proper handling of objections should increase desire and lower cognitive dissonance. The salesperson seeks action in the closing by attempting

◀ **FIGURE 20.3 Personal selling and the AIDA concept.**

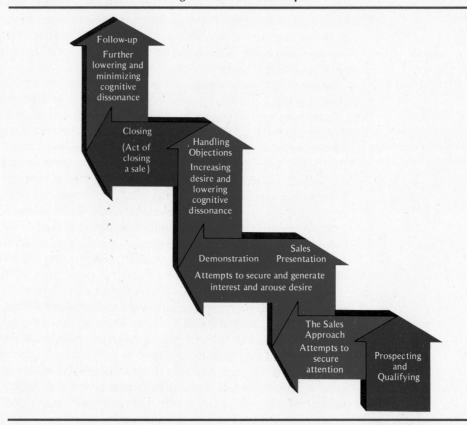

Follow-up
Further lowering and minimizing cognitive dissonance

Closing
(Act of closing a sale)

Handling Objections
Increasing desire and lowering cognitive dissonance

Demonstration   Sales Presentation
Attempts to secure and generate interest and arouse desire

The Sales Approach
Attempts to secure attention

Prospecting and Qualifying

to obtain an agreement to purchase. Follow-up, the final step in selling, not only lowers cognitive dissonance, but may also open up new opportunities to discuss further sales.

PROSPECTING

Before the communication process between the potential buyer and the seller begins, groundwork must be done. This is called **prospecting.** Prospecting is identifying those firms and persons most likely to buy the seller's offerings. Not everyone, of course, is a prospect for a firm's good or service. Nor are all prospects equally likely to purchase. Identification of prospects requires several different sources of information. Some good sources of prospects include: recommendations from customers and business associates, conventions, and advertising leads. Sales representatives selling noncompeting lines are often good sources of potential buyers. Other sources are company records of past purchases, newspapers and trade publications, referrals, and cold canvassing.

THE APPROACH

Once a prospective buyer has been located, the communication process begins. If prospecting has not uncovered the name or names of the decision makers, they must be identified. Sometimes this is as simple as asking the switchboard operator. On other occasions a salesperson may have to contact several people before reaching the "right" prospect.

It is critical that the decision maker be properly identified, or significant time and effort may be wasted. For example, a sales representative for a materials-handling system spent three months with the director of western warehouse operations of a large New York based manufacturing company. This person continually assured the sales representative that he made all the decisions for his area. Unfortunately, the competition got the business for the four regional warehouses because it won over the vice-president of operations in New York, who was in charge of budget approval for all new warehouse systems.

Some companies use **screening committees** or individuals who filter out salespeople offering products that are not compatible with the firm's needs. This is done in order to save the time of the decision maker. As mentioned earlier, the salesperson may find a decision maker with the authority to buy who relies almost exclusively on other individuals to select which product is bought. For example, a secretary may recommend a brand of typewriter or a supervisor may offer advice on a new stamping machine.

A sales letter, telephone call, or any other form of approach may be enhanced through advertising. Advertising informs the prospect about the salesperson's company and product so the salesperson does not "start from scratch" in the information process. Good advertising may generate inquiries that are basically invitations to call. They may come from decision makers who are generally inaccessible to salespeople.

PRESENTATION AND DEMONSTRATION

After the representative has reached the proper person, the sales presentation takes place. If the salesperson understands the key variables that will determine the sale, such as dependable delivery, cost, compatibility with other components or machines, and so forth, he or she is much more likely to succeed. The following is a list of the key elements in a good sales presentation. As you will note, the presentation generally flows from action to analysis to implementation.

◢ *Management summary.* Ties the presentation to the individuals involved in the sale, reflects mutual agreement already touched with top decision makers, and makes note of the customer's criteria for selection.

◢ *Scope.* States the objectives and nature of the problems being solved or challenges being addressed.

◢ *Advantages.* Spells out the advantages in such a way that the presenting company's products or services are made exclusive (they cannot be duplicated by competition).

◢ *Recommended solutions.* Tailors the specific products, services and/or programs to the prospect's requirement, environment, and management objectives.

◢ *Financial analysis and cost justification (reached through mutual agreement).* Shows the economic justification to favor the seller company's method over the prospect's current means of performing the function and over possible proposals from competition.

◢ *Implementation schedule.* Describes the seller's and the prospect's responsibilities, the people to be involved, and dates of completion for the main tasks.

◢ *Contract.* Spells out the terms and conditions of the sale, which have already been discussed with the prospect.

Sales presentations are augmented with visual aids and audiovisual equipment. Movies, brochures, manuals, maps, samples, and slides are commonly used sales aids. Fairchild and Kodak manufacture a simple, briefcase-sized sound projector and screen for "at the desk" audiovisual presentations. Actual demonstrations are excellent supplements to presentations. When a prospect can participate in the presentation by manipulating a product, he or she becomes better acquainted with the product's features and remembers them longer.

HANDLING OBJECTIONS

Rarely does a prospect say "I'll buy it" right after a presentation. Often there are objections or perhaps questions about the presentation and product. The potential buyer may complain that the price is too high, the delivery date is too far away, and the like.

The best way to prepare for objections is to anticipate them and have a reply in mind. A good sales representative handles objections in a relaxed manner and considers them a legitimate part of the purchase decision. They should be viewed as requests for information, not as setting the stage for a confrontation. If the salesperson takes the latter attitude, he or she may lose a sale.

CLOSING THE SALE

If the prospect's objections are handled properly, the salesperson can attempt to close the sale. It might be pointed out that whenever the customer makes a commitment to buy, the close and order processing should begin. But if this does not occur, a number of techniques can be used in an attempt to close the sale. One popular approach is the "assumption close." The salesperson assumes that the prospect is going to buy and says something like, "Which do you want delivered, product A or product B?" or "When do you want the merchandise shipped?"

A second closing technique is to summarize the benefits of the product and ask for the sale. Sometimes a salesperson will withhold a special concession until the end of the selling process and use it in closing the sale. Examples are price cuts, free installation, free service, and trial orders. In today's economy, salespeople can use the "sense" or "urgency" close in many industries. They may say, "Prices will be going up in six weeks" or "We don't anticipate being able to deliver new models for six months owing to component shortages, but we have three of this year's models left."

FOLLOW-UP

A salesperson's responsibilities do not end with making the sale and placing the order. One of the most important aspects of the job is follow-up. The salesperson must make sure delivery schedules are met, that the product or service performs as promised, and that the buyer's employees are properly trained in the use of the product.

Most businesses depend on repeat sales, and repeat sales depend on thorough follow-up. When customers feel that they have been abandoned, cognitive dissonance arises and repeat sales decline. One survey revealed that three out of four sales managers feel that customer service is an increasingly important determinant of long-run sales performance.[10]

CONTRIBUTIONS OF THE BEHAVIORAL SCIENCES

The selling process is not only a communication interaction, but a social situation.

The probability of successfully closing a sale is partially dependent on **social power,** the ability of the salesperson to evoke the behavior desired by the seller. Usually the goal is to obtain an agreement to buy from the prospect. Two important aspects of social power are expert power and referent power.

A sales representative's **expert power** is derived from knowledge, information, and skills related to the product or service. **Referent power** is based on the perceived attraction between the salesperson and prospective purchasers. Similar social backgrounds, convergent personalities, comparable interests, and pleasing physical appearance can enhance referent power. For example, in Phoenix, Arizona, the mode of dress in most business establishments is casual. This is probably due to the heat and the influence of Western styles of dress. An Eastern salesperson who flies into Phoenix and begins calling on customers in a suit complete with tie will probably lose referent power. A tie is the symbol of an outsider — someone who does not understand or relate to the environment of the Southwest. There is less shared identity.

The most extensive research on the impact of social power on the selling process has revealed these major findings:

1. The stronger the expert and referent power bases, the more trustworthy the sales representative is perceived to be by the customer.
2. Expert power is more important than referent power in building trust.
3. Sales representatives with a large amount of referent power have a wider range of influence than those with lower amounts of referent power. In other words, greater referent power enables the salesperson to exert influence in a variety of situations.[11]

These findings have many implications. The importance of product knowledge and training of salespeople is obvious. If a salesperson does not understand the product or service and its applications, he or she has little expert power. Since referent power is particularly important when a sales representative must sell a wide variety of goods and services in a variety of markets, recruitment and screening techniques should be highly refined. Progressive firms recognize the importance of social power in the selling process and have designed recruitment and training programs based on behavioral findings.

Sales management

Just as selling is a person-to-person relationship, so is sales management. The basic function of the sales manager is to maximize sales at a reasonable level of costs. The tasks of sales management are recruiting, training, motivation, organization, and evaluation and control.

RECRUITING AND SCREENING

Salesforce recruitment should be based on an accurate, detailed description of the sales task as defined by the company. The job description, in turn, is developed in light of the salesforce objectives. An accurate job description will tell the sales manager whether he or she should attempt to hire an order taker or an aggressive professional salesperson. Perhaps the job description will indicate a need for a technical specialist, a missionary salesperson, or a detail person.

No single group of demographic or personality characteristics is typical of a successful salesperson. It depends on the needs of the firm. The vice-president of marketing for Remington Rand looks for "an above average student but not an egg-head, a college graduate who worked part-time in school, a person with at least one child." Remington, of course, makes many exceptions to this general profile.

A variety of tools are used to screen sales candidates. The interview is by far the most helpful tool for selecting new salespeople. It is also the most costly screening tool. Rapiston, a manufacturer of materials-handling equipment, attempts to interview applicants in a communication situation similar to the company's selling situation (a committee or group); the interview is conducted as a group meeting. Rapiston believes that shy people are automatically eliminated — some individuals drop out as soon as they see it is a group interview.

What do sales executives look for in new salespeople? One recent survey found enthusiasm to be twice as important as any other characteristic. Other factors, in order of importance, were these: well-organized, obvious ambition, high degree of persuasive ability, general sales experience, and good communication skills.[12]

Recruits can be solicited from a number of sources: colleges, other salespeople, trade journal and newspaper ads, employment agencies, and even competitors. Sometimes companies find that their nonselling employees are attracted to sales. The advantages we have already discussed are offered as reasons for entering the sales field.

SALES TRAINING

After the recruit has been hired and given a brief orientation, training begins. A new salesperson generally receives instruction in five major areas: company policies and practices, selling technique, product knowledge, industry and customer characteristics, and nonselling duties such as account servicing and filling out market information reports. A good training program will build job confidence, improve morale, increase sales, and build better customer relations. Classroom instruction may last several days for company policies and several weeks to a month for actual sales techniques. Trainees are taught everything from how to prospect through servicing the account after the sale. Generally speaking, industrial-goods firms offer more extensive training programs than consumer goods organizations.

Progressive organizations emphasize human interaction in the sales process. For example, **transactional analysis (TA)** is often used to improve sales effectiveness. If you speak to a friend, it is referred to as a transactional stimulus. Your friend's response is a transactional response. Salespeople can act out the customer–salesperson relationship to sharpen their transactional abilities. Closed-circuit television is often used to teach sales recruits how to use TA in lifelike situations. Here is an example of the technique.

In TA, you *communicate* as parent, adult or child and *connect* with the parent, adult or child in another person. The ego states:

- *Parent* is influenced by guidelines of parental or other authority figures.
- *Adult* is data-oriented. It deals with factual reality.
- *Child* incorporates feelings and dependencies of childhood.

Also basic to TA is the *OK-Not OK* position, a person's current total attitude about him/herself and those around him/her. Its variations:

- *I'm not ok, you're ok* is similar to saying: "I can't do anything right, but you can." In a sales situation: "I'm trying as hard as I can, but it's a buyer's market and the customer has all of the advantages."
- *I'm not ok, you're not ok.* You see both others and yourself as deficient. A salesperson may desert his/her territory and take in a movie "because other salespeople do it." In this position, you're likely to run from any kind of a challenge.
- *I'm ok, you're not ok* says "if it weren't for you things would be perfect." This aggressive position, strong in parent content, is often tyrannical. It runs roughshod over everyone and everything on its way to success.
- *I'm ok, you're ok* expresses basic acceptance of yourself and others. The salesperson confident of his/her product is a problem-solver. He/she assumes mutual trust between company and customer.

Under optimum conditions, when the customer expresses unwarranted fears, the salesperson's *adult* recognizes something is troubling the customer's *child*. Until he solves the problem, a production agreement cannot be reached. For example, consider the following interaction:

CUSTOMER: "The shipment was two weeks late." (This is a statement of fact, but the tone is critical. Characteristic of the parent state.)

SALESPERSON: "I know. I pushed production as hard as I could." (The salesperson responds from a child position. His/her own *not-ok* child was connected or hooked. It can, in turn, hook the parent further.)

CUSTOMER: "If I give you another order, how do I know I'll get it on time?" (This is a perfectly normal adult concern. The customer is trying to establish a realistic basis for trust.)

SALESPERSON: "I'll call it in right away and put a rush on it." (The salesperson responded from his/her parent state trying to convince the customer but lacking information to reassure him.)

CUSTOMER: "I'll talk with my boss. I'll let you know." (Adult statement, at least on the surface. The customer fears any commitment at this point and needs reassurance from the boss. An adult response from the salesperson would serve his need to keep it tentative.)

SALESPERSON: "When will you know? This order is really important to me." (Salesperson, in reverting to the child state, seeks order out of sympathy.)

CUSTOMER: "I'll call you just as soon as I can." (Disguised as an adult response, but more likely a "don't call me, I'll call you" — polite child response.)

SALESPERSON: "I'll give you my personal assurance. We'll get the order out on time even if I have to follow it through production myself." (Salesperson, from the parent state, is pressing harder because the Client's child is not convinced.)

CUSTOMER: "Good. I'll call you later." (Polite child. Wants to end the session and probably the relationship but does not want to hurt salesperson's feelings.)[13]

Lectures, demonstrations, films, and other visual aids are used in the next phase of training—building product knowledge. Depending on the firm and the nature of its product line, the salesperson may learn the characteristics and applications of the simpler items first and then be periodically brought in from the field for additional product training. In addition to learning product attributes, salespeople are taught how the product features translate into benefits for the buyer.

The fourth phase of training often incorporates lectures and on-site visits by the trainee with other salespeople. The final step, nonselling activities, is handled either as the last step before field training or as an adjunct to the selling process. After classroom education has ended, on-the-job training continues for many months. A sales representative may start by working with another representative, a missionary salesperson, or a district sales manager. As salespeople gain experience and confidence, they are gradually left on their own. Other companies start sales representatives alone with simple, low-volume accounts and then slowly build up their accounts and territories.

Sales training is expensive. Companies recognize, however, that a properly trained and motivated salesforce will pay dividends for years to come. Training costs vary significantly from one type of company to another. The training programs of industrial firms selling complicated equipment and systems are not only the longest but also the most elaborate and expensive.[14] Consumer products sales training is more fundamental and is relatively short and inexpensive.[15] For example, average training cost per person for an industrial goods company was $19,025 in 1979. For consumer goods, the expense was $13,173.[16]

MOTIVATING THE SALESFORCE

Training equips the salesperson with the necessary tools for selling. Once an individual has acquired sales skills, he or she must be motivated to use them. Research has shown that pay, promotion, working conditions, security, and intrinsic aspects of the job are of primary concern to the average employee.[17]

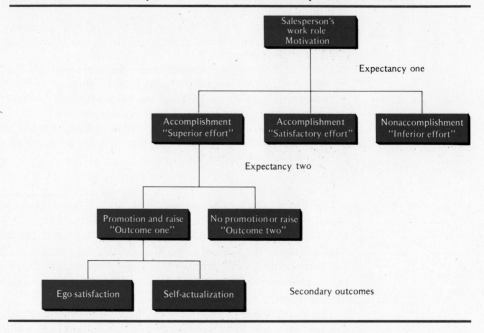

Frederick Herzberg has determined that some job characteristics (achievement, recognition, advancement, growth, and responsibility) lead to job satisfaction. Other factors (salary, working conditions, company policy, and job security) are maintenance factors. When maintenance factors are inadequate, job dissatisfaction will result.

Expectancy theory suggests that motivational force (a salesperson's effort) depends on the expectation that one's behavior will produce certain outcomes and on the attractiveness of those outcomes. For example, a sales representative may expect that selling more than his or her quota will produce a promotion or a salary increase. The degree of motivation will depend on how important a promotion or salary increase is to the sales representative.

Figure 20.4 depicts **expectancy theory** as it applies to the salesforce. A salesperson may study the job description and determine its behavioral demands (loyalty, positive work attitude, and so forth) and subjectively evaluate his or her chances of successfully accomplishing the tasks (expectancy). Next, he or she must subjectively evaluate the probability of being promoted or rewarded. If a tangible reward is received (a maintenance factor), it may enhance intrinsic motivators such as desire for self-actualization. The strength of one's motivation to perform effectively represents a belief that one's efforts can be converted into performance and the net attractiveness of the rewards that are believed to come from good performance.

Nonfinancial motivation. Research has shown that salespeople's performance is dependent on expectancy perceptions.[18] Other studies have shown that the role of the sales manager is very important in developing a salesperson's expectations. The sales manager and company policy are the two most significant factors that determine sales job satisfaction.[19] Income is important, but it ranks only third as determinant of satisfaction.

Researchers have demonstrated that salespeople's performance is based on perceived and expected fulfillment.[20] They found that self-actualization was the most significant factor in the satisfaction of high performers. Salespeople who believe that they are realizing their own potential and doing something intrinsically worthwhile are not only current high performers, but are more likely to perform well in the future.

One technique for building intrinsic satisfaction is to program management functions, such as planning and quota development, into the activities of the salesforce. Other techniques include increasing the amount of interaction between the salesforce and the sales manager, increasing the status and rank of the sales job, and providing public acknowledgments (sales awards) of the value management places on the individual. The following are examples of motivation system.

Bacon, ham, and sausage packer Patrick Cudahy, Inc., Cudahy, Wis., runs a team incentive for its salespeople. If each sells 27 truckloads of product in a nine-week period, all will earn a trip to Acapulco or Las Vegas. "We've taken an average of our sales over a given period. Generally, sales are two to three times greater than average during an incentive period," says Art C. Reimann, vice president, sales and marketing.

Reimann prefers to set team goals and rewards because he believes they are of more benefit to the company. "With individual programs, you'll usually have some stars, and when one or two reach their quotas, others tend to slack off," he says. "With a team program, they urge each other on." A trip or specific items of merchandise are the usual awards in Cudahy programs.

Philip R. Amatucci, vice president, sales and marketing, C. R. Daniels, Ellicott City, Md., doesn't believe in contests and other noncompensation-related incentive programs for his salespeople. But he feels "the right kind of recognition of a job well done is extremely important." To ensure that his salespeople, who sell industrial textiles and materials handling equipment, receive it, Amatucci has instituted not one but two recognition programs.

The first, an annual program, rewards the two salespeople who have done the most outstanding all-around jobs by bringing them and their spouses in to the home office, where they are wined, dined, and listened to by the president and other top executives. The second, called Atta'Boy, is given every six weeks to the salesperson who has done an outstanding job in some specific situation, such as special handling of an account or inquiry, customer problem solving, or new account work.

Financial incentives. The amount that a sales representative is paid is an important factor in job turnover. The method of payment may be a motivator. **Behavior modification theory** can best explain why the role of money is subject to controversy. Simply stated, behavior modification theory involves systematic reinforcement of desirable behavior and nonreinforcement or punishment of unwanted behavior. If the salesperson perceives only an overall "flow of pay" in return for a "flow of work" in a specified period, neither money nor method of compensation will act as a motivator.[21] The stimulus (pay) is too far removed from the response (work) to affect the salesperson's behavior. The money fails to reinforce the particular responses for which it was intended.

The commission system. Although a commission system is consistent with basic behavior modification theory, the commission must be received within a reasonably short period after the sale in order to be a motivator. A typical commission plan provides salespeople with a specified percentage of their sales revenue. If it is a **straight commission plan,** the salesperson receives no revenue until a sale is made. Salespeople must also pay their expenses from the commission.

A book publisher, Holt, Rinehart and Winston, has successfully applied the straight commission plan to achieve behavior modification. Before the commission system was introduced, salaries and commission were equal to 8.3 percent of sales. The new commission plan called for 8 percent on a salesperson's total sales, but the salespeople must pay their own expenses. Expense accountability proved to be a special problem for some salespeople because they were used to giving dozens of free books to professors without knowing whether they would lead to sales. The new plan resulted in a 30 percent decline in sample book costs during the first year.

Sales commission systems require good planning. Some firms that switch from a salary plan to a commission system experience no increase in company profits. Although the new system may seem to motivate some of the salesforce, the remainder may tend to slack off after they reach a perceived acceptable level of income. If the salesperson ceases to be motivated, he or she may not make follow-up calls on good customers.

The advantages of a commission plan are that (1) rewards are tied to productivity; that (2) it is easy to understand; and that (3) sales costs have a direct relationship to sales activity. The disadvantages of the system are (1) It is difficult to get salespeople to engage in nonselling activities, such as marketing research, servicing an account, and training new personnel. (2) There are large variations in incomes among salespeople. (3) Territory may not be fully covered — some salespeople will "skim" a territory to achieve a target level of income. (4) Readjusting territories may meet extreme resistance. (5) Pay may vary with the economy.

Salary and control. Filling out information reports, servicing accounts, calling on smaller customers, and performing any other nonselling task become very unpalatable to the commission salesperson. In contrast, a **straight salary plan** offers maximum control but little incentive to produce. This plan works well when a territory requires an extensive amount of prospecting. In firms that use a team approach and rely on missionary salespeople, it may be difficult to tell who really closed a sale. Thus, a salary system tends to work better than a commission. The advantages of a salary plan are (1) It maximizes control over the salesperson; (2) it offers a steady income; (3) it makes territorial restructuring more palatable for the salesforce; (4) it ensures the performance of nonselling functions. The disadvantages are that (1) it does not motivate the salesforce; (2) it discriminates against highly productive individuals; (3) sales tend to be concentrated in products that are easiest to sell.

Combination plans. In order to achieve the best of both worlds, many companies have turned to a **combination plan.** Virtually all combination plans have a base salary plus an incentive. The incentive is usually a commission or a bonus. Bonuses are often paid as a percentage of salary. They can be based on sales results, market share, sale of specific products, new accounts, nonsales activities, or increased sales from existing accounts.

The advantages of a combination plan are that (1) it offers a minimum stable income (salary) plus an incentive; (2) it provides some degree of security; (3) it compensates for nonselling functions; (4) it maintains control. The problems are that (1) it may be quite complex and difficult for the salesforce to understand; (2) if the bonus is not received shortly after it is earned, it will not be a motivator; (3) it is costly to administer; (4) it may have too many objectives, resulting in few, if any, being fully accomplished.

Trends in sales compensation. More companies are moving away from straight salary and commission plans to a combination plan. The percentage of total compensation that is incentive is also increasing.[22] Thus, it seems that the 1980s is a period of aggressive salesforce motivation, as the example below shows.

Because of the numerous opportunities and difficulties of any compensation plan, none has proved to be entirely satisfactory. As you can see in Table 20.1, a majority of manufacturers and service organizations use a salary plus incentive program. Yet, about one-third were not completely satisfied with the results.

The 800 domestic sales representatives working for Johns-Manville's 10 autonomous divisions share a standardized compensation plan, which replaces several different pay packages that the $1.1 billion Denver company's divisions formerly offered. It is intended to (1) put all sales force compensation on a current basis, (2) motivate sales reps to meet their sales quotas as early in the year as possible in order to qualify for a lucrative "overexpectancy" incentive commission rate, (3) cut the penalty for underachievement in bad years, (4) cut sales costs, and (5) ease the administrative burden and strengthen management control, particularly at the all-important district management level.

◄ TABLE 20.1 Sales Compensation Plans

Plan being used	Percentage using it	Percentage of users satisfied with plan	Percentage dissatisfied	Percentage uncertain or no answer
Service companies				
Salary plus incentive	52.0%	65.4%	34.6%	—
Commission with draw	10.0	80.0[a]	—	20.0%
Commission only	14.0	71.4[a]	28.6[a]	—
Straight salary	24.0	41.7	58.3	—
Number responding: 50[b]				
Manufacturers				
Salary plus incentive	66.3%	53.1%	32.2%	14.7%
Commission with draw	0.8	82.6[a]	17.4[a]	—
Commission only	14.2	80.0	8.6	11.4
Straight salary	18.6	50.0	43.5	6.5
Number responding: 249[b]				

[a] Indicates a small sample—a breakdown of 10 or fewer.
[b] This sample is based upon 449 respondents.
Source: "There Has To Be A Better Way," *Sales and Marketing Management,* November 12, 1979, p. 42. Reprinted by permission from Sales & Marketing Management magazine. Copyright 1979.

J-M sales reps' quotas and compensation packages (other than standard company benefits, such as life insurance) are set by their district managers. The district managers' quotas and budgets are set, in turn, by their division sales managers. Johns-Manville president W. R. Goodwin approves the division's budgets and sales quotas. Each quota, which J-M refers to as a "sales expectancy," is expressed in terms of expected sales volume for the territory, district, or division. It is the responsibility of managers at each level to divide their total assigned expectancy and compensation budget on the basis of the market potential of the individual district or sales territory and the manager's or rep's track record.

The new standardized package for sales reps consists of base salary plus "planned extra compensation," a specific commission rate that applies to all sales up to the expectancy level. Those who surpass that level qualify for an accelerated commission rate. J-M's target is to pay approximately 75% of the sales rep's basic compensation (which it defines as base salary plus "planned extra compensation") in salary and 25% in commission.[23]

ORGANIZING THE SALES EFFORT

Because personal selling is so costly, a sales department cannot afford to be poorly organized. Departmental organizational structures will be discussed in

Chapter 22. In addition to developing the "right" departmental structure, a sales manager must (1) determine the size of the salesforce, (2) develop sales territories, and (3) devise sales quotas.

Size of salesforce. One comon approach to salesforce size is the **workload technique.** The formula for using the workload procedure is

$$\text{Number of salespeople} = \frac{\left[\begin{array}{l}\text{Number of} \quad \text{number of} \\ \text{existing} \quad + \text{potential} \\ \text{customers} \quad \text{customers}\end{array}\right] \times \begin{array}{l}\text{ideal} \\ \text{frequency} \\ \text{of calls}\end{array} \times \begin{array}{l}\text{length} \\ \text{of calls}\end{array}}{\text{Selling time available from one salesperson}}$$

Assume, for example, that a firm has 3000 customers and marketing research has estimated that there are 1000 potential customers. Sales analysis has revealed that sales calls average 1.5 hours and that each customer should be seen 7 times a year. Further examination of records has revealed that each salesperson has 2000 hours of selling time available per year. Thus

$$\text{Number of salespeople} = \frac{[3,000 + 1,000] \times 7 \times 1.5}{2,000} = \frac{42,000}{2,000} = 21$$

If the company now has 18 people in its salesforce, 3 new people should be hired.

The major advantage of the workload approach is its simplicity. Successful application of the technique depends on the sales manager's ability to estimate the ideal frequency of calls and the number of potential customers. Also, the workload approach fails to consider either the cost of increasing the workforce or the costs and profits associated with each sales call.

A second method of ascertaining the size of the sales force is **marginal analysis.** In theory, salespeople are added until the profits generated by the last individual hired equal the costs associated with hiring that person. Companies with good records know the cost of training a salesperson. This cost, plus actual field expenses and the salary of a new person, can be compared with the revenue generated by sales activities. Two drawbacks of marginal analysis are (1) the assumption that a new salesperson will not increase in efficiency as he or she becomes more experienced and (2) the fact that the territorial assignment of the last person hired may have a significant effect on the revenue generated by that person.

Developing territories. Sales territories can also be designated on the basis of marginal analysis. This is done by creating territories so that the marginal profit to sales effort in each territory is equal. If this procedure is followed, all territories will have equal potential. The workload approach can be used by first estimating the ideal frequency of calls and then determining the average length of the sales call. Next, average available sales hours per salesperson are determined. The last step is to locate customers geographically until that amount of time has been used up for one person.

Using our previous example, we estimated that each account should be called upon seven times a year and that each call lasts approximately 1.5

hours. Every salesperson has 2000 hours of selling time available per year. Every customer or potential customer will require 10.5 sales hours per year (7 × 1.5). Therefore each salesperson can handle approximately 190 present and potential customers (2000 ÷ 10.5).

While the workload technique balances sales calls among territories, it does not necessarily equate sales potential between territories. One study has shown that territorial potential is a more important determinant of territorial sales than a sales representative's workload. Assuming that this finding may be generalized, it implies that marginal analysis rather than the workload technique should be used in designating sales territories.

Several computer models have been developed to build sales territories. Xerox Corporation has created a program based upon the expected number of customers in a geographic area, the expected revenue from each customer, and the expected number of calls per day per salesperson.[24] The model then allocates calls sequentially to the customer with the highest revenue per call value until all accounts in an area are called on and all potential realized. Additional areas are combined until the salesperson's maximum time limit is reached. Another model, GEOLINE, builds territories until sales potential or sales workload or both are equal among territories.[25]

What makes the development of sales territories so complex? The wide array of factors that can influence sales potential. Attempting to measure all important variables, their interrelationships, and their subsequent effect on sales is an awesome problem. For example, the following items have been identified as affecting territorial sales: (1) environmental factors, (2) competition (it often varies between territories), (3) company marketing strategies and tactics, (4) salesforce organization policies and procedures; (5) field sales manager characteristics, (6) salesperson characteristics, (7) territory characteristics, and (8) individual customer factors.[26]

Sales quotas. After a sales representative's territory has been delineated, most companies establish a **sales quota.** A quota is simply a statement of a sales objective. It has been estimated that about 75 percent of all sales managers set quotas for the salesforce.[27] The quota is usually based on sales volume alone, but approximately 20 percent of sales managers also use some other measure.[28]

The foundation of a quota is the sales forecast or other sales objective. Most firms accept input from the salesforce before setting quotas. Participation by the sales staff increases the acceptability of the quota to the salesperson and provides the satisfaction of interacting with management. To set sales quotas, managers should (1) select the type, (2) determine the relative importance of each type, and (3) set the level of each type. The most common type of quota is sales volume. Others include key accounts (those with greatest sales potential), new accounts, specific products, and total calls.

After the types of quotas are established, the sales manager should assign weights to each. For example, assume that a firm has two quotas—total sales for a territory and new accounts. If management decides that total sales is five times as important as new accounts, then the weights are 5 to 1. The last step is

▲ TABLE 20.2 Sales Quota Plan

Salesperson	Types	Level	Actual	Percentage obtained	Weight	Weighted attainment percentage
Ann Cox	Sales volume	$400,000	$380,000	95%	5	475%
	New accounts	20	30	150	2	300
	Product X	100	110	110	1	110
						885

$$\text{Overall quota performance} = \frac{885}{8} = 110.63$$

Salesperson	Types	Level	Actual	Percentage obtained	Weight	Weighted attainment percentage
Christopher Reese	Sales volume	$350,000	$297,500	85%	5	425%
	New accounts	15	20	133	2	266
	Product X	80	40	50	1	50
						741

$$\text{Overall quota performance} = \frac{741}{8} = 92.63$$

to set the level of the quota. This is usually a short-range decision and may be set for a quarter of the year or even a month. Levels are usually based on past performance, sales potential, and forecasts. Table 20.2 illustrates the use of a sales quota plan. Note that Ann Cox did not meet her sales volume objective, but still achieved an overall quota performance of over 100 percent. In contrast, Christopher Reese hit 133 percent of his new account target, but still failed to have an overall quota performance of 100 percent.

Quotas are not simply tools for evaluation and control. They also provide a basis for sales planning and can be used as motivators. If a quota is easy to obtain, motivation tends to decline.[29] In fact, it may decline so much that an easier quota is less likely to be attained than a more difficult one. Sales managers should set product or sales quotas at challenging levels and attach great significance to the quota. If the salesforce doesn't perceive quota attainment as being particularly important, motivation will be lacking.

EVALUATION AND CONTROL

The final major tasks of the sales manager are evaluating and controlling the salesforce. Control follows a logical sequence of events. Sales goals are examined, performance standards are established based upon the goals, results are compared with standards, and corrective actions are taken if necessary. Standards are set in three general areas: sales volume, cost, and service of accounts. We will examine the nature of control in Chapter 22.

In addition to sales and costs, sales managers also look at the daily activities of the salesperson. The information is usually reported on a call record form.

▲ TABLE 20.3   How the Sales Manager Can Influence Sales Performance Using Call-Record Data

The salesperson can take the following actions:	These actions of the manager influence the salesperson:
Number of sales calls	Number of salespeople
	Training in territory coverage, routing, and time management
	Standard operating procedures for sales force organization, territory coverage, and routing
	Tools for time-saving
	Motivation and compensation
Quality of sales calls	
Message content	Training in product knowledge and customer operations
	Information flow on customer status, industry trends, and call planning
	Salesperson selection
Communications effectiveness	Training in sales skills, communications, listening, and group presentations
	Standard operating procedures for sales force organization and call planning
	Visual sales aids
Interpersonal relationships	Salespeople selection
	Sensitivity training
	Motivation and compensation

Source: Porter Henry, "Manage Your Sales Force as a System," *Harvard Business Review* (March–April, 1975): 93.

Although call record reports vary from one firm to another, they generally contain information on the number of calls and the quality of those calls. Quality is measured by such yardsticks as calls per order, sales or profits per call, or the percentage of calls that achieve specific objectives. The latter may include sales of products the firm is emphasizing. Improvement in call quality can increase total volume, change the product mix, or decrease sales costs. Table 20.3 shows how the sales manager can use call record data to increase the number of profitable calls and the quality of the calls. Well-managed control systems lead to higher sales productivity.

Selling in a changing economy

Even the most carefully planned control and evaluations systems often must be revised because of major changes in the external environment. Two recent causes of such revisions are shortages and inflation.

SHORTAGES

A study conducted by *Sales and Marketing Management* magazine indicated that fewer sales meetings would be held and that there would be less sales travel in general due to energy shortages.[30] The survey also indicated that many firms planned to prune slow-moving items from their lines. Companies have developed a variety of measures to cope with the energy problem. Georgia-Pacific's fine-paper division took its salespeople off the road for two months and brought them to company headquarters, where they worked on long-range allotment scheduling and new product ideas.

Other companies are seeking new ways of motivating their salespeople during shortages. Diamond Shamrock involves salespeople in deciding what actions the company should take in the future. Some firms have counseled their representatives to keep the customer informed of stock positions and delivery dates, avoid seeking new clients, offer substitute products, take early orders to protect product availability for key accounts, and use the "we're all in this together" approach. The latter position assures the customer that the supplier is not out to gouge him or her but wants to work with the customer until the shortage is over.

INFLATION

Sales managers have been forced to cope with continuing inflation as well as shortages. Often the shortage problem is compounded by customers trying to cope with rising prices by buying in larger-than-normal quantities in anticipation of higher prices in the future.

Even where shortages do not exist, sales managers have had to make major policy changes to meet the problem of inflation. Compensation plans have been revamped to avoid overpaying the salesforce. This is particularly true when sales representatives are paid a fixed percentage of the sales dollar.

Salespeople must bear the brunt of the task of explaining price increases to distraught customers. Al Rinkov, president of Manny Industries, a Los Angeles maker of draperies and bedspreads, says, "Salesmen have become official apologists for what's been happening to prices."[31]

The long-term sales contract has little meaning in an inflationary economy. Most contracts allow for higher prices or lower quantities at the time of delivery. Industrial companies that used to issue a price list every year or two are finding they have to print one each month. Honeywell's Micro Switch Division has inserted price escalator clauses based on the government's wholesale price index into its contracts. Honeywell has also trained its salesforce to suggest less expensive products where possible. Harris, a maker of printing equipment, has instructed its salesforce to limit price quotations to a maximum of six months.

Shortages and inflation seem to be changing the role of the salesforce. More than ever, the salesperson is the company's service agent. He or she must aid the buyer in making an intelligent product selection, explain long delivery times and high prices, and generally act as the buyer's consultant rather than as the seller's salesperson—or as a liaison between the company and the customer.

SUMMARY

We are all salespeople to some extent. We all have to sell ourselves as individuals. Selling is a personalized form of communication with direct feedback.

As the number of potential customers decreases, the complexity of the product increases, and the value of the product grows, the role of personal selling tends to increase. There are about 6 million people engaged in personal selling in the United States. The sales field offers many opportunities for women as well as men. The sales positions open to college graduates include some retail and wholesale positions and others that involve selling to purchasing agents, to committees, professionals, and on a limited basis, directly to the final consumer. Sales support positions are also available. Missionary salespeople stimulate good will within the channel of distribution. Technical specialists have backgrounds in technical fields. They work out the details of custom-made product orders and communicate directly with the customer's technical staff.

The steps in the selling process are (1) prospecting, (2) the approach, (3) the presentation, (4) demonstration, (5) handling objections, (6) the closing, (7) follow-up.

The selling process is a social situation as well as a personal interaction. Sales success is partially dependent upon social power, the ability of the salesperson to evoke the desired action. It depends on expert and referent powers. Referent powers are based on perceived attraction between the salesperson and the prospective purchaser. Expert power is derived from knowledge, information, and skills related to the product or service.

The tasks of sales management are (1) recruiting, (2) training, (3) motivation, (4) organization, and (5) evaluation and control. Salesforce recruitment should be based on an accurate, detailed description of the sales task as defined by the company. Sales training covers the following areas: company policies and practices, selling techniques, product knowledge, industry and customer characteristics, and nonselling duties such as account servicing and filling out market information reports.

Understanding expectancy theory can help a sales manager motivate the salesforce. The theory suggests that a salesperson's effort depends on the expectation that one's behavior will produce certain outcomes and on the attractiveness of those outcomes. Research has shown that salespersons' performance is dependent on such expectations.

The organizational tasks of the sales manager are as follows: (1) determine the size of the salesforce, (2) develop territories, and (3) establish quotas.

Control follows a logical sequence of events. Sales goals are examined, performance standards are established upon the goals, results are compared with the standards, and corrective actions are taken if necessary. Call record reports are a common sales control device.

The prospect of continued shortages of raw materials and other products has led to new roles for the salesforce. A salesperson may now become a good-will ambassador and an allocator rather than a promoter of merchandise. In many companies, the salesperson is becoming a service agent rather than a sales agent.

KEY TERMS

Purchasing agent
Hidden buyer
Detail men
Missionary salespeople
Technical specialists
Prospecting
Screening committees
Social power
Expert power
Referent power

Transactional analysis (TA)
Expectancy theory
Behavior modification theory
Straight commission plan
Straight salary plan
Combination plan
Workload technique
Marginal analysis
Sales quota

REVIEW QUESTIONS

1. Describe the major tasks of a salesperson. Has the role of the salesperson been broadened? Give supporting rationale.
2. Why are missionary salespersons used? Identify their short- and long-run goals. How do they differ from technical specialists?
3. List the steps in the selling process and their relationship to the AIDA framework.
4. What are the objectives of sales management and why must there be coordination with marketing management?
5. Describe the use of the workload technique in setting the size of the salesforce. How can this approach be modified to become more useful?
6. What extended roles must the salesperson assume in times of shortage and inflation?

DISCUSSION QUESTIONS

1. Discuss the role of personal selling in relation to the marketing process.
2. In what ways do the functions and responsibilities of a professional salesperson differ from those of a retail clerk?
3. In what ways do expert and referent power influence salesperson effectiveness? What are the implications of social power with regard to selection and training of salespersons?
4. Discuss the usefulness of expectancy theory in motivating the salesforce. To what extent are nonfinancial rewards important motivators?
5. Is a combination plan of salesperson compensation the normative approach? What accounts for its increased popularity? How do the firm's sales objectives influence the method of compensation?
6. Discuss the use of sales quotas as a means of motivating and evaluating salespeople. How does the sales manager set fair quotas? What factors influence the decision?

NOTES

1. Sally Scanlon, "Pall Hydraulic's Devoted Missionaries," *Sales and Marketing Management,* May 14, 1979, pp. 43–46. Reprinted by permission from Sales & Marketing Management magazine. Copyright 1979.
2. U.S. Department of Commerce, *Statistical Abstract of the United States, 1979* (Washington, D.C.: Government Printing Office, 1979), p. 415.
3. "Sales Jobs Open Up for Women," *Dun's Review,* March 1978, pp. 86–88.
4. Ibid.
5. John E. Swan and Charles M. Futrell, "Men Versus Women in Industrial Sales: A Performance Gap," *Industrial Marketing Management,* July 1978, pp. 369–373. For an overview, see Leslie Kanuk, "Women in Industrial Selling," *Journal of Marketing* 42 (January 1978): 87–91.
6. Paul Busch and Ronald F. Bush, "Women Contrasted to Men in the Industrial Salesforce: Job Satisfaction, Values, Role Clarity, Performance, and Propensity to Leave," *Journal of Marketing Research* 15 (August 1978): 438–448.
7. "Sales Jobs Open . . . ," *Dun's Review,* p. 86.
8. "There's No Place Like Home," *Sales and Marketing Management,* June 18, 1979, p. 85.
9. Mack Hanan, "Join the Systems Sell and You Can't Be Beat," *Sales and Marketing Management,* August 21, 1972, p. 44. Reprinted by permission from Sales & Marketing Management magazine. Copyright 1972.
10. David S. Hopkins and Earl L. Bailey, *Customer Service — A Progress Report* (New York: Conference Board, 1970), p. 1.
11. Paul Busch and David T. Wilson, "An Experimental Analysis of a Salesman's Expert and Referent Bases of Social Power in the Buyer-Seller Dyad," *Journal of Marketing Research* 13 (February 1976): 3–11.
12. Stan Moss, "What Sales Executives Look For in New Salespeople," *1979 Sales and Marketing Plans* (New York: Sales and Marketing Management, 1979), pp. 96–98.
13. Thomas J. Von Der Embse and Thomas D. Dovel, "Take Parent and Child out of Your Selling. Adult to Adult Rings Bell," *Marketing Times,* March–April 1977, pp. 20–22. Reprinted from Marketing Times, business update for the management professional, published by Sales and Marketing Executives International.
14. "Double Digit Hikes in 1974 Sales Training Costs," *Sales Management* 114 (January 6, 1975): 54–55.
15. Ibid.
16. "Sales Meetings and Sales Training," *Sales and Marketing Management,* February 25, 1980, p. 68.
17. Arthur H. Brayfield and Walter H. Crockett, "Employee Attitudes and Employee Performance," *Psychological Bulletin* 52 (September 1955): 396–424.
18. Richard L. Oliver, "Expectancy Theory Predictions of Salesmen's Performance," *Journal of Marketing Research* 11 (August 1974): 243–253.
19. Gilbert A. Churchill, Jr., Neil M. Ford, and Orville C. Walker, Jr., "Measuring the Job Satisfaction of Industrial Salesmen," *Journal of Marketing Research* 11 (August 1974): 254–260.
20. Robert W. Sweitzer and Dev S. Paltrak, "The Self-Actualizing Salesman," *Southern Journal of Business* 7 (November 1972): 1–8.
21. Fred Luthans and Robert Kreitner, "The Role of Punishment in Organizational Behavior Modification," *Public Personnel Management* 7 (May–June 1973): 156–161.

22. "A Better Way," *Sales and Marketing Management,* April 9, 1979, p. 19.

23. Martin Everett, "A Swift Kick in the Pants," *Sales and Marketing Management,* May 14, 1979, p. 34.

24. James M. Comer, "The Computer, Personal Selling, and Sales Management," *Journal of Marketing* 39 (July 1975): 27–33.

25. Ibid., p. 31.

26. Adrian B. Ryans and Charles B. Weinberg, "Territory Sales Response," *Journal of Marketing Research* 16 (November 1979): 453–465.

27. Thomas R. Wotruba and Michael L. Thurlow, "Sales Force Participation in Quota Selling and Sales Forecasting," *Journal of Marketing* 40 (April 1976): 11–16.

28. Ibid.

29. Leon Winer, "The Effect of Product Sales Quotas on Sales Force Productivity," *Journal of Marketing Research* 10 (May 1973): 180–183.

30. "They Say It'll Take 54 Weeks: That's Like No Delivery at All," *Sales Management* 112 (January 21, 1974): 27.

31. Martin Everett, "The Rewards of Hanging in There," *Sales Management* 113 (November 25, 1974): 19–24.

◢ CASES

20.1 Iowa American Telephone Company

Four months ago Robert Perkins, a 24-year-old M.B.A. from the University of Michigan, agreed to participate in a rather unique experiment. After spending six months in Iowa Telephone's junior executive training program, Perkins was offered the position of Council Bluffs district sales manager. The junior executive training program rotates young management candidates through the various departments so that they can work and observe company operations. Wayne McKinney, the sales manager, exuded enthusiasm about Perkins' abilities and reassured him that even though no one had ever been promoted to district sales manager in less than fifteen years, he was sure Perkins could do the job.

American Telephone Company supplies 60 percent of all telephone service in Iowa and is one of the largest independent telephone companies in the nation. The state is divided into three districts, each encompassing approximately one-third of the state. District headquarters are Council Bluffs, Des Moines, and Cedar Rapids, respectively. Each district has a sales manager, a business office manager, a plant and production manager, and a traffic manager (who is in charge of long-distance equipment and operators). Each district manager reports to a state manager in Des Moines. State headquarters for American and Des Moines district offices are located in the same building. Each district manager came up through the ranks, has been with the company approximately 20 years, and is 45 or 50 years old.

The district is served by five communications representatives, or salespeople, who call on commercial accounts to sell switchboards, data communication equipment, tie lines, and similar products. Residential and small-business accounts were handled by the business office. Two salespeople with a combined total of 48 years of experience were stationed in Sioux City; Kelso Smith, with 38 years of experience, and Don Brooks, a new salesman, are headquartered in Des Moines; the remaining salesman, Bill Walker, has 4 years of experience. A bright, aggressive person, he is stationed in Manning.

Perkins realized that he must manage the salesforce with tremendous finesse to obtain their respect, since all except Brooks have far more product knowledge than he does. The past four months have been eye opening for Perkins—he has found few correlations between textbooks and reality. There is no formal prospecting; each salesperson watches the papers and construction reports for new business activity and makes a sales call when the time is right. Some salespeople also keep a card file and periodically call on old accounts. Sales training and hiring is done strictly at the state level; new personnel go through a three-week program on company policies, sales techniques, and product knowledge before being assigned to a district.

All salespeople are paid on a straight-salary basis, which seems to suit them fine. New people who are aggressive and competent, like Bill Walker, normally leave the company after a few years. In fact Perkins suspects Walker of using his sales calls as a way of prospecting for a new job.

Sales quotas for the districts are sent down by McKinney each December in the form of percentage increases over the previous year's figure (traditionally 10 percent). While there is no stated policy, the district sales managers usually add the same percentage to each salesperson's sales for the previous year. Perkins has noticed that under this system Smith seems to work fairly hard one or two days a week and do "busy work" the rest of the time. Perkins also suspects that this phenomenon exists to a lesser degree in Sioux City.

Perkins received a short memo in the morning mail from McKinney asking him to outline what steps could be taken to make the sales operation more efficient in his district.

1. Prepare the memo from Robert Perkins to Wayne McKinney.
2. What can Perkins do to motivate and retain Bill Walker?
3. What should Perkins do about Kelso Smith?
4. Are changes necessary in the firm's hiring and training practices?
5. Should prospecting procedures be implemented?

20.2   National Merchandising Corporation

National Merchandising Corporation is a $6 million company whose independent sales agents sell telephone book cover advertising. It recruits mainly with newspaper ads. Its 28 division managers prescreen respondents by phone, then personally interview likely candidates. Because new-hires are given nine weeks' training, it is especially important to select the right people.

At present, the company attempts to determine whether the candidate will measure up to National's standards. It is thinking about changing its recruiting requirements to force managers to evaluate whether the company can offer the individual the opportunity he or she wants. Those who pass the phone screening would be asked to be prepared to discuss at the interview what they would like to be doing in three to five years. National's present hiring procedure is simply to evaluate the merits of the candidate's background.

1. Should the company alter its hiring objectives?
2. What kind of person should the firm be recruiting?
3. What kind of compensation plan would you recommend for the salesforce? Why?

Eastern State College*

A faculty committee met for the purpose of improving and extending the summer program at Eastern State College, which had been experiencing a summer school enrollment decline for the past four years. The committee was designated the Summer Task Force Committee.

Eastern State College is a four-year public college that had previously been devoted to teacher training but in the past ten years had developed a college of business administration and a school of communications. Moreover, new programs in social work and public administration had been developed. The college has an undergraduate enrollment of approximately 2200 male and 2300 female students. There are about 750 male graduate and 800 female graduate students. There are only about 400 continuing education students. The college operates on a 15-week semester and 12-week summer session basis. Eastern State College is located in a small rural community about 40 miles from a community with a population of over 100,000. The college features a 200-acre campus, field house, student union, and relatively new men's and women's dormitories and apartments.

The curriculum at Eastern State College had developed so that the business, social work, physics, and journalism programs had received national accreditation by their associations. The college offered master's degree programs in the following fields: biology, business, chemistry, counseling, elementary education, English, history, mathematics, physics, reading, social science, and special education. Currently in progress was the development of a master's degree program in computer science.

An analysis of students who were admitted to Eastern State found that 85 percent ranked in the top two-fifths of their high school class. Approximately 50 percent had combined SAT scores above 1000. The middle 50 percent of students accepted for admission had SAT verbal scores between 440 and 540 and SAT mathematical scores between 475 and 585. The college accepted about 300 transfer students annually.

About 90 percent of the students had graduated from an in-state high school. The other students came from adjoining states. There were relatively few foreign students on campus, and these came primarily from South America. The estimated undergraduate enrollment by school was 40 percent in Arts and Sciences, which included the School of Communications; 35 percent in Business Administration; 15 percent in Education; and 10 percent undeclared majors. The faculty-administration complement was about 350.

The Summer Task Force Committee had the following tasks:

1. To identify which students are served by the summer program.
2. To revise the summer program calendar if necessary.
3. To make more effective use of direct mail and other media.
4. To develop a logo.

---

* Case prepared by Professor Ronald D. Michman, Shippensburg State College, Shippensburg, Pennsylvania.

5. To improve teaching and evaluation of promotional efforts.
6. To improve forecasting techniques.

Summer school enrollment was similar to the fall and spring enrollment in the different schools. Students from the School of Arts and Sciences and the School of Business made up approximately 75 percent of the enrollment. However, about 60 percent of the graduate enrollment involved teacher training. The proportion of the undergraduate enrollment in the School of Education had declined from 35 percent in 1976 to 15 percent by 1982. Graduate education in the regular semester had declined from 50 percent of the total to 20 percent. In the summer, graduate education enrollment had declined from 80 percent to 60 percent from 1976 to 1982. Further declines were anticipated.

Approximately 10 percent of the summer school enrollment was from students who lived within commuting distance of the college. Many of these students were surprised to learn that Eastern State College was not primarily a teacher training institution. These students enrolled mostly in the newly created School of Business and in other programs in journalism and public relations. Some of the high school students who had graduated in June were taking basic core courses in order to accelerate their studies, and this source seemed to have promising potential.

The present college calendar consisted of a three-week presummer session, a six-week main session, and a three-week postsummer session. Table 1 shows the credit hour enrollment for pre–, main–, and postsummer sessions. The graduate summer enrollment demonstrated sharp declines. While the undergraduate enrollment had stabilized in some respects, certain environmental conditions were disturbing. First of all, college tuition was increased by the state legislature, and with the recession many students needed to work full time over the summer. Second, the energy situation and the rising costs of gasoline might be especially burdensome for students situated in a rural community without public transportation. Third, more and more families were hard hit by inflation. Many of Eastern State College students were first-generation college students and needed loans in order to attend college.

A number of suggestions were made regarding the summer calendar. Since there were relatively few courses offered in the evening, it was thought that more courses should be placed in the evening session. This would permit students to work during the day. Another thought was that perhaps the length of each session could be extended so that classes would meet only four times a week instead of five. This would give students a long weekend and also reduce traveling expenses. Another option to be investigated would be two five-week sessions. This would have the effect of shortening a twelve-week program to ten weeks. Other

◄ TABLE 1 Credit Hour Production

	1979			1980			1981			1982		
	Pre–	Main–	Post–	Pre–	Main–	Post–	Pre–	Main–	Post–	Pre–	Main–	Post–
UG	2132	3926	1182	2055	4262	1822	1700	4087	1564	2027	4065	1372
G	2348	5315	1264	2020	4424	1103	1779	3930	1154	1316	3297	876

options would be a three week–six week–three week plan, a five week–five week–five week plan, or a three week–four week–five week plan. Naturally, the college could continue the traditional three week–six week–three week schedule. Some objections were raised concerning the four-day plan and schedules that would extend the length of each session. It was believed that perhaps students might be asked to absorb more material than could possibly be learned in a single session, and that this could lead to instructional problems. Another instructional problem would be the longer class periods in a five-week session, which would require restructuring of courses and assignments.

The impact of the present advertising of the summer announcements was also reviewed. The 1981 advertising campaign was studied in order to make effective use of financial resources. Table 2 shows the newspaper advertising for the summer program in 1981. A 36-inch advertisement was used, and the cost computed by multiplying the cost per inch. One advertisement was taken out in each newspaper in communities where summer school students live, and the advertisements were staggered from April 1 to May 15. Some faculty members suggested that perhaps funds should be concentrated for newspaper advertising in areas where the majority of students live rather than using a comprehensive approach. Should this be done, newspapers 5, 6, 7, 10, and 11 would probably be eliminated. A coupon was placed in each advertisement, and 54 coupons were received. These were about equally divided between newspapers 1 through 4.

Another $600 was spent on direct mail advertising. This included mailing program circulars to students who had registered the previous summer and to various schools in order to attract teachers working for master's degrees. A total of about $2500 was allocated in 1981 for advertising, and $3000 would be budgeted for 1983.

There was some sentiment that perhaps television advertising should be used, since a wide audience could be reached. Table 3 shows the costs of advertising on television.

The committee was also charged to develop a logo. Many believed that this was a public relations aspect of the advertising program, since a logo should reflect an image of the college. Some faculty members suggested that a picture of an Indian be used on all stationery and direct mail pieces, since the football team was known as the Red Raiders. Other suggestions included the use of the initials ESC

◢ **TABLE 2   Schedule of Newspaper Advertising April 1–May 15, 1981**

1. Patriot News	$36'' \times \$8.96 = \$$ 322.56
2. Carlisle Sentinel	$36'' \times$ 2.70 = 197.10
3. Public Opinion	$36'' \times$ 2.60 = 93.60
4. News-Chronicle	$36'' \times$ 2.80 = 100.80
5. Gettysburg Times	$36'' \times$ 2.36 = 84.96
6. Herald/Mail	$36'' \times$ 6.11 = 219.96
7. Lewistown Sentinel	$36'' \times$ 2.75 = 99.00
8. York Dispatch	$36'' \times$ 5.74 = 206.64
9. York Record	$36'' \times$ 4.40 = 158.40
10. Lancaster papers	$36'' \times$ 7.56 = 272.16
11. PSU Daily Collegian	$36'' \times$ 3.70 = 133.20
	$1,888.38

▲ **TABLE 3** **Television Advertising**

	Saturday Night Live	MASH	WKRP	Totals
Total households	67,000	70,000	63,000	200,000
Women 18–34	25,000	21,000	16,000	62,000
Men 18–34	26,000	13,000	15,000	54,000
Total 18–34	51,000	34,000	31,000	116,000

Three 30-second spots (Saturday Night Live)	$384
One 30-second spot, MASH	200
One 30-second spot, WKRP	200
TOTAL	$784 + production

in some pictorial way or the use of a picture of the home of a former president of the United States, which was well known and only a few miles away. Still others thought that a picture of one of the modern buildings on campus would show the college to better advantage. The committee appointed a subcommittee to review all these options.

One problem was to develop a method to measure the effectiveness of the summer program advertising. The use of coupons in newspapers really did not reveal that much. The committee was at a loss to make recommendations in this area.

Another facet of developing an effective advertising program was ability to identify the potential market. A commercial organization could furnish a list of about 4 million college students. Students could be selected by home address, school address, by geographic area, and even by field of study. A basic list would cost about $300, with added charges as the list is made more specific.

The committee believed that more information was needed about the characteristics of students who attended the summer session last year. The committee also wanted to know if special programs would stimulate summer attendance. A number of athletic conferences had been held, and these were cited as examples. One faculty member mentioned the use of a computer workshop session of one week for recent high school graduates that was very successful at another college. The committee session concluded with a discussion of the possible development of summer workshops.

1. What procedures should Eastern State College use to identify its target market?
2. How can more effective use be made of media selection?
3. Can you suggest a possible logo?
4. Can you suggest a better promotional mix in this case?
5. How could direct selling be used to sell the summer program?
6. What additional strategies could you recommend for Eastern State College?

PART Seven

Marketing management

21

Marketing planning and forecasting

OBJECTIVES

To realize the importance of marketing planning.

To become acquainted with the procedure for designing a planning system.

To learn the steps involved in tactical planning.

To become aware of the merger of tactical plans into a comprehensive marketing program.

To understand the process and procedures of demand forecasting.

Recently, a gathering of America's largest food retailers were asked the following questions:

1. Are you ready for the working woman who only wants to shop after 6:00 P.M. during the week and on weekends?
2. Are you ready for a shopper who has more money and less time? Will you be ready to get your new customer in and out of the store in half the time and still generate growth?
3. Are you ready to set up sufficient space in your store for ready-to-eat hot meals that can be picked up on the way home from work and brought right to the eating area without ever seeing a pot or a stove—and with sufficient variety?
4. Are you ready with an innovative service to help shoppers who cannot come to the store?
5. Are you prepared to install a switchboard, where operators will take orders that will be picked up or delivered?
6. Are you ready to accommodate a drive-through customer who wants staples in a hurry?
7. Are you ready to offer in-store shopping services, so a customer can leave a list on the way to work in the morning and pick up a ready-to-go package of groceries on the way home from work?
8. Are you ready to switch the theme of your advertising from pricing and specials to service and convenience?[1]

Planning is an essential function of good management. As we mentioned in Chapter 2, marketing managers must understand the ever-changing external environment and plan their marketing strategies accordingly. If the food retailers are going to grow and prosper during the remainder of the decade, they must have a strategic plan and several tactical plans to answer the questions posed above. The food retailers must also prepare accurate forecasts to know when a specific plan should be implemented.

How does one go about planning? What are some of the tools used in forecasting? How is a comprehensive marketing program created? These are the major questions we will address in this chapter.

Developing marketing plans

Planning is a process by which managers visualize and determine future actions that will lead to a realization of company and marketing objectives. **Planning** may be defined as the process of using related facts and future assumptions to arrive at courses of action to be followed in seeking specific goals.

The goal of planning is to help marketing managers make better decisions. Plans can be divided into two categories: strategic and tactical. **Strategic planning** establishes the character of the organization and provides long-run direction. It is normally used with reference to fundamental issues, broad perspectives, and long-term periods (see Chapter 2). Strategic planning is usually performed by upper-level management and supported by input from middle management. **Tactical planning,** on the other hand, is concerned with efficient use of resources to obtain specific objectives. It is generally performed by middle management with support and input by lower-level management.

The longer the planning time span, the more likely the plan is to be strategic. Polaroid's decision to manufacture and market instant cameras involved a considerable amount of strategic planning. Armour-Dial introduced an "updated" version of its Dial soap. This involved tactical planning. The tactical objective was to make sure that retailers had sufficient inventory of the old bars to meet consumer demand through December, but not so much that the company would be hit with returns when the new bars were distributed.

Any firm that engages in long-range planning will be faced with tradeoffs. For example, in one company the end of the fiscal year was rapidly approaching. Sales were off because of an unexpected downturn in the economy, and profit projections were slipping. Pressure was on middle managers to make their profit goals if they expected their normal merit increases. If actual profits were too far below target the manager could expect termination. The situation thus sets up a conflict between the short-run goal of maintaining profits and the long-run goals that may not show an immediate profit.

CONTROLLING CONFLICT

Conflict between long-run and short-run plans usually cannot be escaped (Figure 21.1). The achievement of long-run goals often requires resource commit-

ments, such as new distribution centers and basic research and development funds, that may adversely affect profits in the current period. This is true even though these investments may create major returns in future years. Also, achievement of long-run goals may mean sticking to a strategic plan that creates higher than normal expenses during economic downturns. If, for example, the long-run strategy calls for a full product line, there may be strong pressures to drop slow-selling items during a recession. Although this action may aid in the achievement of short-term profit goals, it can sabotage a long-term strategy of appealing to a broad market segment. Unfortunately, in many businesses there is pressure on operating marketing managers to produce ever-increasing annual profits regardless of the impact on the strategic plan. Firms that accept this posture are not truly strategically oriented.

To minimize short-term versus long-term conflict, the first step is for management to admit that such conflict exists. Second, realistic goals must be established that take potential sources of disagreement into account. Managerial awards must also be tailored to the attainment of long-term as well as short-term objectives. Finally, middle or lower-level marketing managers must be made aware of all aspects of the strategic plan. In conjunction with better communications, management should include some lower-echelon managers in the creation of long-range plans.

THE ADVANTAGES OF GOOD PLANNING

The ultimate aim of strategic planning is better decision making. By forcing managers to assess the marketing environment and forecast future events, it helps them develop a better understanding of various decision alternatives. Management can anticipate changes and have contingency plans (tactical plans) ready in case specific events occur. For example, if competitor X raises prices 10 percent during the next six months, the firm might counter with a 3 percent price increase and a 20 percent increase in promotion stressing its lower price. Having a series of tactical plans derived from a long-run strategic plan helps management react to environmental change calmly and intelligently. Panic and hasty decision making are avoided.

Strategic and tactical planning that is well thought out and is based on inputs from all levels of management typically results in effective plans. Managerial involvement in the process from the bottom up is important because partici-

613

pation leads to better acceptance of the final plan. Lower levels of marketing management do not feel that higher levels are insensitive to their needs. Participation can serve as a form of motivation, since each manager knows where the firm is headed and what the opportunities are. Also, lower levels of management are closer to the "firing line" and may be aware of competitive subtleties that are not recognized by upper management. Other important advantages of good planning are these:

1. Planning provides a framework within which managerial objectives can be pursued through the functions of the manager.
2. Planning opens up multidirectional channels of communication.
3. Planning provides a framework for the decision-making process and leads to the reduction of suboptimal choices.
4. Planning permits the advance identification of opportunities for and threats to the organization.
5. Planning provides a basis for the control of operations in that the standards for control are derived from the objectives contained in the plans.
6. Planning provides a basis for the evaluation of managerial performance through the hierarchy of objectives contained in the plans.
7. Planning leads to a more efficient utilization of scarce resources by focusing attention and efforts on purposeful activities.[2]

WHY PLANNING SOMETIMES FAILS

Although good planning is an invaluable asset, poor planning can be a severe detriment to the firm. Why does planning fail? One reason is the failure to recognize the short-term versus long-term conflict. Other factors include these:

- A lack of realistic goals; without realistic goals, planning becomes an empty exercise.
- Poor communication; a good plan may fail if it is distributed unevenly throughout the managerial ranks.
- Failure to follow through; many failures can be traced to sound marketing plans that were ignored, and not to poor plans.
- A lack of leadership; unless planning receives the necessary leadership from top management, it is probably doomed to failure.

Designing a company planning system

Despite the problems involved, marketing management must have a sound planning system. A firm cannot remain competitive in the long run without effective plans and control systems. Wendy's, the fast food chain, experienced phenomenal growth from its founding in 1969 to its rise to third in the industry in 1980. Yet lack of a good planning system, coupled with an inadequate market information system, resulted in Wendy's failure to make needed strategic changes. Other fast food chains were diversifying their menus to reduce dependence on beef. They also began opening for breakfast. By 1979 Wendy's

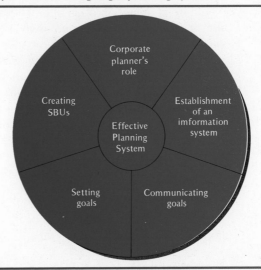

sales volume per restaurant had dropped 10 percent. As one executive noted, "Maybe we got trapped by the fact that everything was working so well, we were afraid to tamper." In other words, previously successful short-term successes created complacency and a failure to recognize the need to plan or establish a planning system.

Unfortunately there is no "off the shelf" planning system suitable for every firm. A planning system is a structured process that organizes and coordinates the activities of the managers who do the planning. Each system must be individually designed to take into account the firm's organizational philosophy, industry characteristics, company size, and so forth. Yet several key issues must be decided while designing a planning system (see Figure 21.2).

COMMUNICATING GOALS

The first issue relates to communication of corporate goals and strategies (if strategies have already been established). In small companies this may not be a problem; in larger firms a mechanism should be established to provide information on corporate goals and strategies to all managers with planning responsibilities.

CREATING SBUs

A second issue is how to divide the corporation (assuming it is fairly large) into strategic business units. As John R. White, vice-president of Arthur D. Little, one of America's largest consulting firms, notes: "Businesses, not corporations, have competition. If you're in a multibusiness company, then you have to decide how to allocate your resources."[3] Typically a **strategic business unit (SBU)** is a reasonably autonomous profit center. Usually an SBU has its own general manager, who reports to corporate top management. The general manager has overall operating authority and responsibility for the SBU.

The exact definition of an SBU will vary from company to company. Some firms define the term rather narrowly as representing a product line or market segment. In other cases, a much broader definition is applied. General Electric, for example, has SBUs that encompass several divisions and have annual sales in excess of $500 million. One reason for the difference is that some corporations believe that an SBU should be fully self-supporting. That is, it should have its own manufacturing, engineering, research and development, and marketing facilities. Others use as the primary criteria for an SBU that it have a clear market focus, identifiable strategy, and a defined set of competitors.[4] If the latter definition is used, the size and scope of the SBU will usually be smaller. One company that has a broad concept of SBUs is the Stanley Works. There SBUs are tools; industrial products, storage systems, and hardware; builder's products; and household products. With their diversity of markets and products, management can shift or allocate resources among various strategic options. General Electric, on the other hand, has 42 SBUs.

RESPONSIBILITY FOR SETTING GOALS

A third issue that must be resolved in creating a planning system is who should set objectives. This question goes beyond whether goal setting should be "top down" or from the "bottom up." Marketing management must decide where in the managerial hierarchy the process should begin. In a large company, "bottom up" is usually most appropriate. The lower-echelon managers of an SBU begin the goal-setting process, since they have the most intimate knowledge of their market, customers, competition, and capabilities. In small companies, goal setting is often "top down." The president of the organization will establish overall goals and then expect marketing and other managers to create plans that will meet the objectives.

ESTABLISHMENT OF AN INFORMATION SYSTEM

Effective marketing requires a good marketing information system. In a broader context, the firm requires a management information system for effective planning. This system can be an extension of the marketing information system that also provides decision-making information to finance, engineering, production, and top management. A planning system has two major functions: to develop an integrated, coordinated, and consistent long-term plan of action, and to facilitate adaptation of the corporation to environmental change.[5]

Thus another issue in creating a planning system is the design of the information system. How the data are to be obtained, who is going to analyze them, and who will receive what information must be determined.

THE CORPORATE PLANNER'S ROLE

The center of formal planning in a company basically determines where planning responsibility will be. In a small company, marketing and other line managers are responsible for planning in their respective areas. In bigger firms, the head of each SBU will be the primary planning officer. Yet even in these organizations, a planning staff usually evolves.

A line manager normally has basic planning responsibility. The **line manager** is the person directly involved in the design, development, production, and marketing of the basic production service offered by the organization. A **staff manager** works to provide specialized services, support, or knowledge to the line managers. Planning jurisdiction and activities in large firms must be resolved between line and staff management.

Steps in tactical marketing planning

After a company planning system has been put into place, marketing managers can actually begin to plan. The strategic marketing planning process was covered in Chapter 2. In this section, we will examine the steps in tactical (sometimes called operational) planning. This type of planning is not necessarily confined to one year or less, but this is the most common time frame. As a newly appointed marketing manager, you will come into contact with and be expected to engage in tactical planning far more often than strategic planning. The basic steps involved in tactical planning are shown in Figure 21.3.

◢ **FIGURE 21.3 Steps in tactical marketing planning.**

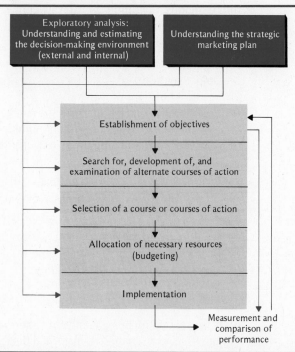

STEP 1. UNDERSTAND THE MARKETING ENVIRONMENT AND THE STRATEGIC MARKETING PLAN

The first step in tactical planning is to understand the internal and external environments of marketing and strategic marketing plan. Until 1980, for example, Holiday Inns defined its mission as being in the travel business. This strategic thinking led to many managerial problems when the firm acquired Trailways, Inc., and Delta Steamship Lines, Inc. Since Holiday Inns was in the travel business, it seemed perfectly logical to acquire a furniture manufacturing operation to supply its motels. It also seemed to make sense that Holiday Inns would buy buses to haul at least some of its customers to its markets.

The furniture manufacturing and bus operation decisions (tactical plans) were made with a reasonable understanding of the strategic plan. Yet these tactical plans were flawed because of lack of knowledge concerning the external environment. For example, management failed to realize that few bus passengers would be willing or able to stay at high- or medium-priced motels. Nor did they understand that motel franchises might balk because Holiday-produced furniture was more expensive than the products of some competitors. Again, successful tactical planning begins with environmental and strategic insights.

STEP 2. ESTABLISH GOALS

After the necessary information is obtained and assimilated, goals can be established. One goal of Holiday Inn, for example, was to provide its motels and hotels with a reliable source of quality furniture while also establishing the furniture-making operation as a profit center. This objective, while impressive, was flawed. Good objectives serve several functions:

1. Objectives provide direction for lower-echelon marketing managers.
2. Objectives serve as motivators. They create something to strive for.
3. Objectives form a basis for control; the effectiveness of a plan can be measured in light of the goals.
4. Objectives telegraph marketing management philosophy. Objectives provide clues to top management thinking and organizational philosophy. They help create a singleness of purpose.

STEP 3. DEVELOP AND EXAMINE ALTERNATIVE COURSES OF ACTION

Portfolio analysis. When goals are created, alternative courses of action can be developed and evaluated. A number of techniques can be used to evaluate alternatives, depending upon the type of decision to be made — price, promotion, product, or distribution (see Figure 21.4). One popular approach for analyzing product/service and market segmentation alternatives is the Boston Consulting Group's portfolio analysis system (see Chapter 8).

PIMS. A second means of analyzing alternatives (or to aid in understanding alternatives) is examination of historical data. Recently a group of over 100 com-

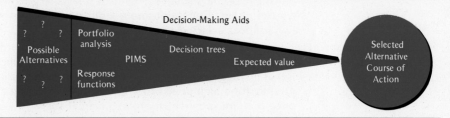

panies and 5 academic institutions has developed a program entitled **profit impact of market strategy (PIMS).**[6]

The objective of PIMS is to provide a business strategy experience data base. The firms have reported over 800 experiences covering a five-year period and involving 300 data items. Each experience describes the marketing strategy, the environment, and the results obtained. Computer analysis of the information has revealed a number of interesting findings. For example, if a company's market position is strong, increased research and development expenditures generally lead to higher profits. The following is a summary of major PIMS findings:

- Capital intensity is strongest of the 37 factors. Market position is second.
- High capital intense businesses don't do well because of the high investment in the ROI ratio but mostly because the process of competition works in a particularly vicious way in such industries—that is, because the sheer fact of capital intensity plus high fixed costs injects a note of desperation into competition to keep the expensive plant loaded. This, in turn, produces price weakness, marketing wars, or other rather expensive forms of competition to get the volume needed.
- If you're highly capital intense, then don't spend a lot of marketing dollars to buy volume. The 42 businesses in the data base which did averaged 0.1 percent pretax ROI. Heavy marketing expense with heavy investment expense is simply too much for any one business to bear.
- If you're highly capital intense, try to segment your market to improve your market position. (It also is a disaster to try to combine a high capital intensity with weak market position.) But if you can succeed in segmenting your market sufficiently well so that you can have a strong position in whatever segments you operate, then you can at least project your profitability into a reasonably good neighborhood.
- A high market share business is considerably more profitable than a low market share business.

- There are two ways in which a business can acquire a strong market position—by being big or by being selective in terms of which specific market segments it selects to go after and concentrating its attentions on establishing a dominant position in those selected segments.

- The high quality producer can be considerably more profitable than the low quality producer regardless of his pricing policy —that is, regardless of whether he sells his high quality product for a high price or for a low price. Charging a low price is an inexpensive way to buy market share.

- Businesses with high quality products and strong market positions also are very profitable, averaging 29 percent ROI.

- At the opposite extreme, low quality and weak position, the average is 6 percent ROI.

- Market position and product quality (remember, it's product quality as perceived by the market and includes the service package as well as the characteristics of the gadget itself) can be used as substitutes for each other—that is, if you're weak in one, you can compensate for it by being strong in the other.

- If your market position is weak, premium pricing doesn't pay. It cuts profitability, even if you have superior product quality. If you have superior quality and weak position, then cash in via volume.

- If your market position is weak, don't do R&D, but do introduce new products by "copying," "stealing," imitating, licensing, or buying them. "Imitation is the natural way of competition for the weak. Innovation is the natural way of competition for the strong."

- If your market position is strong, increase your R&D and profitability will go up. (R&D here is R&D performed by ordinary people, not the "strokes-of-genius" kind.)

- If you've got a low quality product, don't advertise it. If you do, you'll have about a 3 percent pretax ROI. Just quietly put a low price on it and find a segment of the market that responds to it.

- Those who introduce new products at the bottom of a recession find it very profitable, partly because it gives the market a little excitement when it could stand a little and partly because it also insulates the business from the occasionally nasty price competition that develops at the bottom of the cycle. It also helps the business pick up additional market share points at a lower cost per point when the market starts growing again.

- It is unfortunately true that it is never a good idea to spend much more than 10 cents of the sales dollar for all marketing functions. In cosmetics and some other lines, you can't help yourself, but still it's a drag on earnings when you exceed this ratio.

- It is generally true that those businesses with a strong market share are underspending on marketing and could afford to spend more, and those with a weak market position are overspending and would be better off if they spent less.[7]

Response functions. A third analysis technique is the use of **response functions.** These are graphed relationships—curves between a marketing mix, or component of the mix, and sales to a specific market target (see Figure 21.5). Some planners substitute profits for sales when plotting response curves. Part A of Figure 21.5 shows the relationship between intensity of distribution and total sales. In this case, a convenience good was used, thus the resulting "greater the number of outlets—the higher the sales" relationship. If all other elements of the marketing mix were to be held constant, the marketing manager would sub-

▲ **FIGURE 21.5 Using response functions to analyze marketing alternatives.**

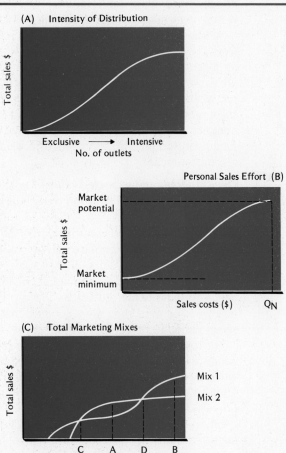

(A)　Intensity of Distribution

Total sales $

Exclusive ⟶ Intensive
No. of outlets

Personal Sales Effort (B)

Total sales $

Market potential

Market minimum

Sales costs ($)　　Q_N

(C)　Total Marketing Mixes

Total sales $

Mix 1

Mix 2

C　A　D　B
Marketing effort ($)

tract the cost of adding the nth outlet from the marginal sales of the nth outlet. As long as this figure was positive (and other costs remained proportional), new stores would continue to be added.

Part B of the chart shows the relationship between personal sales effort and total sales. Note that some sales would be generated without any personal selling due to advertising and sales promotion. This is called the **market minimum.** As salespersons are added, sales will begin increasing at an increasing and then decreasing rate. Finally, sales peak out when Q_N salespersons have been hired. This is the upper limit of sales that can be generated by the salesforce and is called the **market potential.** The difference between the market minimum and the market potential is the **marketing (salesforce) sensitivity of demand.** By allocating additional resources to the sales staff, total revenues can be increased until Q_N. Beyond that point additional personnel do not generate additional sales. The final graph (C) plots the response functions of two marketing mixes. Below expenditure level C, the marketing manager should utilize mix 1. Between expenditures C and D, the manager should choose mix 2. If the firm is fortunate enough to allocate B level of funds to marketing, then management should implement mix 1.

Although response functions are a helpful tool in deciding among alternatives, they are not without an important drawback. A response function is only as good as the assumptions behind the shape of the curve. If the assumptions are wrong, then the curve is wrong. Moreover, even if the assumptions are correct at the time an alternative is chosen, the rapidly changing external environment may alter relationships between variables. Thus alternatives need to be continually reevaluated. Past experience, marketing research, and executive judgment should also be used periodically to reassess the shapes of the response functions.

Decision trees and expected value. Another technique for choosing among alternatives is the use of **decision trees.** Suppose a distributor of important wines was considering whether to introduce a new red, rose, or white wine on the market.[8] Based upon data provided by the marketing information system and the manager's past experience, he appraised the situation as shown in Table 21.1, part A. The columns of the table represent market conditions as they might exist. Listed under each of the possible conditions is the marketing manager's estimate of the probability that a particular market condition exists. For example, the marketing manager feels that 60 percent of the market prefers a sweet wine, 30 percent a medium-dry wine, and 10 percent a dry wine.

The rows of part A represent the alternatives available to the firm. The dollar values within the table are the expected profit or loss given that a particular wine was chosen and that an expected market condition does in fact exist. Thus if a white wine was introduced and the market preferred a sweet wine, the firm would make $150,000. The various decision alternatives can be shown in the form of a decision tree (see Figure 21.6). At the end of each branch is the expected outcome from each alternative. Decision trees can be expanded by using more sophisticated techniques and can help managers visually understand their alternatives.

◢ TABLE 21.1 Using the Decision Tree Technique

Part A. Payoff table for the introduction of a new wine

	Sweet wine $P_1 = .60$	Medium wine $P_2 = .30$	Dry wine $P_3 = .10$
Red	−$100,000	$ 50,000	$200,000
Rosé	$ 50,000	$100,000	$ 50,000
White	$150,000	$ 50,000	−$150,000

Part B. Selection of decision alternatives using three criteria

Decision alternatives	Value of worst outcome	Value of best outcome	Expected value
Red	−$100,000	$200,000	−25,000
Rosé	$ 50,000	$100,000	$65,000
White	−$150,000	$150,000	$90,000

Source: Eli P. Cox III, *Marketing Research Information for Decision Making* (New York: Harper and Row, 1979), p. 119.

◢ FIGURE 21.6 Decision alternatives for introducing a new wine.

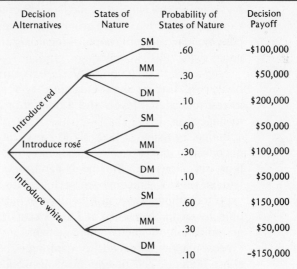

SM = Sweet market preferred by market
MM = Medium market preferred by market
DM = Dry market preferred by market

Source: Eli P. Cox III. *Marketing Research Information for Decision Making* (New York: Harper & Row, 1979), p. 119.

Look at Table 21.1. What alternative should the marketing manager select? If the manager wanted to choose the best possible outcome, the red wine would be marketed. A risk averter might review the alternatives and then pick the one that could do the least damage. In this case, she would introduce the rosé wine, since the value of the worst outcome is still plus $50,000. These two criteria, however, do not take into account the probabilities associated with the various states of the marketplace. This can be overcome by using the expected value approach and selecting the alternative with the greatest expected value. The **expected value** of an alternative is a weighted average of all the possible consequences of the alternative where the weight of a consequence is the estimated probability that it will occur. Therefore, the expected value of the three alternatives is as follows:

$$\text{EV (red)} = -\$100,000 \times .60 + \$50,000 \times .30 + \$200,000 \times .10$$
$$= -\$25,000$$

$$\text{EV (rosé)} = \$50,000 \times .60 + \$100,000 \times .30 + \$50,000 \times .10$$
$$= \$65,000$$

$$\text{EV (white)} = \$150,000 \times .60 + \$50,000 \times .30 - \$150,000 \times .10$$
$$= \$90,000$$

The decision, using expected value, is to introduce the white wine.

STEP 4. SELECT A COURSE OF ACTION AND PREPARE A BUDGET

After alternatives have been chosen and evaluated, a decision must be made. As shown in the wine example, several criteria can be applied: risk aversion, expected value, maximum profits. The criteria chosen will depend upon company policies and philosophies regarding risk-taking, plus the person's managerial style.

After a course of action is selected, resources must be allocated to obtain the objectives. This involves budgeting. Typically, budgets are established at the lowest managerial levels and modified or approved by succeeding levels of management.

Budgeting makes it possible to carry out plans. Without funding, planning becomes an empty exercise. Budgeting also serves as a basis for control. Over time, deviations from the budget can be examined. Deviations are not good or bad per se. Not all events can be anticipated, so some discrepancies should be expected. Budgets may also be used in evaluating managerial performance. If objectives can be reached at a lower cost than the budgeted amount, it is often an indication of effective management.

Most marketing budgets for carrying out tactical plans are revenue and expense budgets. The revenue (or sales) budget must be coordinated with the sales forecast, since revenues from sales define the upper limits of expenses and profits. Some marketing plans call for a capital expenditures budget. An example would be the allocation of funds to increase production of a present product or to manufacture a new product.

In any budget it is important to have some degree of flexibility. For example, a regional sales manager who is experiencing difficulty in meeting sales quotas may have every reason to believe that a market research study would be of help in solving the problem. Yet it may be impossible to conduct the research because there is no money for it in the budget.

STEP 5. IMPLEMENT AND CONTROL THE TACTICAL MARKETING PLAN

After a budget has been established, the planned course of action is ready for implementation. Authority must be granted to the marketing manager or managers who will be responsible for carrying out the plan. Staff personnel need to be informed of their duties as well. Sometimes a major or strategic plan requires task force management. AT&T, for example, established a task force to implement the marketing concept throughout the Bell System. A **task force** is a tightly organized unit under the direction of a manager who usually has broad powers of authority. A task force is established to accomplish a single goal or mission and thus works against a time deadline.

Implementing a plan also has another dimension: gaining acceptance. New plans mean change, and change creates resistance. One reason people resist change is that they feel like they will be losing something. When new product research is taken away from marketing research and given to a new product department, the director of marketing research will naturally feel resistance. He or she is losing part of his or her domain. Misunderstanding or lack of trust also creates opposition to change.

Resistance can be dealt with in several ways:

1. Education and communication regarding the new plan.
2. Participation and involvement by those who will be affected.
3. Giving a group leader such as a marketing research director a key role in the implementation of the change.
4. The worst way to gain compliance is through coercion; people resent forced change.

The last step in the tactical planning process is feedback and control. Control is essentially making sure events conform to the plans, and this is the subject of Chapter 22.

DEVELOPING A COMPREHENSIVE MARKETING PROGRAM

Each tactical marketing plan is ultimately merged into a total marketing program. The marketing program is the responsibility of top marketing management and represents the means by which marketing will accomplish its strategic goals. Holiday Inns' total marketing program includes plans for new hotels and restaurants, as well as casinos. It also plans to spend $950 million between 1980 and 1985 to refurbish many of its hotel and motel rooms to maintain a "fresh image." Continually rising fuel prices are recognized in Holi-

day Inns' strategic plan. Therefore, virtually all new hotels will be built near airports and industrial parks.

The marketing program is only part of the total planning process. Although the marketing program is composed of comprehensive tactical plans, these plans also have planning components (see Figure 21.7). Holiday Inns, for example, is developing elaborate promotional plans for the new casinos. Generally speaking, the planning process is sequential in nature. Management does not develop a complete marketing program until it has a strategic marketing plan. Also, as one moves down the planning hierarchy, planning responsibility is given to succeeding lower levels of management.

It is quite common for marketing managers to be working on several tactical plans at one time. The advertising manager may be responsible for a number of advertising plans (campaigns) for hotels and casinos. This is normally the way to use managerial and other resources well, and yet problems can arise. If planning time or other resources become scarce, decisions have to be made on which plan will suffer.

Forecasting demand for products and services

One aspect of planning that will never change is the importance of forecasting to the planning process. At the exploratory analysis phase of planning, for example, forecasts are used to estimate levels of economic activity; industry sales trends; competitors' market penetrations; the firm's revenues during the next quarter, year, and next five years; sales by product lines; and sales of individual products. These same forecasts are used to develop planning alternatives, evaluate various options, and pick a course of action. Without forecasts, planning becomes an empty process.

Evaluating national trends. Forecasts of sales can be made by starting with overall estimates of economic activity and narrowing them down to a specific product. For example, a forecast might begin with a national economic forecast of GNP (gross national product is the total value of all final goods and services for a specified time period). Unless the company is very large, it will usually obtain GNP forecasts through secondary sources. Major banks, the federal government, consulting firms, and some universities provide GNP forecasts. These are important for most marketers, since sales of goods and services tend to increase when GNP goes up and vice versa.

Forecasting industry sales. After national sales trends have been determined, industry sales are usually estimated. First market sales potential is determined. This is the maximum amount of product or service units that can be sold in a given industry with maximum marketing expenditures under existing marketing mixes within a specific external environment (see Figure 21.8). Obviously market potential will change as the environment changes. The market potential for small cars has increased as the price of gasoline has increased and fuel shortages have occurred. Actual industry sales estimates are normally below sales potential. This is because every firm in the industry usually does not allocate the maximum amount of resources possible to the marketing effort.

Individual product/service sales potential. After actual sales estimates have been made for every industry in which the firm competes, sales forecasts can be made for individual products. Industry sales forecasts place limits on potential product sales. That is, sales for a given product cannot exceed sales of the industry in which the good is sold (unless it is sold in several industries). Also, the competitiveness of each industry will have an impact on sales potential for

FIGURE 21.8 Industry sales potential for small cars under varying conditions.

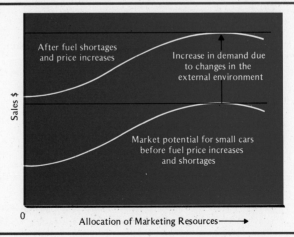

a single product. For example, competition in the fresh pork meat industry became so intense in 1980 that Swift's fresh pork sales forecasts led the company to sell the division.

Company sales forecasts. When forecasts have been completed for each individual product, they are aggregated to form a product line forecast. In larger firms these are summed together to obtain an SBU forecast. Finally, the sales forecasts for the SBUs provide the firm with a company sales forecast.

POPULAR FORECASTING TECHNIQUES

Marketing managers can use a number of tools to estimate sales for products, product lines, companies, and industries. Forecasting GNP levels is a complex task that is rarely the province of the marketing manager. What techniques do marketing managers use most often for forecasting? Table 21.2 shows the methods applied in 175 firms. There are two things to note about this table. First is that most firms do not use high sophisticated quantitative techniques. Second, the listing does not distinguish between methods for forecasting new product sales versus sales of existing products. There is some overlap between the two, but it is not complete. For example, intention-to-buy surveys are associated primarily with new product forecasts, whereas a moving average is generally used for an existing product.

ACCURACY AND MISUSE OF FORECASTS

Although a number of different methods are used to forecast sales, it is better to use one method for the whole company. One survey noted the following:

◀ TABLE 21.2   Sales Forecasting Methods, 175 Firms

Method	Used regularly	Used occasionally	Never tried
Jury of executive opinion	52%	16%	5%
Sales force composite	48	15	9
Trend projections	28	16	12
Moving average	24	15	15
Industry survey	22	20	16
Regression	17	13	24
Intention-to-buy survey	15	17	23
Exponential smoothing	13	13	26
Leading index	12	16	24
Life cycle analysis	8	11	28
Diffusion index	8	11	30
Simulation model	8	8	35
Input/output model	6	8	34

Source: Douglas J. Dalrymple, "Sales Forecasting Methods and Accuracy," *Business Horizons* 18, 6 (December 1975): 71.

Many companies develop a single, objective forecast of sales potential and then establish independently whatever target may be appropriate for their marketing and sales organizations, production divisions, etc. However, we have found companies that use one forecast for establishing sales objectives, a second for projecting earnings and a third for scheduling production, with little consistency among the forecasts.[9]

It is impossible to have an efficient, fully integrated planning system when managers are working with a variety of forecasts to suit their individual needs. A firm should devote its efforts to the creation of a single "best estimate" sales forecast.

How accurate are sales forecasts? It seems to vary widely from company to company and largely depends upon the sophistication of the forecasting method. A Conference Board study reported that a substantial majority of marketing executives were generally satisfied with the usefulness and accuracy of their companies' sales forecasts. Yet the same report indicated that forecast error for a company's "most important product line" ranged from 0.1 to 50 percent, with an average error of about 5 percent.[10] A *Sales and Marketing Management* survey on sales forecast reported similar findings. It also noted that corporate executives felt that efforts to improve forecasting accuracy were well worth the added expense.[11]

FORECASTING TECHNIQUES FOR EXISTING PRODUCTS

Jury of executive opinion. The most popular method of forecasting is to use a **jury of executive opinion.** It is based upon the assumption that a group of "executive experts" can arrive at a better forecast than statisticians using a scientific approach. It relies on the executives' past experience and intuition regarding the future. Often the technique is applied in a group meeting until a consensus is reached. Unfortunately, this simple technique is usually not very reliable.[12] It is used primarily for existing products, and when applied to new goods and services is usually even less accurate. This is especially true if the new product requires an unfamiliar channel of distribution.

Sales force composite. The second most popular technique is also judgmental in nature. The **sales force composite** technique utilizes the opinions of the salesforce to create a forecast. It is assumed that since salespeople are in daily contact with the marketplace, they are in the best position to project future sales. Participating in the establishment of sales estimates can serve as a motivating force to help achieve the objectives. At Minnesota Mining and Manufacturing's Industrial Abrasives Division, forecasting has been described this way:

We rely on our sales force quite heavily and we demand accurate forecasts from our salesmen. The salesman tells us how many units he's going to sell this year compared to last taking into account the inventory levels (and estimated usage) of his customers. We have the data about promotions, new products, pricing and production. And we study the industry models. Then we forecast downward to give the salesman his quota, which is based upon his input and ours.[13]

The sales force composite, like executive judgment, is usually not too reliable. Some marketing managers use a historic inflator or deflator to improve the quality of the estimate. For example, if the salesforce tends to underestimate actual sales by 10 percent (this makes it easier to achieve a quota), then the current estimate can be raised by the same percentage.

Simple average. The easiest form of making trend projections is to use a **simple average** of all past sales. The averaging of the periods of high demand in the past will tend to be offset by corresponding periods of low demand. Assume a new solar irrigation pump had been on the market for four years, with the following annual sales in units: 400, 950, 525, 1100. Using a simple average, the forecast for the fifth year is:

$$\text{Simple average} = \frac{400 + 950 + 525 + 1100}{4 \text{ years}}$$

$$= \frac{2975}{4}$$

$$= 744 \text{ units}$$

One disadvantage of this technique is that underlying demand periods may have changed over time. Also, recent trends are given no more weight in the forecast than those of the first year of operation.

Simple moving average. This problem can be partly overcome by using a **simple moving average.** This technique combines sales data from several of the most recent years and uses an average to obtain next year's forecast. Every year the oldest year in the calculations is dropped and the year just completed is added, hence the term moving average. Assume the solar irrigation pump sold 1500 units in the fifth year. If management uses a four-year moving average, the sales estimate for the sixth year would be as follows:

$$\text{Moving average} = \frac{950 + 525 + 1100 + 1500}{4}$$

$$= \frac{4075}{4}$$

$$= 1019 \text{ units in year 6}$$

Weighted moving average. It may be desirable for the marketing manager to use a moving average but to not weight all periods equally. The firm may have found that the two most current periods are more indicative of future sales than the last two years of the moving average. Thus management has assigned the following weights to the periods: most current, $C_1 = 0.35$, $C_2 = 0.35$, $C_3 = 0.15$, and $C_4 = 0.15$. The **weighted moving average** for the solar irrigation pump would have appeared as follows:

$$\text{Weighted moving average} = .15(950) + .15(525) + .35(1100) + .35(1500)$$
$$= 1131 \text{ units in year 6}$$

Exponential smoothing. **Exponential smoothing** is very similar to the weighted moving average except that it does not use a constant set of weights. Instead, an exponentially decreasing set of weights is applied so that the more recent values receive more weight than older ones. The key to exponential smoothing is selecting an appropriate value for the smoothing constant. One approach is to take some historic sales data and measure the forecasting error created by smoothing constants of different magnitudes. Next, management would pick the one that gave the smallest forecasting error. Exponential smoothing has generally displayed good accuracy, particularly for the most sophisticated forms of the technique.

Regression techniques. Correlation attempts to define a relationship between past sales (a dependent variable) and one or more independent variables such as price, competitor's prices, per capita income, industry advertising expenditures, and new housing starts. Simple regression is a statistical technique that employs only one independent and one dependent variable. This is of limited value to marketing managers because many factors influence a product's sales. It would be unusual for one independent variable such as price to explain much more than half the total variation in a firm's sales from year to year. Therefore marketing managers rely on **multiple regression** to derive a formula that will accurately describe a relationship between sales and several independent values. The value of a multiple regression equation is the degree to which it explains the total variation in sales. Mathematically, this is referred to as the coefficient of multiple determination (R^2) and can range from zero to one. The higher the value of R^2, the greater the percentage of total variance that has been explained and accounted for. For example, a researcher used multiple regression to examine wine consumption in a particular city.[14] The regression equation was as follows:

$$Y = 6.923 + 0.0402X_1 + 0.312X_2$$

where: $Y =$ monthly household wine consumption in quarts
$X_1 =$ annual household income
$X_2 =$ age of head of household

A forecaster can see that a one-year increase in age accounts for a larger portion of the change in wine consumption (0.312 quarts) than does a thousand-dollar increase in annual income (0.0402 quarts). The number 6.923 is a structural coefficient needed to complete the equation. The R^2 for this equation was 0.848. This means that the equation explained 84 percent of the variation in wine consumption, which suggests that the variables included in the equation were in fact the principal determinants of the product's sales. By looking at predicted trends in household incomes and ages of the head of the household, the formula could be used to forecast wine sales in the city in question.

FORECASTING TECHNIQUES FOR NEW PRODUCTS

Forecasting demand for new products presents a different set of problems from estimating sales for existing products. First, there may be no close substitute available for the new product, thus making it difficult to forecast sales potential. Most important, there are no past sales records to use as input into a sales estimate.

Usually new products fall into one of three categories:

Type 1. Line extensions and me-too items—e.g., a new flavor of Campbell soup or IBM's recent "me-too" line of minicomputers.

Type 2. New products that are not easy to classify into existing product categories but require no change in consumer usage habits—e.g., Stove Top Stuffing Mix.

Type 3. New products requiring a change in consumer behavior—e.g., instant coffee, business minicomputers, electronic mail, electronic funds transfer systems.[15]

Concept and product tests. Concept tests that evaluate the feasibility of new ideas and product prototype tests with potential users have been proved to predict trial and first repeat purchase with reasonable reliability.[16] (You may want to review the new product selection process in Chapter 9.) When potential customers are given a product to try, one of the key questions on a call-back questionnaire is purchase intent. It is usually in the following form:

Will you (1) definitely buy
   (2) probably buy
   (3) probably not buy
   (4) definitely not buy
the product you have just tried?

Many researchers add together those who replied definitely and probably will buy to get **purchase intent.** For example, if Kraft is evaluating a new cheese spread and if 18 percent of the respondents answered "definitely will buy" and 34 percent said "probably will buy," the purchase intent is 52 percent. Purchase intent may then be inflated or deflated based upon the company's past experience with similar products or line extensions. For example, Kraft might raise purchase intent by 10 percent based upon experience to get estimated initial trial of 57 percent. If the target market is estimated at 4 million households, the company would forecast initial sales of 2,280,000 tubs of the new cheese spread. Next, historic repurchase rates could be used to obtain a sales estimate for the year.

Regression. Regression models, such as the N. W. Ayer model and the ESP model of the National Purchase Diary, use a sample of past new products to explain variance in initial trial and repurchase patterns. These have been successful only with type 1 new products.[17] Their limited value with the other two categories of new products is due to problems in classifying the product into a known category and uncertainty of the dynamics of the adoption process. Some new type 2 and 3 products obtain high initial purchase plus three or four repurchase cycles, and then die a sudden death. In the snack food area, for example, Bugles, Whistles, and Daisies displayed this pattern. A Carnation Foods new product called "Pastry Shoppe Toast Spread" was a new spread designed to make toast taste like a sweet roll. It was a smashing initial success and triers rebought the product; then suddenly sales came to a grinding halt.[18] The reasons for this phenomenon are still unclear.

Other pretest techniques. Besides regression, some marketers have used laboratory tests to predict sales. Both the Yankelovich, Skelly and White, and COMP (discussed in Chapter 9) tests have been shown successful for type 1 products but not types 2 and 3. The reasons are similar to those already explained. One major problem with such tests is that they rely on posttrial intentions or attitude shifts to predict repeat purchase behavior. Such intentions have not proved to be very reliable beyond the first repeat buy.[19]

Sales wave experiments rely on offering a product at a proposed retail price to a sample of target customers after they have first tried the product in an in-home placement study (see Chapter 9). Although sales waves may take place over several months, it still is not long enough for most type 3 products. Normally type 3 goods have a very slow rate of adoption in the marketplace. Sales waves do tend to be an effective means of forecasting sales for type 2 merchandise. Other techniques described above are less costly and time-consuming for type 1 merchandise.

Test marketing. The most reliable way to predict sales for any type of new product is through test marketing. But test marketing has some important disadvantages. The test markets must be representative of the target market and last long enough to allow repeat purchase patterns to develop. The level of marketing activity (advertising, sales to channel members, couponing, and so forth) should not be greater than that which will exist when the product is "rolled out" nationally. In other words, do not hype sales within a test market, because it will present a distorted picture of national sales potential.

Test marketing is also costly, time-consuming, and enables the competition to get a preview of the firm's offering. But despite these disadvantages, test marketing is normally recommended. The price of product failure is far too great to bypass test marketing of most products and many services. Moreover, the length of test markets today can often be shortened by combining early results with regression models to predict sales success.

SUMMARY

The objective of planning is to help marketing managers make better decisions. Planning is the process of using related facts and future assumptions to arrive at courses of action to be followed in seeking specific goals. Planning can be divided into two categories: strategic and tactical. Strategic planning is long run in nature; tactical planning is concerned with short-run objectives. Strategic planning establishes the character of the organization and provides long-run direction. Conflict between long-run and short-run plans often cannot be escaped. Long-run planning typically requires resource commitments that may adversely affect profits in the short run. Despite potential conflict, however, planning is essential to the managerial process. It helps management delineate alternatives, provides a framework for pursuing objectives, opens communication channels, and provides a framework for decision making.

If planning fails, it is normally the result of one of several factors. These include failure to recognize sources of conflict, a lack of creativity or realistic goals, poor communication, failure to follow through, and/or a lack of leadership.

In order to plan well, there must first be a planning system. A planning system is a structured process that organizes and coordinates the activities of the managers who do the planning. Each system requires customization to take into account organizational philosophy, the industry characteristics, company size, and so forth. A planning system first requires the communication of corporate goals and strategies. In large corporations, the planning system may entail the creation of SBUs. It also requires a mechanism for establishing goals. Next, a management information system must be created, and the corporate planner's role delineated.

After a company planning system has been put into place, marketing managers can begin to plan effectively. The steps in tactical planning are as follows: (1) understand the marketing environment and the strategic marketing plan; (2) establish goals; (3) develop and examine alternative courses of action; (4) select a course of action and prepare a budget; and (5) implement and control the tactical marketing plan. When a tactical marketing plan has been completed, it is ultimately merged into the total marketing program. The marketing program (consisting of all marketing tactical plans) is the responsibility of total marketing management and represents the means by which marketing accomplishes its strategic goals. Ultimately, the marketing program is integrated into the overall corporate planning program.

Good planning is based on accurate forecasting. Forecasting takes place on three different levels: national, industry, and individual product or services. Marketing managers use a number of forecasting techniques. These techniques vary significantly in level of sophistication and accuracy. The most popular techniques are the jury of executive opinion, sales forecast composite, and the simple average. None of these are highly rigorous or particularly sophisticated. More advanced quantitative techniques such as exponential smoothing and regression usually give more reliable forecasts, yet due to their complexity, they are not often used by marketing management. Concept and product tests, as well as laboratory tests, regression analysis, and test marketing are popular forecasting tools for new products.

KEY TERMS

Planning
Strategic planning
Tactical planning
Strategic Business Unit (SBU)
Line manager
Staff manager
Profit impact of market strategy (PIMS)
Response functions
Market minimum
Market potential
Marketing sensitivity of demand

Decision tree
Expected value
Task force
Jury of executive opinion
Sales force composite
Simple average
Simple moving average
Weighted moving average
Exponential smoothing
Multiple regression
Purchase intent

REVIEW QUESTIONS

1. Why is planning of vital importance to marketing management?
2. List and define the steps involved in creating a planning system.
3. What steps are necessary in implementing a tactical marketing plan?
4. What information does a decision tree offer to the marketer?
5. What is forecasting? Why is it necessary?
6. List the various methods of demand forecasting. Outline the advantages and disadvantages of each.

DISCUSSION QUESTIONS

1. Generally, why should strategic plans be adhered to once they have been formulated?
2. What do you think would happen to a firm that made no plans and/or forecasts?
3. Why does a dual planning system implemented by management tend to create conflict?
4. Is no planning better than poor planning? Why or why not?
5. Why do the characteristics of SBUs vary among firms?
6. Which forecasting technique do you believe is best for existing products? For new products? Support your answers.

NOTES

1. "Food Retailers Must Serve America's Kitchenless Society," *Marketing News,* April 17, 1981, p. 22.
2. Adapted from: E. Frank Harrison, *Management and Organizations* (Boston: Houghton Mifflin, 1978), p. 94. Copyright © 1978 by Houghton Mifflin Company. Used by permission.
3. "The New Planning," *Business Week,* December 18, 1978, p. 68.
4. Derek F. Abell and John S. Hammond, *Strategic Marketing Planning Problems and Analytical Approaches* (Englewood Cliffs, N.J.: Prentice Hall, 1979), p. 8.
5. Peter Lorange and Richard F. Vancil, "How to Design a Strategic Planning System," *Harvard Business Review* (September–October 1976), p. 78.
6. "Schoeffler-Cope Team Tells How PIMS Academic-Business Search for Basic Principles Can Get Line Managers into Strategic Planning," *Marketing News,* July 16, 1976, p. 6.
7. Ibid. Reprinted by permission of the American Marketing Association.
8. This example is taken from Eli P. Cox, *Marketing Research Information for Decision Making* (New York: Harper & Row, 1979), pp. 118–120.
9. Robert S. Savesky, "Appraising the Sales Forecast," *Managerial Planning,* November–December 1977, p. 17.
10. *Sales Forecasting Practices: An Appraisal* (New York: National Industrial Conference Board, 1970), pamphlet No. 25.
11. "Is Five Per Cent Error Good Enough?" *Sales and Marketing Management,* December 15, 1976, pp. 41–47.
12. Douglas J. Dalrymple, "Sales Forecasting Methods and Accuracy," *Business Horizons,* December 1978, pp. 69–73.
13. "Executives Roundtable, Forecasting for Higher Profits," *Sales and Marketing Management,* November 17, 1975, p. 12. Reprinted by permission from Sales & Marketing Management magazine. Copyright 1975.
14. The wine example is taken from Harper Boyd, Jr., Ralph Westfall, and Stanley

Stasch, *Marketing Research Text and Cases,* 4th ed. (Homewood, Ill.: Richard D. Irwin, 1977), p. 488.

15. Edward M. Tauber, "Forecasting Sales Prior to Test Market," *Journal of Marketing,* January 1977, pp. 80–84.
16. Ibid.
17. Ibid.
18. Ibid.
19. Ibid.

◢ CASES

21.1 Savin Business Machines

Savin Corporation, headquartered in New York State, has been quite successful in the copying market in recent years. Savin is a highly marketing-oriented organization. Gabriel Carlin, its marketing chief, says: "We put all of our resources into marketing. We design products that customers need in the future and let others manufacture the product."

Savin has been somewhat of a maverick, using product technology, sales strategies, and pricing policies that depart from the rules of the game in the plain-paper copier field. For years Xerox has set the pace with a powdered-toner technique as the basis for plain-paper copying. Savin, after five years of research, brought to market an innovative machine using a liquid-toner transfer method. This gave it several manufacturing and servicing pluses that the firm is trying to convert into marketing advantages. For example, manufacturing costs are low, thus enabling the firm to sell the Savin 750 model at less than half the price of comparable Xerox equipment. The process also gives the machine a degree of reliability unmatched by competitive units.

Savin is now trying to develop its marketing tactics for the 770. According to Carlin, the copying market is changing rapidly. The trend is toward buying relatively inexpensive, slow, convenience machines in order to decentralize copying operations. To avoid long lines at a central location, these smaller units are located on different floors for quicker access. Questions that Carlin is facing right now include the following:

1. Should Savin use a direct selling strategy, like Xerox, or a dealer network? Savin wants to move fast, and developing its own major salesforce could lead to problems of hiring, staffing, and training. Currently it has 26 marketing people directly involved with the dealers; they account for a total of about $7 million worth of business a month. There are also some sales and marketing people in their own branch operations; they average about $3 or $4 million worth of business a month.
2. Should it sell the machines or lease them? If the firm uses a dealer organization, it may have difficulty getting dealers to purchase for resale a machine three to four times as expensive as the coated-paper units they have been handling until now. Few dealers could afford the negative cash flow that can result from renting machines.
3. If Savin uses its own salesforce, the company is considering changing the compensation of sales people from a salary-plus-commission structure to one that is entirely commissions. Carlin realizes that this will increase the turnover rate because

unproductive salespeople will drop out. Yet if the 770 is as good a machine as Savin hopes it will be, selling should not be difficult.

4. A possible by-product of success that Carlin foresees is a steadily expanding customer base and, as a result, new service problems. Savin is concerned about its service response program and the possibility of developing improved training curriculums. It is also considering installing a computer-based information system that will contain the service record for each machine in the field. However, like everything else, this will be an expensive addition.

5. Savin is engaged in a dispute with its Japanese partner, Ricoh, which manufactures the Savin 770. Under the terms of their agreement Ricoh is to pay Savin a royalty on each machine it sells. One scenario depicts Ricoh terminating production so that it can take over the U.S. market for itself. Savin's president discounts this, however, saying: "They do not intend to stop shipping to us." Savin can cut its Ricoh tie over the next few years. However, industry sources doubt that it can find a match for Ricoh's low cost.

6. If Savin is successful and erodes Xerox's market share, how will the industry leader respond? Savin has considered its target market to be primarily a replacement market. Hence, it has gone after prospects that already had copiers, particularly the Xerox 3100. Savin's advertising consistently boasts that half of its replacements knock out Xerox machines.

You have been hired as a marketing consultant for Savin. Your job is to evaluate the marketing environment and advise management on long-range planning.

1. Advise Gabriel Carlin on a new long-range strategy for the Savin Corporation.
2. Develop a tactical strategy for marketing the Savin 770.

21.2 Joseph Garneau Company

The Joseph Garneau Company is an importer of fine wines with such names as Bolla Italian Wines, Cella Lambrusco, Cruse French Wines, and Bols Liqueurs. The Garneau Company uses what it refers to as a "check and double check" sales forecasting process. Central to the process are the company's state managers, who at regular intervals predict and then "repredict" their local sales situation and their product needs. The managers are allowed to review and, if necessary, change their regional manager's refinements and can always make a "fail safe" request for more or less product when the local situation takes a sudden turn. As a result, the company rarely fails to have its product lines fully stocked in stores, bars, and restaurants.

1. How would you categorize the company's forecasting technique? What are the advantages and disadvantages of this technique?
2. What other sales forecasting techniques might be applicable to the Garneau Company? Why?

22 Marketing organization and control

OBJECTIVES

To become aware of the need for an effective marketing organization structure.

To understand the concept and tools of marketing control.

To introduce marketing cost analysis.

To discuss the marketing audit as a tool for control.

To describe the position of the marketing controller.

The 3M Company manufactures about 45,000 products, though much of that list consists of items included numerous times because of variations in size and shape. The output reflects a dazzling diversity—sandpaper and photocopiers, tape and traffic lights, skin lotions and electrical connectors, X-ray film and artificial hips. Yet there is a central wellspring: about 95% of the company's $5.4 billion in 1979 sales involved products related to coating and bonding technology.

Amid this profusion, one startling anomaly bedevils 3M. For all its technical fertility, the company has been a surprisingly lackluster performer in consumer products. Less than 10% of its sales come from consumer goods.

Traditionally, most of 3M's consumer products have been derivatives of industrial products, and somewhat timid afterthoughts at that. Because each division retains control over its products, it has been pretty much free to market its consumer line as it wants.

Understandably, a division whose principal customers are manufacturers of electric appliances does not necessarily have much expertise in selling electrical tape to homeowners. Such a division also lacks a huge budget for consumer advertising. Indeed, the whole costly technique of launching new products in the nation's consumer markets is alien to 3M's traditional strategy. "Our approach is to make a little, sell a little, make a little more," says Robert M. Adams, vice president for research and development.

To a large extent, 3M divisions' approach to consumer marketing has simply been to take items out of a big box that might have gone to an industrial user and separate them into a lot of small boxes. Because the divisions are accustomed to dealing with sophisticated users of their products, the package instructions they write for consumers are apt to be incomplete and laden with jargon.

For years, 3M's divisions used different package designs and assorted versions of the 3M logotype. Several divisions made marine products, such as fishing tackle and non-slip deck coverings, but it was hard for the consumer to tell they were all made by the same company because of the variation in package design.[1]

The manner in which a company is organized can have a major influence on its focus and its success. Proper control systems might have eliminated the 3M logotype problem before it reached the marketplace. What is the relationship between planning and control? What are the components of a control system? Would 3M have been more successful in the consumer products field if marketing had dominated the organization structure? We begin our discussion with an examination of the organization function of marketing management; then we look at control processes and control techniques. The chapter concludes with an explanation of the marketing audit.

Marketing organization

A sound organization structure is required to integrate and utilize marketing resources effectively. Organizing is a three-phase process involving (1) designating tasks and activities, (2) grouping these into subunits and positions, and (3) establishing relationships among the resulting elements. The marketing organization structure is a system of formal and informal relationships that governs the activities of marketing personnel who depend on one another to accomplish marketing goals.

A number of benefits accrue to firms with good organizational structures, for such structures

1. Avoid duplication of work.
2. Minimize conflict between individuals over jurisdiction.
3. Provide a basis for formal communication channels.
4. Establish a base for appraisal of marketing personnel.
5. Provide for smooth, integrated work flows.
6. Increase cooperation when each individual knows what he or she is responsible for and to whom he or she is responsible.
7. Allow resources to be focused and channeled where they are needed to accomplish organizational goals.

TYPES OF ORGANIZATION STRUCTURES

Traditional structures. The first step in creating a sound organization is **functionalization.** This is the division of the total work and activity of the marketing department into separate functions, such as product planning, marketing research, sales. Step 2 is called **departmentation,** which is the process of establishing subunits such as departments, sections, or divisions within the marketing organization. Several common forms of departmentation were explained in Chapters 2 and 9: functional, customer, geographic, venture groups.

Matrix organizations. Companies that use the product manager concept often use matrix structure (see Figure 22.1). Product managers are held accountable

◢ **FIGURE 22.1 A matrix organization structure.**

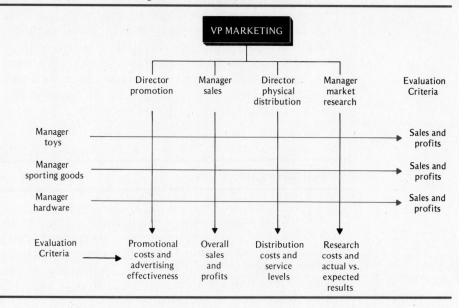

for the sales and profit success of their products, yet they do not always have the authority to, for example, order the advertising manager to develop a certain campaign. Some product managers have relatively little authority; others have complete authority. It depends on the history and nature of the firm.

Matrix organization represents a major departure from traditional structures. The role relationships among various managers are quite different from the norm. Rather than being arranged according to a strict vertical authority-responsibility structure, line and staff functions are mingled. Sometimes an individual may act in a staff capacity; at other times he or she may function as a line manager. The basic idea behind the matrix organization is that resource usage is controlled and directed by two opposing sets of managers.

Corporate marketing staff. In addition to traditional and product-type organization structures, larger companies often create a **corporate marketing staff,** which provides specialized marketing services to the divisions or strategic business units (SBUs), principally in advertising and marketing research, and assists in coordinating certain marketing activities, such as media buying.[2] These services are provided by the corporate marketing staff when it is advantageous to have them centralized, rather than duplicating them at the SBU level. In some large companies, the corporate marketing staff is actively involved in planning and control. At the other extreme are firms whose corporate marketing staff provides purely service functions. Most large organizations tend to fall somewhere between pure service and highly active planning and control. These differences in corporate marketing staff roles stem from

The diversity and the rate and method of growth of the business

The competence of division management

The capabilities of the corporate marketing staff

The background and management style of the chief executive officer[3]

The greater the diversity of the large firms, the more economical it becomes to consolidate services at the corporate level for a review of marketing activities throughout the corporation. If top management's style is highly centralized, it is more likely to use the corporate marketing staff as a source of control.

ESTABLISHING ORGANIZATIONAL RELATIONSHIPS

After tasks have been delineated and a structure determined, the third step in the organizing process is to create organizational relationships. Before discussing the third step, several terms need to be defined. **Formal authority** is a relationship created when the organization officially assigns one person the right to direct or command another. A sales manager, for example, has the right to direct the activities of the salesforce. Power is one person getting another to do something that he or she may not have done otherwise. Power can be derived from authority, expertise, dominant personalities, and a host of other factors. A salesperson who has "been around a long time" may get another salesperson to increase the hours reported on his or her call record sheet for prospecting in order that the "oldtimer" won't look out of line when he was actually goofing off. In this case, seniority acts as a source of power.

Influence is normally considered a more moderate form of power. It exists when one individual can modify or affect another's behavior. Friends tend to influence other friends, but they usually do not control them. Influence takes place in all interpersonal relationships, whereas the use of power is fairly infrequent. Yet power is ultimately the underlying force that structures relationships among people and departments.

Authority and responsibility. **Authority** is the legal right to command; **responsibility** is the obligation to act in response to an order. A marketing supervisor may delegate authority to a subordinate and thus hold the subordinate accountable. Responsibility is shared and never fully delegated. For example, the director of advertising may delegate authority to a creative supervisor or utilize all the resources of the advertising department to create a new campaign. The accountability for the success of the new campaign is not shifted to the creative supervisor. Instead, the director of advertising shares responsibility with the creative supervisor.

Traditionally, it has been considered desirable for authority and responsibility to be equal. If a person is given responsibility for a task, then commensurate authority should also be delegated. This, of course, has been a major problem with the product management form of organization. Another fundamental authority/responsibility principle is to maintain unity of command. A subordinate should report to only one supervisor. Unity of command avoids conflicting instructions and makes an individual fully accountable for the tasks assigned. It also avoids placing the subordinate in a position of having to give one superior's task priority over someone else's. In one large consumer goods firm, for example, the director of marketing research was directly accountable to three group product managers. The position was untenable because each group manager felt his presence deserved priority in time and resources.

Centralization versus decentralization. The amount of authority delegated by a top marketing manager depends upon the firm's philosophy of decentralization. To centralize means to shift much of the organizational decision making to the top levels. As a result, the middle- and lower-level marketing managers have relatively less authority and decision-making responsibility. A decentralized marketing organization has just the opposite effect. The advantages and disadvantages of decentralization may be summarized as follows:

Advantages
1. Executives will be nearer to the point of decision making.
2. There may be a better utilization of the time and ability of executives.
3. The quality of decisions is likely to improve.
4. The amount and expense of paperwork by headquarters staff may be considerably reduced.
5. The expense of coordination may be reduced because of the greater autonomy of decision making.

Disadvantages
1. A lack of uniformity of decisions.
2. Inadequate utilization of specialists.
3. Lack of proper equipment or executives in the field.[4]

An example of overcentralization is discussed below.

Sometimes centralization can work against the firm. In 1976, Standard Brands—makers of Planters Peanuts, Fleischmann Liquors, Chase and Sanborn Coffee, Curtis Candies, and a variety of other products—decided that centralization was the answer to their profitability problems. For years, the company had been milking their "cash cows" and ignored new product development.

The company decided to dramatically increase marketing support for its existing products and establish an aggressive new product development department. A team of well-educated, youthful strategists were brought in to implement and refine the plan. By 1980, the team produced one of the greatest failures in recent food industry history.

The president of Standard Brands, realizing his mistake, disbanded the strategy team. He determined that heavy-handed centralized rule by a small group of corporate planners just wasn't working. Plans need to be implemented by and developed with the aid of experienced operating managers.

INTERACTION WITH OTHER DEPARTMENTS

When management is organizing a new company or reorganizing an existing one like Standard Brands, the question may arise as to what role marketing should play. Perhaps you may be wondering whether marketing literally dominates a company. The answer is No. No single component should have undue influence over the entire structure. Production requirements, financial and engineering questions, and many other facets of the operation must be in harmonious balance.

If marketing controlled or dominated the firm, there might be short production runs (to produce great variety); high inventory levels (no stock outages, since this creates dissatisfaction); minimal credit checks (a source of consumer inconvenience and frustration); and short engineering design lead time (in order to react quickly to changing customer desires). Any or all of these situations can drastically increase costs (see Table 22.1).

Marketing's function is to provide information on customer desires and characteristics. It must work with the other departments to achieve the firm's overall objectives. This often requires compromise and understanding of other departments' needs and goals. Everyone, however, needs to know the importance of the marketing concept. Every member of the firm must work toward customer satisfaction. Without customer satisfaction, there is no market; and if there is no market, there are no jobs.

Marketing control

The management tasks of planning and organizing cannot be effective without control. Control provides the mechanism for correcting actions that are not efficient in aiding the marketing organization reach its objective. Even if a firm is fortunate enough to reach its goals without good controls, the chances are that some resources have been wasted. A good control system keeps marketing programs on track so that they can reach their goals within budget guidelines.

Unfortunately, companies of all sizes have made significant strides in implementing marketing controls, but have often not completed the process.[5] For example, many firms have inadequate controls in the areas of product deletion, marketing cost allocations by functions or product lines, promotion effectiveness, and customer service.[6]

HOW CONTROL WORKS

The concept of a control system was introduced in Chapter 2. The basic control system is shown in Figure 22.2. The control process actually begins while planning is taking place. After goals are established, standards must be developed to aid in performance measurement. When standards have been established, a plan can be put into action. Next, performance is measured to make certain standards are being met. If they are, actions continue. Otherwise, deviations

Department	Their emphasis	Marketing's emphasis
R&D	Basic research	Applied research
	Intrinsic quality	Perceived quality
	Functional features	Sales features
Engineering	Long design lead time	Short design lead time
	Few models	Many models
	Standard components	Custom components
Purchasing	Narrow product line	Broad product line
	Standard parts	Nonstandard parts
	Price of material	Quality of material
	Economical lot sizes	Large lot sizes to avoid stockouts
	Purchasing at infrequent intervals	Immediate purchasing for customer needs
Manufacturing	Long production lead time	Short production lead time
	Long runs with few models	Short runs with many models
	No model changes	Frequent model changes
	Standard orders	Custom orders
	Ease of fabrication	Aesthetic appearance
	Average quality control	Tight quality control
Finance	Strict rationales for spending	Intuitive arguments for spending
	Hard and fast budgets	Flexible budgets to meet changing needs
	Pricing to cover costs	Pricing to further market development
Accounting	Standard transactions	Special terms and discounts
	Few reports	Many reports
Credit	Full financial disclosures by customers	Minimum credit examination of customers
	Low credit risks	Medium credit risks
	Tough credit terms	Easy credit terms
	Tough collection procedures	Easy collection procedures

Source: Phillip Kotler, *Marketing Management: Analysis, Planning, and Control,* 4th edition (Englewood Cliffs, N.J.: Prentice-Hall), 1980, p. 593.

from standards are examined to determine if they fall within acceptable boundaries. If the deviations are not significant, action will continue with minor modifications. When deviations are too large, the plan is brought to a halt and causal analysis is used to revise the plan or perhaps scrap it.

To illustrate a control system, assume that Jane French, the sales manager of Joy Manufacturing—a producer of heavy industrial equipment—decides that key accounts (customers with over $500,000 sales potential per year) are not receiving the attention they deserve from the salesforce. The sales manager's goal is to increase the calls made to key accounts. She decides that rather than slapping a key account quota on the salesforce, she will use positive motivation. A new commission scheme is developed that provides a 2 percent of net

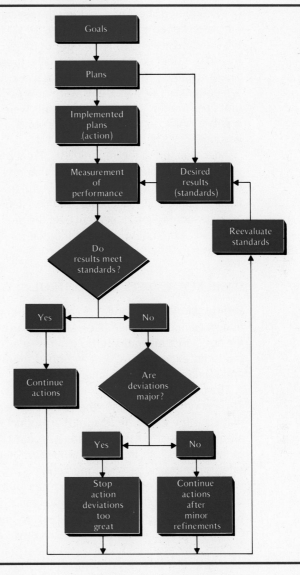

sales bonus on key account sales or $1500, whichever is greater. A letter is sent to each salesperson with a list of key accounts in the territory. The standard established by the sales manager is a minimum average increase in calls on key accounts by 25 percent per month over the same period a year ago. Performance will be measured by examining summary data from individual call record sheets.

During the first six months after the new system was installed, the average increase in calls on key accounts was up 31 percent and key account sales rose 43 percent over the same period a year ago. The plan was conforming to the predetermined standards. During the seventh month, however, the percentage increase slipped to 26 and then fell to 22. Mrs. French felt the deviation from the standard was of concern but not major. Yet the general trend was disturbing, so she notified the eight regional managers to discuss the situation with the salesforce and report back within a week. Essentially, all reports reflected the same situation. Key accounts were now being visited so often (average of three times per month) that many sales calls were unproductive. Thus, the salesforce was beginning to call on other accounts and prospects where sales potential was better.

After examining the reports, Mrs. French was satisfied that the key accounts were getting enough attention and that diverting time to other accounts might be more productive. The key account plan was kept in force to provide incentives to call on key accounts, but the standard was revised downward to an average increase of 15 percent over the previous year. In this example, the general goals were being met, but the control system required a refinement in the standards.

SOME KEY ASPECTS OF CONTROL

Setting standards. **Standards** are bases for measuring how well a marketing activity is being performed. If certain standards are met, benefits should accrue to the firm. High inventory turnover, low sales costs, and low advertising costs per thousand exposures will, it is hoped, translate into increasing sales volume and market share plus higher profitability.

The basis for establishing many standards is a sales and profitability forecast. This becomes the goal for the marketing department. Sometimes forecasts are made for the entire life cycle of a product, as shown in Table 22.2. This example is a long-term forecast for a product that is already in the maturity stage of the cycle. Note that projections have been made for prices, market share, sales, manufacturing costs, marketing costs, and profits. By comparing actual with forecast results, management can pinpoint strengths and weaknesses in the marketing of the product. In the maturity stage, for example, market share was 1 percent higher than forecast, yet selling costs were lower than projected. On the negative side, the selling price was lower than forecast.

Computer models can be used to help marketing managers set standards and budget levels. MIT has developed the ADVISOR model based upon historical data from 27 participating companies such as Du Pont, Goodyear, and Owens Corning.[7] A total of 197 industrial products have been examined, along with their marketing budgets. An ADVISOR report may tell a manager that a product's $105,000 advertising budget compares poorly to products with similar characteristics whose budgets average $357,000 in a range of $245,000 to $520,000.

Measuring performance results. Results have to be measured at various intervals once the plan has been implemented. The method of information gather-

Product: Tape **Introduction:** February 1968 to October 1968
Current Period: April 1, 1982 **Latest Revision:** May 10, 1981

	Introductory period Year 1		Growth period Years 2–5		Maturity period Years 6–10		Decline period Years 11+	
	Forecast	Actual	Forecast	Actual	Forecast	Actual	Forecast	Actual
Average market share	5%	7%	30%	36%	40%	41%	20%	—
Average price per unit	$1.75	$1.65	$1.50	$1.47	$1.40	$1.30	$1.35	—
Sales:								
In units	10,000	14,000	300,000	360,000	400,000	410,000	100,000	—
In dollars	$17,500	$23,100	$450,000	$529,200	$560,000	$533,000	$135,000	—
Manufacturing costs— dollars per unit	0.75	0.72	0.68	0.68	0.67	0.67	0.67	—
Selling costs— dollars per unit	0.35	0.32	0.18	0.18	0.06	0.05	0.04	—
Distribution costs— dollars per unit	0.30	0.30	0.30	0.30	0.30	0.30	0.30	—
Advertising and promotional support:								
Dollars	3,000	5,600	150,000	162,000	80,000	61,500	—	—
Dollars per unit	0.30	0.40	0.40	0.30	0.20	0.15	—	—
Net contribution to profit:								
Dollars	2,000	2,240	—	2,880	320,000	348,500	64,000	—
Dollars per unit	0.20	0.16	—	0.08	0.80	0.85	0.64	—

ing for measurement purposes may range from simple observations by a salesperson to a complex management information system of which marketing may be only one of many areas of interest. This step in the control process is complicated by problems inherent to any measurement system. Questions to be answered by the marketing manager include (1) the determination of specific units to be measured; (2) the selection of measurement intervals—to ensure timeliness of information; (3) selection of quantity of information to be included; (4) relevance, reliability, and validity of information; and (5) choice of proper authority to receive information gathered. Although measurement is not always precise, continuous monitoring improves corrective actions and thus improves management effectiveness.

Comparison and evaluation of actual performance. For the control process to be effective, deviations from standards have to be evaluated for relevance and significance. Positive as well as negative deviation can provide useful information to management. For example, if a sales manager finds one of his salespersons continuously exceeding her sales quota, an examination of her technique may be usefully applied to other salespersons. A deviation that falls beyond tolerance limits requires the immediate attention of management.

Marketing managers usually follow the **exception principle** of control (see Figure 22.3). This means that only major variations are examined (plus or minus

FIGURE 22.3 Control by the exception principle.

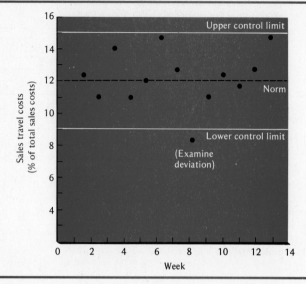

a certain percent from target). To examine the causal factors of each deviation from the established norm would be inefficient. For example, assume that a sales manager expects travel costs to be around 12 percent of total sales costs. A standard is established to examine all call record and expense sheets where travel costs are greater than 15 percent or less than 9 percent. High travel costs may indicate that a salesperson is zigzagging across his or her territory, rather than following an efficient routing plan. Low travel expenses may reveal that a person is not calling on all his or her accounts within the territory as often as desired.

Corrective action. The final step in the control process is the determination and implementation, based upon need, of corrective action. Prior to taking any corrective action, it is necessary to determine if such actions are advantageous. Costs as well as effects on the overall marketing plan have to be evaluated before any actions can be taken. Once it has been decided that corrective action is necessary, such action must be implemented. The effectiveness of the entire control function depends on timely implementation of corrective action when necessary.

THE RELATIONSHIP OF PLANNING, ORGANIZATION, AND CONTROL

The normal sequence of the marketing management process is planning, organizing, and then control. Effective organization is the basis for putting a plan into action. The control function helps assure that resources are used effectively to reach marketing goals. The control system also calls for the frequent reexamination of plans and objectives. This in turn becomes the first step in the next sequence, which leads to another sequence, and then to another.

Tools of marketing control

SALES ANALYSIS

All marketing plans of profit-oriented firms (and of many nonprofit firms) involve sales of a product or service. Therefore, most organizations have goals and objectives that are sales related. Sales analysis is the effort to evaluate the firm's success in the marketplace. Sales volume analysis and market share analysis are two of the most common tools used for this purpose.

Sales volume analysis. **Sales volume analysis** is the simplest and therefore the most common type of analysis performed by marketing management. It reflects the target market's reactions to the firm's offering and the achievement of the goals and objectives of the organization.

Total sales volume, which is called **macrosales analysis,** is an indicator of aggregate market performance. **Microsales analysis** subdivides total sales volume by some other bases, such as territory or product, for a more introspective examination of sales.

By examining aggregate sales performance, the marketing manager can determine trends in total sales activity. Usually company sales are compared to those of the industry to see how well the firm or SBU is performing relative to the competition. Table 22.3 shows that total sales for Rely Equipment Company increased $2.5 million from 1979 to 1980. Sales grew at an annual rate of 25 percent from 1980 through 1982, but the increase for 1983 was only 15 percent.

Further insight can be gained by looking at column 6 in Table 22.3, which shows the rate of growth for the industry during the same periods. Rely outperformed the industry in 1981 and 1982, yet fell behind in 1983. In fact, 1983 seems to have been a problem year. Sales were $1.6 million, or 7 percent below Rely's forecast. Similarly, the firm achieved only 89 percent of its

◢ **TABLE 22.3   Sales of Rely Equipment Company**

Year	Company volume ($ millions)	Increase (%)	Company sales forecast ($ millions)	Variance (+ or −) ($ millions)	Industry volume ($ millions)	Increase (%)	Estimated market share (%)	Actual market share (%)	Variance (+ or −) (% of market)
1983	$22.4	15%	$24.0	$−1.6	$158.3	25.0%	16.0%	14.2%	−1.8%
1982	19.5	25	19.4	+0.1	126.6	15.5	15.0	15.4	+0.4
1981	15.6	25	15.6	−	109.6	21.0	14.0	14.2	+0.2
1980	12.5	25	12.0	+0.5	90.0	30.0	14.0	13.9	−0.1
1979	10.0	−	9.5	+0.5	69.1	−	13.0	14.5	+1.5

TABLE 22.4 Sales by Territory—Rely Equipment Company

Territory	Estimated sales ($ millions)	Actual sales ($ millions)	Sales variance ($ millions)
1	$ 8.0	$10.0	+2.0
2	12.0	8.4	−3.6
3	4.0	4.0	—
	$24.0	$22.4	

forecasted market share (14.2 ÷ 16.0). Market share is company sales as a percentage of industry sales. A macro sales analysis such as this provides warning signals that further analysis is necessary. Something went wrong in 1983, and Rely needs to uncover the cause.

The shortfall in 1983 of $1.6 million in Rely's sales can be further examined through allocating sales volume by territory and product. Table 22.4 shows that the sales staff met the forecast in territory 3 and went 25 percent over the company estimate in territory 1. Territory 2 achieved only 70 percent of its estimate. Thus, the problem seems to lie in territory 2.

The next step is to analyze sales in territory 2 by product line (see Table 22.5). The culprit is the pump product line. Rely manufacturers specialty pumps used by the construction and petroleum industry for pumping waste water that is heavily laden with silt and gravel. Territory 2 encompasses the West Coast and the Southwestern states. Further inquiry by top management revealed that a San Francisco manufacturer sales representative was now selling an imported pump designed for the same market Rely served. The imported pump had a better service record, developed more horsepower per unit of energy, and cost 30 percent less than the Rely model. Since the product was so specialized, the manufacturer's representative knew virtually all potential buyers west of the Mississippi. Although Rely had many loyal customers, they could not pass up a significantly better pump at a much lower price.

The 80–20 rule. One of the primary benefits of these control tools is the recognition and correction of misdirected sales efforts. The **80–20 rule** exemplifies misplaced marketing efforts. Many companies discover that approximately 20

TABLE 22.5 Sales by Product Line, Territory 2

Product line	Estimated sales ($ millions)	Actual sales ($ millions)	Sales variance ($ millions)
Industrial cable	$ 3.5	$ 3.6	$+0.1
Fasteners	4.9	4.8	−0.1
Pumps	3.6	-0-	−3.6
	$12.0	$ 8.4	

percent of their customers account for 80 percent of sales volume, gross margin, and profits. The other 80 percent of the customers, therefore, are responsible for only 20 percent of the marketing results. If the marketing efforts of the firm have been evenly distributed among all customers, its efforts have been misdirected. A reallocation of resources to concentrate on key customers may increase sales and profits.

Market share analysis. Volume sales analysis measures performance in absolute terms but does not measure the company's activities relative to the overall market; nor does it take the competition into account. An increase in market share usually indicates that the firm's marketing mix is more effective than that of its competitors. A declining market share may serve as a basis for investigation of potential problem areas. Like sales analysis, **market share analysis** is generally most meaningful when data are broken down by sales territory, customer type, and product category. A marketing manager may find, for example, that an overall sales increase in market share is due to increased sales to a particular type of customer.

Problems with sales and volume analysis. The macro analysis process is not without its problems and limitations. Not only does sales information have to be available, but it also needs to be presented in sufficient detail. Total sales volume is often too generalized to pinpoint problem areas. So marketing managers do not rely on sales analysis alone. Sales analysis is complemented by marketing cost analysis.

Conducting several types of analysis allows marketing managers to avoid the entrapment of the **iceberg principle.** An iceberg has 10 percent of its mass visible above the surface of the water, with the other 90 percent submerged below the water level. Analysis of sales volume in current dollars may be misleading if inflation rates have been high. For example, a 15 percent increase in total dollar sales of a product may be reduced to an effective 5 percent increase due to a 10 percent inflation. Marketing administrators may find sales analysis by units a necessary consideration during periods of rapidly changing prices.

MARKETING COST ANALYSIS

A basic concept in accounting is the **matching concept** — the matching of revenues and the costs incurred in generating those revenues. We have examined sales revenue; now we look at costs. Cost analysis is one of the most important techniques for maintaining marketing control. It is based on the allocation of marketing costs by products, customers, channel of distribution, or territories to measure the efficiency of the firm's marketing mix. The marketing mix is a basis for direct costs of many types, such as advertising costs, market test expenses, and salesforce expenses. In turn, marketing costs play an important role in determining the profitability of a product or product line.

Accounting information has become more readily available in recent years due to more sophisticated accounting systems and more common use of the computer. For accounting information to be present in a manner that will be useful for marketing cost analysis, it must be reallocated not once, but twice.

Sales	$75,000	
Cost of goods sold	−$44,000	
Gross margin		$31,000
Expenses:		
Salaries	$13,000	
Office supplies	$ 4,000	
Rent	$ 3,500	
Insurance	+$ 2,000	
Total expenses		−$22,500
Net profit		$8,500

The first reallocation is from natural to functional accounts, and the second is from functional accounts to market segments. These reallocations provide a basis for marketing cost analysis, and profit analysis as well.

Natural accounts to functional accounts. **Natural accounts** are accounts that carry the name of the subject for which the expenditure was made, such as rent, salaries, office supplies, insurance, and equipment. **Functional accounts,** on the other hand, are classified according to the particular marketing activity. The number and name of the account will vary with the individual firm. Examples of typical functional accounts include personal selling, advertising, storage, packaging, shipping, order filling, billing, market research, and delivery.

It is important to allocate funds from natural to functional accounts to determine the profitability of performing specific marketing activities. Most marketing expenditures are made to accomplish a specific task—to develop a specific product, to promote a specific product, or to deliver a specific product. Marketing management needs to know whether or not such activities are increasing or decreasing the profitability of the firm. Assume that Metroplex Locksmiths, a small commercial locksmith, had a net profit of $8,500, as shown in Table 22.6.

The first step is to allocate the expenditures from natural accounts to functional accounts, as shown in Table 22.7. Most of the salary expense ($8,000) went to a commissioned salesperson, $2,000 went to a freelance artist doing advertising layouts, $1,500 went to the warehouse stock person, and $1,500 went to a delivery person who works after school. Half the office supplies were consumed in the sales effort, and the remainder were used for advertising, recordkeeping, and delivery. Since storage takes up half the building, it is charged with half the rent ($2,000), and the remainder is allocated using the same principle. The storage facility insurance payments are $1,000 per year and allocated accordingly. Drafting equipment and tables used to prepare advertisements are insured for $500, and the delivery vehicle for $500.

John Smith, owner of Metroplex, is concerned that the three markets he serves may not all be profitable. He decides to continue his analysis by allocat-

TABLE 22.7   Reallocation of Costs from Natural to Functional Accounts

Natural accounts		Functional accounts			
		Personal selling	Advertising	Storage	Delivery and installation
Salaries	$13,000	$ 8,000	$2,000	$1,500	$1,500
Office supplies	4,000	$ 2,000	$1,000	$ 500	$ 500
Rent	3,500	–	$1,000	$2,000	$ 500
Insurance	2,000	–	$ 500	$1,000	$ 500
	$22,500	$10,000	$4,500	$5,000	$3,000

ing the functional costs to customer type, as shown in Table 22.8. Since 67 percent of the sales are made to industrial customers, this percentage of cost of goods sold is allocated to the industrial market ($29,333). The same process is followed for the retail and institutional markets. The sales representative spent 70 percent of his time calling on industrial accounts, 25 percent calling on retailers, and 5 percent calling on institutional customers. Therefore, personal selling is allocated as follows: industrial, $7,000; retail, $2,500; and institutional, $500. Advertising is strictly direct mail, and Mr. Smith's files reveal that 623 pieces were sent to industrial customers, 222 to retailers, and 455 to institutional customers for a total of 1,300 advertising pieces. Thus, $2,157 of advertising expense was allocated to the industrial customers (623/1,300 = 0.4792 × $4,500 = $2,157). The same procedure was followed for allocating advertising costs to retail and institutional accounts. Storage and delivery costs were distributed using the percentage of sales accounted for by each market.

Using the allocation procedure, Mr. Smith finds that his firm is earning a 12 percent profit in the industrial market, 14 percent in the retail market, and losing money in the institutional area. What action should Smith take at this point? Several alternatives deserve further consideration:

TABLE 22.8   Metroplex Locksmith: Reallocated Profit and Loss Statement

		Marketing segment – customer type		
		Industrial	Retail	Institutional
Sales	$75,000	$50,000	$20,000	$5,000
Cost of goods sold	44,000	29,333	11,733	2,934
Gross margin	$31,000	$20,667	$ 8,267	$2,066
Expenses (functional):				
Personal selling	$10,000	$ 7,000	$ 2,500	$ 500
Advertising	4,500	2,157	768	1,575
Storage	5,000	3,333	1,333	334
Delivery	3,000	2,000	800	200
Total expenses	$22,500	$14,490	$ 5,401	$2,609
Net profit	$ 8,500	$ 6,177	$ 2,866	($543)

1. Drop out of the institutional market. Since the market is currently unprofitable, Smith could avoid serving institutional customers.
2. The advertising expenditures to sales ratio is very high in the institutional market. Smith could examine his promotional program and attempt to raise institutional advertising effectiveness.
3. Only 5 percent of the sales effort is being devoted to the institutional market. A stronger sales effort coupled with a more effective promotion program might make the institutional market profitable.

This customer analysis clearly illustrates the iceberg principle described earlier. Although Metroplex is a profitable company as a whole, an in-depth analysis revealed that only the industrial and retail customer markets were generating profits. Serving institutional accounts was actually lowering overall profitability. Before Mr. Smith takes any action, he should also consider future trends in the institutional market. If, for example, the number of competitors is expected to increase and the average size of an insitutional account to decrease, it may hasten his decision to leave the market.

CONTROL SYSTEM INFORMATION FLOWS

Mr. Smith was fortunate because he had the information necessary to evaluate costs. Marketing managers must be sure when designing control systems to obtain the necessary cost and other data needed for effective control. Two examples of the information problems a marketing manager can experience are discussed below.

A sportings goods manufacturer designed a promotion pack and display piece for use in department stores, although, for legal reasons, the offer had to be extended to all types of accounts. Post-sales analysis indicated that total sales in one area increased significantly while another region showed only a slight increase. Because the company's information system could not break out data on sales and shipments of the display piece by type of account, the marketer decided to forgo a detail analysis of the promotion pack's effectiveness in department stores and relied instead on field salesmen's weekly reports of market conditions.

A major toilet goods manufacturer prepared a detail budget of all marketing activities by sales territory and by month. Although the accounting department received information on actual expenditures by area (advertising dollars by market from the advertising agency, promotional shipments from sales invoices, selling costs from the territory sales personnel), the data were not compiled into the territory classifications for comparison with budget. The marketer recognized that he did not, in fact, control the actual expenditures by territory and season.[8]

Nonfinancial controls: the marketing audit

Not all marketing controls center on financial forecasts and analysis. A typical example of nonfinancial control information is a complaint report. Such data can be used as a basis for quality control and maintenance of customer satisfaction. Table 22.9 is a complaint disposition form for a company selling pre-cooked T-bone steaks. Note that complaints are recorded over a particular period. Also, the complaint disposition is reported along with the cost of making an adjustment. A quick glance at the report tells management that the Miami plant seems to be overtenderizing the meat (4 percent of total shipments). This cost the company $30,000 during a six-month period.

The complaint process, like other forms of control, needs to be based on a comprehensive control policy. In this case, responsibility for handling and resolving complaints must be defined. Authority must be spelled out to enable a manager to resolve the problem efficiently and courteously. Procedures for recording and analyzing the complaints must be determined, and standards must be established.

Perhaps the broadest control device available to marketing management is the marketing audit. This tool incorporates both financial and nonfinancial reporting and is primarily futuristic in nature. It is designed to aid management in allocating marketing resources efficiently. A **marketing audit** may be defined as a thorough, systematic, periodic evaluation of the goals, strategies, organization, and performance of the marketing organization. A marketing audit is not preoccupied with past performance, but looks to the future allocation of marketing resources. Table 22.10 gives an outline of the types of information gathered and analyzed in the audit.

Marketing audits are not designed solely for firms that are having difficulty meeting their marketing objectives. All companies should utilize the audit system to uncover potential weaknesses and identify cost-cutting opportunities. In one survey of marketing organizations, 28 percent conducted one form or another of marketing audit.[9] The survey also showed that the marketing audit was not restricted to any single form of organizations. Small and large organizations, service firms and manufacturers all rely on the marketing audit. As companies continue to place more emphasis on strategic planning, the use of the marketing audit should increase.

A typical marketing audit begins with an examination of the external environment. The major target markets currently being served are scrutinized for growth trends and changing characteristics. Competitive challenges and expected responses to the firm's strategy are forecast. Uncontrollable elements of the marketing environment (see Chapter 3) are analyzed to determine their impact on the marketing mix. Internally, marketing objectives are reviewed and updated. Plans and programs are studied in order to see how effectively they are reaching objectives. The degree of management participation in planning and implementing new programs is also examined. The final stage of the marketing audit is a thorough review of each element of the marketing mix.

TABLE 22.9 Returns and Complaints Report

Summary of complaints by source	Number of customer complaints received					
	1/83	2/83	3/83	4/83	5/83	6/83
Miami plant						
Precooked T-bone						
Overtenderized/mushy	25	22	20	25	30	35
Tough/uncuttable	15	13	14	10	8	3
Wrong size	8	7	7	8	7	6
Other	3	2	2	2	3	4
Subtotal	51	44	43	45	48	48
Chicago plant						
Precooked T-bone						
Overtenderized/mushy	50	55	48	52	48	47
Tough/uncuttable	28	25	30	29	31	26
Wrong size	11	10	13	12	14	12
Other	7	8	6	6	6	9
Subtotal	96	98	97	99	99	94

Plant shipments (total cases)	January to June			Cost/Adjustments— January to June		
	Complaints	Percent[a]	Adjustments	Percent[b]	Actual	Per case shipped
100,000	4,000	4.0%	3,000	3.0%	$30,000	$0.30
	1,000	1.0	250	0.3	2,500	0.03
	500	0.5	—	—	—	—
	500	0.5	—	—	—	—
	6,000	6.0%	3,250	3.3%	$32,500	$0.33
250,000	5,000	2.0	2,500	1.0	25,000	0.10
	3,500	1.4	1,750	0.7	17,500	0.07
	1,000	0.4	—	—	—	—
	1,000	0.4	—	—	—	—
	10,500	4.2%	4,250	1.7%	$42,500	$0.17

[a] Number of cases involved in a complaint as a percentage of shipments; includes duplications of reasons.

[b] Number of cases actually adjusted as follow-up to complaints as percentage of shipments.

Source: Information for Marketing Management (New York: National Association of Accountants, 1981), p. 34.

When the audit has been completed, the results should be conveyed to top management and all levels of marketing management. The marketing audit and market share and cost analysis are useless if corrective action is not taken. Ideally, remedial steps should be taken immediately after the source of the problem has been identified. Rapid action can often help prevent costly mistakes.

Part I. The Marketing Environment Audit

Macroenvironment

A. *Economic-demographic*
   1. What does the company expect in the way of inflation, material shortages, unemployment, and credit availability in the short run, intermediate run, and long run?
   2. What effect will forecasted trends in the size, age distribution, and regional distribution of population have on the business?

B. *Technology*
   1. What major changes are occurring in product technology? In process technology?
   2. What are the major generic substitutes that might replace this product?

C. *Political-legal*
   1. What laws are being proposed that may affect marketing strategy and tactics?
   2. What federal, state, and local agency actions should be watched? What is happening in the areas of pollution control, equal employment opportunity, product safety, advertising, price control, etc., that is relevant to marketing planning?

D. *Social-cultural*
   1. What attitudes is the public taking toward business and toward products such as those produced by the company?
   2. What changes are occurring in consumer life styles and values that have a bearing on the company's target markets and marketing methods?

Task environment

A. *Markets*
   1. What is happening to market size, growth, geographical distribution, and profits?
   2. What are the major market segments? What are their expected rates of growth? Which are high opportunity and low opportunity segments?

B. *Customers*
   1. How do current customers and prospects rate the company and its competitors, particularly with respect to reputation, product quality, service, sales force, and price?
   2. How do different classes of customers make their buying decisions?
   3. What are the evolving needs and satisfactions being sought by the buyers in this market?

C. *Competitors*
   1. Who are the major competitors? What are the objectives and strategy of each major competitor? What are their strengths and weaknesses? What are the sizes and trends in market shares?
   2. What trends can be foreseen in future competition and substitutes for this product?

D. *Distribution and dealers*
   1. What are the main trade channels bringing products to customers?
   2. What are the efficiency levels and growth potentials of the different trade channels?

E. *Suppliers*
   1. What is the outlook for the availability of different key resources used in production?
   2. What trends are occurring among suppliers in their pattern of selling?

F. *Facilitators*
   1. What is the outlook for the cost and availability of transportation services?
   2. What is the outlook for the cost and availability of warehousing facilities?
   3. What is the outlook for the cost and availability of financial resources?
   4. How effectively is the advertising agency performing? What trends are occurring in advertising agency services?

Part II. Marketing Strategy Audit

A. *Marketing objectives*
  1. Are the corporate objectives clearly stated, and do they lead logically to the marketing objectives?
  2. Are the marketing objectives stated in a clear form to guide marketing planning and subsequent performance measurement?
  3. Are the marketing objectives appropriate, given the company's competitive position, resources, and opportunities? Is the appropriate strategic objective to build, hold, harvest, or terminate this business?

B. *Strategy*
  1. What is the core marketing strategy for achieving the objectives? Is it a sound marketing strategy?
  2. Are enough resources (or too much resources) budgeted to accomplish the marketing objectives?
  3. Are the marketing resources allocated optimally to prime market segments, territories, and products of the organization?
  4. Are the marketing resources allocated optimally to the major elements of the marketing mix, i.e., product quality, service, salesforce, advertising, promotion, and distribution?

Part III. Marketing Organization Audit

A. *Formal structure*
  1. Is there a high-level marketing officer with adequate authority and responsibility over those company activities that affect the customer's satisfaction?
  2. Are the marketing responsibilities optimally structured along functional, product, end user, and territorial lines?

B. *Functional efficiency*
  1. Are there good communication and working relations between marketing and sales?
  2. Is the product-management system working effectively? Are the product managers able to plan profits or only sales volume?
  3. Are there any groups in marketing that need more training, motivation, supervision, or evaluation?

C. *Interface efficiency*
  1. Are there any problems between marketing and manufacturing that need attention?
  2. What about marketing and R&D?
  3. What about marketing and financial management?
  4. What about marketing and purchasing?

Part IV. Marketing Systems Audit

A. *Marketing information system*
  1. Is the marketing intelligence system producing accurate, sufficient, and timely information about developments in the marketplace?
  2. Is marketing research being adequately used by company decision makers?

B. *Marketing-planning system*
  1. Is the marketing-planning system well conceived and effective?
  2. Is sales forecasting and market-potential measurement soundly carried out?
  3. Are sales quotas set on a proper basis?

C. *Marketing control system*
  1. Are the control procedures (monthly, quarterly, etc.) adequate to insure that the annual-plan objectives are being achieved?
  2. Is provision made to analyze periodically the profitability of different products, markets, territories, and channels of distribution?
  3. Is provision made to examine and validate periodically various marketing costs?

D. *New product development system*
1. Is the company well organized to gather, generate, and screen new product ideas?
2. Does the company do adequate concept research and business analysis before investing heavily in a new idea?
3. Does the company carry out adequate product and market testing before launching a new product?

Part V. Marketing Productivity Audit

A. *Profitability analysis*
1. What is the profitability of the company's different products, served markets, territories, and channels of distribution?
2. Should the company enter, expand, contract, or withdraw from any business segments and what would be the short- and long-run profit consequences?
B. *Cost-effectiveness analysis*
1. Do any marketing activities seem to have excessive costs? Are these costs valid? Can cost-reducing steps be taken?

Part VI. Marketing Function Audits

A. *Products*
1. What are the product line objectives? Are these objectives sound? Is the current product line meeting these objectives?
2. Are there particular products that should be phased out?
3. Are there new products that are worth adding?
4. Are any products able to benefit from quality, feature, or style improvements?
B. *Price*
1. What are the pricing objectives, policies, strategies, and procedures? To what extent are prices set on sound cost, demand, and competitive criteria?
2. Do the customers see the company's prices as being in line or out of line with the perceived value of its offer?
3. Does the company use price promotions effectively?
C. *Distribution*
1. What are the distribution objectives and strategies?
2. Is there adequate market coverage and service?
3. Should the company consider changing its degree of reliance on distributors, sales reps, and direct selling?
D. *Salesforce*
1. What are the organization's salesforce objectives?
2. Is the salesforce large enough to accomplish the company's objectives?
3. Is the salesforce organized along the proper principle(s) of specialization (territory, market, product)?
4. Does the salesforce show high morale, ability, and effort? Are they sufficiently trained and are there sufficient incentives?
5. Are the procedures adequate for setting quotas and evaluating performances?
6. How is the company's salesforce perceived in relation to competitors' salesforces?
E. *Advertising, sales promotion, and publicity*
1. What are the organization's advertising objectives? Are they sound?
2. Is the right amount being spent on advertising? How is the budget determined?
3. Are the ad themes and copy effective? What do customers and the public think about the advertising?
4. Are the advertising media well chosen?
5. Is sales promotion used effectively?
6. Is there a well-conceived publicity program?

Source: Phillip Kotler, *Marketing Management Analysis Planning and Control,* 4th ed. (Englewood Cliffs, N.J.: Prentice-Hall, 1980), pp. 652–655. By permission of Prentice-Hall, Inc. © 1980.

Quick reaction time implies that control information is funneled to the proper decision maker. If, for example, the promotional mix needs to be modified, this information should not flow upward through four or five layers of management. Instead, the data should go directly to the person with the authority to take the needed action. Good control mechanisms can lose their effectiveness without timely reporting and action.

The marketing controller

In the marketing audit survey cited above, 29 percent of the firms relied on an outside auditor, whereas the remainder utilized internal personnel.[10] If the company decides to conduct an audit using its own resources, the person given responsibility for the audit should be the marketing controller.

The basic function of the marketing controller has been described this way:

This person will administer the broad corporate financial/marketing planning function, its related programs, and the preparation of such analyses as are requested. Attendant to this is a broad-based necessity to maintain liaison with the operating functions of the company with particular emphasis on providing assistance and advice to marketing in regard to plans, budgets, and selected analyses.[11]

Suggested duties include these:

Establish a record of adherence to profit plans.
Maintain close control of media expense.
Prepare brand managers' budgets.
Advise on optimum timing for strategies.
Measure the efficiency of promotions.
Analyze media production costs.
Evaluate customer and geographic profitability.
Present sales-oriented financial reports.
Assist direct accounts in optimizing purchasing and inventory policies.
Educate the marketing area in the financial implications of decisions.
Conduct the marketing audit on regularly scheduled basis.[12]

At the present time, most companies do not have a marketing controller. Those that do are typically very large, such as Nestlé, Johnson & Johnson, and American Cyanamid. One study, however, showed that many companies had either just embarked, or were about to embark, on the creation of the position of marketing controller.[13] The skills required for the job are a unique blend of marketing, finance, and quantitative training. Perhaps this will be a significant career field for MBA's during the late 1980s.

SUMMARY

A sound organization structure is required for marketing management to integrate and utilize the firm's resources to accomplish predetermined objectives. Organizing is a three-phase process involving: (1) designating tasks and activities, (2) grouping these subunits into positions, and (3) establishing relationships among the resulting elements. A good organization structure avoids duplication of work, minimizes conflict, serves as a basis for formal communication channels, provides for smooth, integrated work flows, establishes a means for appraisal of marketing personnel, and allows resources to be focused and channeled.

Two important aspects of establishing organizational relationships are the authority and responsibilities assigned to various personnel and the issue of centralization versus decentralization. In addition, management must consider marketing's interaction with other departments. It is important that marketing not dominate the organization. A marketing-controlled firm often results in short production runs, high inventory levels, minimal credit checks, and short engineering design lead time. These situations can drastically increase total costs.

The management task of planning and organizing cannot be effective without control. Control is the basis for correcting actions that are not efficient in aiding the organization to reach its objectives. The control process actually begins while planning is taking place. After goals are established, standards must be developed to aid in performance measurement. When standards have been established, a plan can be put into action. Performance is then measured to make certain standards are being met. If standards are being met actions continue. Otherwise, deviations are examined to see if they fall within acceptable boundaries. If the deviations are too large the marketing plan is brought to a halt, and causal analysis is used to revise the plan or perhaps scrap it.

Marketing managers tend to rely on a number of tools for marketing control. Among the most popular are sales analysis, volume analysis, market share analysis, and marketing cost analysis. It is often found that the 80–20 rule applies when conducting sales analysis. Many companies discover that approximately 20 percent of customers account for 80 percent of sales volume, gross margin, and profits. In addition to financial controls, marketing managers also utilize a number of nonfinancial controls. Complaint reports are a common form of nonfinancial control; another, and the broadest control device, is the marketing audit. This tool incorporates both financial and nonfinancial reporting and is primarily futuristic in nature. A marketing audit helps management allocate marketing resources efficiently and is not used strictly for firms that are experiencing marketing difficulties. All companies should utilize the audit system to uncover potential weaknesses and identify the sources of problems. The audit includes a thorough review of each element of the marketing mix plus other internal and external factors. Some companies are assigning the responsibility for the marketing audit to the marketing controller. The marketing controller administers the marketing planning function and prepares marketing analyses as requested by top management.

KEY TERMS

Functionalization

Departmentation

Matrix organization

Corporate marketing staff

Formal authority

Authority

Responsibility

Standard

Exception principle

Sales volume analysis

Macrosales analysis

Microsales analysis

80–20 rule

Market share analysis

Iceberg principle

Matching concept

Natural account

Functional account

Marketing audit

REVIEW QUESTIONS

1. What does the process of organization involve?
2. Explain the difference between centralization and decentralization. What are the advantages and disadvantages of each?
3. For what reasons is control desirable?
4. Outline some of the techniques used for maintaining marketing control.
5. Why is it necessary to distinguish natural accounts from functional accounts?
6. What is a marketing audit? Explain the purpose and scope of such an audit.

DISCUSSION QUESTIONS

1. What determines the type of organizational structure a firm utilizes?
2. What is the relationship between planning and control?
3. Should the marketing department dominate the structure of the firm? Why or why not?
4. Formulate an illustration of the iceberg principle as it relates to marketing.
5. How does the matching concept of accounting relate to marketing?
6. Do you think it is better for a firm to hire an outsider or to employ a marketing controller for purposes of conducting a marketing audit? Explain the advantages and disadvantages of each alternative.

NOTES

1. Adapted from Lee Smith, "The Lures and Limits of Innovation," *Fortune,* October 20, 1980, pp. 85–94.
2. Watson Snyder, Jr., and Frank B. Gray, *The Corporate Marketing Staff: Its Role and Effectiveness in Multi-Division Companies* (Cambridge, Mass.: Marketing Science Institute, April 1971).
3. Ibid.
4. Ernest Dale, *Planning and Developing the Company Organization Structure* (New York: American Management Association, 1973).
5. Fred W. Morgan, Jr., "Marketing Control Systems: Their Relationship to Company Size," in *Proceedings 1977 Southern Marketing Conference,* eds. Henry Nash and Donald Robin, Southern Mississippi University, pp. 90–91.
6. Ibid.

7. "Keeping Up with the Marketing Jones," *Industrial Marketing,* March 1980, pp. 76–84.

8. *Information for Marketing Management* (New York: National Association of Accountants, 1981), pp. 21–22.

9. Louis M. Copella and William S. Sekely, "The Marketing Audit: Usage and Application," *Proceedings 1978 Southern Marketing Association Annual Conference,* eds. Robert S. Franz, Robert M. Hawkins, and Al Toma, University of Southern Louisiana, pp. 411–414.

10. Ibid.

11. Sam R. Goodman, *The Marketing Controller Concept: An Inquiry into Financial/Marketing Relationships in Selected Consumer Companies* (Cambridge, Mass.: The Marketing Science Institute, 1970), p. 48.

12. Ibid., p. 39. List modified by the author.

13. Ibid., p. 41.

◢ **CASES**

22.1 Intel Corporation

Intel Corporation is a California semi-conductor manufacturer that grew more than a hundredfold during the 1970s. By 1980 it was number 4 in the integrated-circuit business. Its plans for the decade of the 1980s include a device complex enough to put an entire large mainframe computer on a handful of silicone chips. The company also plans to produce and market most of the software (the instructions telling the computer what to do) that would put this computer power to work, a job semi-conductor producers have typically left for others. The integrated circuits at the heart of the family Intel proposes to produce will each contain the equivalent of more than 100,000 individual transistors.

The organization structure at Intel is unique, to say the least. Due to unprecedented growth, about half of its people have typically been there a year or less. Intel has never bothered with staff positions except in a few specialized areas of finance and law. At Intel, workers may have dozens of bosses, depending on the problem at hand. Instead of staff specialists for purchasing, market research, and so forth, Intel has committees or "councils." There are about 90 of these at the present, making decisions and enforcing standards. These coordinating bodies are overlaid on a grid of 24 strategic business units (SBUs) that do product planning. Intel's top management would like to see virtually all decisions handled at the council or SBU level, but the flood of new employees and the proliferation of markets during the past few years have made this concept difficult to sustain. Moreover, Intel is in the midst of a massive decentralization of its physical facilities, with major operations now in Portland, Oregon, and Phoenix, Arizona, as well as its home base in Santa Clara, California.

1. How would you describe the Intel organization structure?
2. If you were brought in as an organizational consultant to aid in establishing an efficient marketing structure, what would you recommend? Why?

22.2 Thompson Engineering Laboratories

Thompson Engineering Laboratories, located in Stamford, Connecticut, is a manufacturer of electronic instruments and instrumentation systems. The company was founded in 1977 by two former General Electric engineers. Since capital was a problem in the early years, the firm decided to rely on manufacturers' representatives. Company sales doubled annually through 1980 and were probably going to continue at that pace through 1985. The company president felt the organization might be growing too fast for him to monitor the performance of 50 manufacturers' representatives and representative organizations that sold the company's product lines.

Essentially, Mr. Thompson, the president, waits for the representatives to turn in the orders and hopes that sales this month will be higher than last month. There was no control system per se. The company had no idea which manufacturers' representatives were giving Thompson a fair share of their time. Even though sales might be growing from a particular representative, this does not necessarily mean that the representative is putting a lot of time and effort into the account. At present, since the firm does not have a sales tracking system or control system, it often waits several months before noticing a sales decline on a specific product. A recently instituted cost accounting system revealed that some of its products were much more profitable than others. Mr. Thompson wondered if he could institute a system to provide representatives with incentives to sell certain items and then monitor the success of the incentive program.

1. You have been hired as a consultant for Thompson Engineering Laboratories. Suggest a control system that will provide the necessary data to monitor the activities of the sales organization. Justify your recommendations.
2. What type of control system could be implemented to make certain that desired products are being promoted?

Baxter Corporation*

The Baxter Corporation is contemplating the adoption of a new organizational structure in order to obtain greater control over its operations. Baxter is primarily engaged in the manufacture of kitchen products such as range hoods, built-in cooking appliances, compact freezers and refrigerators, and fluorescent fixtures. Kitchen product sales in 1980 were about $20 million, and fluorescent fixture sales were approximately $18 million.

The Baxter Corporation has reviewed its past 10-year sales record and was concerned that private-brand sales to retailers grew at a more rapid rate than Baxter-brand sales in the period. Sales to other manufacturers and private-brand sales by retailers actually exceeded those of Baxter in 1980 for the first ime. This occurred because of the changing nature of the fluorescent lighting business and the demand by retailers for private-label kitchen products. During the past 10-year period, Baxter produced basic fluorescent fixtures for residential markets. However, in 1980 a shift in production began from utility lights for the home to decorative residential fixtures, which are much more profitable. Higher production costs and costs of materials were important reasons for decreased profits in the past year.

The Baxter Corporation sells its products to over 2500 customers throughout the United States and Canada. Most of the customers are department stores, discount houses, and specialty shops. Baxter employed 32 salespeople to handle sales activities. These salespeople were granted exclusive territories and were paid on a straight commission basis after two years' employment. Salespeople turnover with Baxter was about average for the industry. The firm advertises on a material level in various women's and fashion magazines, such as *Vogue* and *Redbook*. Advertising in trade papers is used extensively, and Baxter generally reserves a booth at trade shows. Baxter has a cooperative advertising program with its retailers and generally will match expenditures in local media.

Baxter had not developed the industrial market and was considering how to contact contractors and developers of housing communities. However, prices of the decorative residential fixtures might pose a problem, since they were higher than for competitive brands but at the same time of higher quality. The Baxter Corporation also believed that many of its kitchen products and lighting fixtures could be sold to federal, state, and municipal government units. The process of selling to government would be different, since competitive bidding was utilized in this market.

For some years the product planning function had been under the engineering department, which reported to the vice-president of research and development. Baxter's engineers were outstanding in the industry. Two of them had been honored by receiving industry awards. Their ability to design kitchen products at competitive prices and higher quality was instrumental in helping the company to achieve a position of prominence in the industry.

---

* Case prepared by Professor Ronald D. Michman, Shippensburg State College, Shippensburg, Pennsylvania.

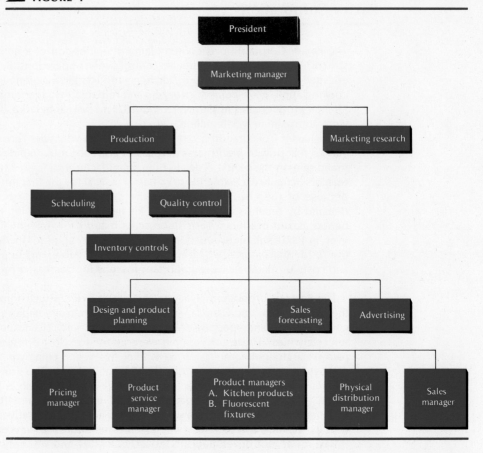

The pricing function had been placed under the accounting department. Baxter had gained a reputation for charging fair prices and extending favorable terms for payment. The accounting department was proud of its record for the extension of credit to retailers. However, the budget for sales efforts was developed by the finance department. Baxter had a reputation as a conservative firm and rarely overextended itself in the development of new territories. The finance department projected the sales forecast for each of the firm's products on an annual basis. On some occasions sales did exceed the forecast, except for the past two years.

Sales and advertising were performed by separate departments. Both the sales and advertising managers had been with Baxter for more than ten years and were respected within the company. A marketing manager had been hired three years ago. He had been an assistant marketing manager of a large competitor of Baxter, and although he was young, he was considered competent.

Baxter wanted the marketing manager to be given more control of its opera-

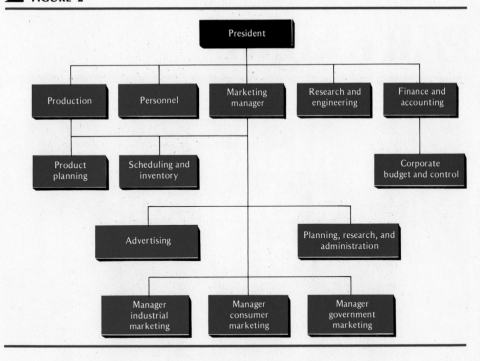

tions. Specifically, the marketing manager should have more control over product planning, making production scheduling requests, and controlling finished products inventory. Other responsibilities would include developing sales terms and discounts for customers, supervising advertising and sales, and guiding product and marketing services.

The marketing manager and a consulting firm were both asked to submit reorganization plans. Figure 1 is the reorganization plan of the marketing manager. Under the present organization, the production department decides how and what to produce. The reorganization proposal would have the marketing manager responsible for the products to be manufactured and for consulting with the production department on scheduling.

The consulting firm, however, submitted Figure 2, which emphasizes a market organizational approach. This approach designs the marketing organization around the markets served. It also includes a liaison relationship with the production department.

1. What arrangements should Baxter make in its organization for product planning?
2. What should be the relationship of the marketing manager to the production departments?
3. Which new organization structure plan should the Baxter Corporation adopt? What are the limitations of both plans?

PART Eight

Marketing in a changing world

23

Consumerism and marketing's social responsibility

OBJECTIVES

To understand the meaning of consumerism.

To present a brief overview of the consumer movement.

To understand the nature of micro and macro marketing concerns with regard to consumerism.

To examine the response of business to consumerism.

To understand the nature of social responsibility.

To become aware of the different ways in which marketing meets its social responsibilities.

In early 1980 the Children's Advertising Review Unit of the National Advertising Division (NAD) of the Council of Better Business Bureaus came down hard on a comic-book advertising campaign for Casper Fuzzy accessories (which . . . are mostly decorative pins bearing the likeness of a TV cartoon character named Casper). Says a recent NAD release: "The Children's Unit was . . . concerned that the advertisement . . . might convey to a child the sense that by owning a Fuzzy, the child could be better than his or her peers."

In the past, it has questioned the Hasbro Industries campaign for the Sno-Cone Machine, a device that helps our little friends to make flavored ice. The question here was whether the advertisements encouraged the owners to share the flavored ice with their chums in a democratic and participative spirit. The NAD ultimately let Hasbro off the hook on this one, but only after insisting that future commercials communicate an "ambience of sharing."[1]

Should a Fuzzy be removed from the marketplace? Are Sno-Cone Machines little more than status symbols? Or has government and self regulation in response to consumerism gone too far? Where does social responsibility fit in? What caused the rise of consumerism? Let us begin with the last question.

What is consumerism?

Florence Skelly, vice president of Yankelovich, Skelly and White, one of America's leading social research organizations, says: "The public's current generalized suspicion of and hostility toward business as an institution is an important element in the consumerist movement."[2] Her company has determined that the public feels business places too much emphasis on self-interest and on profits. More than half of the American people (including educated and sophisticated consumers) believe they cannot identify or deal with false or misleading advertising, and they cannot judge the quality, value, or adequacy of many products.[3] In short, they find many aspects of our business system frustrating. Mistrust of business generates the support for the consumerism movement. Skelly's research has also revealed widespread public support for protective regulatory action, even when consumers know they will ultimately pay for it.

Consumerism is a struggle for power between buyers and sellers. It is a social movement seeking to augment the rights and powers of buyers in relation to sellers. The rights and powers of both groups are presented in the following list:

Sellers have the right to introduce any product in any size and style they wish into the marketplace so long as it is not hazardous to personal health or safety; or, if it is, to introduce it with the proper warnings and controls.

Sellers have the right to price the product at any level they wish provided there is no discrimination among similar classes of buyers.

Sellers have the right to spend any amount of money they wish to promote the product, so long as it is not defined as unfair competition.

Sellers have the right to formulate any message they wish about the product provided that it is not misleading or dishonest in content or execution.

Sellers have the right to introduce any buying incentive schemes they wish.

Buyers have the right not to buy a product that is offered to them.

Buyers have the right to expect the product to be safe.

Buyers have the right to expect the product to turn out to be essentially as represented by the seller.

Additional rights consumers want:

Buyers want the right to have adequate information about the product.

Buyers want the right to additional protections against questionable products and marketing practices.

Buyers want the right to influence products and marketing practices in directions that will increase the "quality of life."[4]

Although consumerism can be viewed as a struggle for power, the specific issues are not always clear. In fact, the relevant issues vary according to the group that describes them. One study revealed that businesspeople view consumerism as primarily an informational problem (see Table 23.1).[5] That is, it is

Issues	Students (N = 241)	Nonemployed women (N = 55)	Businesspeople (N = 71)
Information (such as more informative advertising, clearly written warranties, etc.)	82.2%	89.1%	95.8%
Health and safety (such as testing and evaluation of drugs, stronger auto bumpers, etc.)	80.1	92.7	83.1
Repair and servicing (such as improved servicing of appliances and automobiles)	70.1	85.5	71.8
Pricing issues (such as the high price of food, insurance, hospital care)	59.3	81.8	63.4
Pollution in the environment (such as dirty air, water, excessive billboards)	61.8	47.3	36.6
Market concentration (such as lack of competition in the marketplace)	26.1	45.5	42.3
Product quality (such as frequent obsolescence, product breakdowns)	72.2	89.1	78.9
Consumer representation in government (such as a lack of consumer representation in government agencies)	58.5	69.1	52.1

Source: Norman Kangun, Keith Cox, James Higginbotham, and John Burton, "Consumerism and Marketing Management," *Journal of Marketing* 39 (April 1975): 5. Reprinted by permission of the American Marketing Association.

a matter of getting factual and timely warranties and advertising to the consumer. Nonemployed women believe that health and safety factors are the most important issues. Students tend to agree with businesspeople regarding the importance of good information. However, the student group is almost twice as likely as businesspeople or nonemployed women to mention pollution as a consumer issue.

The history of consumerism

THE EARLY YEARS

Contrary to popular opinion, consumerism is not new. The first consumer protection law was passed in 1872; it made it a federal crime to defraud consumers through the mails.[6] Other piecemeal laws passed before 1900 prohibited the sale of unwholesome tea (1883) and barred the importation of adulterated food and drink (1890). Between 1879 and 1905, more than 100 bills were introduced in Congress to regulate interstate production and sale of foods and drugs. A largely apathetic public (and, therefore, Congress) plus strong business opposition resulted in the failure of those bills to pass.

Perhaps the first general consumer outcry came in February 1906 with the publication of Upton Sinclair's *The Jungle,* a devastating exposé of the meat-packing industry in the United States. Consider the following paragraph:

These rats were nuisances, and the packers would put poisoned bread out for them and they would die, and then rats, bread and meat would go into the hoppers together. . . . Men, who worked in the tank rooms full of steam . . . fell into the vats; and when they were fished out, there was never enough of them to be worth exhibiting—sometimes they would be overlooked for days, till all but the bones of them had gone out to the world as Durham's Pure Leaf Lard![7]

The book helped assure the passage of the Pure Food and Drug Act of 1906.

World War I dulled the consumer thrust. New fuel for the movement came with the publication in 1927 of *Your Money's Worth,* by Stuart Chase and F. J. Schlink. The book attacked advertising and high-pressure salesmanship and called for scientific testing and product standards to provide consumers with the technical information they needed to make purchase decisions. World War II also slowed the growth of consumerism. Little activity occurred until the middle 1950s when the modern consumer movement began. In *The Hidden Persuaders,* Vance Packard charged that advertisers were using motivation research and subliminal advertising to manipulate consumers. Similarly, Rachel Carson's *The Silent Spring* described the damage to the environment and the food chain caused by the use of pesticides. State governments began to get involved, indicated by the organization of the Office of Consumer Council in the state of New York in 1955, and similar organizations in the Office of the Governor in California and Connecticut. In 1960, the Consumer Advisory Council was formed to advise the Council of Economic Advisors on consumer affairs. However, the CAC and other federal regulatory agencies concerned with consumer protection were not effective because they were understaffed, lacked sufficient funds, and had no direct access to the president.

One major blow to the modern consumer movement came in February 1978, when Congress soundly defeated a proposal to create an Agency for Consumer Advocacy and thus give consumers a permanent spokesperson within the federal government. Working as a tightly knit coalition, the Chamber of Commerce, the Business Roundtable, the National Association of Manufacturers, the National Federation of Independent Business, and most major farm groups launched a sophisticated campaign against the proposed agency. The coalition called instead for "beefing up" departmental consumer offices. The early 1980s finds consumerism returning to grassroots issues throughout the country, sponsored by such groups as the National Council of Churches. In 1980 Ralph Nader promoted "Big Business Day" to expose the abuses of corporations.

Lack of public interest limited the success of the affair. More important, consumer advocates were appointed to chair the Civil Aeronautics Board, the Equal Employment Opportunity Commission, the National Highway Traffic Safety Administration, the Occupational Safety and Health Administration, and the Federal Trade Commission. Consumers now have a growing voice in Washington's inner councils and in the world, as these examples show.

Today, consumerism has assumed worldwide stature. In April 1960, the International Organization of Consumers Unions (IOCU) was launched at a conference in The Hague. The charter members were Consumers Union of U.S., Inc.; Consumers Association, London; Australian Consumers' Association; Consumenten Bond, The Hague; and Association des Consommateurs, Brussels.

It provided an interchange of educational materials and established a technical committee to represent consumers on international standardization bodies. It also moved to assist consumers in less developed nations by obtaining consultative status with the Food and Agriculture Organization, the Economic and Social Council, and UNESCO, agencies of the UN concerned with raising living standards in less developed countries.

The development of consumer standards and consumer testing also extended into Eastern Europe. Yugoslavia has a federal board on the family and the household to strengthen the role of consumers. Hungary recently entered the consumer testing field. The Soviet Union established a consumer institute which undertakes comparative testing.[8]

The marketing forces behind the consumer movement

A number of factors gave rise to the growth and permanence of today's consumer movements. We begin with an examination of the macro factors.

MACRO FORCES

Marketing efficiency. The question of the efficiency of our marketing system is not new. A popular book written in 1939 aroused public concern by asking the question "Does distribution cost too much?"[9] Consumers are aware of all too frequent price increases when they are shopping. The natural tendency is to point a finger at the retailer. The retailer in turn blames the wholesaler, who criticizes the manufacturer. Rising transportation costs, inefficient handling systems, and corporate bureaucracy are often mentioned as causes of the problem. Is the macro marketing system inefficient? The answer to this question is not easy.

Efficiency may be defined as the ratio of useful output to the total input of the marketing system. The more productive the system, the greater its efficiency. The productivity of a warehouse operation might be measured by looking at the relationship between labor input (man-hours worked) and output (volume of goods moved through the warehouse). Productivity would obviously increase if: (1) a fixed number of man-hours led to an increase in volume moved; (2) an increase in man-hours led to a proportionately greater increase in volume moved; or (3) a reduction in man-hours led to a proportionately smaller reduction in volume moved.[10] This is called physical productivity. A second aspect of productivity is economic productivity. It is measured by the highest dollar value of output (or costs) for a specific dollar value of input. An example is lower costs of distribution centers versus the traditional warehouse.

These examples relate to distribution, but marketing is concerned with other variables. Moreover, the other variables are difficult to conceptualize and measure in terms of productivity. How does one measure the productivity of pricing in a macro context? A second problem is sometimes called the **macro-micro dilemma:** what is efficient for the firm may be inefficient for society. If a firm develops a very creative advertising campaign it may be able to increase sales, raise prices, and improve profits. In short, the firm has used promotion effectively. From a macro perspective, however, the efficient firm's competitors may have to operate at a lower volume of sales. Production efficiencies for the competitors decline and costs rise. Management may then increase prices to compensate for the higher costs. Therefore, the net macro effects may be higher industry prices and lower total industry outputs.

Marketers have undertaken two types of studies when attempting to answer the question of efficiency. The first are cost studies, which focus on distribution activities.[11] Results have shown a slight decline in distribution's share of the consumer's dollar from 51 percent in 1929 to 46 percent in 1958. Still, almost half of that dollar goes to distribution expenses. Is this bad? You get what you want in most cases without exerting a lot of time or effort. It is sanitary and packed in convenient packages. No other system in the world offers greater variety or convenience. A second type of study that attempts to answer the efficiency question measures output per man-hour.[12] This research has shown a slow but steady growth in labor productivity over the years. The studies also show vast differences in labor productivity from industry to industry.

So is macro marketing inefficient? The answer is no. It delivers one of the world's highest standards of living at a cost that is slowly declining. Man-hour productivity is slowly growing, promising even lower costs in the future.

The fairness of the marketing system. A second criticism leveled at marketing is that it is unfair. The obvious question is, "unfair to whom?" The consumer buys what he or she wants and avoids other goods and services. Nothing is forced upon the buyer. But although products are not arbitrarily allocated to consumers, it is also true that Americans do not equally share the wealth. Poor Americans receive a disproportionately smaller share of goods and services due to lower levels of purchasing power. More important, one study found that they pay more for what they receive than their affluent counterparts.

A second study found no significant differences in prices charged by food stores located in low-income areas versus those charged by stores in higher-income areas, when the same types of stores (chains, large independents, small independents), the same quality of food, and the same sizes of packages are compared.[13] Further research has found that the poor pay more when they shop at inefficient ghetto stores rather than large national chains.[14] Part of the problem is the lack of mobility of ghetto residents. Many national chains have moved out of low-income areas, forcing the poor to trade with small ghetto merchandisers. Slum residents in large cities often lack private transportation and find public transit systems inadequate, inconvenient, unsafe, or nonexistent.

A fair system is a just and equitable system. One way to determine if our system is fair to the poor is to examine what it takes to be a good consumer and see if the poor are afforded such opportunities. Being a good consumer requires:

1. Buying necessities first and luxuries last. The poor generally do this with one or two exceptions, e.g., television sets.
2. Getting the best quality at the lowest price. As shown above this cannot always be done.
3. Budgeting incomes and planning purchases ahead. A lack of education has usually meant poor money management. Also, many poor people lead a hand to mouth existence.
4. Meeting needs through home production. The poor rely less on home growing of food and home repairs than others. Urban crowding is partially accountable for this phenomenon. A lack of interest or a lack of ability also is partially responsible.
5. Taking advantage of consumer benefits. Although legal, medical, and other forms of aid are usually available to the poor the facilities are often underutilized.[15]

Can the ghetto dweller be a good consumer? In most cases, the answer would be a qualified no. Since the opportunity to be a good consumer is denied to the poor, it may be said that the macro marketing system is not fair to one group of consumers.

The macro marketing mix as a problem. In addition to questions regarding fairness and efficiency, there is also the question of the impact of the macro marketing mix. The **macro marketing mix** consists of aggregate promotion, product, distribution, and pricing activities. The factor most often attacked is advertising. As we noted in Chapter 18, advertising is accused of creating economic concentration, increasing consumer prices, and posing a barrier to entry into some industries. It is also viewed by some to be wasteful and deceptive. Critics have claimed that advertising causes people to buy things they do not really need and shifts spending from public goods to private consumption.

In the product area, questions regarding utilization of resources and pollution are raised. It is said, for example, that planned product obsolescence wastes precious natural resources. **Planned product obsolescence** is deliberately making an existing product that is still serviceable obsolete by bringing out new models. The automobile and major appliance industries have followed this practice for years. It is defended by noting that economies of scale and lower prices cannot be achieved except through high volumes. Without the additional demand created by planned obsolescence, prices would be much higher. Also, there is a secondhand market for used goods that helps to "recycle" the supposedly obsolete items.

Critics have also complained about inadequate product safety, poor and unintelligible warranties, complex labels (or lack of labeling information), and littering. Each of these items was discussed in Chapter 10.

The major charge against distribution has been its lack of efficiency. I feel that this is unwarranted for the reasons discussed above. It is true that there are, in some instances, too many retailers. In the 1960s and early 1970s it was common to find four service stations at an intersection. Today you may find two supermarkets within the same block or several specialty clothing shops in a mall carrying essentially the same brands and prices. Needless duplication in our distribution system should be eliminated if the goal is to increase distribution efficiency.

The macro pricing complaint centers on inflation, which was discussed in Chapter 3. Inflation is a complex phenomenon that goes far beyond a marketing cause and effect relationship. While marketing may sometimes contribute to inflation or even to lower prices, there are numerous other factors involved, such as government spending and taxation policies, actions of OPEC and other cartels, technological advantages, and so forth.

MICRO MARKETING FORCES

Public dissatisfaction with marketing also reaches the micro level. Individual firms and industries, although a small percentage of the total number of companies, have been criticized on every aspect of the marketing mix.

Product. Firms have been accused of making products that (1) do not meet the needs of the marketplace, (2) are of poor quality, and (3) are sometimes dangerous. Ralph Nader's Center for Study of Responsive Law conducted 2419 interviews with consumers throughout the United States on the subject of product problems. Here is a sample of the responses:

> Battery operated toys use the batteries up too fast.
> The doll's hair fell out four days after Christmas.
> I bought a hearing aid for $350. They told me it was new. Then I found out it was second-hand.
> They cut the legs off my new sofa when they came to deliver it. They should have measured the front door better.
> The turntable cover is too flimsy. It should be stronger, or it should have instructions that you have to handle it very gently.
> Radial tires were expensive, and then when they wore out within the 40,000 mile guarantee time, the company didn't honor the promise.
> Vacuum cleaner has poor suction, can't fit under appliances, its handle slips.
> [Car] seats are uncomfortable, light switch is hard to use, battery wore out after six months, thin paint, springs are starting to poke through the seats.

> Bought outside antenna for TV set. The display in the store isn't like the real unit. They installed it sloppily. Might be a fire hazard.[16]

Many consumers don't bother to complain even when they perceive a problem; it is estimated that only about one-third of the problems are reported.[17] The importance of this statistic can be appreciated when one realizes that the Better Business Bureau alone processes over a half-million complaints a year (70 percent involve service or repair problems).[18]

Price. Price complaints against companies fall into several categories. First is **bait and switch.** Local appliance and furniture stores use bait and switch advertising year after year in some communities because of lax law enforcement or lack of public concern. Even some of America's largest companies such as Sears have been accused in the recent past by the FTC of using bait and switch pricing. Levitz Furniture has been indicted in more than one community for the same violation.

A second price tactic used by companies is the **low ball price.** A low price is quoted by a salesperson over the telephone to get a potential buyer into a store or showroom. The salesperson then informs the consumer that the sales manager won't let him or her sell the merchandise for such a low price. High pressure is then used to convince the consumer to buy the item.

Another pricing tactic is the use of a **stripped-down price.** An automobile, for example, will be prominently advertised at a very low price. Upon inquiry, the consumer finds that the price does not include wheel covers, air conditioning, power steering or brakes, and so forth. In order for the buyer to get what he or she wants, the seller may increase the price several thousand dollars.

Promotion. Promotion is also a major source of consumer complaints. The most obvious is deceitful or misleading advertising. While corrective action has been taken by the FTC against Horizon Bread and Listerine and a few others, it is largely an overlooked enforcement tool. Advertising credibility is relatively low in many industries simply because the product or service cannot live up to its claims. STP oil treatment, for example, advertised for years that the additive would reduce oil consumption. The FTC claimed that it did not and fined the firm $700,000. Other examples of misleading advertising include these:

> A new bathroom tissue is "softer," the advertisers claim. (Sure, they made it "softer" by cutting down the number of tissues per roll and fluffing out the rest.)
> A fabric softener bottle "bounced" off the nice, soft towels in a commercial. (It did that because the advertisers put foam rubber on the bottom of the bottle.)
> A vegetable soup appears to be full to the brim with vegetables in ads. (By putting marbles in the bowl, ad people forced the contents to the top.)
> A shaving cream could shave sandpaper, according to one advertising claim. But in the commercial, it was really sand glued to Plexiglas.[19]

After advertising draws customers into some stores, high pressure personal selling takes over. The potential buyer is cajoled, intimidated, and even threatened. In one automobile showroom in Phoenix, hidden microphones were installed in the sales offices. After initial negotiations, the salesperson would leave the room on the pretext of speaking with the sales manager. During this time, the manager would listen to the conversation (if husband and wife or father and son were present) to determine the most the buyer would pay. Aggressive selling was then used to exact that price from the consumer. Eventually the dealership lost its franchise.

High pressure is not the only problem. Congress has refused to take action against telephone selling. Thus the number of annoying, monotone telephone sales presentations is increasing. Often a ploy of "You have just won a valuable prize" or "Hello, I am conducting a marketing research study" is used to begin the conversation.

Sales promotion techniques used by some companies have also generated complaints. Contests are run where prizes are never delivered or chances of winning are not fully explained. Coupons are offered with very short life spans. Purchasers at trade shows sometimes receive lower-quality merchandise than that which was demonstrated. Trading stamps increase the costs of merchandise. These are but a few of the types of complaints leveled against sales promotion.

Distribution. Consumers are also not happy with some retailers. Because of the rise in labor costs, many retailers have moved more heavily into self-service during the past twenty years. Self-service is, of course, a very impersonal system. There is no longer a close, caring personal relationship between most retailers and their customers. Before the advent of self-service, retailers knew the needs of their customers and even developed personal friendships.

In contrast, a person can walk into a chain store and be hard-pressed to locate a clerk. If someone can be located, chances are that the clerk will know less about the merchandise than the potential buyer. After a purchase is made, a long line often awaits at central checkout. Paying for an item with a check is often akin to a police lineup. Not only will the buyer be required to show multiple forms of identification, but the clerk will often be required to call a supervisor for approval. After an examination of the check, a few more questions, and a visual check of your appearance (do you look responsible), the purchaser will be allowed to leave with the merchandise.

Physical distribution is also the subject of verbal and written consumer abuse. How many times have you ordered something only to have it delivered broken? Sometimes orders are lost or filled incorrectly. JS and A, a mail order sales firm that specializes in electronic merchandise, was accused by the FTC of cashing checks without rapid delivery (30 days) of ordered merchandise. JS and A is a reputable firm that experienced computer and other difficulties which delayed delivery. Other mail order organizations go into business every year with the intent of bilking customers. One such firm promoted a guaranteed roach killer. The unsuspecting buyer received a small block of wood and a miniature wooden mallet. The instructions read "catch the roach, place it on the wooden block. . . ."

The business response to consumerism

Only a small portion of firms have been guilty of consumer abuse. Literally billions of satisfactory exchanges occur every day. Since most exchanges are satisfactory, many businesses choose to ignore consumerism. The attitude seems to be, "we're not causing problems, so why get involved." One study found that 63 percent of the industrial firms polled indicated that they had not been affected by consumerism.[20] Approximately half the consumer goods companies claimed that consumerism had affected them.

The 1980s have led to a more positive approach to consumerism. General Mills, for example, felt the sting of consumer activists during much of the 1970s. First there was a highly publicized list that ranked cereals by their nutritional value. Some of General Mills' brands, which ranked high, improved in sales. Other products that did not fare as well, such as Mr. Wonderful's Surprise and Total, experienced a sharp drop in dollar volume. Next came reports from such groups as The Safe Food Institute (how can a firm possibly oppose such a well-chosen and official-sounding name), which issued such statements as "the food industry is literally killing us producing foods that cause cancer and heart disease."[21]

To counteract such irresponsible statements, General Mills initiated a new strategy. The company felt that it would no longer stand idly by while the activists had a field day. The firm was also concerned that the public was receiving a biased story. Accordingly, General Mills took the following steps:

1. Organized a top-level management team to identify the issues, define corporate consumerist objectives and strategies, and assign duties.
2. Initiated a comprehensive fact-finding mission to become fully knowledgeable about consumerist issues.
3. Identified key target audiences that the firm wished to reach. These included government officials, media, academics, and others who exert influence on public policy.
4. Discussed the issues with General Mills employees and stockholders. These two key groups must understand what is being said by activists, why it is being said, and what is being done to countermand it.
5. We launched an aggressive communications campaign, utilizing key executives.
6. Attempted to create positive industry momentum by demonstrating in the public media that many arguments on the issues are emotional in nature and not supported by facts.[22]

The steps taken by General Mills were designed to protect the firm against propaganda. One activist theme, for example, was "It's about time for the FTC to stop Kelloggs from lying to our children."[23] Yet when the emotionalism is stripped away, there are often real problems that need attention. Solving these problems requires much more than a media campaign. First, it takes a broad sense of social responsibility from top management that permeates the entire organization. Consumerism should be viewed as only one dimension of social responsibility. Next, a system is required to monitor potential consumer and social factors that may impinge upon the firm. Corrective action then needs to be taken before a problem develops.

Social responsibility

The term **social responsibility** has many dimensions:

The term is a brilliant one; it means something, but not always the same thing, to everybody. To some it conveys the idea of legal responsibility or liability; to others it means socially responsible behavior in an ethical sense; to still others the meaning transmitted is that of "responsible for," in a causal mode; many simple equate it with a charitable contribution; some take it to mean socially conscious; many of those who embrace it almost fervently see it as a mere synonym for "legitimacy," in the context of "belonging" or "being proper or valid"; a few see it as a sort of fiduciary duty imposing higher standards of behavior on businessmen than on citizens at large. Even the antonyms, socially "irresponsible" and "nonresponsible," are subject to multiple interpretations.[24]

Social responsibility means different things to different people. Here we will use the following general definition: Social responsibility is business concern for social welfare.

SOCIAL RESPONSIBILITY AND ETHICS

Is social responsibility an ethical issue for the individual businessperson, or is it an issue that concerns the role the corporation should play in society? A *Harvard Business Review* study of 1227 business executives found that they think it is both.[25] Responsibility for both the individual and the corporation tends to be defined in terms of the social arrangements and obligations that make up the structure of our society (for example, a pledge to hire the hard-core unemployed). Ethics concerns the rules by which those responsibilities are carried out. Hiring hard-core unemployed for jobs that management plans to abolish in the near future would be poor ethics. Thus it is extremely hard to separate the rules of the game from the game itself. What are the rules of the game? The World Marketing Control Group met in Verona, Italy, in 1976 to create a marketing creed that would define ethics for the marketing manager. The result of this work is shown in Table 23.2.

Milton Friedman, the noted economist, and Theodore Levitt, a marketing philosopher, argue that social responsibility is something quite different from what we have defined here. They say that social responsibility means (1) having high ethical standards and (2) earning an adequate return for the stockholders. Levitt says that business should take care of the material aspects of welfare while government should handle the general welfare. The business of business is earning profits. Friedman reinforces this by claiming the sole responsibility of business is to employ its resources in activities that yield profits,

1. I hereby acknowledge my accountability to the organization for which I work and to society as a whole to improve marketing knowledge and practice and to adhere to the highest professional standards in my work and personal relationships.

2. My concept of marketing includes as its basic principle the sovereignty of all consumers in the marketplace and the necessity for mutual benefit to both buyer and seller in all transactions.

3. I shall personally maintain the highest standards of ethical and professional conduct in all my business relationships with customers, suppliers, colleagues, competitors, governmental agencies and the public.

4. I pledge to protect, support and promote the principles of consumer choice, competition and innovative enterprise, consistent with relevant legislative public policy standards.

5. I shall not knowingly participate in actions, agreements or marketing policies or practices which may be detrimental to customers, competitors or established community social or economic policies or standards.

6. I shall strive to ensure that products and services are distributed through such channels and by such methods as will tend to optimize the distributive process by offering maximum customer value and service at minimum cost while providing fair and equitable compensation for all parties.

7. I shall support efforts to increase productivity or reduce costs of production or marketing through standardization or other methods, provided these methods do not stifle innovation or creativity.

8. I believe prices should reflect true value in use of the product or service to the customer, including the pricing of goods and services transferred among operating organizations worldwide.

9. I acknowledge that providing the best economic and social product value consistent with cost also includes:

a. Recognizing the customer's right to expect safe products with clear instructions for their proper use and maintenance

b. Providing easily accessible channels for customer complaints

c. Investigating any customer dissatisfaction objectively and taking prompt and appropriate remedial action

d. Recognizing and supporting proven public policy objectives such as conserving energy and protecting the environment

10. I pledge my efforts to assure that all marketing research, advertising, sales presentations of products, services or concepts are done clearly, truthfully and in good taste so as not to mislead or offend customers. I further pledge to assure that all these activities are conducted in accordance with the highest standards of each profession and generally accepted principles of fair competition.

11. I pledge to cooperate fully in furthering the efforts of all institutions, media, professional associations and other organizations to publicize this creed as widely as possible throughout the world.

Source: "Marketing Creed," Marketing Times, August 1977, p. 11.

so long as business stays within the framework of law established by society.[26] Others have picked up upon this theme by pointing out that one business can only have a minuscule effect on a problem such as illiteracy or training the hard-core unemployed. If each business tries to define what is socially responsible, there will be a lack of common direction or thrust. Another argument is that if one firm spends too much money on social problems, it will lower earnings to the point that the company can no longer attract capital for investment.

CONTEMPORARY SOCIAL RESPONSIBILITY

Despite arguments to the contrary, most large corporations feel that their social responsibility extends beyond simply earning profits. The power of social opinion is against those firms not taking overt social actions. Business options are increasingly restricted as a result of the changing climate of opinion on socially permissible conduct. Earning an adequate return is still considered the firm's primary social responsibility. If the company receives enough "dollar votes" for its goods and services to meet profit objectives, it must mean that the firm's output is meeting the material needs of society. But contemporary social responsibility also means development of environmental controls, providing equal employment opportunities, and much more.

Edward G. Harness, chairman of the board of Procter & Gamble, made the following comments about corporate responsibility to Procter & Gamble management:

The state provides a corporation with the opportunity to earn a profit if it meets society's needs. It follows inevitably that reported profits are the primary scorecard that tells the world how well a corporation is meeting its basic responsibility to society. . . .

For example, corporations in the United States pay nearly 40 percent of all the taxes collected at the federal, state, and local levels. Corporations in this country furnish over half of all the jobs, generate about two-thirds of the gross national product, and a similar share of the payroll dollars. I take real issue with the critics when they propose that corporations must put their other citizenship responsibilities ahead of their responsibility to earn a fair return for the owners. The only way in which corporations can carry their huge and increasing burden of obligations to society is for them to earn satisfactory profits. If we cannot earn a return on equity investment which is more attractive than other forms of investment, we die. I am not aware of any bankrupt corporations which are making important social contributions. . . . The corporation's proper role is to produce economic goods or services in the pursuit of profit. It takes no managerial skill to employ two people instead of one to generate the same quantity of goods or services. But how is society served if Procter & Gamble has twice as many people on the payroll and must pay them each only half as much because we have not increased sales?[27]

Another reason often given for social responsibility involving more than just earning a profit is the concept of **social power.** Keith Davis, a well-known management scholar, claims that social responsibility arises from social power.[28] He feels that the business community has immense social power. Its social responsibility therefore arises from concern about how its actions will affect society. Davis feels that business is obligated to take actions that protect and enhance society's interests. Social power exists, according to Davis, because the counsel of businesspeople is sought by government, and what businesspeople say and do influences their community. This type of influence is social power. It comes to businesspeople because they are leaders, intelligent people of affairs, people with a record of accomplishing projects successfully, and managers of vast economic resources. Power is a social resource which can be used for good or evil, and for social gain or loss.

If, in the long run, business does not use social power in a manner society considers responsible, it will lose that power. In other words, governmental regulation will supplant private enterprise. For example, the charging of excessive interest rates led to truth-in-lending legislation. Another example would be the creation of the Consumer Products Safety Commission. Business did not incorporate a sufficient number of safety features into new products to meet the needs of society, so the commission was created by legislation. Now product decision-making boundaries are constrained by laws and regulations on product safety.

THE ROLE OF GOVERNMENT

The multitude of laws and regulations issued by various levels of government have reduced the degree of voluntary social responsibility on the part of business. For example, laws, on nonreturnable containers have eliminated such containers in some states. The issue is no longer subject to decision by the bottlers. The growth of institutionalization via government decree is a major reason why executive interest in the issue may be waning. Efforts to demonstrate or "showcase" social responsibility have abated since the early 1970s. Instead, the prevalent attitude is, "Let's get on with it" in a no-nonsense fashion.

What should be the government's role in the consumerism phase of social responsibility? The *Harvard Business Review* survey discussed earlier suggests that the main function of government is to protect consumers against fraud, deceit, and the like (see Table 23.3). The consumer's responsibility is to be informed and to develop buying priorities. Business's major task, in turn, is to provide accurate decision-making information.

Government protects consumers through a variety of laws and agencies. You will recall, for example, our discussion of the legislation that deals with pricing —and that's only a single variable in the marketing mix. The major governmental bodies that handle consumer complaints are the following:

◢ States' attorney general's office.
◢ The Federal Office of Consumer Affairs (a catchall agency for complaint referrals).
◢ The Consumer Product Safety Commission (gives and receives much information on unsafe products).
◢ The Food and Drug Administration (similar to the CPSC, but for ingestibles).

- The Interstate Commerce Commission (handles household moving and shipping claims).
- The Civil Aeronautics Board is supposed to handle air travel complaints, but it simply refers them to the offending airline.

◀ **TABLE 23.3 Business, Government, and Consumer Responsibilities for Consumer Protection**

Consumer protection area	Group assigned primary responsibility for each consumer protection area[a]		
	Business	Government	Consumers
Providing adequate information to assist consumers in making purchase decisions	90%	6%	6%
Protecting consumers from abuses (e.g., fraud and deceit)	32	58	13
Protecting consumers from their own buying mistakes (e.g., a cooling-off period on door-to-door sales)	27	33	43
Protecting consumers from their own views of appropriate buying priorities	11	7	83

[a] Data sum to more than 100% across because of tie first-place votes.

Source: Stephen Greyser and Steven Diamond, "Business Is Adapting to Consumerism," *Harvard Business Review,* September–October 1974, p. 54. Copyright © 1974 by the President and Fellows of Harvard College; all rights reserved.

◀ **TABLE 23.4 Companies Responding Effectively to Consumer Pressures**

Company	Percentage of respondents mentioning company
American Motors	21.5%
Sears, Roebuck	13.0
Ford	12.9
General Motors	7.6
AT&T	6.4
General Electric	5.2
Whirlpool	4.1
IBM	2.4
Procter & Gamble	2.4
J. C. Penney	2.2
Zenith	1.9
Volkswagen	1.8
Xerox	1.8
Exxon	1.7
Maytag	1.7

Source: Stephen Greyser and Steven Diamond, "Business Is Adapting to Consumerism," *Harvard Business Review,* September–October 1974, p. 56. Copyright © 1974 by the President and Fellows of Harvard College; all rights reserved.

▲ FIGURE 23.1 An example of overzealous consumer protection: a person would have
to drink 1250 cans of Diet Pepsi a day to ingest the dose of saccharin
that is considered carcinogenic in rats.

Source: Courtesy of Pepsico, Inc.

As you can see, there is no shortage of sympathetic ears. Of course the costs of
protection are eventually passed on to the consumer in the forms of higher
prices and taxes. Also, not all regulations and decrees seem to be based on intelligent decisions making. Witness the public reaction to the proposed ban of
saccharin. A person must consume approximately 1250 diet soft drinks a day
to take in an amount of saccharin equivalent to the dose at which some rats develop bladder cancer (see Figure 23.1).

SOCIALLY RESPONSIBLE BUSINESSES

Many companies are taking the initiative in social responsibility rather than
waiting for governmental actions. Referring once more to the *Harvard Business
Review* study, Table 23.4 indicates which firms are perceived to be doing the

best job in responding to consumerism. These examples only scratch the surface, however. Many other firms provide a variety of social services, often with little fanfare. A few examples include these:

- Pennsylvania Power and Light Company pioneered the utility-consumer conference concept. It now conducts regular meetings between all PP&L departments and consumer panels.
- Shell Oil Company has distributed over 250 million driving and car booklets.
- Whirlpool Corporation spends over $500,000 annually operating a nationwide toll-free complaint line.
- Polaroid Corporation maintains a 300-person consumer services department to perform such tasks as rewriting ads that might mislead buyers and dropping in on Polaroid camera repair centers to check on quality.
- The American Association of Advertising Agencies has done extensive work to overcome functional illiteracy by establish the AAAA Literacy Center.

Organizing for marketing social responsibility

To engage in a program such as that of Polaroid requires planning and organization. It also required the efforts of the entire corporation and not just marketing. However, we will confine our discussion to the marketing aspects of social responsibility.

CONSUMER AFFAIRS DEPARTMENT

The vehicle for carrying out marketing social responsibilities is the consumer affairs department. Historically, these departments were created to handle consumer complaints and to develop and disseminate consumer-education materials. Some education programs are directed solely toward company products and services, such as S. C. Johnson and Sons booklets on decorating, gift-making, and antique furniture. Other departments take on broader social causes, such as the advertisement in Figure 23.2 from the American Council of Life Insurance. The progressive consumer affairs departments of the 1980s are monitoring company advertisements, providing input for product design, researching consumer satisfaction, developing warranties and guarantees, increasing product safety, overseeing product packaging and labeling, selecting suppliers, and improving quality control.[29]

The chief consumer affairs officer in many companies is taking on expanded policy-making duties. Decision areas where the head consumer affairs officer has a significant influence are shown in Table 23.5, which is based on survey responses by 153 consumer affairs executives.[30] During the remainder of the 1980s, consumer affairs departments will grow in influence over marketing activities. There will be an increase in the number of firms where the top

FIGURE 23.2 Consumer education as part of marketing's social responsibilities.

Source: Courtesy of American Council of Life Insurance.

consumer affairs person reports directly to the company's chief executive officer. Concurrently, consumer affairs departmental budgets will grow to meet new and expanding responsibilities.

TOP MARKETING EXECUTIVES' SOCIAL RESPONSIBILITIES

At the top echelon of marketing management, policies for social responsibility must be established and a marketing social responsibilities audit must be periodically undertaken.

Social responsibility policy. An example of broad social responsibility policies for marketing managers includes these tasks:

Change corporate practices that are perceived as deceptive. The consumer affairs division should identify corporate practices that are perceived as deceptive and/or antagonistic by consumers. These practices should be reviewed and a viable resolution of the problem developed. Examples of such corporate practices include packaging, credit, advertising, warranties, and the like.

Educate channel members to the need for a consumerism effort throughout the channel system. Recognition of the need for a consumerism effort by all members of the channel will aid in the development of an industry consumerism program which will enhance performance of the channel system and provide better customer satisfaction. Moreover, a firm must be willing to eliminate an organization from its overall channel system if that organization is unwilling or unable to work within the constraints of corporate policy.

Decision area	Percentage of consumer affairs officers indicating that they had "much" influence
Handling consumer inquiries	93.3%
Processing consumer complaints	86.8
Consumer education programs	79.4
Researching consumer satisfaction	74.3
Developing consumer orientation among executives	72.5
Improving employee attitudes toward consumers	72.2
Public relations programs	65.7
Product safety	51.1
Developing consumer orientation among dealers and distributors	46.4
Developing warranties and guarantees	44.2
Advertisements	43.5
Packaging and labeling	40.2
Quality control	38.2
Training service personnel	31.4
Establishing industry standards	23.8
Product design	22.9
Training sales personnel	22.0
Selecting suppliers	17.8

Source: Richard T. Hise, Peter L. Gillett, and T. Patrick Kelly, "The Corporate Consumer Affairs Effort," *MSU Business Topics,* summer 1978, p. 22. Reprinted by permission of the publisher, Division of Research Graduate School of Business Administration, Michigan State University.

Incorporate the increased costs of consumerism efforts into the corporate operating budget. Unless the consumer affairs division is budgeted sufficient money to carry out its mission, it will be little more than a facade and its effectiveness will be hampered. These costs will be reflected either in higher prices or lower margins unless the consumer program affects sales sufficiently to lower costs commensurately. To date little or no research exists to document the market responses to such programs. However, it does seem apparent that substantial costs will be incurred by firms not meeting their responsibilities to the consumer because of both governmental and legal actions.[31]

Social responsibility audit. After policies have been established, top marketing managers should conduct a periodic **social audit** to measure the gap between social objectives and social performance. One way to accomplish this is to examine the relationship between marketing efforts and social goals. This will aid in determining if the "right" amount of emphasis is being placed on desired social goals. The top half of Table 23.6 shows one evaluation framework.[32] Retail price, for example, can be important to the health and safety of customers if it is applied to a health care product. Packaging can be very important if misuse by adults or consumption by children could cause physical harm. Utility companies can use promotion to show consumers how to be more energy efficient.

Desired relationships between selected marketing variables and primary social goals[a]

Selected marketing variables	Primary social goals					
	Health and safety	Education, skills, and income level	Housing and recreational opportunities	Arts, science, nature, beauty	Leisure time	Freedom and harmony
Product planning						
Packaging, labeling	1	2	1	2	3	3
Physical product	1	2	1	2	2	3
Service	1	2	3	3	2	3
Distribution						
Transportation	1	3	2	2	3	3
Channels of distribution	3	2	3	2	2	3
Price						
Price level	2	3	2	3	3	3
Credit terms	3	2	3	3	3	3
Discount and allowances	3	3	3	3	3	3
Promotion						
Advertising	1	1	1	2	3	3
Personal selling	1	2	2	2	3	3
Sales promotion	2	2	2	3	3	3

Desired relationships between selected marketing variables and consumer rights[b]

Selected marketing variables	Consumer rights			
	Right to safety	Right to be informed	Right to choose	Right to be heard
Product planning	1	2	2	3
Distribution	2	3	2	3
Price	3	2	1	3
Promotion	1	1	1	2

[a] Key: 1 = maximum importance, 2 = moderate importance, 3 = minimum importance.

Source: A. H. Kizilbash, William O. Hancock, Carlton A. Maile, and Peter Gillett, "Social Auditing for Marketing Managers," *Industrial Marketing Management,* August 1979, pp. 4–5.

Another approach that is useful for the marketing manager is to determine which consumer rights are best protected through the marketing mix. By examining the relationship between the importance of specific consumer rights and the marketing mix, the social audit can help determine if the firm is maximizing the safeguarding of consumer interests. The lower half of Table 23.6 shows where a hypothetical firm feels it should place its emphasis to maximize consumer rights. It can then compare actual marketing emphasis to desired emphasis. For example, the primary emphasis in product planning should be protecting the consumer's right to safety. The actual audit might reveal that the organization is devoting more resources and time to product line extensions (the right to choose) than to product safety. The audit might also reveal that not enough emphasis is being placed on informative promotion that explains how to use a product properly and various safety precautions.

A broad social responsibility audit will help top managers determine if resources are properly allocated to maximize the firm's social responsibility efforts. The audit will also help to determine if new social responsibility policies need to be created, or if old policies need redirection. The broad social responsibility audit must be undertaken by top marketing managers. They have the responsibility for guiding the accomplishment of marketing's social objectives and creating a philosophy of sensitivity to social concerns throughout the marketing organization.

SUMMARY

Consumerism is essentially a struggle for power between buyers and sellers. However, the specific issues are not always clear. Consumerism is not new; the first consumer laws were passed in 1872. Modern consumerism is generally considered to have begun after World War II. President Kennedy's message on the rights of consumers (the right to safety, the right to be informed, the right to choose, and the right to be heard) provided the foundation for today's consumerism. The Federal Trade Commission is a major force overseeing the interests of all consumers. Today, consumerism seems to be returning to grassroots issues throughout the country.

A number of factors, both macro and micro, gave rise to the growth and permanence of today's consumerism. These include variables such as marketing efficiency, problems in measuring marketing output, fairness of the marketing system, and abuses in all areas of the marketing mix. At the micro level, individual firms are accused of not offering products and services that meet the needs of the marketplace, and of producing poor-quality merchandise and sometimes even products which are dangerous.

The business community's response to consumerism has not been overwhelming. Most industrial goods firms responded in a survey that they have not been affected at all by consumerism. Only half of the consumer goods companies stated that consumerism affected their organization. However, many organizations are taking a more positive approach to consumerism. They are organizing top-level management teams to identify consumer issues; key audiences are identified that they wish to reach regarding consumerism; and management often launches aggressive communication campaigns to defend their organizations.

Consumerism is closely tied to social responsibility. Social responsibility is business's concern for social welfare. Most large corporations feel that social responsibility extends beyond simply earning profits. The power of social opinion seems to be against those firms not taking overt social actions. Philosophically, social responsibility arises from social power. The business community has extensive social power and must therefore exercise it in a reasonable fashion or be subject to further government regulations.

Meeting social responsibilities requires both planning and organization. The vehicle for carrying out social responsibilities in large companies is the consumer affairs department. Historically these departments were little more than consumer complaint departments. Today, consumer affairs departments monitor company advertisements, provide input for product design, do research on consumer satisfaction, help develop warranties and guarantees, provide input for improving product safety, often oversee product packaging and labeling, may have input into supplier selection, and work to improve quality control.

Top marketing executives should be involved in social responsibility programs. They must establish social responsibility policies and conduct periodic social audits to measure the gap between social objectives and social performance.

KEY TERMS

Consumerism	Low ball pricing
Macro-micro dilemma	Stripped down price
Macro marketing mix	Social responsibility
Planned product obsolescence	Social power
Bait and switch pricing	Social audit

REVIEW QUESTIONS

1. What is consumerism?
2. What does social responsibility mean to you?
3. What is the social responsibility of the large corporation?
4. What is social power?
5. How has government become involved in the social responsibility of business?
6. In your own words, describe how a social responsibility audit may be undertaken.

DISCUSSION QUESTIONS

1. Have you ever been the "victim" of any of the tactics described in the chapter? If so, relate the incident and what you did in the situation. If not, choose a tactic and describe how you think you would react.
2. Do you agree with the view of consumerism being a balance of power? Why or why not?
3. Do you agree with the idea of consumer rights? What do you feel are your rights as a consumer?
4. How can the marketing department benefit from engaging in social responsibility programs?

NOTES

1. Excerpted from "Fuzzy Thinking on Madison Avenue," *Fortune,* June 16, 1980, pp. 73–76.
2. Florence Skelly, "Measuring Public Policy Pressures on Marketers," speech before the San Francisco Chapter of the American Marketing Association, March 11, 1976.
3. Ibid.
4. Philip Kotler, "What Consumerism Means for Marketers," *Harvard Business Review* 49 (May–June 1971): 48–49. Copyright 1971 by the President and Fellows of Harvard College; all rights reserved.
5. Norman Kangun, Keith Cox, James Higginbothom, and John Burton, "Con-

sumerism and Marketing Management," *Journal of Marketing* 39 (April 1975): 3–10.

6. Ralph Gaedeke, "The Muckraking Era," in Ralph Gaedeke and Warren Etcheson, eds., *Consumerism: Viewpoints from Business, Government, and the Public Interest* (San Francisco: Harper & Row, 1972), pp. 57–59.

7. Robert Herrmann, "The Consumer Movement in Historical Perspective," in David Aaker and George Day, eds., *Consumerism: Search for the Consumer Interest*, 2nd ed. (New York: Free Press, 1974), pp. 10–18; the original passage is from Upton Sinclair, *The Jungle* (Garden City, N.Y.: Doubleday, 1906).

8. This material is condensed from Colston Warne, "The Worldwide Consumer Movement," in Gaedeke and Etcheson, *Consumerism*, pp. 17–19.

9. Paul W. Stewart and J. Frederic Dewhurst, *Does Distribution Cost Too Much?* (New York: The Twentieth Century Fund, 1939).

10. Reed Moyer and Michael D. Hutt, *Macro Marketing*, 2nd ed. (New York: Wiley, 1978), p. 23.

11. Examples of distribution studies include: Stewart and Dewhurst, *Does Distribution Cost Too Much?* and Reavis Cox, *Distribution in a High Level Economy* (Englewood Cliffs, N.J.: Prentice-Hall, 1965). See also Harold Barger, *Distribution's Place in the American Economy* (Princeton, N.J.: Princeton University Press, 1955).

12. See Victor R. Fuchs, *Productivity Trends in the Goods and Services Sectors, 1929–61* (New York: National Bureau of Economic Research, 1964). Louis P. Bucklin, "A Synthetic Index of Marketing Productivity," paper presented at the Fifty-eighth International Marketing Conference of the American Marketing Association, Chicago, Illinois, April 1975, and Louis P. Bucklin, *Productivity in Marketing* (Chicago: American Marketing Association, 1978).

13. U.S. Bureau of Labor Statistics, "A Study of Prices Charged in Food Stores Located in Low and Higher Income Areas of Six Large Cities," February 1966, reproduced in *National Commission on Food Marketing, Technical Study No. 10,* June 1966, p. 122.

14. Howard Kunreuther, "Why the Poor May Pay More for Food: Theoretical and Empirical Evidence," *Journal of Business* 46 (July 1973): 368–383.

15. These factors are from Moyer and Hutt, *Macro Marketing*, pp. 138–139. Reprinted by permission of John Wiley & Sons, Inc.

16. Arthur Best and Alan Andreasen, *Talking Back to Business: Voiced and Unvoiced Consumer Complaints* (New York: Center for the Study of Responsive Law, 1976), p. 19; see also "Consumer Response to Unsatisfactory Purchases: A Survey of Perceiving Defects, Voicing Complaints and Obtaining Redress," *Law & Society Review* 11 (1977): 701.

17. Ibid., p. 39.

18. "Marketing Briefs," *Marketing News*, March 26, 1976, p. 3.

19. Christopher Gilson and Harold W. Berkman, *Advertising Concepts and Strategies* (New York: Random House, 1980), p. 65.

20. Frederick Webster, Jr., "Does Business Misunderstand Consumerism?" *Harvard Business Review* 51 (September–October 1973): 89–97.

21. "How To Deal With Professional Consumer Activists," *Marketing News*, August 10, 1979, p. 1.

22. Ibid.

23. Ibid.

24. Dow Votaw, "Genius Becomes Rare: A Comment on the Doctrine of Social Responsibility, Part I," *California Management Review* 15 (1972): 25. © 1972 by the Regents of the University of California. Reprinted only by permission of the Regents.

25. Steven Brenner and Earl Molandes, "Is the Ethics of Business Changing?" *Harvard Business Review* 55 (January–February 1977): 57–71.

26. See Milton Friedman, *Capitalism and Freedom* (Chicago: University of Chicago Press, 1962), and Theodore Levitt, "The Dangers of Social Responsibility," *Harvard Business Review* 36 (September–October 1958): 41–50.

27. Speech by Edward G. Harness entitled "Views on Corporate Responsibility," presented to Procter & Gamble management on December 8, 1977, at Cincinnati, Ohio.

28. Keith Davis, "Five Propositions for Social Responsibility," *Business Horizons,* June 1975, pp. 19–24.

29. Richard T. Hise, Peter L. Gillett, and J. Patrick Kelly, "The Corporate Consumer Affairs Effort," *MSU Business Topics,* summer 1978, pp. 17–26.

30. Ibid.

31. Richard Buskirk and James Rothe, "Consumerism—An Interpretation," in Gaedeke and Etcheson, *Consumerism,* p. 88.

32. A. H. Kizilbash, William O. Hancock, Carlton A. Maile, and Peter Gillett, "Social Auditing for Marketing Managers," *Industrial Marketing Management,* August 1979, pp. 1–6.

◢ CASES

23.1 Nestlé Incorporated

Everyone, including the infant-formula industry, agrees that breast feeding provides the best and cheapest nutrition for babies. Because mothers who are lactating are less likely to conceive, breast feeding also helps to space out births.

In the least developed parts of the Third World, breast feeding still prevails, but an overworked and poorly fed mother who is rearing many children in an urban slum without the help and support of the traditional family is often unable to continue producing enough milk to nourish her baby. At this point the question is not whether supplementary foods are needed, but which ones to use. The superiority of infant formula over all other infant foods other than breast milk is beyond dispute. Some substitutes, such as skim milk, lack sufficient fat and can cause dangerous dehydration.

Nestlé has about one-third of the Third World market for infant formula. Activists have accused Nestlé of deliberately "hooking" Third World mothers on formula by giving free samples to doctors and hospitals. The mothers stop lactating but cannot long afford a product that costs 50 cents for a day's ration. They charge that Nestlé is destroying the precious bond between the breast-feeding mother and her baby. As one activist puts it, "It links the capitalistic system and the way it organizes our lives to people's very personal existence." For several years now, the activists have been boycotting all Nestlé products. In fact, the campaign has gained support among some groups such as congressional staffs, research organizations, and even the bureaucracies of the federal government and the United Nations. One university professor said that scientific evidence left "no room" for doubt that Nestlé was guilty of for-profit infanticide.

1. How could Nestlé have prevented this public outcry in the first place?

2. You are a consultant to Nestlé. Outline a program to offset the claims made by the activists.
3. Do you think Nestlé is socially responsible? Why or why not?

23.2 East–West Manufacturing

East–West Manufacturing, one of the largest corporations in the United States, is a major manufacturer of consumer appliances as well as electrical engines, power plants, aircraft engines, and virtually any other product that makes or uses electricity. Hoping to capitalize on the ecology movement, it has come up with a new line called "homecology products." These items include an electric can opener for cleaner food (according to its ad) and an electric water conditioner for cleaner water. One new product that East–West touts is a small new electric washer/dryer combination that cleans clothes using less detergent.

Environmentalists have jumped on East–West with both feet. They say that its advertising comes suspiciously close to making the same old sales pitches in an ecologically fashionable vocabulary. The critics feel that such advertising is especially ironic when it comes from companies whose products or manufacturing facilities increase the demand for electric power (the production of which is a major, if indirect, source of pollution) or whose products wind up as substantial quantities of solid waste.

A few of the critics say that such promotion is blatantly false; others just say it is subtly deceptive. The cost of such advertising, they say, in some cases may far exceed the amount of money the companies are spending to directly reduce pollution or other environmental damage caused by their products and production facilities.

East–West defends its brand-new advertising campaign on the ground that the products advertised "create a better home environment." Also, the company says that its new washer unit uses 150 watts of electricity—less than a conventional washer. In response to the observation that the three new electrical products in the campaign use a total of 185 watts, or 35 watts more than the washer saves, an East–West spokesman says, "That's nitpicking."

Ann Boswell, vice-president for consumer affairs at East–West, is concerned about the adverse publicity that the new advertising campaign has generated. The president of East–West shares her concern. Yesterday he sent a memo to Boswell asking for a new policy whose goal is to make certain that this does not happen again. He also asked for a general procedure that would enable the company to take the initiative in matters related to consumerism rather than simply reacting to critics. He has asked Boswell to prepare a strategy that aggressively promotes East–West's good deeds and avoids mention of any negative actions by the company.

1. Prepare Ann Boswell's memo to the president.
2. How would you respond to the critics of East–West's new campaign? Is it reasonable for East–West to assume that there is a market for ecology-related products? If so, how should that market be approached? Part of Boswell's plan is to develop a social responsibility audit for the company. What should be included in a social responsibility audit?

24

Marketing in nonprofit organizations

OBJECTIVES

To learn how marketing can aid nonbusiness organizations.

To become aware of the unique characteristics of nonbusiness marketing.

To understand the process of implementing the marketing concept in a nonbusiness setting.

To gain awareness of the control problems and ethics of the nonbusiness organization.

With the help of the Ford Foundation, the Robert Sterling Clark Foundation, and the New York Community Trust, five dance companies developed a unique cooperative approach to ticket pricing, subscription offers, promotional planning, and budgeting for performances at the City Center. The program is called "Masters of American Dance."

Several distinct direct-mail subscription offers were tested to determine the popularity of different ticket combinations and the prices different groups of people will pay for them. This enabled the dance companies to target their subscription offers more effectively.

Multiple-offer testing lowered the risk associated with traditional ticket-selling techniques by allowing the public to indicate its purchase preference. It also increased subscription mailing cost effectiveness and accurately projected anticipated expenses and revenue.

In forming the cooperative, the five dance companies feel they can still "preserve artistic individuality," while affording themselves an opportunity to use techniques traditionally associated with profit-oriented marketing efforts.

The success of the program was due to enthusiastic receptiveness to the dance offer from outside the traditional dance market. The concept tapped a totally new market, a market not necessarily sophisticated with respect to modern dance, that is interested in sampling the companies at an attractive price.

One of the most popular options was the "$99 Subscription For Two." This provided two top-dollar seats to five dance performances for $99, a $50 savings off regular box office ticket prices.

Murray Louis, artistic director of the Murray Louis Dance Co., said that "this utilization by the arts of modern marketing techniques is long overdue."

"Marketing is a prime area where cost efficiencies can be enhanced without impairing artistic quality. For us, initiating an approach of this kind is vital to the preservation of City Center's long-standing policy of high artistic quality at moderate ticket prices."[1]

The Masters of American Dance program illustrates how marketing can help nonbusiness organizations accomplish their tasks effectively and efficiently. Ten years ago the broadened concept of marketing was in its infancy; today it is fully accepted by the academic community and by an increasing number of organizations.[2] Is profit and nonprofit marketing essentially the same thing? How about social marketing? Where does it come into the picture? How is the marketing mix actually applied in a nonbusiness environment? These are some of the major questions we will consider in this chapter.

The broadened concept of marketing

The **broadened concept of marketing** expanded the applications of marketing principles and techniques into the nonprofit sector. Within the nonprofit sector are organizations such as public transit companies and universities that are not attempting to further social causes. The New York Transit Authority, for example, is seeking more riders on its low-volume routes. It is not espousing social ideas. The Masters of American Dance must attract sufficient funds (donations and ticket sales) to pay performers, utility bills, set designers, and others. Even though they are nonprofit, nonbusiness organizations must meet expenses. This must be the primary objective, or the group will cease to exist. A secondary goal is maximum exposure to the target audience.

A second dimension of nonprofit marketing is **social marketing.** Social marketing has both macro and micro components. From a macro perspective, social marketing includes effecting social change (lowering the birth rate), furthering social causes (supporting your local police), and evaluating marketing and society relationships ("Should society allow politicians to be sold like candy bars?"). At the micro level are individual units and large groups (for example, The Southern Baptist Radio and Television Convention) that also have social goals, such as promoting brotherhood and good will. Such groups are concerned with the following marketing problems:

1. Defining target audiences.
2. Offering the right social products or services.
3. Developing the "right" promotions for social causes.
4. Distributing social goods and services.
5. Remaining financially solvent.

The uniqueness of nonprofit marketing

The tasks outlined above sound strikingly similar to those of a profit-oriented institution, but there are some important distinctions that make nonbusiness marketing (with or without social objectives) unique (see Figure 24.1).

ORGANIZATION STRUCTURE

One of the most important distinctions between profit and nonprofit groups is in organization structures. At General Motors, for example, the board delegates operating authority to the chief executive officers of the firm. These people, in turn, are held directly accountable for accomplishing the strategic goals of the company. Authority is vested in GM's top management to carry out the required tasks. Top management delegates authority to lower-level management to conduct day-to-day operations for which they are responsible.

Confused accountability. In nonbusiness groups there is often lack of direct line accountability, and it is often unclear to whom "management" is accountable.[3] Some nonbusiness organizations offer a service that can be delivered only by a professional staff. These might be professors at a university, musicians for an opera company, or doctors at a hospital. Professional leadership such as a medical board or university administration usually reports to a board of trustees, thus creating a direct line of accountability. Yet there may be other groups to which the professionals are accountable. Moreover, these groups are not accountable to the board of trustees, or the public, or the consumers of the service. Examples are a state medical board and the American Association of Collegiate Schools of Business (AACSB). The latter group "accredits" schools of business administration.

Conflicting goals. It is not uncommon for the goals of outside groups and the board of trustees to conflict. The board of trustees of a university might endorse a strategic plan to increase the number of night business students and to staff this growth with part-time instructors. But although this action would improve the university's financial position, it would also violate AACSB standards and thus jeopardize its accreditation.

In some organizations boards assume management responsibilities and volunteers occupy important line and staff positions. There may also be a hierarchy of volunteers, such as a service group within a hospital. These groups have their own leadership and staff and are rarely directly accountable to a paid administrative staff. At Boy Scouts of America there are assistant troop leaders, troop leaders, and district leaders, who are all volunteers. The volunteers are not responsible to the paid scouting staff that guides, assists, and helps motivate the volunteers.

Three lines of accountability. Thus nonprofits may have three different lines of accountability—voluntary workers, outside organizations, and the paid administrative hierarchy. From a marketing perspective these parallel and interacting networks sharing responsibility for delivery of a product or service can create many managerial problems. It is very hard to clarify accountability for delivery of the goods or services or to receive feedback about the quality of the service.

Each line of accountability may be working with different standards because goals are not congruent. The standard for the number of camping trips a scout troop takes per month might be set at one by a volunteer district scout leader. He or she realizes that if it is set much higher, the troop will lose its leaders. On the other hand, top scout executives (paid staff) have found through market research that camping is the primary factor that gets boys into scouting. Thus they may set a goal of two trips per month. Yet because there is no single line of authority, the executives are powerless to enforce the higher standard.

DUAL-TARGET MARKETS

Nonbusiness groups have **dual-target markets.** First, the organization must satisfy its sources of funds market target. Without funds, the second target market (receivers of services) becomes irrelevant.

◀ **FIGURE 24.2 Dual target audiences of nonprofit organizations.**

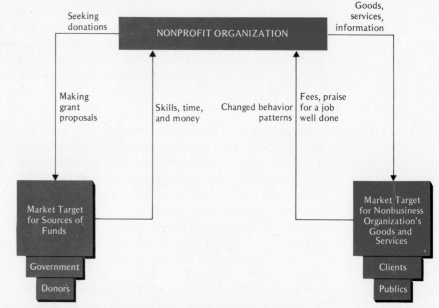

Chapter 24 MARKETING IN NONPROFIT ORGANIZATIONS

Funds target market. Sources of funds may be donors, government, or both (see Figure 24.2). The Department of Health and Human Services dispenses funds for many social programs. To tap this source, an organization must understand the various types of programs currently being funded, the project officer, how to write a grant proposal, and the political nuances in getting a proposal accepted.

Nonbusiness organizations must also understand their donor target market. Who are the "heavy donors"? What are their life style and demographic characteristics? What appeals unlock the coffers? Republican party fundraisers, for example, maintain lists of heavy donors. This is broken out by "interest areas," such as international relations and taxation, and by geographic regions. Candidates can buy the lists and send the target donors a "personalized" computer letter. It is important not only to identify the target donor, but also to make the right appeals (see Figure 24.3). Otherwise contributions will be fewer and smaller.

In addition to money, some organizations need people to volunteer their

---

◄ **FIGURE 24.3 UNICEF — "Voluntary Contributions" campaign.**

UNICEF Volunteers Across America

Across the United States, from the Hawaiian Islands to northern Maine, Anchorage to Key West, you will find hardworking, dedicated groups of UNICEF volunteers. UNICEF volunteers coordinate fund-raising campaigns and Greeting Card Sales programs, and also contribute their time and talent for community organizing, public speaking, education programs, and office work.

There are no typical UNICEF volunteers, only people who share one concern—children! Supporters range from the seven-year-old down the block who rings your doorbell on Halloween, to such celebrities as Pearl Bailey and the Bee Gees. Businessmen and homemakers, flight attendants and student councils—these are the people UNICEF is privileged to work with in helping to bring the neediest children in the world a better start in life.

UNICEF Greeting Cards

A holiday greeting . . .

a birthday wish . . . a note of thanks . . .

a postcard message . . . a gift for a child . . .

UNICEF Greeting Card sales fill these needs—but the profits fill the needs of UNICEF's children.

You may buy cards for yourself through our mail order catalog. Better still, you can sell UNICEF cards, gifts and stationery through consignment. Each year over 1000 groups, civic organizations, commercial outlets and individuals sell UNICEF greeting cards, gifts and stationery in their communities. Obviously, the potential is much, much greater! UNICEF "shops" may be set up in banks and schools, in office building lobbies and private homes, at street fairs and flea markets, in church and temple bazaars . . . just about anywhere, any place and any time of the year. Our consignment brochure will help you decide where you can best help.

The UNICEF Gift Card Program

You can add special meaning to any occasion—and help a child—through the UNICEF Gift Card Program. Celebrate birthdays, anniversaries, graduations, weddings, Mother's Day, Father's Day, the birth of a new baby—or convey feelings of sympathy—with a UNICEF Gift Card. You may make a donation to UNICEF in the name of a friend or relative and we will send an appropriate card announcing your gift. Send for the new gift card brochure and order form.

National UNICEF Day

Declared National UNICEF Day by Presidential proclamation, October 31 is the day when millions of Americans show their concern for the world's children by rallying to support the work of UNICEF. For more than 25 years, money raised from the traditional Trick or Treat collection and innumerable hunger banquets, benefit sports events, shopping center collections, carnivals and other activities have helped to insure a brighter future for children all over the world. Activity outline sheets, posters, leaflets and publicity kits are available free of charge to help you organize your school, group or community for National UNICEF Day.

Music for UNICEF

. . . is a gift of song. Started by the Bee Gees, MUSIC FOR UNICEF activities are being held across the United States to benefit the Children's Fund. A special kit (tips on how to plan and publicize a MUSIC FOR UNICEF benefit event, suggested activities, sample press releases and radio spots, posters and basic information) is available, free, so that you, too, can help put music to work for children.

Adopt-A-Project

. . . at UNICEF Day or any other time of the year! Your group can now select a UNICEF-assisted project and earmark funds raised for that project. Special country / project information kits are available at no cost on selected UNICEF-assisted countries and worldwide child care projects. All kits include a photo wallsheet and detailed study guide. Accompanying slide sets are also available at a slight charge.

Here's how the funds you raise will help children:

$1.00 Provides enough high-dose Vitamin A capsules to protect 50 toddlers against nutritionally-caused blindness for one year

$5.00 Stocks a rural village pond with baby fish for a potential protein supply

$30.00 Will buy a baby scale for a mother-child health center

$100.00 Supplies five midwifery kits for village birth attendants who are trained to teach mothers the importance of good prenatal nutrition

$311.00 Provides one set of applied nutrition equipment so that nutrition workers can teach rural mothers to cook better-balanced meals.

Source: "How Can I Help UNICEF's Children's Program?" (New York: U.S. Committee for UNICEF), 1980.

699

THE UNIQUENESS OF NONPROFIT MARKETING

time. This also requires identifying the target volunteer and appealing to him or her. The Campfire Girls know that mothers of elementary school children are prime prospects for Campfire leaders. In one city, Campfire Girls hold coloring contests (coloring is a Campfire activity) to build child and ultimately parent interest. At the beginning of the school year an organizational meeting is held to recruit new members and adult leaders. Attendance is enhanced by announcing the coloring contest winners and giving prizes. Before the awards ceremony, a professional multimedia presentation is made about the merits of being a Campfire leader. In this manner, the organization meets its volunteer needs.

Service user target market. In most cases the beneficiary of the nonprofit organization's services or goods is not a primary financial contributor. A primary goal of most groups is to increase the number of transactions between the target market and the organization. A transit company must identify characteristics of potential bus riders and develop a marketing mix that will meet their needs. A politician must find out who the "swing voters" (not heavily committed to the party) are, his image among this group, and the issues that concern them. A consumer education group may define its user target audience as Spanish-speaking families in cities of over 500,000 population, with total family incomes of under $12,000.

What is the return to nonbusiness organizations? The consumer education group, for example, trains community leaders in "how to be a more efficient consumer." The leaders, in turn, go into the residential areas and conduct consumer education seminars. One of their "products," offered at no charge, is where to obtain the least costly sources of credit. Another booklet explains various types of life insurance. What is the payback? It is better-educated consumers. It is knowing that people are better off because of the organization's efforts. In this case, the rewards and returns are psychic rather than monetary.

NONPROFIT OBJECTIVES

A third major distinction between profit and nonprofit organizations is lack of a profit orientation. Instead of profit, the nonbusiness organization has goals such as social benefits and services. This means that success or lack thereof cannot be measured in financial terms. The Methodist Church, for example, does not gauge its success by the amount of money in the offering plates. The Museum of Science and Industry does not base its performance evaluations on the number of dollar tokens put into the turnstile.

On the other hand, revenues are always a factor. If an organization is running at a deficit something must usually be done, at least in the long run, to correct the situation. When an organization such as The Humane Society charges a fee for spaying a pet or your adopting one of its animals, it may still have expenses greater than revenues. If the United Way continually covers the Humane Society deficit each year, it means that the "social profit" from providing the service is greater than the financial costs. This means that the public sector, through its representatives, such as the board of directors of the

United Way, has a line of authority over the nonbusiness organization. If the external board is not in agreement with the organization goals, next year's funding may not be forthcoming.

GOODS AND SERVICES

Profit-making firms produce goods and services that are generally marketed as private property. A television set, a will, or new suit are all purchased as private property. The satisfaction is divisible among individual purchasers. If you do not buy a new suit, you do not experience the pleasure of having new clothes. So in the private profit-oriented sector, a good or service is normally available exclusively to the individual. You do not have to share your suit with anyone else. Of course, you may share the style and material with many other purchasers of identical articles of clothing!

The nonbusiness sector usually offers services, instead of goods, which are often collectively consumed. Usually such services are socially beneficial and/or recognized as aiding groups, the community, or society as a whole. We collectively consume a prettier environment brought forth by the Keep America Beautiful antilitter campaign. A country club membership results in collective social payoffs for the group. A community gains better health care when it establishes its own nonprofit hospital.

CONCERN FOR SOCIAL COSTS

A fifth distinction between business and nonbusiness organizations is concern or sensitivity about social costs. Obviously nonbusiness organizations with social goals, such as the American Heart Association and the American Cancer Society, strive to make sure that the social costs of their groups are minimal and that net social benefits will be consistent with the long-run interests of society. Even in nonbusiness organizations that have something other than social considerations as their primary objective, there is still awareness of and concern about social costs. Many police departments, for example, burn propane rather than gasoline to help lower the demand for gasoline and minimize environmental pollution. A number of fine arts groups give free concerts or showings to the aged and the underprivileged. Universities offer inexpensive noncredit courses to help people within the community to broaden their interests and horizons.

PUBLIC SCRUTINY

The final distinction between business and nonbusiness organizations is the degree of public scrutiny. Government marketing activities such as recruiting by the armed services, setting new postage rates, tourism campaigns by cities and states, and the "services" offered by a national park are open to public review. Not all nonbusiness groups provide a public service. Yet where public services are provided, they must generally meet society's "standards," since the taxpayer is footing the bill. For example, there was a great public outcry when parts of Yosemite National Park were closed to automobile traffic. The city of Miami Beach came under fire when its travel posters were considered "too risqué."

Political pressures can also influence the nonbusiness organization. Amtrack routes, for example, continue to go through highly unprofitable areas. But they do pass through states where powerful politicians reside. The U.S. Postal Service continues Saturday mail delivery and maintains many rural post offices in thinly populated areas partially due to political pressures. Austin, Texas, was the beneficiary of many new federal regional offices during the Johnson administration. The LBJ ranch is less than 90 miles from Austin.

Applying the marketing concept in a nonprofit setting

Despite the differences between business and nonbusiness organizations, general marketing principles apply in both areas (see Figure 24.4).

PLANNING

The first step in implementing a marketing program is to develop a strategic marketing plan. The marketing manager must define the organization's mission by asking "What service are we attempting to offer?" A political organization may define its mission as "the election of Albert Jackson to the presidency."

◀ FIGURE 24.4 The marketing concept in a nonprofit environment.

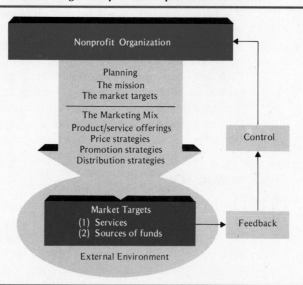

The March of Dimes changed its mission from "the fight against polio" to "the fight against birth defects." The Campfire organization broadened its mission from "serving young girls" to "serving young children." A large Texas country club decided it was not just in the "country club business," but in the "social, educational, and recreational business." With the new mission agreed upon, the group bought a used airliner to take its members on private tours, to football games, and so forth.

The target market. Both business and nonbusiness organizations need a clear definition of their target audience. Often nonbusiness groups define their target audiences in terms that do not allow for effective planning. To say "we are here to serve the community" or "we want to help all people" is useless. For virtually every good or service there are those who are "heavy users," or persons with "greater needs," versus those with "moderate needs." Even in the area of cancer screening, there are some people with greater needs than others, as demonstrated in the example below.

The target market may be segmented into two groups: the health consumers and the supporting agents. The health consumer market includes the potential screenees and the general adult public. Potential screenees are the ultimate consumers, while the general adult public, which serves as a powerful influence group, comprises potential screenees and younger people not yet old enough to qualify for periodic screening tests. These groups are differentiated in terms of their roles. For example, potential screenees are asked to participate in the screening program, whereas the general adult public is encouraged to initiate and promote participation of friends and relatives who are eligible for screening.

Potential screenees include consumers who fit the risk profile for a particular disease. This population can be broadly identified according to age, sex, geographic location, socioeconomic level, race, and religion. Cancer screening programs are generally aimed at men and women over the age of 40, who live within the catchment area of the health facility. Forty is considered the appropriate starting point because this is the age at which screening for early detection is most effective in breast, colon, and uterine cervical cancers, which begin to appear in significant numbers.

The market of supporting agents includes external and internal groups that provide credibility, approval, and the support needed by a screening service. Of the possible sites for screening, consider the example of a hospital-based service. Here, external groups may include the media, potential donors, social and civic organizations [and so forth]. . . . Internal groups may include organizational governing committees and administration, medical staff and employees, the Board of Trustees, the Development Office, the Health Education Department. . . .[4]

Another example of target market definition in the health care field is in family planning. The primary target was defined as "low-income, underprivileged, fecund females between the ages of 15 and 44." It was further segmented by urban and rural customers and various age groups. This was because urban and rural customers and younger women demonstrated different behavioral patterns. Thus the approaches to each group varied.[5]

Information systems aid planning. Using segmentation to identify market targets requires solid market information. Market research, for example, can help identify segments, measure attitudes toward existing services, and aid in the creation of an effective marketing mix. Attitudes toward various modes of transportation were used as a basis of segmenting potential users of mass transit. The research suggested a strong link between perceptions of modal attributes and the selection of a particular mode of transportation. For example, existing transit users had a much more favorable attitude toward bus travel than nonusers.[6] For most attributes there was a significant difference in attitudes of the two groups (see Figure 24.5). This type of data can be very useful when planning the marketing mix.

PRODUCT/SERVICE OFFERINGS

The product/service offering is the heart of marketing for both businesses and nonbusinesses. The product may be social interaction, education, health care, toys for poor children at Christmas. But whatever it is, it must satisfy the needs of the target market. If the product/service is not delivering "value" (either social or economic), then donor or government funds will ultimately dry up. This means that the business mission and goals must be properly defined and target markets accurately identified. The American Cancer Society, for example, is in the business of fighting cancer. Its product line includes research, treatment, informing the public, and working with governmental regulatory agencies.

The U.S. Postal Service has defined its mission in several areas: First, it is in the communications business with message transfer services like first class mail. Second, it is in the media business by using the mail to deliver advertising messages. Third, it is in the material handling business with products and services like parcel post. Fourth, it is in the financial business. The Postal Service has the best-selling money order brand in the country.[7] By conceptualizing its lines of business, what is feasible, and its strengths and weaknesses, the Postal Service has developed several new product offerings. Examples include Mailgrams, Express Mail, and Control Pack. Each new service was first conceptualized through market research and then refined via test marketing.

Research has also been used to help create a better "product line" for the church.[8] One major denomination used surveys to ascertain what topics would be of major interest to its flock (see Table 24.1). Answers were also broken out by type I members (leaders in their individual churches) and type II members (random selections from church rolls). Additional statistical techniques applied to the data enable church leaders (managers) to see how members (consumers)

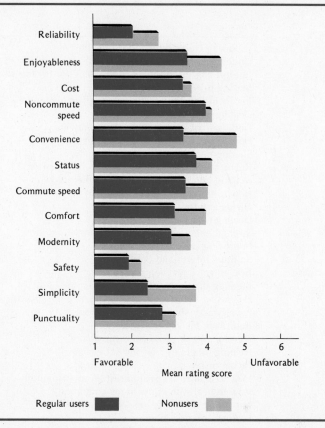

Regular users ▮   Nonusers ▮

Source: Christopher H. Lovelock, "A Market Segmentation Approach to Transit Planning, Modeling, and Management," in *Readings in Public and Nonprofit Marketing,* eds. Christopher H. Lovelock and Charles B. Weinberg (New York: The Scientific Press, 1978), p. 107.

viewed the interrelationships of the various topics. Church management was able to identify seven "educational packages" that were essentially unrelated in the eyes of consumers.

McCollum/Speilman Advertising Agency has created a Health Message Testing Service for assessing audience response to public service messages. The product being offered is public interest information. Research helps the agency create the "right" product for message impact. McCollum/Speilman has found that it is quite effective to confront the public with the victim of a severely debilitating ailment. In one striking 30-second message from the United Way, a man speaking from his hospital wheelchair thanked the public for the contributions that were making possible his recovery. A dramatic opening line, "Have you any idea what it's like to have a stroke?" was an important factor in getting the viewers' attention.

Topic area	Mean rating[a]
Following God's direction for my life	1.9
Understanding other people's ideas and feelings	2.0
Interpreting the meaning of the Bible for my life	2.0
Making prayer more meaningful	2.0
Improving communication among family members	2.0
Dealing with drug abuse	2.1
Finding what is most important in my life	2.1
How to make decisions about right and wrong	2.1
Sharing my faith with others	2.1
Facing personal crises	2.2
Helping people without "putting them down"	2.2
How to find the best in people	2.2
Giving and receiving affection	2.2
Dealing with conflicts	2.2
Strengthening my ability to counsel with people	2.2
Improving services of worship	2.3
Spiritual rebirth and conversion	2.3
How to solve problems	2.3
Meeting the needs of people in a community	2.4
Expressing my ideas and feelings	2.4
Poverty and what can be done about it	2.5
Improving my skills as a teacher	2.5
Developing my own leadership ability	2.5
Helping others to plan and set goals	2.5
Facing death	2.5
How to deal with social unrest in my community	2.6
How to deal with crime in my community	2.6
Improving my ability to speak in public	2.7
Ecology and pollution	2.7
Developing my ability to lead small groups	2.7
Improving community health care	2.7
Improving participation in an organization	2.7
Famous and ordinary people talking about their lives and faith	2.7
Issues of war and peace	2.7
How to plan for my old age	2.8
The prison system	2.8
Improving my ability to use arts and news media in working with others	2.8
How to build and use a family budget	2.9
Great religious leaders of the past	3.0
Equal employment opportunity	3.0
The meaning of sex	3.0
Population problems	3.0
The religions of the world	3.0
Integrating a community	3.2
The history of minority groups	3.3
Becoming involved in political action	3.4
Women's rights and liberation	3.6

[a] Mean Rating for each topic area is simply the mean importance given that topic area by all respondents. 1.0 = of highest importance; 5.0 = of little importance.

Source: James L. Ginter and Wayne Talarzyk, "Applying the Marketing Concept to Design New Products," *Journal of Business Research,* January 1978, pp. 51–66.

In a similarly oriented effort, in a 60-second spot sponsored by the High Blood Pressure Education Program, a hospitalized victim reminded the public that he was "proof positive" of the serious consequences of not taking high blood pressure medication during periods of temporary well-being or remission. Research showed that highly charged human interest in both messages had strong emotional impact which translated into significantly positive attitudinal changes.[9]

DISTRIBUTION

In addition to offering the "right product/service" mix, nonbusiness organizations must have good channels of distribution. Service distribution channels, whether profit or nonprofit, are usually short. The provider of the services typically offers them directly to the user. This is not always true, however; one example is the case of Montgomery Ward selling memberships in the U.S. Auto Club.

Marketing-oriented nonprofit organizations attempt to locate the source of the services close to potential users. Medical clinics are often set up in low-income areas to meet the health care needs of the neighborhood. Branch libraries are established to make obtaining books less trying. Universities set up extension courses in downtown office buildings and even on commuter trains. Public transportation routes are changed to meet population migration patterns.

Fund solicitations also require good channels of distribution. That is, monies must flow upward to the nonbusiness organization (**reverse-flow channel**). The Salvation Army places its kettles in high foot traffic areas during the Christmas season. The donations then flow primarily to local units, with a small amount going to the national office. Perhaps the most sophisticated fund channel is the annual Jerry Lewis MD Telethon. Thousands of local telephone numbers are used to collect pledges at the grassroots level. Totals are then aggregated by the state or regional area, which provides the "local talent and personalities" for the local portion of the annual program. Finally, the total gifts are reported nationally in Las Vegas, where Jerry Lewis and his staff coordinate the "superstar" entertainment portion of the program.

PRICING

Nonprofit firms do not have to create black ink on the ledger sheet, but they are expected to be financially responsible. Sometimes the services they provide are free or provided at low prices. A number of nonprofit operations attempt to charge enough to meet their operating expenses—wages, costs of supplies, utilities. They want donors or taxpayers to cover their fixed plant and equipment costs. As long as the social benefits are justified, donors and government will continue to provide long-term capital and even operating funds.

It may be very desirable for an organization to charge enough for services to "break even." If an organization can avoid the need for donations or government largess, it can avoid at least one line of accountability within the organization structure. Management will not have to spend large amounts of time and effort defining target donors or government agencies, creating proposals and funds solicitation programs, and so forth. It will not have to worry about justifying its existence to a third party.

Museums, symphonies, and hospitals charge a fee, but many organizations, such as the National Safety Council, cannot. If services such as those of a family planning clinic are provided free but are still underutilized, managers must determine if there are psychic costs involved that discourage use. Long waiting lines, rude and disinterested employees, location, and hours of operation may be creating the problem. These are considered **psychic costs** that discourage use. There may also be a **psychic price** a person is expected to pay if he or she uses a service. For example, Alcoholics Anonymous charges a "psychic price" of a commitment not to drink and a public admission of one's problem. Some rescue missions demand that a person sing religious songs and pray before they offer a hot meal and a place to sleep.

Not all persons charged a fee pay the same amount. Family counselors who work for state and local governments charge according to total family income. Sometimes organizations such as legal clinics give price breaks to students and the elderly. Many hospitals will charge a patient little or nothing if he or she will donate a pint of blood for every one received. In a different sense, wealthy donors are expected to contribute more to a group than others.

PROMOTION

Some nonprofit organizations place their primary marketing emphasis on promotion. Keep America Beautiful, political campaigns, and groups dedicated to encouraging people to have themselves checked (or check themselves) for various diseases, are largely promotional organizations. Their ultimate goal is to persuade someone to change behavior or take some action. These campaigns are conducted through the mass media and rely on public service time and space (see Figure 24.6), or they are paid announcements.

Social marketing promotion campaigns do not seek interaction with an individual. They are not asking donations or for someone to purchase or use their goods and services. The "Drive 55" and "Arrive Alive" programs are examples of social marketing campaigns.

Personal selling. Not all promotion by nonbusiness organizations is through the mass media. Representatives of the armed services travel to college campuses to recruit volunteers. United Way campaigns choose community leaders for their boards of directors. These leaders are expected to sell the merits of the United Way organization to other prominent members of the community. Colleges and universities usually have an individual on staff who is a professional fundraiser. He or she visits wealthy alumni and others within the community for major donations. Four percent of the contributors to the Harvard College Fund account for 70 percent of the total contributions.[10] Some religious organizations rely very heavily on personal selling. Missionaries and evangelists often "spread the word" among the unholy. Mormons and the Jehovah's

FIGURE 24.6 Public service advertisement for Boy Scouts of America.

When you help start a Scout troop, there's no guarantee one of the Scouts will grow up to be in the Movies.

But you never know.

For all the facts on how your organization can support a Scout troop, call Boy Scouts of America. The sponsors of Troop 3, Indiana Pennsylvania did, and look what they've got to show for it.

SCOUTING USA

Prepared as a Public Service by Foote Cone & Belding Inc

Jimmy Stewart, actor

Source: Courtesy of Boy Scouts of America.

Witnesses use young church people to do little but "sell" the church for a period of time.

Sales promotion. Another form of promotion used by these organizations is sales promotion. Handicraft groups sometimes have catalogs; many organizations pass out brochures that explain their activities and advantages; states set up travel booths at sport and recreation shows; the National Safety Council offers free films to schools and other groups. A number of states have also used sweepstakes as a source of funds. Observing the success of the state lotteries, the National Foundation for Cancer Research decided to follow suit, as described below.

The National Foundation for Cancer Research (NFCR) sent out 3,000,000 sweepstakes packets at a cost of $400,000. Among the 128 donated prizes were a two-week vacation in Bermuda and Acapulco, a new car, $5,000, console stereos, color TVs, watches, pocket calculators and cameras.

While the use of a sweepstakes may be an effective fund-raising tool, it is frowned upon when used by nonprofit organizations. According to the National Information Bureau, an independent, nonprofit, watchdog agency which oversees fund-raising activities of 300 companies, the NFCR does not meet its standards.

The bureau advises fund raisers to solicit contributions "without payment of commissions or undue pressure, such as mailing unordered tickets or merchandise, general telephone solicitation and use of identified government employees as solicitors."

The bureau noted that sweepstakes mailings are considered the same as sending "unordered tickets and merchandise." In addition, the added cost of printing sweepstakes tickets takes money away from research. A spokesperson from the NFCR countered that if the foundation had an additional $1,000,000— above its anticipated revenue—a cure for cancer would be imminent.[11]

Although the National Foundation for Cancer Research relies heavily on promotion, many public organizations have traditionally been opposed to using this marketing tool. The idea was, "if people want our service, they will come and get it." Also, the value of promotion campaigns was hard to measure and thus hard to justify. Some nonprofit organizations considered promotion nothing more than "crass commercialism." This attitude seems to be changing, however, as more organizations become marketing-oriented.

CONTROLLING THE MARKETING MIX

The growing emphasis on marketing has also meant that more attention is being paid to control. The basic control procedure discussed in Chapter 22 is the same for both profit and nonprofit organizations. Historically, many managers of nonprofit organizations have been motivated to enter their fields by altruism. The desire to "help someone" or "make the world a better place to live" often led to the assumption that the manager would do the "right thing" or take action for the "good of the organization." Unfortunately, lack of management training on the part of both paid administrators and volunteers led to poor and sloppy control systems.

Part of the problem is that the output of many nonprofit organizations cannot be measured in financial returns. A program designed to improve the image of the local police department has no direct financial return, since consumers are not purchasing a service. Because programs are not measured by financial returns, some managers have used this as an excuse for not establishing control systems. Yet lack of a control system can create a serious misuse of funds or inadequate service to the target audience:

The director of a large social service agency in a New England state was told at fiscal midyear that unexpectedly lower tax revenues had forced a 5% reduction in his budget (or about $100 million). The distribution of the cut among the different programs was left to his judgment, but he couldn't respond to the order in a reasonable manner because he lacked the resources that would have given him the needed information.

Lacking relevant information, he had to make a judgment solely on the basis of political considerations. He chose to cut the budgets of those programs affecting people with the least political influence—abandoned children and the mentally retarded.[12]

This situation could have been avoided with clear, measurable objectives, realistic standards, and a good feedback system. When goals are set, care must be taken to establish standards that will insure activities geared toward goal accomplishment. For example, the U.S. Department of Labor developed some elaborate objectives to train the hard-core unemployed and place them in jobs that would be meaningful and long-lasting. The primary standard was the number of people placed in jobs. Local directors of manpower programs got the message: they accepted applications only from people temporarily unemployed or those with a high probability of being placed. The placement rate was high, but those who really needed help were ignored.

When a nonprofit group is attempting to build awareness or change attitudes, the standard advertising tests discussed in Chapter 18 are often used as control devices. These tests are also used in fund drives. For example, an objective of the March of Dimes was to increase consumer association of birth defects with the March of Dimes. A precampaign audit yielded a 30.9 percent combined aided and unaided recall for the March of Dimes and birth defects. A second audit conducted a week after a direct mail campaign showed that the figure had risen to 45.3 percent (a 50 percent increase). A third audit, conducted a week after a mothers' march, yielded a recall figure of 61.2 percent (a 100 percent increase from the pretest). Donations increased by one-third over the previous year.[13] By setting recall standards for each promotion activity and then measuring results, March of Dimes management has developed a valuable control system.

Ethics in nonprofit marketing

To some people in nonprofit organizations, marketing is synonymous with selling. In their eyes, selling is "high-pressure persuasion" and manipulating people. Thus it is not uncommon to find persons within nonprofit groups who perform most or all of the activities of a marketing manager without the title. This person may be called program director, business manager, public relations officer — anything but what the person really is.

It is unfortunate that administrators and the general public do not place marketing in a proper perspective. Marketing is simply a managerial philosophy (with commensurate tools) to aid organizations in accomplishing their goals. It is not enough for management to be "socially concerned." To get the job done, there must also be good managers. This is true whether the person is managing a free medical clinic, hospital, country club, or the Army's recruitment program.

The question of what marketing techniques are ethical for nonprofit organizations is difficult to ascertain. Is it unethical, for example, for the National Foundation for Cancer Research to administer a sweepstakes? What if the sweepstakes earnings led to a major breakthrough in cancer research? One German campaign showed a simple headshot of an apparently benevolent, grandfatherly old man. Under his picture was a multiple-choice question: "Is this a picture of a stamp collector / grocer / chess player / child molester?" Another ad used brutal shots of a man's hand groping for his fly, and of the spraddled legs and torn panties of a recently raped little girl.[14] Are both or either of these ads unethical, or are they simply in poor taste? On the other hand, does it take this kind of "shock promotion" to drive home the importance of the problem?

The question of what is ethical marketing behavior for nonprofit organizations engaged in social marketing depends upon whom one is asking (see Table 24.2). It also appears difficult to separate the ethics of applying marketing techniques to social ideas and programs from the ethics of the ideas themselves. This is particularly true from the point of view of nonmarketers. All groups within the study whose results are shown in Table 24.2 agreed that if marketers assist nonprofit organizations to diffuse social issues or ideas, the marketers should be held accountable for their actions. For example, the Indian government, during Indira Gandhi's first administration, sponsored systematic communications campaigns to promote family planning. Since this idea was not popular with the public, those helping disseminate the concept, as well as the sponsors, were held in some contempt.[15]

Ethical questions vary not only by those being asked, but also by country and time. The child molester campaign mentioned above would not be shown in the United States today. It would probably be considered unethical by most Americans. Yet time can change that which is considered unethical. During the gasoline shortages, "topping off" your gas tank was viewed by many as unethical.

SUMMARY

The broadened concept of marketing first expanded the application of marketing principles and techniques into the nonprofit sector. The second dimension of nonprofit marketing has been social marketing, which has both macro and micro components. At the macro level, it includes how to affect social change, such as lowering the birth rate or furthering social causes. It also includes evaluating marketing and society relationships. At the micro level, individual organizations, such as churches, also have social goals like promoting brotherhood, peace, and understanding. These organizations must (1) find their target audiences, (2) offer the right social products and services, (3) develop the right promotions for social causes, (4) distribute social goods and services, and (5) remain financially solvent.

Nonprofit organizations are unique for several reasons. First, their organization structures are quite different from those of profit-making institutions. Nonprofit organizations may have three different lines of accountability: voluntary workers, outside organizations such as accreditation groups, and the paid administrative hierarchy. Each line of accountability may be working with different standards because goals are not synonymous. A second factor that distinguishes nonprofit from profit-making organizations is dual target markets—a funds target and a service target. The third major distinction between profit and

Statement	Ethicians (n = 71)	Economic historians (n = 80)	Social psychologists (n = 70)	Marketing practitioners (n = 88)	A priori test significance between 4 groups	Ex post facto test marketing practitioners vs. all others
A. The utilization of marketing techniques with respect to social issues or ideas will help communicate these causes in a more effective manner.	3.8	3.8	4.0	4.5	.001	.001
B. The application of marketing techniques to diffuse social issues and ideas is not a beneficial development.	3.4	3.0	2.5	2.0	.001	.001
C. The application of marketing techniques to diffuse social issues and ideas raises significant ethical questions.	4.8	4.4	4.5	3.8	.001	.001
D. The application of marketing techniques to social issues and ideas is a step toward a society wherein the opinions held by the population can be manipulated.	4.2	4.1	4.0	3.7	.001	.001
E. Marketers who assist others in diffusing social issues or ideas should be held strictly accountable for their actions.	4.7	4.5	4.6	4.2	.005	.005
F. A professional certification board which would "license" marketers (much like the American Bar Association certifies attorneys) should be formulated to control marketers working to diffuse social issues or ideas.	2.9	1.6	3.3	2.0	.001	not tested
G. Marketers working to diffuse social issues or ideas should be regulated by a new government review board.	2.5	1.4	2.5	1.3	.001	not tested
H. When judging the application of marketing techniques to social programs or ideas in terms of their ethical appropriateness, one cannot separate the techniques from the ideas themselves.	4.1	3.4	3.8	2.3	.001	.001

Note: Numbers in table are median responses to a five point scale with (1) = strongly disagree, (2) = moderately disagree, (3) = neither agree nor disagree, (4) = moderately agree, and (5) = strongly agree. Significance level is for a one-way Kruskal-Wallis analysis of variance.

Source: Gene R. Laczniak, Robert F. Lusch, and Patrick E. Murphy, "Social Marketing: Its Ethical Dimensions," *Journal of Marketing,* spring 1979, p. 31.

nonprofit organizations is the lack of a profit orientation. A fourth distinction is that nonprofit organizations usually offer services rather than goods, and these services are collectively rather than individually consumed. A final distinction is that nonprofit organizations tend to be subject to more public scrutiny than private institutions.

The marketing concept in a nonprofit setting is applied in essentially the same manner as within a profit-making organization. First there must be strategic planning to establish the mission of the group. The dual market targets must be identified and analyzed, and an information system must be established to monitor the external environment. Next, a marketing mix is created to reach target markets. A control system is established to monitor the marketing mix.

Sometimes an ethical question may arise as to which marketing techniques should be used. For example, is it ethical for a museum to hold a lottery to raise funds? Is it ethical to show mutilated accident victims in an attempt to get people to "drive 55"? It is difficult to separate the ethics of applying marketing techniques to social ideas and programs from the ethics of the ideas themselves. If marketers assist nonprofit organizations to achieve their objectives, then the marketers should be held accountable for their actions.

KEY TERMS

Broadened concept of marketing
Social marketing
Dual-target market

Reverse-flow channel
Psychic costs
Psychic price

REVIEW QUESTIONS

1. What are some of the objectives of nonprofit organizations?
2. How does the concept of "value" relate to nonprofit functions?
3. Distinguish between psychic costs and psychic prices.
4. What is the goal of social marketing campaigns?
5. How can control be maintained within the nonprofit organization?
6. How can a college, faced with declining enrollments and increasing costs, use the marketing concept to its advantage?

DISCUSSION QUESTIONS

1. What are some of the problems caused by the uniqueness of nonprofit organizations?
2. Why do nonprofit organizations need to segment their publics?
3. How are marketing ethics determined within the nonprofit organization?
4. What are some marketing principles applied by the following groups?
    a. United Way
    b. Religious groups
    c. Educational foundations
    d. Public libraries
    e. American Red Cross
    f. Museums
5. For what reasons does the nonprofit organization need to engage in marketing research?

NOTES

1. Adopted from "New Marketing System Increases Revenue for Modern Dance Group," *Marketing News,* October 5, 1979, p. 11.

2. William G. Nickels, "Conceptual Conflicts in Marketing," *Journal of Economics and Business,* winter 1974, pp. 140–143.

3. See Cecily Cannan Selby, "Better Performance from Non Profits," *Harvard Business Review* 56 (September–October 1978): 92–98.

4. Evelyn Gutman, "Effective Marketing of a Cancer Screening Program," in *Marketing in Nonprofit Organizations,* ed. Patrick J. Montana (New York: AMACOM, a division of American Management Associations, 1978), pp. 134–135.

5. Adel El-Ansary and Oscar L. Kramer Jr., "Social Marketing: The Family Planning Experience," *Journal of Marketing,* July 1973, pp. 1–7.

6. Christopher H. Lovelock, "A Market Segmentation Approach to Transit Planning, Modeling, and Management," in *Readings in Public and Nonprofit Marketing,* eds. Christopher H. Lovelock and Charles B. Weinberg (New York: The Scientific Press, 1978), pp. 101–110.

7. "Now the 'Postman' Hustles for His Piece of the Business," *Government Executive,* October 1974, pp. 17–19.

8. James L. Ginter and Wayne Talarzyk, "Applying the Marketing Concept to Design New Products," *Journal of Business Research,* January 1978, pp. 51–66.

9. "Communicating Health Information to the Public," *Topline* (Great Neck, N.Y.: McCollum/Speilman and Company, June 1979), p. 1.

10. Benson P. Shapiro, *Marketing in Nonprofit Organizations* (Cambridge, Mass.: Marketing Science Institute, September 1972), p. 24.

11. Louis A. Fanelli, "Cancer Research Sweepstake Breeds Controversy," *Advertising Age,* May 21, 1979. Copyright 1979 by Crain Communications, Inc. Reprinted with permission.

12. Regina Herzlinger, "Why Data Systems in Nonprofit Organizations Fail," *Harvard Business Review* 55 (January–February 1977): 81.

13. This example is taken from William A. Mindak and H. Malcom Bybee, "Marketing's Application to Fund Raising," *Journal of Marketing,* July 1971, pp. 13–18.

14. Elspeth Durie, "Is Government Persuasion in Advertising Acceptable?" *Advertising Age,* March 13, 1978, p. 196.

15. Gene R. Laczniak, Robert F. Lusch, and Patrick E. Murphy, "Social Marketing: Its Ethical Dimensions," *Journal of Marketing,* spring 1979, pp. 29–36.

◢ **CASES**

24.1 Johnson Hospitals

Johnson Hospitals is a nonprofit corporation whose mission is to provide the best health care possible for its patients. At present it has nine hospitals in the upper Midwest and is planning to build at least three new ones each year during the remainder of the 1980s.

Johnson attempts to cater to privately insured patients because they can be charged whatever the market will bear. When one of the hospitals has empty beds, Medicare and Medicaid patients are accepted, and the nonprofit corporation charges off every penny of overhead that the government will allow. Johnson's locational strategy is to build the facility in the suburbs, where young working families are having lots of babies. They are more likely to be privately insured and in need of surgery, which makes the most money. The babies then provide a second generation of customers. In general, the shorter the stay, the more profitable the case. Diagnostic tests, operating room services, and intensive care facilities are used during the first few days of hospitalization and produce the highest revenues. After that, a hospital charges patients mainly for room and board. By attracting young, privately insured customers, Johnson lowers the probability of having to deal with diseases such as cancer that are four or five times more expensive to treat than a fracture or gall bladder operation.

To attract the "right" patients, Johnson tries to sell the "right" doctors on its services. Doctors usually decide where patients are to be hospitalized. Family doctors funnel the most potential patients to Johnson because they see the most patients. Specialists are a second source of patients, and Johnson tries to influence the decisions of specialists with the greatest number of young, privately insured patients—gynecologists, neurologists, general surgeons, and so forth.

Johnson often puts up office buildings next to its hospitals and offers doctors space at a discount. It also helps the physicians find office staffs, furnishings, and even partners. To encourage physicians to practice in close proximity to their hospitals, Johnson guarantees them first-year incomes of up to $60,000. If a doctor earns less, Johnson makes up the difference. Recently, in several cities municipally owned hospitals which are also nonprofit have charged the Johnson chain with skimming off the money-making patients, leaving them with poor people and the costliest ailments. Johnson has replied that it is not attempting to serve that particular market segment.

1. Does Johnson have the marketing concept? Why or why not?
2. Do you feel that Johnson is acting in a socially responsible manner? Defend your position.
3. Should there always be a strong correlation between nonprofit organizations and social responsibility? Why?

24.2   Southeastern State University

Southeastern State University is a tax-supported institution located in the middle of a major southeastern metropolitan area. Total enrollment is approximately 13,000 students. During the past four years there has been a 5 percent decline in enrollment each academic year. Enrollment is important to Southeastern State because the university receives appropriations from the state legislature partly based on student credit hours. Also, decreasing enrollment may affect the university's image. Central administration, concerned over the decline in enrollment, decided to undertake a survey of graduating high school seniors in the metropolitan area.

The most important factors in college selection were (in order): (1) excellence in subject of interest, (2) good academic reputation, (3) location, (4) low tuition costs, (5) being able to meet the admissions requirements, (6) warm, friendly campus, (7) good student activities program, (8) recommendation by friend or relative, (9) scholarship offer, and (10) friends going there. Among five area universities, Southeastern State ranked first in (1) most of their friends were going there, (2) best location, (3) lowest tuition costs, (4) simple admission requirements, and (5) excellence in subjects of interest. It ranked lowest in (1) most difficult admission requirements and (2) best student activities. The central administration, upon seeing the results of the survey, decided now was the time for action. At this point, an unusual phenomenon occurred; the central administration decided to seek counsel from its own marketing department prior to taking action.

1. You are a member of Southeastern State's marketing department. How would you respond to central administration?
2. Does Southeastern State have the marketing concept? Defend your answer.
3. Was a survey the place to begin solving the problem? If not, what action should have been taken initially?

25 International marketing

OBJECTIVES

To understand the importance of international marketing.

To become aware of the impact of multinationals on the world economy.

To learn the various ways of entering the international market.

To gain an understanding of the external environment facing international marketers.

To become aware of the basic elements underlying the development of an international marketing mix.

To learn about the forms of organization used in international marketing.

Gillette is trying to sell razor blades all around the world, but in many lands the company has to sell people on its idea of shaving.

The competition for Gillette razors overseas ranges from pairs of coins used as tweezers to honed edges on broken soda bottles. The company is patiently spreading the word in less-developed nations that shaving can be more comfortable and easier than traditional methods of removing facial hair. And it also is introducing the local equivalent to America's time-honored "Super Blue."

One of Gillette's more popular marketing devices in Africa and Asia is a giant shaving brush.

The brush is carried from village to village in vans equipped with wash basins, towels, and razors. When the native show persons who travel in the van attract a crowd, the big brush is produced and used to paste a volunteer with a facefull of shaving cream.

He then is shaved and, in an atmosphere of great hilarity, other villagers are invited into the van to try their hand at lather and blade.

"It's a long process, developing a market," said Rodney Mills, assistant general manager of Gillette International.

The Boston-based firm has been developing overseas markets since it first sold razor blades to the British 75 years ago. Today its international division sells toiletries in 22 countries and operates 29 foreign plants. The operation accounted for two-thirds of Gillette's $1.98 billion in sales last year. . . .

To sell its blades [in Indonesia], which carry the Indonesian trademark "Goal," Gillette must sell the idea of shaving—no easy feat in lands where men tweeze out facial hair with coins or shave with a double-edge blade held between the fingers.

Mills said another popular shaving instrument is a broken soft-drink bottle honed down on one side, but is quick to point out that "neither Coca Cola nor Gillette would consider each other a competitor."

In Indonesia, billboards and store posters sell blades with advertising techniques out of the 1930s. Quality and economy are stressed, but the blades also are portrayed as keys to romance and success.

"We try to sell the shaving habit and a factor of social consciousness," Mills said. "We have ads showing the clean-shaven man getting the good job or winning the girl."[1]

The Gillette story illustrates a number of important aspects about international marketing. First, it can be very lucrative for the company; two-thirds of Gillette's revenues come from its international division. Second, the marketing mix often varies dramatically from that used in the United States and also from country to country. A third point is that markets sometimes must be created, but once demand has been stimulated, the results can be financially rewarding. A final point is that the external environment (culture, level of technology, economic factors, and so forth) require thorough understanding in order for a company's effort to be successful. Success in international marketing requires a high level of marketing sophistication, just as in domestic marketing. And accomplishing marketing objectives often requires a radically different approach from domestic strategies.

How does a firm enter the international market? What roles do multinational firms play in the world today? How does a marketing manager develop an international marketing mix? We begin with an overview of international marketing and the multinational firm.

International marketing: a macro perspective

In the broadest sense, international marketing has many advantages. Economic advantages can accrue from foreign trade. As people engage in international commerce, there can be greater mutual understanding. Interdependence among nations means that they have a stake in one another's future. J. Paul Austin, former president of Coca-Cola, says:

Greater opportunities for free trade mean greater assurance of world-wide freedom. The commitment of international business, or world traders headquartered on all the continents, calls for an open interchange of goods, services, communications, and ideas. Increasingly, this will mean a dynamic force toward world peace.[2]

International marketing is by no means a panacea for the world's problems. Yet if it generates closer cooperation and better understanding among people everywhere, it will have performed an invaluable service for all of us.

THE IMPORTANCE OF TRADE TO THE UNITED STATES

American imports, exports, and direct investment in foreign lands are shown in Table 25.1. America is a full participant in world trade, yet it is less dependent on external trade than any other industrialized nation. Our exports and imports average only 7 percent of our GNP, compared to over 20 percent for West Germany and the United Kingdom.[3]

Even though exports have exceeded imports each year except 1980, the United States balance of payments typically reveals a deficit. This is due to mil-

▲ **TABLE 25.1 U.S. International Transactions, 1960–1980 (in millions of dollars)**

Type of transaction	1960	1965	1970	1975	1980
Exports of goods and services	$27,595	$39,548	$62,483	$155,721	$335,956
Imports of goods and services	23,555	32,443	59,545	132,761	336,224

Source: U.S. Department of Commerce, *Statistical Abstract of the United States, 1980* (Washington, D.C., 1980), p. 860.

itary and other expenditures abroad by the federal government. American exports consist primarily of agricultural products and manufactured goods. The latter include many manufactured goods ready for sale in foreign markets as well as component parts and intermediate products used in manufacturing. Rolls-Royce, for example, admits that the drivetrain that propels the wheels of the world famous Rolls is made by Oldsmobile and that its automatic transmission is by Borg-Warner.

MULTINATIONALS

Firms that are heavily engaged in international trade are called **multinational corporations.** These firms move resources, goods, services, and skills across national boundaries without regard to the country in which the headquarters office is located. Yet a multinational is more than a business entity. As Neil Jacoby puts it:

The multinational corporation is, among other things, a private "government," often richer in assets and more populous in stockholders and employees than are some of the nation-states in which it carries on its business. It is simultaneously a "citizen" of several nation-states, owing obedience to their laws and paying them taxes, yet having its own objectives and being responsive to a management located in a foreign nation. Small wonder that some critics see in it an irresponsible instrument of private economic power or of economic "imperialism" by its home country. Others view it as an international carrier of advanced management science and technology, an agent for the global transmission of cultures bringing closer the day when a common set of ideals will unite mankind.[4]

The size of the multinationals is enormous. Table 25.2 indicates the sales and income of the 50 largest multinationals. The sales of Exxon, Royal Dutch/ Shell Group, and General Motors were larger than the GNP of all but 14 nations in the world.[5] Today more than half the earnings of such well-known American companies as Colgate-Palmolive, Heinz, Hoover, Mobil, National Cash Register, and Exxon come from international operations.

The role of multinational corporations in developing nations is a subject of much controversy. Their ability to tap financial, physical, and human resources from all over the world can be of benefit to any country. Multinationals usually have the competence to combine these resources in an economically feasible and profitable fashion. They also often possess and can transfer the most up-to-date technology to complex problems facing developing as well as developed

TABLE 25.2   The 50 Largest Multinational Corporations in the World

1980 Rank	1979 Rank	Company	Headquarters	Sales ($000)	Net income ($000)
1	1	Exxon	New York	103,142,834	5,650,090
2	3	Royal Dutch/Shell Group	The Hague/London	77,114,243	5,174,282
3	4	Mobil	New York	59,510,000	3,272,000
4	2	General Motors	Detroit	57,728,500	(762,500)
5	7	Texaco	Harrison, N.Y.	51,195,830	2,642,542
6	6	British Petroleum	London	48,035,941	3,337,121
7	8	Standard Oil of California	San Francisco	40,479,000	2,401,000
8	5	Ford Motor	Dearborn, Mich.	37,085,000	(1,543,300)
9	13	ENI	Rome	27,186,939	98,046
10	9	Gulf Oil	Pittsburgh	26,483,000	1,407,000
11	10	International Business Machines	Armonk, N.Y.	26,213,000	3,562,000
12	14	Standard Oil (Ind.)	Chicago	26,133,080	1,915,314
13	15	Fiat	Turin (Italy)	25,155,000	n.a.
14	11	General Electric	Fairfield, Conn.	24,959,000	1,514,000
15	16	Francaise des Pétroles	Paris	23,940,355	946,772
16	21	Atlantic Richfield	Los Angeles	23,744,302	1,651,423
17	12	Unilever	London/Rotterdam	23,607,516	658,820
18	26	Shell Oil	Houston	19,830,000	1,542,000
19	22	Renault	Paris	18,979,278	160,165
20	29	Petróleos de Venezuela	Caracas	18,818,931	3,450,921
21	18	International Telephone & Tel.	New York	18,529,655	894,326
22	32	Elf Aquitaine	Paris	18,430,074	1,378,222
23	20	Philips' Gloeilampenfabrieken	Eindhoven (Netherlands)	18,402,818	165,210
24	19	Volkswagenwerk	Wolfsburg (Germany)	18,339,046	170,964
25	36	Conoco	Stamford, Conn.	18,325,400	1,026,195
26	23	Siemens	Munich	17,950,253	332,434
27	24	Daimler-Benz	Stuttgart	17,108,100	605,149
28	17	Peugeot	Paris	16,846,434	(348,998)
29	25	Hoechst	Frankfurt	16,480,551	251,605
30	27	Bayer	Leverkusen (Germany)	15,880,596	356,342
31	28	BASF	Ludwigshafen on Rhine	15,277,348	197,641
32	31	Thyssen	Duisburg (Germany)	15,235,998	61,611
33	47	Petrobrás (Petróleo Brasileiro)	Rio de Janeiro	14,836,326	767,419
34	●	PEMEX (Petróleos Mexicanos)	Mexico City	14,813,514	17,316
35	33	Nestlé	Vevey (Switzerland)	14,615,187	407,785
36	30	Toyota Motor	Toyota City (Japan)	14,233,779	616,051
37	38	Nissan Motor	Yokohama (Japan)	13,853,503	461,647
38	39	E.I. du Pont de Nemours	Wilmington, Del.	13,652,000	716,000
39	49	Phillips Petroleum	Bartlesville, Okla.	13,376,563	1,069,614
40	42	Imperial Chemical Industries	London	13,290,347	(46,510)
41	43	Tenneco	Houston	13,226,000	726,000
42	38	Nippon Steel	Tokyo	13,104,996	496,205
43	46	Sun	Radnor, Pa.	12,945,000	723,000
44	37	Hitachi	Tokyo	12,871,328	503,385
45	44	Matsushita Electric Industrial	Osaka (Japan)	12,684,404	541,923
46	34	U.S. Steel	Pittsburgh	12,492,100	504,500
47	48	Occidental Petroleum	Los Angeles	12,476,125	710,785
48	●	United Technologies	Hartford	12,323,994	393,383
49	45	Western Electric	New York	12,032,100	693,200
50	●	Standard Oil (Ohio)	Cleveland	11,023,196	1,811,224
		TOTALS		**1,203,998,984**	**53,281,324**

● = Companies were not in the top 50 in 1979.

Source: "The 50 Largest Industrial Companies in the World," *Fortune,* August 10, 1981, p. 205.

nations. On the negative side, critics claim that the wrong kind of technology is often transferred. Usually, it is **capital-intensive** (high capital cost per worker), and thus does not substantially increase employment. A "modern sector" emerges, employing a small proportion of the labor force at relatively high productivity and income levels and with increasingly capital-intensive technologies. In addition, multinationals sometimes support reactionary and oppressive regimes if it is in their best interests. Other critics say that the firms take more wealth out of developing nations than they bring in, thus widening the gap between rich and poor nations.[6]

Although Table 25.2 shows that 22 of the top 50 multinationals are American firms, the U.S. competitive edge among world multinationals has been eroding rapidly. In 1959, an American company was the largest in the world in 11 out of 13 major industries into which manufacturing activity plus commercial banking can be grouped—namely, aerospace, automotive, chemicals, electrical equipment, food products, general machinery, iron and steel, metal products, paper, petroleum, pharmaceuticals, textiles, and commercial banking. By 1976, the United States was leading in only 7 out of 13. Three of the non-American leaders in 1976 were German, one was British-Dutch, one was British, and one was Japanese.

The number of U.S. companies among the world's top 12 declined in all industry groups except aerospace between 1959 and 1976. U.K. companies displaced other countries' in three industries, but lost ground in three others. Continental European companies increased their representatives among the top 12 in 9 out of 13 industries; the Japanese scored gains in 8.

Why has this happened? During the 1960s and 1970s there was much more rapid growth in industrial productivity in both Japan and the Continent than in the United States and the United Kingdom (not to mention Continental and Japanese attention to after sales service, product quality and design, delivery schedules, and stable labor relations).

Continental European and Japanese capabilities in product and process innovation have grown considerably relative to those of the United States and the United Kingdom.

Still another part of non-U.S. companies' success appears to be due to their comparatively greater ability to negotiate, live, and collectively work with governments, unions, and competitors. In 1971, 60% of the foreign ventures of Continental European companies and 90% of those of Japanese companies were joint ventures, whereas 60% of U.S. and of British companies' foreign operations were wholly American or British.

A final factor has been the dramatic increase in oil prices during the 1970s and early 1980s. This has given a tremendous boost to the demand for energy-saving products and processes—and resource-short Europe and Japan had them first.[7]

International marketing: the individual firm

A company does not have to be a huge multinational organization to enter international marketing. There are a wide variety of techniques for penetrating global markets, and a variety of risk levels as well (see Figure 25.1). Actually, international marketing can be relatively risk-free and uncomplicated, yet 95 percent of America's firms do not make an effort to sell their products overseas.[8] Reluctance to enter the international scene may stem from several factors. First, international operations are usually characterized by greater uncertainty than domestic operations. A second problem is that of obtaining good information in foreign markets. Lack of good information, of course, increases the difficulty of decision making. A third factor is the price increases in many petroleum-based products during the 1970s and early 1980s. Oil-importing nations have been forced to adopt policies aimed at conserving hard currencies, and this has tended to discourage importation of nonessential consumer products. In Europe, America's biggest customer, lingering uncertainties over unemployment and inflation have caused consumers to cut back drastically on unnecessary spending.

EXPORTING

If, despite such difficulties, a company decides to pursue international opportunities, exporting is usually the least complicated of those opportunities. Sales can be made through individuals or firms located in America known as **buyers for export.** A buyer for export is usually treated as a domestic customer and is served by the domestic salesforce. The buyer for export is essentially a middleman who assumes all the risks and sells internationally for its own account. The

◄ FIGURE 25.1 Methods of entry and risk levels for international marketing.

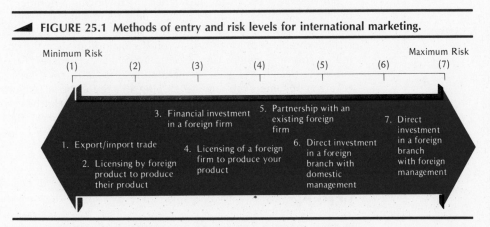

Source: From Richard D. Robinson, *International Business Policy.* Copyright © 1964 by Holt, Rinehart and Winston, Inc. Reprinted by permission of Holt, Rinehart and Winston.

American firm is involved only to the extent that its products are ultimately purchased in foreign markets.

Direct exporting is the preferred alternative for the firm that wants to maintain control over its export activities and also avoid middleman fees. The producer deals directly with foreign customers by using traveling salespeople or appointing foreign firms as representatives. Sometimes foreign sales offices are established if there is sufficient demand to justify the expenditure. Sometimes a company decides that a foreign sales agent-distributor is the most economical means of obtaining direct international sales. The U.S. Department of Commerce has an agent-distributor service that each year helps about 5000 American companies find an agent or distributor in virtually every country in the world. Direct exporting (with or without an agent-distributor) often requires patience and ingenuity, as described in the Fieldcrest Mills example below.

Fieldcrest Mills' bed and bath division decided in 1976 to export its "boutique" marketing system to Western Europe and Japan. "It seemed an obvious thing to do," the president explains. "Department stores in those countries were decades behind the U.S. They still looked on towels and sheets as mundane products with no fashion pizzazz whatever. And just like our stores decades ago, they were selling unattractive products at virtually no profit, sort of like a public service to customers."

The firm embarked on a campaign to convince department stores in Europe and Japan that they could, like their U.S. counterparts, make money by selling high-fashion (that is, high-markup) towels and sheets. At first there was considerable resistance to Fieldcrest's selling efforts. The owner of a Stuttgart department store flatly rejected Tracy's offer of a written guarantee that installation of a Fieldcrest boutique would double the profits generated on that floor space within two years.

But Fieldcrest eventually succeeded in convincing a number of overseas department stores to take a fling. Stores in Hamburg, Munich, London and Tokyo agreed to install boutiques in especially favorable locations—usually on the main floor near the cosmetics counters, where customer traffic is heavy. Fieldcrest provided the design and even the lighting systems at its own cost. Foreign consumers are now developing a taste for those fashionable U.S. bed and bath products. At London's famed Harrods, the Fieldcrest boutique has become one of the most successful profit centers. As a result of its boutique concept, Fieldcrest's exports jumped in 1980 by a most respectable 58 percent.[9]

LICENSING

A more aggressive move into the international market without direct manufacturing is **licensing.** The licensor agrees to let another firm use its manufacturing process, trademark, patents, trade secrets, or other knowledge of a proprietary nature. The licensee agrees, in turn, to pay the licensor a royalty or fee agreed upon by both parties.

Licensing is sometimes used to test the international waters before a company engages in manufacturing or in joint ventures. Culligan, the water softener company, began its international operations in 1958 by establishing a Belgium licensee. After four years of growth, the firm reached the conclusion that European manufacturing operations were necessary to offset the high costs of freight from the United States. Today Culligan markets its products in 92 countries.

Care must be taken by the licensor to make certain it can exercise the control over the licensee's activities necessary to ensure proper quality levels, pricing structure, adequacy of distribution, and so forth. Licensing may create a new competitor in the long run if the licensee decides to void the license agreement. International law is often ineffective in prohibiting such actions. One common way of maintaining effective control is to shop one or more critical components from the United States. If the licensee does not possess the technology or facilities to produce the parts, control will be maintained. A second control technique is local registration of patents and trademarks by the U.S. firm, not by the licensee. Some companies add a provision in the licensing agreement for renegotiating contracts to cover new products and improvements in technology.

International franchising is a form of licensing. Franchising has been most successful in developed countries that have full-fledged service economies. In addition to the traditional product franchises, such as fast food restaurants (see Figure 25.2) and automotive products, service franchising has been growing rapidly in industrialized nations. These franchises include accounting services, credit and collection agencies, employment services, printing services, hotels, laundry and cleaning, and vehicle rental agencies. Despite the growth of international franchising, a number of formidable problems have had to be overcome:

Official limitations on royalty payments or licensing and trademark contracts. In some cases, royalties on trademarks and brand names are taxable and payable by the franchisor whether he is domiciled in or out of that particular country.

Problems may exist in the protection of trademarks, as no facility exists for their registration.

In some cases, franchising arrangements remain solely the concern of the contracting parties and there are no regulations to safeguard franchising agreements. Tie-in arrangements are discouraged and sometimes forbidden.

In some countries, a significant percentage of ownership share of the business activity is required by nationals; in others, aliens cannot own real estate property and in others they cannot own retail businesses.[10]

To avoid many of these problems, franchisors often enter countries they "understand." Canada continues to be the dominant foreign franchising market, followed by the United Kingdom and Japan.

Source: Photo by Wilson Brown, courtesy of Naples Editing Services.

CONTRACT MANUFACTURING

Firms that do not want to become involved in licensing arrangements or want to become more heavily involved in international marketing may engage in **contract manufacturing.** This is simply private-label manufacturing by a foreign company. The foreign company produces a certain volume of products to specifications, with the domestic firm's brand name affixed to the goods. Marketing is usually handled by the domestic company.

Contract manufacturing enables the domestic firm to broaden its international market base without direct investment in new plant and equipment. Often foreign manufacturing, particularly in labor-intensive industries, results in significant cost savings. These savings enable the domestic company to compete internationally on a price basis, something that would otherwise be impossible. Using cheap labor enables the firm to sell the product at a lower price. Contract manufacturing may enable a company to build a market position and develop brand loyalty. After a solid base has been established, the domestic firm may switch to direct investment or a joint venture.

JOINT VENTURES

Joint ventures are quite similar to licensing agreements except that the domestic firm assumes an equity position in a foreign company. Naturally, this is more risky than the options just discussed. It does, however, give management a voice in company affairs that it might not have under licensing.

The key to a successful joint venture is selecting the right foreign company and then maintaining effective communications. Attitudes toward marketing, production, financial, and growth policies must be clearly delineated. Governmental restrictions should be fully explored before the joint venture agreement is made final. A number of countries require that the local firm maintain at least 51 percent ownership in any joint arrangement.

DIRECT INVESTMENT

Direct investment in wholly owned manufacturing and marketing subsidiaries offers the greatest potential rewards. Naturally, the possibility of substantial rewards means greater risk. Firms may make direct investments because no suitable local partner can be found; others form wholly owned operations in order to maintain control.

Countries that lack strong nationalistic policies may offer foreign companies substantial tax concessions and/or make long-term loans at favorable interest rates. Puerto Rico, for example, not only makes significant tax concessions, but will also construct the plant when necessary. It then leases the plant to the investor and assists in recruiting local managerial personnel as well as a workforce. Direct investment may be discouraged or prohibited in some countries, such as Japan or Chile. In other countries, the firm may have difficulty repatriating profits. Argentina and Brazil allow a maximum of 12 percent of profits to be remitted to the home country. Multinationals sometimes develop ingenious schemes to extract a much greater level of profits from their foreign operations. For example, Volkswagen sent $100 million back to Germany as payments for its parent's technical advice and expertise over a ten-year period.

The biggest threat to direct investment is expropriation of assets. As nationalistic feelings rise throughout the world, the possibility of expropriation increases. Cartels such as OPEC continue to develop in terms of basic commodities and raw materials. As they grow, these organizations often expropriate the assets of the multinationals operating in their territory.

The external environment facing the international marketer

One major reason why firms have their assets expropriated or are not successful in the international market is a failure to understand the external environment. The same factors operate internationally as in the domestic market. They include culture, level of economic development, political and legal structure, technological level, demographic makeup, and natural resource shortages (see Figure 25.3).

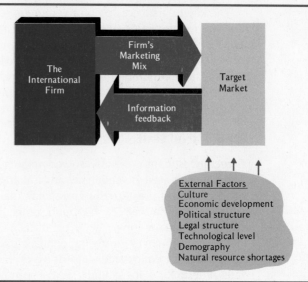

CULTURE

Central to any country is a common set of values shared by its members that determine what is socially acceptable. Culture also forms the basis for the family, the educational system, or the social class system. The network of social organizations generates different overlapping roles and status positions. The Swiss housewife, for example, considers the performance of household chores such as washing dishes or cleaning floors central to the housewife's role. She finds it difficult to accept the idea of labor-saving machines or commercial products, and she rejects commercial appeals emphasizing time and effort saved in performing household tasks.

Social institutions also develop conventions, rituals, and practices governing behavior at different times, such as when entertaining family or friends, or during holidays. In the United States, bringing a bottle of wine for the host at a dinner party is likely to please; in France, such a gift would be considered an insult to the host's choice of wine, and a bouquet of flowers for the hostess is considered more appropriate.[11]

Without understanding a country's culture, a firm has little chance of effectively penetrating the market. A few additional examples illustrate the importance of cultural knowledge:

In England, Germany and Scandinavia, beer is generally perceived as an alcoholic beverage. In Mediterranean lands, however, beer is considered like soft drinks. Therefore, a study of the competitive status of beer in Northern Europe would have to build in questions on wine and liquor. In Italy, Spain, or Greece, the comparison would have to be with soft drinks.

In Italy, it is common for children to have a bar of chocolate between two slices of bread as a snack. In France, bar chocolate is often used in cooking. But a West German housewife would be revolted by either practice.

A third of all German and Dutch businessmen take their wives with them on business trips, as opposed to only 15 percent of their English and French counterparts. As a study for one hotel delicately put it, the criteria each group uses in judging hotels and the services they offer are clearly different.

A summary of some important cultural considerations is given in Table 25.3. A number of additional examples will be discussed in the section on the marketing mix.

LEVEL OF ECONOMIC DEVELOPMENT

A second major factor in the external environment facing the international marketer is level of economic development. In order to appreciate marketing opportunities (or lack of them), it is helpful to examine the stages of economic growth: the traditional society, the preindustrial society, the takeoff economy, the industrializing society, and the fully industrialized nation.

The traditional society. If we make the assumption that all nations are either developed or developing, then countries in the traditional stage would be in the embryonic phase of developing. The traditional society is largely agrarian. Its social structure is hierarchical, and the value system is geared to a sort of

◢ **TABLE 25.3 Important Cultural Considerations in International Marketing**

Differences in these cultural factors	Affect a people's values and habits relating to:
1. Assumptions and attitudes	Time One's proper purpose in life The future This life versus the hereafter Duty, responsibility
2. Personal beliefs and aspirations	Right and wrong Sources of pride Sources of fear and concern Extent of one's hopes The individual versus society
3. Interpersonal relationships	The source of authority Care or empathy for others Importance of family obligations Objects of loyalty Tolerance for personal differences
4. Social structure	Interclass mobility Class or caste systems Urban-village-farm origins Determinants of status

Source: Avind Phatak, *Managing Multinational Corporations* (New York: Praeger, 1974), p. 139. Reprinted by permission.

fatalism. The country is custom-bound and unproductive due to backward or no technology. Typically, the traditional country is ruled by an authoritarian personality. The system may be highly stable and require a powerful disruptive force to initiate economic growth.

One example of misplaced technology and strong central control is Ghana. There, a tollway 16 miles long and six lanes wide, which would seem excellent as a basis for distribution, goes from nowhere to nowhere. At a Ghanian port, giant silos reach skyward. Cocoa beans were to be stored in them, but it gets so hot inside that the beans would cook, so they stand empty.

The preindustrial society. The second stage, the preindustrial society, involves economic and social change. A rising middle class with an entrepreneurial spirit begins to emerge. They are risk-takers who view economic growth as desirable. Nationalism may begin to rise, with resulting restrictive policies toward multinational organizations. The rate of capital accumulation rises above the rate of population growth, and the training of labor for large-scale production begins. Countries such as North Korea and Chile are in this stage. Effective marketing in these countries is extremely difficult. They lack the modern distribution and communication systems American marketers often take for granted. Peru, for example, did not establish a television network until 1975.

The takeoff economy. The third stage, economic takeoff, is the period of transition from developing to developed nation. New industries arise, and a healthy sociopolitical climate emerges. Usually takeoff lasts about twenty years.

Eastern European countries such as Poland, Bulgaria, Romania, and Hungary have entered the takeoff phase with little emphasis on marketing. Typically, their emphasis is on increasing production without regard to distribution, product quality, or promotion. Poland, for example, has many small retailers that lack efficient assortments. Prices and margins are still centrally fixed. Yet since 1970, Karl Marx University in Budapest has offered a specialization in market research and marketing. Latin American countries such as Ecuador, Peru, and Colombia are proceeding through the takeoff period with a stronger marketing orientation. Colombia, for example, pushes exports with tax incentives and is easing important restrictions.

The industrializing society. The fourth phase of economic development is the industrializing society. Historically, this phase has lasted about forty years. During this era, technology spreads from the leading sectors of the economy that powered the takeoff to the remainder of the nation. Hong Kong, Brazil, and Mexico are in this phase of development.

Countries in the industrializing stage begin to produce capital goods and consumer durable products. Demands for component parts and materials to fuel the capital goods and durable goods assembly lines create many secondary industries, such as tire manufacturing, motors for refrigerators, and electronic components. These industries also foster economic growth. As a result, a large middle class begins to emerge, and demand for luxuries and services grows. These markets become increasingly attractive to large multinational firms.

The industrialized society. The industrialized society is an exporter of manufactured products. A large percentage of these goods are based upon high technology, such as automobiles, computers, airplanes, oil exploration equipment, and telecommunications gear. Great Britain, Japan, West Germany, and the United States fall into this classification.

The wealth of the industrialized nations creates tremendous market potential. As a result, extensive trading occurs between the industrialized countries. Also, industrial nations usually ship manufactured goods to developing countries in exchange for raw materials, such as petroleum, precious metals, and bauxite.

POLITICAL AND LEGAL STRUCTURE

A third important uncontrollable variable facing the international marketer is political considerations. Government policies run the gamut from no private ownership or individual freedom to little central government and maximum personal freedom. As rights of private property increase, government-owned industries and centralized planning tend to decrease. Rarely will a political environment be at one extreme or the other. India, for instance, is a republic, but it has shades of socialism, monopoly capitalism, and competitive capitalism in its political ideology. In countries such as Greece and Spain, individual freedoms are highly restricted but private enterprise is allowed to flourish almost unhindered.

Failure to understand foreign governments and their modes of operation can lead to marketing failures like this one:

A major pharmaceutical manufacturer a number of years ago developed a process for coating rice with vitamin A that could withstand cooking. The company believed, with considerable justification, that a serious public health problem endemic to the Far East could be alleviated through this process.

The Philippine government welcomed the process, promising total cooperation, and went to the extent of enacting legislation to compel all rice millers to incorporate the process.

When the rice millers refused en masse to go along with the new government regulation, it was learned that the Philippine authorities had really intended that the vitamin A program provide a means of determining quantities of rice that were milled, thereby enabling the government to collect its taxes, which the millers had evaded successfully for years.[12]

Failure to appreciate emerging nationalist feelings can ultimately result in expropriation. Such problems can be avoided by allowing citizens of the host country equity participation in the operation. In other situations, industries are nationalized to infuse more capital into their development, such as airlines in Italy and Volvo in Sweden. They are also nationalized to assist domestic corporations by selling goods and services below cost. For example, for many years France has been supplying coal to users at a loss. Two state-owned banks have lent the loss-ridden French steel industry billions of francs. Figure 25.4 shows the scope of state ownership in industrializing and industrialized countries.

FIGURE 25.4 Scope of state ownership.

	Posts	Tele-communi-cations	Electricity	Gas	Oil production	Coal	Railways*	Airlines	Motor industry	Steel	Ship-building
Australia	●	●	●	●	○	○	●	◕	○	○	NA
Austria	●	●	●	●	●	●	●	●	●	●	NA
Belgium	●	●	◔	◔	NA	○	●	●	○	◐	○
Brazil	●	●	●	●	●	●	●	◕	○	◕	○
Britain	●	●	●	●	◔	●	●	◕	◐	◕	●
Canada	●	◔	●	○	○	○	◕	◕	○	○	○
France	●	●	●	●	NA	●	●	◕	◐	◕	○
West Germany	●	●	◕	◐	◕	◐	●	●	●	◕	◕
Holland	●	●	◕	◐	NA	NA	●	●	○	◕	◕
India	●	●	●	●	●	●	●	●	○	◕	●
Italy	●	●	◕	●	NA	NA	●	●	◕	◕	●
Japan	●	●	○	○	NA	○	◕	◕	○	○	○
Mexico	●	●	●	●	●	●	●	◐	◕	◕	●
South Korea	●	●	◔	○	NA	◔	●	●	○	◕	○
Spain	●	◐	○	◔	NA	◐	●	●	○	◐	◕
Sweden	●	●	◐	●	NA	NA	●	◕	○	◕	◕
Switzerland	●	●	●	●	NA	NA	●	◔	○	○	NA
United States	●	○	◔	○	○	○	◔*	○	○	○	○

○ Privately owned: all or nearly all   ● Publicly owned: all or nearly all   ◕ 75%   ◐ 50%   ◔ 25%

*Including Conrail.
NA: Not applicable or negligible production.
Source: Adapted from a chart in *The Economist* (London), December 30, 1978, and reprinted with special permission.

Closely related and often intertwined with political factors are legal considerations. Legal structures are designed to encourage or to limit trade.

Tariffs. The most common means of limiting trade is through a **tariff,** a tax levied on goods entering a country. It may be a specific tariff assessed per unit of import, such as $300 per imported car. In other cases it will be an ad valorem tariff based upon the value of the import. The effect of any tariff is to make the imported merchandise more expensive, thereby discouraging consumption. In recent years, progress has been made in reducing tariffs throughout the Western world. The **General Agreement on Tariffs and Trade (GATT)** has provided a forum for negotiating multilateral tariff reductions among the member nations. Although GATT has met with success, nationalistic tendencies have prevented many tariffs from being eliminated or lowered.

Quotas. A second means of restricting trade is by imposing import quotas. A **quota** places a limit on the amount of a specific product that can enter a country. The quota usually has an absolute limit, so that importation of the good stops when the quota is filled. A second common form of quota is combined with a tariff. When the quota limit is reached, the tariff increases substantially. A more severe form of trade barrier is the **boycott.** This measure excludes all products from certain countries or companies. Some Arab countries have boycotted American firms for their dealings with Israel. In 1980, Iran boycotted all American products and also refused to sell petroleum to the United States.

Exchange control. Another means of regulating foreign trade is **exchange control,** a government monopoly on all dealings in foreign exchange. It works as follows:

A national company earning foreign exchange from its exports must sell this foreign exchange to the control agency, usually the central bank. A company wishing to buy goods from abroad must buy its foreign exchange from the control agency rather than in the free market. Exchange control always means that foreign exchange is in scarce supply, and therefore the government is rationing it according to its own priorities rather than letting higher prices ration it.

Firms producing within the country have to be on the government's favored list to get exchange for imported supplies; or, alternatively, they may try to develop local suppliers, running the risk of higher costs and indifferent quality control. The firms exporting to that nation must also be on the government's favored list. Otherwise they will lose their market if importers can get no foreign exchange to pay them. Generally, exchange control countries favor the import of capital goods and necessary consumer goods but avoid luxuries.[13]

Trade agreements. Not all government efforts are meant to stifle imports or investment by foreign corporations. The GATT is a good example of an organization whose objective is to increase international trade. GATT has been most successful in fostering trade between industrialized and industrializing nations. Developing countries encouraged the formation of the United Nation's Conference on Trade and Development (UNCTAD) in 1964. The objective of UNCTAD is to further the growth of developing nations through trade. UNCTAD seeks to improve the prices of primary goods exports through commodity agreements. The idea is to control supply, which in turn means higher prices. UNCTAD has not been overly successful; about the only commodity agreement that has achieved its objectives is that for international coffee.

Market groupings. Trade is also encouraged through **market groupings**— countries creating common trade alliances. Integrating several markets into a common unit has several advantages:

1. Increased growth for the region.
2. Growth in income within the region can lead to increased exports for both member and nonmember countries.
3. Trade creation and diversion possibilities may lead international businesses to invest in production and marketing facilities within the region in order to get behind the tariff wall and to minimize nontariff barriers.[14]

The best-known market grouping is the European Economic Community (EEC), often called simply the Common Market. Its members are Belgium, France, West Germany, Italy, Luxembourg, the Netherlands, Denmark, Ireland, and the United Kingdom. The EEC has as its goal the gradual reduction of tariffs among member nations until free trade is achieved. It also has the goal of ultimately creating a single external tariff for the EEC. Another important marketing grouping is the European Free Trade Association (EFTA), which represents Sweden, Ireland, Norway, Portugal, Switzerland, and Finland. EFTA represents over 40 million people and contains several countries (Sweden, Switzerland, and Norway) that have some of the highest per capita incomes in the world. Two other significant groups are the Council for Mutual Assistance (COMECON), which represents the East European nations, and the Latin American Free Trade Association (LAFTA). LAFTA has faced serious problems due to differences in the economic structures of the Latin American nations and a general lack of political support.

LEVEL OF TECHNOLOGICAL DEVELOPMENT

Technology is a fourth major factor in the external environment that can influence the success of the international firm. Just like legal factors, technology can sometimes block trade (or cause the firm to lose sales to a higher or lower level of technology), or it can open up markets.

Technology levels sometimes must be lowered in order to make a product attractive for developing nations. Singer, for example, still sells vast quantities of foot-pumped sewing machines throughout the world. General Motors has "designed down" cars in developing nations to make repairs easier. A firm that has technological knowhow but fails to appreciate a country's culture may experience a sales disaster. The LTV Corporation developed a completely amphibious, half-ton capacity, all-purpose vehicle called the "Kid" to replace the water buffalo in agriculture and transportation in the Far East. In demonstrations, the Kid traveled about 20 miles per hour on land and cost only $1500. It was a total flop. First, the price equaled up to ten years' wages for some Southeast Asian farmers. Second, there was no real need for the speed offered by the Kid. Third, the Kid had a gasoline engine. Not only was gasoline difficult to obtain in rural areas, but the peasant farmers couldn't afford it. Fourth, the water buffalo produced manure that could be used to fertilize the crops. Finally, when a water buffalo is too old to work, it is butchered for food. This option for the Kid would be palatable only to those with bizarre appetites. Although LTV recognized the huge number of farmers in the Far East, the company did not examine the cultural factors adequately.

DEMOGRAPHY

The five most populous nations in the world are China, India, the USSR, the USA, and Indonesia.[15] Yet population per se is often a poor indicator of market potential. Density of population is also an important consideration. Oceania has only 5 people per square mile. Egypt has about 94 persons per square mile (the United States has 57), but virtually all the people live along the Nile River. The remainder of Egypt is desert. Thus, average density figures can be misleading unless the population is rather equally distributed throughout the land mass.

Just as important as population is the amount and distribution of incomes in a country. The wealthiest countries in the world include the United States, Switzerland, Sweden, Canada, West Germany, and several of the Arab oil-producing nations. At the other extreme are countries like Kenya and India, with 6 and 7 percent, respectively, of the per capita purchasing power of an American consumer. Even in countries with low per capita incomes, wealth is often not evenly distributed. There are pockets of upper- and middle-class consumers in just about every country of the world. The demand for luxury goods is present, but often limited by the number of affluent buyers.

NATURAL RESOURCE SHORTAGES

A final factor in the external environment that has become more evident in the past decade is natural resource shortages. Petroleum shortages have created huge amounts of wealth for countries such as Argentina, Saudi Arabia, and Liberia. Both consumer and industrial markets have blossomed in these countries. Industrial areas such as Japan, the United States, and much of Western Europe have experienced rampant inflation and an enormous transfer of wealth to the petroleum-rich nations. Coal seems to be the only energy source that offers any serious hope of greatly reducing the industrialized world's dependence on oil during the 1980s. If this transfer happens, it will have a positive impact on the American trade balance, since the United States has immense deposits of coal and is the world's low-cost producer.

Energy is not the only form of natural resource shortage that will affect international marketing in the 1980s. Lack of water and/or warm weather will mean that many of Africa's countries and the Soviet Union will be major importers of foodstuffs. America, on the other hand, must rely on African countries for many precious metals. Japan relies heavily on America for timber and logs. The list could go on, but the point is clear. Vast differences in natural resource assets create international dependencies, huge shifts in wealth, inflation and recessions, export opportunities for countries with abundant resources, and even a stimulus for military intervention.

Developing an international marketing mix

INTERNATIONAL MARKET RESEARCH

When marketing managers understand how external variables can affect the firm's marketing mix, their chances of reaching international marketing goals are enhanced. The first step in creating a marketing mix is developing a thorough understanding of the international marketing target. This can be accomplished in one of two ways, or with a combination of both: (1) analysis of secondary data and (2) marketing research.

Secondary data have the same advantages in the international market as they do at home. They are relatively inexpensive and can usually be obtained more rapidly than primary data. National economic statistics and industry analyses published by the U.S. Department of Commerce are excellent sources of secondary information (a more detailed source list is shown in Table 25.4).

International marketing research utilizes the same tools, techniques, and theory as domestic research. Yet it is done in vastly different environments. In some countries, a woman would never consider being interviewed by a male interviewer. Drawing samples based on known population parameters is often difficult owing to lack of secondary data. In some cities in South America, Mexico, and Asia, street maps are unavailable; in some large metropolitan areas of the Near East and Asia, streets are not identified and houses are not numbered.

Despite the difficulties often faced in conducting international research, some information is always better than none. Sunbeam, for example, failed to do research and only after lack of sales of its toaster in Italy found that although most Europeans eat toast, Italians do not. Sunbeam also was first in the Italian market with a ladies electric shaver. Again no research was done (after all, it was a quality product and sold well in the United States). The shaver bombed. Sunbeam later learned that Italian men like their women with hair on their legs. Good market information is essential for developing the "right" product offerings.

PRODUCT CONSIDERATIONS

After research information has been obtained, the marketing mix can be developed. Marketing managers can select from several product-communications alternatives:[16]

- One product, one message
- Product invention
- Product extension–communication adaptation
- Product adaptation–communication extension

◄ **TABLE 25.4   Information Sources for the International Market**

Reference services (available on a fee or subscription basis):

The Gallatin Annual of International Business. Annual report on 134 countries, updated monthly.

Investing, Licensing and Trading Conditions in 50 Countries. Annual specific report of legal and economic conditions.

Economist Intelligence Unit. Quarterly reports of an economic and political nature on 57 different foreign countries.

Rundt's Market Reports. 30 reports or more per year on major countries, of which more than half are on Latin America.

U.S. government publications:

Several series of publications have been prepared on a country-by-country basis by the Department of Commerce. These include

Overseas Business Reports.

The Market for U.S. Products in . . .

Investment in . . . The most comprehensive series covering investment factors in many countries.

Doing business in [specific countries].

Reports of U.S. trade missions that have visited various countries.

Publications issued by the government of the country being studied:

Many foreign governments publish booklets providing general business information about their country. Most of these booklets are prepared specifically for circulation in foreign countries, particularly the United States. It is definitely worthwhile to contact the nearest consulate or the consulate general of the country being analyzed. A general inquiry about doing business in the country will usually bring a collection of booklets that have been prepared to answer such inquiries.

These publications are often distributed by foreign chambers of commerce in this country. Such semi-official bodies play much the same role as the consulates in attempting to promote trade and investment in their country. Chambers of commerce usually publish periodicals which are of interest to the potential international marketer. These take two forms: a monthly magazine with general articles and a newsletter that may be restricted to the members. Many of these newsletters contain worthwhile information.

Other general publications of interest on specific countries:

Contimart Reports, Zurich, Switzerland. A series of detailed market studies on the major European and Scandinavian markets.

Information Guides for Those Doing Business Outside the U.S. A useful series prepared by Price Waterhouse & Co. which deals with various legal and tax aspects of doing business in foreign countries.

The British Board of Trade has published two series of pamphlets, the *Hints to Businessmen* series and the *Overseas Economic Surveys.*

Important banks in foreign countries often publish promotional booklets describing business conditions in their country. A short letter to each of the important banks should determine whether such material is available.

The larger international advertising agencies periodically publish country studies.

Source: Export Marketing for Smaller Firms, 3rd ed. Small Business Administration, 1978, pp. 23–25.

One product, one message. The simplest strategy is to offer the same product and the same message throughout the world. For example, PepsiCo offers the same product and uses the same promotional theme everywhere. Wrigley's chewing gum and Levi's follow the same philosophy. The advantages of using this strategy include economies of scale in production; marketing economies (uniform sales training and promotion); and universal availability for mobile consumers.

Product invention. Often, however, a single product is not feasible. Incomes will not justify a mass market. Moreover, consumers use products differently. For example, in many countries clothing is worn much longer between washings than in America. Thus the fabric must be more durable. Goodyear developed a tire to handle the tough driving conditions on Peru's roads. It contained a higher percentage of natural rubber than tires manufactured elsewhere and had better treads. As a result, Peruvians preferred it to other tires. National Cash Register developed the NCR80, a crank-operated cash register. It is selling thousands of NCR80s in the Philippines, the Orient, Latin America, and Spain. With about half the parts of more advanced registers, the machine sells for about half the price of the cheapest models available in America.[17] Some typical product modifications and the factors causing the change are shown in Table 25.5.

Product extension–communication adaptation. It may be possible to maintain the same basic product but alter the communication strategy. Bicycles and motorcycles are primarily pleasure vehicles in America. In many parts of the world, however, they are a family's major mode of transportation. Promotion in

◢ **TABLE 25.5   Product Characteristics**

Key factor	Design change
Level of technical skill	Product simplification
Level of labor costs	Automation or manualization of product
Level of literacy	Remaking and simplification of product
Level of income	Quality and price change
Level of interest rates	Quality and price change (investment in high quality might not be financially desirable)
Level of maintenance	Change in tolerances
Climatic differences	Product adaptation
Isolation (heavy repair, difficult and expensive)	Product simplification and reliability improvement
Differences in standards	Recalibration of product and resizing
Availability of other products	Greater or lesser product integration
Availability of materials	Change in product structure and fuel
Power availability	Resizing of product
Special conditions	Product redesign or invention

Source: S. B. Prasad and Y. Krishna Shetty, *An Introduction to Multinational Management* (Englewood Cliffs, N.J.: Prentice-Hall, 1976), p. 154. © 1976. Reprinted by permission.

these countries can stress durability and efficiency. American advertising, in contrast, may emphasize escaping and having fun.

Product adaptation–communication extension. A fourth strategy is to utilize the same promotional theme throughout the world and alter the product to meet local conditions. Campbell Soup learned this lesson the hard way. The familiar red-and-white label was sacrosanct, and the company's communications mix and product remained the same. In England the company failed to explain how to prepare its condensed soups. No one told people to add water to the small can of condensed soup. Since the can looked relatively more expensive next to larger cans of ready-to-eat soup, sales suffered. In this case the product change was an entirely new label explaining how to prepare condensed soup. Campbell lost an estimated $30 million in sales before the problem was corrected. On the other hand, one of the world's largest multinational firms, Exxon, has used the "Put a Tiger in Your Tank" theme successfully throughout the world. The gasolines, of course, are blended for local conditions and engine specifications.

PRICING

Once an international product strategy has been determined, the remainder of the marketing mix can be selected. Pricing presents some unique problems in the international sphere—in fact, the technicalities of export-import pricing are far beyond the scope of this book.

Selling to developing nations often poses special pricing problems owing to lack of mass purchasing power. Sometimes products can be simplified, as in the NCR example, to enable the firm to lower prices substantially. However, the firm must not assume that low-income countries are willing to accept lower quality. The nomads of the Sahara, although they are extremely poor, purchase expensive cloth to make their clothing. Their very survival in harsh conditions and extreme temperatures require this expense. At least a small number of expensive luxury items can be sold almost anywhere. The Lamborghini car sells for over $30,000. The country with the lowest per capita income in Europe is Portugal. Yet the largest single market for Lamborghinis is Portugal. Portuguese are very status-conscious, and the wealth of the country is highly stratified.

Some companies overproduce certain items and end up dumping them in the international market. Government tariffs and decrees further confuse pricing. In addition, fluctuation in international monetary exchange rates can make a product relatively "cheap" overnight. Conversely, it can price a product that was at a competitive level almost out of the market. This was the case with Japanese and German automobiles in the United States during the early 1970s. Some companies are avoiding the pricing issue by returning to direct bartering. For example:

> The Brazilians are considering buying Russian turbines for a dam on the Itapi River. Brazil hopes to pay for the turbines with shoes.
> Morocco and the Soviet Union agree to exchange capital equipment and fresh oranges for a new phosphate plant.[18]

PROMOTION

Much of the international advertising and promotion function tends to be highly standardized among multinational firms, according to a 1975 study.[19] Headquarters develops a prototype campaign and then lets the various subsidiary operations adapt it to local conditions. Goodyear has used this method successfully in developing localized ads based on a worldwide theme, approach, and format. In contrast to centralized campaigns, probably the least standardized of all marketing decisions is the media strategy.[20] Commercial television time, for example, is readily available in Canada, severely restricted in Germany, and totally unavailable in Sweden.

Some cultures view a product as having less value "if it has to be advertised." The hard-sell tactics and sexual themes so common in America are taboo in many countries. Sometimes media are controlled by the government, which restricts or eliminates advertising. An example of failure to understand a country's culture in a promotional campaign follows.

A leading producer of farm equipment was particularly pleased with the success of a North American advertising campaign which was built around the testimonials of small farmers. . . . Thus the testimonial campaign was introduced into Europe. The advertising vice president was dismayed to receive an urgent telex from the largest distributor organization demanding that the campaign be withdrawn after only two weeks. The distributor had been flooded with telegrams from his dealers. They all found the campaign to be insulting and described it like this: "Most of our farms in Europe are small to begin with. When you stress 'smallness' so much, our customers think you are talking about peasants. And who likes advice from them?"[21]

Language barriers and translation problems have generated numerous headaches for international marketing managers, as the following examples show.

Chrysler Corp. was nearly laughed out of Spain when it copied the U.S. theme advertising, "Dart is Power." To the Spanish, the phrase implied that buyers lack but are seeking sexual vigor. Ford goofed when it named its low-cost "third world" truck "Tiera" which means "ugly old woman" in Spanish. American Motors has had its problems too. Market research showed that AMC's "Matador" name meant virility and excitement, but when the car was introduced in Puerto Rico it was discovered that the word meant "killer"—an unfortunate choice for Puerto Rico, which has an unusually high traffic fatality rate.[22]

DISTRIBUTION

Solving promotion, price, and product problems does not guarantee international marketing success. The firm still has to obtain adequate distribution. The Japanese system is considered the most complicated in the world. Imported goods wind their way through layers of agents, wholesalers, and retailers. "Our trade distribution channels are historical, traditional ones," a trade ministry official says, "and it will be extremely difficult for the Japanese government to change such traditional channels."

Kentucky Fried Chicken Japan observes that "everything in Japan starts in Tokyo." Its three initial stores in Osaka were a mistake. Fay Weston, chairperson of KFC Japan, notes, "We goofed—you can't start in Osaka and expect to creep into Tokyo. All three stores were a total disaster."

For a variety of reasons, American-type retail outlets are not practical in developing countries. For example, supermarkets encounter many cultural taboos. Many foods are highly perishable, since the use of preservatives is uncommon. Thus shoppers do not welcome packaged goods because they believe that food in a package would be spoiled. Also, most consumers do not have the storage space to keep food for several days. Refrigerators, when available, are usually small and do not allow for bulk storage.

Sometimes channels simply do not exist. This is true not only in developing nations, but in industrialized countries as well. Procter & Gamble sells soap and other products from door to door in the Philippines, Iran, and a number of developing countries. Lack of storage facilities and adequate highway and road systems also complicate international distribution.

Political and governmental actions can hinder distribution. In Central America, cargo moving by truck must be unloaded at the border of each country. It is then placed on a truck registered in the country being entered.

Cartels can block distribution channels. General Tire was forced out of Europe because the tire cartel would not tolerate its presence and made its channels ineffective. Israel's huge wholesaler, Hamashber Hamerkazi, handles about one-fifth of the country's wholesale trade and maintains partial ownership of twelve major industrial firms. The company has tremendous political and economic clout in Israel's distribution system.

Not only are channels of distribution often inadequate in developing nations, but so is the physical infrastructure. China, for example, is a growing trading partner with the United States. Yet Chinese modes of transportation are primitive:

The vast bulk of all transport is carried on poles or human backs, in wheelbarrows and hand carts and, increasingly (and this is an important advance), on bicycles. Much effort has gone in recent years into extending the rail system, but many of the new lines have primarily strategic rather than commercial value; and most trains are still pulled by steam locomotives. The line between the two largest industrial centers, Shanghai and Tientsin, was only double-tracked in 1976. The road system is even more limited. Some communities have no road access at all and some of the main highways do not have all-weather surfaces.[23]

Organizing for international marketing

Effective marketing in an international setting requires good planning. A key issue that arises early in the decision process is degree of centralization. Some companies centralize marketing decision making at company headquarters; others favor a decentralized structure. The tremendous dissimilarities among nations speak strongly for at least some degree of local autonomy. Yet integration of talent and resources, as well as overall control, requires a certain amount of centralization.

The trend among large multinationals in the 1980s is back to centralization. As one executive says:

The whole idea of setting up the regional office was to exercise control and coordination. We think it's more efficient to have some highly qualified senior guys here at headquarters who get more involved in subsidiary operations than to duplicate management skills at the country level. It's a way of life for us now and the subsidiaries are accepting it more and more.[24]

Companies selling "culture-free" products such as transistors can usually centralize more readily than those that offer "culture-bound" products such as food that require significant adaptation to local conditions.

Translating centralization versus decentralization into an organization structure means grappling with three major problems:

How to encourage a predominantly domestic organization to take full advantage of growth opportunities abroad.

How to blend product knowledge and geographic area knowledge most efficiently in coordinating worldwide business.

How to coordinate activities of foreign units in many countries while permitting each to retain its own national identity.[25]

Most large multinational firms have at least some degree of regionalization in their organization structure. From this point, they are structured along product, functional, or matrix lines. Armco Steel, for example, uses a basic geographical organization modified to emphasize worldwide product coordination. All Armco products with international potential are grouped together under Armco Enterprises. The international division is responsible for the operations of 27 overseas affiliates, administering the international licensing program, and export sales. Operating units in each country have wide latitude in the marketing of locally produced Armco products. Each operation not only adapts to local conditions, but acts as a profit center as well.

Armco is just one example of a well-organized multinational firm. There is no one structure that will solve all international problems. It depends upon the firm's philosophy of centralization, its human and physical resources, and its fund of international experience.

SUMMARY

There are a number of reasons for engaging in international marketing. From a macro point of view, international marketing may offer the potential for achieving a "better world." When exchange occurs between countries, it builds stronger ties between those nations.

The firms that are responsible for most of the activity in international trade are the multinationals. A multinational corporation is one that moves resources, goods, services, and skills across national boundaries. Many multinational organizations are huge organizations.

There are a variety of techniques for pursuing international trade. Perhaps the simplest form is the exporting of goods. A more aggressive technique is licensing. Firms that do not want to become involved in licensing arrangements may engage in contract manufacturing, private label manufacturing by a foreign company. The foreign organization produces merchandise to specifications with the domestic firm's brand name affixed to the merchandise. Joint ventures are similar to a licensing agreement except that the domestic firm assumes an equity position in a foreign company. Direct investment in wholly owned foreign manufacturing and marketing subsidiaries usually offers the greatest potential reward. Naturally, the possibility of substantial reward also means great risk. Countries with strong nationalistic policies may extract substantial tax concessions and other controls from the manufacturer. At the extreme level, the assets of the foreign corporation may be nationalized.

In order to be effective in international trade, it is necessary to understand the external environment within which the firm is operating. One of the most important aspects of the external environment is a country's culture. In addition to understanding a country's culture, the international marketer needs to have an appreciation for its economic development. One way to examine the level of economic development is to apply the stages of economic growth theory: the traditional society, the preindustrial society, the takeoff economy, the industrialized society, and the fully industrialized nation.

A third important uncontrollable variable facing international marketers is political considerations. In some cases, governments actively encourage foreign investment; in others, they engage in just the opposite behavior. Closely related and often intertwined with political factors are legal considerations. The legal considerations are designed to encourage trade or to limit trade.

Technology is the fourth major factor in the external environment that can influence the success of the international firm. American multinational firms have long prided themselves as being technological leaders. Yet technology levels sometimes must be lowered in order to make a product attractive and a price competitive for developing nations.

Demographics is another major consideration in the external environment. Although many countries such as China and India have huge populations, their relatively low per capita incomes mean that there is not a huge mass market for moderate- to high-priced consumer goods. Yet within virtually every country in the world there are "pockets of wealth" that offer opportunities for the astute marketer.

A final factor in the external environment is natural resource shortages. Energy is not the only form of natural resource shortages that will affect international marketing during the remainder of the 1980s. A lack of water and/or warm weather will mean that many African countries and the Soviet Union will be major importers of foodstuff. America, on the other hand, is a major importer of petroleum and precious metals.

After a company's marketing manager has a thorough understanding of the external environment, he or she must then develop a marketing mix. The development of the mix often entails conducting marketing research abroad. While the process is generally the same as conducting a domestic marketing research study, cultural differences and a lack of secondary marketing data often impede the efficient completion of a research project.

The international marketing mix typically begins with product considerations. Basic product strategies are these: one product, one communication message; product inventions; product extension–communication adaptation; or product adaptation–communication extension.

Pricing presents some unique problems in international marketing. Expensive products are sometimes bought by poor people who do without other goods and services in order to make certain purchases. Credit and inflation further complicate international pricing.

Promotion is the most highly standardized marketing function in many multinational firms. Often the headquarters of a multinational firm develops a prototype campaign and lets the various subsidiary operations adapt it to local situations. Media strategy varies markedly from one country to another because of great differences of media availability.

In many countries, distribution is primitive. In others it is tradition-bound. Thus it is often difficult to build adequate channels. Sometimes channels simply do not exist. In other situations, political and government actions can hinder distribution through tariffs, embargoes, and shipment regulations.

Putting the international marketing mix into operation requires good planning. Some companies centralize marketing decision making; others use a decentralized structure. The great socioeconomic and cultural differences between various nations suggest the need for some degree of decentralization. However, the resultant lack of control has resulted in many of the large multinationals recentralizing some of their marketing operations.

KEY TERMS

Multinational corporation
Capital-intensive technology
Buyer for export
Licensing
International franchising
Contract manufacturing
Joint ventures

Tariff
General Agreement on Tariffs and
   Trade (GATT)
Quota
Boycott
Exchange control
Market groupings

REVIEW QUESTIONS

1. What is international marketing?
2. Which method of entering the international market is most risky? Least risky? Why?
3. Why is control by the domestic firm of such importance in international marketing? How can control be maintained?
4. What environmental factors affect the international marketing mix?
5. What is the purpose of a tariff? Why is it necessary?

6. What are some of the problems encountered in international marketing research?
7. Briefly outline the different product–communications alternatives available to international marketers.
8. What are some of the problems encountered in international distribution activities? Give a few examples.

DISCUSSION QUESTIONS

1. Why do you think America is less dependent on external trade than other industrialized countries?
2. Briefly outline and explain the economic evolution of a country and its impact on marketing.
3. Explain some of the cultural factors that affect international marketing. Can you think of some examples?
4. Assume that Pizza Hut wants to expand to Kuwait. What elements of the marketing mix would it have to alter?
5. Small Chemical manufactures a chemical that could have limited usefulness in several Asian countries. Assume you are the firm's marketing manager. How would you go about trying to exploit this market? Give reasons for your answer.
6. Outline the advantages to be gained through centralized international marketing as compared to a decentralized structure. Which organization form would be more suitable for marketing the following products?
   a. Calculators.
   b. Special steel tubing.
   c. Soft drinks.
   d. Sporting equipment.

NOTES

1. "What's in a Name Sales Game?" *Dallas Morning News,* August 3, 1980, pp. 3, 11. Reprinted by permission of the Associated Press, New York.
2. J. Paul Austin, "World Marketing as a New Force for Peace," *Journal of Marketing* 30 (January 1966): 1–3.
3. Susan R. Silver and Jules T. Schwartz, "The U.S. Industrial Marketer's Position in International Trade," *Industrial Marketing Management,* June 1977, pp. 337–352.
4. Neil Jacoby, "The Multinational Corporation," *Center Magazine* 3 (May 1970): 37. Reprinted by permission from *The Center Magazine,* a publication of the Center for the Study of Democratic Institutions, Santa Barbara, California.
5. Robert Stauffer, *Nation Building in a Global Economy: The Role of the Multinational Corporation* (Beverly Hills, Calif.: Sage Publications, 1973), p. 13.
6. Irgo Walter, "Developing Lands Seek Ways to Control or Bypass Transnational Enterprises," *Marketing News,* November 5, 1976, p. 6.
7. Lawrence G. Franko, "Multinationals: The End of U.S. Dominance," *Harvard Business Review* 56 (November–December 1978): 93–101.
8. F. R. Lineaweaver, "Key to Company Growth: Effective Export Distribution," *Distribution Worldwide,* October 1970, p. 55.
9. Herbert E. Meyer, "How U.S. Textiles Got To Be Winners in the Export Game," *Fortune,* May 5, 1980, pp. 261–262.
10. Wray O. Candiles, "The Growth of Franchising," *Business Economics,* March 1978, p. 16.

11. Susan Douglas and Bernard Dubois, "Looking at the Cultural Environment for International Marketing Opportunities," *Columbia Journal of World Business,* winter 1977, p. 103.

12. John Liebman, "Planning for Foreign Marketing Takes both Learning and Unlearning," *Industrial Marketing,* May 1974, p. 52.

13. Vern Terpstra, *International Marketing,* 2nd ed. (Hinsdale, Ill.: Dryden Press, 1978), p. 34. Copyright © 1978 by The Dryden Press, a division of Holt, Rinehart and Winston, Publishers. Reprinted by permission of Holt, Rinehart and Winston.

14. Ruel Kahler and Roland L. Kramer, *International Marketing,* 4th ed. (Cincinnati: South-Western, 1977), p. 138.

15. Terpstra, *International Marketing,* p. 57.

16. See Warren Keegan, "Multinational Product Planning: Strategic Alternatives," *Journal of Marketing* 33 (January 1969): 58–62.

17. Both the Goodyear and National Cast Register examples are taken from Vern Terpstra, *International Marketing* (Hinsdale, Ill.: Dryden Press, 1972), pp. 248–249.

18. These examples are from Robert E. Weigand, "International Trade without Money," *Harvard Business Review* 55 (November–December 1977): 28–56.

19. Ralph Sorenson and Ulrich Wiechmann, "To What Extent Should a Consumer Goods Multinational Corporation Vary Its Marketing from Country to Country?" *Harvard Business Review* 53 (May–June 1975): 42.

20. Ibid.

21. James Killough, "Improved Payoffs from Transnational Advertising," *Harvard Business Review* 56 (July–August 1978): 103.

22. Philip Cateora and John Hess, *International Marketing,* 3rd ed. (Homewood, Ill.: Irwin, 1975), pp. 402–403.

23. Guy M. Sayer, "The China Market," *Across the Board,* April 1978, p. 50.

24. Ulrich Wiechmann, "Integrating Multinational Marketing Activities," *Columbia Journal of World Business,* winter 1974, p. 10.

25. Michael Duerr and John Roach, *Organization and Control of International Operations* (New York: The Conference Board, 1973), p. 5.

 CASES

25.1 Household Finance Corporation

Extending credit to the prosperous Japanese seemed like an excellent opportunity for Household Finance Corporation. It would compete with a local industry whose operating methods were antiquated and whose reputation was very negative. The Japanese press called their own country's lenders "the world's deadliest loan sharks" because they often charge as much as 110 percent a year interest. Firms that offered loans in Japan became known as *sarakin,* which is a combination of the words for "salaried man" and "money." One steel mill employee got fired because *sarakin* collectors interrupted his work 40 times and annoyed his colleagues. Police were reporting an average of one "*sarakin* suicide" a day during the late 1970s.

The market looked highly attractive because Japan's population is about one-half that of the United States, yet with about one-seventh of the American level of consumer debt. Most Japanese consumers, however, hate to borrow. Traditionally, no one writes personal checks, and credit cards provide only temporary credit, since charges are paid in full each month. An average Japanese white-collar worker earns about as much as his American counterpart, but faces a chronic cash shortage. In 1978 Household Finance Corporation set out to get a major position in the developing Japanese market.

The results of Household Finance's efforts have been unique, to say the least. In a typical Japanese family, the wife is supposed to manage the household and its finances. A husband is given an allowance of about $7 a day. If he cannot live on his allowance, the *sarakin* is close to a necessity. *Sarakin* require no security, nor do they require answers to a lot of questions, such as usually required by Household Finance.

When Household Finance and other American loan companies entered the market, they did what was expected. They drove the initial interest rates down to 48 percent, and Japanese *sarakin* soon followed. The American companies immediately attracted many Japanese applicants—those already mired in debt to the *sarakin*. When *sarakin* had a collection problem, they would drive the customer over to an American firm, wait outside, and then take the money he borrowed.

Americans also found no central credit bureau in the country, and had to set up their own (with little Japanese cooperation). One applicant, for example, had 47 loans outstanding. Household Finance had trouble building up a sizable and dependable clientele. The company generally requires wives to sign applications, which happens to be a tremendous blow to the Japanese ego. To make matters worse, the negative reputation of the *sarakin* rubbed off on the American companies. The Finance Ministry issued an "administrative guidance" to banks against providing substantial amounts to loan companies that charge high interest rates and use harsh collection practices. Banks chose to interpret that order as applying to the American companies as well. In a show of self-reform to avoid additional government regulation, the 170 largest Japanese loan companies which belonged to the Japan Consumer Finance Association developed a new code of ethics in the late 1970s. Many of the advertising media decided to accept ads only from members of the association, which excluded foreigners. A Household Finance Corporation executive said, "The people don't know HFC except as a *sarakin* company, and we can't advertise to explain that we're different."

1. Could the problems experienced by Household Finance Corporation have been avoided? How?
2. If you were an executive of Household Finance Corporation, what action would you recommend? Defend your position.

25.2 Goldman Microwave Corporation

A microwave system is divided into three components, the transmitter, the receiver, and the repeater stations between the transmitter and the receiver. The microwave repeater units must be placed about every 30 miles, with each unit making a link in a chain as the microwave signal or message is passed from one location to another. The microwaves are used for a variety of purposes, such as telecommunications and television signal transmission.

Goldman Microwave Corporation is considering entering the Mexican market.

At present there are two main purchasers of microwave systems in Mexico, the Secretaria de Comunicaciones y Transportes, and Telefonos de Mexico. These two organizations make up most of the projected sales within the next ten years. The Mexican oil company, Pemex, now has only a small percentage of sales, but has excellent future potential. Presently, Goldman manufactures the microwave systems in the United States in the unitary form, ships the components to the foreign buyer, and then sends technicians from the United States to assemble the final product. This procedure will probably be unacceptable to the Mexican government, as it does not provide employment for Mexican workers, as would the manufacture of the microwave systems in Mexico.

Goldman has a connection with a Nogales, Mexico, organization that is capable of manufacturing the microwave systems. This firm utilizes Mexican labor that is managed by Americans, and has a special agreement with the Mexican government that allows the manufactured products and profits to flow from Mexico without restriction because of its border location. This organization would perhaps not be considered acceptable to the Mexican government. A second alternative would be for Goldman to build a plant for the manufacture of the microwave system in Mexico. The plant could be managed by American and Mexican managers, with the final managerial control initially resting with the Goldman Corporation. Over a period of time, if the plant is properly managed, control of the business would be shifted to the managers of the Mexican plant. This would involve a decreasing level of control by Goldman as the business developed.

Goldman company executives agree that the timing of the plant is critical, for if the plant is built too early there will not be enough demand for the product to make a sufficient profit for a number of years. If the company delays too long, potential market share might be lost. Goldman is in a quandary as to what action to take. Should it attempt to sell the government on the Nogales concept? Should it build a plant in Mexico? A third alternative is simply to stay out of the market altogether.

1. Discuss the advantages and disadvantages of the alternatives facing the Goldman Microwave Corporation.
2. If you were the president of Goldman, what would you do? Why?

The Darling Doll Corporation*

The Darling Doll Corporation was started by George and Jane Mason in 1950 and enjoyed a reputation as a quality manufacturer of dolls within the industry. By 1960 sales volume had reached a high of $10 million. However, because of the decline in the birth rate, sales volume stabilized in 1972 at about $8 million. Although the firm had achieved a place of eminence in the industry for making a wide range of dolls, sales last year were only $7 million.

The toy industry is characterized by a large number of relatively small firms. Mattel and Marx are two of the largest firms in the industry. A number of new firms enter the industry each year, since entry costs are low. Many of these small firms declare bankruptcy due to undercapitalization and inexperience. There is keen price competition because of these marginal producers. Some producers charge prices very close to actual costs.

The toy industry traditionally has experienced a highly seasonal sales pattern. Toy sales start to rise in October and reach a peak in November and December. It has been estimated that at least 50 percent of the toy sales occur over the Christmas season.

The Darling Doll Corporation was not a diversified toy company. George and Jane Mason had a line of dolls made from a wide variety of materials. Their most successful item was a Raggedy Ann doll. Other products that sold well recently were dolls dressed in costumes of foreign countries. The firm manufactured approximately 75 dolls representing foreign nations. The Darling Doll Corporation also manufactured clothes for these dolls, and a complete wardrobe reflecting the seasonal dress of the various nations was available. The dolls were expensive and sold very well in gift stores located in airports and hotels. The Raggedy Ann dolls sold very well in discount stores, variety stores, and drugstores. The firm also made up a line of stuffed animals. These were sold in hotel shops, specialty stores, and department stores. The stuffed animals were exceedingly profitable.

The Darling Doll Corporation used wholesalers to distribute its dolls to department stores and variety stores. Rack jobbers were used to distribute to supermarkets and drugstores. The firm sold direct to stores in hotels and airports. Approximately 50 percent of the firm's sales volume came from department and variety stores. Stores located in hotels and airports accounted for another 25 percent. Supermarkets and drugstores accounted for only 10 percent. The balance of sales came from discount stores, stationery and book stores, and gift shops.

About 50 percent of the Darling Doll Corporation's market was situated in large metropolitan areas and their suburbs. This was especially true for sales of stuffed animals. In recent years, Darling Doll found that as much as 40 percent of sales volume was derived from the sale of stuffed animals. Department stores were the major sellers of this item.

The woman in the family was the largest purchaser of the products of the Darling Doll Corporation; women accounted for approximately two-thirds of the purchasers. In many instances, men purchasers were adding to a collection of

---

* Case prepared by Professor Ronald D. Michman, Shippensburg State College, Shippensburg, Pennsylvania.

foreign dolls. Many children themselves purchased the less expensive dolls, especially in the variety stores.

The Darling Doll Corporation wanted to produce a giant Raggedy Ann doll about 3 feet in height that would have mechanical movement in its arms and head. The doll would not have any mechanized movement in its legs, except that the child would be able to walk the doll. To achieve this objective, realistic leather-soled shoes were constructed. The Darling Doll Corporation entered into an agreement with a firm in Hong Kong to manufacture the doll, which would be distributed under the brand name China Doll in the United States. There were several reasons for this arrangement. First of all, the Hong Kong firm would be licensed to produce and sell all the Darling Doll stuffed animals in Hong Kong and Japan, where they have a branch. The license would include patents, trademarks, product standards, and production and marketing techniques. Second, the Darling Doll Corporation did not have any mechanical products, and the Hong Kong firm could produce the China Doll at lower cost, even considering customs and import fees.

The Consumer Product Safety Act aims at reducing or eliminating product hazards. Under the act, importers are not permitted to bring a foreign product into the United States, even under customs bonds, while the product is undergoing safety tests. The findings and purposes of the Consumer Product Safety Act are found in Table 1, along with a section of the act pertaining to product safety information and research. The China Doll product passed the safety tests, and the Darling Doll Corporation distributed the doll to discount houses such as K-Mart, Nichols, and Woolco throughout the United States.

A few months later, after the doll had been distributed to retailers through toy wholesalers, *Consumer Reports* devoted a section to the results of its tests on mechanical dolls of this type selling from $20 to $25, which included the China Doll. The report revealed that if the child walked the doll and moved the feet on a cement surface, it would cause enough friction on the soles of the shoes to generate sparks and might possibly ignite clothing. Executives at the Darling Doll Corporation were shocked upon learning of this report. The China Doll was selling well in large metropolitan areas in the discount stores, but not in the suburbs, medium sized, or small towns.

The China Doll was not meant to be walked in the manner described in *Consumer Reports*. Executives of Darling Doll pointed to the fact that the doll had passed tests administered by the Consumer Product Safety Commission and that the purposes and objectives for product safety and research as described in Table 1 seem quite rigorous. Therefore the executives could not understand how *Consumer Reports* could issue such a report. The executives believed that a harmful incident developing from playing with the China Doll was a million to one chance.

Some of the executives wondered about the importance of the rating by *Consumer Reports*. How many potential buyers of the doll would read this report and not make the purchase? Some executives believed that *Consumer Reports* would be of minor importance in affecting consumer demand. Others believed that a poor rating would be of much greater significance if the product were a major appliance. However, one executive pointed out that the China Doll sold for $20 in discount houses, and that since the product was expensive, a source of consumer information might be consulted. The majority of executives disagreed

Findings and Purposes

Sec. 2.   (a) The Congress finds that—

(1) an unacceptable number of consumer products which present unreasonable risks of injury are distributed in commerce;

(2) complexities of consumer products and the diverse nature and abilities of consumers using them frequently result in an inability of users to anticipate risks and to safeguard themselves adequately;

(3) the public should be protected against unreasonable risks of injury associated with consumer products;

(4) control by state and local governments of unreasonable risks of injury associated with consumer products is inadequate and may be burdensome to manufacturers;

(5) existing Federal authority to protect consumers from exposure to consumer products presenting unreasonable risks of injury is inadequate; and

(6) regulation of consumer products the distribution or use of which affects interstate or foreign commerce is necessary to carry out this Act.

(b) The purposes of this Act are—

(1) to protect the public against unreasonable risks of injury associated with consumer products;

(2) to assist consumers in evaluating the comparative safety of consumer products;

(3) to develop uniform safety standards for consumer products and to minimize conflicting State and local regulations; and

(4) to promote research and investigation into the causes and prevention of product-related deaths, illnesses, and injuries.

Product Safety Information and Research

Sec. 5.   (a) The Commission shall—

(1) maintain an Injury Information Clearinghouse to collect, investigate, analyze, and disseminate injury data, and information, relating to the causes and prevention of death, injury, and illness associated with consumer products; and

(2) conduct such continuing studies and investigations of deaths, injuries, diseases, other health impairments, and economic losses resulting from accidents involving consumer products as it deems necessary.

(b) The Commission may—

(1) conduct research, studies, and investigations on the safety of consumer products and on improving the safety of such products;

(2) test consumer products and develop product safety test methods and testing devices; and

(3) offer training in product safety investigation and test methods, and assist public and private organizations, administratively and technically, in the development of safety standards and test methods.

Source: Consumer Product Safety Act PL 92-573, pp. 1400, 1404.

and contended that neither a favorable nor an unfavorable rating by consumer testing services would increase or decrease sales significantly. Therefore, nothing was done to correct the condition affecting the China Doll.

A few months later, one of the employees of the Darling Doll Corporation reported that her five-year-old daughter had been playing with the China Doll on the sidewalk and it had ignited, damaging the doll's clothing. Fortunately, no one was hurt. The incident had happened while the little girl was walking the China

Distributors

According to Section 3 (a) (5) of the CPSA, a distributor is any person to whom a consumer product is delivered or sold for purposes of distribution in commerce, unless that person is a manufacturer or retailer. Included in this definition, would be wholesalers and any other middlemen involved in the sale of consumer products.

Distributors are basically held to all of the requirements of manufacturers, with the notable exception for the product safety standards that relate to the actual production of consumer products.

1. They may not distribute banned products.
2. They must allow inspection of their premises.
3. They are subject to such record-keeping rules as the Commission may prescribe.
4. They are required to inform the Commission of any product defects they observe.
5. They may be ordered to notify the public of product hazards and remedies.

Also, if a distributor is a manufacturer as well, he is subject to the Act's requirements involving certification of product safety and labeling. If not, he is not subject to these rules.

Retailers

Under Section 3 (a) (6) of the Act, a retailer is defined as a person to whom a consumer product is delivered or sold for purposes of sale or distribution to a consumer. This would include both independent or chain retail outlets, as well as mail order houses.

Generally, retailers are held to all of the provisions of the CPSA, such as dealing with the distribution of nonconforming or banned goods or the seizure of hazardous products. However, they are not subject to the provision dealing with labeling, but they are required to inform the Commission whenever they obtain information that a consumer product fails to comply with an applicable safety standard or contains a substantial product hazard.

Doll and moving its feet, thereby causing friction. Several employees of the Darling Doll Corporation had been given the China Doll as gifts, and this was the only reported incident.

The sections of the act shown in Table 2 concerning distributors and retailers were carefully read. Some executives did not believe that the Darling Doll Corporation had any responsibility to report the incident to the Consumer Product Safety Commission, since the product had passed its laboratory tests. They did not want to make too much of one reported incident. However, the marketing manager was requested to determine the extent of the Darling Doll Corporation's liability, should such information be needed.

1. What are the advantages and limitations of arrangements with foreign firms to produce a product and to subsequently import the product into the United States?
2. Do you agree or disagree with the approach used by the Darling Doll Corporation?
3. What is the extent of the liability of the Hong Kong firm, Darling Doll, and wholesalers and retailers, should this product be recalled?

Epilogue:
Marketing–its future

By now, you should have a firm grasp of the fundamental concepts and theories of marketing. Although this material marks the conclusion of the text, however, it is not the end, but actually the beginning. For marketing is a fertile source of job opportunities. If you are considering marketing as a career field you should be aware of some of the key economic trends that may affect you as a marketing manager.

Broad economic trends

CONTINUED HIGH RATES OF INFLATION

In the 1980s, inflation will continue to be a significant problem. For many Americans, the cost of living will continue to outstrip income. Housing and energy expenses will be leading the inflationary charge. This means that the inflationary psychology of "Buy it today, because it will cost more tomorrow. Borrow to buy, you can repay with cheaper dollars" will continue. Inflation pushes many consumers (and businesses) beyond good judgment in managing debt. Inflation also discourages investment that could improve productive efficiency and create new job opportunities.

MORE SHORTAGES

As a marketing manager in this decade, you will also have to cope with shortages, both real and threatened. The energy problem is the most apparent area of shortages—technology will not find an effective solution during the 1980s. The synfuel programs, solar and geothermal development, and others will not have a significant impact until the following decade. This means greater emphasis on the manufacture, distribution, and use of energy-efficient products. Other important shortages will be minerals and forest products. Shortages coupled with inflation will make it increasingly difficult for consumers to maintain the quality of life they once knew. It also means that more firms will, from time to time, become demarketers; they will be forced to implement strategies designed to discourage consumption.

CONTINUED TECHNOLOGICAL CHANGE

The technological revolution, particularly in the fields of electronics and communication, shows no signs of abating. Microprocessors, the computers on a silicon chip, will continue to proliferate, making industrial and consumer goods "smarter." Firms that do not keep up with this and other technological developments will soon find themselves by the wayside.

Two-way communication between homes and businesses, and companies and other firms through cable TV and CRT terminals will offer many new challenges and opportunities. Marketing is usually more efficient in moving products than it is in moving people. That is, it is more efficient to get products to people rather than people to products. It is also more efficient to move information rather than products. The communications revolution moves information, thus making marketing more efficient. For example, rather than moving large quantities of goods to a number of retail stores, catalog information can be flashed to potential buyers on home TV screens. When the consumers see something they like, they can press buttons on a terminal to either charge the merchandise or have the cost deducted from a checking account. The goods can then be shipped from a central warehouse. The growth of information technology may mean a decline in personal selling as we now know it. Make no mistake, in-store shopping will not disappear soon. Some products and many services will be bought in stores. People will always want to try on new clothes, squeeze the produce, and go out to get their hair styled.

OTHER IMPORTANT TRENDS

In addition to inflation, shortages, and technological advancement, other significant changes will also affect marketing management during the remainder of the 1980s. New mores, societal values, and priorities will evolve, requiring alterations in the marketing mix. It would be foolish for me to try to predict what these social changes will be. I can say with authority that social change will take place. Government regulation and bureaucratic red tape will continue to plague marketing managers, although the deregulation of the airlines, trucking, and the railroads, plus the tempered zeal of the FTC, does give cause for hope. However, the issues of consumerism and social responsibility will remain with us, and the pressures are likely to increase.

Social and nonprofit marketing will continue to grow in stature and importance. Health care and university marketing will continue to be in the forefront in the nonprofit sector. Their successful application of the marketing concept will induce a wider variety of nonprofit groups to take the plunge into marketing.

Many marketers will also rely more heavily on desegmentation to meet profit objectives. Shortages and inflation will force buyers to accept goods marketed under desegmentation strategies since they will probably be less expensive, albeit not an ideal fit between consumer needs and desires and product specifications. Desegmentation will also help American firms compete more effectively in the international sphere. Increased governmental assistance and better marketing intelligence data will also help the American international marketer.

Marketing opportunities

The remainder of the 1980s will offer many excellent opportunities as well as challenges. Even though inflation is a problem, real household income should rise about 2 percent per year for the remainder of the decade.[1] This means greater real purchasing power and new markets to serve. By 1990, more than half of total family income will be controlled by families in the $25,000 and above income categories, based upon 1977 dollars.[2] Higher family incomes translate into greater demand for luxury items and quality merchandise. Moreover, this market will not be small. Over 40 percent of all households will earn $25,000 and above (1977 dollars) by 1990.[3]

During the second half of the 1980s, the consumer will be better educated, more cosmopolitan, and older. The average age will be around 40 by 1990, and over 27 million persons will qualify as senior citizens.[4] As consumers get older, many marketers will change their marketing mix to tap the more mature segment. Gross national product will have a top range of real growth of about 3.4 percent during the 1980s.[5] This is better than the 1970s, but below that of the 1960s. As GNP increases, industrial marketing opportunities will also grow.

So, there you have it—my assessment of the challenges and opportunities for the rest of the decade. If you are looking for a career that tests your abilities but provides tremendous rewards and fast-track advancement, I suggest you consider marketing. It will not necessarily be easy, but it can be exciting and satisfying.

NOTES

1. "Lucrative Marketing Opportunities Will Abound in the 'Upbeat' 1980's," *Marketing News,* July 11, 1980, p. 14.
2. Ibid.
3. Ibid.
4. Bob Middendorf, "Your Marketing Plan Cannot Ignore Working Women in the 1980's," *Marketing Times,* January–February 1980, p. 30.
5. Joseph J. Ingolia, "Problems We Have, But We've Beat Problems Before. What We Really Need: Better Leadership," *Marketing Times,* January–February 1980, p. 28.

Appendix:
A career in marketing

Personal selling

There are perhaps more marketing jobs available to college graduates in sales than any other career field. Usually, the most challenging positions are with industrial goods manufacturers or wholesalers and entail calling on purchasing agents or buying committees. Large consumer goods manufacturers such as Procter & Gamble also hire marketing majors to act as local sales representatives. These reps visit retail stores (perhaps as many as 15 per day), rotate stock, assemble displays, and take orders. This entry-level position can often lead to a rewarding career in sales management.

Another type of sales position is called "detailing." These representatives call on doctors, dentists, hospitals, and pharmacies for pharmaceutical or medical equipment manufacturers. The job offers pleasant working conditions and calling on a professional clientele. There is little actual "selling"; instead, the detailer dispenses samples and information about new products.

Many other sales positions are available to the college graduate. Sales jobs often give the individual an opportunity to travel, plenty of free time without close supervision, advancement opportunities, and rewards closely associated with effort and results. However, extensive travel can be a detriment to family life, and a commission plan may mean lean times for the person just starting out. He or she will also face indifferent or hostile prospects from time to time. But if you like people and personal freedom, a sales career might be for you.

Advertising

Advertising is the glamour area of marketing, yet it presents relatively few job openings. The entire industry employs only about 200,000 people. Marketing majors entering advertising are likely to start as assistant account executives. An account person acts as a liaison between the advertising agency and the client. It is that person's responsibility to keep the client organization satisfied so that it remains with the agency. It is his or her job to sell new campaigns or campaign concepts to the advertiser and also explain client needs to the agency's creative staff (artists and copywriters).

Another career path is in media. A media person develops plans that show how different media will be used to meet each client's marketing plan. The media person also buys and schedules broadcasting time, newspaper or magazine space, or billboard space. A third area for marketing students to consider is agency research. A researcher engages in copy testing, runs focus groups for concept evaluation, does advertising tracking studies, and performs any type of market research the client requests. But the number of research positions with advertising agencies is quite limited. It is rare, for example, to find an agency with billings of under $30 million with an employee whose function is strictly research.

Marketing research

Many students, particularly those with a quantitative flair, become interested in careers in marketing research. Jobs in this area, however, are even more limited (although growing) than in advertising. If you decide to pursue a career with a research firm, you are probably going to have to live in New York, Chicago, Los Angeles, or San Francisco, because this is where most of the firms are located. In any case, the number of applicants is usually far greater than the number of openings, so salaries are typically low. Also, many jobs specify an MBA as a minimum requirement.

A second alternative is to join the research department of a large retailer or manufacturer. This will offer a wider choice of geographic locations and probably better pay. The size of most marketing research departments is quite small (less than 10 people), even for large firms. Most industrial goods manufacturers with sales under $25 million and consumer goods producers with sales under $10 million do not have marketing research departments.

In a marketing research firm, you may start as an assistance account executive. In this position, you would be expected to "sell" research projects to potential and existing clients and act as a liaison between the research firm and the client. A second path to consider is starting as an assistant project director. This person works with the account executive to design the sampling frame and select a sampling technique, determine sample size, select the statistical tools to be used in the analysis, analyze the data, and prepare the final report. The report is then presented by the account executive, the assistant project director, or both. Career advancement is usually from assistant account executive or project director to account executive or project director. From this point, promotion is typically into higher management. If you choose to work for a large manufacturer or retailer, you would probably start as an assistant project director. In a smaller company, it would be assistant director of research.

Retailing

If marketing research does not present a sufficient number of openings in the part of the country in which you wish to live, you might examine a retailing career. One of the most exciting places to begin is as an assistant buyer or department manager. Here, you will learn how to plan displays, supervise salespeople, evaluate vendors, order merchandise, and so forth. The assistant buyer is more involved in the purchasing aspect of retailing; the assistant department manager supervises personnel and learns store operations. The next step is buyer or department manager, which is more entrepreneurial in nature and closely akin to running your own business. From this point, a person is promoted to store manager or senior buyer.

As an alternative to working for someone else, you might elect to own your own retail business. Unless you are well-financed and have plenty of skilled help, you may be the buyer, personnel manager, advertising director, salesperson, credit analyst, company planner, and janitor. Capital investments do not always have to be large, particularly if you decide to open a service business. Although you may work long hours, being your own boss can be rewarding. Not only will you reap the financial fruits of your labors, but you will also experience the satisfaction that results from personal accomplishment and growth.

Product management

Product management is viewed by many to be one of the most challenging and exciting jobs in marketing. There are a number of positions available, and they are often a route to a top marketing position within the firm. A product manager is usually placed in a matrix organization structure, meaning that the position is not fully line or staff, yet the manager is fully accountable for the product's success. A good product manager is skillful at planning and public relations, and is usually well paid for his or her successses. A college graduate normally begins as an assistant product manager, then becomes a product manager, and finally a group product manager. The next promotion is into general marketing management.

Getting started

It would be impossible to list and discuss all the career paths in marketing. Those mentioned here are only a sample of what is available. Other possibilities include purchasing, traffic and physical distribution, wholesaling, brokering and agent work, public relations, customer service, sales promotion, and new product development. A number of other jobs can be found in nonprofit areas such as government, museums, hospitals, universities, and charities.

If one of these fields appeals to you, ask your faculty advisor or the university placement service to provide you with more information. It is also wise to speak with someone in the field, if you have the opportunity. After you have decided where you would like to begin your marketing career, do not forget to apply the marketing principles you have learned to yourself.

Think about product differentiation. What skills and training do you have that will provide unique advantages over other candidates? Also consider product development. Take courses that will appeal to a potential employer. If you are going into marketing research, for example, be sure to take a number of quantitative courses. If sales is where you want to begin, join student organizations and try to develop your interpersonal and leadership skills. A retailer might be more interested in you if you have had part-time retailing jobs while attending school.

Do not forget the "consumer orientation" of marketing. Learn all you can about your potential employer. Ask questions that reveal your insight into the company. Do some library research before the job interview. Read the company's annual reports. Make the interviewer realize you are truly interested in the company. Before the first interview, talk with the university placement service. Let a counselor guide you in preparing a résumé and with tips on an effective job interview. You might rehearse the first interview with someone knowledgeable about the interviewing process. This will help you to relax, and to be ready for standard interview questions, and to get the job you want.

Author index

Subject index